DSM-5
Learning Companion for Counselors

Stephanie F. Dailey ◆ Carman S. Gill
Shannon L. Karl ◆ Casey A. Barrio Minton

AMERICAN COUNSELING
ASSOCIATION
5999 Stevenson Avenue ◆ Alexandria, VA 22304
www.counseling.org

DSM-5
Learning
Companion
for Counselors

10   9   8   7   6   5   4   3   2   1

American Counseling Association
5999 Stevenson Avenue
Alexandria, VA 22304

Associate Publisher ♦ Carolyn C. Baker

Production Manager ♦ Bonny E. Gaston

Copy Editor ♦ Elaine Dunn

Editorial Assistant ♦ Catherine A. Brumley

Cover and text design by Bonny E. Gaston.

Library of Congress Cataloging-in-Publication Data
Dailey, Stephanie F.
    DSM-5 learning companion for counselors / Stephanie F. Dailey, EdD, Carman S. Gill, PhD, Shannon Karl, PhD, Casey A. Barrio Minton, PhD.
        pages cm
    Includes bibliographical references and index.
    ISBN 978-1-55620-341-1 (alk. paper)
    1. Mental health counseling—Study and teaching. 2. Mental health counselors—Education. 3. Diagnostic and statistical manual of mental disorders. 5th ed. I. Gill, Carman S. II. Karl, Shannon (Shannon L.) III. Barrio Minton, Casey A. IV. Title. V. Title: Diagnostic and statistical manual of mental disorders, fifth edition, learning companion for counselors.
    RC466.D35 2014
    362.2'04251—dc23   2013046898

*This book is dedicated to professional counselors
who draw upon the art and science of counseling in a
courageous attempt to serve and foster growth in those seeking
relief, wellness, and personal empowerment.*

Table of Contents

Foreword   xi
Acknowledgments   xiii
About the Authors   xv

Chapter 1
Introduction and Overview   1
   Counseling Identity and Diagnosis   2
   Why We Wrote This *Learning Companion*   2
   The Revision Process   3
   Revision Feedback   4
   Organization of the *DSM-5 Learning Companion for Counselors* 5
   References   6

Chapter 2
Structural, Philosophical, and Major Diagnostic Changes   9
   History of the *DSM*   9
   DSM-5 Structural Changes   11
   DSM-5 Philosophical Changes   16
   Major Diagnostic Highlights   20
   Implications of the *DSM-5*   22
   Future of the *DSM-5*: Where Will It Go From Here?   24
   References   24

Introduction to Diagnostic Changes
Part One to Part Four Overview   29

Part One
Changes and Implications Involving Mood, Anxiety,
and Stressor-Related Concerns
♦ ♦ ♦
Part One Introduction   31

Chapter 3
Depressive Disorders   33
   Major Changes From *DSM-IV-TR* to *DSM-5*   33
   Differential Diagnosis   34

Etiology and Treatment   34
Implications for Counselors   34
Disruptive Mood Dysregulation Disorder   35
Major Depressive Disorder, Single Episode and Recurrent Episodes   38
Persistent Depressive Disorder (Dysthymia)   41
Premenstrual Dysphoric Disorder   44
Substance/Medication-Induced Depressive Disorder   47
Depressive Disorder Due to Another Medical Condition   48
Other Specified and Unspecified Depressive Disorders   49
Specifiers for Depressive Disorders   49

Chapter 4
Bipolar and Related Disorders   **53**
Major Changes From *DSM-IV-TR* to *DSM-5*   53
Differential Diagnosis   54
Etiology and Treatment   54
Implications for Counselors   54
Bipolar I Disorder   55
Bipolar II Disorder   58
Cyclothymic Disorder   61
Substance/Medication-Induced Bipolar and Related Disorder   63
Bipolar and Related Disorder Due to Another Medical Condition   63
Other Specified and Unspecified Bipolar and Related Disorders   64
Specifiers for Bipolar and Related Disorders   65

Chapter 5
Anxiety Disorders   **69**
Major Changes From *DSM-IV-TR* to *DSM-5*   70
Differential Diagnosis   70
Etiology and Treatment   70
Implications for Counselors   71
Separation Anxiety Disorder   71
Selective Mutism   73
Specific Phobia   74
Social Anxiety Disorder (Social Phobia)   75
Panic Disorder   78
Panic Attack Specifier   79
Agoraphobia   80
Generalized Anxiety Disorder   81
Substance/Medication-Induced Anxiety Disorder   83
Anxiety Disorder Due to Another Medical Condition   84
Other Specified and Unspecified Anxiety Disorders   85

Chapter 6
Obsessive-Compulsive and Related Disorders   **87**
Major Changes From *DSM-IV-TR* to *DSM-5*   88
Differential Diagnosis   88
Etiology and Treatment   89
Implications for Counselors   89
Obsessive-Compulsive Disorder   90
Body Dysmorphic Disorder   93
Hoarding Disorder   95
Trichotillomania (Hair-Pulling Disorder)   98
Excoriation (Skin-Picking) Disorder   99
Substance/Medication-Induced Obsessive-Compulsive and Related Disorder   101
Obsessive-Compulsive and Related Disorder Due to Another Medical Condition   102
Other Specified and Unspecified Obsessive-Compulsive and Related Disorders   104

Chapter 7:
Trauma- and Stressor-Related Disorders   **105**
Major Changes From *DSM-IV-TR* to *DSM-5*   105
Essential Features   106

Differential Diagnosis 107
Etiology and Treatment 107
Implications for Counselors 107
Reactive Attachment Disorder 108
Disinhibited Social Engagement Disorder 109
Posttraumatic Stress Disorder 111
Acute Stress Disorder 119
Adjustment Disorders 122
Other Specified and Unspecified Trauma- and Stressor-Related Disorders 124

Chapter 8
Gender Dysphoria in Children, Adolescents, and Adults **125**
Major Changes From *DSM-IV-TR* to *DSM-5* 126
Essential Features 128
Differential Diagnosis 130
Etiology and Treatment 131
Implications for Counselors 132
Coding, Recording, and Specifiers 133

Part One References **135**

Part Two

Changes and Implications Involving Addictive,
Impulse-Control, and Specific Behavior-Related Concerns

♦ ♦ ♦

Part Two Introduction **147**

Chapter 9
Substance-Related and Addictive Disorders **149**
Major Changes From *DSM-IV-TR* to *DSM-5* 150
Substance-Related Disorders 151
Substance Intoxication and Withdrawal 153
Specific Substance-Related Disorders Overview 157
Gambling Disorder 161

Chapter 10
Disruptive, Impulse-Control, and Conduct Disorders **165**
Major Changes From *DSM-IV-TR* to *DSM-5* 166
Differential Diagnosis 167
Etiology and Treatment 168
Implications for Counselors 169
Oppositional Defiant Disorder 170
Intermittent Explosive Disorder 172
Conduct Disorder 173
Pyromania 175
Kleptomania 177

Chapter 11
Specific Behavioral Disruptions **179**
Feeding and Eating Disorders 179
Specific Feeding Disorders 184
Pica 184
Rumination Disorder 186
Avoidant/Restrictive Food Intake Disorder 187
Specific Eating Disorders 188
Anorexia Nervosa 188
Bulimia Nervosa 191
Binge-Eating Disorder 194
Elimination Disorders 196
Enuresis 197
Encopresis 199

Sleep-Wake Disorders   199
    Insomnia Disorder   200
    Hypersomnolence Disorder and Narcolepsy   201
    Breathing-Related Sleep Disorders   202
    Parasomnias   203
    Circadian Rhythm Sleep-Wake Disorders   204
    Restless Legs Syndrome   205
    Substance/Medication-Induced Sleep Disorder   205
    Additional Resources for Sleep Disorders   205
Sexual Dysfunctions   205
    Delayed Ejaculation   208
    Erectile Disorder   209
    Female Orgasmic Disorder   210
    Female Sexual Interest/Arousal Disorder   211
    Genito-Pelvic Pain/Penetration Disorder   211
    Male Hypoactive Sexual Desire Disorder   212
    Premature (Early) Ejaculation   213
    Substance/Medication-Induced Sexual Dysfunction   214
Paraphilic Disorders   214
    Pedophilic Disorder   216
    Exhibitionistic Disorder   218
    Voyeuristic Disorder   220
    Frotteuristic Disorder   220
    Sexual Masochism Disorder and Sexual Sadism Disorder   221
    Fetishistic Disorder   223
    Transvestic Disorder   223

Part Two References   **225**

Part Three
Changes and Implications Involving Diagnoses Commonly Made by Other Professionals

♦ ♦ ♦

Part Three Introduction   **235**

Chapter 12
Neurodevelopmental and Neurocognitive Disorders   **239**
Neurodevelopmental Disorders   239
    Intellectual Disabilities   241
    Intellectual Disability (Intellectual Developmental Disorder)   242
    Global Developmental Delay   242
    Communication Disorders   242
    Language Disorder   243
    Speech Sound Disorder   243
    Childhood-Onset Fluency Disorder (Stuttering)   243
    Social (Pragmatic) Communication Disorder   244
    Autism Spectrum Disorder   244
    Attention-Deficit/Hyperactivity Disorder   247
    Specific Learning Disorder   249
    Motor Disorders   249
    Developmental Coordination Disorder   249
    Sterotypic Movement Disorder   250
    Tic Disorders   250
Neurocognitive Disorders   251
    Delirium   252
    Major Neurocognitive Disorder   253
    Mild Neurocognitive Disorder   254
    Major and Mild Neurocognitive Disorders   254

Chapter 13

Schizophrenia Spectrum and Other Psychotic Disorders   **257**
Major Changes From *DSM-IV-TR* to *DSM-5*   258
Differential Diagnosis   259
Etiology and Treatment   260
Implications for Counselors   262
Delusional Disorder   263
Brief Psychotic Disorder   263
Schizophreniform Disorder   264
Schizophrenia   265
Schizoaffective Disorder   265
Substance/Medication-Induced Psychotic Disorder   266
Psychotic Disorder Due to Another Medical Condition   266
Catatonia   267

Chapter 14

Dissociative Disorders   **269**
Major Changes From *DSM-IV-TR* to *DSM-5*   270
Differential Diagnosis   270
Etiology and Treatment   271
Implications for Counselors   272
Dissociative Identity Disorder   273
Dissociative Amnesia   273
Depersonalization/Derealization Disorder   274

Chapter 15

Somatic Symptom and Related Disorders   **277**
Major Changes From *DSM-IV-TR* to *DSM-5*   277
Differential Diagnosis   278
Etiology and Treatment   279
Implications for Counselors   280
Somatic Symptom Disorder   280
Illness Anxiety Disorder   281
Conversion Disorder (Functional Neurological Symptom Disorder)   281
Psychological Factors Affecting Other Medical Conditions   282
Factitious Disorder   282

Part Three References   **285**

Part Four
Future Changes and Practice Implications for Counselors
◆ ◆ ◆

Part Four Introduction   **291**

Chapter 16

Looking Ahead: Personality Disorders   **293**
Major Changes From *DSM-IV-TR* to *DSM-5*   295
Essential Features   295
Special Considerations   295
Differential Diagnosis   296
Paranoid Personality Disorder   296
Schizoid Personality Disorder   297
Schizotypal Personality Disorder   298
Antisocial Personality Disorder   299
Borderline Personality Disorder   300
Histrionic Personality Disorder   302
Narcissistic Personality Disorder   303
Avoidant Personality Disorder   304

Dependent Personality Disorder   305
Obsessive-Compulsive Personality Disorder   306
Summary   307
Alternative Model for Diagnosing Personality Disorders   308
Using the Alternative *DSM-5* Model   313
Conclusion   315

Chapter 17

Practice Implications for Counselors   **317**

Diagnosis and the Counseling Profession   317
Other Specified and Unspecified Diagnoses   320
Coding and Recording   320
Diagnostic Assessment and Other Screening Tools   323
Cultural Formulation Interview   324
The Future of the *DSM*   325

Part Four References   **327**

Index   **331**

Part Four References   **327**

Index   **331**

Foreword

The *Diagnostic and Statistical Manual of Mental Disorders, Fifth Edition* (*DSM-5*), published in 2013 by the American Psychiatric Association, is a dense book that spans 947 pages and describes hundreds of mental disorders. Keeping abreast of the manual's evolving changes is a tedious but necessary task for counselors. In their text *DSM-5 Learning Companion for Counselors,* Dailey, Gill, Karl, and Barrio Minton provide readers with an exceptionally practical, straightforward, and, most important, readable summary of the *DSM-5*.

One of the many highlights of the text is its focus on clinical utility and counselor practice implications. Care is taken to ensure readers understand what the changes from the *DSM-IV-TR* to *DSM-5* mean to them and how these changes can be applied in their day-to-day practice.

Structural changes to the *DSM-5*, diagnostic changes, and newly added disorders are discussed, and Dailey and colleagues take care to avoid distracting readers with diagnostic material that has not changed. While it is easy to feel overwhelmed by the sheer volume of diagnostic changes presented in the *DSM-5*, the authors ease this transition by highlighting the changes that relate to disorders counselors more commonly treat (e.g., depressive, anxiety, obsessive-compulsive disorders). Attention is also paid to emerging diagnostic trends, such as the proposed personality disorders continuum, which provide readers with information that may be foundational to future *DSM* changes. The authors' understanding of the manual's evolutions is obvious, and their discussion of this in Chapter 2 is a must-read for all practicing counselors.

The final chapter is a gem and explains practical *DSM-5* resources that will inform practitioners' counseling. In terms of assessment, the updated diagnostic coding processes, the diagnostic interview, culturally informed assessments (specifically the Cultural Formulation Interview), and the World Health Organization Disability Assessment Schedule are discussed; these are excellent counselor resources and can serve to enrich counselors' diagnostic practices. Essential information regarding the upcoming Health Insurance Portability and Accountability Act changes to require *International Statistical Classification of Diseases and Related Health Problems, 10th Revision* (*ICD-10*) diagnoses is also provided and deepens readers' understanding of the emerging, broader landscape of diagnosis, beyond just the *DSM* system.

The material in this *Learning Companion* is presented in a highly engaging format. The authors address and clearly explain the changes from the *DSM-IV-TR* to *DSM-5*. They use lively case studies to illustrate the diagnostic features of the new *DSM-5* disorders. They also provide "notes" that highlight the information to which readers should pay special attention. These aforementioned features help readers connect with the essential information they need to successfully use the newest edition of the *DSM*. The case examples especially are quite thought provoking and serve to bring the newest *DSM* disorders to life.

In addition, and consistent with counselors' values and practices, the authors pay close attention to the developmental considerations that have been integrated into the *DSM-5* as well as the situational and environmental contexts that relate to the changes. Paralleling the increased emphasis placed on culture in the *DSM-5*, cultural considerations relating to the diagnoses are also addressed.

The authors are to be commended on providing a resource that is thorough and comprehensive, yet engaging and highly readable—a tall order for a topic as detailed and complex as the *DSM* system of diagnosis. This book is an essential read for all practicing counselors who wish to stay contemporary in their practices and stay connected with the current edition of the *DSM*!

—*Victoria E. Kress, PhD*
Youngstown State University

Acknowledgments

We wish to acknowledge the following individuals for making this book possible: Vanessa Teixeira, Allison Sanders, Colleen O'Shea, and Vickie Hagan.

We also wish to acknowledge those who touch not only our lives but also our hearts:

Stephanie F. Dailey
To my husband, Peter, and my son, Cameron,
for being my best friends.

Carman S. Gill
To Roberta and Tara for your
humor, patience, and friendship.

Shannon L. Karl
To my daughter, Arianna Ray, for her steadfast support
and keen editing suggestions.

Casey A. Barrio Minton
To Joel, for his infinite patience,
optimism, and affirmation.

♦ ♦ ♦

About the Authors

Stephanie F. Dailey, EdD, LPC, NCC, ACS, is an assistant professor of counseling at Argosy University in Washington, DC. Dr. Dailey is a licensed professional counselor in Virginia as well as a national certified counselor and an approved clinical supervisor. She specializes in working with individuals and groups from a wide range of multicultural backgrounds on counseling issues ranging from normal situational and developmental issues to living and coping with severe and persistent mental illness. As a certified American Red Cross disaster mental health responder and liaison to the American Red Cross disaster mental health partners for the American Counseling Association (ACA), she is also trained to work with disaster survivors, first responders, and emergency preparedness personnel. Dr. Dailey has published and presented regionally and nationally on the American Psychiatric Association's 2013 *Diagnostic and Statistical Manual of Mental Disorders, Fifth Edition* (*DSM-5*) as well as counseling assessment, diagnosis, and treatment planning. Dr. Dailey is a member of the ACA Ethics Committee; sits on the executive board for the Association for Spiritual, Ethical and Religious Values in Counseling (ASERVIC); and serves as chair of the ASERVIC Ethics Committee.

Carman S. Gill, PhD, LPC, NCC, ACS, is an associate professor and chair of the counselor education program at Argosy University, Washington, DC. She has worked with client populations, including individuals who are dually diagnosed, individuals with chronic mental illness, children, and those experiencing acute mental health crises. She has published book chapters and journal articles in the areas of spirituality, wellness, forgiveness, and assessment. Dr. Gill has served as a member of ACA's DSM-5 Task Force and as president of ASERVIC.

Shannon L. Karl, PhD, LMHC, NCC, CCMHC, is an associate professor with the Center for Psychological Studies at Nova Southeastern University. She has extensive clinical mental health experience and is a licensed mental health counselor in the state of Florida as well as a national certified counselor and a clinically certified mental health counselor. Dr. Karl has published and presented regionally, nationally, and internationally on the *DSM-5*. She was a member of the ACA DSM-5 Task Force from 2011 to 2013, an ACA DSM-5 Series webinar presenter, and has conducted numerous workshops and trainings on the *DSM-5*.

Casey A. Barrio Minton, PhD, NCC, is an associate professor and counseling program coordinator at the University of North Texas. Her clinical experiences include serving clients in a range of outpatient, residential, intensive outpatient, and inpatient mental health settings with a focus on crisis intervention and stabilization. She has authored multiple book chapters and journal articles focused on counselor preparation and mental health issues. Dr. Barrio Minton is founding editor of the *Journal of Counselor Leadership and Advocacy* and has served as president for the Association for Assessment and Research in Counseling and Chi Sigma Iota International.

◆ ◆ ◆

Chapter 1

Introduction and Overview

Regardless of background, training, or theoretical orientation, professional counselors need to have a thorough understanding of the fifth edition of the *Diagnostic and Statistical Manual of Mental Disorders* (*DSM-5*), published by the American Psychiatric Association (APA; 2013). The *DSM-5* and its earlier editions have become the world's standard reference for client evaluation and diagnosis (Eriksen & Kress, 2006; Hinkle, 1999; Zalaquett, Fuerth, Stein, Ivey, & Ivey, 2008). Most important, the manual allows professional counselors to break down the complexity of clients' presenting problems into practical language for practitioners and clients alike. Sometimes referred to as the "the psychiatric bible" (Caplan, 2012; Kutchins & Kirk, 1997; Perry, 2012), the *DSM* is intended to be applicable in various settings and used by mental health practitioners and researchers of differing backgrounds and orientations.

Because of the prevalent use of the *DSM*, professional counselors who provide services in mental health centers, psychiatric hospitals, employee assistance programs, detention centers, private practice, or other community settings must be well versed in client conceptualization and diagnostic assessment using the manual. For those in private practice, agencies, and hospitals, a diagnosis using *DSM* criteria is necessary for third-party payments and for certain types of record keeping and reporting. Of the 50 states and the U.S. territories, including the District of Columbia, that have passed laws to regulate professional counselors, 34 include diagnosis within the scope of practice for professional counselors (American Counseling Association [ACA], 2012). Even professionals who are not traditionally responsible for diagnosis as a part of their counseling services, such as school or career counselors, should understand the *DSM* so they can recognize diagnostic problems or complaints and participate in discussions and treatment regarding these issues. Although other diagnostic nomenclature systems, such as the World Health Organization's (WHO; 2007) *International Statistical Classification of Diseases and Related Health Problems* (*ICD*), are available to professional counselors, the *DSM* is and will continue to be the most widely used manual within the field. For these reasons, the ability to navigate and use the *DSM* responsibly has become an important part of a professional counselor's identity.

Counseling Identity and Diagnosis

By definition, counseling is a "professional relationship that empowers diverse individuals, families, and groups to accomplish mental health, wellness, education, and career goals" (ACA, 2013, para. 2). To accomplish this role, practitioners often incorporate diagnosis as one component of the counseling process. Therefore, it is not surprising that ethical guidelines for the profession and accreditation standards for counselor education programs encourage counselors to have an understanding of diagnostic nomenclature. For example, the *ACA Code of Ethics* (ACA, 2014) Section E.5.a., Proper Diagnosis, requires counselors to "take special care to provide proper diagnosis of mental disorders" (p. 11). The Council for Accreditation of Counseling and Related Educational Programs (CACREP; 2009) requires that counselors learn strategies for collaborating and communicating with other human service providers as part of their common core curricular experiences. Thus, learning outcomes for clinical mental health counselors require demonstrated knowledge regarding the most recent edition of the *DSM*. Ask any professional counselor and he or she is likely to agree that a thorough understanding of the *DSM* is an essential aspect of interdisciplinary communication.

Despite widespread guidance encouraging counselors to be familiar with the *DSM*, utilization of the manual is not without challenges and controversy. Many professional counselors feel unprepared or uncomfortable when faced with the task of assigning clients a diagnosis (Mannarino, Loughran, & Hamilton, 2007). Other professionals are conflicted about the *DSM*'s focus on psychopathology and feel the mechanistic approach reduces "complex information about people into a few words . . . describing a person's parts (symptoms) as static" (Mannarino et al., 2007). As counselors are only too aware, clients cannot be encapsulated into fixed categories. Each client comes to counseling with numerous sociocultural issues that the counselor must consider prior to making a diagnosis and putting together an approach for treatment. This is also particularly important given a large body of research that provides support for the far-reaching impact of poverty and social class on psychological and emotional well-being (e.g., American Psychological Association, 2007; Belle & Doucet, 2003; Groh, 2006). For example, studies of children and adolescents from lower socioeconomic families report higher instances of emotional and conduct problems, including chronic delinquency and early onset of antisocial behavior (McLoyd, 1998). Low income has also been correlated to higher levels of family distress and discord as well as higher rates of parental mental illness.

Finally, many counselors believe the "medicalization" of clients ignores the strengths-based, developmental, wellness approach that is the hallmark of the counseling profession (see Chapter 16 of this *Learning Companion* for information on the wellness vs. the medical model). The introduction of the *DSM-5* adds to this controversy, presenting counselors with a new challenge—the application of a new nomenclature system.

Why We Wrote This *Learning Companion*

We wrote this *Learning Companion* to make the *DSM-5* accessible to professional counselors by breaking down the complexity of the changes and additions found within the revised manual. Because the CACREP 2009 Standards require that programs "provide an understanding of the nature and needs of persons at all developmental levels and in multicultural contexts, . . . including an understanding of psychopathology and situational and environmental factors that affect both normal and abnormal behavior" (p. 9), we believe it essential that new and seasoned professional counselors, counselor educators, and counseling students have easily accessible and accurate information regarding the *DSM-5* and implications of changes for current counseling practice.

To understand changes from the *DSM-IV-TR* (APA, 2000) to the *DSM-5* (APA, 2013), we believe it is important for the reader to first understand the revision process. In the following section, we describe the revision process of the *DSM-5* and the role counselors took in its inception. Readers will find a comprehensive description of structural and philosophical changes to the manual, including a history of the manual's iterations, in Chapter 2.

The Revision Process

The *DSM-5*, after 14 years of debate and deliberation, was intended to be the most radical revision to date (Frances & First, 2011; Jones, 2012b; Miller & Levy, 2011). Beginning in 1999, a year before the *DSM-IV-TR* was published, APA began collaboration with the National Institute of Mental Health (NIMH) on a new edition. The intent of these meetings was to develop a more scientifically based manual that would increase clinical utility while maintaining continuity with previous editions (APA, 2012a). The process began with an initial DSM-5 Research Planning Committee Conference, held in 1999, in which APA and NIMH deliberated on a research agenda and priorities for the new manual. Additional conferences, sponsored by APA, NIMH, and WHO, took place in 2000 and resulted in the formation of six work groups. These initial work groups focused on nomenclature, neuroscience and genetics, developmental issues and diagnosis, personality and relational disorders, mental disorders and disability, and cross-cultural issues. In 2002, a series of six white papers was published with the intent of "providing direction and potential incentives for research that could improve the scientific basis of future classifications" (Kupfer, First, & Regier, 2002, p. xv). Two final manuscripts were published in 2007. One focused on mental disorders in infants, young children, and older persons and the other on gender, cultural, and spiritual issues.

After the release of the initial research agenda for the *DSM-5*, it became clear that further deliberation was needed with regard to nomenclature, neuroscience, developmental science, personality disorders, and the relationship between culture and psychiatric diagnoses (APA, 2000; Kupfer et al., 2002). Steered by APA, NIMH, and WHO, 13 conferences were held between 2004 and 2008 in which participants discussed relevant diagnostic questions and solicited feedback from colleagues and other professionals regarding potential changes. Findings from these conferences facilitated the research base for proposed revisions for the *DSM-5* and fueled the agenda of the *DSM-5* work groups (see Kupfer et al., 2002, for the full *DSM-5* research agenda).

In 2007, APA officially commissioned the DSM-5 Task Force, made up of 29 members, including David J. Kupfer, MD, chair, and Darrel A. Regier, MD, MPH, vice-chair (APA, 2012a). The DSM-5 Task Force expanded the work groups from six to 13. These included attention-deficit/hyperactivity disorder (ADHD) and disruptive behavior disorders; anxiety, obsessive-compulsive spectrum, posttraumatic, and dissociative disorders; childhood and adolescent disorders; eating disorders; mood disorders; neurocognitive disorders; neurodevelopmental disorders; personality disorders; psychotic disorders; sexual and gender identity disorders; sleep-wake disorders; somatic symptoms disorders; and substance-related disorders. Although each of these work groups investigated specific disorders, cross-collaboration was common. Kupfer and Regier provided clear direction to the work groups to, among other things, eradicate the use of not otherwise specified (NOS) diagnoses within categories, do away with functional impairments as necessary components of diagnostic criteria, and use empirically based evidence to justify diagnostic classes and specifiers (Gever, 2012; Regier, Narrow, Kuhl, & Kupfer, 2009). With these marching orders, each work group proposed draft criteria and changes for the new manual.

Three rounds of public comment regarding proposed changes took place between April 2010 and June 2012. An estimated 13,000 mental health professionals commented on the proposed criteria (APA, 2012c, 2012d). Additionally, mental health professionals conducted field trials to "assess the feasibility, clinical utility, reliability, and (where possible) the validity of the draft criteria and the diagnostic-specific and cross-cutting dimensional measures being suggested for *DSM-5*" (APA, 2010, p. 1). Two field trial study designs were administered (APA, 2010, 2011b). The first trial, held between April 2010 and December 2011, took place in 11 large academic or medical centers and involved a total of 279 clinicians (APA, 2012b, 2012c). The second trial, which included solo or small group practices, took place between October 2010 and February 2012. APA recruited a volunteer sample of psychiatrists, psychologists, licensed clinical social workers, licensed counselors, licensed marriage and family therapists, and licensed psychiatric mental health nurses to participate in the second field trial (APA, 2012b, 2012c). Feedback from public comment periods and field trials was shared with work group members, who edited proposed criteria as indicated. The final version of the *DSM-5* went before the APA Board of Trustees in December 2012 and was released in May 2013. The following outlines the complete timeline of the development of the *DSM-5*.

Timeline of *DSM-5*

1999–2001	Development of the *DSM-5* research agenda
2002–2007	APA/WHO/NIMH *DSM-5/ICD-11* research planning conferences
2006	Appointment of DSM-5 Task Force
2007	Appointment of DSM-5 work groups
2007–2011	Literature review and data reanalysis
2010–2011	First phase field trials
2010–2012	Second phase field trials
July 2012	Final draft of *DSM-5* for APA review
May 2013	*DSM-5* released to the public

Revision Feedback

Although no professional counselor was invited to serve on the DSM-5 Task Force, ACA served as an important advocate for professional counselors during the revision process. Through advocacy efforts of the ACA Professional Affairs Office and the ACA DSM-5 Revisions Task Force, two ACA presidents sent letters to APA indicating concern over proposed changes. The first was sent by Dr. Lynn E. Linde, ACA 2009–2010 president, to Dr. David J. Kupfer, DSM-5 Task Force chair. The letter indicated that ACA members had concerns regarding five areas of particular importance to professional counselors: (a) applicability across all mental health professions, (b) gender and culture, (c) organization of the *DSM-5* multiaxial system, (d) lowering of diagnostic thresholds and combining diagnoses, and (e) use of dimensional assessments. The second letter was sent by Dr. Don W. Locke, ACA 2011–2012 president, informing Dr. John Oldham, APA president, that licensed professional counselors were the second largest group to routinely use the *DSM-IV-TR*. He noted uncertainty among professional counselors about the quality and credibility of the *DSM-5* and included a prioritized list of concerns APA should consider before publishing the *DSM-5*. APA responded to this letter on November 21, 2011 (APA, 2011a).

In addition to feedback provided by ACA, several divisions of the American Psychological Association voiced concern about the writing process of the *DSM-5* (Jones, 2012a). As a result, the Society for Humanistic Psychology, Division 32 of the American Psychological Association, sponsored a petition outlining its concerns and inviting other mental health professionals, including counselors, to sign this petition (for a review of these concerns, see British Psychological Society, 2011). It is important to note that nine out of 19 ACA divisions endorsed this petition, including the Association for Adult Development and Aging; Association for Creativity in Counseling; American College Counseling Association; Association for Counselor Education and Supervision; Association for Humanistic Counseling; Association for Lesbian, Gay, Bisexual and Transgender Issues in Counseling; American Rehabilitation Counseling Association; Association for Specialists in Group Work; and Counselors for Social Justice.

Professional counselors are responsible for understanding changes and using the *DSM-5* in a manner consistent with the mission of our profession and the *ACA Code of Ethics* (ACA, 2014). A thorough understanding of the revision process, changes, rationale for changes, and impact of changes will help professional counselors decide how they would like to continue to use the *DSM-5* in practice, consider possibilities for future revisions, and ensure advocacy so counselors have a greater voice in the next revision of the *DSM*.

Organization of the *DSM-5 Learning Companion for Counselors*

In Chapter 2 of this *Learning Companion*, we outline major structural and philosophical changes adopted for the *DSM-5*, such as the elimination of the multiaxial system. We also outline major diagnostic changes, such as the removal of the bereavement clause from major depressive disorder. In addition, we discuss major changes that influence numerous chapters within the *DSM-5*, for example, the removal of NOS and the inclusion of other specified and unspecified disorders to replace all NOS diagnoses.

Following Chapter 2, this *Learning Companion* includes four separate parts, grouped by diagnostic similarity and relevance to the counseling profession. In each of the four parts, we provide a basic description of the diagnostic classification and an overview of the specific disorders covered, highlighting essential features as they relate to the counseling profession. We also provide a comprehensive review of specific changes, when applicable, from the *DSM-IV-TR* to the *DSM-5*. When specific or significant changes to a diagnostic category or diagnosis have not been made, we provide a general review of either the category or the diagnosis, but we refrain from providing the reader with too much detail because the purpose of this *Learning Companion* is to focus on changes from the *DSM-IV-TR* to the *DSM-5*. For example, we do not go into great detail about personality disorders, found in Part Four, because the diagnostic criteria for these disorders have not changed. What we do focus on, however, is the proposed model for diagnosing personality disorders that may significantly affect how counselors diagnose personality disorders in future versions of the *DSM*.

Readers will find, within each part of the book, individual chapters that highlight key concepts of each disorder (including differential diagnoses), new or revised diagnostic criteria, and implications for professional counseling practice. We provide "Notes" to highlight significant information and include case studies to assist counselors in further understanding and applying the new or revised diagnostic categories. All case studies are fictitious composites and do not depict real clients. Any similarity to any person or case is simply coincidental.

Readers should also note that we provide more detail for disorders that counselors are more likely to see in their clients. Therefore, because this *Learning Companion* is organized in order of diagnoses counselors are most likely to diagnose, each consecutive part of the book provides the reader with less specific detail about each diagnostic grouping. For example, Part One includes a detailed synthesis for key disorders, including cultural considerations, differential diagnosis, and special considerations for counselors. We have also included a description of other specified and unspecified diagnoses for each diagnostic class. Conversely, Part Three provides less detail about neurodevelopmental disorders because these diagnoses are typically made by other professionals.

Part One, Changes and Implications Involving Mood, Anxiety, and Stressor-Related Concerns, includes chapters regarding depressive disorders, bipolar and related disorders, anxiety disorders, obsessive-compulsive and related disorders, trauma- and stressor-related disorders, and gender dysphoria. We listed this section first because these disorders, both within and outside of the counseling profession, are some of the highest reported mental disturbances within the United States (Centers for Disease Control and Prevention [CDC], 2011). Readers will note that this is the only section in which other specified and unspecified diagnoses are listed.

Part Two, Changes and Implications Involving Addictive, Impulse-Control, and Specific Behavior-Related Concerns, includes chapters focused on behavioral diagnoses such as substance use and addiction disorders; impulse-control and conduct disorders; and specific behavioral disruptions consisting of feeding and eating, elimination, sleep-wake, sexual dysfunction, and paraphilic disorders. Similar to the disorders found in Part One, counselors are often exposed to the disorders listed in Part Two within clinical practice, but these disorders frequently manifest through more visible, external behavioral concerns rather than less visible, internal experiences (i.e., depression vs. sexual dysfunction). Moreover, counselors may or may not diagnose these disorders. This is not to say that counselors do not frequently diagnose substance use disorders. However, compared with depression and anxiety disorders, substance use disorders are more often diagnosed by a combination of counselors and other health professionals.

Part Three, Changes and Implications Involving Diagnoses Commonly Made by Other Professionals, includes chapters focused on neurodevelopmental, schizophrenia spectrum, and other psychotic, dissociative, neurocognitive, and somatic disorders. Many of these disorders, specifically neurodevelopmental and somatic issues, require highly specialized assessment or extensive medical examination by physicians or other qualified medical professionals. These chapters focus on helping professional counselors understand major changes and the potential impact of these changes on the clients counselors serve. We do not provide a detailed description of each disorder in this chapter; rather, we address major changes, if applicable, and considerations for counselors.

Part Four, Future Changes and Practice Implications for Counselors, addresses future changes to the *DSM* as well as clinical issues related to professional counseling. Whereas all parts of the book focus on professional counselors, this part highlights clinical utility of the *DSM-5* as well as future changes that may affect the counseling profession. For example, Chapter 16 addresses the personality disorders section of the *DSM-5*. Although personality disorders did not change from the *DSM-IV-TR* to the *DSM-5*, proposed changes were included in Section III of the *DSM-5*. If these changes were implemented, they would significantly alter the way counselors diagnose and treat clients with these disorders.

Chapter 17 addresses issues such as the diagnostic interview, the nonaxial system, cultural inclusion, and assessment instruments such as the WHO Disability Assessment Schedule (Version 2.0; WHO, 2010). This chapter also contains information regarding diagnostic coding and changes counselors can expect with the October 2014 revision to the *ICD-10-Clinical Modification* (*ICD-10-CM*; CDC, 2014) coding required for Health Insurance Portability and Accountability Act of 1996 (HIPAA) purposes. We also explore ways in which counselors can continue to be an active part of future revisions of diagnostic nomenclature systems.

References

American Counseling Association. (2012). *Licensure requirements for professional counselors: A state-by-state report.* Alexandria, VA: Author.

American Counseling Association. (2013). *What is professional counseling?* Retrieved from http://www.counseling.org/learn-about-counseling/what-is-counseling

American Counseling Association. (2014). *ACA code of ethics.* Alexandria, VA: Author.

American Psychiatric Association. (2000). *Diagnostic and statistical manual of mental disorders* (4th ed., text rev.). doi:10.1176/appi.books.9780890423349

American Psychiatric Association. (2010). *Protocol for DSM-5 field trials in academic/large clinic settings.* Retrieved from http://www.DSM5.org/Research/Documents/Forms/AllItems.aspx

American Psychiatric Association. (2011a). *DSM-5: APA responds to American Counseling Association concerns.* Retrieved from http://www.psychiatrictimes.com/dsm-5-0/dsm-5-apa-responds-american-counseling-association-concerns#sthash.PiLWpxod.dpuf

American Psychiatric Association. (2011b). *Protocol for DSM-5 field trials in routine clinical practice settings.* Retrieved from http://www.DSM5.org/Research/Documents/Forms/AllItems.aspx

American Psychiatric Association. (2012a). *DSM: History of the manual.* Retrieved from http://www.psychiatry.org/practice/DSM/DSM-history-of-the-manual

American Psychiatric Association. (2012b). *DSM-5 development: Timeline.* Retrieved from http://www.dsm5.org/about/Pages/Timeline.aspx

American Psychiatric Association. (2012c). *DSM-5 field trials.* Retrieved from http://www.dsm5.org/Research/Pages/DSM-5FieldTrials.aspx

American Psychiatric Association. (2012d). *DSM-5 overview: The future manual.* Retrieved from http://www.dsm5.org/about/Pages/DSMVOverview.aspx

American Psychiatric Association. (2013). *The diagnostic and statistical manual of mental disorders* (5th ed.). Arlington, VA: Author.

American Psychological Association. (2007). *Report of the APA Task Force on Socioeconomic Status.* Retrieved from http://www.apa.org/pi/ses/resources/publications/index.aspx

Belle, D., & Doucet, J. (2003). Poverty, inequality, and discrimination as sources of depression among U.S. women. *Psychology of Women Quarterly, 27,* 101–113.

British Psychological Society. (2011). *Response to the American Psychiatric Association: DSM-5 development.* Retrieved from http://apps.bps.org.uk/_publicationfiles/consultation-responses/DSM-5%202011%20-%20BPS%20response.pdf

Caplan, P. J. (2012, April 27). Psychiatry's bible, the *DSM,* is doing more harm than good. *Washington Post Opinions.* Retrieved from http://www.washingtonpost.com/opinions/psychiatrys-bible-the-DSM-Is-doing-more-harm-than-good/2012/04/27/gIQAqy0WlT_story.html

Centers for Disease Control and Prevention. (2011). *Burden of mental illness.* Retrieved from http://www.cdc.gov/mentalhealth/basics/mental-illness/depression.htm

Centers for Disease Control and Prevention, National Center for Health Statistics. (2014). *The international classification of diseases, 10th revision, clinical modification (ICD-10-CM).* Retrieved from http://www.cdc.gov/nchs/icd/icd10cm.htm

Council for Accreditation of Counseling and Related Educational Programs. (2009). *2009 standards.* Retrieved from http://www.cacrep.org/doc/2009%20Standards.pdf

Eriksen, K., & Kress, V. E. (2006). The *DSM* and the professional counseling identity: Bridging the gap. *Journal of Mental Health Counseling, 28,* 202–216.

Frances, A., & First, M. B. (2011). Hebephilia is not a mental disorder in *DSM-IV-TR* and should not become one in *DSM-5. Journal of American Academy of Psychiatry and the Law, 39,* 78–85.

Gever, J. (2012, May 10). *DSM-5: What's in, what's out.* Retrieved from http://www.medpagetoday.com/MeetingCoverage/APA/32619

Groh, C. J. (2006). Poverty, mental health, and women: Implications for psychiatric nurses in primary care settings. *Journal of the American Psychiatric Nurses Association, 13,* 267–274.

Health Insurance Portability and Accountability Act of 1996, Pub. L. 104–191, 110 Stat. 1936.

Hinkle, J. S. (1999). A voice from the trenches: A reaction to Ivey and Ivey (1998). *Journal of Counseling & Development, 77,* 474–483.

Jones, K. D. (2012a). A critique of the *DSM-5* field trials. *Journal of Nervous and Mental Disease, 200,* 517–519.

Jones, K. D. (2012b). Dimensional and cross-cutting assessment in the *DSM-5. Journal of Counseling & Development, 90,* 481–487.

Kupfer, D. J., First, M. B., & Regier, D. A. (2002). *A research agenda for DSM-V.* Washington, DC: American Psychiatric Association.

Kutchins, H., & Kirk, S. A. (1997). *Making us crazy: DSM: The psychiatric bible and the creation of mental disorders.* New York, NY: Free Press.

Mannarino, M. B., Loughran, M. J., & Hamilton, D. (2007, October). *The professional counselor and the diagnostic process: Challenges and opportunities for education and training.* Paper presented at the Association for Counselor Education and Supervision Conference, Columbus, OH.

McLoyd, V. C. (1998). Socioeconomic disadvantage and child development. *American Psychologist, 53,* 185–204.

Miller, J. D., & Levy, K. N. (2011). Personality and personality disorders in the *DSM-5*: Introduction to the special issue. *Personality Disorders: Theory, Research, and Treatment, 2,* 1–3.

Perry, S. (2012, May 4). Last chance to comment on psychiatry's controversial diagnostic "bible." *Minnesota Post.* Retrieved from http://www.minnpost.com/second-opinion/2012/05/last-chance-comment-psychiatrys-controversial-diagnostic-bible

Regier, D. A., Narrow, W. E., Kuhl, E. A., & Kupfer, D. J. (2009). The conceptual development of *DSM-5. American Journal of Psychiatry, 166,* 645–650.

World Health Organization. (2007). *International statistical classification of diseases and related health problems, 10th revision.* Geneva, Switzerland: Author.

World Health Organization. (2010). *WHO Disability Assessment Schedule 2.0–WHODAS 2.0.* Geneva, Switzerland: Author.

Zalaquett, C. P., Fuerth, K. M., Stein, C., Ivey, A. E., & Ivey, M. N. (2008). Reframing the *DSM-IV-TR* from a multicultural/social justice perspective. *Journal of Counseling & Development, 86,* 364–371. doi:10.1002/j.1556-6678.2008.tb00521.x

Chapter 2

Structural, Philisophical, and Major Diagnostic Changes

In this chapter, we highlight major structural modifications of the *DSM-5* (APA, 2013), including removal of the multiaxial system and changes to chapter order; philosophical changes, such as the proposed use of dimensional and new cross-cutting assessments; and major diagnostic changes from the *DSM-IV-TR* to the *DSM-5*. To help readers better understand the revision process and the philosophy behind it, we begin with a brief description of the historical background and evolution of the *DSM*.

History of the *DSM*

The original *DSM*, published by the APA in 1952, was psychiatry's first attempt to standardize the classification of mental disorders. Developed by the APA Committee on Nomenclature and Statistics, the *DSM-I* (APA, 1952) served as an alternative to the sixth edition of the *ICD* (WHO, 1949), which, for the first time, included a section for mental disorders (APA, 2000). Differing slightly from the *ICD*, which primarily served as an international system to collect health statistics, the *DSM-I* focused on clinical utility and was grounded in psychodynamic formulations of mental disorders (Sanders, 2011). This version highlighted prominent psychiatrist Adolf Meyer's (1866–1950) psychobiological view, which posited that mental disorders denoted "reactions" of the personality to biological, psychological, or social aspects of client functioning (APA, 2000). The *DSM-I* included three categories of psychopathology (organic brain syndromes, functional disorders, and mental deficiency) and 106 narrative descriptions of disorders in about as many pages. Only one diagnosis, adjustment reaction of childhood/adolescence, was applicable to children (Sanders, 2011).

Meyer's influence was abandoned in the initial revision of the *DSM-II* published in 1968. This version contained 11 categories and 182 disorders (APA, 1968). Similar to the previous version, the development of the *DSM-II* coincided with the development of the WHO's (1968) revised *ICD-8*. Although only incremental changes were evident, the focus of the manual shifted from causality to psychoanalysis, as evidenced by the removal of the word *reactions* and retention of terms such as *neuroses* and *psychophysiologic disorders* (Sanders, 2011). With the intent on reform, this shift was significant because separation meant removing unverified or speculative diagnoses from the manual. Critics, however, argued that actual separation of diagnostic labels from etiological origins would not actually occur until the next revision (Rogler, 1997).

Work on the third version, *DSM-III*, began in 1974 and continued until the edition was published in 1980. A considerable divergence from previous editions, the *DSM-III* represented a dramatic shift with inclusion of descriptive diagnoses and emphasis on the medical model (APA, 1980; Wilson, 1993). This profound reframing introduced a biopsychosocial model to diagnostic assessment with an emphasis on empirical evidence that represented a clear follow-through on previous attempts to separate the *DSM* from psychoanalytic origins. Supporters claimed "theoretical neutrality" of the *DSM-III* (Maser, Kaelber, & Weise, 1991, p. 271). As Rogler (1997) argued, "The *DSM-III* was an official attempt to abruptly, not gradually, reduce reliance on the vagaries of the diagnosticians' subjective understandings by specifying sets of diagnostic criteria" (p. 9).

With the publication of the *DSM-III*, mental health professionals repositioned themselves toward positivistic, operationally defined symptomatology based on specific descriptive measures (Wilson, 1993). This modification included the introduction of explicit diagnostic criteria (i.e., a checklist) as opposed to narrative descriptions. The *DSM-III* also introduced the multiaxial system and diagnostic classifications free from specific theoretical confines or etiological assumptions. This version integrated demographic information such as gender, familial patterns, and cultural features into diagnostic classifications (Sanders, 2011). On the basis of these philosophical changes, professional counselors began to emphasize the structured interview and insisted on empirically validating *DSM-III* diagnostic criteria. The age of empirically based treatments had arrived, and widespread use of the *DSM-III*, as opposed to the *ICD-9* (WHO, 1975), became commonplace. Wilson (1993) wrote,

> The biopsychosocial model [alone] did not clearly demarcate the mentally well from the mentally ill, and this failure led to a crisis in the legitimacy of psychiatry by the 1970s. The publication of *DSM-III* in 1980 represented an answer to this crisis, as the essential focus of psychiatric knowledge shifted from the clinically-based biopsychosocial model to a research-based medical model. (p. 399)

Intended only to be a minor change to the third version, the revised *DSM-III-R* (APA, 1987) renamed, added, and deleted categories; made changes to diagnostic criteria; and increased reliability by incorporating data from field trials and diagnostic interviews (APA, 2000; Blashfield, 1998; Scotti & Morris, 2000). Despite these innovations, the *DSM-III* and *DSM-III-R* were profoundly criticized. The manual had increased from 106 to 297 diagnoses (APA, 1987). Descriptions of Axis I disorders topped at 300 pages whereas explanations of Axis IV and V disorders totaled only two pages, leading many to question the multiaxial system (Rogler, 1997). Additionally, critics questioned field trials and claimed lack of objectivity among researchers, further contributing to strong criticism of the *DSM-III* and *DSM-III-R*.

Heavy critique of the *DSM-III* and its revision led to relatively mild changes to the *DSM-IV*, published in 1994. Despite few changes, the revision process was considerable and involved a steering committee, 13 work groups, work group advisors, extensive literature reviews, and numerous field trials to ensure clinical utility. The *DSM-IV* (APA, 1994) included 365 diagnoses; and at 886 pages, it was almost 7 times the length of the *DSM-I*. A "text revision" (*DSM-IV-TR*) was published in 2000 and included additional empirically based information for each diagnosis as well as changes to diagnostic codes for the purpose of maintaining consistency with the *ICD* (APA, 2000). In the *DSM-IV-TR* (APA, 2000), wording of the manual was modified in an attempt to differentiate people from their diagnoses. For example, phrases such as "a schizophrenic" were modified to read "an individual with schizophrenia" (Scotti & Morris, 2000).

Like their predecessors, the *DSM-IV* and *DSM-IV-TR* were heavily critiqued by help-ing professionals (Eriksen & Kress, 2006). Many felt the manual leaned too heavily on the medical model with its rigid classification system, despite claims of diagnostic neutrality (Eriksen & Kress, 2006; Ivey & Ivey, 1998; Scotti & Morris, 2000). Issues of comorbidity, questionable reliability, and controversial diagnoses were hot topics among critics; the mul-tiaxial system continued to be controversial (Houts, 2002; Malik & Beutler, 2002). Because of the changing nature of how the *DSM* was being used and by whom, many practitioners began demanding that a more holistic or dimensional approach be used and that psycho-metrically sound assessments be included (Kraemer, 2007). Other critics, specifically those directly involved in writing the *DSM-5*, advocated for incorporating scientific advances from psychiatric research, genetics, neuroimaging, cognitive science, and pathophysiology (functional changes associated with or resulting from disease or injury) into diagnostic nosology (Kupfer & Regier, 2011).

Some counselors, in particular, believed that overreliance on *DSM* diagnoses can "narrow a counselor's focus by encouraging the counselor to only look for behaviors that fit within a medical-model understanding of the person's situation" (Eriksen & Kress, 2006, p. 204). In contrast to those who support the medical model, many counselors use diagnosis as only one aspect of understanding the client. Most counselors view individuals as having strengths and difficulties across myriad emotional, cognitive, physiological, social, occu-pational, cultural, and spiritual areas. Counselors recognize the whole person and nurture a strength-based approach to achieve wellness, not simply reduce symptomatology. Myers, Sweeney, and Witmer (2000) defined wellness as

> A way of life oriented toward optimal health and well-being, in which body, mind, and spirit are integrated by the individual to live life more fully within the human and natural commu-nity. Ideally, it is the optimum state of health and well-being that each individual is capable of achieving. (p. 252)

The controversial issues of rigid classification, comorbidity, questionable reliability, and controversial diagnoses were the driving force of numerous structural and philosophical changes included in the *DSM-5*. Information regarding these major changes is provided in the next section.

DSM-5 Structural Changes

The *DSM-5* includes approximately the same number of disorders as the *DSM-IV-TR*. This goes against a popular trend within health care to increase, rather than decrease, the num-ber of diagnoses available to practitioners (APA, 2013). Despite being similar in number, several major changes affect the manual as a whole. Unlike the previous version that was organized by 16 diagnostic classes, one general section, and 11 appendixes, the *DSM-5* is divided into three sections, 20 diagnostic classes, two general sections for medication-induced problems and other conditions that may be a focus of clinical attention, and seven appendixes. It also lists two sets of *ICD* codes, using *ICD-9-CM* (CDC, 1998) codes as the standard coding system with *ICD-10-CM* (CDC, 2014) codes in parentheses. *ICD-10-CM* codes are included because as of October 1, 2014, all practitioners must be in alignment with HIPAA, which requires use of *ICD-10-CM* codes. For more information, Part Four of this *Learning Companion* comprehensively reviews how diagnostic coding systems will change and implications of these modifications for counselors.

Section Overview

Section I of the *DSM-5* provides a summary of revisions and changes as well as information regarding utilization of the revised manual. Section II includes all diagnoses broken into

20 separate chapters ordered by similarity to one another. Because comorbid symptoms are clustered together, counselors can now better differentiate between disorders that are distinctively different but have similar symptom characteristics or etiology (e.g., body dysmorphic disorder vs. obsessive-compulsive disorder; acute stress disorder vs. adjustment disorder). Section III includes conditions that require further research before they can be considered for adoption in an upcoming version of the *DSM*, dimensional assessment measures, an expanded look at how practitioners can better understand clients from a multicultural perspective, and a proposed model for diagnosing personality disorders.

Cultural Inclusion

Section III (see pp. 749–759 of the *DSM-5*) includes special attention to diverse ways in which individuals in different cultural groups can experience and describe distress. The manual provides a Cultural Formulation Interview (pp. 750–757 of the *DSM-5*) to help clinicians gather relevant cultural information. Expanding on information provided in the *DSM-IV-TR*, the Cultural Formulation Interview calls for clinicians to outline and systematically assess cultural identity, cultural conceptualization of distress, psychosocial stressors related to cultural features of vulnerability and resilience, cultural differences between the counselor and client, and cultural factors relevant to help seeking. The *DSM-5* also includes descriptions regarding how different cultural groups encounter, identify with, and convey feelings of distress by breaking up what was formerly known as culture-bound syndromes into three different concepts. The first concept is *cultural syndromes*, a cluster of co-occurring symptomatology within a specific cultural group. The second is *cultural idioms of distress*, linguistic terms or phrases used to convey suffering within a specific cultural group. The third concept is *cultural explanation or perceived cause*, mental disorders unique to certain cultures that serve as the reason for symptoms, illness, or distress. This breakdown improves clinical utility by helping clinicians more accurately communicate with clients, so that they are able to differentiate disorders from nondisorders when working with clients from varied backgrounds.

Personality Disorders

Section III of the *DSM-5* also provides an alternative model for diagnosing personality disorders. This model is a radical change from the current diagnostic structure, introducing a hybrid dimensional-categorical model, which evaluates symptomatology and characterizes five broad areas of personality pathology. As opposed to separate diagnostic criteria, this proposed model identifies six personality types with a specific pattern of impairments and traits. We review this model and the Cultural Formulation section in Part Four of this *Learning Companion*.

Adoption of a Nonaxial System

One of the most far-reaching structural modifications to the *DSM-5* is the removal of the multiaxial system and discontinuation of the Global Assessment of Functioning (GAF) scale. Table 2.1 includes a comparison of the traditional multiaxial and the new nonaxial system. Axes I, II, and III are now combined with the assumption that there is no differentiation between medical and mental health conditions. Rather than list psychosocial and contextual factors affecting clients on Axis IV, counselors will now list V codes or 900 codes (used for conditions related to neglect, sexual abuse, physical abuse, and psychological abuse) as stand-alone diagnoses or alongside another diagnosis as long as the stressors are relevant to the client's mental disorder(s). An expanded listing of V codes is included in the *DSM-5*. Although the *DSM-5* does not include direction for formatting, counselors may also use special notations for psychosocial and environmental considerations relevant to the diagnosis. Similarly, counselors will no longer note a GAF score on Axis V. Rather, the *DSM-5* advises that clinicians find ways to note distress and/or disability in functioning, perhaps using the World Health Organization Disability Assessment Schedule 2.0 (WHO-

Table 2.1
Comparison of Multiaxial Versus Nonaxial Systems

DSM-III *and* DSM-IV *Multiaxial System*	DSM-5 *Nonaxial System*
Axis I: Clinical disorders and other conditions that are the focus of treatment *Axis II:* Personality disorders and intellectual disability (i.e., mental retardation) *Axis III:* General medical conditions	Combined attention to clinical disorders, including personality disorders and intellectual disability (i.e., mental retardation); other conditions that are the focus of treatment; and medical conditions continue to be listed as a part of the diagnosis.
Axis IV: Psychosocial and environmental stressors	Special notations for psychosocial and contextual factors are now listed by using V codes or *ICD-10-CM* Z codes. An expanded list of V codes has been provided in the *DSM-5*. In rare cases where psychosocial and contextual factors are not listed, counselors can include the specific factor as it is related to the client's diagnosis.
Axis V: Global Assessment of Functioning (GAF)	Special notations for disability are listed by using V codes or *ICD-10-CM* Z codes. The World Health Organization Disability Assessment Schedule 2.0 (WHODAS 2.0) has been included in Section III and is listed on APA's website (www.psychiatry.org) within the online assessment measures section.

DAS 2.0; WHO, 2010) as a dimensional assessment of functioning. Again, the manual does not include directions for formatting or presenting this assessment.

Note

Counselors are not qualified to diagnose medical conditions. However, it is important to record all historical medical information. Counselors must work closely with medical professionals to identify any medical conditions.

Once *ICD-10-CM* is implemented (October 2014), all codes in the Other Conditions That May Be a Focus of Clinical Attention chapter of the *DSM-5* will change. Z codes will replace V codes, and T codes will replace 900 codes. The only exception is V62.89 borderline intellectual functioning, in which the *ICD-10-CM* code is R41.83. (See APA, 2013, pp. 715–727.)

♦ ♦ ♦

The advantage to dropping the multiaxial system confirms what counselors from a wellness perspective have been claiming for decades—that differentiation among emotional, behavioral, physiological, psychosocial, and contextual factors is misleading and conveys a message that mental illness is unrelated to physical, biological, and medical problems. Combining these axes has the potential to be more inclusive, embracing more aspects of client functioning. However, practitioners will need to be intentional and systematic when incorporating more holistic assessments and notations into the diagnostic process so that their diagnoses do not become a simple listing of primary *DSM-5* disorders.

Note

The *DSM-5* has dropped the GAF scale because of a lack of clinical utility and reliability. The WHODAS 2.0 (WHO, 2010) has been included in Section III of the manual. This scale is used in the *ICD* as a standardized assessment of functioning for individuals diagnosed with mental disorders. The *DSM-5* notes, however, that "it has not been possible to completely separate normal and pathological symptom expressions contained in diagnostic criteria" (APA, 2013, p. 21). Counselors who use the WHODAS 2.0 are responsible for ensuring they do so in accordance with the *ACA Code of Ethics* (ACA, 2014); this includes ensuring appropriateness of instruments through review of psychometric properties, appropriateness for client population, and appropriate use of interpretation. This is particularly important because the *DSM-5* does not include information regarding the validity or reliability of the WHODAS 2.0.

♦ ♦ ♦

Critics of the multiaxial system argued that the system is cumbersome and ambiguous, thus providing poor clinical utility (Bassett & Beiser, 1991; Jampala, Sierles, & Taylor, 1986; Paris, 2013). Furthermore, many clinicians will agree that although the multiaxial system was well intentioned, client reports typically stopped at Axis I. In cases where Axis II was listed, some clients would feel stigmatized by their diagnostic label (Aviram, Brodsky, & Stanley, 2006; Fritz, 2012). Enhanced attention to V codes within the nonaxial system may also help counselors emphasize a client's entire worldview and systemic context in a way that informs the therapeutic process. If used intentionally, movement to a nonaxial system may help increase client understanding, remind counselors that medical and psychosocial issues are just as important as mental health diagnoses, and reduce stigma.

Challenges of moving to a nonaxial system include conceptual lack of clarity regarding how clinicians are going to implement the nonaxial system. If clinicians struggled to use holistic assessment within a multiaxial system that essentially required some attention to psychosocial and environmental issues and overall distress and disability, will they actually take the time to incorporate these elements into a more ambiguous format? We anticipate problems with interpretation, specifically regarding the combination of Axes I, II, and III, within the counseling profession and among interdisciplinary teams. Although counselors can include subjective descriptors next to the client's diagnosis, there is no telling whether these will carry over to the next clinician or if they will make sense to a different party. Other challenges include delays as insurance companies and governmental agencies update their claim forms and reporting procedures to accommodate *DSM-5* changes. Major challenges for both counselors and clients are to be expected as helping professionals, insurance and service providers, and public or private institutions move toward nonaxial documentation of diagnosis.

With these new changes, diagnoses will be cited listing the primary diagnosis first, followed by all psychosocial, contextual, and disability factors. For example, a client presents with depressive symptoms during withdrawal of a severe cocaine use disorder. She has just revealed that she is being sexually abused by her husband who just kicked her out of her home. This client would receive a diagnosis of 292.84 cocaine-induced depressive disorder, with onset during withdrawal. An additional diagnosis of 304.20 severe cocaine use disorder would also be recorded, as well as 995.83 spouse violence, sexual, suspected, initial encounter and V60.0 homelessness. Any subsequent notations related to a mental health diagnosis would follow. More information regarding recording diagnoses can be found in Chapter 17 of this *Learning Companion*.

Chapter Organization

Overall organization of chapters within the *DSM* changed significantly to reflect a developmental approach to listing diagnoses. Diagnoses are now ordered in terms of similar symptomatology with presumed underlying vulnerabilities grouped together. This organization is indicative of the life-span (i.e., developmental) approach taken by the DSM-5 Task Force. Readers will notice that disorders more frequently diagnosed in childhood, such as intellectual and learning disabilities, are renamed as neurodevelopmental disorders and appear at the beginning of the manual. Diagnoses more commonly seen in older adults, such as neurocognitive disorders, appear at the end of the *DSM-5*. This modification more closely follows the *ICD* and was intended to increase practitioners' use of the manual for differential diagnosis.

Other structural changes include significant modifications to overall classification of disorders. The mood disorders section has been separated into two distinct classes: depressive disorders and bipolar and related disorders. Anxiety disorders have been broken out into three separate diagnostic chapters: anxiety disorders, obsessive-compulsive and related disorders, and trauma- and stressor-related disorders. In another large structural and philosophical change, the *DSM-5* eliminated disorders usually diagnosed in infancy, childhood, or adolescence. Disorders within this section were incorporated into a new neurodevelopmental disorders chapter or, if not presumed to be neurodevelopmental in nature, relocated to other specific sections of the *DSM-5*. The DSM-5 Task Force justified this change because many of the disorders in this section are also seen in adulthood (e.g., ADHD; Jones, 2013), and many disorders seen in childhood may be precursors to concerns in adulthood. This section, originally created for convenience, led clinicians to erroneously believe there was a clear distinction between "adult" and "childhood" disorders. Critics felt this division was confusing and prevented clinicians from diagnosing children with "adult" disorders such as major depression or posttraumatic stress disorder (PTSD). Likewise, adults diagnosed with disorders such as ADHD have reported feeling stigmatized with limited treatment options (Katragadda & Schubiner, 2007). In terms of structure, diagnoses that were removed from this section, such as childhood feeding and eating disorders, can now be found within their associated sections, just later in the manual. For example, the feeding and eating disorders section of the *DSM-5* now includes pica and rumination.

Other comprehensive structural changes include the removal of labeling disorders as *not otherwise specified* (NOS) so practitioners can be more specific and accurate in their diagnosis. As a replacement, the *DSM-5* has two options for cases in which the client's presenting condition does not meet the criteria for a specific category: other specified disorder and unspecified disorder. The use of *other specified disorder* allows counselors to identify the specific reason why the client does not meet the criteria for a disorder. *Unspecified disorder* is used when a clinician chooses not to specify a reason for not diagnosing a more specific disorder or determines there is not enough information to be more specific. This is also supportive of dimensional, rather than categorical, classification (this idea is expanded on in the next section, *DSM-5* Philosophical Changes). Finally, language throughout the *DSM-5* changed so that medical conditions, previously referred to as general medical conditions, are renamed *another medical condition*. This change reflects the philosophical assumption that mental health disorders *are* medical conditions.

Note

Clinical judgment is the driving force for whether the client's presenting condition should be "other specified" or "unspecified." APA is very clear in that the use of either is the decision of the clinician.

◆ ◆ ◆

Readers will also note that the *DSM-5* includes both *ICD-9-CM* and *ICD-10-CM* codes. This inclusion is a response to a mandate from the U.S. Department of Health and Human Services that required all health care providers to use *IDC-10-CM* codes by October 2014. To ease this transition, the *DSM-5* lists both code numbers in the Appendix section. This will aid in standardization among mental health care providers and will also allow for easier transition to the new *ICD-10-CM* codes and revised billing processes.

The following list is a summary of the major structural changes in the *DSM-5*:

- removal of the multiaxial system;
- modification to chapter order to reflect a developmental approach;
- division into three sections: Section I: *DSM-5* Basics; Section II: Diagnostic Criteria and Codes; and Section III: Emerging Measures and Models;
- replacement of the first diagnostic chapter of the *DSM-IV-TR*, Disorders Usually First Diagnosed in Infancy, Childhood, or Adolescence, with a new Neurodevelopmental Disorders chapter;
- inclusion of both *ICD-9-CM* and *ICD-10-CM* codes;
- modifications to the classification of disorders: Bipolar and related disorders and depressive disorders are now stand-alone chapters; anxiety disorders was separated into three distinct categories (anxiety disorders, obsessive-compulsive and related disorders, and trauma- and stressor-related disorders); and
- removal of NOS and inclusion of other specified and unspecified disorders.

Note

Whereas *ICD* code numbers were originally created for statistical tracking of diseases, not reimbursement, most medical systems within the United States use these codes for billing purposes. The *DSM-III* was coordinated with the development of the *ICD-9*. Other versions of the *DSM* continued to use the *ICD-9* codes, despite that fact that the *ICD-10* was first published in 1992.

◆ ◆ ◆

DSM-5 Philosophical Changes

Two philosophical changes, spearheaded by the DSM-5 Task Force, have modified the way in which counselors will approach diagnosis when using the *DSM-5*. The first philosophical change involves a shift in focus from phenomenological interpretations (i.e., symptom identification and behavioral observations—a medical model) to identifiable pathophysiological origins (i.e., functional changes associated with or resulting from disease or injury—a biological model). The second philosophical change involves the use of dimensions as opposed to diagnostic categories. Although these two changes are theoretically similar, each philosophy has a unique impact on the way in which counselors approach diagnosis, treatment planning, and interdisciplinary communication.

Regarding the first shift, the DSM-5 Task Force decided that using a bioecological perspective, as opposed to identifying symptomatology, was a more empirically sound way to approach diagnostic classifications (Kupfer & Regier, 2011). Neurobiologists believe that problems with growth and development of the brain or central nervous system adversely affect behavioral patterns, learning, and social interactions. Officially included in the *DSM-5 Research Agenda* (Kupfer, First, & Regier, 2002), the idea that disorders should be grouped by underlying neurobiological similarities rather than phenomenological observations (i.e., criteria) is not a new one (Kupfer & Regier, 2011). Supporters of a pathophysiologic (i.e., biological) approach to mental illness emphasize findings from genetics, neuroimaging, cognitive science, and pathophysiology need to drive psychiatric diagnosis. Followers claim the overuse of NOS diagnoses and problems with comorbidity as key indicators that previous versions of the *DSM* relied too heavily on "psychodynamic, a priori hypotheses" rather than "external, empirical indicators" (Kupfer & Regier, 2011, p. 672). Kupfer and Regier, respectively the chair and vice-chair of the DSM-5 Task Force, even proposed "keeping the *DSM* as a 'living document' that can be readily updated to reflect changes in our understanding of neuroscience and pathophysiology in a world of (sometimes) rapid and dramatic neuroscience discovery" (Kupfer & Regier, 2011, p. 674).

The impact of this philosophical shift on the current *DSM* is not as significant as proponents would have hoped. With regard to grouping disorders by underlying pathophysiological similarities, Kupfer and Regier (2011) stated,

> We realized from our *Research Agenda* conference series that we would not be able to accomplish by the *DSM-5*'s deadline all of the things we set out to and, in fact, that portions of that agenda related to advances in neurosciences were already being addressed in other arenas . . . [which] will be very informative for subsequent versions: *DSM-5.1, DSM-5.2*, and beyond. (p. 673)

Although not as significant as some would have liked, this movement has affected the current *DSM* and will most certainly have an impact on future iterations of the manual. First, the way in which disorders are grouped, as previously mentioned, has changed. By listing diagnoses in terms of clinical expressions across the life span, the DSM-5 Task Force highlighted neurodevelopmental disorders such as autism and ADHD as having biological origins. This movement led the task force to eliminate the first section because they felt using a bioecological perspective to focus on the first 2 decades of life, when rapid changes in behavior, emotion, and cognition occur, was more empirically sound. Although critics claim that removal of disorders usually diagnosed in infancy, childhood, or adolescence points too heavily to a biological basis of behavior and deemphasizes sociocultural variations, this position is in alignment with the pathophysiologic movement adopted by the DSM-5 Task Force.

Within the narrative sections of the *DSM-5*, readers will notice inclusion of neurobiologic findings, such as genetic and physiologic risk factors, and life-span development and course alongside diagnostic criteria. Proponents claim this biological and life-span information, in conjunction with current criteria, will allow practitioners to better understand the role of genetic and physiologic risk factors, prognostic indicators, and biologic markers in shaping client risk and prognosis.

The DSM-5 Task Force did not fully accept or wholly incorporate classification of all mental illness from a neurodevelopmental and biological perspective. However, even the slightest movement toward adoption of this philosophy has had a significant impact on the current manual, as evidenced by the changes just described. Moreover, this movement has fueled another philosophical shift: recognition that categorical systems found within the *DSM-IV-TR* should be supplemented with dimensional models of assessment.

Although professional counselors may find themselves flipping through the *DSM-5* in search of reorganized diagnoses, we suspect they may be most affected by the shift from categorical to dimensional assessment. The philosophical change and resulting implications are addressed throughout the remainder of this chapter. We begin the discussion with a historical overview of categorical and dimensional assessment along with explanation of philosophical challenges of dimensional assessment; we conclude by explaining dimensional assessments within the *DSM-5*.

From Categorical to Dimensional Assessment

In the 1960s and 1970s, scholars criticized psychiatric diagnosis for lack of diagnostic reliability, meaning there was little diagnostic agreement among helping professionals who evaluated the same individual (Spitzer & Fleiss, 1974). Revisions to the *DSM*, beginning with the *DSM-III*, provided practitioners and researchers with a more reliable common language for diagnostic criteria (Scotti & Morris, 2000). Rather than providing only narrative descriptions regarding manifestation of disorders, the *DSM-III* and *DSM-IV* included discrete clinical criteria that, when considered together, allowed professionals to identify the presence or absence of a disorder (APA, 2000; Jones, 2012a; Scotti & Morris, 2000). This system was intended to help users better understand complex and obscure phenomena of mental illness. In turn, creators of the system assumed a categorical approach would help mental health professionals find a common language for treatment, select empirically based interventions, calculate course and prognosis, and differentiate between clients who present with a mental health disorder and those who do not (First, 2010; Jones, 2012b). This philosophical shift resulted in etiologically based treatment options that integrated seemingly varied symptoms into a particular diagnosis (Millon, 1991). Even researchers were affected, as the *DSM* now serves as an important foundation for research conceptualization.

Several professionals have applauded modifications to this categorical classification system for allowing clinicians to plan treatments tailored to the special needs of the client (Bedell, Hunter, & Corrigan, 1997; Millon, 1991; Widiger & Frances, 1985). Categorical diagnoses have also assisted with accountability and record keeping, treatment planning, communication between helping professionals, and identification of clients with issues beyond one's areas of expertise (Hinkle, 1999). These revisions have been praised for including more empirically based criteria, thus allowing for what was assumed to be a more scientifically sound classification system (Maser et al., 1991). Although the categorical system was a vast improvement over the descriptive categories of *DSM-I* and *DSM-II*, the categorical approach poses several important limitations that DSM-5 Task Force members attempted to address.

Challenges to the Categorical Philosophy

Categorical diagnosis assumes that all individuals diagnosed with a given disorder have similar symptoms and attributes (First, 2010; Jones, 2012a). This system also presumes that mental disorders have little variation, that populations are relatively homogeneous, and that diagnoses are objective, discrete phenomena. However, the absoluteness of this yes/no approach has caused significant problems in terms of clinical utility among researchers and clinicians (Brown & Barlow, 2005; Demjaha et al., 2009; First, 2010). Critics of the categorical system point to significant limitations in terms of diagnostic agreement and dispute the assumption that there is a clear-cut line between having and not having a mental disorder (Kraemer, Noda, & O'Hara, 2004). Overuse of NOS diagnoses is sufficient evidence that the line between diagnosis and no diagnosis is not as clear as practitioners would like it to be. Specifically among counselors, there is excessive use of the NOS specifier when clients face significant distress or impairment but do not meet all criteria for a given disorder (Jones, 2012a).

Other problems with categorical diagnosis include disproportionate comorbidity among disorders and disputes regarding psychological constructs. For example, epidemiologic researchers argue that comorbidity between depressive and anxiety disorders is aberrantly high (Kessler et al., 1996; Mineka, Watson, & Clark, 1998). Magee, Eaton, Wittchen, McGonagle, and Kessler (1996) reported agoraphobia, simple phobia, and social phobia to be highly comorbid. Researchers also found that individuals with coexisting disorders experience more severe symptomatology. Diagnostic concurrence has also been identified between substance abuse and mood, anxiety, somatoform, personality, and eating disorders (Andrews, Slade, & Issakidis, 2002; Mineka et al., 1998; Subica, Claypoole, & Wylie, 2011; Widiger & Coker, 2003). In response to these findings, Jones (2012b) claimed, "It seems that diagnostic comorbidity is more the norm rather than the exception" (p. 482). Because the limitations of a purely categorical approach are widely documented, APA introduced dimensional assessments within the *DSM-5*.

Dimensional Assessments in the DSM-5

The *DSM-5* has proposed specific assessment tools to help mental health professionals diagnose disorders. This philosophy, seen throughout the manual, moves beyond categorical description and considers etiological, biological, and behavioral dimensions of psychopathology. Dimensional assessments are a significant change to the philosophy of previous versions of the *DSM* in that the *DSM-5* attempts to capture characteristics such as frequency, duration, and severity of individuals' experiences with disorders.

Although the categorical model has not been abandoned, dimensional assessments have been included in some areas to allow clinicians to evaluate clients on a full range of symptoms. This approach also allows clinicians to gather additional information to diagnose, create individualized treatment plans, and, as opposed to categorical models, evaluate client outcomes more effectively. Severity ratings for anxiety and depression as well as guidance for assessing suicide risk can now be found within the new manual. Beginning in Chapter 3, Depressive Disorders, of this *Learning Companion*, we provide several examples of assessments that measure severity (i.e., dimensional assessments). These can also be found on APA's website under Online Assessment Measures (www.psychiatry.org/practice/dsm/dsm5/online-assessment-measures).

Readers should note that the use of dimensional assessments is in its infancy. A dimensional approach to rating severity for the core symptoms of schizophrenia spectrum and other psychotic disorders, for example, is included in the *DSM-5*'s Section III, Emerging Measures and Models. Under the previous categorical model followed in *DSM-III* and *DSM-IV*, a client diagnosed with schizophrenia who was experiencing severe positive symptoms such as persecutory hallucinations would have no way for this to be included as a part of his or her diagnostic classification. With the proposed rating system, counselors can indicate levels of severity on various criteria so that they can document concerns more effectively and determine the degree to which the client is experiencing decreases in symptomatology as a result of treatment (APA, 2013). Because disorders present with different degrees of severity and in the company of comorbid symptoms, the *DSM-5* includes several standardized dimensional assessments proposed for future iterations of the manual. Similar to the idea of incorporating pathophysiological etiologies, these ideas need to evolve through research and continued advancements within psychiatry and counseling. To date, only one dimensional assessment is included in the *DSM-5*.

Critics of Dimensional Assessment

Some counselors speculate that introduction of dimensional assessments will bring about considerable potential for diagnostic inflation, claiming that APA-approved dimensional assessments are cumbersome, are difficult to administer, and lack rigorous psychometric validation (First, 2010; Jones, 2012a). Zimmerman and McGlinchey (2008) analyzed data from more than 300 psychiatrists and found that, despite the wide availability of assessments, fewer than 20% of the participants used depression scales to evaluate depression. Participants clearly identified three reasons why they did not administer a scale: (a) lack of confidence in scale utility, (b) lack of training, and (c) lack of time to administer an assessment. Although some studies have documented improvements in clinical care as a result of assessment (Trivedi et al., 2006), First (2010) expressed concerns that "clinicians are likely to view dimensional measures more as an administrative burden than as a clinically useful tool" (p. 471).

Critics also warn that severity specifiers already included in some *DSM* diagnoses lack clinical utility (First, 2010). For example, the *DSM-III-R* introduced severity and course specifiers for all but eight diagnoses. These specifiers were ignored by clinicians and, with the exception of specifiers for major depressive and manic episodes, were removed from the *DSM-IV-TR*. Research has provided little insight into why clinicians continue to ignore these specifiers (First, 2010; First et al., 2004). Given these criticisms and potential shortcomings of the *DSM-5*, we are intentional about highlighting dimensional components of diagnoses and incorporating implications in case studies and associated learning activities throughout this *Learning Companion*.

Cross-Cutting Assessments in the *DSM-5*

In addition to incorporating dimensional assessments for specific diagnoses, the *DSM-5* has also included several cross-cutting assessment measures in Section III of the manual (APA, 2013, pp. 733–748). Although they are not required for use at this time, the measures are included for research and exploration purposes. These measures are not specific to any individual disorder, taking into consideration symptoms characteristic of clients in nearly all clinical settings (APA, 2013; Jones, 2012a). These assessments evaluate symptoms that are of high importance to all clinicians, such as suicidal ideation, depressed mood, sleep disturbance, and substance abuse. Cross-cutting assessment scales included in the *DSM-5* were developed by the National Institutes of Health Patient-Reported Outcomes Measurement Information System and consist of two levels. The first level includes self-report measures that evaluate major clinical domains. Clients rate items on a Likert-type scale ranging from 0 (*none–not at all*) to 4 (*severe–nearly every day*). If any Level 1 area is considered clinically significant, counselors will follow up with a Level 2 measure. Level 2 measures provide a more detailed assessment of specific symptoms identified by the Level 1 measure. Like dimensional assessments, these measures are in their infancy; researchers do not yet know how use of the measures will influence diagnostic process and clinical utility. Still, it is likely that future editions of the *DSM* will include enhanced attention to cross-cutting assessments.

Critics of cross-cutting assessments claim there is a lack of psychometric data backing up some of these measures (Widiger & Samuel, 2008). A hot topic of debate, concerns over the utilization of cross-cutting assessments include lack of clinical utility due to the complexity and time-consuming nature of the assessments, need for extensive training for counseling professionals, and variance in validity and reliability of specific instruments (First, 2010; Jones, 2012a). These constraints, as well as the potential cost for procuring the assessments, fuel skepticism regarding the cross-cutting assessment approach.

We realize these structural and philosophical changes are significant. Readers will note that we include focused commentary regarding how philosophical shifts, structural changes, and specific diagnostic changes affect the counseling profession. In the next section, we highlight major diagnostic changes found within the *DSM-5*. Each of these changes will be explored in greater depth throughout this book.

Major Diagnostic Highlights

Although the following changes will be addressed comprehensively in subsequent chapters, we provide a general idea of the major changes readers should anticipate while reading this *Learning Companion*.

1. Mental retardation is now referred to as intellectual disability (intellectual developmental disorder). Severity of disability is now determined by adaptive functioning rather than IQ score. New criteria include severity measures for mild, moderate, severe, and profound intellectual disability. Intellectual developmental disorder is placed in parentheses to reflect the term used in the *ICD*.
2. Communication disorders have been restructured to include social communication disorder (SCD). SCD is intended to identify persistent difficulties in the social use of verbal and nonverbal communication. Individuals diagnosed under the *DSM-IV-TR* with pervasive developmental disorder NOS may meet criteria for SCD.
3. Two diagnostic categories have been added to communication disorders: language disorder and speech disorder. Language disorder combines *DSM-IV-TR* expressive and mixed receptive-expressive language disorders.
4. Phonological disorder is now referred to as speech sound disorder.
5. Stuttering is now referred to as childhood-onset fluency disorder.
6. Autism, Asperger's disorder, childhood disintegrative disorder, and pervasive developmental disorder have been replaced with one umbrella diagnosis: autism spectrum disorder. The purpose of this change is to improve diagnostic efficacy, accuracy, and consistency.
7. Specific learning disorders have been expanded to represent distinct disorders that involve problems with the acquisition and/or use of one of more of the following skills: oral language, reading, written, and/or mathematical operations. Now referred to as specific learning disorder, this diagnosis is intended to combine reading disorder, mathematics disorder, disorder of written expression, and learning disorder NOS.
8. Schizophrenia spectrum and other psychotic disorders remove special treatment of bizarre delusions and hallucinations involving conversations or commentary. Schizophrenia no longer includes attention to five subtypes.
9. Disruptive mood dysregulation disorder is added with the intent of addressing overdiagnosis of bipolar disorder in children. Symptoms include persistent irritability and persistent outbursts three or more times a week for a year.
10. Premenstrual dysphoric disorder is added to depressive disorders.
11. The *DSM-5* eliminates Criterion E, also known as the "grief exclusion," for a major depressive episode. Individuals who have experienced the loss of a loved one can now be diagnosed with depression if they meet other criteria for a major depressive episode.

12. Depressive and bipolar disorders include new specifiers such as *with catatonia, with anxious distress*, and *with mixed features*. These specifiers are intended to account for experiences often comorbid with mood disorders yet not part of standard criteria.

13. Anxiety disorders include separate diagnostic categories for agoraphobia and panic disorder. Clients no longer need to experience panic to be diagnosed with agoraphobia.

14. The anxiety disorders section includes diagnostic criteria for panic attacks. The specifier *with panic attacks* may now be used across all diagnostic categories of anxiety and within other sections of the *DSM-5*.

15. A new chapter on obsessive-compulsive and related disorders groups disorders such as obsessive-compulsive disorder, body dysmorphic disorder, and trichotillomania together as opposed to having them scattered throughout the manual. It also includes several new disorders including excoriation (skin-picking) disorder and hoarding disorder. Hoarding disorder is characterized by persistent difficulty disposing of possessions, regardless of monetary or personal value.

16. A new chapter on trauma- and stressor-related disorders groups disorders related to trauma and/or situational stress factors such as reactive attachment disorder, disinhibited social engagement disorder, PTSD, acute stress disorder, and adjustment disorder.

17. PTSD was revised to include four distinct diagnostic clusters (as opposed to three in the *DSM-IV-TR*); the section includes considerable attention to developmentally appropriate criteria for children and adolescents.

18. The feeding and eating disorders section includes a new disorder, binge eating disorder.

19. The personality disorders section has not changed and will maintain the same 10 categories as the *DSM-IV-TR*. However, Section III on emerging measures and models includes a framework for diagnosing personality disorders using trait-specific methodology.

20. The previous sexual and gender identity disorders section is now divided into three separate sections: sexual dysfunctions, gender dysphoria, and paraphilic disorders. Pedophilia disorder is now referred to as pedophilic disorder.

21. The sleep-wake disorders section includes revisions with enhanced attention to biological indicators for diagnosis of many disorders.

22. The substance-related and addictive disorders section is expanded to include addictive disorders; however, only gambling disorder falls in this category. Previous substance dependence and substance abuse criteria are combined into one overarching disorder: substance use disorders. Significant changes have been made to coding, recording, and specifiers for these disorders.

23. The chapter on neurocognitive disorders (previously cognitive disorders) removes language regarding dementia, includes enhanced attention to a range of impairment as evidenced by incorporation of major and mild neurocognitive disorders, and includes additional attention to neurological assessment and basis of the condition.

24. Section III includes several new disorders for study, such as attenuated psychosis syndrome (which describes individuals at high risk for psychosis who do not meet the criteria for a psychotic disorder), Internet gaming disorder, nonsuicidal self-injury, and suicidal-behavioral disorder.

25. Section III also contains a detailed discussion of culture and diagnosis, including tools for in-depth cultural assessment and a description of some common cultural syndromes, idioms of distress, and causal explanations relevant to clinical practice.

26. Within each diagnostic category, the NOS diagnosis has been replaced with other specified and unspecified diagnoses. The other specified category is used in situations in which the clinician chooses to communicate the specific reason that the presentation does not meet the criteria for the specific disorder.

Note

Readers will notice that only in Part One of this *Learning Companion* are other specified and un-specified diagnoses included. Readers can find more information on other specified and unspecified diagnoses in Chapter 17.

◆ ◆ ◆

Implications of the *DSM-5*

Implications for Clients

The *DSM-5* changes outlined in this chapter and in the remainder of this *Learning Companion* are likely to have significant implications for clients who experience mental health concerns. While some believe the shift toward viewing mental illness as organic, with less focus on environmental precipitants of symptoms, could potentially reduce the stigma associated with mental disorders (Yang, Wonpat-Borja, Opler, & Corcoran, 2010), others wonder whether this philosophy will lead individuals to be viewed as fundamentally flawed rather than human beings who are struggling with developmental and environmental life tasks (Ben-Zeev, Young, & Corrigan, 2010; Frances, 2012b). In addition, the potential for dimensional criteria to lower diagnostic thresholds may increase the number of individuals diagnosed and boost false positives, increase labeling and associated stigma, and raise health care costs within the general population (Ben-Zeev et al., 2010; Frances, 2010; Jones, 2012a, 2013). Loosening criteria for diagnosis also raises the potential for an increase in unnecessary pharmaceutical treatment among those who seek first-line treatment from medical providers (First, 2011; Frances, 2010, 2012b). Thus, counselors need to be especially careful not to overpathologize symptoms that could be better explained by factors external to individuals (Jones, 2011). Conversely, some proponents of the *DSM-5* believe a more dimensional system could normalize mental health concerns and facilitate help seeking and access to care among consumers (Andrews et al., 2007; Rosenbaum & Pollock, 2002).

Initial research on new diagnostic thresholds seems to indicate an increase in the rates of diagnosis for the general population, particularly in the areas of behavioral addictions and psychosis, as well as depressive, anxiety, eating, and neurocognitive disorders (Frances, 2010; Jones, Gill, & Ray, 2012; Mewton, Slade, McBride, Grove, & Teesson, 2011). For example, under the new combined substance use disorders, prevalence rates may increase to a staggering 12.4% (Jones et al., 2012). Similarly, lower diagnostic thresholds for ADHD have been noted as areas of concern among mental health professionals (British Psychological Society, 2011). Although these are all legitimate concerns, the reality of lower diagnostic thresholds remains to be seen.

In response to worries regarding loosened criteria, APA (2012) published documentation regarding reliability and prevalence of some diagnoses based on the field trials. However, this attempt at clarifying the anticipated increase in diagnoses has been met with strong criticism from scholars who believe the research is not adequate (Frances, 2011, 2012a; Jones, 2011). It is hoped implementation of the *DSM-5* will result in data that help mental health professionals clarify usefulness of diagnostic thresholds for reaching consumers without artificially inflating diagnostic prevalence rates. Note that, throughout this *DSM-5 Learning Companion*, we provide information regarding diagnostic prevalence based on research using *DSM-IV-TR* criteria.

Concerns regarding potential increases in medications accompany concerns around the shift toward viewing mental illness as organic. In particular, many mental health professionals fear that lowering diagnostic thresholds and viewing symptoms as biological will end in more medications prescribed to newly diagnosed clients (Frances, 2010, 2012b; Jones, 2011). This is of particular concern given questions about financial relationships between task force members and pharmaceutical companies (Moisse, 2012). Although essential for some clients, the long- and short-term effects of medications are often unknown. For clients, the outcome could be an increase in the recommendation to take medications with less focus on other types of empirically supported treatments that are, by nature, less invasive. Finally, some frequently assigned disorders such as substance abuse, substance dependence, and disorders within NOS categories will no longer be included in the *DSM-5*, resulting in reevaluation and perhaps reassignment of long-standing diagnoses.

Implications for Counselors

Changes in the *DSM-5* have potential widespread implications for counselors. Without understanding current diagnostic nomenclature, counselors may have trouble with re-imbursement and thus suffer reduced credibility and potentially lose the opportunity to help clients. Whether counselors agree or disagree with the philosophy and nomenclature, there is no disputing the *DSM* "is the key to millions of dollars in insurance coverage for psychotherapy, hospitalization, and medications" (Kutchins & Kirk, 1997, p. 12).

The *DSM-5* represents the first major structural change to the diagnostic classifications (including the layout, biopsychological model, and collapsing of the multiaxial system) since the publication of the *DSM-III* in 1980. As a result, there is a need for comprehensive training for counselors across settings. These radical changes affect seasoned counselors as well as new professionals, counselor educators, and counseling students (Jones, 2013).

Because of the pathophysiological model purported in the *DSM-5*, there are extant concerns regarding potential increases in psychopharmacological treatment (Mewton et al., 2011). The potential for a concomitant reduction in psychotherapeutic treatments may significantly affect provision of counseling services and holistic client care (First, 2011; Frances, 2010, 2012b). Because the psychiatric profession as a whole is trained in the medical model, the importance of retaining the efficacy of psychotherapy is critical. Counselors can and should advocate on community, state, and national levels in addition to actively engaging in research on evidenced-based practices.

A primary concern for counseling professionals is the lowering of diagnostic thresholds. The criteria for PTSD, acute stress disorder, ADHD, and substance use disorders have all been lowered (Frances, 2010; Jones et al., 2012; Mewton et al., 2011). There is concern that this could lead to vast overdiagnosis (Jones et al., 2012). According to Mewton et al. (2011), reducing the number of the criteria for diagnosis in the *DSM-5* could increase prevalence rates of alcohol use disorders by 61.7%. As previously stated, however, the credibility of these studies remains to be seen as others have found low or no impact on prevalence rates (Beesdo et al., 2011; Pardini, Frick, & Moffitt, 2010). In response to these critiques, David Kupfer, chair of the DSM-5 Task Force, stated:

> Charges that *DSM-5* will lower diagnostic thresholds and lead to a higher prevalence of mental disorders are patently wrong. Results from our field trials, secondary data analyses, and other studies indicate that there will be essentially no change in the overall rates of disorders once *DSM-5* is in use. For most disorders, including the addictive disorders that recently drew headlines, thresholds will remain the same or will increase. With other disorders, diagnostic criteria are being refined to hone specificity. The challenge is to balance specificity and sensitivity, to make sure that the language characterizes a disorder as accurately as possible. (Kupfer, 2012, p. 1)

There is also a concern of pathologizing normal behavioral patterns that lead to potential deleterious effects. The extant stigma of incurring a mental health diagnosis, including the cultural and spiritual impact it holds, should be carefully addressed across helping professions. The cost of treatment and ensuing medications can be burdensome as well. Because evidenced-based practices support the efficacy of psychotherapeutic treatment, medication can potentially be unnecessary and even dangerous (Olfson & Marcus, 2010). All of these factors hold specific implications for counselors across all levels of training.

Future of the *DSM-5:* Where Will It Go From Here?

Even as we work to understand implications of the *DSM-5*, others are already speculating on changes to upcoming iterations of the *DSM*. Research on the utility and efficacy of new diagnostic categories, cross-cutting and dimensional assessments, lowered threshold, and collapsing of the multiaxial system will affect the future direction of the manual. The ramifications of this, positive and negative, will not be fully understood until the *DSM-5* is fully implemented across a multitude of settings. In the final section of this *Learning Companion*, we include a summary chapter regarding research and practice implications for counselors. We hope to provide avenues for counseling professionals to have an active voice in upcoming revisions to the *DSM-5*.

References

American Counseling Association. (2014). *ACA code of ethics.* Alexandria, VA: Author.

American Psychiatric Association. (1952). *Diagnostic and statistical manual of mental disorders.* Washington, DC: Author.

American Psychiatric Association. (1968). *Diagnostic and statistical manual of mental disorders* (2nd ed.). Washington, DC: Author.

American Psychiatric Association. (1980). *Diagnostic and statistical manual of mental disorders* (3rd ed.). Washington, DC: Author.

American Psychiatric Association. (1987). *Diagnostic and statistical manual of mental disorders* (3rd ed., rev.). Washington, DC: Author.

American Psychiatric Association. (1994). *Diagnostic and statistical manual of mental disorders* (4th ed.). Washington, DC: Author.

American Psychiatric Association. (2000). *Diagnostic and statistical manual of mental disorders* (4th ed., text rev.). Washington, DC: Author.

American Psychiatric Association. (2012). *DSM-5 field trials.* Retrieved from http://www.dsm5.org/Research/Pages/DSM-5FieldTrials.aspx

American Psychiatric Association. (2013). *Diagnostic and statistical manual of mental disorders* (5th ed.). Arlington, VA: Author.

Andrews, G., Brugha, T., Thase, M. E., Duffy, F. F., Rucci, P., & Slade, T. (2007). Dimensionality and the category of major depressive episode. *International Journal of Methods in Psychiatric Research, 16,* S41–S51.

Andrews, G., Slade, T., & Issakidis, C. (2002). Deconstructing current comorbidity: Data from the Australian National Survey of Mental Health and Well-Being. *British Journal of Psychiatry, 181,* 306–314.

Aviram, R. B., Brodsky, B. S., & Stanley, B. (2006). Borderline personality disorder, stigma, and treatment implications. *Harvard Review of Psychiatry, 14,* 249–256.

Bassett, A. S., & Beiser, M. (1991). *DSM-III:* Use of the multiaxial diagnostic system in clinical practice. *Canadian Journal of Psychiatry, 36,* 270–274.

Bedell, J. R., Hunter, R. H., & Corrigan, P. W. (1997). Current approaches to assessment and treatment of persons with serious mental illness. *Professional Psychology: Research and Practice, 28,* 217–228.

Beesdo, K., Winkel, S., Pine, D., Hoyer, J., Lieb, R., & Wittchen, H. U. (2011). The diagnostic threshold of generalized anxiety disorder in the community: A developmental perspective. *Journal of Psychiatric Research, 45,* 962–972. doi:10.1016/j.jpsychires.2010.12.007

Ben-Zeev, D., Young, M. A., & Corrigan, P. W. (2010). *DSM-V* and the stigma of mental illness. *Journal of Mental Health, 19,* 318–327.

Blashfield, R. K. (1998). Diagnostic models and systems. In A. S. Bellack, M. Herson, & C. R. Reynolds (Eds.), *Clinical psychology: Assessment* (Vol. 4, pp. 57–79). New York, NY: Elsevier Science.

British Psychological Society. (2011). *Response to the American Psychiatric Association: DSM-5 development.* Retrieved from http://apps.bps.org.uk/_publicationfiles/consultation-responses/DSM-5%202011%20-%20BPS%20response.pdf

Brown, T. A., & Barlow, D. H. (2005). Dimensional versus categorical classification of mental disorders in the fifth edition of the *Diagnostic and Statistical Manual of Mental Disorders* and beyond: Comment on the special section. *Journal of Abnormal Psychology, 114,* 551–556.

Centers for Disease Control and Prevention, National Center for Health Statistics. (1998). *The international classification of diseases, ninth revision, clinical modification (ICD-9-CM)*. Atlanta, GA: Author.

Centers for Disease Control and Prevention, National Center for Health Statistics. (2014). *The international classification of diseases, 10th revision, clinical modification (ICD-10-CM)*. Atlanta, GA: Author.

Demjaha, A., Morgan, K., Morgan, C., Landau, S., Dean, K., Reichenberg, A., . . . Dazzan, P. (2009). Combining dimensional and categorical representation of psychosis: The way forward for the *DSM-V* and *ICD-11*? *Psychological Medicine, 39,* 1943–1955. doi:10.1017/S0033291709990651

Eriksen, K., & Kress, V. E. (2006). The *DSM* and the professional counseling identity: Bridging the gap. *Journal of Mental Health Counseling, 28,* 202–217.

First, M. (2010). Clinical utility in the revision of the *Diagnostic and Statistical Manual of Mental Disorders* (DSM). *Professional Psychology: Research and Practice, 41,* 465–473. doi:10.1037/a0021511

First, M. (2011). *DSM-5* proposals for mood disorders: A cost–benefit analysis. *Current Opinion in Psychiatry, 24,* 1–9.

First, M., Pincus, H., Levine, J., Williams, J., Ustun, B., & Peele, R. (2004). Clinical utility as a criterion for revising psychiatric diagnoses. *American Journal of Psychiatry, 161,* 946–954.

Frances, A. (2010, February 11). Opening Pandora's box: The 19 worst suggestions for *DSM-5*. *Psychiatric Times,* 1–3.

Frances, A. (2011, June 3). Who needs *DSM-5*? A strong warning comes from professional counselors. *Psychology Today.* Retrieved from http://www.psychologytoday.com/blog/dsm5-in-distress/201106/who-needs-dsm-5

Frances, A. (2012a, October 30). *DSM 5* field trials discredit APA. *Psychology Today.* Retrieved from http://www.psychologytoday.com/blog/dsm5-in-distress/201210/dsm-5-field-trials-discredit-apa

Frances, A. (2012b, December 2). *DSM 5* is guide not bible—Ignore its ten worst changes. *Psychology Today.* Retrieved from http://www.psychologytoday.com/blog/dsm5-in-distress/201212/dsm-5-is-guide-not-bible-ignore-its-ten-worst-changes

Fritz, J. C. (2012). *"She's such a borderline": Exploring the stigma of borderline personality disorder through the eyes of the clinician* (Unpublished doctoral dissertation). Smith College, School for Social Work.

Health Insurance Portability and Accountability Act of 1996, Pub. L. 104–191, 110 Stat. 1936.

Hinkle, J. S. (1999). A voice from the trenches: A reaction to Ivey and Ivey (1998). *Journal of Counseling & Development, 77,* 474–483.

Houts, A. C. (2002). Discovery, invention, and the expansion of the modern *Diagnostic and Statistical Manuals of Mental Disorders*. In M. L. Malik & L. E. Beutler (Eds.), *Rethinking the DSM: A psychological perspective* (pp. 17–65). Washington, DC: American Psychological Association.

Ivey, A. E., & Ivey, M. B. (1998). Reframing *DSM-IV*: Positive strategies from developmental counseling and therapy. *Journal of Counseling & Development, 76,* 334–350.

Jampala, V. C., Sierles, F. S., & Taylor, M. A. (1986). Consumers' views of *DSM-III*: Attitudes and practices of U.S. psychiatrists and 1984 graduating psychiatric residents. *American Journal of Psychiatry, 143,* 148–153.

Jones, K. D. (2011). *American Psychological Association divisions criticize DSM-5* [Web blog]. Alexandria, VA: American Counseling Association. Retrieved from http://my.counseling.org/2011/10/24/american-psychological-association-divisions-criticize-dsm-5/

Jones, K. D. (2012a). A critique of the *DSM-5* field trials. *Journal of Nervous and Mental Disease, 200,* 517–519.

Jones, K. D. (2012b). Dimensional and cross-cutting assessment in the *DSM-5*. *Journal of Counseling & Development, 90,* 481–487.

Jones, K. D. (2013). *American Counseling Association DSM-5 webinar.* Retrieved from http://www.counseling.org/Resources/Webinars.aspx

Jones, K. D., Gill, C. S., & Ray, S. (2012). Review of the proposed *DSM-5* substance use disorder. *Journal of Addictions & Offender Counseling, 33,* 115–123. doi:10.1002/j.2161-1874.2012.00009.x

Katragadda, S., & Schubiner, H. (2007). ADHD in children, adolescents, and adults. *Primary Care: Clinics in Office Practice, 34,* 317–341. doi:10.1016/j.pop.2007.04.012

Kessler, R. C., Nelson, C. B., McGonagle, K. A., Liu, J., Swartz, M., & Blazer, D. G. (1996). Comorbidity of *DSM-III-R* major depressive disorder in the general population: Results from the U.S. National Comorbidity Survey. *British Journal of Psychiatry, 168*(Suppl. 30), 17–30.

Kraemer, H. C. (2007). *DSM* categories and dimensions in clinical and research contexts. *International Journal of Methods in Psychiatric Research, 16,* S8–S15.

Kraemer, H. C., Noda, A., & O'Hara, R. (2004). Categorical versus dimensional approaches to diagnosis: Methodological challenges. *Journal of Psychiatric Research, 38,* 17–25.

Kupfer, D. J. (2012, June 1). Dr. Kupfer defends *DSM-5*. *Medscape*. Retrieved from http://www.medscape.com/viewarticle/764735_2

Kupfer, D. J., First, M. B., & Regier, D. A. (Eds.). (2002). *DSM-5 research agenda*. Washington, DC: American Psychiatric Association.

Kupfer, D. J., & Regier, D. A. (2011). Neuroscience, clinical evidence, and the future of psychiatric classification in *DSM-5*. *American Journal of Psychiatry, 168,* 672–674.

Kutchins, H., & Kirk, S. A. (1997). *Making us crazy: DSM—The psychiatric bible and the creation of mental disorders*. New York, NY: Free Press.

Magee, W. J., Eaton, W. W., Wittchen, H. U., McGonagle, K. A., & Kessler, R. C. (1996). Agoraphobia, simple phobia, and social phobia in the National Comorbidity Survey. *Archives of General Psychiatry, 53,* 159–168.

Malik, M. L., & Beutler, L. E. (2002). *Rethinking the* DSM: *A psychological perspective*. Washington, DC: American Psychological Association.

Maser, J. D., Kaelber, C., & Weise, R. E. (1991). International use and attitudes toward *DSM-III* and *DSM-III-R*: Growing consensus in psychiatric classification. *Journal of Abnormal Psychology, 100,* 271–280.

Mewton, L., Slade, T., McBride, O., Grove, R., & Teesson, M. (2011). An evaluation of the proposed *DSM-5* alcohol use disorder criteria using Australian national data. *Addiction, 106,* 941–950. doi:10.1111/j.1360-0443.2010.03340.x

Millon, T. (1991). Classification in psychopathology: Rationale, alternatives, and standards. *Journal of Abnormal Psychology, 100,* 245–261.

Mineka, S., Watson, D., & Clark, L. A. (1998). Comorbidity of anxiety and unipolar mood disorders. *Annual Review of Psychology, 49,* 377–412.

Moisse, K. (2012, March 13). *DSM-5* criticized for financial conflicts of interest. *ABC News*. Retrieved from http://abcnews.go.com/Health/MindMoodNews/dsm-fire-financial-conflicts/story?id=15909673

Myers, J. E., Sweeney, T. J., & Witmer, M. (2000). Counseling for wellness: A holistic model for treatment planning. *Journal of Counseling & Development, 78,* 251–266.

Olfson, M., & Marcus, S. C. (2010). National trends in outpatient psychotherapy. *American Journal of Psychiatry, 167,* 1456–1463.

Pardini, D. A., Frick, P. J., & Moffitt, T. E. (2010). Building an evidence base for *DSM-5* conceptualizations of oppositional defiant disorder and conduct disorder: Introduction to the special section. *Journal of Abnormal Psychology, 119,* 683–688.

Paris, J. (2013). *The intelligent clinician's guide to the DSM-5*. New York, NY: Oxford University Press.

Rogler, L. H. (1997). Making sense of historical changes in the *Diagnostic and Statistical Manual of Mental Disorders*: Five propositions. *Journal of Health Social Behavior, 38,* 9–20.

Rosenbaum, J. F., & Pollock, R. (2002, June 20). *DSM V*: Plans and perspectives. *Medscape Psychiatry*. Retrieved from http://www.medscape.org/viewarticle/436403

Sanders, J. L. (2011). A distinct language and a historic pendulum: The evolution of the *Diagnostic and Statistical Manual of Mental Disorders*. *Archives of Psychiatric Nursing, 25,* 394–403. doi:10.1016/j.apnu.2010.10.002

Scotti, J. R., & Morris, T. L. (2000). Diagnosis and classification. In M. Hersen & R. T. Ammerman (Eds.), *Advanced abnormal child psychology* (pp. 15–32). Mahwah, NJ: Erlbaum.

Spitzer, R., & Fleiss, J. L. (1974). A re-analysis of the reliability of psychiatric diagnosis. *British Journal of Psychiatry, 125,* 341–347.

Subica, A. M., Claypoole, K. H., & Wylie, A. M. (2011). PTSD's mediation of the relationships between trauma, depression, substance abuse, mental health, and physical health in individuals with severe mental illness: Evaluating a comprehensive model. *Schizophrenia Research, 136,* 104–109. doi:10.1016/j.pain.2011.04.019

Trivedi, M., Rush, A., Wisniewski, S., Nierenberg, A., Warden, D., Ritz, L., . . . Fava, M. (2006). Evaluation of outcomes with citalopram for depression using measurement-based care in STAR*D: Implications for clinical practice. *American Journal of Psychiatry, 163,* 28–40.

Widiger, T. A., & Coker, L. A. (2003). Mental disorders as discrete clinical conditions: Dimensional versus categorical classification. In M. Hersen & S. M. Turner (Eds.), *Adult psychopathology and diagnosis* (4th ed., pp. 3–35). New York, NY: Wiley.

Widiger, T. A., & Frances, A. (1985). The *DSM-III* personality disorders: Perspective from psychology. *Archives of General Psychiatry, 42,* 615–623.

Widiger, T. A., & Samuel, D. B. (2008). Diagnostic categories or dimensions? A question for the *Diagnostic and Statistical Manual of Mental Disorders–fifth edition. Journal of Abnormal Psychology, 114,* 494–504. doi:10.1037/0021-843X.114.4.494

Wilson, M. (1993). *DSM-III* and the transformation of American psychiatry: A history. *American Journal of Psychiatry, 150,* 399–410.

World Health Organization. (1949). *International statistical classification of diseases, 6th revision.* Geneva, Switzerland: Author.

World Health Organization. (1968). *International statistical classification of diseases, 8th revision.* Geneva, Switzerland: Author.

World Health Organization. (1975). *International statistical classification of diseases, 9th revision.* Geneva, Switzerland: Author.

World Health Organization. (2007). *International statistical classification of diseases and related health problems, 10th revision.* Geneva, Switzerland: Author.

World Health Organization. (2010). *World Health Organization Disability Assessment Schedule 2.0–WHODAS 2.0.* Geneva, Switzerland: Author.

Yang, L. H., Wonpat-Borja, A. J., Opler, M. G., & Corcoran, C. M. (2010). Potential stigma associated with inclusion of the psychosis risk syndrome in the *DSM-V:* An empirical question. *Schizophrenia Research, 120,* 42–48. doi:10.1016/j.schres.2010.03.012

Zimmerman, M., & McGlinchey, J. (2008). Why don't psychiatrists use scales to measure outcome when treating depressed patients? *Journal of Clinical Psychiatry, 69,* 1916–1919.

Introduction to Diagnostic Changes:
Part One to Part Four Overview

In the remaining chapters, we provide an overview of changes to the diagnostic criteria from the *DSM-IV-TR* to the *DSM-5* as well as render comprehensive information for all new diagnoses. We help readers understand these changes and additions by highlighting similarities and differences among diagnostic clusters, explaining common differential diagnoses, and providing case studies and questions to enhance clinical utility. Because we are licensed professional counselors, we present this information in a way that closely relates to the work that our readers, as counselors, typically perform.

In terms of organization of this *Learning Companion*, the reader will find diagnostic classifications presented in a sequence of what counselors or counselors-in-training typically encounter. For example, mood and anxiety disturbances are addressed before diagnoses commonly made by other professionals, such as neurodevelopmental disorders. Our intent is to target areas that will most significantly affect counselors. While no guidebook can speak to the myriad tasks that counselors perform or the wide range of settings in which counselors work, we did organize this *Learning Companion* in such as way that it is useful and relevant to work typically performed by counselors. Rather than adhering to the developmental format of the *DSM-5* or ordering our chapters by prevalence within the general population, we have organized this book by what counselors most frequently diagnose. With the role of a counselor in mind, the *Learning Companion* is divided, by relevance, into four sections:

Part One: Changes and Implications Involving Mood, Anxiety, and Stressor-Related Concerns

Part Two: Changes and Implications Involving Addictive, Impulse-Control, and Specific Behavior-Related Concerns

Part Three: Changes and Implications Involving Diagnoses Commonly Made by Other Professionals

Part Four: Future Changes and Practice Implications for Counselors

The goal of this organizational structure is to assist counselors in their everyday work. For example, the first chapter in Part One addresses depressive disorders because depression is one of the most prevalent mental illness worldwide. The second chapter in Part One addresses anxiety, which is, to date, the most common class of mental illness present in the general population. Aside from being relevant to the work that most counselors perform, this layout parallels the *DSM-5* by grouping together diagnoses that have higher rates of co-occurrence. Although all diagnoses have clinical utility within a counseling setting, we aimed to organize this *Learning Companion* in a way that is most relevant to the actual work that counselors do. In keeping with our aim of making this *Learning Companion* an accessible and handy guidebook for readers, we have grouped the references of related chapters at the end of each part of the book.

♦ ♦ ♦

Part One

Changes and Implications Involving Mood, Anxiety, and Stressor-Related Concerns

Part One Introduction

The disorders covered in Part One are divided into six chapters: Chapter 3: Depressive Disorders; Chapter 4: Bipolar and Related Disorders; Chapter 5: Anxiety Disorders; Chapter 6: Obsessive-Compulsive and Related Disorders; Chapter 7: Trauma- and Stressor-Related Disorders; and Chapter 8: Gender Dysphoria in Children, Adolescents, and Adults. This part includes diagnoses, such as major depressive disorder (MDD) and PTSD, that involve affective distress commonly seen by counselors across various work settings and client populations. In each chapter, readers will find a basic description of the diagnostic classification, an overview of specific disorders covered, highlights and essential features of each disorder (including differential diagnoses), and a comprehensive review of specific changes, when applicable, from the *DSM-IV-TR* (APA, 2000) to the *DSM-5* (APA, 2013a). For newly minted disorders and disorders commonly seen by counselors, we present case studies to help counselors understand and apply diagnoses. In keeping with our intent to discuss conditions relevant to counselors, we discuss pervasiveness of disorders among the general population as well as etiology and treatment. Unless explicitly stated, prevalence rates are based on *DSM-IV-TR* criteria.

Major changes to look for in Part One include the removal of the *DSM-IV-TR* major depression "bereavement exclusion" (APA, 2013d, p. 1). This change recognizes recent research revealing little to no systematic differences between individuals who develop a major depression in response to bereavement and those who develop major depression in response to other severe stressors, such as being physically assaulted or betrayed by a spouse (Wakefield & First, 2012; Zisook, Shear, & Kendler, 2007). Removal is consistent with the *ICD*, which has never had a grief exclusion criterion for major depression. Counselors will also see changes to traumatic stress disorders such as PTSD and acute stress disorder, which have added exposure criteria and taken away the requirement for individuals to experience extreme fear reactions such as horror and helplessness.

Major additions to look for in this section include the addition of disruptive mood dysregulation disorder, addition of premenstrual dysphoric disorder, and renaming dysthymic disorder to persistent depressive disorder within the chapter on depressive disorders. Also look for the addition of hoarding disorder, excoriation (skin-picking) disorder, and disinhibited social engagement disorder under the chapter on trauma and stressor-related disorders. As with the *DSM-IV-TR*, panic attack criteria are provided. However, counselors can now use this specifier for disorders throughout the *DSM-5*. Finally, readers will note gender dysphoria replaces the previously termed gender identity disorder, and separate criteria are listed for children. Readers will also notice the separation of gender dysphoria from paraphilias and sexual dysfunctions, which strongly supports the idea that this diagnosis is not a pathological disorder. For gender dysphoria, the separation of criteria sets for children from those for adolescents and adults more accurately captures the experience of children, adolescents, and adults struggling with gender identity issues.

◆ ◆ ◆

Chapter 3

Depressive Disorders

Depression refers to a sustained condition of prolonged emotional dejection, sadness, and withdrawal. This persistent affective state "colors a person's perception of the world" (Reid & Wise, 1995, p. 145). Depressive disorders are diagnosed when a person's depressed mood is prolonged enough to interfere with regular daily functioning (APA, 2013a; NIMH, 2012).

Differing from addiction, impulse control, and behavioral concerns, depressive disorders primarily affect individuals through disturbance of mood and anxious symptoms that are often co-occurring (NIMH, 2013a, 2013b). Prevalence among the general population is extremely high in comparison with other mental health disorders. The Anxiety and Depression Association of America (ADAA; 2013), for example, posits that close to 50% of individuals diagnosed with an anxiety disorder also meet the criteria for a depressive disorder. Because the prevalence of depression in the general population is approximately 10%, these diagnoses are frequently the focus of clinical attention for counselors (ADAA, 2013; CDC, 2010).

Major Changes From *DSM-IV-TR* to *DSM-5*

The Depressive Disorders chapter of the *DSM-5* contains diagnoses that were previously listed within the Mood Disorders chapter of the *DSM-IV-TR*. It is noteworthy that the DSM-5 Task Force separated mood disorders into two distinct classes: depressive and bipolar. Therefore, the Depressive Disorders chapter no longer contains any disorders related to mania. These disorders are now included in a separate chapter titled Bipolar and Related Disorders in the *DSM-5* (see Chapter 4 of this *Learning Companion*).

Aside from distinguishing between depressive and bipolar disorders, the most prevalent change to the Depressive Disorders chapter of the *DSM-5* is the addition of disruptive mood dysregulation disorder (DMDD) and premenstrual dysphoric disorder (PMDD). Other changes include the exclusion of bereavement as part of a major depressive episode, reconceptualization of dysthymic disorder as persistent depressive disorder including chronic cases of MDD, and clarifications to help counselors differentiate between depression and events involving significant loss such as bereavement or financial devastation

(APA, 2013a, 2013d). The *DSM-5* continues to use three groups of criteria to diagnose depressive disorders: (a) episodes, (b) specific disorders, and (c) specifiers indicating the most recent episode and course.

Differential Diagnosis

Comorbidity is more so the rule rather than the exception with anxiety and depressive disorders. For example, symptoms for MDD and generalized anxiety disorder (GAD) converge in several specific areas, including excessive fatigue, difficulty concentrating, and sleep disturbance (Aina & Susman, 2006). The National Comorbidity Survey found that 60% of clients diagnosed with MDD also have symptoms related to anxiety disorder (Kessler et al., 2003). However, there are specific differences among these disorders. For example, individuals who have depressive disorders typically do not display marked fear and uncertainty common with anxiety. Moreover, clients diagnosed with anxiety disorders do not usually display persistent feelings of sadness, hopelessness, and anhedonia typically observed by counselors within the context of depressive disorders. As we discuss below, the *DSM-5* includes a new *with anxious distress* specifier in hopes of capturing overlapping features of depressive and anxiety disorders.

Etiology and Treatment

There are multiple theories as to the etiology of depressive disorders, including biological factors, personality factors, neurochemistry, developmental processes, and environmental factors (Barlow, 2002; Kessler et al., 2003; Saveanu & Nemeroff, 2012). Treatments for these disorders are most successful when started early in the course of the disorder, and counselors should always recommend a medical assessment to rule out physical causes. The most common and effective forms of treatment for depressive disorders combine medication and psychotherapy (Keller et al., 2000; NIMH, 2013a). Counselors will find numerous online assessment measures for depressive disorders, such as the Patient Health Questionnaire, for adults, on APA's website. Counselors should note that these assessments are still under review and should only be used to enhance clinical decision making, not as stand-alone diagnostic tools.

In terms of treatment outcomes, research indicates that depressive disorders typically respond to psychotherapeutic interventions (Hausmann et al., 2007; NIMH, 2013a, 2013b). NIMH (2013a, 2013c) and the ADAA (2013) have identified cognitive behavior therapy (CBT) and interpersonal therapy as the two most efficacious psychotherapeutic treatment modalities for depressive disorders. CBT assists individuals with restructuring and reframing negative thought processes, and interpersonal therapy helps them understand and work through discordant relationships (Corey, 2013; Ivey, D'Andrea, & Ivey, 2012).

Implications for Counselors

The counselor's ability to recognize depressive disorders is important because nearly 10% of the adult population in the United States meets the criteria for a depressive disorder at any given point in time (CDC, 2010). Depressive disorders are more prevalent in women than in men, and although persons from any racial or social class background can be affected, these disorders are more commonly diagnosed in individuals of African American or Latino decent, individuals who are unemployed or unable to work, individuals who have previously been married, and individuals without health insurance. Clients who have a family history of depression also present at higher risk (CDC, 2010; Morrison, 2006).

Depression is the leading cause of disability in the United States and can account for as many as 50% of clients within a typical mental health practice (CDC, 2010; Morrison, 2006). Counselors often make the mistake of overlooking underlying symptoms of depression, focusing rather on the client's chief complaint, such as problems with mood or adjustment difficulties. Counselors should always inquire about other problems, such as substance abuse, somatic complaints, or recent changes in medical status. Failure to do so can result in the assumption that a depressive disorder is the client's only presenting problem.

To help readers better understand changes from the *DSM-IV-TR* to the *DSM-5*, the rest of this chapter outlines each disorder within the Depressive Disorders chapter of the *DSM-5*. Readers should note that we have focused on major changes from the *DSM-IV-TR* to the *DSM-5*; however, this is not a stand-alone resource for diagnosis. Although a summary and special considerations for counselors are provided for each disorder, when diagnosing clients, counselors need to reference the *DSM-5*. It is essential that the diagnostic criteria and features, subtypes and specifiers (if applicable), prevalence, course, and risk and prognostic factors for each disorder are clearly understood prior to diagnosis.

296.99 Disruptive Mood Dysregulation Disorder (F34.8)

No one gets me, especially my dad. I do the right thing and I get in trouble. That's why I get mad all the time and sometimes I get in fights. My little sister is so stupid that I can't help but get mad at her. When she does dumb stuff I yell at her, and sometimes I yell at my teachers too. I shouldn't have to do homework because I know all this stuff anyway, and I get so mad when they try to make me. They keep telling me I yell all the time, but it's not my fault. They just don't understand. —Barry

Disruptive mood dysregulation disorder (DMDD) was not listed in the *DSM-IV-TR* but was added to the *DSM-5* as a response to the rise in children diagnosed with bipolar disorder (Blader & Carlson, 2007; Moreno et al., 2007). Explanations for the increasing rates of bipolar disorder diagnosis in children and youth vary; however, some practitioners believe underdiagnosis was related to a lack of developmentally appropriate diagnostic criteria. Issues with diagnosing bipolar disorder in children and youth include a lack of clarity regarding how counselors should operationalize manic or hypomanic episodes, especially those shorter than 4 days duration. Additionally, counselors were concerned whether severe nonepisodic irritability was developmental as opposed to a diagnosable pathological disorder. The inclusion of DMDD aims to clarify these issues and allows for an appropriate diagnosis of children who do not fit well into the diagnoses of either conduct disorder or bipolar disorder. It is interesting to note that the placement of DMDD is not within either bipolar disorder or impulse disorder. Because of the characteristic feature of mood dysregulation, the DSM-5 Task Force decided the best placement for DMDD was within depressive disorders.

Essential Features

DMDD is a depressive disorder diagnosis intended for children and adolescents between the ages of 6 and 18 with onset before the age of 10 (APA, 2013a). The disorder is marked by severe, recurrent outbursts of temper, either verbal or behavioral, that are significantly out of proportion in intensity and duration with situational factors and the developmental stage of the individual. The individual's mood between temper outbursts is persistently irritable or angry. Frequency must average at least three times per week for at least 12 months or more, and the behavior must be observable by others (e.g., parents, teachers, peers). The behaviors must occur in at least two settings (e.g., school and home) and must be severe in at least one of these settings. The individual cannot be free from severe recurrent temper outbursts for longer than 3 months (APA, 2013a). See the Diagnostic Criteria section below for a complete listing of DMDD criteria.

Special Considerations

Counselors diagnosing DMDD need to consider whether symptoms of an abnormally elevated or expansive mood have ever been present most of the day during the course of 1 day or have a duration of longer than 1 day. If so, counselors need to consider the presence of grandiosity or inflated self-esteem, decreased need for sleep, pressured speech, flight of ideas, distractibility, increase in goal-directed activity, or excessive involvement in activities with a high potential for painful consequences. If these symptoms are present, a diagnosis of bipolar disorder might be warranted. Special care should also be taken to differentiate abnormally elevated mood from developmentally appropriate mood elevation because the latter could occur in the context of anticipation or participation in a special event.

Note

Although initially proposed, criteria regarding hyperarousal were removed because these symptoms could be accounted for by assigning an additional diagnosis of ADHD.

◆ ◆ ◆

Cultural Considerations

Unlike some other depressive disorders, such as Bipolar I disorder, rates of DMDD are higher in male children in clinical settings than within the general population (APA, 2013a). Although there is little research regarding DMDD from a cultural perspective, research indicates that individuals diagnosed with DMDD do not have high familial rates of bipolar disorder (Leibenluft, 2011).

Differential Diagnosis

DMDD cannot be diagnosed if behavioral concerns are exclusively present during a major depressive episode or are better accounted for by another diagnosis. Additionally, DMDD cannot be diagnosed alongside oppositional defiant disorder (ODD) or bipolar disorder, although it can coexist with ADHD, conduct disorder, and substance use disorder. Only DMDD should be assigned if the client meets the criteria for this disorder as well as ODD. Finally, counselors must ensure that no other explanation, such as a medical or neurological condition, better accounts for the behavior.

Note

If an individual has ever experienced a manic or hypomanic episode, the diagnosis of DMDD should not be assigned.

◆ ◆ ◆

Coding, Recording, and Specifiers

There is only one diagnostic code for DMDD: 296.99 (F34.8). There are no specifiers for this diagnosis.

Diagnostic Criteria for DMDD 296.99 (F34.8)

A. Severe recurrent temper outbursts manifested verbally (e.g., verbal rages) and/or behaviorally (e.g., physical aggression toward people or property) that are grossly out of proportion in intensity or duration to the situation or provocation.
B. The temper outbursts are inconsistent with developmental level.
C. The temper outbursts occur, on average, three or more times per week.
D. The mood between temper outbursts is persistently irritable or angry most of the day, nearly every day, and is observable by others (e.g., parents, teachers, peers).
E. Criteria A–D have been present for 12 or more months. Throughout that time, the individual has not had a period lasting 3 or more consecutive months without all of the symptoms in Criteria A–D.
F. Criteria A and D are present in at least two of three settings (e.g., at home, at school, with peers) and are severe in at least one of these.
G. The diagnosis should not be made for the first time before age 6 years or after age 18 years.
H. By history or observation, the age at onset of Criteria A–E is before 10 years.

I. There has never been a distinct period lasting more than 1 day during which the full symptoms criteria, except duration, for a manic or hypomanic episode have been met.

Note: Developmentally appropriate mood elevation, such as occurs in the context of a highly positive event or its anticipation, should not be considered as a symptom of mania or hypomania.

J. The behaviors do not occur exclusively during an episode of major depressive disorder and are not better explained by another mental disorder (e.g., autism spectrum disorder, posttraumatic stress disorder, separation anxiety disorder, persistent depressive disorder [dysthymia]).

Note: This diagnosis cannot coexist with oppositional defiant disorder, intermittent explosive disorder, or bipolar disorder, though it can coexist with others, including major depressive disorder, attention-deficit/hyperactivity disorder, conduct disorder, and substance use disorder. Individuals whose symptoms meet criteria for both disruptive mood dysregulation disorder and oppositional defiant disorder should only be given the diagnosis of disruptive mood dysregulation disorder. If an individual has ever experienced a manic or hypomanic episode, the diagnosis of disruptive mood dysregulation disorder should not be assigned.

K. The symptoms are not attributable to the physiological effects of a substance or to another medical or neurological condition.

 Example

Angelo is a 16-year-old Latino American high school student living with his biological, married parents in a middle-class urban environment. He has no siblings and reports feeling particularly close to his mother. Angelo's dad has traveled extensively for work for the past 7 years, and Angelo reports not having a close relationship with him. Angelo presents as physically healthy although slightly underweight and generally small in stature. His physical appearance is unkempt, his clothes are soiled, and he appears to have problems with personal hygiene. His mother states that getting Angelo to complete daily living activities is often very difficult; she does not push him unless she feels it is very important. When asked about his personal hygiene, Angelo reports that showering is stupid because he is just going to get dirty again, and he feels he looks fine. Aptitude testing suggests Angelo is of above-average intelligence. However, he is in danger of not passing the 11th grade, mainly because of his refusal to turn in homework and failure to attend class. Angelo states that school is pointless because he will never use the information in real life. He frequently gets into verbal conflicts with his teachers.

Angelo reports that he has had many acquaintances over the years but none who are long-term friends. When asked why, he reports that "they are idiots and don't do what I tell them to do so I stop hanging out with them." Angelo admits to wanting to hit people when they make him angry. He has been suspended from school for fighting. Angelo is active in sports and excels in baseball, for which he has a high batting average. However, school reports indicate he is frequently left out of the lineup or removed from the game because of excessive anger and verbal aggression toward other players. His coach states that he could have a future in baseball, but his reputation for poor sportsmanship prohibits him from progressing in the sport. He is not friends with any of his teammates.

Angelo's mother states that beginning at approximately 9 years of age, Angelo began showing signs of undue irritability and outbursts. These outbursts included yelling, throwing objects, and refusing to engage in social or daily living activities. This behavior occurred both at home and at school. Over the course of the past year, Angelo's outbursts have occurred at least three times per week, with 3 weeks the longest Angelo has gone without an outburst. He has been required to speak to the school counselor two times over the course of the year because of his outbursts. When asked about his mood, Angelo reports feelings of sadness, helplessness, and hopelessness but denies any thoughts of harm to himself. Angelo has never experienced symptoms of a manic episode. Angelo has no history of previous clinical diagnosis or substance utilization.

◆ ◆ ◆

Diagnostic Questions

1. Do Angelo's presenting symptoms meet the criteria for a depressive disorder? If so, which disorder?
2. Based on the disorder identified in Question 1, which symptom(s) led you to select that diagnosis?
3. What would be the reason(s) a counselor may not diagnose Angelo with ODD?
4. Would Angelo be more accurately diagnosed with bipolar disorder? If so, why? If not, why not?
5. What rule-outs would you consider for Angelo's case?
6. What other information may be needed to make an accurate clinical diagnosis?

296._ _ Major Depressive Disorder, Single Episode (F32._) and Recurrent Episodes (F33._)

I just didn't want to live anymore. The feelings of worthlessness and hopelessness were overwhelming. I couldn't get off the sofa. The exhaustion was crushing, and all I wanted to do was sleep. I lost a lot of weight because I just didn't care about food or much of anything else anymore. This went on for days, and nothing seemed to help. I just felt depressed. —Angela

Major depressive disorder (MDD) has a long history of inclusion in the *DSM* diagnostic system and is one of the most frequently diagnosed mental disorders among health professionals (NIMH, 2013a). The NIMH (2013a) estimates that 6.7% of the U.S. population suffers from MDD in any given year. The Substance Abuse and Mental Health Services Administration (SAMHSA; 2008) reports that only 64.5% of people experiencing MDD actually seek treatment.

Note

Blank spaces (i.e., "_ _") in the *ICD-9-CM* (CDC, 1998) and *ICD-10-CM* (CDC, 2014) diagnostic codes represent frequency and severity specifiers clinicians must select to properly record diagnoses. These codes are listed throughout this *Learning Companion*. Complete *ICD-9-CM* and *ICD-10-CM* codes can be found in the Appendixes section of the *DSM-5* by alphabetical and numerical listing.

◆ ◆ ◆

MDD is characterized by nearly universal—meaning everyday nearly almost all day—feelings of sadness and loss of interest in previously enjoyed activities. Many individuals will experience loss of appetite, fatigue, problems with sleep, and suicidal ideation. Others may also experience agitation, trouble with concentration, and excessive feelings of guilt. Because feelings of worthlessness predominate for individuals with MDD, low self-esteem and excessive guilt (either real or imagined) are not uncommon. Major depression can lead to a variety of emotional and physical problems and is considered a chronic illness that may require long-term mental health and psychopharmaceutical treatments.

Major Changes From *DSM-IV-TR* to *DSM-5*

A major and somewhat controversial change to the *DSM-5* is the removal of the bereavement exclusion. In the *DSM-IV-TR*, the diagnosis of major depression was excluded for individuals who experienced depression for up to 2 months after the death of a loved one. The idea of excluding bereaved individuals from diagnosis began with the *DSM-III*, which noted that "uncomplicated bereavement" is not the same as major depression (Kendler, Myers, & Zisook, 2008). However, researchers and the DSM-5 Task Force have since made the argument that bereavement-related depression does not differ significantly from other stressor-related depressive episodes such as those related to divorce or job loss (APA, 2013c, 2013d). This change is also consistent with long-standing *ICD* criteria for depression.

Kendler et al. (2008) studied individuals who experienced depression related to various types of stressful life events. They compared responses of those reporting bereavement-related depressive episodes with those who reported other life events as a trigger. The results did not differ significantly in frequency or duration of symptoms, nor did they differ significantly in the number of Criterion A symptoms identified. Participants with bereavement-related depressive symptoms were more likely to be women and tended to be older at age of symptomatology onset. These participants tended to seek treatment less frequently and expressed more fatigue and loss of interest but less guilt than peers who experienced depression related to another stressful event. Because of these and similar research findings, the bereavement exclusion was not carried over to the *DSM-5* (APA, 2013c, 2013d).

In response to criticism that removal of bereavement could pathologize a normal grieving process, APA stated that bereavement does not always lead to a diagnosis of MDD. Whereas a natural grieving process can occur without a diagnosis of MDD, individuals who experience clinically significant and impairing symptoms deserve appropriate care for concerns related to bereavement and depression. In recognition of this difficult balance, the *DSM-5* includes language that advises practitioners to carefully differentiate normal grieving from MDD.

Essential Features

MDD can be diagnosed at any age, but the likelihood of onset increases significantly once an individual reaches puberty (APA, 2013a). Although prevalence rates in the U.S. population peak for people in their early 20s, it is not uncommon for the first episode of major depression to occur in mid or later life. The disorder is marked by a single or recurrent major depressive episodes, which must consist of at least five of nine criteria. These criteria differ from an individual's normal functioning and include

- depressed mood almost every day, with irritable mood more often noted in children and adolescents;
- a marked diminished interest or pleasure in activities almost every day;
- a significant change in daily appetite or a significant weight change (e.g., either a weight gain or loss of more than 5% body weight in 1 month not due to dieting; in children, failure to make expected weight gains is also considered);
- sleep disturbance, either insomnia or hypersomnia, nearly every day;
- a change in normal physical pace, either psychomotor agitation or retardation, and in addition to a self-report, psychomotor problems must be observable by others;
- noteworthy energy loss or fatigue almost every day, not including guilt or self-blame related to being ill;
- excessive or inappropriate guilt, which can be delusional, or feelings of worthlessness;
- reduced ability to concentrate, focus, or make decisions almost daily, as reported by self or others; and
- frequent suicidal thoughts or ideation with or without a specific plan for committing suicide or attempting suicide (APA, 2013a).

The symptoms must persist for a 2-week period. Counselors should not include symptoms that are related to another medical condition when diagnosing (e.g., difficulty concentrating because of a traumatic brain injury).

Note

Many people with chronic illness experience depression. In fact, depression is one of the most common complications of chronic illness. It is estimated that up to one third of individuals with a serious medical condition experience symptoms of depression.

◆ ◆ ◆

Special Considerations

MDD is associated with high rates of mortality. As many as 40.3% of individuals diagnosed with MDD within a calendar year considered suicide, and 10.4% make an attempt (Office of Applied Research, 2006). Certainly, it is critical that counselors understand issues and criteria related to this condition, particularly when developing and implementing evidence-based treatments for reducing symptoms.

Counselors who work with clients at risk for MDD need to use depression screening and suicide assessment instruments, closely monitoring clients with moderate to severe depressive symptoms. Counselors should also be aware of risk and protective factors unique to each client struggling with MDD. Should a higher level of care, such as inpatient hospitalization, be warranted, counselors must be aware of their ethical obligations in accordance with the *ACA Code of Ethics* (ACA, 2014), organization policies for accessing care, and related laws and procedures in their local practice areas.

Cultural Considerations

In a postmodern, multicultural society, it is challenging to provide cultural norms for how different communities experience any depressive disorder. Despite this, we can provide general guidelines that counselors can use to better understand the role of culture when diagnosing MDD (or any depressive disorder). First, counselors should understand that many people recognize depression as a physical rather than a psychological problem. Patterns of somatization are common among Latinos, Mexican Americans, Puerto Ricans, and Cuban Americans (Guarnaccia, Martinez, & Acosta, 2013). In many ways, however, somatic experience of symptoms is universal across cultures. For example, the inability to sleep and feelings of fatigue are commonly reported and included in diagnostic criteria. Still, individuals in some cultures may be more likely to experience MDD as physical or somatic in nature. Depressive symptoms in many Asian cultures are experienced as physical rather than psychological ailments (Kleinman, 2004). Many Asian clients do not express sadness or tearfulness; instead, they report dullness, uneasiness, feelings of inner pressure, physical aches, dizziness, or feeling tired. Counselors may also discover that Asian immigrants find the idea of mental illness morally offensive and futile (Kleinman, 2004). Although this cultural pattern changes depending on one's acculturation, counselors must become aware of how depressive symptoms manifest and are reported among diverse cultural groups.

Depression tends to be more prevalent for women and older adults, with 70% of the reported cases being female (NIMH, 2013c). Depression is noted as the most significant mental health issue of later life (Myers & Harper, 2004), and almost 50% of those living in nursing homes report depressive symptoms (Koenig & Blazer, 1996). Although most studies indicate that depression is more prevalent among the European American population (Riolo, Nguyen, Greden, & King, 2005), many researchers agree that MDD is underreported or underdiagnosed among many populations, particularly African Americans (Black, Gitlin, & Burke, 2011).

With regard to specific multicultural populations, Latinas and Latinos may be more susceptible to depressive symptoms, especially recent immigrants or those who have had problems with acculturation (Letiecq, Bailey, & Kurtz, 2008; Robison et al., 2009). High-risk factors for Latino Americans, compared with other cultural groups, include economic stressors and a lack social support. Native Americans are another important cultural group to consider (Letiecq et al., 2008) because they have an increased risk of lifetime prevalence of MDD (19.17%). The second most widely reported group are Caucasian Americans (14.58%), followed by Latino Americans (9.64%), African Americans (8.93%), and Asian Americans/Pacific Islanders (8.77%; see Hasin, Goodwin, Stinson, & Grant, 2005).

Counselors need to understand that culture influences not only clients' experience of symptoms but also the language used to report them and clients' decisions about how they will approach treatment. Counselors must also be aware of how culture may affect the likelihood of clients' risk-taking or suicide behavior and influence how clients interact with mental health professionals. First-generation immigrants may be uncomfortable with a client-directed model of counseling; they may need a more directive, hierarchical thera-peutic relationship. Finally, whether working with depression, trauma, or any mental health disorder, counselors must be sensitive to institutional racism and be aware that mental health professionals can unintentionally convey a sense of stigma to clients. Counselors can avoid this by understanding their own biases and refraining from stereotypical behavior. Counselors should always attempt to better understand the cultural worldview of the client.

Differential Diagnosis

Individuals experiencing MDD will have clinically significant distress or impairment in at least one area of daily functioning, such as social, occupational, or other important areas (APA, 2013a), not resulting from a medical condition or substance use. Additionally, the symptoms are not more consistent with another diagnosis, such as schizoaffective disor-der, and are not masking another disorder, such as delusional disorder or other specified schizophrenia spectrum or psychotic disorder. If clients have previously experienced manic or hypomanic episodes not related to medication, substance, or a medical condition, a diagnosis of bipolar disorder may be more appropriate (APA, 2013a). Counselors should differentiate MDD related to a stressor from adjustment disorders with depressed mood by ensuring that full criteria for MDD are met.

Coding, Recording, and Specifiers

Coding and recording for MDD are contingent on single or recurrent episodes and sever-ity, such as *mild, moderate, severe*, and *with psychotic features*, as well as specifiers to note unique features and course. The diagnostic code for a single MDD episode is 296.__ (F32._) and for a recurrent episodes is 296.__ (F33._). Note that the *ICD-9-CM* code is the same for both single and recurrent episodes. The blank spaces indicate specifiers that must be selected by the counselors prior to giving a diagnosis of MDD. Because these specifiers apply to all depressive disorders, we discuss them (and their associated codes) at the end of this chapter. Readers will note, however, that to be considered recurrent, there must be 2 consecutive symptom-free months between episodes in which the criteria are not met. Whereas number of episodes, severity, and course specifiers are always listed following the MDD diagnosis code, there are specifiers without codes that may be used as applicable (APA, 2013a). These are also listed at the end of this chapter.

300.4 Persistent Depressive Disorder (Dysthymia) (F34.1)

I remember being very happy at times as a teenager but that was years ago. I'm sad most days now. Sometimes I just eat and eat and can't stop myself. I don't like the way I look or act, and I feel tired most of the day. Naps don't help, even though I take a lot of them. This has gone on for so long I feel like it will never end. I just don't have any hope anymore. —Matt

Persistent depressive disorder (PDD), known in the *DSM-IV-TR* as dysthymic disorder, was originally called neurotic depression and then relabeled dysthymic disorder in the

DSM-III (Sprock & Fredendall, 2008). In reality, PDD is a consolidation of the *DSM-IV-TR* chronic MDD and dysthymia. A person with PDD presents with depressed mood more days than not for at least 2 years (APA, 2013a). For children, the disorder can appear as a chronic irritable mood, and the mood disturbance must last 1 year or more. Counselors should note it is not uncommon for MDD to precede PDD, as one criterion for PDD is that MDD may be continuously present. This will be noted in the Coding, Recording, and Specifiers section.

Major Changes From *DSM-IV-TR* to *DSM-5*

In previous editions of the *DSM*, dysthymia was considered a long-term, low-grade depression. New *DSM-5* criteria allow for concurrent major depressive episodes, thus leading to a much greater range of experience to be captured within this disorder. In addition to modifying the name, the *DSM-5* no longer excludes the presence of a major depressive episode in the first 2 years of onset. Thus, a diagnosis of PDD may be applied for clients who experience 2 years of long-term, low-grade depression characterized by, for example, depressed mood, low self-esteem, and low energy, as well as clients who have experienced several years of a continuous major depressive episode. The *DSM-5* provides a number of specifiers that allow counselors to denote the specific nature of the PDD experience for any given client.

Essential Features

For a diagnosis of PDD to be assigned during the experience of the depressed mood, the individual will report at least 2 years of depressed mood in which he or she experiences at least two symptoms among the following: (a) poor appetite or overeating, (b) insomnia or hypersomnia, (c) low energy or fatigue, (d) low self-esteem, (e) poor concentration or difficulty making decisions, or (f) feelings of hopelessness (APA, 2013a). However, clients may experience symptoms in excess of these minimal criteria. In children, the disturbance may include irritable rather than depressed mood and need only last 1 year. In either case, the individual may not be free of symptoms for more than 2 consecutive months. Age of onset is typically in childhood, adolescence, or early adulthood (APA, 2013a).

Special Considerations

Authors have noted many similarities between PDD and MDD, but counselors should be aware of distinct differences in the diagnostic criteria. The most notable discrepancy is that PDD is a chronic, ongoing condition rather than one that is experienced through episodes. Previously, the depressive symptoms experienced in PDD were considered to be less severe than major depressive episodes. This is no longer true given the major revision to this disorder.

Cultural Considerations
Research on PDD is based on criteria for the old dysthymic disorder. Affecting 1.5% of the population (NIMH, 2005), dysthymia is frequently seen in clients in counseling sessions, with a high prevalence of this disorder noted among older adults (Zalaquett & Stens, 2006) and in the African American community (Vontress, Woodland, & Epp, 2007). Vontress et al. (2007) underscored the importance of noting culturally relevant factors when conceptualizing this disorder in African Americans.

Differential Diagnosis

The diagnosis of dysthymia in the *DSM-IV-TR* required that the individual be free of any major depressive episodes in the first 2 years of the experience. However, changes to PDD criteria in the *DSM-5* stipulate that the disorder may involve the presence of a major depressive episode at any point in the experience. The *DSM-5* provides extensive guidelines for differentiating between MDD and PDD and includes numerous specifiers in which the major depressive episode is or is not present alongside the disorder (see APA, 2013a, pp. 168–171).

PDD cannot be diagnosed if symptoms occur only during the course of schizophrenia spectrum or other psychotic disorders or if a client has ever experienced a manic episode, hypomanic episode, or cyclothymic disorder. Clinically significant impairment or distress in important areas of functioning, such as problems with interpersonal relationships or holding onto a job, must be evident. Additionally, the symptoms are not better accounted for by the direct effects of substance or medication use. Finally, counselors need to be sure there is no other explanation for the behavior, such as another medical or neurological condition.

Coding, Recording, and Specifiers

There is only one diagnostic code for PDD (dysthymia): 300.4 (F34.1). However, counselors are asked to indicate current severity of *mild*, *moderate*, or *severe* and other specifiers in writing. It is important that counselors note specifiers to describe the client's chronic mood state (i.e., *with anxious distress, with mixed features, with melancholic features, with atypical features, with mood-congruent psychotic features, with mood-incongruent psychotic features,* or *with peripartum onset*) and indicate if the client is in *partial remission* or *full remission*. Counselors must also identify if the client is *early onset* (i.e., before the age of 21) or *late onset* (i.e., after the age of 21) and whether the following apply: *with pure dysthymic syndrome, with persistent major depressive episode, with intermittent major depressive episodes (with current episode),* or *with intermittent major depressive episodes (without current episode;* APA, 2013a).

 Example

> Anthony is 37-year-old African American man who is attending counseling for the first time at the insistence of Willa, his wife of 10 years. Willa states that she has been dealing with Anthony's "chronic negativity" for at least 6 years and that he "wasn't always like this." Recently, it has been much worse and she says she has had enough. She has told Anthony that if he does not get help, she is not going to stay in the marriage. As a result, Anthony has made an appointment for an intake during which he tells you "nothing is going to help."
>
> Anthony presents as underweight and neatly dressed but unshaven. His affect is blunted and he speaks only to answer direct questions. During the intake, he appears to be thinking about other things and frequently seems distracted. He reports that he is simply tired a lot and doesn't want to waste his energy on things that aren't important, such as shaving and showering. He does these things when his wife "nags" him, which he states she does a lot and particularly when he doesn't feel like eating. Anthony reports working the same full-time job for the past 10 years. He has never put in for a raise or promotion because "it's a lot of effort and very competitive." He frequently leaves early or takes sick time because he feels "down" and needs a break.
>
> Anthony can recall a time when he had more energy and was at an average weight. He states this was about 5 years ago, but then he went through a time when "things were really bad." When asked about this time frame, Anthony states he never had thoughts of hurting someone else but did think about killing himself. He reports feeling so depressed that he just didn't want to live anymore. His wife reports that he had difficulty getting out of bed during this time period and lost a lot of weight. She reports that he had no sexual interest in her and

says negative things about himself. She states she should have "made" him get help at the time but he seemed to be getting better so she just "let it go."

When asked, Anthony states that he does have friends and most of them are life-long. He says he doesn't spend a lot of time with them because he is tired and feels down. He also reports that they call him "Eeyore" and they are probably right. He is currently well oriented and denies thoughts of harm to himself or anyone else. A recent medical workup indicates that he is in good health. He reports drinking the occasional beer with his friends but denies other substance use. He states he wants to become more positive and to have more energy so that his wife won't leave him.

♦ ♦ ♦

Diagnostic Questions

1. Do Anthony's presenting symptoms meet the criteria for a depressive disorder? If so, which one?
2. What would be the reason(s) a counselor would not diagnose Anthony with PDD?
3. Would Anthony be accurately diagnosed with major depressive episodes?
4. What rule-outs would you consider for Anthony's case?
5. What other information may be needed to make an accurate clinical diagnosis?

625.4 Premenstrual Dysphoric Disorder (N94.3)

I learned to count the days and dread that time of the month. I wouldn't make plans around the time I would have my period. I would avoid family and friends because I was so afraid of what I would say. My boyfriend dreads it because I am so sensitive, depressed, and angry. I couldn't concentrate at work and I wanted to eat all the time. I felt horrible and was often so swollen I couldn't even put my jewelry on. —Molly

Premenstrual dysphoric disorder (PMDD) is a depressive disorder exclusive to women and is characterized by intense emotional and physical symptoms that occur in the days prior to the onset of menses and often continuing into menstruation (Daw, 2002). This disorder was originally adopted into the *DSM-III-R* (APA, 1987) as "late luteal phase dysphoric disorder" and changed to premenstrual dysphoric disorder in the *DSM-IV* (Cunningham, Yonkers, O'Brien, & Eriksson, 2009), in which it was listed and coded as depressive disorder NOS. Whereas for most women, mild physical and emotional symptoms can occur near and during menstruation—frequently referred to as premenstrual syndrome, or PMS—about 8% of menstruating women report symptoms distressing enough to cause impairment in daily functioning (Pilver, Desai, Kasl, & Levy, 2011).

Major Changes From *DSM-IV-TR* to *DSM-5*

Although previous editions of *DSM* included reference to PMDD within the NOS category, this is the first time PMDD is appearing as an official disorder within the *DSM*.

Essential Features

PMDD presents with symptoms that begin in the week before menstruation, improve in the days after menstruation starts, and dissipate as menstruation ends. The individual must experience at least five symptoms, including at least one of the following: (a) severe mood swings (affective lability), including feeling suddenly sad or tearful or becoming overly sensitive to rejection; (b) increased interpersonal conflicts or significantly increased anger or irritability; (c) feelings of hopelessness, self-critical thoughts, or distinctly depressed mood; or (d) noticeable anxiety, tension, or feeling of edginess (APA, 2013a).

Additional symptoms that can be considered include lack of interest in normal activities, self-reported problems with concentration, fatigue or lack of energy, changes in eating habits to include under- or overeating and/or cravings, sleep disturbance, feeling of loss of control or being overwhelmed, and physical symptoms such as tenderness in the breasts, pain in the muscles or joints, swelling, bloating, or weight gain (APA, 2013a). Moreover, the symptoms must occur in most menstrual cycles the year before this diagnosis is given and must result in clinically significant impairment in social, work, school, or usual activities.

Special Considerations

Concerns regarding the inclusion and diagnosis of PMDD in the *DSM* have been part of the research and discourse process since its inception (Daw, 2002). These concerns include stigmatizing or targeting women as a result of their normal biological functions, pathologizing normal reproductive functioning (APA, 2013a), and relying on medication therapy for treatment (Daw, 2002). The DSM-5 Mood Disorders Work Group responded to the concerns, stating that statistics on the prevalence indicate that PMDD affects a small portion of women and symptoms should not be generalized to all women. Furthermore, in acknowledging this as a diagnosis, the APA believes this conveys that PMDD does not typically occur for menstruating women and is only clinically impairing for a few (APA, 2013a). Certainly, counselors must be careful about stigma and inherent biological processes. In addition, counselors are encouraged to take into account the likelihood of abuse having occurred and adjust assessment treatment for this factor as needed.

Cultural Considerations

A portion of the etiology of PMDD can be attributed to a combination of physiological factors, including hormones, neurotransmitters, and variations in a specific estrogen receptor (Cunningham et al., 2009; Girdler et al., 2007; Pearlstein & Steiner, 2008). However, cultural considerations are still important. Cunningham et al. (2009) reported risk factors for this disorder include stress and high body mass index. Girdler et al. (2007) reported that women diagnosed with PMDD are at least 60% more likely to have experienced physical or sexual abuse over their lifetime when compared with women who have not received this diagnosis. They posited that traumatic events, particularly early life trauma, could contribute to dysregulation in stress-responsive systems, which may be a risk factor for PMDD. Additionally, Pilver et al. (2011) found a relationship between symptoms of PMDD and lifetime discrimination.

Differential Diagnosis

When diagnosing PMDD, counselors should ensure that the symptoms associated with it are not better explained by normal hormonal fluctuations or exacerbation of symptoms related to another previously diagnosed disorder. Counselors should also clarify that symptoms are not directly related to substance use or other medical issues. The symptoms of this disorder are primarily affective or anxiety related, so counselors should not give this diagnosis when an underlying depressive or anxiety disorder already exists. Rather, these symptoms could be considered a premenstrual exacerbation of the already existing disorder and happen most commonly with dysthymia (now PDD), MDD, panic disorder, and GAD (Pearlstein & Steiner, 2008). This can be a particularly difficult issue because women diagnosed with PMDD are more likely than other women to have co-occurring disorders such as PTSD or anxiety disorder. Furthermore, comorbidity is complicated by symptom overlap for some disorders, which makes diagnosis even more difficult (Cunningham et al., 2009).

Coding, Recording, and Specifiers

There is only one diagnostic code for PMDD: 625.4 (N94.3). While there are no specifiers, if there has not been a daily rating of symptoms for at least two cycles, a provisional diagnosis must be noted after the name (APA, 2013a).

Diagnostic Criteria for PMDD 625.4 (N94.3)

A. In the majority of menstrual cycles, at least five symptoms must be present in the final week before the onset of menses, start to *improve* within a few days after the onset of menses, and become *minimal* or absent in the week postmenses.

B. One (or more) of the following symptoms must be present:
  1. Marked affective lability (e.g., mood swings; feeling suddenly sad or tearful, or increased sensitivity to rejection).
  2. Marked irritability or anger or increased interpersonal conflicts.
  3. Marked depressed mood, feelings of hopelessness, or self-deprecating thoughts.
  4. Marked anxiety, tension, and/or feelings of being keyed up or on edge.

C. One (or more) of the following symptoms must additionally be present, to reach a total of *five* symptoms when combined with the symptoms from Criterion B above.
  1. Decreased interest in usual activities (e.g., work, school, friends, hobbies).
  2. Subjective difficulty in concentration.
  3. Lethargy, easy fatigability, or marked lack of energy.
  4. Marked change in appetite; overeating; or specific food cravings.
  5. Hypersomnia or insomnia.
  6. A sense of being overwhelmed or out of control.
  7. Physical symptoms such as breast tenderness or swelling, joint or muscle pain, a sensation of "bloating," or weight gain.

  Note: The symptoms in Criteria A–C must have been met for most menstrual cycles that occurred in the preceding year.

D. The symptoms are associated with clinically significant distress or interference with work, school, usual social activities, or relationships with others (e.g., avoidance of social activities; decreased productivity and efficiency at work, school, or home).

E. The disturbance is not merely an exacerbation of the symptoms of another disorder, such as major depressive disorder, panic disorder, persistent depressive disorder (dysthymia), or a personal disorder (although it may co-occur with any of these disorders).

F. Criterion A should be confirmed by prospective daily ratings during at least two symptomatic cycles.

  Note: The diagnosis may be made provisionally prior to this confirmation.)

G. The symptoms are not attributable to the physiological effects of a substance (e.g., a drug of abuse, a medication, other treatment) or another medical condition (e.g., hyperthyroidism).

From *Diagnostic and Statistical Manual of Mental Disorders, Fifth Edition*, 2013, pp. 171–172. Copyright 2013 by the American Psychiatric Association. All rights reserved. Reprinted with permission.

 Case Example

Shara is a 32-year-old Asian American woman who presents to counseling services at the insistence of her girlfriend, Dani. Shara reports that they have a good relationship for the most part, but once a month they get in horrible fights. She states that she is aware that she has always had difficulty around the time of menstruation, but lately she has become more aware of the impact on her life.

Shara reports that prior to starting her period, she becomes physically very uncomfortable. She states that she experiences pain and swelling. At that point, she easily becomes tearful, is easily stressed out, and may "snap people off" at any moment. Occasionally, she leaves work early or refuses to leave her house or talk to anyone because she is afraid of what she may do or say. Shara reports these symptoms have been consistent since her early 20s but for some reason seem to be getting worse.

♦ ♦ ♦

Diagnostic Questions

1. Do Shara's presenting symptoms meet the criteria for PMDD?
2. What would be the reason(s) a counselor would not diagnose her with PMDD?
3. What are the treatment approaches that a counselor could use when working with Shara?
4. What rule-outs would you consider for her case?
5. What other information may be needed to make an accurate clinical diagnosis?

Substance/Medication-Induced Depressive Disorder

Substance/medication-induced depressive disorder, titled substance-induced mood disorder in the *DSM-IV-TR*, is a depressive disorder in which there is evidence that a substance or medication physiologically caused the onset of depressive symptoms. The symptoms must be in excess of what is expected with the substance and must last a month or more after substance intoxication or withdrawal. There are no changes from the *DSM-IV-TR* to the *DSM-5* except for the name (APA, 2013a).

Essential Features

Substance/medication-induced depressive disorder presents with symptoms that are consistent with those of a depressive disorder. However, evidence demonstrates that symptoms for this disorder develop during or within a month of use or withdrawal from a particular substance known to produce depressive symptoms. Verification can be produced by using history, laboratory findings, or physical examination of the client (APA, 2013a).

This disorder should not be diagnosed if depressive symptoms precede the onset of substance use or withdrawal. If the symptoms continue for a month or more after cessation of the substance use or end of the withdrawal period, the symptoms may be better accounted for by an independent mood disorder (APA, 2013a). Moreover, the depressive symptoms should not occur concomitant with delirium alone and must result in clinically significant impairment in key functional areas.

Special Considerations

Given the presumed physiological connection between substance use and development of depressive episodes, this diagnosis should be made by a physician or in consultation with a physician who has expertise to determine etiology. Counselors should be aware that substance/medication-induced depressive disorder that involves alcohol, heroin, or cocaine has specific implications for treatment. For example, Samet et al. (2012) found that individuals with substance-induced depressive disorders had much greater risk of relapse compared with those diagnosed with MDD. These authors reported their findings to be consistent with neurobiological research on addiction positing that brain changes that occur during dependence, presenting as depressive symptoms, can linger long after withdrawal and well into the maintenance stage. Therefore, counselors working with clients who meet the criteria for this disorder should be aware of the high risk of relapse. Evidence-based treatments for addressing mood concerns, treating substance use disorders, and teaching coping are essential. Informing clients about the symptoms and implications of this disorder and developing relapse prevention plans and strategies for coping with relapse are important as well.

Differential Diagnosis

Substance/medication-induced depressive disorder should be diagnosed instead of substance intoxication and substance withdrawal only when depressive symptoms are prominent and the condition is clinically impairing for the client. In addition, counselors must be careful to assess for co-occurring substance use disorder.

Coding, Recording, and Specifiers

Because specific diagnostic codes will vary based on the class of substances for *ICD-9-CM* codes, no coding numbers have been identified for this disorder. In addition to variation based on substance class, the *ICD-10-CM* further differentiates coding procedures based on whether or not a comorbid substance use disorder is present for the same class of substance. Specifiers for this disorder include *with onset during intoxication* and *with onset during withdrawal*. For example, a woman experiencing depressive symptoms during withdrawal of a severe cocaine use disorder would receive a diagnosis of 292.84 cocaine-induced depressive disorder, with onset during withdrawal. An additional diagnosis of 304.20 severe cocaine use disorder, severe, would also be recorded.

When more than one substance class is judged to be clinically significant, counselors would list each substance separately. When recording substance/medication-induced disorders, counselors must reference the criteria set and the corresponding recording procedures for the specific substance-specific codes, also being sure to record the name of the substance. For substances that do not fit into any category, counselors should use the code of other substance. Likewise, if counselors are unaware of the name of the substance, the code for unknown substance should be used. The codes for both of these classes is the same, but counselors do need to specify whether the substance is other (meaning it is not included in the listing) or unknown.

293.83 Depressive Disorder Due to Another Medical Condition (F06._ _)

Depressive disorder due to another medical condition differs from substance/medication-induced depressive disorder in that the former diagnosis applies when symptoms are consistent with MDD and are presented as exclusively relating to a medical condition (APA, 2013a). There are no changes to this section from the *DSM-IV-TR* to the *DSM-5*.

Essential Features

During a depressive disorder due to another medical condition, the individual will typically present with a significant mood change, that can be connected directly to a medical condition through physical examinations, laboratory findings, or history that give evidence linking the two conditions (APA, 2013a). The mood change will include noticeable depressed mood or diminished interest in usual pleasures. Another condition or mental disorder cannot better explain the symptoms, and there must be clinically significant impairment, distress, mental health hospitalization, or psychotic features. The symptoms cannot occur only during delirium (APA, 2013a).

Special Considerations

For diagnosis of this disorder, it is important to ensure that the related medical condition can cause depressive symptoms. This determination should be made by a physician who is qualified to diagnose the medical condition and determine etiology. Some medical conditions associated with depressive symptoms include hypothyroidism, stroke, Huntington's disease, Parkinson's disease, and traumatic brain injury. Depressive symptoms can present as early as 1 day after a stroke and occur fairly early in conjunction with Huntington's disease. The symptoms tend to precede impairments related to the advancement of Parkinson's and Huntington's disease.

Cultural Considerations

The APA (2013a) notes that certain diseases run along gender lines; in some cases, such as with strokes, which occur more often in men, the medical condition is known to be more likely to cause depressive symptoms. Although there are considerable data to suggest a link between physical illness and depression (Østergaard & Foldager, 2011), there is limited research on depressive disorder due to another medical condition and culture. This may be because of difficulty in assessing, diagnosing, and determining the actual etiology of depressive symptoms.

Differential Diagnosis

Differentiating this disorder from a depressive disorder not related to a medical condition can be challenging. Counselors need to determine if a depressive episode has ever occurred or if this episode began before the onset of the medical condition. It is also important to ensure that the medical condition the client is experiencing can cause the symptoms of a depressive disorder. Furthermore, monitoring the course of the symptoms can confirm the diagnosis is related to a medical condition, especially if the symptoms lessen or disappear as the medical condition resolves (APA, 2013a).

Because most medical conditions that could create depressive symptoms are also treated with medication that may do the same, counselors should consider medication-induced depressive disorder in the differential. Certain medical conditions (such as a stroke) can present significant life stressors for individuals. If the medical condition is known to have caused the depression *and* the client is experiencing difficulty adjusting to the diagnosis, adjustment disorders should be considered as an additional diagnosis. However, if the depression is a response to the diagnosis or its implications and does not meet full criteria for another depressive disorder, adjustment disorders may be the more appropriate diagnosis.

Coding, Recording, and Specifiers

There is no specific *DSM-5* code identified for this disorder. Instead, the *ICD-9-CM* code of 293.83 is listed. The medical condition can be coded and listed before this disorder and then 293.83 with the specific condition following this code within the disorder name. However, the *ICD-10-CM* introduces a specific code for each condition, such as 293.83 (F09.31), depressive disorder due to (list condition) with depressive features. The specifiers may also include 293.83 (F09.32), *with major depression–like symptoms* or 293.83 (F09.34) *with mixed features* (APA, 2013a).

Other Specified and Unspecified Depressive Disorders

This category is new to the *DSM-5*. Whereas the *DSM-IV-TR* allowed for an NOS diagnosis, the *DSM-5* includes other specified and unspecified depressive disorders. The other specified depressive disorder (311.0 [F32.8]) category is provided for symptom presentations that lead to clinically significant distress or impairment but do not meet full criteria for a specific depressive disorder. The counselor can specify one of the three types: recurrent brief depression, short duration depressive episode (4–13 days), and depressive episode with insufficient symptoms (APA, 2013a). There is one code for this diagnosis (311 [F32.8]). The counselor should indicate this code, followed by the disorder name, and finally the specific designation, such as short-term depressive episode (APA, 2013a). The unspecified depressive disorder (311 [F32.9]) diagnosis can be assigned when an individual presents with symptoms of a depressive disorder but the counselor does not have access to more specific diagnostic information or chooses not to diagnose a specific depressive disorder.

Specifiers for Depressive Disorders

The following is an all-inclusive listing of specifiers for depressive disorders. We have chosen to include these because of the requirement for counselors to accurately identify and list specifiers to further clarify the course, severity, or special features of the identified depressive disorder. The major change to this section is the addition of *with anxious distress* and *with mixed features* as specifiers (APA, 2013c).

Severity specifiers are used throughout the Depressive Disorders chapter of the *DSM-5*. These specifiers are based on the most recent episode and are identified by the number of symptoms, symptom severity, and degree of impairment. For a specifier of *mild*, few additional symptoms are noted, they are manageable, and they result only in minor impairment. For *severe*, there are multiple excess symptoms, they are intensely distressing and unmanageable, and there is a marked interference with functioning. *Moderate* occurs when symptom number, intensity, and impairment fall between mild and severe (APA, 2013a).

For diagnoses of MDD and PDD, the *DSM-5* allows for the specifier of *with anxious distress* if, during most days of a current or most recent experience of MDD or PDD, two of the following symptoms are reported: being keyed up or tense, increased restlessness, excessive worry that leads to difficulty concentrating, irrational fear that something negative is about to occur, and fear of loss of self-control. Symptom severity can be identified for this specifier. If two symptoms are noted, *mild* severity is indicated. For three symptoms, *moderate* is indicated; if four or more symptoms are present, *moderate-severe* is used.

Note

The specifier *with anxious distress* has been added to both MDD and bipolar disorder because of its prominence in mental health and special care settings. Additionally, anxious distress has been related to higher risk of suicide in these setting. The APA (2013a, 2013b) encourages clinicians to be aware of severity levels of anxious distress and to assess and plan appropriately.

◆ ◆ ◆

Another specifier that can be associated with MDD and PDD is *with mixed features*. For this specifier to be given, the individual must experience three manic/hypomanic symptoms almost every day during the depressive episode. These include inflated self-esteem or grandiosity; elevated mood; pressured speech or increased talkativeness; racing thoughts or flight of ideas; increased energy or goal-directed activity; involvement in high-risk, high-consequence behaviors; and decreased need for sleep (APA, 2013a). These symptoms are not related to medication or substance use and must be noticeable to others. If symptoms meet full criteria for either mania or hypomania, the appropriate bipolar disorder diagnosis should be given.

Note

It is important to note the specifier where appropriate because of the strong link between it and a future diagnosis of bipolar disorder.

◆ ◆ ◆

For the specifier of *with melancholic feature* to be applicable, during the most severe period of the episode, the individual must experience lack of pleasure in almost all or all activities or lack of response to pleasurable events. Three or more additional symptoms must be experienced from the following: distinct depression that may include deep despondency, despair, glumness, or empty mood; increased depression in the morning that can be accompanied by early waking, at least 2 hours earlier than normal; noticeable slowing or psychomotor agitation; significant weight fluctuation; and overwhelming guilt. The changes are noticeable, and psychomotor changes are almost always present. Furthermore, the condition occurs more frequently in individuals who also have psychotic features and is more likely to occur in severe depressive episodes requiring inpatient treatment (APA, 2013a). The *with melancholic features* criteria cannot be met during the same episode as *with catatonia* (APA, 2013a).

The *with atypical features* specifier is applicable when the individual spends most days of the current or most recent major depressive episode experiencing mood reactivity and two or more additional features, which include significant weight gain or increased appetite, constant daytime sleepiness, feeling of heaviness in the arms or legs, and a history of social or occupational issues related to extreme sensitivity to being rejected. This sensitivity to rejection begins early in life and can occur even when the individual is not experiencing depressive symptoms but can be worse during a depressive episode.

For the specifier of *with psychotic features* to be given, the individual will experience delusions or hallucinations during the depressive episode. *With mood-congruent psychotic features* or *without mood-congruent psychotic features* should be diagnosed if psychotic features are present. When the psychotic features are mood-congruent, they will be consistent with the depressive themes (e.g., guilt, death, punishment). When this does not occur or the content is mixed, a specifier of *with mood-incongruent psychotic features* should be included (APA, 2013a).

With catatonia is specified when catatonic features are present during most of the episode for a depressive episode. Criteria for catatonia associated with a mental disorder are given in the Schizophrenia Spectrum and Other Psychotic Disorders chapter.

The specifier of *with peripartum onset* can be used when the beginning of mood symptoms is during pregnancy or in the 4 weeks after delivery. Whereas mood episodes can begin before or after delivery, about half of women begin experiencing these symptoms prior to delivery, and as such, the specifier is *peripartum*. Symptoms associated with this can be severe, and for some women this includes anxiety, panic attacks, and psychotic features, which can be extreme and include command hallucinations to harm or kill the child. Between one in 500 women and one in 1,000 women experience postpartum episodes with psychotic features (APA, 2013a). The risk of experiencing peripartum or postpartum symptoms increases with prior history of symptoms, with family history, and with history of depressive or bipolar diagnosis (APA, 2013a).

Note

The APA (2013a) reports that between 3% and 6% of women will experience a depressive episode during pregnancy or following the delivery.

◆ ◆ ◆

When an MDD, recurrent, occurs in a pattern over the life span, coinciding with a specific season, the specifier *with seasonal pattern* may apply. The depressive episode will have a consistent temporal relationship to a particular time of year, unrelated to outside stressors (such as difficult holiday events), and will not occur outside the seasonal pattern for at least 2 years. The symptomatology may diminish or change as the seasons change, and the seasonal episodes will outnumber the nonseasonal episodes over the life span. In MDD, recurrent, with seasonal pattern, the depressive episodes tend to occur more often in fall and winter and are not typical in the summer. The symptoms appear more often in younger individuals who live in higher latitudes (APA, 2013a).

If the symptoms of the current episode are still ongoing but do not meet full criteria, or if the individual has experienced no significant symptoms for 2 months, *in partial remission* can be specified. If there are no significant symptoms, *in full remission* is applicable.

Chapter 4

Bipolar and Related Disorders

Bipolar refers to fluctuations of a good or irritable mood (APA, 2013a; NIMH, 2012). The swings between mania and depression can sometimes be quite severe. Although bipolar was not officially included in the *DSM* until the third edition (APA, 1980), writers as far back as the ancient Greeks referred to *melancholia* and *mania* related to behavior. Aretaeus of Cappadocia wrote of individuals who displayed high levels of energy and euphoria followed by periods of melancholy (Burton, 2012). During the 19th century, psychiatric professionals used terms such as *manic-depressive* and *affective psychosis* as descriptive for this phenomenon (APA, 2013a). Kraepelin (1921) theorized that these symptoms were separate from psychosis and conceptualized them on a spectrum, emphasizing outcome as a criterion. Originally termed *manic depressive illness* in the first *DSM*, the diagnosis was renamed bipolar disorder in the *DSM-III* because of the stigma associated with manic depression and the attempt to explain the polarity of disorder rather than simply focus on symptomatology. Currently, theorists debate the need for conceptualization of bipolar disorder on a spectrum (Merikangas et al., 2007; Paris, 2009).

Since the *DSM-III*, the diagnosis of bipolar disorder has increased rapidly, particularly for adolescents, for whom claims of increase fall between 10% and 40% (Jenkins, Youngstrom, Washburn, & Youngstrom, 2011). CNN (see Gardner, 2011) reported that 4.4% of individuals in the United States will be diagnosed on the bipolar spectrum in their lifetimes, making the United States the highest in the world for bipolar disorder diagnosis. NIMH (2012) reported bipolar disorder as the sixth leading cause of disability worldwide. Individuals diagnosed with bipolar disorder have the highest rates of suicide and premature death related to medical disorders (Merikangas et al., 2007), with a 10–20 times increased risk of suicide compared with the U.S. population in general (Jenkins et al., 2011).

Major Changes From *DSM-IV-TR* to *DSM-5*

The major changes to the Bipolar and Related Disorders chapter in the *DSM-5* include its strategic location. Whereas in the *DSM-IV-TR* bipolar disorders were presented within the mood disorders section, the *DSM-5* includes bipolar and related disorders as a stand-alone chapter, located between schizophrenia spectrum and other psychotic disorders and depressive disorders (APA, 2013a). In addition, the mixed episode criteria have been discontinued and reorganized into a new specifier. Bipolar II is no longer considered a milder diagnosis than Bipolar I, because of the intensity of the impairment experienced by clients with this disorder and the length of time depressive symptoms are experienced. Both mania and hypomania criteria now emphasize changes in activity or energy, and other specified bipolar and related disorders have been added as a category (APA, 2013c).

Differential Diagnosis

As with depressive disorders, comorbidity seems to be the rule rather than the exception for bipolar and related disorders. Because individuals tend to seek treatment more frequently when they are experiencing depression, bipolar and related disorders are frequently mistaken for depression or anxiety. Furthermore, symptoms consistent with hypomania are often unreported or misdiagnosed as anxiety. Together, it is estimated that between 20% and 30% of individuals being treated for depression and anxiety symptoms have a bipolar disorder (Manning, 2010). In other cases, bipolar disorder may go completely unrecognized. Das et al. (2005) screened individuals at a primary care facility for bipolar disorder. Of the 81 individuals who qualified for a bipolar disorder diagnosis, just 9% had been diagnosed with bipolar or related disorders. Remaining participants were undiagnosed or carried depressive, substance use, and anxiety disorder diagnoses. Manning (2010) posited that thorough history, accurate assessments, and a good therapeutic alliance, including multiple contacts with the client, might be key to accurately diagnosing bipolar and related disorders.

Etiology and Treatment

Although no one single explanation can be given, researchers and theorists posit a variety of contributors to bipolar disorder, including life stress, genetic predisposition, neurobiological factors, psychosocial factors, environmental issues, brain structure, ion activity, and impaired executive functioning (Alloy, Abramson, Urosevic, Bender, & Wagner, 2009; R. J. Comer, 2013; Hankin, 2009). Understanding the factors that contribute to bipolar symptoms can inform well-rounded, evidence-based treatments.

Traditionally recommended treatment for bipolar and related disorders includes psychotherapy in conjunction with mood-stabilizing medication. Psychoeducation, CBT, family-focused therapy, and interpersonal and social rhythm therapy have been shown to be effective in treating the symptoms of bipolar disorder (Steinkuller & Rheineck, 2009). Lithium and other mood stabilizers have had high success rates in decreasing manic episodes and symptoms; however, individuals who discontinue medication are at very high risk of relapse (R. J. Comer, 2013). Psychoeducation can emphasize the importance of lifestyle management and regular medication use and assist with social skills and relationship building (R. J. Comer, 2013).

Implications for Counselors

Because of the impact of bipolar disorder on the individual, family, and community, it is critical that counselors are able to recognize the disorder. Individuals who experience bipolar disorder tend to have more health problems, experience relationship issues, and are at risk for suicidal ideation and attempts (R. J. Comer, 2013; Steinkuller & Rheineck, 2009). Because of issues with comorbidity, many clients in mental health centers may not be fully treated for the symptoms of bipolar disorder (Manning, 2010). Rather than attend solely to initial presenting problems (which may be depressive or anxious in nature), counselors need to attend to the possibility of bipolar disorder through a full and complete assessment, which may be over several sessions.

To help readers better understand changes from the *DSM-IV-TR* to the *DSM-5*, the rest of this chapter outlines each disorder within the Bipolar and Related Disorders chapter of the *DSM-5*. Readers should note that we have focused on major changes from the *DSM-IV-TR* to the *DSM-5*; however, this is not a stand-alone resource for diagnosis. Although a summary and special considerations for counselors are provided for each disorder, when diagnosing clients, counselors need to reference the *DSM-5*. It is essential that the diagnostic criteria and features, subtypes and specifiers (if applicable), prevalence, course, and risk and prognostic factors for each disorder are clearly understood prior to diagnosis.

296. _ _ Bipolar I Disorder (F31._ _)

The constant energy was amazing. It felt like I was connected to everything and everyone all at once. Everything I saw was beautiful, and I bought everything I wanted. But after about a week or so, the crash would come and I would be miserable. The misery would increase over time until I didn't want to live anymore. No one understood. My wife eventually left, and I can't pay for all things that I bought. —Richard

With a lifetime prevalence of 0.8% (Merikangas et al., 2007), Bipolar I disorder is characterized by the presence of at least one manic episode. This episode can precede or follow major depressive or hypomanic episodes. Most individuals who meet full criteria for manic episodes also experience major depressive episodes. Although major depressive episodes are not required for diagnosis, it is atypical for manic episodes to occur without a history of depression (APA, 2013a).

Essential Features

At least one episode of mania is required for a Bipolar I disorder diagnosis. Symptoms of a manic episode will occur for at least a week, almost every day, with symptoms being present most of the day. During this time, the individual will experience abnormally increased goal-directed activity or heightened energy levels along with persistently elevated, irritable, or expansive mood (APA, 2013a). The individual will experience some additional symptoms that represent a noticeable change from usual behavior. If the mood is irritable only, he or she will experience at least four of the following symptoms (for other mood presentations, three or more of the following are required): exaggerated self-esteem or grandiosity; limited need for sleep; pressured speech or abnormally talkative self-report of racing thoughts or flight of ideas; inability to concentrate or easily distractible as indicated by self or others; significant increase in psychomotor agitation or goal-directed activity that is often social, work, or sexually related; and increased involvement in high-risk behavior or activities that could result in painful consequences (APA, 2013a).

In addition to current or historical presence of a manic episode, individuals with Bipolar I disorder often have histories involving major depressive and hypomanic episodes. Contrary to popular belief regarding the nature of bipolar disorder as involving rapid mood swings, mood episodes may go on for weeks or months at a time, resolve, and then be followed several months (or more) later with another mood episode.

Special Considerations

As with MDD, Bipolar I disorder is associated with high rates of lethality. Some researchers speculate that between 25% and 50% of individuals suffering from this disorder attempt suicide (Jamison, 2000), and APA (2013a) estimates the suicide risk to be 15 times that of the general population. The length of depressive episodes and previous suicide attempts are related to elevated risk. In addition, individuals who are experiencing a manic episode often engage in risky, even life-threatening, behaviors as part of the course. Counselors need to be particularly aware of these risk factors and engage clients who have bipolar disorder in risk assessments and crisis planning.

Counselors also need to be aware of the impact of Bipolar I disorder on the family system. R. J. Comer (2013) noted that the "roller coaster ride" (p. 224) of bipolar emotions results in dramatic impact on the individual's friends and family. Health care costs for an individual with Bipolar I disorder are 3 times higher than costs for other individuals because there are significantly more hospital visits, doctor visits, and medications (Chatterton, Ke, Lewis, Rajagopalan, & Lazarus, 2008). As a result of their symptoms, individuals with this disorder experience higher divorce rates and chronic relationship instability. Because of this disruption and the impact on functioning, family members should be included in the therapeutic process whenever possible (Steinkuller & Rheineck, 2009).

Although it may require lifelong management, there are effective treatments for Bipolar I disorder. Mood-stabilizing medications have been shown to be effective for treatment, and many researchers agree that a combination of psychotherapy and medications is the most effective treatment (R. J. Comer, 2013; Culver, Amow, & Ketter, 2007; Steinkuller & Rheineck, 2009). Evidence-based interventions for treating Bipolar I disorder include psychoeducation, CBT, family-focused therapy, and interpersonal and social rhythm therapy (Steinkuller & Rheineck, 2009). Counselors can use these interventions for assisting clients with Bipolar I disorder.

Cultural Considerations

Although Bipolar I disorder occurs as frequently in women as in men, women tend to experience more rapid cycling and depressive episodes than men (R. J. Comer, 2013; Ketter, 2010). Concurrent with Bipolar I, women also experience higher rates of eating disorders and substance use disorders (APA, 2013a). In terms of cultural variation, individuals diagnosed with Bipolar I disorder often have lower socioeconomic status, higher rates of disability, and lower life expectancy (R. J. Comer, 2013; Ketter, 2010). Despite being one of the most distinct diagnoses in mental health treatment, there is sparse information on how Bipolar I disorder manifests in different populations (APA, 2013a; Belmaker, 2004). Some studies have indicated higher levels of prevalence in African American and Caucasian samples (APA, 2013a), whereas other studies have claimed little variation in rates of bipolar disorder across cultures (R. J. Comer, 2013; Ketter, 2010). This discrepancy is most easily explained by the hallmark symptom of Bipolar I disorder, mania, which varies significantly according to culture, country of residence, and socioeconomic class. More research on the cultural presentation of this disorder is needed.

Differential Diagnosis

For Bipolar I disorder diagnosis, the manic episodes cannot be better explained by substance use or a medical condition and must be severe enough to result in significant impairment in functioning, include psychotic features, or require hospitalization. The APA (2013a) notes that if an individual experiences a manic episode while receiving antidepressant treatment, the diagnosis is warranted as long as the episode continues with full criteria met after the effects of the treatment are over. Symptoms of Bipolar I disorder must present in an episode and represent a marked difference in one's baseline functioning, thus differentiating Bipolar I disorder from symptoms of a personality disorder. A personality disorder should never be diagnosed during a manic episode (APA, 2013a).

Moreover, symptoms of mania or hypomania can occur along with MDD. If the episodes are shorter in duration than required or have fewer symptoms than is necessary for a Bipolar I disorder diagnosis to be given, MDD or Bipolar II disorder can be diagnosed. Anxiety disorder and panic symptoms should be explored through careful determination of the episodic nature of the client's symptoms. Gathering a thorough history of symptoms can be crucial to helping differentiate panic or anxiety from a true experience of mania (APA, 2013a).

Because onset for this disorder usually occurs between 15 and 44 years of age (R. J. Comer, 2013), counselors will need to differentiate between mania and ADHD, especially in adolescents (APA, 2013a). Whereas ADHD symptoms are continuous, Bipolar I symptoms should be episodic, which will help counselors to differentiate between the two. Severe irritability can present a similar challenge, particularly in children; a diagnosis of DMDD may be more appropriate if an episode of mania is not clearly present (APA, 2013a).

Coding, Recording, and Specifiers

The diagnostic code for Bipolar I disorder is 296. _ _ (F31._ _). Coding for Bipolar I disorder is based on the current or most recent episode only. Counselors must also specify severity, whether psychotic features are present, and whether the client is in partial or full remission. If psychosis is present, the specifier *with psychotic features* is given. If the episode includes psychotic features, that code is given rather than specifying severity. Severity indicators are listed as *mild, moderate,* or *severe.* Remission status includes *in partial remission* or *in full remission.* An *unspecified episodes* specifier may also be given (APA, 2013a). As shown in the table on pages 126–127 of the *DSM-5,* all coding numbers for these specifiers are based on whether the most recent or current episode is manic, hypomanic, or depressed. When the name of the diagnosis is given, Bipolar I is stated or written first, followed by the type of episode (i.e., manic, hypomanic, or depressed), and finally any and all the noncoded specifiers that apply. We discuss additional specifiers for bipolar and related disorders at the end of this chapter. Readers can also see pages 149–154 in the *DSM-5* for more information regarding specifiers for bipolar and related disorders.

Counselors should note that the *DSM-5* incorrectly published coding numbers for Bipolar I disorder, current or most recent episode hypomanic, with the *in partial remission* and *in full remission* specifiers. As published, the second decimal point of the *ICD-10-CM* code is incorrect. For the Bipolar I disorder, current or most recent episode hypomanic, in partial remission, the diagnostic code is published as F31.7**3** but should be F31.7**1**. For the Bipolar I disorder, current or most recent episode hypomanic, in full remission, the diagnostic code is published as F31.7**4** but should be F31.7**2**. The accurate diagnostic codes for this disorder with these specifiers should be:

- 296.45 (F31.71) Bipolar I disorder, current or most recent episode hypomanic, in partial remission
- 296.46 (F31.72) Bipolar I disorder, current or most recent episode hypomanic, in full remission

 Example

Vincent is a 28-year-old African American man who has just completed a major work project. He and his team were contracted to complete the project within a 2-month timeframe. Vincent bragged, however, that he is good enough to get the work done in half the time. About 2 weeks into the project, his energy level "went on high" as it has done in the past. Vincent states that he slept a couple of hours a day, working at fevered pitch. He states that he was the best contractor ever hired and that, even though his colleagues told him he was edgy and difficult most of the time, he knew this was not the case because women were "all over him." In fact, he bragged about taking a different woman home almost every night. After a little over a week, his energy level slowly returned to normal and the work was completed early, as he predicted, making his employer very happy.

Because he had done such a great job and received a sizable bonus, Vincent's coworkers were surprised when he began missing work. He told them he wasn't feeling well and didn't want to get out of bed. When his family didn't hear from him in over week, his sister stopped by to check on him. She found him unkempt; he had eaten very little in a week and had considered ingesting a bottle of aspirin. Vincent explained this to you as you complete his intake at the inpatient psychiatric facility where you work. He stated that he has experienced elevated energy levels before but never felt this sad afterward. He doesn't want to live if he has to feel like this again.

♦ ♦ ♦

Diagnostic Questions

1. Do Vincent's presenting symptoms meet the criteria for a bipolar disorder? If so, which one?
2. What would be the reason(s) a counselor would not diagnose Vincent with Bipolar I disorder?
3. Would Vincent be accurately diagnosed with manic episodes?
4. What rule-outs would you consider for Vincent's case?
5. What other information may be needed to make an accurate clinical diagnosis?
6. Are there any assessments available that might help you determine symptom severity?

296.89 Bipolar II Disorder (F31.81)

The extra boost of energy was great. While my colleagues were downing coffee and energy drinks, I could easily handle all the workload and then some. I didn't need as much sleep either so could get up early to work as well. I was so much better at my job than they were, and my boss would be so happy with me. But the downside was that blues would get really bad at times, and I lost my last job because I was so sad I couldn't leave the house for days. —Cecilia

Bipolar II disorder is characterized by at least one hypomanic episode and at least one major depressive episode and has been recognized as a unique diagnosis since the 1970s (Swartz, Levenson, & Frank, 2012). The lifetime prevalence of this disorder is estimated to be 0.4% to 0.5% (Merikangas et al., 2007), slightly less than Bipolar I disorder. Although it has been conceptualized as a mild bipolar disorder or mild mania, this disorder is phenomenologically distinct from Bipolar I disorder (APA, 2013a; Swartz et al., 2012). There is no experience of full mania or psychosis; however, the lifelong impact can include poor health-related outcomes, higher rates of suicide, and significant psychosocial impairment (Swartz et al., 2012). There are no major changes from the *DSM-IV-TR* to the *DSM-5*.

Essential Features

Bipolar II disorder requires an individual to experience at least one hypomanic episode and one major depressive episode in the absence of any history of manic episodes. A hypomanic episode is described as a period of time lasting at least 4 consecutive days in which the person will present with an abnormal mood described as persistently elevated, expansive, or irritable. During this time, the person will experience heightened energy or unusually increased activity (APA, 2013a). Although the specific symptoms for hypomania are identical to those for mania with the expectation of the minimum time period required, the hypomanic symptoms cannot cause marked impairment, be associated with hospitalization, or involve psychotic symptoms. Because these symptoms may be more subtle, they must be observable to others and not simply a return to normal mood. Counselors should note that Bipolar II is not a milder form of Bipolar I, because both cause significant impairment within individuals.

Special Considerations

Counselors need to keep in mind some unique circumstances surrounding Bipolar II disorder. Individuals experiencing Bipolar II disorder tend have higher rates of "rapid cycling" than do those with Bipolar I disorder (Swartz, Frank, Frankel, Novick, & Houck, 2009). Rapid cycling occurs when the individual experiences four or more mood episodes, either hypomanic or depressed, within a 12-month period, and this occurs in 5% to 15% of cases (APA, 2013a).

As with Bipolar I disorder, interpersonal relationships and occupational status may be difficult for these individuals to maintain. Furthermore, high rates of suicidal ideation occur in both groups (Weinstock, Strong, Uebelacker, & Miller, 2009). APA (2013a) reports that one third of individuals who have this disorder will attempt suicide; people with Bipolar II disorder tend to make more lethal attempts than those diagnosed with Bipolar I disorder. As a result, counselors must be vigilant with risk assessment and prevention when working with these individuals.

Evidence-based treatments for working with individuals who have Bipolar II disorder include cognitive therapy, CBT, psychoeducation, family-focused therapy, and case management, in conjunction with medication (Swartz et al., 2012). Swartz and colleagues also found preliminary evidence that interpersonal and social rhythm therapy can be effective for working with this population.

Cultural Considerations

As with Bipolar I disorder, Bipolar II disorder is more common in women than in men. The average age of onset for this disorder is somewhat later than that for Bipolar I disorder (APA, 2013a). Bipolar II disorder tends to be more prevalent in the population than Bipolar I disorder (Akiskal, 2002; APA, 2013a) and has a more chronic course (Swartz et al., 2012). This is likely because episodes of hypomania have seemingly less severe consequences, such as hospitalization, which are customary to Bipolar I disorder. The misconception that Bipolar II disorder is a milder form of bipolar disorder (Akiskal, 2002) needs to be clarified by mental health professionals so laypersons and individuals diagnosed with this disorder can be better educated about manifestations of this illness and courses of treatment. Also relevant is a thorough understanding of the cultural context in which the client reports symptoms.

As stated previously, individuals diagnosed with mental disorders experience symptoms grounded within the framework of their cultural beliefs, values, and norms (National Alliance on Mental Illness, 2009; Warren, 2007). Misunderstanding this worldview can lead to high rates of misdiagnosis, delayed diagnosis, or a lack of recognition and treatment of comorbid conditions. Aside from clients not receiving proper treatment, these problems negatively affect the way in which they are able to function and interact with others (Vázquez et al., 2011). These problems also can lead to psychosocial issues, such as high rates of unemployment and problems with physical health. All of these contribute to stigma, especially among different cultural groups. Mental health settings that are incompatible with the cultural background of the clients they serve deter these clients from seeking mental health support services or following through with treatment (National Alliance on Mental Illness, 2009).

Understanding cultural norms is essential when working with clients diagnosed with Bipolar II disorder. When describing symptoms, clients must recount rapid fluctuations in mood and behavior. These descriptions may be laden with culturally relevant innuendos. A Latino American client, for example, may state he or she is "feeling *loco*" (i.e., crazy) when experiencing cycling between mania and depression. A culturally competent counselor would understand the client's cultural context and be able to recognize the signs and symptoms of hypomania (e.g., feeling *loco* means feeling crazy, which can often accurately describe rapid mood swings). Counselors, therefore, need to be sensitive to cultural differences in clients' behavior and emotional expression and be aware of their own biases and stereotyping.

Differential Diagnosis

For a diagnosis of Bipolar II disorder, the symptoms must represent a distinct change from the individual's normal functioning; must cause clinically significant impairment in social, occupational, or other important areas of functioning; and must be observable by others. If a person experiences a hypomanic episode during antidepressive treatment, the symptoms must continue beyond the effects of the treatment to be considered for this diagnosis. Symptoms cannot be better explained by another medical condition or abuse of a substance. They cannot be better explained by schizoaffective disorder, schizophrenia, schizophreniform, delusional, or any other disorder on the schizophrenia spectrum (APA, 2013a). Although psychosis may occur during a major depressive episode, psychotic features cannot occur within hypomania. The symptoms of a hypomanic episode will not be severe enough to warrant hospitalization, nor will they result in marked impairment in social or work functioning (APA, 2013a).

Mental health professionals may struggle to differentiate Bipolar II disorder from MDD or Bipolar I disorder. Determining whether the specific episode meets full criteria and length for hypomania will assist the counselor in determining an accurate diagnosis. Recognizing symptoms as part of a specific episode, rather than chronic irritability associated with depression only, occurs more effectively when a thorough evaluation of symptoms is given. A diagnosis of cyclothymic disorder may be more appropriate if hypomanic and depressive episodes are noted but the individual does not meet full criteria for major depressive and hypomanic episodes (APA, 2013a).

Coding, Recording, and Specifiers

There is only one diagnostic code for Bipolar II disorder, 296.89 (F31.81), unless the specifier of *with catatonia*, 293.89 (F06.1), is appropriate. However, counselors can indicate current severity (*mild, moderate, severe*), course, and other specifiers in writing. For example, for a client who presents with severe Bipolar II disorder with catatonic features, the diagnostic code would be written as 293.89 Bipolar II, with catatonia, severe. Unlike Bipolar I disorder, severity and course specifiers do not have specific codes associated with them. The most recent episode (either hypomanic or depressed) should be given as well as severity and all the following specifiers that apply: *with anxious distress, with mixed features, with rapid cycling, with mood-congruent psychotic features, with mood-incongruent psychotic features, with peripartum onset,* and *with seasonal pattern* (APA, 2013a). We discuss additional specifiers for bipolar and related disorders at the end of this chapter. See pages 149–154 in the *DSM-5* for more information regarding specifiers for bipolar and related disorders.

 Case Example

Sue is a 24-year-old Caucasian elementary school teacher who started coming to see you for counseling 3 months ago because she was experiencing moderate depressive symptoms. When she originally presented for counseling, she reported a history of depression. You have been working with her using CBT and teaching her coping skills for depression. Sue came in for her regularly scheduled appointment and was accompanied by her husband, Zion, who is extremely worried about her.

Sue's husband states that, for several days including this weekend, she was not herself. He reports that she didn't sleep much but wasn't tired. She was highly "keyed up," talking constantly. Zion reports that she couldn't seem to focus on anything and was fixated on the idea that something awful was going to happen. She told him she doesn't want him or the children out of sight. Zion states that there is no reason to expect that something awful would happen, but Sue was too upset and distracted to listen to reason. When pressed, he states that her symptoms lasted all day for 4 days but definitely not for a full week. Sue has never used drugs and is not on medication.

◆ ◆ ◆

Diagnostic Questions

1. Do Sue's presenting symptoms meet the criteria for a bipolar disorder? If so, which one?
2. What would be the reason(s) a counselor would not diagnose Sue with Bipolar I disorder?
3. Would Sue be accurately diagnosed with manic episodes? Why or why not?
4. What rule-outs would you consider for Sue's case?
5. Are there any specifiers that apply?
6. What other information may be needed to make an accurate clinical diagnosis?

301.13 Cyclothymic Disorder (F34.0)

Ever since my mid-20s, I've been described as moody. My friends and family members seem to test the waters before hanging out with me, and I know it's because they want to avoid me when I'm down. When I'm happy and energetic, we always have good times. But I cycle through the energy and start feeling down pretty regularly. I wish I could control it. —Justin

Cyclothymic disorder, originally introduced in the *DSM-II* (APA, 1968) as an affective personality disorder, was reported under bipolar disorder when this category was renamed in the *DSM-III* (APA, 1980). Having been noted as far back as the 1880s when German psychiatrist Karl Kahlbaum coined the term *cyclothymia* (Van Meter, Youngstrom, & Findling, 2012), this subthreshold form of bipolar disorder is characterized by cycles of hypomanic symptoms and depressive symptoms that occur at distinctly different times within at least a 2-year period for adults and 1 year for children. About 0.4% to 1% of the general population experiences this disorder (APA, 2013a; R. J. Comer, 2013). Individuals rarely seek treatment for cyclothymic disorder; when they do, it is typically during a depressive cycle (Van Meter et al., 2012). The disorder usually presents in late adolescence or early adulthood and can be a precursor to other mood disorders (APA, 2013a).

Essential Features

Cyclothymic disorder is diagnosed when, over the course of 2 years for adults or 1 year for children and adolescents, the individual experiences multiple periods of depressive symptoms that do not meet criteria for major depressive episodes and multiple periods of elevated mood that do not meet criteria for hypomania (APA, 2013a). During this time frame, the individual cannot be symptom free for more than 2 months, and the symptoms must be present more days than not. The disorder should not be diagnosed if the symptoms can be better explained by another medical condition or substance use. In addition, the symptoms cannot be better explained by another bipolar or related disorder, schizoaffective disorder, schizophrenia, schizophreniform, delusional, or any other disorder on the schizophrenia spectrum (APA, 2013a).

Special Considerations

Although individuals with cyclothymic disorder tend to seek treatment more frequently when experiencing depressive symptoms, counselors need to be aware that both mood presentations have a significant impact on the client's functioning. The depressive symptoms can include irritability, explosive episodes, low self-esteem, and guilt. Although the description of the disorder appears mild, cyclothymia may be more treatment resistant than MDD or Bipolar II disorder (Van Meter et al., 2012). Furthermore, hypomanic symptoms associated with this disorder can include impulsivity and uninhibited friendliness. Suicidality is a critical issue with individuals diagnosed with cyclothymic disorder, and these clients should be monitored carefully. Because of the chronic change in mood presentation, social functioning can be severely affected (Fava, Rafanelli, Tomba, Guidi, & Grandi, 2011; Van Meter et al., 2012). Therapies including CBT and CBT in conjunction with well-being therapy have been shown to reduce mood instability and increase quality of sleep (Fava et al., 2011; Van Meter et al., 2012). Cultural considerations for individuals with cyclothymic disorder do not vary considerably from those for individuals with MDD. Although the prevalence is the same, more women than men get treatment (APA, 2013a).

Cultural Considerations

In the general population, there is no significant difference in lifetime prevalence of cyclothymic disorder according to gender (APA, 2013a). Studies investigating cyclothymic disorder in children are rare. Van Meter et al. (2012) examined individuals with familial patters of cyclothymic and bipolar disorders and found that individuals with cyclothymic disorder experienced greater irritability and were more likely to have a family history of bipolar disorder. In a study of cyclothymic temperament in adults with ADHD, researchers discovered individuals were more likely to have lower levels of education and higher levels of occupational problems (Landaas, Halmoy, Oedegaard, Fasmer, & Haavik, 2012).

Because the symptoms of cyclothymic disorder are similar to those of bipolar disorders, clients must describe fluctuations in mood and behavior. As described previously in the Cultural Considerations section of Bipolar II disorders, counselors must be aware of cultural innuendos regarding mania, hypomania, and depression to accurately understand what the client is experiencing. Descriptions of these symptoms can vary significantly depending on a client's culture, so counselors should be sure to investigate the client's cultural worldview and consider it in diagnosis and treatment planning.

Differential Diagnosis

When diagnosing cyclothymic disorder, counselors should ensure that the client does not meet the criteria for MDD, mania, or a full hypomanic episode. In addition, counselors should differentiate this disorder from the rapid cycling presentation of Bipolar I and II disorders; because of frequent shifts in rapid cycling, both of these disorders may resemble cyclothymic disorder. A thorough assessment of presenting symptoms and history will assist counselors in determining if full criteria for a depressive episode, manic episode, or hypomanic episode have been met. If at any point the full symptoms of these episodes have been met, the cyclothymic disorder diagnosis can be dropped and the more appropriate mood disorder assigned (APA, 2013a).

Because this disorder was originally included in the chapter on personality disorders, referred to as cyclothymic temperament, it can be confused for borderline personality disorder (Van Meter et al., 2012). The APA (2013a) acknowledges this change and suggests that marked shifts in mood can be associated with both disorders, and both disorders can be diagnosed if the full criteria for each have been met.

Coding, Recording, and Specifiers

There is only one diagnostic code for cyclothymic disorder: 301.13 (F34.0). If applicable, coding is recorded along with the specifier of *with anxious distress*. See the end of this chapter for more information on this specifier. Because mood symptoms are considered mild by nature, there is no specifier for mild, moderate, and severe.

__.__ Substance/Medication-Induced Bipolar and Related Disorder (__.__)

This is a diagnosis that presents with the same essential features as those of manic, hypomanic, and depressive episodes. The symptoms are very similar to those of a bipolar disorder; however, they are related directly to the use of a substance or a medication and subside when those factors are removed. If an individual continues to experience symptoms of mania or hypomania after the effects of medication, treatments, or substance have subsided, a bipolar or related disorder may be diagnosed (APA, 2013a)

Essential Features

Substance/medication-induced bipolar disorder is characterized by clinically significant changes in mood that include elevated, expansive, or irritable mood or lack of interest in pleasurable activities or all activities. This may or may not include depressive symptoms. The mood disturbance must occur during or soon after substance intoxication or withdrawal or after taking medications. The substance or medication must be able to cause the symptoms, and the disturbance does not only occur when the individual is experiencing delirium (APA, 2013a). Furthermore, the symptoms must result in clinically significant distress or impairment in functioning.

Special Considerations

Etiology is the key to understanding this particular disorder. As a result, when making this diagnosis, counselors should take steps to ensure that an independent bipolar or related disorder does not exist and better explain the observed symptoms. This will almost always involve a consultation with a physician who is qualified to determine etiology of symptoms. If the symptoms occurred before the substance or medication was ingested or continue for a month or more afterward, it is likely that the condition is not related to substance use or medication (APA, 2013a).

Differential Diagnosis

The side effects of some psychotropic medications can account for symptoms consistent with mania and hypomania. Unless the person meets the full criteria for a bipolar disorder, independent of these medications or treatments, a bipolar diagnosis is not warranted (APA, 2013a). If mania occurs while the person is receiving treatments but extends well beyond the cessation of treatment, Bipolar I disorder can be diagnosed. However, in the case of hypomanic symptoms that extend well beyond the end of treatment, a depressive episode must have occurred previously for Bipolar II disorder to be diagnosed (APA, 2013a).

Coding, Recording, and Specifiers

For substance/medication-induced bipolar and related disorder, *ICD-9-CM* and *ICD-10-CM* codes are used. The name of the substance causing the symptoms is used to identify the code and is in the written name as well. The code can include .1, .2, or .9 to indicate *with use disorder, mild*; *with use disorder, moderate*; or *without use disorder*, respectively. Additionally, specifiers of *with onset during intoxication* and *with onset during withdrawal* should be indicated after the code and name (APA, 2013a). See pages 142–143 of the *DSM-5* for more information.

293.83 Bipolar and Related Disorder Due to Another Medical Condition (F06.3_)

Differing from substance/medication-induced bipolar and related disorders, the diagnosis of bipolar and related disorder due to another medical condition applies when symptoms consistent with mania present related exclusively to a medical condition. Typically, the symptoms are seen on the onset of the medical condition but can occur as part of the relapse of a medication condition or as the course of the condition intensifies (APA, 2013a).

Essential Features

During a bipolar disorder due to another medical condition, the individual will typically present with a significant mood change, which can be connected directly to a medical condition through physical examinations, laboratory findings, or history with evidence linking the two conditions (APA, 2013a). The mood change will include unusually elevated or expansive mood or chronic irritability, along with increased energy levels or activities. Another condition or mental disorder cannot better explain the symptoms and there must be clinically significant impairment, distress, mental health hospitalization, or psychotic features. The symptoms cannot occur only during delirium (APA, 2013a).

Special Considerations

Consistent with substance/medication-induced bipolar and related disorders, etiology is the key to diagnosing this disorder. Although these individuals are most often seen in medical setting first, counselors need to be aware that certain medical conditions can cause bipolar symptoms (e.g., multiple sclerosis, stroke, and Cushing's disease; APA, 2013a). Furthermore, because symptoms are consistent with mania, counselors should monitor carefully for suicidal ideation and collaborate with physicians who are qualified to make diagnoses related to etiology of the condition.

Differential Diagnosis

Because medical conditions that can induce manic symptoms may be treated by medications that do the same, it is important to determine the etiology when differentiating the two (APA, 2013a). An assessment that assists in identifying the timing of symptom onset can be helpful. In addition, presence of symptoms for delirium, catatonia, and acute anxiety should be noted when considering a differential diagnosis.

Coding, Recording, and Specifiers

The code for this disorder is determined through *ICD-9-CM* or *ICD-10-CM*. For the *ICD-9-CM*, there is a stand-alone code for the disorder, 293.83, with the specific medical condition and related code noted after the *ICD* code. Specifiers, such as *with manic features, with manic or hypomanic-like episode*, and *with mixed features*, are added at the end as needed. Codes for the *ICD-10-CM* are related to the specifier (APA, 2013a). These include F06.33, *with manic features*; F06.33, *with manic- or hypomanic-like episode*; or F06.34, *with mixed features*. As with all diagnostic coding related to instances in which another medical condition is clinically significant, the name of the medical condition should be included in the name of the disorder. In addition to the mental disorder, the medical condition should also be coded and listed immediately before the mental disorder. For example, if a client has bipolar disorder due to hyperthyroidism, with manic features, this would be coded: 242.90 (E05.90) hyperthyroidism; 293.83 (F06.33) bipolar disorder due to hyperthyroidism, with manic features. Of course, counselors are not going to be diagnosing medical conditions; however, knowledge regarding placement is critical for interdisciplinary communication and enhanced client care.

Other Specified and Unspecified Bipolar and Related Disorders

The other specified bipolar and related disorder (296.89 [F31.89]) category may be used for diagnosis if the counselor wants to identify the specific reason that the full diagnosis for a bipolar or related disorder is not met. There are four specifiers for this diagnosis: *short-duration hypomanic episodes and major depressive episodes, hypomanic episodes with insufficient symptoms and major depressive episodes, hypomanic episode without prior major depressive episode*, and *short-duration cyclothymia (less than 24 months)*. There is one code for this diagnosis (296.89 [F31.89]). The counselor should indicate this code, followed by the disorder name, and finally the specific designation, such as *short-term cyclothymia*. The unspecified bipolar and related disorder (296.80 [F31.9]) diagnosis can be given when an individual presents with symptoms of a bipolar or related disorder but does not meet the full criteria and the counselor does not have the information to diagnose other specified bipolar and related disorder.

Specifiers for Bipolar and Related Disorders

The following is an all-inclusive listing of specifiers for bipolar and related disorders. We have chosen to include these because of the requirement for counselors to accurately identify and list specifiers to further clarify the course, severity, or special features of the identified bipolar disorder. The major change to this section includes the addition of *with anxious distress* and *with mixed features* as specifiers.

Essential Features

If the symptoms of the current episode are still ongoing but do not meet full criteria, or if the individual has experienced no significant symptoms for 2 months, *in partial remission* can be specified. If there are no significant symptoms, *in full remission* is applicable. Severity specifiers can also be identified based on the number of symptoms, symptom severity, and degree of impairment. For a specifier of *mild*, few additional symptoms are noted, they are manageable, and they result in only minor impairment. For *severe*, there are multiple excess symptoms, they are intensely distressing and unmanageable, and there is a marked interference with functioning. *Moderate* occurs when symptom number, intensity, and impairment fall between mild and severe (APA, 2013a).

For the diagnosis of bipolar and related disorders, counselors can identify specifiers as appropriate. The *DSM-5* allows for the *with anxious distress* if, during most days of a current or most recent episode of mania, hypomania, or depression, two of the following symptoms are reported: feeling keyed up or tense, increased restlessness, excessive worry that leads to difficulty concentrating, irrational fear that something negative is about to occur, and fear of loss of self-control. Symptom severity can be identified for this specifier as well. If two symptoms are noted, *mild* severity is indicated. For three symptoms, *moderate* is indicated, and *moderate-severe* is indicated if four or more symptoms are present.

Note

The specifier *with anxious distress* has been added to both MDD and bipolar disorder because of its prominence in mental health and special care settings. Anxious distress has been related to higher risk of suicide. The APA (2013a) encourages clinicians to be aware of severity levels, assess, and plan appropriately.

◆ ◆ ◆

Another specifier associated with the manic, hypomanic, or depressive episode of Bipolar I and II disorder is *with mixed features*. The criteria for the *with mixed features* specifier differ depending on the current mood episode. For this specifier to be given as a *manic or hypomanic episode, with mixed features*, the individual will have experienced a full manic or hypomanic episode, and during the majority of days this occurs, he or she also experiences at least three of the following additional symptoms: lack of interest or pleasure in all or almost all activities; depressed mood or noticeable dysphasia; noticeable slowing of movement, or psychomotor retardation; lack of energy or constant fatigue; guilt or feeling of being worthless; and unusual preoccupation with dying, thoughts of suicide, a plan for suicide, or an attempt. These symptoms are not related to medication or substance use and must include change that is noticeable to others. If the individual meets all the criteria for both mania and depression at the same time, manic episode with mixed features should be assigned.

For the specifier of *depressive episode, with mixed features* to apply, the individual will have met all the criteria for a major depressive episode with a minimum of three of the manic/hypomanic symptoms occurring most days during the episode. The manic/hypomanic criteria include exaggerated self-esteem or grandiosity; expansive or elevated mood; limited need for sleep; pressured to speak or abnormally talkative; self-report of racing thoughts or flight of ideas; inability to concentrate or easily distractible as indicated by self or others; significant increase in psychomotor agitation or goal-directed activity that is often social, work, or sexually related; and unusually increased involvement in high-risk behavior or activities that could result in painful consequences (APA, 2013a). Furthermore, the symptoms are not related to a medical condition, medication, or substance and must differ from typical behavior in a way that is noticeable to others.

The specifier of *with rapid cycling* may be present in both Bipolar I and II disorder. The individual will have at least four mood episodes within a 12-month period and these will meet the criteria for manic, hypomanic, or major depressive episodes. These episodes can switch polarity (mania and hypomanic are on the same pole) and will have either partial or full remission for at least 2 months. The episodes may occur in any order and meet the time frames and full criteria for manic, hypomanic, or major depressive episodes, with the only difference being that rapid cycling episodes occur more frequently. The episodes cannot be influenced or better accounted for by substance use (APA, 2013a).

For the specifier of *with melancholic features* to be applicable, during the most severe period of the major depressive episode, the individual must experience lack of pleasure in almost all or all activities or lack of response to pleasurable events. Three or more additional symptoms must be experienced from the following: distinct depression that may include deep despondency, despair, glumness, or empty mood; increased depression in the morning that can be accompanied by early waking, at least 2 hours earlier than normal; noticeable slowing or psychomotor agitation; significant weight fluctuation; and overwhelming guilt. The changes are noticeable, and the psychomotor changes are almost always present. Furthermore, the condition occurs more frequently in individuals who also have psychotic features and is more likely to occur in severe depressive episodes requiring inpatient care (APA, 2013a).

With atypical features is applicable when the individual spends most days of the current or most recent major depressive episode experiencing mood reactivity and two or more additional features. The additional features include significant weight gain or increased appetite, constant daytime sleepiness, feeling of heaviness in the arms or legs, and a history of social or occupational issues related to extreme sensitivity to being rejected. This sensitivity to rejection begins early in life and can occur even when the individual is not experiencing depressive symptoms but can be worse during a depressive episode.

Note

Whereas the term *atypical depression* was historically acknowledged as the traditional presentation of depressive symptoms, depression is no longer a rarely diagnosed condition, as the name may imply.

◆ ◆ ◆

For the specifier *with psychotic features* to be given, the individual will experience delusions or hallucinations during the episode. *With mood-congruent psychotic features* or *without mood-congruent psychotic features* should be diagnosed if psychotic features are present. When the psychotic features are mood-congruent, they will be consistent with the manic themes (e.g., grandiosity), but there may also be paranoia surrounding whether or not others believe the grandiose statements or the individual's capacities. When this does not occur, a specifier of *with mood-incongruent psychotic features* should be included.

With catatonia is specified when catatonic features are present during most of the episode for either a manic or a major depressive episode. Criteria for catatonia associated with a mental disorder are given in the Schizophrenia Spectrum and Other Psychotic Disorders chapter.

The specifier of *with peripartum onset* can be used when the beginning of mood symptoms is during pregnancy or in the 4 weeks after delivery for current or most recent episode of mania, hypomania, or major depression in Bipolar I or Bipolar II disorder. Whereas mood episodes can begin before or after delivery, about half of women begin experiencing these symptoms prior to delivery, and as such, the specifier is *with peripartum onset*. Symptoms associated with this can be severe, and for some women this includes anxiety, panic attacks, and psychotic features that can be extreme and include command hallucinations to harm or kill the child.

When a mood episode, whether manic, hypomanic, or depressive, occurs regularly over the life span, in conjunction with a specific season, the specifier of *with seasonal pattern* may apply. Although other mood episodes can occur, the type of episode referred to by this specifier has a consistent temporal relationship to a particular time of year, unrelated to outside stressors (such as difficult holiday events), and will not occur outside the seasonal pattern for at least 2 years. The symptomatology may either diminish or change as the seasons change, and the seasonal episodes will outnumber the nonseasonal episodes over the life span.

Chapter 5

Anxiety Disorders

Anxiety is defined as "a state of intense apprehension, uncertainty, and fear resulting from the anticipation of a threatening event or situation, often to a degree that normal physical and psychological functioning is disrupted" (*American Heritage Medical Dictionary*, 2007, p. 38). The APA (2013a) purports that each of the anxiety disorders shares features of fear and anxiety, which it defines as follows: "*Fear* is the emotional response to real or perceived imminent threat, whereas *anxiety* is anticipation of future threat" (p. 189). People who experience anxiety often have physiological symptoms such as muscle tension, heart palpitations, sweating, dizziness, or shortness of breath. Emotional symptoms include restlessness, a sense of impending doom, fear of dying, fear of embarrassment or humiliation, or fear of something terrible happening. People with anxiety disorder worry more than others and display excessive or persistent fear and anxiety (Kessler, Berglund, et al., 2005).

Prevalence of anxiety among the general population is high. Each year, anxiety disorders affect approximately 18%, or 40 million, adults in the United States (NIMH, 2013b, 2013d). Anxiety disorders have a lifetime prevalence of approximately 30% (Kessler, Berglund, et al., 2005). Close to 50% of individuals diagnosed with an anxiety disorder also meet the criteria for a depressive disorder. Anxiety and depression are highly comorbid and share genetic predispositions (Batelaan et al., 2010). It is important for counselors to accurately diagnose anxiety disorder as they respond to clinical interventions (ADAA, 2013).

Anxiety manifests in multiple ways, including fear for the future on a cognitive level, muscle tension on a somatovisceral level, and situational avoidance on a behavioral level. This symptomatology holds pervasive impact for the functioning of the individual, including varying degrees of difficulty in establishing and maintaining interpersonal relationships (Hickey et al., 2005). Anxiety disorders often persist over time, thus representing ongoing challenges for the many people living with them (Beard, Moitra, Weisber, & Keller, 2010; Rubio & Lopez-Ibor, 2007; Wittchen, 2002). Because the prevalence of anxiety in the general population is so high, these diagnoses are frequently the focus of clinical attention for counselors and are often diagnosed within counseling settings (ADAA, 2013).

Major Changes From *DSM-IV-TR* to *DSM-5*

The DSM-5 Anxiety, Obsessive-Compulsive Spectrum, Posttraumatic, and Dissociative Disorders Work Group separated what had been traditionally known as anxiety disorder into three distinct chapters: anxiety disorders, obsessive-compulsive and related disorders, and trauma- and stressor-related disorders. This represents an overall shift in the organization of the manual that includes clustering comorbid symptoms together. Specific changes to the Anxiety Disorders chapter include removing panic attack as a specifier for agoraphobia, including selective mutism and separation anxiety disorder, and changing the name of social phobia to social anxiety disorder (APA, 2013a). Panic attack criteria are also provided, along with the provision that the specifier may be applied to a wide array of *DSM-5* diagnoses.

Differential Diagnosis

APA's (2013a) decision to cluster anxiety disorders within one chapter, separate from obsessive-compulsive disorder (OCD) and other stressor-related disorders, affects clinicians' differential diagnosis. Stein, Craske, Friedman, and Phillips (2011) posited that clinical attention should focus on the discernment of disorders enumerated within this chapter. Perhaps the best way for counselors to accurately diagnose anxiety disorders is to have a clear framework for the specifics of each diagnosis as well as common differential and comorbid diagnoses.

Differential diagnosis of anxiety disorders can be challenging, especially considering the comorbidity of anxiety disorders with depressive disorders. One way to differentiate the two is for counselors to keep in mind that depressive disorders are sometimes viewed as "anxious-misery" with high incidences of sadness and anhedonia; this distinguishes them from anxiety disorders, which often include anxious anticipation, uncertainty, and fear (Craske et al., 2009). Anhedonia and lowered affect are more commonly symptoms of depression than anxiety, whereas sleep disturbance, overall fatigue, and difficulty with concentration can be symptoms of both (APA, 2013a). The high comorbidity rates between depression and anxiety often make discernment a difficult task for counselors and researchers alike; clear understanding of the distinctions in sequelae of both disorders can assist with accurate differential diagnosis.

Counselors can also consider the propensity of individuals diagnosed with anxiety disorders to worry more about future events and individuals with depressive disorders to be generally sad or morose. Across the spectrum of anxiety disorders, there are heightened responses to threats (real or perceived), increased responses to stress, and reactivity of the amygdala. Common overarching features of anxiety and depressive disorders include inability to focus, appetite or sleep disturbance, and negative impact on self-efficacy (APA, 2013a; Craske et al., 2009).

Etiology and Treatment

Close to 50% of individuals diagnosed with an anxiety disorder also meet criteria for a depressive disorder (ADAA, 2013). Because of their high prevalence rate, these diagnoses are frequently the focus of clinical attention for counselors. Over the course of a lifetime, an individual's diagnosis can migrate from anxiety to depression and vice versa. Therefore, it is important for counselors to view the treatment of these disorders from a longitudinal perspective (Batelaan et al., 2010).

Anxiety disorders contain myriad psychobiological factors that include genetic predisposition, social and cultural contexts, and life events. Kessler, Petukhova, Sampson, Zaslasvky, and Wittchen (2012) discussed the lifetime morbid risk (LMR) for anxiety disorders; LMR represents the portion of people who will eventually develop the disorder at some time in their life, regardless of risk factors such as comorbid diagnoses. In the United States, specific phobia (18.4%) and social phobia (13.0%) have the highest LMR and agoraphobia has the lowest (3.7%). Women are more likely than men to have coexisting anxiety and depression (Friborg, Martinussen, Kaiser, Overgard, & Rosenvinge, 2013).

Although tending toward chronicity, anxiety disorders are responsive to psychotherapeutic treatment modalities. It is important for counselors to note that severe anxiety is a risk factor for suicide (Fawcett, 2013); therefore, assessment of suicide risk should be incorporated into treatment for all clients. Additionally, anxiety disorders are the most common disorders among youth (Sood, Mendez, & Kendall, 2012) and have a median age of onset of 11 years. Additional research is needed for the treatment of anxiety disorders in young people because, at the current time, only CBT has evidenced-based treatment efficacy (Mohr & Schneider, 2013).

Implications for Counselors

Because of the prevalence of anxiety disorders in the general population, their diagnoses are frequently the focus of clinical attention for counselors and are common within counseling settings (ADAA, 2013). Individuals with anxiety disorders generally respond well to clinical intervention with effective treatments, including CBT, behavior therapy, and relaxation training (ADAA, 2013). Numerous research studies reveal that positive treatment outcomes for anxiety disorders are maintained longer for individuals, including children and adolescents, who have participated in CBT and behavior therapy (Hausmann et al., 2007; Hofmann & Smits, 2008; Silverman, Pina, & Viswesvaran, 2008). Because anxiety disorders are often diagnosed in counseling settings, it is important for counselors to focus on ongoing assessment and monitoring.

To help readers better understand changes from the *DSM-IV-TR* to the *DSM-5*, the rest of this chapter outlines each disorder within the Anxiety Disorders chapter of the *DSM-5*. Readers should note that we have focused on major changes from the *DSM-IV-TR* to the *DSM-5*; however, this is not a stand-alone resource for diagnosis. Although a summary and special considerations for counselors are provided for each disorder, when diagnosing clients, counselors need to reference the *DSM-5*. It is essential that the diagnostic criteria and features, subtypes and specifiers (if applicable), prevalence, course, and risk and prognostic factors for each disorder are clearly understood prior to diagnosis.

309.21 Separation Anxiety Disorder (F93.0)

> I know it is irrational but every time my partner begins to get ready for work, I start to feel horrible. I am certain that something bad will happen as soon as he leaves. It may be a car wreck or a heart attack, but I just know something bad will happen. I get physically ill. Sometimes I throw up. Often, I go to work with him. It's causing problem for him, and he has become very frustrated with me because this has gone on for so long.—Benjamin

Separation anxiety disorder has been listed as a mental disorder since the publication of the *DSM-III* in 1980. In the *DSM-5*, separation anxiety disorder was moved from the Disorders Usually First Diagnosed in Infancy, Childhood, or Adolescence chapter of the *DSM-IV-TR* to the Anxiety Disorders chapter, and the age-of-onset requirement ("before age 18 years") was dropped, thus allowing for diagnosis of separation anxiety disorder in adults (Mohr & Schneider, 2013).

Essential Features

The essential feature for separation anxiety disorder includes developmentally inappropriate nervousness and fear related to separation from the primary caregiver. In addition to fear and anxiety, physical symptoms can include headaches, stomachaches, and cardiovascular symptoms in adolescents and adults. These emotional and somatic symptoms can develop in childhood and persist into adult life. The fear and worry is focused on potential harm to attachment figures. This leads to reluctance on the part of these individuals to be alone or away from loved ones. Typical behaviors are "clinging" or "shadowing" (APA, 2013a, p. 191), with sleep disturbances commonly affecting both children and adults.

Special Considerations

Separation anxiety disorder can be extant through the life course, although it must last 6 months or longer for diagnosis in adults. For children, there is a minimum duration of 1 month. Prevalence rates are 4% for children, 1.6% for adolescents, and 0.9% to 1.9% for adults. Separation anxiety disorder is the most prevalent anxiety disorder in children, with girls more susceptible than boys. Functionality in school, work, or social settings is often impaired (APA, 2013a).

Although considered a diagnosis primarily seen in childhood, separation anxiety disorder also affects adults, with the key features similar across the age spectrum: fear of separation from or harm befalling loved ones (Manicavasagar, Silove, Curtis, & Wagner, 2000). Adults with separation anxiety disorder typically display more covert behaviors, such as staying home or in close proximity to loved ones as well as engaging in frequent check-ins (Marnane & Silove, 2013). In contrast to APA prevalence reports, the National Comorbidity Survey Replication found a lifetime prevalence of separation anxiety disorder in adulthood of 6.6%, indicating that it is one of the most commonly occurring anxiety disorders (Shear, Jin, & Ruscio, 2006).

Cultural Considerations

Expectations for physical and emotional closeness in relationships are culturally linked, and counselors must be careful not to pathologize behaviors of individuals from more collectivist cultures, especially cultures in which parents and children are rarely separated. Sood et al. (2012) studied help seeking among Indian American, Puerto Rican, and European American mothers who had children diagnosed with separation anxiety disorder. Puerto Rican mothers were more likely to view the symptoms as resulting from a physical health condition and were thus less likely to seek psychological treatment. Acculturation was directly correlated with help-seeking behaviors, and those with strongly held religious beliefs were more likely to seek assistance from a religious leader. Sood et al.'s study highlights the need to examine cultural variables in addressing perception and treatment.

Differential Diagnosis

When considering separation anxiety disorder, counselors must distinguish between developmentally and culturally appropriate reactions to separation and abnormal reactions to separation. Common differential diagnoses for separation anxiety disorder include GAD, panic disorder, agoraphobia, conduct disorder, PTSD, illness anxiety disorder, bereavement, depressive and bipolar disorder, ODD, psychotic disorder, and personality disorder. With separation anxiety disorder, the thrust of the anxiety is focused on separation from attachment figures (APA, 2013a). It differentiates from GAD and social anxiety disorder in this regard. GAD's predominant features are diffuse anxiety, whereas social anxiety disorder is specific to social situations.

Panic disorder, with its unexpected panic attacks, is distinguishable from separation anxiety disorder in that the unexpected and incapacitating panic attacks are not extant. PTSD centers around intrusive thoughts about and avoidance of memories related to the traumatic event; the worries central to separation anxiety disorder are related to harm to loved ones. With illness anxiety disorder, depressive disorder, bipolar disorder, and ODD, there is no predominant concern in being separated from attachment figures. Psychotic disorders contain hallucinations; this is not an evident feature of separation anxiety disorder (APA, 2013a).

Coding, Recording, and Specifiers

There is only one diagnostic code for separation anxiety disorder: 309.21(F93.0). There are no specifiers for this diagnosis.

313.23 Selective Mutism (F94.0)

Camilla didn't speak to anyone but me for 2 months after the accident. No one knew what to do. Clearly, she had the ability to talk, but she just refused to do so. I didn't want to constantly punish her, and it didn't seem to be helping anyway. I promised her rewards, but she didn't respond to that either. The students in her kindergarten class really teased her.—Jules (Camilla's mom)

Selective mutism represents the voluntary refusal to speak (typically occurring outside of the home or immediate family). Elective mutism, first identified as a mental disorder in the *DSM-III*, was relabeled to selective mutism in the *DSM-IV-TR*. This is a new diagnosis in the Anxiety Disorders chapter of the *DSM-5*, because of the restructuring of the chapters and the removal of the chapter on disorders usually first diagnosed in infancy, childhood, or adolescence (APA, 2013a).

Essential Features

The essential feature of selective mutism is a refusal to verbally communicate outside of the home or with people other than immediate family members or caregivers not due to speech/language difficulties. Children with selective mutism may speak only to immediate family members and will sometimes communicate with nonverbals such as nodding or grunting; these children do not usually possess language deficits. Selective mutism typically has an age of onset of under 5 years and is often first noticed in school settings (APA, 2013a).

Special Considerations

Selective mutism can manifest in adolescents and adults but is much less frequent (APA, 2013a). Excessive shyness is a personality trait often seen with selective mutism. Children diagnosed with selective mutism have high diagnostic comorbidity with other anxiety disorders, most frequently social anxiety disorder (APA, 2013a). Children with selective mutism frequently suffer significant impairment in social and school situations. Social isolation and academic impairment both occur.

Cultural Considerations

Cultural formulations play a critical role in the diagnosis of selective mutism. Hollifield, Gepper, Johnson, and Fryer (2003) discussed the ease of misdiagnosis when culture is not integrally considered in diagnosing selective mutism. It is important to assess language acquisition (especially if a child is living in a country whose native language is not his or her own). Further research on cultural contexts and the diagnosis of selective mutism is needed.

Differential Diagnosis

Counselors who are considering a diagnosis of selective mutism must consider the child's developmental and contextual functioning so they do not pathologize normal developmental transitions and adjustments. Common differential diagnoses for selective mutism include communication disorders, neurodevelopmental disorders, schizophrenia and other psychotic disorders, and social anxiety disorder. It is important to note that with selective mutism, the communication disorders are not specific to social situations and are more pervasive. Selective mutism should be diagnosed only when a child has readily demonstrated speaking ability in certain situations, such as the home environment. This is distinct from neurodevelopmental disorders, schizophrenia, and other psychotic disorders for which there may be impairment in communication regardless of the setting. Finally, it is not uncommon for social anxiety disorder to occur concomitantly with selective mutism; when this occurs, both disorders should be given (APA, 2013a).

Coding, Recording, and Specifiers

There is only one diagnostic code for selective mutism: 313.23 (F94.0). There are no specifiers for this diagnosis. Counselors should note that the original *DSM-5* mistakenly published the code 312.23 (F94.0) for selective mutism. This is incorrect, and the code of 313.23 (F94.0) should be used.

300.29 Specific Phobia (F40._ _ _)

> Ever since I was a child, I've been terrified of needles. My friends got their ears pierced but I refused to go near the salon. I avoid the doctor for the same reason, even when I know I should go. Last time I got sick, I waited until the last minute to go in. When the nurse started talking about taking my blood, my stomach started hurting, my heart started pounding in my ears, and I got light-headed. I refused to let her draw blood. It's been so long since I had blood work, I can't even remember my blood type. —Marin

Specific phobias represent the existence of fear or anxiety in the presence of a specific situation or object. This is called the "phobic stimulus" (APA, 2013a, p. 198). This fear or anxiety must be markedly stronger than the actual threat of the object or situation (e.g., likelihood of being stuck on a well-maintained elevator). Specific phobias were first identified as such in the *DSM-III-R* (APA, 1987) and carry a lifetime prevalence rate of 9.4% to 12.5% (Marques, Robinaugh, LeBlanc, & Hinton, 2011).

Essential Features

The main feature of specific phobia is an inappropriate fear response to a specific object or situation that is incongruent with the danger or threat and out of proportion to the danger posed. Specific phobias can develop after a traumatic event or from witnessing traumatic events. Individuals with specific phobia will avoid situations of exposure to the stimulus. The fear or anxiety happens every time the person is exposed to the stimulus and may include symptoms of a panic attack. The median age of onset for a diagnosis of specific phobia is 13 years (APA, 2013a).

Special Considerations

Physiological arousal responses resulting from specific phobia may include feeling faint, accelerated heart rate and blood pressure, and hyperarousal. Quality of life is negatively affected, and impairment in overall functioning is common. Early intervention is key because the recovery rate for specific phobia in children has been shown to be as high as 60% after CBT (Mohr & Schneider, 2013).

Cultural Considerations

It is important to take sociocultural context into account when assessing specific phobia because in some contexts fear of a stimulus is real and proportionate (e.g., being bitten by a poisonous snake in certain geographic locations). African Americans have the highest lifetime prevalence of specific phobia, with Caucasians ranking second among ethnic groups within the United States (Marques et al., 2011). Generally, Asians and Latinos possess overall lower rates of specific phobia than other groups (Marques et al., 2011).

Differential Diagnosis

When considering whether to diagnose a specific phobia, counselors are wise to consider the degree to which the fear and response to the fear are consistent with one's developmental level and cultural context. This diagnosis should not be made if the fear is seen as culturally appropriate. Similarly, counselors must consider the degree of distress and impairment associated with the phobia. Common differential diagnoses for specific phobia include agoraphobia, social anxiety disorder, separation anxiety disorder, panic disorder, OCD, trauma and stressor-related disorders, eating disorders, and schizophrenia spectrum and other psychotic disorders. Agoraphobia has many fears that overlap with specific phobias. The counselor should diagnose agoraphobia when more than one condition/situation is feared. Social anxiety disorder should be diagnosed instead of specific phobia when social situations are the cause of the fear. Panic attacks can occur in conjunction with specific phobia; however, the diagnosis of panic disorder would supersede the diagnosis of specific phobia if the attacks are unexpected. A diagnosis of specific phobia would not be given if the fear results from delusional thought processes such as those disorders in the schizophrenia spectrum and other psychotic disorders (APA, 2013a).

Coding, Recording, and Specifiers

There is one *ICD-9-CM* diagnostic code for specific phobia: 300.29. Counselors using the *ICD-10-CM* will assign the appropriate diagnostic code based on the phobia specifier. These specifiers for specific phobia include *animal, natural environment, blood-injection injury, situational,* and *other.* Blood-injection injury includes four subtypes: *fear of blood, fear of injections and transfusions, fear of other medical care,* and *fear of injury.* If more than one specific phobia is present, the counselor codes all of those present using the *ICD-10-CM* diagnostic codes. Approximately 75% of individuals diagnosed with specific phobia fear more than one object. When this occurs, more than one diagnosis is given. The following is a complete list of codes and specifiers for specific phobia.

300.29 (F40.218)	Animal
300.29 (F40.228)	Natural environment
300.29 (F40.23x)	Blood-injection injury
F40.230	Fear of blood
F40.231	Fear of injections and transfusions
F40.232	Fear of other medical care
F40.233	Fear of injury
300.29 (F40.248)	Situational (e.g., airplanes, elevators, enclosed places)
300.29 (F40.298)	Other (e.g., situations that may lead to choking or vomiting; in children, e.g., loud sounds or costumed characters)

In cases in which individuals experience panic attacks in response to their phobia, counselors should add *with panic attacks* to the diagnosis.

300.23 Social Anxiety Disorder (Social Phobia) (F40.10)

> I was so relieved when I was told I could work from home. Even though my job is working on computer programs, the anxiety around interacting with the people in the other cubes was overwhelming. I don't think they liked me anyway because I always said the wrong things. I thought my boss was going to fire me because I had such a hard time going into work, but I am good at my job so she made this arrangement. My family members seem concerned though because I almost never leave my house. —Ryan

Social phobia was originally classified as a mental disorder in the *DSM-III* and has been renamed social anxiety disorder in the *DSM-5*. It is one of the most common mental disorders with a lifetime prevalence rate of slightly greater than 10%; the majority of diagnoses are made during childhood or early adolescence (Kerns, Comer, Pincus, & Hofmann, 2013; Marques et al., 2011). Social anxiety disorder is often seen in conjunction with MDD, other anxiety disorder, and substance use disorder (APA, 2013a).

Essential Features

The main feature of social anxiety disorder is ongoing fear and worry surrounding myriad social situations (Kerns et al., 2013). Individuals with social anxiety disorder often fear negative evaluation (e.g., being humiliated, embarrassed, or rejected) by others (either unfamiliar or familiar) in performance, interaction, or observation situations. A *performance only* specifier has been added for social anxiety disorder in the *DSM-5* and includes a minimum duration of 6 months. Children, adolescents, and adults now share the same criteria for duration, and the criterion for adult insight has been dropped (Mohr & Schneider, 2013).

Special Considerations

Women tend to be diagnosed with social anxiety disorder more often than men, but both genders experience lifelong consequences from the symptoms. Individuals with social anxiety disorder tend to never marry or have children. They often drop out of school, have difficulties maintaining continuous employment, and experience low socioeconomic status. Although individuals with this disorder tend to seek mental health care after suffering for 15 to 20 years, being unemployed is frequently a trigger for initiating treatment (APA, 2013a).

Cultural Considerations

Across cultural demographics, social anxiety disorder is highest among Caucasian and Native American adults; however, studies have shown it to also be high among Latino and Caucasian youth (Marques et al., 2011; Martinez, Polo, & Carter, 2012). In an article examining Asian cultural constructs, Hsu et al. (2012) posited that reticence and social restraint may appear as social anxiety when, in fact, they are normalized behaviors in Asian culture. As such, it is important for counselors to carefully assess social constructs in diagnosing social anxiety disorder.

Differential Diagnosis

Common differential diagnoses of social anxiety disorder are normative shyness, agoraphobia, panic disorder, GAD, separation anxiety disorder, specific phobias, selective mutism, MDD, body dysmorphic disorder (BDD), delusional disorder, autism spectrum disorder (ASD), personality disorder, and ODD. It is important to note that shyness is viewed as a personality trait and is not pathological in nature; a diagnosis of social anxiety disorder is unwarranted unless there is impairment in functioning. Individuals with social anxiety disorder are fearful of negative evaluation from others; they are not fearful of nor do they worry about separation from loved ones as seen in separation anxiety disorder. Conversely, individuals with specific phobias do not typically worry about being judged in social situations.

Selective mutism is differentiated from social anxiety disorder in that individuals diagnosed with selective mutism are not fearful in social situations where they are not required to speak. For individuals with BDD, fear and avoidance are specifically caused by thoughts about their own appearance. In contrast to individuals diagnosed with ASD, individuals with social anxiety disorder display capacity for age-appropriate interactions and social relationships; however, they avoid them or endure them with intense distress.

Finally, individuals with MDD, personality disorder, and ODD typically are not worried about negative social evaluations. A key differentiating feature of individuals with social anxiety disorder from those with delusional disorder is that individuals diagnosed with social anxiety disorder typically display insight into the disproportionate fear or worry they have in social situations (APA, 2013a).

Coding, Recording, and Specifiers

There is only one diagnostic code for social anxiety disorder: 300.23 (F40.10). Social anxiety disorder has a *performance only* specifier, which is given if anxiety is specific to speaking or performing in public. Individuals diagnosed with the *performance only* specifier are mainly impaired in their occupational environments or in school situations where public speaking is a requirement. These individuals are not afraid of and do not avoid other social situations. If individuals experience panic attacks in conjunction with social anxiety disorder, the specifier *with panic attacks* should be added to the diagnosis.

 Example

Adam is an 11-year-old fifth grader who is the fourth out of seven children born into an Orthodox Jewish family. Adam is one of five boys in his family. His father is loving and attentive but also works a lot; Adam's mother does most of the hands-on parenting. At home, Adam is quiet and serious but takes time to read to his younger siblings and occasionally plays outside with his brothers. At school, Adam stays by himself and rarely interacts with his classmates. Adam will make excuses to stay in the classroom during recess (such as wanting extra time to study) and prefers to study after school in lieu of extracurricular activities.

Adam is a quiet, serious child who obeys the rules and rarely displays upset emotions or anger. Adam's mom is busy raising seven children and is grateful that Adam has no disciplinary issues and performs well academically. She does not see a problem with his behaviors. His teacher has referred Adam to the school counselor because of his reluctance to work on any group projects or engage with peers. Adam tells his counselor that he has no friends other than his siblings and that he doesn't want any. Adam says that he enjoys studying and playing games with his brothers but "doesn't have time for friends." Upon questioning, Adam discloses that he has never had any peer friendships and gets nervous in most all situations outside of his home. Unlike his siblings, he does not look forward to religious services although he enjoys his religious studies. Adam generally avoids social interactions and is afraid to travel outside of his hometown. He reports feeling sick to his stomach when his routine changes. At home, although quieter than his brothers, Adam laughs, jokes, and interacts with all of his siblings. He tells his counselor that he would like to have one or two close friends to hang out with but also is "fine" the way things are.

Adam's presenting symptoms include worry that he will embarrass himself, freezing in unfamiliar situations, avoidance of social situations, and emotional distress outside of his home environment. These feelings and behaviors have been extant since he began elementary school and have increased in severity over the course of the past year.

◆ ◆ ◆

Diagnostic Questions

1. Do Adam's presenting symptoms meet the criteria for an anxiety disorder? If so, which one?
2. Based on the disorder identified in Question 1, which symptom(s) led you to select the diagnosis?
3. What would be the reason(s) a counselor may not diagnose Adam with GAD?

4. Would Adam be more accurately diagnosed with ASD? Why or why not?
5. What rule-outs would you consider for Adam's case?
6. What other information may be needed to make an accurate clinical diagnosis?

300.01 Panic Disorder (F41.0)

I never knew when it was going to hit me, and that made it even worse. My heart would start pounding, my hands shook, and I would start sweating. I couldn't breathe. I felt like the world was going to end and I was going to die at any moment. I felt like I was going crazy. —Mabel

Panic disorder is defined as recurrent, unexpected panic attacks and was initially classified in the *DSM-III*. There is a median age of onset ranging from 20 to 24 years, with a small percentage of individuals first diagnosed in childhood. Panic disorder is not usually first seen in individuals over the age of 45. There is an annual U.S. prevalence rate of 2.1% to 2.8%; this is one of the highest prevalence rates worldwide (Marques et al., 2011).

Essential Features

The essential features of panic disorder are persistent fear or concern of inappropriate fear responses, with recurrent and unexpected panic attacks including physiological changes, such as accelerated heart rate, sweating, dizziness, trembling, and chest pain. Worry and behavioral changes may also accompany the diagnosis. Panic disorder has physical and cognitive symptoms and involves numerous, unexpected panic attacks (although it is important to note that individuals with panic disorder can have expected panic attacks too). Worry typically focuses on physical symptoms or concern regarding mental functioning such as losing control (APA, 2013a).

Special Considerations

Up to 50% of individuals diagnosed with panic disorder will have nocturnal panic attacks or waking up in a "state of panic" (APA, 2013a, p. 210). Childhood abuse (sexual and physical) is a risk factor, and there is scientific evidence of genetic predisposition, with women being more likely to receive the diagnosis of panic disorder than men.

Cultural Considerations

Individuals with panic disorder display specific variations in physical symptoms based on cultural contexts (Marques et al., 2011). Cultural expectations can lead to the experience of panic attack such as *ataque de nervios* ("attack of nerves"; see Glossary of Cultural Concepts of Distress Appendix in the *DSM-5*, p. 833) in Latin Americans that involves trembling, screaming, crying, aggression, depersonalization, and possible suicidal behavior. African American and Afro-Caribbean groups generally have lower rates of panic disorder. Fears related to the symptoms of panic disorder vary across cultures. Although Caucasians have a higher prevalence rate of panic disorder, they typically have less functional impairment than African Americans; this highlights the need for counselors to carefully assess severity with African American clients (APA, 2013a).

Differential Diagnosis

By themselves, panic attacks are not a diagnosable condition; a diagnosis of panic disorder is only made if one's response to unexpected panic attacks includes persistent worry or behavioral changes associated with the attacks. Common differential diagnoses for panic disorder are other specified or unspecified anxiety disorder, anxiety disorder due to another medical condition, substance/medication-induced anxiety disorder, and other mental disorders with panic attacks as an associated feature. Illness anxiety disorder, formerly known as hypochondriasis, often shares features with or is comorbid with panic disorder (Starcevic, 2013). It is the unexpected nature of the panic attacks that makes panic disorder distinct from panic attacks occurring within the context of another anxiety disorder. If an unexpected panic attack has not occurred, the diagnosis of panic disorder is not appropriate and is also not diagnosed if the panic attack results from a medical condition or utilization of a substance (APA, 2013a).

Coding, Recording, and Specifiers

There is only one diagnostic code for panic disorder: 300.01(F41.0). However, there is extensive information about the one specifier, *panic attack*. See the next section regarding the *panic attack* specifier. Note that the *panic attack* specifier is not a mental disorder and is not assigned a diagnostic code.

Panic Attack Specifier

Panic attacks are not classified as a mental disorder and do not have a diagnostic code. Panic attacks are abrupt surges of intense fear; they can occur with mental disorders such as depressive and anxiety disorders and also be extant with physical disorders. *Panic attack* is a specifier for both mental and physical disorders; however, the elements of panic attack are contained within the criteria for panic disorder so it is not a specifier for that diagnosis. An example of panic attack used as a specifier is social anxiety disorder, *with panic attacks* (APA, 2013a).

Essential Features

Panic attacks represent intense fear or discomfort that occurs abruptly and peaks rapidly. Physical symptoms predominate and must include a minimum of four out of the 13 identified symptoms. These mostly physical symptoms occur and reach their zenith within minutes. Panic attacks have an 11.2% annual prevalence rate in the general U.S. population (APA, 2013a). See page 214 of the *DSM-5* for a list of physical symptoms.

Special Considerations

The rapid time to reach peak intensity distinguishes panic attacks from general or ongoing anxiety. Panic attacks are associated with higher rates of suicidal ideation and attempts. As such, individuals presenting with panic attacks should be carefully screened for suicide risk. Panic attacks are rare in young children and occur more frequently in women than men (APA, 2013a).

Cultural Considerations
There are culturally distinct symptoms that do not count toward four of the 13 symptoms needed for use of the *panic attack* specifier. Cultural context can also lend to the difference between expected and unexpected panic attacks and may also cause fear of specific situations. The *DSM-5* includes an Appendix titled the "Glossary of Cultural Concepts of Distress" that provides specific information about the cultural syndromes (APA, 2013a).

Differential Diagnosis

Common differential diagnoses for the *panic attack* specifier include other paroxysmal episodes, anxiety disorder due to another medical condition, and substance/medication-induced anxiety disorder. For appropriate application of the *panic attack* specifier, abrupt surges of intense fear or discomfort must occur in the individual. This distinguishes panic attack from emotional reactions such as grief or anger. Multiple medical conditions, as well as myriad substance intoxication and withdrawal, can cause panic attacks. If the age of onset for panic attacks is older than 45 years or if there are unusual symptoms occurring during the panic attack, it is important to carefully consider the possibility of the panic attack being caused by a medical condition or substance use (APA, 2013a).

300.22 Agoraphobia (F40.00)

I didn't leave my condo for 2 weeks. I even arranged to have my groceries delivered. The fear has been bad for years, but that was the worst. Obviously, I lost my job. But I was certain that if I went out, something awful would happen. —Devin

Agoraphobia is a newly codable disorder in the *DSM-5* and represents an intense fear that results from real or imagined exposure to a wide range of situations. There is a 1.7% prevalence rate for the diagnosis of agoraphobia for adolescents and middle-age adults; it is less prevalent in young children and older adults (0.4%; APA, 2013a). Agoraphobia leads to moderate to severe impairment in functioning, with more than 33% of individuals diagnosed with agoraphobia restricted to home environments (APA, 2013a).

Essential Features

Agoraphobia represents fear of situations in which escape from bad things is difficult. The fear may fluctuate depending on exposure to the event; it may also result from anticipation of an event. This response happens almost every time an individual is exposed to the situation or event (it is not agoraphobia if the response occurs only some of the time). Avoidance of the event or situation must also be present and can include cognitive or behavioral aspects (APA, 2013a).

Special Considerations

A diagnosis of agoraphobia is given regardless of whether the individual meets the criteria for panic disorder. If criteria for both conditions are met, both diagnoses are given. It is important to note that agoraphobia can impair functioning to the level that an individual becomes homebound. The mean age of onset of agoraphobia is 17 years, and onset during childhood is rare. Females are twice as likely to be diagnosed with agoraphobia than males. Most people who are given the diagnosis of agoraphobia have comorbid mental disorders, including a higher likelihood of other anxiety disorders (APA, 2013a).

Cultural Considerations
There is a need for research focusing on the cultural considerations of agoraphobia. The *DSM-5* does not include cultural information specific to the diagnosis.

Differential Diagnosis

Common differential diagnoses for agoraphobia include the following: specific phobia, situational type, separation anxiety disorder, social anxiety disorder, panic disorder, acute stress disorder, PTSD, MDD, and other medical conditions. A diagnosis of agoraphobia can be given in conjunction with that of another disorder if the criteria for both are met unless the fears result from the sequelae of another disorder. MDD can leave an individual homebound, but this is predominantly from apathy or anhedonia. One of the main challenges is differentiating agoraphobia from specific phobia. Acute stress disorder and PTSD can be distinguished from agoraphobia in that the avoidance occurs only from situations that trigger a memory of the traumatic event, such as a driving or riding in a car after a motor vehicle accident (APA, 2013a).

Coding, Recording, and Specifiers

There is only one diagnostic code for agoraphobia: 300.22 (F40.00). The specifier *with panic attacks* may be added if individuals experience panic attacks associated with agoraphobia.

 **Example**

Daryl is a 40-year-old Native American woman of Navajo descent and a married mother of two teenage sons. During the course of her 19-year marriage, she has rarely worked outside of the home. During the past 5 years, Daryl has gradually given up engaging in most of the leisure and social activities she previously enjoyed, such as painting, making pottery, and attending concerts. She has developed feelings of worry about many bad things happening to her if she leaves her home, including car accidents, robbery, becoming lost, and falling ill. These feelings have increased in intensity and frequency over the course of the past 13 months. Daryl has relied on her husband and children to purchase groceries and household necessities. She no longer paints and has not used her outdoor pottery kiln, a lifelong hobby and a source of income, in over a year. Although she regularly engages in yard work, she no longer receives the enjoyment from it she previously did.

Daryl's husband is worried about her, and her relationships with her sons have suffered because she no longer attends their extracurricular events. Despite repeated attempts at various relaxation and calming techniques, Daryl cannot force herself to reengage in any of these activities.

Daryl reports that she fears situations that include being outside of her home or yard, being in a crowd, standing in a line, crossing a bridge, and driving or riding in a car. Daryl has no prior history of panic attacks or previous trauma.

◆ ◆ ◆

Diagnostic Questions

1. Do Daryl's presenting symptoms meet the criteria for an anxiety disorder? If so, which one?
2. Based on the disorder identified in Question 1, which symptom(s) led you to select the diagnosis?
3. What would be the reason(s) a counselor may not diagnose Daryl with GAD?
4. Would Daryl be more accurately diagnosed with a depressive disorder? Why or why not?
5. What rule-outs would you consider for Daryl's case?
6. What other information may be needed to make an accurate clinical diagnosis?

300.02 Generalized Anxiety Disorder (F41.1)

I constantly felt tense and jumpy. For months I lived with excessive worry and fears that something was wrong or something bad was going to happen. My friends described me as high-strung. I just wished I could sleep through the night. —Trey

Generalized anxiety disorder (GAD), in existence since the *DSM-III*, is one of the most common of all mental disorders with an annual prevalence rate of 2.9% among adults in the United States (APA, 2013a; J. S. Comer, Pincus, & Hoffman, 2012). Excessive worry or anxiety about a number of events is the key feature of GAD, with the experience of the anxiety or worry in discord with the actual or expected event.

Essential Features

Although the DSM-5 Task Force proposed changes to GAD that would have resulted in a lowered diagnostic threshold, this disorder remains largely unchanged from the *DSM-IV-TR*. Essential features include anxiety or worry that takes place across a number of settings and more days than not for at least 6 months. The individual finds it difficult to control the worry and experiences at least three characteristic symptoms, including restlessness or feeling keyed up or on edge, being easily fatigued, difficulty concentrating or mind going blank, muscle tension, irritability, and sleep disturbance (APA, 2013a).

Special Considerations

The predominant symptom of GAD is pathological worry. What distinguishes GAD from nonclinical levels of anxiety are the intensity of the worry and its resultant impairment in functioning. These worries can be consuming, marked, and cause considerable concern to the individual suffering from them. Physical and somatic symptoms often accompany GAD; these include muscle tension, sweating, nausea, diarrhea, accelerated heart rate, and dizziness. As with other disorders enumerated in this chapter, women are more likely than men to receive the diagnosis (Friborg et al., 2013).

Cultural Considerations

Cultural considerations include previous exposure to traumatic events occurring environmentally or geographically. In the United States, GAD is highest among Caucasian and Native American populations; it is most notable in younger individuals. Asian, Latino/a, African, and Caribbean Black populations have lower rates of GAD (Marques et al., 2011). Although it may manifest differently, the overall worry and anxiousness associated with GAD is extant across all cultures.

Differential Diagnosis

Common differential diagnoses for GAD are anxiety disorder due to another medical condition, substance/medication-induced anxiety disorder, social anxiety disorder, OCD, PTSD, adjustment disorders, and depressive, bipolar, and psychotic disorders. The clear distinction between GAD and anxiety disorder due to another medical condition is that the substance must be etiologically related to the anxiety. Those with GAD have diffuse worry that focuses on events that have yet to happen; this separates individuals with GAD from individuals living with social anxiety disorder, PTSD, OCD, and adjustment disorders. Adjustment disorders also do not persist for 6 months or more beyond the termination of the stressor or its consequences. If inordinate worry occurs only during the course of depressive, bipolar, and psychotic disorders, GAD should not be diagnosed (APA, 2013a).

Owing to lack of specificity in the criteria, differential diagnosis can be a challenge. Many of the anxiety disorders outlined in this chapter, along with OCD, PTSD, adjustment disorders, depressive disorders, and psychotic disorders possess, similar features to GAD. It is likely that individuals with GAD have, have had, or will develop other anxiety or depressive disorders (APA, 2013a).

Coding, Recording, and Specifiers

There is only one diagnostic code for GAD: 300.02 (F41.1). There are no specifiers for this diagnosis, although counselors may choose to use the *with panic attacks* specifier if appropriate.

 Case Example

Jean is a 65-year-old African American divorced mother and grandmother. She has a successful career in real estate and enjoys good physical health. Throughout her childhood and adulthood, Jean has been characterized as a nervous and high-strung person. She typically worries excessively about all aspects of her life and often lets her fear of the worst keep her from enjoying activities. Jean is very good at putting on a "game face" and masking her anxiety with humor and good cheer. However, Jean's fear and worry keep her from traveling to family reunions and impede her ability to relax.

Over the past year, Jean's worries have increased in intensity and frequency. She has been canceling appointments on occasion in order to "not have to deal with the stress." Never one to drink much alcohol, Jean will have a glass of wine before bed several times a week to "take the edge off." She has also experienced some physical symptoms, such as difficulty falling asleep, needing to urinate frequently, and muscle tension.

Jean's emotional symptoms include worrying about many things, having difficulty concentrating, and being irritable, and these symptoms occur multiple times daily. She tires easily and sometimes feels so overwhelmed she does not want to get out of bed. Jean states she has trouble stopping her worrisome thoughts and reports that her family is concerned about her and has encouraged her to see a counselor. Although Jean would like to feel better, she expressed doubt that counseling could be helpful and believes this is just the "way she is." Jean has been treated for depression in the past and reports that she doesn't feel "depressed" now.

◆ ◆ ◆

Diagnostic Questions

1. Do Jean's presenting symptoms meet the criteria for an anxiety disorder? If so, which one?
2. Based on the disorder identified in Question 1, which symptom(s) led you to select the diagnosis?
3. What would be the reason(s) a counselor may not diagnose Jean with agoraphobia?
4. Would Jean be more accurately diagnosed with a depressive disorder? Why or why not?
5. What rule-outs would you consider for Jean's case?
6. What other information may be needed to make an accurate clinical diagnosis?

Substance/Medication-Induced Anxiety Disorder

Anxiety caused by substance use is the primary criterion for the diagnosis of substance/medication-induced anxiety disorder. Panic or anxiety must have developed during or soon after substance/medication usage and be in excess of what would be expected to be associated with intoxication or withdrawal from that specific substance. Prevalence rates for this disorder are reportedly low (0.002%), although it is difficult to assess accurate rates because of diagnostic challenges in differentiating it from other anxiety or substance disorders. It is important for counselors to tease out substances used to self-medicate anxious symptoms with anxiety resulting from substance use or withdrawal (APA, 2013a).

Essential Features

Essential features of substance/medication-induced anxiety disorder are that the symptoms occur during intoxication, during withdrawal, or after medication use. The anxiety must be severe enough to cause a need for clinical intervention.

Special Considerations

Laboratory tests can be helpful in assessing substance/medication-induced anxiety disorder (e.g., urinalysis). There are a number of medications that can cause symptoms of anxiety. These include, but are not limited to, antidepressant medications, antihypertensive and cardiovascular medications, corticosteroids, anticonvulsants, antihistamines, oral contraceptives, insulin, and bronchodilators. Counselors are responsible for consulting with physicians to determine whether an anxiety disorder may be physiologically caused by use of a substance or medication.

Differential Diagnosis

Common differential diagnoses for substance/medication-induced anxiety disorder include substance intoxication and substance withdrawal, anxiety disorder not induced by a substance/medication, delirium, and anxiety disorder due to another general medical condition. A diagnosis of substance/medication-induced anxiety disorder is only used when anxiety symptoms are predominant. If panic or anxiety symptoms occur exclusively during the course of delirium, they are not separately addressed.

Coding, Recording, and Specifiers

The extensive coding chart for substance/medication-induced anxiety disorder can be found on page 227 of the *DSM-5*. When using this chart, counselors will notice specifiers for substance/medication-induced anxiety disorder, including *with onset during intoxication, with onset during withdrawal*, and *with onset after medication use*, with severity indicators of accompanying substance use disorder. Again, counselors may use the *with panic attacks* specifier at their discretion. The specifier follows the name of the disorder. The *ICD-9-CM* uses a separate diagnostic code for substance use disorder and substance/medication-induced anxiety disorder when a substance use disorder is comorbid. An example of *ICD-9-CM* coding is 292.89 opioid-induced anxiety disorder, *with onset during intoxication*. The same example with *ICD-10-CM* coding is F11.188 mild opioid use disorder with opioid-induced anxiety disorder *with onset during intoxication*. A second diagnosis of F11.10 opioid use disorder, mild, is also given.

293.84 Anxiety Disorder Due to Another Medical Condition (F06.4)

Medical conditions can cause the development of an anxiety disorder, but they must cause clinically significant distress. APA (2013a, p. 231) reports "unclear" prevalence rates of anxiety disorder due to another medical condition because of the extreme difficulty with differential diagnosis for this category. It is especially important for counselors to carefully rule out differential diagnoses and consult with a physician before using the diagnosis of anxiety disorder due to another medical condition.

Essential Features

Marked anxiety attacks occur and can be directly attributed to an existing medical condition. The development of the anxiety can parallel the course of the illness. Examples of medical conditions that cause anxiety disorder due to another medical condition include endocrine disease, cardiovascular disorders, respiratory illness, metabolic disturbance, and neurological illness (APA, 2013a).

Special Considerations

Because prevalence rates are not clear for this disorder, it is important to track the course of the illness to be able to chart the concomitant course of the anxiety. This is a key consideration within the older adult community because older adults often experience chronic illnesses. Counselors also need to be aware of the possibility of the development of anxiety disorder not related to physical illness.

Differential Diagnosis

Common differential diagnoses are substance intoxication, substance withdrawal, delirium, anxiety disorder due to another medical condition, and adjustment disorders. Anxiety symptoms, such as panic, must be predominant and demand separate clinical assessment. It is important for counselors to rule out the existence of anxiety disorders that have developed during the course of a medical condition but are not resultant from direct effects of the medical condition. Anxiety that occurs during the course of a delirium does not qualify the individual for the diagnosis of anxiety disorder due to another medical condition. The key to discerning anxiety disorder due to another medical condition is that the anxiety symptoms must be attributed to the physiological effects of the medical condition (APA, 2013a).

Coding, Recording, and Specifiers

There is only one diagnostic code for anxiety disorder due to another medical condition: 293.84 (F06.4). Although counselors may specify *with panic attacks*, there are no other specifiers for this diagnosis.

Other Specified and Unspecified Anxiety Disorders

The other specified anxiety disorder and the unspecified anxiety disorder categories in the *DSM-5* replace the NOS category of the *DSM-IV-TR*. The other specified anxiety disorder, 300.09 (F41.8),

> applies to presentations in which symptoms characteristic of an anxiety disorder that cause clinically significant distress or impairment in social, occupational, or other important areas of functioning predominate but do not meet the full criteria for any of the disorders in the anxiety disorder diagnostic class. The other specified anxiety disorder category is used in situations in which the clinician chooses to communicate the specific reason that the presentation does not meet the criteria for any specific anxiety disorder (e.g., "generalized anxiety not occurring more days than not"). (APA, 2013a, p. 233)

The unspecified anxiety disorder code, 300.00 (F41.9),

> is used in situations in which the clinician chooses *not* to specify the reason that the criteria are not met for a specific anxiety disorder, and includes presentations in which there is insufficient information to make a more specific diagnosis (e.g., in emergency room settings). (APA, 2013a, p. 233)

Obsessive-Compulsive and Related Disorders

The term *obsessive-compulsive disorder* (OCD) refers to unwanted and repeated mental rituals, including thoughts, feelings, ideas, sensations, or observable behaviors (i.e., obsessions) that make an individual feel driven to do something (i.e., compulsions; National Library of Medicine, 2013; Stein, 2002). Examples of obsessions include excessive counting, skin picking, ruminating about physical flaws, and hoarding (see Table 6.1). Rituals are very common among individuals diagnosed with OCD and may include frequent checking of doors or locks, recurrent hand washing, or avoidance of certain situations. An example would be a person who has persistent and uncontrollable thoughts that he is soiled, polluted, or otherwise unclean. To mitigate stress, he washes his hands numerous times throughout the day, gaining temporary relief from these thoughts. For his behavior to be considered an OCD, it must be disruptive to his everyday functioning, such as washing to the point of excessive irritation of his skin.

Disorders listed in this chapter have the common feature of obsessive preoccupation and engagement in repetitive behaviors. These disorders are considered similar enough to be grouped in the same diagnostic classification but distinct enough to subsist as separate disorders. Some of the disorders in this chapter have historically been included as part of what was considered the "obsessive-compulsive spectrum."

Table 6.1
Common Obsessions and Compulsions

Obsessions	*Commonly Associated Compulsions*
Fear of contamination	Washing, cleaning
Need for symmetry, precise arranging	Ordering, arranging, balancing, straightening until "just right"
Unwanted sexual or aggressive thoughts or images	Checking, praying, "undoing" actions, asking for reassurance
Doubts (e.g., gas jets off, doors locked)	Repeated checking behaviors
Concerns about throwing away something valuable	Hoarding

Major Changes From *DSM-IV-TR* to *DSM-5*

OCD, previously classified in the *DSM-IV-TR* as an anxiety disorder, is now the first disorder listed in a stand-alone chapter in the *DSM-5* titled Obsessive-Compulsive and Related Disorders. The fundamental features of obsession and compulsion, rather than anxiety, served as the driving force for moving OCD and other related disorders to a separate chapter (APA, 2013a). This also follows revisions within *ICD-10-CM* that classifies OCD separately from anxiety disorder. As with the *ICD-10-CM*, which keeps OCD and anxiety disorder in the same larger category, the sequential order of this chapter reflects the close relationship between OCD and anxiety disorder. Separating obsession and compulsion from anxiety received more support from psychiatrists than other mental health professionals, as only 40% to 45% of other mental health professionals supported the move (Mataix-Cols, Pertusa, & Leckman, 2007). Some counselors opposed the move because treatment protocols are similar for anxiety and obsessive-compulsive and related disorders and, just like anxiety and depression, comorbidity is more often the rule than the exception (Stein et al., 2010).

New disorders in this chapter include hoarding disorder, excoriation (skin-picking) disorder, substance/medication-induced obsessive-compulsive and related disorder, and obsessive-compulsive and related disorder due to another medical condition. The *DSM-IV-TR* diagnosis of trichotillomania is now termed *trichotillomania (hair-pulling disorder)* and has been moved from a *DSM-IV-TR* classification of impulse-control disorders to obsessive-compulsive and related disorders in *DSM-5* (APA, 2013a).

Aside from moving OCD out of the anxiety chapter and adding new diagnoses, most changes to this section are semantic. For example, the *DSM-5* has modified the word *impulse* to the word *urge*. This change more accurately reflects the origin of obsessive disorders (i.e., behaviors that can be modified as opposed to an irresistible compulsion). The word *impulse* seems to have a strong biological component, thus insinuating that these disorders are involuntary. This modification is backed by numerous studies that demonstrated that obsessive-compulsive and related disorders can be treated and, in many cases, extinguished (Simpson et al., 2008; Tenneij, Van Megen, Denys, & Westenberg, 2005; Tolin, Maltby, Diefenbach, Hannan, & Worhunsky, 2004; Tundo, Salvati, Busto, Di Spigno, & Falcini, 2007).

Other semantic changes include amending references to *inappropriate* behaviors or feelings to *unwanted* behaviors or feelings. The reason for this change is culturally based, because cultural norms regarding appropriate versus inappropriate behaviors are very different. Finally, the new diagnostic classifications of obsessive-compulsive and related disorders have removed the criterion that people must recognize their obsessions or compulsions as unreasonable or excessive. Although people must realize the obsessive thoughts, mental images, or urges are a product of their own minds, it is no longer required that they understand the behavior or mental rituals are excessive.

Differential Diagnosis

As with anxiety disorders, the decision of APA (2013a) to cluster obsessive-compulsive and related disorders within one chapter, separate from anxiety and trauma and stressor-related disorders, influences differential diagnosis. Stein et al. (2011) posited that clinical attention should focus on the discernment of disorders enumerated within this chapter. One way to differentiate OCD is the common feature of obsessive preoccupation and repetitive behaviors. Once this has been established, counselors can then distinguish between the disorders in this chapter.

Note

To help differentiate between obsessive-compulsive and related disorders and anxiety disorders, counselors can ask clients, "Do you ever have thoughts or images that you can't get out of your mind?" and "Are there things that you can't resist doing over and over again?"

◆ ◆ ◆

Differential diagnosis of obsessive-compulsive and related disorders is challenging because of comorbidity with other diagnoses. It is not uncommon for individuals diagnosed with an obsessive-compulsive or related disorder to also exhibit symptoms of depressive and anxiety disorders; somatoform disorder; hypochondrias; eating disorder; impulse-control disorder, especially kleptomania; and ADHD (Pallanti, Grassi, Sarrecchia, Cantisani, & Pellegrini, 2011). There is also a significant amount of literature dedicated to comorbidity between OCD and Tourette's syndrome. In a clinical population of children ages 7 to 18 years diagnosed with Tourette's syndrome, approximately 30% also met diagnostic criteria for OCD (Sukhodolsky et al., 2003). In terms of commonality, counselors should look for mood disorders, specifically depression, social and simple phobias, eating disorders, panic disorder, and Tourette's syndrome. Counselors should be aware that comorbidity with schizophrenia and other psychotic disorders is relatively uncommon; in cases in which a client is unable to recognize that the obsession is a product of his or her own mind, the obsession may be better classified as a delusion. In that case, a schizophrenia spectrum or other psychotic disorder may be a more appropriate diagnosis.

Etiology and Treatment

Exact etiology for obsessive-compulsive and related disorders has not been determined. However, there is a considerable amount of research that suggests abnormalities in serotonin (5-HT) and dopamine neurotransmission are responsible for mental rituals and compulsive behaviors (Bloch et al., 2006; Greist, Jefferson, Kobak, Katzelnick, & Serlin, 1995; Kobak, Greist, Jefferson, Katzelnick, & Henk, 1998). Twin studies have suggested a strong genetic influence (van Grootheest, Cath, Beekman, & Boomsma, 2005), and a considerable amount of literature supports the idea that obsessive-compulsive and related disorders are stress responsive, meaning symptoms increase with stress. However, stress in and of itself is not seen as an etiologic factor (Abramowitz, Khandker, Nelson, Deacon, & Rygwall, 2006; Lin et al., 2007).

The most commonly reported treatment for obsessive-compulsive and related disorders involves a combination of psychopharmacological treatments and psychotherapy (Simpson et al., 2008; Tenneij et al., 2005; Tolin et al., 2004). In some trials, CBT has been identified as more effective than drug treatment (Blatt, Zuroff, Bondi, & Sanislow, 2000; Melville, 2013) or as a suitable replacement once medication has reduced symptomatology (Tundo et al., 2007). The International Obsessive-Compulsive Disorder Foundation (IOCDF; 2012) specifically recommends exposure and response prevention (ERP), a type of CBT, citing that ERP may reduce symptoms by 60% to 80% if clients are active participants in treatment (Melville, 2013). ERP confronts thoughts, images, objects, and situations that make a person experience anxiety and uses "response prevention" to encourage clients to choose not to engage in a compulsive behavior.

Implications for Counselors

The ability for counselors to recognize obsessive-compulsive and related disorders is important because studies have indicated that nearly one in 100, approximately 2 to 3 million adults, currently have OCD (IOCDF, 2012; Kessler, Chiu, Demler, & Walters, 2005). Numbers for children are also alarming, with nearly 1 in 200, or 500,000 children and adolescents, diagnosed with OCD (Ruscio, Stein, Chiu, & Kessler, 2008). These numbers only apply to OCD and do not include other related disorders. Rates of BDD among community samples are between 0.7% and 1.1% of the general population (Phillips, 2004). Hoarding affects 4% of the general population (Samuels et al., 2008). Trichotillomania affects 2.5 million individuals within the United States (Diefenbach, Reitman, & Williamson, 2000), and 3.8% of college psychology students exhibited signs of excoriation (Misery et al., 2012).

To help readers better understand changes from the *DSM-IV-TR* to the *DSM-5*, the rest of this chapter outlines each disorder within the Obsessive-Compulsive and Related Disorders chapter of the *DSM-5*. Readers should note that we have focused on major changes from the *DSM-IV-TR* to the *DSM-5*; however, this is not a stand-alone resource for diagnosis. Although a summary and special considerations for counselors are provided for each disorder, when diagnosing clients, counselors need to reference the *DSM-5*. It is essential that the diagnostic criteria and features, subtypes and specifiers (if applicable), prevalence, course, and risk and prognostic factors for each disorder are clearly understood prior to diagnosis.

300.3 Obsessive-Compulsive Disorder (F42)

I couldn't do anything without counting. It invaded every aspect of my life and really bogged me down. I would wash my hair three times as opposed to once because 3 was a good luck number and 1 wasn't. It took me longer to read because I'd count the lines in a paragraph. When I set my alarm at night, I had to set it to a number that wouldn't add up to a "bad" number. —Cathey

Obsessive-compulsive disorder is characterized by "recurrent, persistent, and intrusive anxiety-provoking thoughts or images (obsessions) and subsequent repetitive behaviors (compulsions)" (den Braber et al., 2008, p. 91). These thoughts, beliefs, ideas, or mental rituals dominate an individual's life. Compulsions are the acts that relieve this distress and can be simple (e.g., thinking of a word) or extraordinarily complex (e.g., engaging in an elaborate washing routine that takes hours to complete). Most individuals have both obsessions and compulsions, although it is not unheard of for clients to report obsessions only. Once considered a rare and eccentric disorder, OCD has risen considerably in visibility since the NIMH conducted a study in 1988 that recognized a 2.5% lifetime prevalence of OCD in the U.S. population (Karno, Golding, Sorenson, & Burnam, 1988). There have been no major changes to this disorder in the *DSM-5*.

Essential Features

The most common pattern of obsessions and compulsions is a fear of contamination, which causes excessive washing of an individual's hands or body (Morrison, 2006). Also common are persistent doubts such as "Did I lock the door?" that lead a person to repetitively check the locks. There is also a strong need to have things in a particular order, which causes significant distress when objects are perceived as disorganized. These thoughts and behaviors significantly influence clients' lives, sometimes to the point of interfering with work, school, family relationships, or social obligations. Individuals exhibiting symptoms of OCD often realize that these thoughts and behaviors are irrational and often have a strong desire to resist the obsessive thoughts and compulsive behaviors. Because of a lack of cognitive awareness, children have never been required to recognize obsessive-compulsive behaviors as unreasonable.

Special Considerations

Having some degree of obsessive thoughts or compulsive behaviors is not rare; in fact, 70% to 80% of the general population may experience some features of OCD (den Braber et al., 2008). A clinical diagnosis of OCD, however, requires substantial distress or impairment. Counselors should pay close attention to whether the symptoms significantly interfere with a person's daily routine. For example, clients can have a fear of blurting out obscenities or insults, but until this fear prevents them from engaging in activities of daily living or from engaging in a regular routine at work, home, or school or in social situations, it cannot be diagnosed as OCD.

Counselors should be aware that the level of insight among adults, and even children, varies considerably. There is a specifier *with poor insight* that can be applied to this diagnosis, but it is not unusual for adults to vary considerably in their ability to recognize a mental ritual or behavior as unreasonable. This is particularly common when the disorder coexists with another psychological disorder such as MDD or social anxiety disorder. Because avoidance of certain situations, such as one that might make an individual dirty, is common, evading objects or scenarios that provoke obsessions or compulsions may begin to seem ordinary as opposed to excessive (Morrison, 2006; National Library of Medicine, 2013). Counselors who work with individuals diagnosed with OCD must be on the lookout for situations that restrict functioning severely.

Cultural Considerations

OCD is more common among individuals with higher socioeconomic status and higher levels of intelligence. Culturally appropriate ritualistic behavior, such as rituals to ward off bad luck, may have distinct parallels to OCD but are not indicative of OCD unless the behavior exceeds cultural norms. Counselors must be sure they are familiar with the cultural context of the client before determining that a ritualistic behavior is obsessive-compulsive. OCD will typically manifest before the age of 25, with symptoms becoming more prevalent as the individual ages (Morrison, 2006). Many clients will report that obsessive hand washing, for example, began with a 3- to 4-minute wash routine using only soap. Gradually, however, clients may report that they began to use nail brushes, surgical soap, and washing for 15 minutes per arm numerous times per day.

Gender does not seem to be an indicator of prevalence. In children, however, OCD is more common in boys than in girls. Whereas the *DSM-5* (APA, 2013a) states the age of onset is earlier for boys, research has indicated a wider age of onset, with symptoms appearing between ages 6 and 15, and women typically experience symptoms between the ages of 20 and 29 years (Mancebo et al., 2008). Familial patterns for OCD are higher in first-generation biological relatives than in the general population. Pathophysiologic findings provide evidence of a familial pattern with OCD; studies of monozygotic twins have revealed concordance rates as high as 87% and nearly half that for dizygotic twins (den Braber et al., 2008). Symptoms may fluctuate and increase with emotional stressors. For example, during flu season, a client may experience constant worry about becoming contaminated and exhibit persistent OCD symptoms, but these symptoms may decrease or even disappear during the summer months.

Differential Diagnosis

Counselors must be sure to distinguish OCD from anxiety disorder due to another medical condition. For example, counselors working with children experiencing a sudden onset of obsessions, compulsions, or tics need to work with a medical professional to rule out pediatric autoimmune neuropsychiatric disorder associated with streptococcal infections. If a substance is the source of the obsession or compulsion, counselors need to rule out substance/medication-induced anxiety disorder. Counselors should be aware that OCD could occur within the context of other psychological disorders. However, if content is distinctly related to another disorder, such as fixation with one's appearance as in BDD or preoccupation with a fear-based object or situation as in specific phobia or social anxiety disorder, OCD cannot be diagnosed unless there are symptoms that are unrelated to the other disorder. In this case, both disorders would be diagnosed. Finally, an important criterion that distinguishes OCD from psychotic disorders is the ability of the individual to recognize, at some point, that the obsessions or compulsions are unreasonable. Although levels of insight occur on a continuum, counselors who detect a presence of psychotic features should consider assessing for schizophrenia spectrum and other psychotic disorder instead of or in addition to OCD.

Note

As many as half of individuals diagnosed with OCD have a comorbid psychiatric disorder. It is not uncommon for clients to display only OCD symptoms when they are experiencing a major depressive episode. Counselors should be careful to assess for accompanying disorders.

◆ ◆ ◆

Coding, Recording, and Specifiers

There is only one diagnostic code for OCD: 300.3 (F42). However, there are two specifiers. The first specifier indicates the client's current level of insight (*with good or fair insight, with poor insight,* or *with absent insight/delusional beliefs*). The second specifier, *tic-related,* denotes whether an individual has a current or past history of a tic disorder. These specifiers do not have specific codes associated with them.

Note

The same diagnostic code is used for both OCD and hoarding. Hoarding is a new disorder in the *DSM-5* and is not listed specifically as a diagnosable disorder in the *ICD.* Therefore, the *DSM-5* uses the same diagnostic code for OCD.

◆ ◆ ◆

 Example

Anuj is a 15-year-old Indian American boy who lives with his mother in a lower-middle-class neighborhood bordering a major metropolitan area. He is an only child and attends the 10th grade at a local public high school. Anuj recently had a full physical for school and the doctor reported no medical problems. His mother states that Anuj has a great deal of difficulty concentrating on and completing any of his schoolwork.

Anuj reports he is constantly distracted by powerful and strange thoughts, such as counting how many times he blinks and how many steps it takes to get to the hallway. He feels compelled to avoid stepping on any floor tiles with dirt on them because he does not want to get germs on his feet. The possibility that germs could be on door handles or windows also forces him to avoid touching them unless he first uses a cloth (which he always carries with him) to clean them off. In fact, if he misplaces or forgets to bring a clean cloth with him, he feels a great deal of anxiety, feels paralyzed, and may get physically ill.

Anuj realizes that his behavior does not make sense, and it frustrates him that he cannot overcome these powerful thoughts. His compulsive behaviors have become increasingly frequent over the past 2 years, although he has always had a lot of unusual fears and behaviors associated with cleanliness. Other classmates make fun of him and call him crazy.

Anuj has been staying home from school because he is embarrassed and upset with himself. His mother is concerned about his absences from school but does not know how to make him go to school. His teachers are concerned about his absences and poor academic performance. They support Anuj as much as they can, but they do not understand his behavior either.

◆ ◆ ◆

Diagnostic Questions

1. Do Anuj's presenting symptoms meet the criteria for an OCD? If so, which disorder?
2. Based on the disorder identified in Question 1, which symptom(s) led you to select that diagnosis?
3. What would be the reason(s) a counselor may not diagnose Anuj with the disorder identified in Question 1?

4. Would Anuj be more accurately diagnosed with obsessive-compulsive personality disorder? If so, why? If not, why not?
5. What rule-outs would you consider for Anuj's case?
6. What other information may be needed to make an accurate clinical diagnosis?]

300.7 Body Dysmorphic Disorder (F45.22)

You could say that all my life I've been semi-obsessed with being perfect. I often did not think I looked pretty enough. What's amazing to me is, I know that I am very attractive, and yet, whenever I glance at myself in public or something, I kind of see everything wrong with me. It's very frightening. Most of all, I fear that people are judging me for the imagined flaws that I see staring back at me. —Ester

Body dysmorphic disorder (BDD), previously included in the somatoform disorders section of the *DSM-IV-TR*, involves excessive concern with how one looks, specifically with the shape or appearance of one's body or a specific body part. Common concerns often involve breasts, genitalia, hair, nose, or some other portion of the face. Distress is not focused on worry about the presence of an unknown medical condition, as with illness anxiety disorder (previously known as hypochondriasis), or excessive concern with body weight, as with eating disorder. Historically, this disorder was referred to as *dysmorphophobia*, but this term was changed in the *DSM-IV* because it implies a phobia rather than an OCD. Because individuals diagnosed with BDD do not present with persistent and irrational fear of their body or body part, a more accurate term is *dysmorphia*, which refers to preoccupation rather than irrational fear.

Note

When working with clients who have concerns about their bodies, counselors should carefully consider whether a delusional disorder, illness anxiety disorder, or feeding or eating disorder is present.

◆ ◆ ◆

Essential Features

Common concerns for individuals with BDD are skin imperfections such as wrinkles, scars, or acne. Hair concerns can be due to the lack of hair or too much hair. Individuals may also obsess about their weight, height, or the shape of a body part. Although most individuals can point out some feature of their appearance that they would like to change, BDD is a devastating disorder in which individuals repeatedly obsess about their body or a part of their body. For example, they will spend hours a day engaged in activities to camouflage their "defect" or repeatedly check themselves in a mirror. It is not uncommon for some clients to seek out surgical interventions to correct perceived flaws; however, these individuals seldom feel satisfied with the results of surgery and often attempt other surgical procedures or look for other ways in which they can modify the perceived imperfection (Nietzel, Speltz, McCauley, & Bernstein, 1998).

BDD is an underrecognized yet relatively common disorder affecting 2.5% of women and 2.2% of men in the general population (Bjornsson, Didie, & Philips, 2010; Koran, Abujaoude, Large, & Serpe, 2008). Prevalence of BDD in clinical settings is high, including 9% to 12% of individuals in dermatological settings and up to 53% of clients seen by cosmetic surgeons. There have been no major changes to this disorder.

Special Considerations

BDD is associated with increased occupational and social impairment, hospitalization, and suicide attempts. Counselors should not assume BDD is simply a symptom of depression. Although this diagnosis often coexists with depression, it should always be considered a stand-alone diagnosis if diagnostic criteria are met (Phillips, 1999).

Cultural Considerations

BDD usually begins in early adolescence, with an age onset of 16 to 22 years (Mancebo et al., 2008). This diagnosis affects males and females equally but with different manifestations. Phillips and Diaz (1997) identified males as more likely to be preoccupied with their physique, genitals, and loss of hair. Females are more likely to have a comorbid eating disorder, hide perceived defects with various camouflaging techniques, frequently check mirrors, and pick their skin as a symptom of BDD. In terms of psychosocial functioning, males fared worse than females and were more likely to be unemployed and receiving disability payments. The *DSM-5* states that "the disorder may have more similarities than differences across races and cultures but that cultural values and preferences may influence symptom content to some degree" (APA, 2013a, p. 245).

Differential Diagnosis

For a diagnosis of BDD, the symptoms must represent disproportionate concerns about real or imagined flaws related to one's appearance (APA, 2013a). Counselors should consider the degree to which one's concern with appearance may be culturally or developmentally expected (even if unhealthy). Counselors must rule out eating disorders when a client is only concerned with weight and feeling "fat." Counselors should also strongly consider depressive, anxiety, psychotic, and other obsessive-compulsive related disorders such as OCD (Frances, 2013). Ensuring that the client's obsessions and symptomatology focus only on appearance will help ensure accurate diagnosis (APA, 2013a).

Coding, Recording, and Specifiers

There is only one diagnostic code for BDD: 300.7 (F45.22). However, there are two specifiers, the first of which indicates extreme preoccupation with one's body build and the second an individual's level of insight. Counselors should use the specifier *with muscle dysmorphia* if clients are significantly troubled by the idea that their body build is too small. This specifier is also used if the clients are preoccupied with other body areas, such as one's breasts. Counselors should indicate current insight (*with good or fair insight, with poor insight*, or *with absent insight/delusional beliefs*) specifiers assessing the degree to which clients accept their beliefs as true.

 **Example**

> Becca, a 32-year-old single Hispanic woman, had been obsessed with her "huge" nose and "acne-scarred" skin since junior high school. She reported being "absolutely convinced" that she looked "deformed and atrocious." When others tried to tell her she was pretty, she would not budge. Becca was convinced that others talked about her "hideous" nose and "grotesque" skin. Because of her self-loathing, Becca became severely depressed. She could not work or leave home. She has a history of two suicide attempts and was hospitalized after both attempts.
>
> Although her friends and family strongly advised against it, Becca received two rhinoplasties for a nose that outwardly appeared normal. She also received a course of isotreninoin (Accutane). These treatments left Becca even more obsessed with her appearance and feeling more depressed because her "last hopes" had not cured her perceived ugliness.

◆ ◆ ◆

Diagnostic Questions

1. Do Becca's presenting symptoms meet the criteria for BDD? Which symptom(s) led you to select that diagnosis?

2. What rule-outs would you consider for Becca's case?
3. What course of treatment would you recommend for Becca?

300.3. Hoarding Disorder (F42)

I've always had trouble throwing things away. Magazines, newspapers, old clothes. What if I need them one day? I don't want to risk throwing something out that might be valuable. The large piles of stuff in our house keep growing so it's difficult to move around and sit or eat together as a family. My wife is upset and embarrassed, and we get into horrible fights. I'm scared when she threatens to leave me. My children won't invite friends over, and I feel guilty that the clutter makes them cry, but I get so anxious when I try to throw anything away. I don't know what's wrong with me, and I don't know what to do. —Ben

Hoarding is defined as "persistent difficulty discarding or parting with possessions, regardless of their actual value" (APA, 2013a, p. 247). Historically referred to as pathological or compulsive hoarding, this disorder has extremely detrimental emotional, social, and financial effects on individuals and their loved ones. Because of their avoidance of or difficulty with getting rid of possessions, individuals diagnosed with hoarding disorder are consumed with fears related to losing important information or objects of emotional significance (IOCDF, 2012).

Major Changes From *DSM-IV-TR* to *DSM-5*

Hoarding, commonly associated with OCD and previously listed in the *DSM-IV-TR* as one of eight concurrent criteria for obsessive-compulsive personality disorder (OCPD), is now a stand-alone diagnosis in the *DSM-5*. The DSM-5 Task Force decided to include hoarding as a discrete disorder because individuals with hoarding symptoms may not display any other symptoms of OCD and are often nonresponsive to traditional treatments for OCD or OCPD, such as exposure therapy or psychopharmaceutical treatments (see Pertusa et al., 2010; Samuels et al., 2008). Moreover, correlational studies only identified a small to moderate relationship between hoarding and OCD (Abramowitz, Wheaton, & Storch, 2008; Wu & Watson, 2005). Two strong indicators that hoarding is a distinct disorder rather than a component of OCD are that hoarding is the only OCD symptom that increases with age and that distress and disability often appear late in the course of the disorder (Ayers, Saxena, Golshan, & Wetherell, 2010).

Essential Features

Individuals with hoarding disorder typically have living spaces and personal surroundings cluttered to the point of being useless for their intended purpose (e.g., a bathroom or bedroom). Hoarding behaviors often cause a considerable amount of distress for the individual and family members, caregivers, neighbors, and friends who attempt to clear spaces. It is important to note that diagnostic criteria for hoarding, like other obsessive-compulsive and related disorders, include symptoms that cause significant impairment in social, occupational, or other essential areas of functioning.

Prevalence of hoarding among the general population is 2% to 5%, with older adults more likely to exhibit hoarding behaviors. Hoarding typically manifests in childhood with symptoms worsening as clients become older. Some researchers claim that as the geriatric population increases, so will the number of adults diagnosed with a hoarding disorder (Ayers et al., 2010). Symptoms often are associated with other psychological disorders such as depression, anxiety, and substance abuse. Although epidemiological research is limited, some researchers have identified a familial pattern (Samuels et al., 2008).

Special Considerations

A client's ability to maintain a safe living environment, free of any public health consequences, is often a major indicator for counselors considering this diagnosis. Counselors should not diagnose hoarding simply because a person owns an abnormal amount of things. Counselors should keep in mind the following three behaviors regarding hoarding: (a) acquisition of numerous possessions, many of little value; (b) difficulty discarding these possessions; and (c) significant difficulty organizing possessions. In contrast to people with hoarding problems, people who collect items often keep their property well organized. Collectors often display items for others to appreciate, whereas those with hoarding disorder overrun living areas with items and can create problems such as financial obligations of paying for storage space.

When collecting behaviors lead to health or safety problems or cause significant distress, hoarding becomes a diagnosable disorder. For example, a major feature of hoarding is the large amount of disorganized clutter that creates chaos in the home or office. Individuals diagnosed with hoarding disorder often have rooms that can no longer be used as they were intended, moving through the home is challenging, exits are blocked, and life inside the home becomes difficult (Frances, 2013; Morrison, 2006). Counselors should pay close attention to health and safety concerns, especially in older adult clients. Client safety (e.g., falling over items in one's home or illnesses due to contaminated food or infestation) is the number one concern for counselors working with individuals diagnosed with a hoarding disorder.

Cultural Considerations

It is not uncommon for individuals who hoard to have a history of trauma or have experienced significantly stressful life events (Hartl, Duffany, Allen, Steketee, & Frost, 2005; Samuels et al., 2008). Some studies have linked symptom onset or exacerbation to traumatic events. Although some researchers have identified material deprivation (e.g., lack of money, food, adequate clothing, or shelter during their lifetime) as an environmental risk factor, general consensus among scholars is that there is no clear link between a lack of material items and hoarding disorder (Landau et al., 2011). People with hoarding disorder are typically older, yet most have trouble discarding items early on in their lives. They are also less likely to be married, which may relate to functional impacts associated with the disorder.

Differential Diagnosis

Researchers have identified important phenomenological differences between hoarding and prototypical OCD symptoms, which can help counselors differentiate between hoarding disorder and OCD (Landau et al., 2011). Thoughts associated with hoarding are not intrusive, and typically no ritualistic attributes are associated with hoarding behaviors. Researchers have also discovered that failure to discard possessions is more of a passive behavior than an active attempt to neutralize unwanted thoughts, images, or impulses (Pertusa et al., 2010; Steketee & Frost, 2003). Counselors must be sure to rule out MDD, schizophrenia, or any neurocognitive disorder such as ASD because the presentation of any one of these could result in an inability for a client to be able to get rid of objects or clear clutter (APA, 2013a; Frances, 2013). Hoarding is often comorbid with ADHD-inattentive type (Hartl et al., 2005).

Coding, Recording, and Specifiers

There is only one diagnostic code for hoarding disorder: 300.3 (F42). Because hoarding is not directly mentioned in either the *ICD-9* or the *ICD-10*, the diagnostic code for OCD is used. There are two specifiers, the first of which indicates extreme hoarding and the second an individual's level of insight. Counselors should use the *with excessive acquisition* specifier if attainment of items is extreme and individuals are unable to discard large numbers of possessions. In addition, counselors should use insight specifiers (e.g., *with good or fair insight*, *with poor insight*, or *with absent insight/delusional beliefs*) to indicate the degree to which the individual is able to understand the hoarding beliefs and behaviors as problematic. These specifiers do not have specific codes associated with them.

Diagnostic Criteria for Hoarding 300.3 (F42)

A. Persistent difficulty discarding or parting with possessions, regardless of their actual value.
B. This difficulty is due to a perceived need to save the items and to distress associated with discarding them.
C. The difficulty discarding possessions results in the accumulation of possessions that congest and clutter active living areas and substantially compromises their intended use. If living areas are uncluttered, it is only because of the interventions of third parties (e.g., family members, cleaners, authorities).
D. The hoarding causes clinically significant distress or impairment in social, occupational, or other important areas of functioning (including maintaining a safe environment for self and others).
E. The hoarding is not attributable to another medical condition (e.g., brain injury, cerebrovascular disease, Prader-Willi syndrome).
F. The hoarding is not better explained by the symptoms of another mental disorder (e.g., obsessions in obsessive-compulsive disorder, decreased energy in major depressive disorder, delusions in schizophrenia or another psychotic disorder, cognitive deficits in major neurocognitive disorder, restricted interests in autism spectrum disorder).

Specify if:
With excessive acquisition: If difficulty discarding possessions is accompanied by excessive acquisition of items that are not needed or for which there is no available space.

Specify if:
With good or fair insight: The individual recognizes that hoarding-related beliefs and behaviors (pertaining to difficulty discarding items, clutter, or excessive acquisition) are problematic.
With poor insight: The individual is mostly convinced that hoarding-related beliefs and behaviors (pertaining to difficulty discarding items, clutter, or excessive acquisition) are not problematic despite evidence to the contrary.
With absent insight/delusional beliefs: The individual is completely convinced that hoarding-related beliefs and behaviors (pertaining to difficulty discarding items, clutter, or excessive acquisition) are not problematic despite evidence to the contrary.

 Example

Barrett, an articulate 69-year-old Caucasian male retiree, first came to the attention of the Community Services Board when a neighbor complained to the police about the mounds of trash she could see through his windows. A staff person from the Fire Department visited Barrett but was unable to investigate the complaint because he would not allow the investigator to enter his home. The fire official was able to persuade Barrett to meet with a case manager from Adult Protective Services, who evaluated Barrett and found him to be competent and able to refuse services. Over the next 10 years, neighbors complained about Barrett's hoarding behavior approximately every 2 years. Complaints included references to a car that was so stuffed full of things that it was unsafe to drive, rodents on the property, and trash piled up in the backyard.

When Barrett was not seen at his volunteer job for several days, his supervisor requested that police check on his welfare. Police found Barrett unconscious in a corner of his bedroom where he had landed after tripping over a pile of papers. Barrett was hospitalized and received treatment for an infection of both legs. During this time, the fire marshal condemned his home. In the hospital, a counselor met with Barrett to help him cope with being removed from his home and begin exploring a plan for moving forward.

◆ ◆ ◆

Diagnostic Questions

1. Do Barrett's presenting symptoms meet the criteria for an OCD? If so, which disorder?
2. Based on the disorder identified in Question 1, which symptom(s) led you to select that diagnosis?
3. What would be the reason(s) a counselor may not diagnose Barrett with OCD or OCPD?
4. Would Barrett be more accurately diagnosed with an anxiety disorder? If so, why and which one? If not, why not?
5. What rule-outs would you consider for Barrett's case?
6. What other information may be needed to make an accurate clinical diagnosis?

312.39 Trichotillomania (Hair-Pulling Disorder) (F63.3)

I eat my hair. I know I am a freak, but I don't even realize I am doing it. I just pull at my hair and, one day, just started swallowing it. I have tried to stop, but I cannot. Even the thought of trying to stop again makes my heart start racing. —Allyia

Previously identified in the *DSM-IV-TR* as an impulse-control disorder, trichotillomania (TTM), or hair-pulling disorder, is characterized by the compulsive urge to pull out, and sometimes ingest, one's own hair (APA, 2013a). TTM leads to noticeable hair loss and, as characteristic of all obsessive-compulsive and related disorders, causes distress or functional impairment (APA, 2013a; Chamberlain, Menzies, Sahakian, & Fineberg, 2007). The *ICD-10* classifies TTM as a habit and impulse disorder in the section on disorder of adult personality and behavior. Both the *ICD* and the *DSM* describe TTM as recurrent and noticeable by others.

Essential Features

Hair pulling often occurs without focused attention, meaning individuals are typically not aware they are doing it (APA, 2013a). This is different from OCD, in which people may have a high level of insight into their behavior (Chamberlain et al., 2007). Hair pulling occurs in response to a wide range of negative moods, such as anger, boredom, sadness, or stress. Although there were not many changes to this disorder, aside from moving it from the Impulse-Control Disorders Not Elsewhere Classified chapter in the *DSM-V-TR* to the new Obsessive-Compulsive and Related Disorders chapter, the *DSM-5* includes a new criterion that addresses attempts to resist hair pulling.

The hallmark feature of TTM is pleasure, gratification, or relief experienced by the client as a result of pulling out one's hair (APA, 2013a; Chamberlain et al., 2007). In the *ICD-10*, this disorder is described as "preceded by mounting tension [that] is followed by a sense of relief" (WHO, 2010, p. 87). It is the defining characteristic of relief, as opposed to pleasure, that caused this disorder to be recategorized. Impulse disorders, such as pyromania and kleptomania, give pleasure to the person and are not typically carried out for the purpose of relief (Gershuny et al., 2006; Stein, Chamberlain, & Fineberg, 2006). Prevalence of TTM is 1% to 2% of adults and adolescents in the general population (APA, 2013a).

Special Considerations

Counselors should be aware that the reference to "mania" in trichotillomania implies an interest or enthusiasm for the hair-pulling behavior. Since this is not the case, a more neutral reference to "hair-pulling disorder" has been included in the *DSM-5*. The typical age of onset is between 12 and 13, and the disorder affects mostly females (APA, 2013a; Chamberlain et al., 2007). Cases of TTM in toddlers and young children, referred to as pediatric TTM, have been reported with onset between the age of 18 months and 4 years. Pediatric TTM is often short term (Tolin, Franklin, Diefenbach, Anderson, & Meunier, 2007). Behavior therapy, CBT, and selective serotonin reuptake inhibitors have been found to be effective for the treatment of TTM (Blatt et al., 2000; Chamberlain et al., 2007; Melville, 2013).

Cultural Considerations
Unfortunately, little is known regarding cultural considerations and features of TTM.

Differential Diagnosis

A TTM diagnosis should not be made if there is a preexisting dermatological problem, another medical condition, or if the hair pulling is in response to a delusion, hallucination, or another mental health disorder (APA, 2013a; Chamberlain et al., 2007). TTM has a high rate of comorbidity, with some studies reporting up to 60% of individuals diagnosed with TTM having another mental health disorder (see Chamberlain et al., 2007). It is not uncommon for individuals also to be diagnosed with MDD, GAD, social phobia, OCD, or other impulse-control disorder and substance use disorder.

Coding, Recording, and Specifiers

There is only one diagnostic code for TTM (hair-pulling) disorder: 312.39 (F63.3). There are no specifiers for this disorder. Counselors should note that the original *DSM-5* mistakenly published the code 312.39 (F63.**2**) for TTM (hair-pulling disorder). This is incorrect, and the code of 312.39 (F63.**3**) should be used.

698.4 Excoriation (Skin-Picking) Disorder (L98.1)

> First it was occasional picking at scabs and acne on my face. Then I started just sitting at home picking at my fingers and arms. Now, I spend hours nearly every day obsessed with picking the skin on my face, arms, and hands. I think about it all the time. I can't even go to work sometimes because I am either embarrassed about the scabs and scars on my skin or because I am so consumed with the need to keep picking at myself. —Meagan

Excoriation (skin-picking) disorder is characterized by repetitive and compulsive picking of skin, resulting in tissue damage (Odlaug & Grant, 2010). Sometimes called neurotic excoriation, compulsive skin-picking, dermatillomania, or psychogenic skin-picking, symptoms of excoriation can also include skin rubbing, squeezing, lancing, and biting (APA, 2013a; Stein et al., 2010). Individuals with excoriation disorder may use their fingers, fingernails, tweezers, or other objects. These individuals spend a considerable amount of time picking, and the disorder can continue for months or years. This disorder may be accompanied by a range of behaviors or rituals, typically does not occur in the presence of others, and has the potential to cause significant distress in several areas of functioning (APA, 2013a).

Major Changes From *DSM-IV-TR* to *DSM-5*

Excoriation disorder is new to the *DSM-5*; symptoms of it were previously classified by clinicians as impulse-control disorder NOS because there was no other appropriate diagnostic classification. As the *DSM-5* was being developed, there were serious deliberations as to whether this disorder should be included as an impulse-control disorder or as a body-focused repetitive behavioral disorder (Stein et al., 2010). Before inclusion in the *DSM-5*, excoriation was considered clinically similar to substance abuse or impulse-control disorders, rather than a disorder related to obsessive-compulsive behavior. However, similar to TTM, the core feature of excoriation is repetitive feelings of tension, anxiety, or agitation immediately preceding the picking episode (i.e., obsessive) and feelings of relief during or following picking (i.e., compulsive). Thus, the diagnosis was included within the Obsessive-Compulsive and Related Disorders chapter.

The DSM-5 Anxiety, Obsessive-Compulsive Spectrum, Posttraumatic, and Dissociative Disorders Work Group determined there was clinical utility in conceptualizing excoriation as part of the OCD spectrum because of comorbidity of excoriation and OCD and treatment approaches that have been strongly influenced by research on OCD (Stein et al., 2010).

Essential Features

Six core features characterize excoriation: (a) recurrent and repetitive picking resulting in noticeable tissue damage; (b) intrusive urges to pick skin; (c) feelings of tension, anxiety, or agitation immediately preceding the picking episode; (d) feelings of pleasure, relief, or satisfaction during or after picking; (e) the picking cannot be accounted for by another medical (e.g., scabies, eczema) or mental disorder (e.g., cocaine or amphetamine use disorders); and (f) the individual suffers significant distress or social or occupational impairment as a result of the picking behavior (APA, 2013a). Clients most frequently report picking at the face, but the fingers, arms, torso, hands, legs, back, and stomach are also common areas for picking.

Special Considerations

Counselors should be sensitive to the needs of clients who engage in skin picking. This behavior may result in skin discoloration or scarring. In more serious cases, severe tissue damage and visible disfigurement can result. Although skin picking is typically not related to other physical or mental disorders, it is essential for counselors to help clients identify whether picking is a symptom of another problem, for example, dermatological disorders, autoimmune problems, BDD, or psychosis. Because clients are often embarrassed about their problem, they may avoid treatment (Flessner & Woods, 2006). In a study of 31 patients with pathological skin picking, only 14 (45%) had ever sought treatment, and only six of the 31 had ever received dermatological treatment. The largest concern for counselors is significant medical complications such as scarring and infection. As with TTM, common interventions include behavioral approaches (i.e., habit reversal) and psychopharmaceutical treatments.

Note

Clients are typically embarrassed about hair-pulling or skin-picking disorders. Therefore, if you do not see evidence of the disorder, you are not likely to hear about associated symptoms.

◆ ◆ ◆

Cultural Considerations

Age of onset is bimodal, beginning in either young adulthood or between the ages of 30 and 45. Mostly identified in females, prevalence rates of excoriation range from 1.4% to 5.4% in the general population (Odlaug & Grant, 2010).

Differential Diagnosis

Comorbidity is not uncommon. For example, in an examination of clients with BDD, 44.9% reported skin-picking behaviors (Grant, Menard, & Phillips, 2006). Also common is the existence of another body-focused repetitive behavior, such as excessive washing seen in individuals diagnosed with OCD. Somatic symptoms, such as a factitious disorder, should be ruled out as should any other substance/medication-induced disorder (APA, 2013a).

Coding, Recording, and Specifiers

There is only one diagnostic code for excoriation (skin-picking) disorder, 698.4 (L98.1), and there are no specifiers for this disorder. Readers will note the *ICD-10-CM* code for excoriation begins with an "L" as opposed to the commonly seen "F." The reason is because the *ICD-10* classifies excoriation under other disorders of skin and subcutaneous tissue, not elsewhere classified (WHO, 2007).

 Example

> Adrianne, a 38-year-old European American single woman, picks her arms on a daily basis. Although she had previously picked at her face, particularly her nose, her arms have been her main focus for the past 2 years. Her picking sometimes lasts as long as 3 hours each day and is so intense that her arms are scarred and covered with scabs. Touching her arms creates an irresistible urge to pick. Sometimes when she walks and her hands touch her thighs she has to stop what she is doing and pick.
>
> Adrianne started picking her face when she was 14 years old. Because of the time she spent picking, she missed a significant amount of high school and could not graduate. Since then, because of the facial scarring, Adrianne started focusing on her arms. Scarring and the consistent bleeding caused Adrianne to avoid going out in public, working, or socializing. She lives alone at home on medical disability. She had never sought help for her picking until just recently when she was hospitalized for septicemia, a life-threatening infection as a result of skin picking.

◆ ◆ ◆

Diagnostic Questions

1. Do Adrianne's presenting symptoms meet the criteria for excoriation (skin-picking) disorder?
2. Which symptom(s) led you to agree with this diagnosis?
3. What rule-outs would you consider for Adrianne's case?
4. What other information may be needed to make an accurate clinical diagnosis?

Substance/Medication-Induced Obsessive-Compulsive and Related Disorder

Substance/medication-induced obsessive-compulsive and related disorder is characterized by obsessive-compulsive symptoms as a direct result of substance use (APA, 2013a). For an individual to meet the criteria for substance/medication-induced obsessive-compulsive and related disorder, symptoms must have occurred during or soon after substance or medication intoxication or withdrawal; must be in excess of what is expected during intoxication or withdrawal for the specific substance; and must subside after the effects of the medication, treatments, or substance have been removed.

Major Changes From *DSM-IV-TR* to *DSM-5*

The *DSM-IV-TR* included a specifier *with obsessive-compulsive symptoms* in the diagnoses of substance-induced anxiety disorder, but the *DSM-5* now classifies this as a distinct disorder given that obsessive-compulsive and related disorders are now a distinct category. This change is consistent with the intent of *DSM-IV-TR* and reflects the recognition that substances, including medications, can present with symptoms similar to primary obsessive-compulsive and related disorders.

Special Considerations

Counselors should ensure that the substance or medication deemed to be responsible for symptoms directly caused the disturbance; this effect does not only occur when the individual is experiencing delirium (APA, 2013a). Moreover, the symptoms must in some way result in clinically significant distress or impairment to functioning.

Coding, Recording, and Specifiers

Similar to all substance/medication-induced disorders in the *DSM-5*, the *ICD-9-CM* and *ICD-10-CM* codes are used. An extensive coding chart for substance/medication-induced obsessive-compulsive and related disorder can be found on page 258 in the *DSM-5*. As with all substance/medication-induced disorders, the name of the substance causing the symptoms is used to identify the appropriate code and is included within the written name of the disorder, for example, 292.89 (F15.288) amphetamine-induced obsessive-compulsive and related disorder.

Three different types of substances are classified as applicable to obsessive-compulsive and related disorders. These are amphetamines/stimulants, cocaine, or other/unknown substance. Specifiers indicating *with onset during intoxication, with onset during withdrawal,* or *with onset after medication use* can be indicated after the code and name but, as with all specifiers in this chapters, do not have specific codes associated with them (APA, 2013a). Counselors using the *ICD-10-CM* diagnostic codes should note specific coding procedures when there is a comorbid substance use disorder present for the same class of substance. For example, if a mild substance use disorder is comorbid with the substance/medication-induced obsessive-compulsive related disorder, the fourth position character should be a "1"; if the comorbid substance use disorder is considered heavy, the fourth position character should be a "2." If there is no comorbid disorder, the fourth position character should be a "9" and only the substance-induced obsessive-compulsive and related disorder would be recorded (APA, 2013a).

Note

Counselors should reference page 482, Table 1, Diagnoses Associated With Substance Class, in the Substance-Related and Addictive Disorders chapter of the *DSM-5* to fully understand which mental health diagnoses are associated with specific substances classes.

◆ ◆ ◆

294.8 Obsessive-Compulsive and Related Disorder Due to Another Medical Condition (F06.8)

Medical conditions can cause the development of an obsessive-compulsive or related disorder, but symptoms must cause clinically significant distress in order to be diagnosed. Symptoms can include a wide range of obsessive-compulsive features (e.g., obsessions, compulsions, preoccupation with appearance, hoarding, skin picking), but there is direct pathophysiological evidence of a medical condition. The characteristic features of obsessive-compulsive and related disorder due to another medical condition is that symptoms are not better explained by another obsessive-compulsive related disorder and are deemed to be the result of direct pathophysiological consequence of a medical condition (APA, 2013a).

Major Changes From *DSM-IV-TR* to *DSM-5*

Obsessive-compulsive and related disorder due to another medical condition is now a distinct disorder. It was previously a specifier in the diagnoses of anxiety disorder due to a general medical condition in the *DSM-IV-TR*. This reflects the recognition that medical conditions can present with symptoms similar to OCD.

Essential Features

A medical condition, as evidenced by laboratory findings, physical examination from a medical professional, or physical health history, must be present when diagnosing a client with obsessive-compulsive and related disorder due to another medical condition. Furthermore, the condition cannot be better explained by another medical condition or use of a substance/medication. As with any obsessive-compulsive and related disorder, symptoms must cause significant impairment to social, occupational, or other essential areas of functioning.

Special Considerations

Two medical conditions that are of significance are (a) pediatric autoimmune neuropsychiatric disorder associated with streptococcal infections (PANDAS), with the rapid onset of OCD symptoms or tics as a result of strep throat or scarlet fever; and (b) pediatric acute-onset neuropsychiatric syndrome (PANS), a broader condition similar to PANDAS but not related to a strep infection (APA, 2013a). Clients with a history of these disorders are prone to obsessive-compulsive traits.

Cultural Considerations

There is limited information on cultural considerations for this disorder because these are typically relevant to the underlying medical illness rather than the psychiatric diagnosis. However, as with any medical disorder, counselors should consult with health professionals for information related to the development and course of the medical disorder as it relates to the client's cultural background.

Differential Diagnosis

It is especially important for counselors to rule out differential diagnoses, such as a primary diagnosis of OCD or an illness anxiety disorder (i.e., hypochondriasis), and consult with a physician to determine physiological etiology before using the diagnosis of obsessive-compulsive and related disorder due to another medical condition.

Coding, Recording, and Specifiers

There is only one diagnostic code for obsessive-compulsive and related disorder due to another medical condition: 294.8 (F06.8). When coding this disorder, counselors should be sure to indicate the medical condition alongside the diagnosis (e.g., obsessive-compulsive and related disorder due to PANDAS). There are five specifiers associated with this diagnosis that are relatively self-explanatory because they relate to the diagnoses found within this chapter. These include *with obsessive-compulsive disorder–like symptoms*, *with appearance preoccupations*, *with hoarding symptoms*, *with hair-pulling symptoms*, and *with skin-picking symptoms*. There are no specific codes assigned to these specifiers.

Note

Proper recording procedures should include the separate coding and listing of the medical condition immediately before the obsessive-compulsive and related disorder due to another medical condition diagnosis.

◆ ◆ ◆

Other Specified and Unspecified Obsessive-Compulsive and Related Disorders

The other specified obsessive-compulsive and related disorder (300.3 [F42]) category, along with the unspecified criterion, replaces the NOS category in the *DSM-IV-TR*. This disorder may include conditions such as body-focused repetitive behavior disorder and obsessional jealousy. Body-focused repetitive behavior disorder, for example, is characterized by recurrent behaviors other than hair pulling and skin picking (e.g., nail biting, lip biting, cheek chewing) and repeated attempts to decrease or stop the behaviors. Obsessional jealousy is characterized by nondelusional preoccupation with a partner's perceived infidelity.

The other specified obsessive-compulsive and related disorder category is used in situations in which the counselor chooses to communicate the specific reason that the presentation does not meet the criteria for any specific anxiety disorder (e.g., "body dysmorphic-like disorder with actual flaws"; APA, 2013a, p. 263). The example given would indicate BDD, except the client's preoccupation involves a physical imperfection that is evident to other persons. When coding other specified obsessive-compulsive and related disorder, counselors will use one diagnostic code, 300.3 (F42), being sure to indicate the specific reason for choosing this diagnosis in the name. If the counselor chooses *not* to specify the reason the criteria are not met, then the unspecified obsessive-compulsive and related disorder (300.3 [F42]) category is used. In either case, symptoms cause clinically significant impairment or distress. This diagnosis is also commonly used when counselors are unable to distinguish whether a medical illness or substance has played a causal role in the manifestation of obsessive-compulsive symptoms.

Note

The diagnostic code for specified and unspecified obsessive-compulsive and related disorder is the same.

♦ ♦ ♦

Chapter 7

Trauma- and Stressor-Related Disorders

The term *trauma* refers to an emotional response to a severely distressing event such as combat, sexual assault, a severe accident, abuse, or exposure to a natural or human-caused disaster (Halpern & Tramontin, 2007; Norris & Elrod, 2006; Ursano, McCaughey, & Fullerton, 1994). Traumatic or stressful events or circumstances may be physically or emotionally harmful to an individual and can involve a single experience or a long-lasting or repetitive event or events. Trauma and stress affect clients in a variety of ways, all of which can threaten their physical, social, cognitive, emotional, or spiritual well-being (Gerrity & Flynn, 1997; Halpern & Tramontin, 2007; Norris et al., 2002). There is one common factor encompassing all traumatic experiences—these situations overwhelm a person's ability to cope (Halpern & Tramontin, 2007; Norris & Elrod, 2006).

Major Changes From *DSM-IV-TR* to *DSM-5*

The Trauma- and Stressor-Related Disorders chapter in the *DSM-5* is a new chapter of disorders that includes PTSD, acute stress disorder, adjustment disorders, reactive attachment disorder (RAD), and a new category, disinhibited social engagement disorder (DSED). In the *DSM-IV-TR*, PTSD and acute stress disorder were categorized as anxiety disorders; RAD was categorized as disorders usually first diagnosed in infancy, childhood, and adolescence; and adjustment disorders had its own diagnostic category. The *DSM-5* placed these disorders together based on their common roots in external events or triggers (APA, 2013a). Categorizing these disorders according to common etiology (i.e., trauma or psychological stressors preceding the disorder), as opposed to common phenomenology, has both clinical utility and heuristic value (First, 2010; First et al., 2004). Because many of these disorders are similar enough to be grouped together but distinct enough to subsist as separate disorders, counselors can more easily distinguish them from one another. For example, including PTSD and adjustment disorders in the same diagnostic classification allows counselors to more easily identify marked differences between these diagnoses. Second, because these disorders are grouped according to cause as opposed to symptoms, researchers can easily create testable theoretical explanations for trauma-based disorders (Friedman et al., 2011).

Aside from being an entirely new chapter, the most significant change for this section is the stressor criterion for acute stress disorder and PTSD. Acute stress disorder and PTSD now note that a traumatic event can be either directly or indirectly experienced or witnessed (APA, 2013a). This means that a traumatic event that was experienced by a close family member or friend can result in possible PTSD or acute stress disorder for the client. There have also been significant changes for children in this chapter. The diagnostic threshold for PTSD has been modified to include children and adolescents, and the *DSM-5* contains developmentally appropriate criteria for children 6 years or younger. The childhood diagnosis RAD formerly had two subtypes, *inhibited* and *disinhibited*. However, in the *DSM-5*, these subtypes are now separate disorders, RAD and DSED. Both disorders address a child's ability to form meaningful/secure attachments as a result of social neglect or other stressors and have common etiology of gross neglect from caregivers. The difference, however, is that children diagnosed with DSED can have some form of attachment to their caregivers. Unlike children diagnosed with RAD, children diagnosed with DSED struggle to conform to social boundary norms and can be in danger of inappropriate interactions with strangers. Most other changes to disorders within this section are primarily semantic.

Essential Features

Potentially traumatic events include combat, sexual and physical assault, robbery, being kidnapped or taken hostage, terrorist attacks, torture, disasters, severe automobile accidents, child abuse, and life-threatening illnesses (Frances, 2013; Halpern & Tramontin, 2007). Trauma also extends to witnessing death or serious injury by violent assault, accidents, war, or disaster. References to stressor-related events in the *DSM-5* include circumstances that cause less adverse emotional effects for a shorter period of time (APA, 2013a). Whereas these events can still markedly disturb an individual, sometimes to the point of social or occupational impairment, adverse emotional effects decrease once the stressor is removed (APA, 2013a). Examples of stressor-related events include relationship breakups, business difficulties or loss of a job, marital problems, or living in a crime-ridden neighborhood. Developmental events, such as going away from school or retiring, can also cause serious stress.

Note

Counselors should note that different people will react differently to similar events. One person may experience an event as traumatic whereas another person would not suffer trauma as a result of the same event. Not all people who experience a potentially traumatic event will become psychologically traumatized.

♦ ♦ ♦

As with many disorders found within Part One of this book, prevalence of trauma-based disorders among the general population is high (APA, 2013a; Morrison, 2006). According to the National Comorbidity Survey Replication (Kessler, Berglund, et al., 2005), the past year prevalence of PTSD was 3.5%, with a 3.6% lifetime prevalence among men and 9.7% prevalence among women. Currently, no population-based epidemiological studies have been conducted to examine prevalence rates in children; however, children who have been exposed to specific traumatic events are at greater risk of prevalence of PTSD. Depending on the trauma or stressor, prevalence rates for acute stress disorder vary from 6% to 94% (Gibson, 2007). The prevalence of RAD is estimated to be 1% of children under age 5 (Widom, Czaja, & Paris, 2009). However, children who are orphaned or placed in foster care at an early age have a higher chance of developing RAD. The prevalence of adjustment disorders has been reported to be between 2% and 8% in community samples of children, adolescents, and older adults (Portzky, Audenaert, & van Heeringen, 2005). In general hospital settings, 12% of inpatients are referred to mental health treatment for adjustment disorders, compared with 10% to 30% of individuals in mental health outpatient settings.

Individuals from low socioeconomic status backgrounds have a higher chance of being treated for adjustment disorders due to increased exposure to life stressors (Portzky et al., 2005).

Differential Diagnosis

The onset of trauma-related disorders discussed in this chapter can be associated with increased risk of anxiety, depression, disordered eating, sleep disturbances, substance use problems, and suicidal ideation (APA, 2013a; Friedman et al., 2011). It is not uncommon for individuals diagnosed with a traumatic disorder to also exhibit symptoms of somatic symptom disorder, impulse-control disorder, and ADHD. Symptoms of these disorders have also been linked to dissociative disorders. Many survivors of traumatic events, especially children, are often misdiagnosed with ADHD (Gibson, 2007; Widom et al., 2009). Children diagnosed with RAD are often mistaken for children with ADHD or ODD and often have behavioral problems during childhood and adolescence (Widom et al., 2009).

Etiology and Treatment

In the *DSM-I* (APA, 1952), individuals were diagnosed with gross stress reaction resulting from psychological problems that arose as a result of military or civilian experiences (Friedman et al., 2011). However, the concept of gross stress reaction was criticized for not providing a solid foundation for diagnosing criteria. The *DSM-II* (APA, 1968) disposed of that diagnosis and developed the alternative diagnosis of, situational reaction. Clinicians felt this diagnosis captured both traumatic and unpleasant events resulting from traumatic exposure. Both gross stress reaction and situational reaction were identified as being reversible and temporary disorders. However, in the late 1970s, mental health clinicians noticed patients were presenting with severe, chronic, and irreversible symptoms as a result of exposure to traumatic events. This resulted in the *DSM-III* (APA, 1980) diagnostic criteria for PTSD that remain in existence until now. Through the development of the diagnostic criteria for PTSD, the possible symptoms increased from 12 to 17 and the symptom clusters shifted (Friedman et al., 2011).

Implications for Counselors

It is important that counselors understand that the fundamental feature of trauma rather than anxiety served as the driving force for the movement of trauma- and stressor-related disorders into a separate chapter. This modification follows revisions within *ICD-10* that also separate trauma from anxiety disorder (WHO, 2007). However, unlike the *ICD-10*, which keeps trauma and anxiety disorder in the same larger category, the sequential order of this chapter in the *DSM-5* following anxiety disorders and obsessive-compulsive and related disorders reflects the close relationship between trauma and anxiety disorders. In addition to diagnostic similarities, these disorders were also grouped together in an effort to increase clinical utility (First, 2010).

The new Trauma- and Stressor-Related Disorders chapter will require counselors to closely examine traumatic and stressor-related experiences and closely evaluate new diagnostic criteria to categorize trauma and stressor-related impairments. With the lower diagnostic threshold for acute stress disorder and PTSD, counselors will need to be on alert for diagnostic inflation, especially as it relates to children under the age of 6 (Frances, 2013).

To help readers better understand changes from the *DSM-IV-TR* to the *DSM-5*, the rest of this chapter outlines each disorder within the Trauma- and Stressor-Related Disorders chapter of the *DSM-5*. Readers should note that we have focused on major changes from the *DSM-IV-TR* to the *DSM-5*; however, this is not a stand-alone resource for diagnosis.

Although a summary and special considerations for counselors are provided for each disorder, when diagnosing clients, counselors need to reference the *DSM-5*. It is essential that the diagnostic criteria and features, subtypes and specifiers (if applicable), prevalence, course, and risk and prognostic factors for each disorder are clearly understood prior to diagnosis.

313.89 Reactive Attachment Disorder (F94.1)

We adopted John when he was 6 years old. He has never known his birth parents and, prior to our adoption, was shuffled from institution to institution. After having been with us for 1 year, John continued to be severely withdrawn, refusing any forms of affection even when he is upset. He doesn't seem to interact with any other children or seems fearful of anyone getting close to him. Even when others try to interact with him or comfort him he doesn't respond.—Emma (John's mom)

Reactive attachment disorder (RAD) is characterized by markedly disturbed and developmentally inappropriate social relatedness in children before the age of 5 (APA, 2013a; Schechter & Willheim, 2009; Widom et al., 2009). There is broad consensus among clinicians that this disorder results from an extremely inadequate caregiving environment and is directly associated with grossly pathological care. Children diagnosed with RAD continuously fail to initiate or respond to social interactions.

Essential Features

Typically seen before the age of 5, children diagnosed with RAD have not had the opportunity to form stable attachments and have experienced persistent disregard of their basic physical and emotional needs for comfort, stimulation, and affection (APA, 2013a; Schechter & Willheim, 2009; Widom et al., 2009). Symptoms of RAD include detachment, unresponsiveness or resistance to comforting, holding back emotions, withdrawal from others, and a mixture of approach and avoidance behaviors (APA, 2013a; Zeanah & Gleason, 2010). Children diagnosed with RAD have no developmental delays. Little epidemiological data exist for this disorder, but it is relatively uncommon. Only a minority of children with severe caretaking deficiencies or abnormalities develop RAD.

Major Changes From *DSM-IV-TR* to *DSM-5*

Formerly located within the Disorders Usually First Diagnosed in Infancy, Childhood, or Adolescence chapter in the *DSM-IV-TR*, RAD included two specifiers: inhibited and disinhibited type. *Disinhibited type*, characterized by indiscriminate social skills marked by a child's inability to exhibit appropriate attachments, is no longer included as a criterion for this disorder (APA, 2013a; Zeanah & Gleason, 2010). This specifier has been moved to a separate disorder (see next section).

Special Considerations

RAD is not diagnosed when children, despite abuse or maltreatment, can still form attachments and are not markedly maladjusted (Schechter & Willheim, 2009; Zeanah & Gleason, 2010). RAD should be differentiated from ASD, which can develop within a relatively supportive setting (APA, 2013a). Although RAD can present like ADHD, it is different because children who are diagnosed with ADHD will form attachments (Zeanah & Gleason, 2010). RAD is not applicable to children with developmental delays or neurological damage. Finally, RAD does not apply to rebellious behavior, which develops in preadolescent and adolescent children who previously had strong attachments with caregivers. Critics of this diagnosis point to limited research with contradictory findings (cf. Chaffin et al., 2006; Hanson & Spratt, 2000).

Common approaches to treating RAD are based on attachment theory and concentrate on increasing the responsiveness and sensitivity of the caregiver, or if that is not possible, placing the child with a different caregiver (Prior & Glaser, 2006). Prevention programs are also important, especially to target problematic early attachment behaviors in both children and caregivers. Cohen et al. (2010) identified important parameters mental health practitioners should focus on when working with children diagnosed with RAD. The first goal is ensuring the child is in a safe and stable environment that can provide for physical and emotional needs. The second goal focuses on how the child can begin to develop an appropriate, healthy attachment with his or her primary caregiver(s).

Counselors should be aware that neglected children are often at risk for developmental delays, dialectical deficits/disorders, and neglect of medical concerns (Prior & Glaser, 2006). Counselors must remember that all cases of abuse, neglect, and exploitation must be reported. Therefore, counselors need to be familiar with their local and state laws regarding mandated reporting, and their actions need to be in compliance with the *ACA Code of Ethics* (ACA, 2014).

Cultural Considerations

As stated previously, there has been little research on RAD (Zeanah & Gleason, 2010). This means that counselors should pay particular attention when making a diagnosis of RAD, especially for cultural groups in which attachment has not been thoroughly studied (APA, 2013a). Because attachment behavior varies greatly from one cultural group to another, counselors must use caution to ensure that the child's attachment behavior is markedly disturbed and developmentally inappropriate as defined by the child's cultural norms.

Differential Diagnosis

Pervasive developmental disorders or developmental delays are commonly considered as differential diagnoses from RAD (APA, 2013a). However, criticisms of RAD are that the criteria from the *DSM-IV-TR* focused too much on social behavior and not attachment behavior, for example, how a child seeks comfort, support, nurturance, and protection from a preferred attachment figure in times of fear or distress. Focusing on social behavior runs the risk of overlapping with ASD rather than an attachment disorder.

Coding, Recording, and Specifiers

There is only one diagnostic code for RAD: 313.89 (F94.1). There are two specifiers for this disorder: *persistent*, which is used when the disorder has been present for more than 12 months, and *severe*, when there is evidence of all symptoms and each has a relatively high level of occurrence. There are no codes associated with these specifiers.

313.89 Disinhibited Social Engagement Disorder (F94.2)

We do not know what to do. Jamaal runs up to strangers and is willing to run away with anyone. One day he even got into a stranger's car while we were at the supermarket. He is distant from us and has been ever since we adopted him 1 year ago. I worry about his safety while at school or away from my partner and I.—Jamaal's father

Disinhibited social engagement disorder (DSED) is a new diagnosis in the *DSM-5* (APA, 2013a; Zeanah & Gleason, 2010). This disorder represents the indiscriminately *social/disinhibited* subtype of the *DSM-IV-TR* childhood diagnosis of RAD (Zeanah & Gleason, 2010). Now considered a distinct disorder, DSED is characterized by a pattern of behavior in which the child actively approaches and interacts with unfamiliar adults (APA, 2013a; Zeanah & Gleason, 2010).

Essential Features

Children diagnosed with DSED do not exhibit developmentally appropriate discretion with unfamiliar adults and may engage in overly familiar behavior with strangers (APA, 2013a; Zeanah & Gleason, 2010). In familiar or unfamiliar settings, these children may venture away from a primary caregiver and often are willing to go off with an unfamiliar adult with minimal or no hesitation. Like RAD, the origin of these symptoms is grossly inadequate caregiving that failed to meet the child's basic emotional or physical needs and safety (Schechter & Willheim, 2009; Widom et al., 2009). Risk factors for DSED include repeated changes in caregivers or being raised in unconventional settings, such as an orphanage or institution that severely limited the child's ability to form secure attachments.

Special Considerations

Counselors need to be careful not to overdiagnose RAD or DSED in children who are adopted, living in a foster home, or have been mistreated by their caregiver (APA, 2013a). Children with RAD and DSED are presumed to have grossly disturbed internal models for relating to others; therefore, treatment should involve both the caretaker and the child (Prior & Glaser, 2006). Counselors should not attempt to change the child but rather should focus on changing the child's surroundings and creating positive interactions with caregivers. As with RAD, counselors must be sure the child with DSED is in a safe and stable environment where he or she can get appropriate care, and counselors should always be aware that neglected children are often at risk for developmental delays, dialectical deficits/disorders, and neglect of medical concerns (Prior & Glaser, 2006). All cases of abuse, neglect, and exploitation must be reported, and counselors need to be familiar with mandated reporting laws as well as the *ACA Code of Ethics* (ACA, 2014).

Cultural Considerations

There has been little research on DSED (Zeanah & Gleason, 2010). Similar to RAD, counselors should pay particular attention when making a diagnosis of DSED in cultures in which attachment has not been studied. Because attachment behavior varies greatly from one cultural group to another, counselors must use caution to ensure that the child's attachment behaviors are inappropriate as defined by the child's cultural norms.

Differential Diagnosis

DSED can be mistaken for ADHD (APA, 2013a; Frances, 2013). Although the symptoms of DSED are inattentiveness and impulsivity, the etiology of DSED, inadequate caregiving and neglect, is what differentiates this disorder from other impulse-control disorders or ADHD (Zeanah & Gleason, 2010). As with RAD, counselors must be sure to distinguish DSED from pervasive developmental disorders (Zeanah & Gleason, 2010). Counselors should also be sure the client does not have the genetic disorder Williams syndrome, characterized by mild to moderate intellectual disability (Zeanah & Gleason, 2010). Children with Williams syndrome have unique facial features and distinct personality traits of overfriendliness, anxiety, and high levels of empathy (National Institute of Neurological Disorders and Stroke, 2008).

Note

Counselors must be careful to differentiate RAD and DSED from PTSD. To do so, look for emotional regulation problems and aggression, as these are not core symptoms of either RAD or DSED. Whereas maladaptive care can be defined as trauma, problems with attachment to caregiver prior to 5 years old are distinct features of RAD and DSED and should not be misdiagnosed as PTSD.

◆ ◆ ◆

Coding, Recording, and Specifiers

There is only one diagnostic code for DSED: 313.89 (F94.2). Counselors will note the same *ICD-9-CM* code is used for RAD and DSED (i.e., 313.89). A similar code, with .2 as opposed to the .1 given for RAD, is listed under the *ICD-10-CM*. The reason these are the same in the *ICD-9-CM* but not the *ICD-10-CM* is because the *disinhibited type* specifier, formerly listed under RAD in the *DSM-IV-TR*, has now been included the *DSM-5* and the *ICD-10-CM* as a separate diagnosis. There are two specifiers for this disorder. The specifier *persistent* is used when the disorder has been present for more than 12 months, and *severe* is used when there is evidence of all symptoms and each has a relatively high level of occurrence. There are no codes associated with these specifiers.

309.81 Posttraumatic Stress Disorder (F43.10)

About a year ago, I was in a major car accident. Although I sustained only minor injuries, two of my friends were killed. At first, the accident seemed like just a bad dream. Then the nightmares started. Now, the sights and sounds of the accident haunt me all the time. I have trouble sleeping at night, and during the day I feel "on edge." I jump whenever I hear a siren or screeching tires, and I avoid TV altogether as I might find a program that shows a car chase or accident scene. I avoid driving when possible. —Amanda

Posttraumatic stress disorder (PTSD) applies only if someone has been exposed to one or more traumatic or stressful events or circumstances. Without severe trauma, a diagnosis of PTSD cannot be made. A *traumatic stressor* is defined by the *DSM-5* as "any event (or events) that may cause or threaten death, serious injury, or sexual violence to an individual, a close family member, or a close friend" (APA, 2013a, p. 830). Critics have argued that this definition does not include nonviolent trauma such as emotional abuse; therefore, counselors should be careful if considering traumas such as emotional neglect and verbal abuse as triggering stressors for PTSD (Frances, 2013).

As mentioned earlier, the past year prevalence of PTSD was 3.5%, with a 3.6% lifetime prevalence among men and 9.7% among women. No population-based epidemiological studies have been conducted to examine the prevalence rates in children; however, children who have been exposed to specific traumatic events are at greater risk of prevalence of PTSD.

Major Changes From *DSM-IV-TR* to *DSM-5*

PTSD was previously classified in the *DSM-IV-TR* as an anxiety disorder, but the criteria for it have undergone substantial changes in the *DSM-5*. Compared with the *DSM-IV-TR*, *DSM-5* diagnostic criteria for PTSD include more explicit attention to what represents, and does not represent, a traumatic event. Within the diagnostic features description, APA (2013a) lists exposure to war as a combatant or civilian, childhood physical abuse, and threatened or actual sexual violence, with a wide range of examples, to give a clearer picture of traumatic exposure. References to concentration camps and being diagnosed with a life-threatening illness were removed, but the *DSM-5* does clarify that medical illnesses in which a shocking or catastrophic event occurs (e.g., waking during surgery or anaphylactic shock) may be considered traumatic (APA, 2013a; Frances, 2013).

The *DSM-5* also offers clarification in Criterion A.3, which states that accidental or violent traumatic events, such as automobile fatalities, in which a close family member or friend is involved can be traumatic (APA, 2013a). This clarification, although technically not new to the *DSM*, is controversial because of the potential for exploitation in forensic proceedings, which often use the diagnosis of PTSD for determination of disability or damages compensation. Because the symptoms of PTSD are entirely based on client self-reports, counselors should caution against the misuse of the PTSD diagnosis in forensic settings (Frances, 2013).

New to the *DSM-5* is Criterion A.4, which includes recurring or intense exposure, such as extreme traumas frequently witnessed by police officers and first responders (APA, 2013a). The addition of this criterion is in response to research that supports the idea that individuals who have regular exposure to traumatic events, such as persons who handle the deceased and other first responders, are at risk for developing PTSD (Halpern & Tramontin, 2007; Ursano, 2004). Although this criterion does not apply to media, television accounts, photos, or movies, occupational exposure to events (e.g., exposure of reporters to traumatic events) is included.

Other major changes are the introduction of four, as opposed to three, diagnostic clusters. The change is a result of splitting up *DSM-IV-TR* Criterion C, avoidance and numbing, into two criteria: avoidance (Criterion C) and negative alterations in cognitions and mood (Criterion D). Avoidance and numbing were separated because of empirical evidence and clinical experiences that indicated at least one avoidance symptom (e.g., evasion of activities, thoughts, feelings, or conversations related to the event) was needed for an accurate PTSD diagnosis (Friedman et al., 2011). The cognition and mood criterion was added because research indicates that shifts in cognition and emotion dysregulation are common to all individuals diagnosed with PTSD. See Table 7.1 for a breakdown of the four clusters and associated examples.

Other changes to PTSD are related to subtypes. The *DSM-5* includes the addition of two new subtypes: the *preschool* subtype and the *dissociative* subtype (APA, 2013a). The first,

Table 7.1
Diagnostic Criteria of Posttraumatic Stress Disorder (PTSD)

PTSD Diagnostic Clusters	Commonly Associated Examples
Exposure (Criterion A): Direct experience; witnessing the event(s) in person; learning that a friend or close family member was directly affected by a traumatic event; repeated exposure to averse details of a traumatic event (exposure to electronic media is not considered repeated exposure).	
Cluster 1 (Criterion B): Intrusion	Recurrent, involuntary, and intrusive distressing memories or dreams of the traumatic event and dissociative reactions (i.e., flashbacks). In children, trauma-specific reenactment may occur in play. Intense distress or marked physiological reactions because of exposure to internal or external cues that symbolize or resemble an aspect of the traumatic event.
Cluster 2 (Criterion C): Avoidance (one or both)	Avoidance or attempts to avoid distressing memories, thoughts, or feelings or external reminders about or closely associated with the traumatic event.
Cluster 3 (Criterion D): Negative alterations in cognitions or mood (two or more)	Inability to recall an important aspect of the traumatic event, persistent negative beliefs of oneself, persistent distorted cognitions about the cause or consequences of the traumatic event, persistent negative emotional state, diminished interest in significant activities, or persistent inability to experience positive emotions. Represents myriad feelings a survivor can experience. Includes, but is not limited to, persistent and distorted sense of blame of self and others, estrangement, markedly diminished interest in activities, and problems remembering.
Cluster 4 (Criterion E): Arousal and reactivity (two or more)	Irritability and angry outbursts, recklessness, hypervigilance, exaggerated startle response, problems with concentration, or sleep disturbances.

PTSD *preschool* subtype, is used for children under 6 years old. One of the most significant changes for counselors working with children is the inclusion of PTSD criteria for children 6 years and younger. Overall, counselors will find that the *DSM-5* diagnostic threshold has been lowered for children. As opposed to the criteria for individuals over 6 years of age, the criteria for children 6 years and younger emphasize the impact of traumatic events on children when primary caregivers are involved (see Criterion A.2 for children 6 years and younger), clarify that play reenactment may serve as a catalyst for recurrent or intrusive memories, and only require that either persistent avoidance of stimuli or negative alterations in cognitions and mood be present. This is in contrast to the diagnostic criteria for individuals over the age of 6, which require that individuals avoid stimuli and have negative alterations in cognition and mood. The criteria for children under 6 also remove references related to recollection of the event and negative beliefs of self. For example, children under 6 are not necessarily capable of expressing feelings related to their negative beliefs or expectations of self. Problems related to work-related events and reckless, self-destructive behavior were also not included in this diagnostic set because they are not applicable to children.

The *dissociative* subtype is used when PTSD is seen with prominent dissociative symptoms, which are categorized as either depersonalization or derealization. *Depersonalization* includes feelings of detachment from one's own mind or body, "as if one were an outside observer of one's mental processes or body" (APA, 2013a, p. 272). *Derealization* includes experiences in which the world seems unreal, illusory, or distorted. Sometimes referred to as "complex PTSD," these subtypes would most likely be seen when an individual has been exposed to multiple traumas, particularly in childhood, that result in a complex range of symptoms.

Another significant change in the *DSM-5* was removal of what was formerly known in the *DSM-IV-TR* as Criterion A.2. This criterion mandated that a response of intense fear, helplessness, or horror to the event must be present to diagnose PTSD. This language was deleted because the reactions of intense fear, helplessness, or horror do not predict the onset of PTSD (APA, 2013c). Understanding a person's reaction to trauma is a complex task because emotional responses, like traumatic events, vary considerably; counselors should never attempt to identify a "normal" reaction to traumatic stress. Ursano et al. (1994) summarized this exposure well by stating, "Overall, most individuals exposed to traumatic events and disasters do quite well . . . but for some psychiatric illness, behavioral change, or alterations in physical health result. Certainly, no one goes through profound life events unchanged" (p. 5). Finally, what *DSM-IV-TR* called *delayed onset* is now called *delayed expression*.

Essential Features

Characteristic PTSD symptoms include daytime memories, images, or flashbacks of the event(s) (APA, 2013a). Individuals may experience physiological or emotional stress when they encounter reminders of the event, and any potential triggers, even if only remotely related to the event, must be avoided. Many persons with PTSD also become disconnected from others, find little meaning in life or the future, are indifferent in their relationships, have trouble sleeping and concentrating, and may seem to be constantly tense or "on guard." Nightmares and survivor guilt are also common. Symptoms must be present for more than 1 month and, like most clinical diagnoses, cause significant impairment or distress.

Note

For a diagnosis of PTSD, there must be exposure to severe trauma. In addition, stress must be relived in some fashion and clients must attempt to avoid stimuli associated with the trauma, including memories or external reminders of the trauma. Clients must also have cognitive problems and marked changes in their emotional state. Symptoms must last over 1 month, and stress must cause significant distress or impairment. None of these issues may be due to a substance or medical condition.

◆ ◆ ◆

Counselors should pay particular attention to ensure that all criteria are met for PTSD, not just exposure to an extreme stressor. These additional criteria, as stated previously, include intrusion, avoidance, negative alteration in cognitions and mood, and alterations in arousal and reactivity. These additional criteria are often referred to as "clusters" and are discussed in detail in the next section and outlined in Table 7.1.

Special Considerations

The new Trauma- and Stressor-Related Disorders chapter requires counselors to closely examine premorbid experiences and the new diagnostic criteria to categorize distress and functional impairments. Because all individuals respond to trauma differently, it is important that counselors understand that symptoms of PTSD manifest in various ways. Some clients will reexperience the trauma through nightmares and violent flashbacks, others will be unable to experience pleasure or will have negative core beliefs about themselves, and some others will display a combination of symptoms.

An important inclusion for counselors are the risk and prognostic factors in the *DSM-5*, which indicate a predictable pattern of elements that either place clients at risk or serve as protective factors. Separated by pre- and posttrauma, these include emotional, environmental, and genetic or physiological factors. Pretraumatic emotional factors include temperamental or psychiatric problems. Environmental factors include socioeconomic status, education level, and previous exposure to trauma. Genetic factors include gender and age. Inclusion of these elements is based on research that indicates factors such as age (Green & Solomon, 1995), gender (Rubonis & Bickman, 1991), ethnicity (Perilla, Norris, & Lavizzo, 2002), socioeconomic status (Bolin, 1986; Epstein, Fullerton, & Ursano, 1998), and marriage and familial status (Gleser, Green, & Winget, 1981; Solomon & Smith, 1994) can be predictive of survivor mental health outcomes. For example, racial/ethnic minority groups, females, younger adults, and individuals with a history of trauma often do not fare as well as their counterparts (Green et al., 1990; Norris & Elrod, 2006). It is important to note that these populations are also more frequently exposed to such stressors as rape, domestic violence, and acculturative stress.

Cultural Considerations

In addition to the risk and prognostic factors described previously, counselors should also carefully consider culture-related variation in the type of exposure, severity, and clinical expression of symptoms as well as the ongoing sociocultural context in relation to the client's diagnosis. Counselors must not forget that clinical presentation of symptoms is culturally specific and may significantly affect clinical expression, particularly with respect to avoidance/numbing and somatic symptoms (Hinton & Lewis-Fernández, 2010). For example, post-9/11 studies of Latino Americans found higher rates of panic attacks (13.4% to 16.8%), a risk factor for PTSD, compared with non-Latinos (5.5%; Hinton & Lewis-Fernández, 2010). This can primarily be explained by *ataque de nervios* (attack of nerves), a relatively common manifestation of distress among Latino Americans. Commonly reported symptoms include uncontrollable shouting, attacks of crying, and trembling. Also common are dissociative symptoms; seizure-like or fainting episodes and suicidal gestures are also prominent. Moreover, there is a cultural perception among some Latino Americans that older members of the community need to always maintain control of their emotions; this may account for instances of dissociation regarding emotional responses. For example, when asked about emotional responses to trauma, some Latino clients will respond "*ese no era yo*," which translates to "that was not me" (Lewis-Fernández, Guarnaccia, Patel, Lizardi, & Diaz, 2005). Other examples include mental health clinicians working with Cambodians who experienced the torture and brutality inflicted by the Khmer Rouge regime (Van de Put & Eisenbruch, 2004). Some of the survivors described themselves as "thinking too much" (Van de Put & Eisenbruch, 2004, p. 137), which later was described as "Cambodian sickness" (p. 137). Although this study was conducted in the early 1980s, clinicians later noted their symptoms bore similarities to PTSD (Van de Put & Eisenbruch, 2004).

Studies such as these reveal how imperative it is for counselors to develop multicultural expertise when working with trauma survivors and to include cultural considerations in all diagnostic assessments.

Differential Diagnosis

PTSD cannot be diagnosed if symptoms are present for less than 1 month. Instead, a diagnosis of acute stress disorder is made if symptoms are present for less than a month. Adjustment disorders should be assigned for clients who have experienced traumatic stress but do not express all other diagnostic criteria for a diagnosis of PTSD or, conversely, if a client presents with PTSD criteria but the stressor is not extreme enough to meet Criterion A (e.g., divorce, losing one's job, or business difficulties). Counselors should also consider other anxiety, depressive, dissociative, or psychotic disorders or traumatic brain injury. In terms of comorbid diagnoses, clients with PTSD are 80% more likely to meet diagnostic criteria for other psychiatric diagnosis (Kessler, Sonnega, Bromet, Hughes, & Nelson, 1995). Substance use disorder and conduct disorders are common and, among those who have experienced traumatic brain injury, co-occurrence of PTSD is 48%. Comorbidity is also high in children with PTSD, with ODD and separation anxiety disorder most frequently seen. Finally, counselors should look for neurocognitive disorders because clients who experience head injuries may experience a number of overlapping symptoms (APA, 2013a).

Coding, Recording, and Specifiers

There is only one diagnostic code for PTSD: 309.81 (F43.10); however, counselors must indicate whether the diagnosis is for an adult or for a child under 6 in the written name of the disorder. Counselors may also select two specifiers, as applicable, for both adults and children under 6 years old. The first specifier indicates whether an individual has persistent and recurrent symptoms of dissociation. When indicating *with dissociative symptoms*, counselors will also identify a subtype of depersonalization or derealization. The specifier subtype will be indicated in the written name of the disorder, for example, 309.81 (F43.10) PTSD for children 6 years and younger, *with dissociative symptoms, depersonalization*. The second specifier for PTSD is *with delayed expression*, formerly known as *delayed onset*. Whereas the typical course of symptoms begins within the first 3 months, this newly renamed specifier recognizes that there may be a delay of months or even years before full criteria for PTSD are met. For counselors, this means that in the aftermath of the trauma, an individual may meet the criteria for acute stress disorder (see next section) rather than PTSD. There are no codes assigned to either of these specifiers. If panic attacks are present with PTSD, counselors may add the specifier *with panic attacks*.

Diagnostic Criteria for PTSD 309.81 (F43.10)

The following criteria apply to adults, adolescents, and children older than 6 years. For children 6 years and younger, see corresponding criteria below.

A. Exposure to actual or threatened death, serious injury, or sexual violation, in one (or more) of the following ways:
1. Directly experiencing the traumatic event(s).
2. Witnessing, in person, the event(s) as it occurred to others.
3. Learning that the traumatic event(s) occurred to a close family member or close friend. In cases of actual or threatened death of a family member or friend, the event(s) must have been violent or accidental.
4. Experiencing repeated or extreme exposure to aversive details of the traumatic event(s) (e.g., first responders collecting human remains; police officers repeatedly exposed to details of child abuse).

Note: Criterion A.4. does not apply to exposure through electronic media, television, movies, or pictures, unless this exposure is work related.

B. Presence of one (or more) of the following intrusion symptoms associated with the traumatic event(s), beginning after the traumatic event(s) occurred:

1. Recurrent, involuntary, and intrusive distressing memories of the traumatic event(s).

Note: In children older than 6 years, repetitive play may occur in which themes or aspects of the traumatic event(s) are expressed.

2. Recurrent distressing dreams in which the content and/or affect of the dream are related to the traumatic event(s).

Note: In children, there may be frightening dreams without recognizable content.

3. Dissociative reactions (e.g., flashbacks) in which the individual feels or acts as if the traumatic event(s) were recurring. (Such reactions may occur on a continuum, with the most extreme expression being a complete loss of awareness of present surroundings.)

Note: In children, trauma-specific reenactment may occur in play.

4. Intense or prolonged psychological distress at exposure to internal or external cues that symbolize or resemble an aspect of the traumatic event(s).

5. Marked physiological reactions to internal or external cues that symbolize or resemble an aspect of the traumatic event(s).

C. Persistent avoidance of stimuli associated with the traumatic event(s), beginning after the traumatic event(s) occurred, as evidenced by one or both of the following:

1. Avoidance of or efforts to avoid distressing memories, thoughts, or feelings about or closely associated with the traumatic event(s).

2. Avoidance of or efforts to avoid external reminders (people, places, conversations, activities, objects, situations) that arouse distressing memories, thoughts, or feelings about, or that are closely associated with, the traumatic event(s).

D. Negative alterations in cognitions and mood associated with the traumatic event(s), beginning or worsening after the traumatic event(s) occurred, as evidenced by two (or more) of the following:

1. Inability to remember an important aspect of the traumatic event(s) (typically due to dissociative amnesia and not to other factors such as head injury, alcohol, or drugs).

2. Persistent and exaggerated negative beliefs or expectations about oneself, others, or the world (e.g., "I am bad," "No one can be trusted," "The world is completely dangerous," "My whole nervous system is permanently ruined").

3. Persistent, distorted cognitions about the cause or consequences of the traumatic event(s) that lead the individuals to blame himself/herself or others.

4. Persistent negative emotional state (e.g., fear, horror, anger, guilt, or shame).

5. Markedly diminished interest or participation in significant activities.

6. Feelings of detachment or estrangement from others.

7. Persistent inability to experience positive emotions (e.g., inability to experience happiness, satisfaction, or loving feelings).

E. Marked alterations in arousal and reactivity associated with the traumatic event(s), beginning or worsening after the traumatic event(s) occurred, as evidenced by two (or more) of the following:

1. Irritable behavior and angry outbursts (with little or no provocation) typically expressed as verbal or physical aggression toward people or objects.

2. Reckless or self-destructive behavior.

3. Hypervigilance.

4. Exaggerated startle response.

5. Problems with concentration.

6. Sleep disturbance (e.g., difficulty falling or staying asleep or restless sleep).

F. Duration of the disturbance (Criteria B, C, D, and E) is more than 1 month.

G. The disturbance causes clinically significant distress or impairment in social, occupational, or other important areas of functioning.

H. The disturbance is not attributable to the physiological effects of a substance (e.g., medication, alcohol) or another medical condition.

Specify whether:

With *dissociative symptoms:* The individual's symptoms meet the criteria for posttraumatic stress disorder, and in addition, in response to the stressor, the individual experiences persistent or recurrent symptoms of either of the following:

1. *Depersonalization:* Persistent or recurrent experiences of feeling detached from, and as if one were an outside observer of, one's mental processes or body (e.g., feeling as though one were in a dream; feeling a sense of unreality of self or body or of time moving slowly).

2. *Derealization:* Persistent or recurrent experiences of unreality of surroundings (e.g., the world around the individual is experienced as unreal, dreamlike, distant, or distorted).

Note: To use this subtype, the dissociative symptoms must not be attributable to the physiological effects of a substance (e.g., blackouts, behavior during alcohol intoxication) or another medical condition (e.g., complex partial seizures).

Specify if:

With *delayed expression:* If the full diagnostic criteria are not met until at least 6 months after the event (although the onset and expression of some symptoms may be immediate).

Posttraumatic Stress Disorder for Children 6 Years and Younger

A. In children 6 years and younger, exposure to actual or threatened death, serious injury, or sexual violence, in one (or more) of the following ways:

1. Directly experiencing the traumatic event(s).

2. Witnessing, in person, the event(s) as it occurred to others, especially primary caregivers.

Note: Witnessing does not include events that are witnessed only in electronic media, television, movies or pictures.

3. Learning that the traumatic event(s) occurred to a parent or caregiving figure.

B. Presence of one (or more) of the following intrusion symptoms associated with the traumatic event(s) , beginning after the traumatic event(s) occurred:

1. Recurrent, involuntary, and intrusive distressing memories of the traumatic event(s).

Note: Spontaneous and intrusive memories may not necessarily appear distressing and may be expressed as play reenactment.

2. Recurrent distressing dreams in which the content and/or affect of the dream are related to the traumatic event(s).

Note: It may not be possible to ascertain that the frightening content is related to the traumatic event.

3. Dissociative reactions (e.g., flashbacks) in which the child feels or acts as if the traumatic event(s) were recurring. (Such reactions may occur on a continuum, with the most extreme expression being a complete loss of awareness of present surroundings.) Such trauma-specific re-enactment may occur in play.

4. Intense or prolonged psychological distress at exposure to internal or external cues that symbolize or resemble an aspect of the traumatic event(s).

5. Marked physiological reactions to reminders of the traumatic event(s).

C. One (or more) of the following symptoms, representing either persistent avoidance of stimuli associated with the traumatic event(s) or negative alterations in cognitions and mood associated with the traumatic event(s), must be present, beginning after the event(s) or worsening after the event(s):

Persistent Avoidance of Stimuli

1. Avoidance of or efforts to avoid activities, places, or physical reminders that arouse recollections of the traumatic event(s).
2. Avoidance of or efforts to avoid people, conversations, or interpersonal situations that arouse recollections of the traumatic event(s).

Negative Alterations in Cognitions

3. Substantially increased frequency of negative emotional states (e.g., fear, guilt, sadness, shame, confusion).
4. Markedly diminished interest or participation in significant activities, including constriction of play.
5. Socially withdrawn behavior.
6. Persistent reduction in expression of positive emotions.

D. Alterations in arousal and reactivity associated with the traumatic event(s), beginning or worsening after the traumatic event(s) occurred, as evidenced by two (or more) of the following:

1. Irritable behavior and angry outbursts (with little or no provocation) typically expressed as verbal or physical aggression toward people or objects (including extreme temper tantrums).
2. Hypervigilance.
3. Exaggerated startle response.
4. Problems with concentration.
5. Sleep disturbance (e.g., difficulty falling or staying asleep or restless sleep).

E. The duration of the disturbance is more than 1 month.

F. The disturbance causes clinically significant distress or impairment in relationships with parents, siblings, peers, or other caregivers or with school behavior.

G. The disturbance is not attributable to the physiological effects of a substance (e.g., medication or alcohol) or another medical condition.

Specify whether:

With *dissociative symptoms:* The individual's symptoms meet the criteria for post-traumatic stress disorder, and the individual experiences persistent or recurrent symptoms of either of the following:

1. *Depersonalization:* Persistent or recurrent experiences of feeling detached from, and as if one were an outside observer of, one's mental processes or body (e.g., feeling as though one were in a dream; feeling a sense of unreality of self or body or of time moving slowly).
2. *Derealization:* Persistent or recurrent experiences of unreality of surroundings (e.g., the world around the individual is experienced as unreal, dreamlike, distant, or distorted).

Note: To use this subtype, the dissociative symptoms must not be attributable to the physiological effects of a substance (e.g., blackouts) or another medical condition (e.g., complex partial seizures).

Specify if:

With *delayed expression:* If the full diagnostic criteria are not met until at least 6 months after the event (although the onset and expression of some symptoms may be immediate).

Note

The dissociative and preschool subtypes are not mutually exclusive. An individual can be diagnosed with both the preschool and dissociative subtypes if criteria for both are met. In a forensic setting, it is recommended that the diagnosis of PTSD only be used when the individual has directly experienced the event (Frances, 2013).

♦ ♦ ♦

 Example

Officer Teixeira was referred to mental health support services by her husband, who is concerned about her "unpredictable mood swings" and nightmares. He stated these have been going on for about 9 months and seem to be getting worse. In addition, although no formal action has been taken, Officer Teixeira has had two complaints of using unwarranted force in apprehending offenders. When she comes into counseling, she reports she is seriously at risk of losing her current position. When asked if there are any recent events that might have contributed to her rapid change in behavior, she states she just hasn't been herself since one "horrific case" that took place 9 months ago involving a teenage girl.

Officer Teixeira vividly recalls the details of this case. "She was only 15 when she was attacked by a group of men on the way home from school. They took turns screaming abuse at her and then they each raped her. Finally, they tried to stab her to death and would almost certainly have succeeded had we not arrived on the scene. I don't know what is worse, the fact that this happened to her or the fact that this is by no means the worse case I have seen."

She reports being unable to keep the memories of the attack out of her mind. At night, she has terrible dreams of rape and often wakes up screaming. She has had significant difficulty policing her route, especially those areas in which she has seen violence. Because of this, she has volunteered to take a desk job, something she never thought she would do. She also avoids any cases in which the victims have been raped, beaten, or abused. Despite these actions, she still feels as if her emotions are numbed and that she has no real future in the police force. At home, she is anxious, tense, and easily startled. She is unable to concentrate on anything and reports feeling helpless and shamed that she can't do more to help these victims.

♦ ♦ ♦

Diagnostic Questions

1. Do Officer Teixeira's presenting symptoms meet the criteria for PTSD?
2. Which symptom(s) led you to select that diagnosis?
3. What rule-outs would you consider for Officer Teixeira's case?
4. What other information may be needed to make an accurate clinical diagnosis?

308.3 Acute Stress Disorder (F43.0)

I just don't know what has happened to Marie. A week ago she was completely normal, then all of a sudden she is a mess! Ever since she saw that apartment on fire she has been a complete wreck. She can't sleep, she can't work, and she seems like she is in a daze all the time.—Ronald (Marie's husband)

Introduced in the *DSM-IV* (APA, 1994), acute stress disorder identifies individuals experiencing acute stress responses, as opposed to transitory stress, as a result of exposure to a traumatic event. The inclusion of acute stress disorder was a major diagnostic landmark in the early 1990s because, for nearly a century, the presentation of trauma-like symptoms was referred to only in military populations. Terms such as "shell shock," "war hysteria," or "war neurosis" (Van der Kolk, McFarlane, & Weisaeth, 1996) were commonly used to describe soldiers' reactions to combat.

In addition to identifying acute stress reactions, the overarching goal of acute stress disorder in the *DSM-IV-TR* was to identify people who may be at risk for PTSD. More recent studies, however, have questioned the capacity of acute stress disorder to sufficiently identify persons at risk for PTSD (Bryant, Friedman, Spiegel, Ursano, & Strain, 2011). Therefore, counselors should not assume that acute stress disorder is a predictor of PTSD and instead use the criteria presented to help identify acute stress reactions and people who may benefit from early intervention. Research that acute stress disorder does not necessarily predict PTSD as well as evidence that acute posttraumatic reactions are exceedingly heterogeneous fueled changes to acute stress disorder in the *DSM-5*.

Major Changes From *DSM-IV-TR* to *DSM-5*

As is the case with PTSD, the exposure criterion (Criterion A) for acute stress disorder has changed from *DSM-IV-TR* to *DSM-5*. A diagnosis of acute stress disorder now requires that exposure to an extreme stressor must meet the following criteria: experiencing the event directly; witnessing the event in person; learning that an event occurred to a close family member or friend; or having repeated, first-hand experience with trauma that is not the result of non-work-related media, pictures, television, or movies (APA, 2013a). As with PTSD, the *DSM-5* has expanded Criterion A for acute stress disorder to include repeated or extreme exposure and dropped the requirement for an emotional response of fear, helplessness, or horror.

Because of evidence that acute posttraumatic reactions are significantly varied and that the *DSM-IV-TR*'s emphasis on dissociative symptoms was overly restrictive, acute stress disorder now requires the presence of nine out of 14 symptoms within five categories (APA, 2013a). There is no longer a requirement for individuals to have three or more dissociative symptoms. These categories, which do not differ from those associated with PTSD, include intrusion, negative mood, dissociative, avoidance, and arousal. Whereas these symptoms have not radically changed in the *DSM-5*, removing the requirement for dissociative symptoms represents a significant change to the diagnostic criteria and the way in which counselors conceptualize acute stress reactions.

Since the inclusion of acute stress disorder in the *DSM*, there have been many concerns regarding the dissociative requirements. First, results from research regarding dissociative symptoms as a predictor of PTSD are not conclusive (Breh & Seidler, 2007; Bryant et al., 2011; van der Velden et al., 2006). Second, requiring dissociative symptoms has the potential for disregarding other high-risk persons from being identified, thus limiting services that may be available (Bryant, 2003; Bryant et al., 2011). Third, there is significant literature that highlights dissociative symptoms as a common transient stress response not indicative of psychopathology (Bryant, 2007; Bryant et al., 2011). This argument is also applicable to arousal, which is often observed as a normal stress response and not pertinent to either acute stress disorder or PTSD.

Like other modifications made to the *DSM-5*, revised criteria for this disorder more closely match the definition of acute stress reaction in the *ICD-10-CM*. This more comprehensive description of acute stress is believed to be more useful because the focus is on symptoms—rather than specific clusters—that may warrant intervention (e.g., sleep disturbances) but do not necessarily predict PTSD. The *ICD-10-CM* goes further to claim that acute stress reactions cannot be categorized into specific response sets (Bryant et al., 2011); therefore, clusters are not useful in the detection of acute posttraumatic stress.

Essential Features

The clinical presentation for acute stress disorder is equivalent to PTSD with two exceptions. First, symptom duration of acute stress disorder is more than 3 days but less than 1 month (APA, 2013a). Second, acute stress disorder does not require symptom clusters. Although clinical presentation varies from person to person, it is not uncommon for those diagnosed with acute stress disorder to have some form of reexperiencing (e.g., flashbacks) or hypervigilance. Detachment or strong reactivity, whether physiological or emotional, is typical when survivors are exposed to reminders of the event. Others can experience reactivity in the form of heightened emotional responses, such as anger, aggression, grief, or problems with concentration (Bryant et al., 2011). Because of the short duration, acute stress disorder has no specifiers; it can be diagnosed in both children and adults.

Special Considerations

Recognizing the heterogeneity of stress responses among individuals, the *DSM-5* diagnosis of acute stress disorder serves to help practitioners differentiate between transient stress responses, which are normal, and acute stress reactions, which may require clinical attention. Counselors must remember that strong emotional, behavioral, cognitive, physiological, and spiritual responses are common among survivors of traumatic events. Although these responses vary significantly from individual to individual, feelings of distress are common and are often normal reactions to a catastrophic event. Differentiating what is a normal reaction from an abnormal one can help counselors better determine which clients may require interventions or, in some cases, be at risk for developing PTSD.

Cultural Considerations

Children and adolescents who were diagnosed with acute stress disorder have been found to have a greater range of emotional difficulties when they experienced a trauma (Salmond et al., 2011). There may also be a difference in the level or duration of trauma examined in Western and non-Western studies. Western studies often focus on one-time events such as an accident or some similar event in which the sample is selected from a hospital, whereas many non-Western studies tend to focus on events that might be ongoing and do not have a specific start and stop time. The situations and environments between Western and non-Western studies are likely to lend themselves to looking at trauma from different perspectives (Bryant et al., 2011).

Differential Diagnosis

Counselors who work with clients who have experienced a brain injury in the context of the traumatic event will need to ensure symptoms are not better accounted for by a diagnosis of neurocognitive disorder attributable to traumatic brain injury. Panic attacks are not uncommon in clients who present with acute stress. If these attacks are unexpected and there is considerable anxiety about future attacks, then counselors will want to consider whether a diagnosis of panic disorder better accounts for the client's symptom profile.

It is also important to consider both duration of symptoms and the type of stressor when diagnosing acute stress disorder. In doing so, counselors must consider whether symptoms have been present for more than 1 month, so as to a rule out PTSD. Counselors must also consider whether the associated stressor meets the criteria for acute stress disorder as opposed to an adjustment disorder. The diagnosis of adjustment disorder is used when the stressor does not meet Criterion A for exposure to actual or threatened death, serious injury, or sexual violence. For example, a person losing his or her job would not meet Criterion A for acute stress disorder. Acute stress symptoms (as described in Criterion B) may be more appropriately diagnosed as an adjustment disorder when an individual does not meet or exceed the symptom profile for acute stress disorder. This is especially true for anger, guilt, and depressive symptoms, which are common to both acute stress disorder and adjustment disorders (APA, 2013a).

Coding, Recording, and Specifiers

There is only one diagnostic code for acute stress disorder: 308.3 (F43.0). There are no specifiers associated with this disorder; however, counselors may add *with panic attacks* if the client experiences panic attacks concurrent with acute stress disorder.

 Example

Vanessa, a 46-year-old television reporter, was part of a small group of journalists who were chosen to witness an execution by lethal injection. For several years, she had been following stories of capital punishment. This story was very personal to her, because she had interviewed members of the victim's family and covered their experiences as the inmate approached execution.

When asked to describe the experience, she stated it was ghastly. "His face turned an ash color, then purple. He seemed to be gasping for air and grimacing. At one point his body convulsed. It took approximately 20 minutes. All of which I will never forget." Vanessa reported she was hoping she could remain objective since she was a reporter and had been covering capital punishment for quite some time.

Vanessa reported that since the execution nearly 2 weeks ago, she has had problems concentrating on her work. She can't stop thinking about the execution and finds herself replaying the scene where the person grimaced over and over in her mind. She has felt detached, almost like she was in a dream watching herself. She has problems sleeping and also problems getting along with her husband. "He just doesn't understand that I need to be left alone right now."

◆ ◆ ◆

Diagnostic Questions

1. Do Vanessa's presenting symptoms meet the criteria for a stress disorder? If so, which disorder?
2. Based on the disorder identified in Question 1, which symptom(s) led you to select that diagnosis?
3. Would Vanessa be more accurately diagnosed with an adjustment disorder? If so, why? If not, why not?
4. What rule-outs would you consider for Vanessa's case?
5. What other information may be needed to make an accurate clinical diagnosis?

309. _ _ Adjustment Disorders (F43. _ _)

Two months ago was when it happened. My department announced budget cuts, and five out of eight of us were asked to leave. After 13 years I was just asked to go. No party, no compensation package, not even a good-bye. I don't know what I am going to do. I can't seem to do anything now; even getting out of bed is useless. I just sit around all day and cry. The rejection is unbearable. Getting another job and even being able to pay my mortgage just seems hopeless. —Patrick

Introduced in the *DSM-III* (APA, 1980) to describe individuals who did not meet the criteria for a mental disorder but experienced marked distress and impairment because of a life stressor, adjustment disorders focus on individuals who have difficulty coping with a particular source of stress. The stressor can include major life changes, such as retirement or going to school, or loss of something, such as the ending of an important relationship. Events that do not meet the criteria for acute stress disorder or PTSD but still cause marked distress, such as a business crisis or marital problems, are also included.

Major Changes From *DSM-IV-TR* to *DSM-5*

Previously listed as a separate chapter in the *DSM-IV-TR*, adjustment disorders are now integrated in the *DSM-5* with other disorders in which an identifiable stressor precedes symptom onset. What differentiates adjustment disorders from other stressor-related disorders is that the identifiable stressor is not considered traumatic. The stressor may be a sole occurrence, such as losing one's job or ending a relationship, or may be a continuous set of stressful circumstances, such as relationship or occupational problems. Similar to acute stress disorder, adjustment disorders may be predictive of subsequent impairment. Therefore, the new location of this diagnosis helps increase clinical utility simply by its placement in the *DSM-5*.

Essential Features

Individuals diagnosed with adjustment disorders have impaired relationships in their personal or occupational life or have stress symptoms that exceed what would be expected as a result of the stressor. Reactions need to be somewhat inflated but temporary, with symptom reduction within 6 months once the stressor and its consequences have been removed.

Note

There is no "normal" reaction to a traumatic event. Counselors must remember that adjusting to life stressors is not indicative of mental illness. This category should only be used when an individual encounters a difficult life event and criteria of marked distress and significant impairment are met.

◆ ◆ ◆

Adjustment disorders occur at all ages; however, symptomatology differs in children and adolescents. These differences are noted in the symptoms experienced, severity and duration of symptoms, and the outcome. Adolescent symptoms of adjustment disorders are more behavioral, such as conduct problems and temper tantrums, whereas adults experience more depressive symptoms, such as tearfulness and loss of pleasure in previously enjoyed activities.

Special Considerations

A major limitation of the diagnostic criteria for adjustment disorders is the amount of ambiguity within diagnostic criteria. Critics posit that there is too much room for interpretation (Frances, 2013; Paris, 2013). Therefore, counselors need to approach assigning a diagnosis of adjustment disorder with caution. Counselors should also keep in mind that adjustment disorders can accompany many mental disorders as well as medical illnesses. For example, individuals with adjustment disorders often have symptoms of tearfulness, feel loss of hope, and experience a lack of interest in work or social activity. Whereas many of these symptoms mirror MDD, unlike MDD, adjustment disorders are always triggered by an outside stressor and generally go away once the individual has been able to cope with the situation or the stressor has been removed.

Cultural Considerations

Stressors and the signs associated with the stressor will vary on the basis of the client's cultural influences. Individuals who routinely experience a high level of stress may be at greater risk for an adjustment disorder.

Differential Diagnosis

Adjustment disorders can be differentiated from acute stress disorder or PTSD because the stressor does not necessarily include exposure to actual or threatened death, serious injury, or sexual violence (Criterion A for PTSD and acute stress disorder). Counselors also need to consider MDD, personality disorder, or any other mental illness or medical condition that would reduce a client's ability to cope with life stressors. In the event that clients meet criteria for more stringent mental disorders, even in the face of a known stressor, counselors should diagnose the more stringent disorder. Counselors should also consider whether the symptom profile is a normative reaction to an unfortunate event. If the client's reaction is normative and expected, adjustment disorders should not be diagnosed.

Coding, Recording, and Specifiers

There is no diagnostic code for adjustment disorders. Coding and recording are contingent on the counselor choosing one of six specifiers: 309.0 (F43.21) *with depressed mood*; 309.24 (F43.22) *with anxiety*; 309.28 (F43.23) *with mixed anxiety and depressed mood*; 309.3 (F43.24) *with disturbance of conduct*; 309.4 (F43.25) *with mixed disturbance of emotions and conduct*; and 309.9 (F43.20) *unspecified*. Because depressed mood, anxiety, and disturbance of conduct are common to clients diagnosed with adjustment disorders, counselors must assign one of these specifiers to an adjustment disorder diagnosis. If an individual experiences mixed anxiety and depression, the counselor would choose the *mixed* specifier. Similarly, if an individual (most likely a child or adolescent) experiences mixed disturbance of conduct and emotion, the counselor would indicate these symptoms using the *mixed* specifier. For reactions that do not meet any of the aforementioned specifiers, the counselors would choose *unspecified*.

Because adjustment disorders are associated with a known stressor, counselors should also include reference to the stressor by using *ICD-9-CM* V codes or *ICD-10-CM* Z codes located in Other Conditions That May Be a Focus of Clinical Attention. For example, an adolescent experiencing depression and anxiety related to an unexpected pregnancy may be diagnosed with "309.28 (F43.23) adjustment disorder with mixed anxiety and depressed mood and V61.7 (Z64.0) problems related to unwanted pregnancy."

Other Specified and Unspecified Trauma- and Stressor-Related Disorders

Other specified trauma- and stressor-related disorder (309.89 [F43.8]), along with the unspecified criterion (309.9 [F43.9]), replaces the NOS category in the *DSM-IV-TR*. The other specified category may now be used for diagnosis if the counselor wants to identify the specific reason that the full diagnosis is not met, for example, 309.89 (F43.8) other specified trauma- and stressor-related disorder, *ataque de nervios*.

The unspecified trauma- and stressor-related disorder (309.9 [F43.9]) diagnosis is used when clients have prominent trauma- and stressor-related symptoms but do not meet criteria for any of the specific disorders listed in this chapter. This diagnosis is also used in situations when the counselor chooses not to specify the reason that the criteria are not met. In either case, symptoms cause clinically significant impairment or distress. This diagnosis is also commonly used when counselors are unable to distinguish whether a medical illness or substance has played a causal role in the manifestation of symptoms.

Note

The *ICD-9-CM* diagnostic code for unspecified trauma and stressor-related disorder and unspecified adjustment disorder (309.9) is the same.

◆ ◆ ◆

Chapter 8

Gender Dysphoria
in Children, Adolescents, and Adults

I was taught early on what I "should" be doing as a boy. I remember asking my mother why God made me a boy when I wanted to be a girl. She took me to a counselor who told me I was too young to know what I wanted. He simply gave me medication for anxiety and suggested I participate in team sports. That was years ago. Since then, I have not admitted to anyone that I want to be a woman. I feel so alone and isolated. —Jacob

Men and women typically display different behaviors related to their assigned genders. These differences in cultural and social behaviors are looked at as constructs and norms in which the two genders are expected to act and behave within the boundaries of society (Diamond, 2002). Identification of these gender differences in behavior starts in early childhood (Balleur-van Rijn, Steensma, Kreukels, & Cohen-Kettenis, 2012). As children age, they develop friendships and participate in activities with other children who are of the same sex. If an individual does not display behaviors considered congruent with his or her natal gender, or the gender assigned at birth, this may cause confusion and discomfort for the individual. This incongruence may lead to a misidentification of one's gender role and how society expects one to act (Diamond, 2002).

In addition to behavioral differences, gender is also often displayed through physical appearances (Balleur-van Rijn et al., 2012). For example, whether a person has long or short hair is often an indicator of gender. Physical features, such as breasts or facial hair, and clothing are also common determinants. Children learn at a young age how each gender has certain physical attributes as well as different kinds of behaviors (Dragowski, Scharron-del Rio, & Sandigorsky, 2011). If a child is experiencing discrepancies between his or her assigned and expressed gender, the child might likely identify with or adopt physical characteristics (i.e., clothing, hairstyles) of his or her expressed, rather than natal, gender (Perrin, Smith, Davis, Spack, & Stein, 2010).

To help readers better understand both diagnostic categories of gender dysphoria in adults and gender dysphoria in children and adolescents, as well as major changes from the *DSM-IV-TR* to the *DSM-5*, we have included major changes and the diagnostic criteria for gender dysphoria at the beginning of this chapter. After presenting the reader with the diagnostic criteria, as with other chapters of this *Learning Companion*, we then present essential features, special considerations, implications for counselors, differential diagnoses, and two case studies to facilitate a better understanding of gender dysphoria among all age ranges.

Major Changes From *DSM-IV-TR* to *DSM-5*

Gender dysphoria replaces the previously termed *gender identity disorder* in the *DSM-IV-TR*. Changing from *disorder* to *dysphoria* reduces the notion that an individual has a disorder because he or she identifies with a gender other than the one he or she was born into (APA, 2013b, 2013c). Although there was considerable debate from the lesbian, gay, bisexual, and transgender community about keeping gender dysphoria in the *DSM*, APA advocated that retaining this as a mental disorder will promote treatment: "To get insurance coverage for the medical treatments, individuals need a diagnosis. The Sexual and Gender Identity Disorders Work Group was concerned that removing [gender dysphoria] as a psychiatric diagnosis—as some had suggested—would jeopardize access to care" (APA, 2013b, p. 2). For example, clients can advocate for hormonal and surgical treatments such as gender reassignment surgery because of the clinically significant distress associated with this condition (APA, 2013b; Megeri & Khoosal, 2007).

Counselors must recognize these changes as major symbolic shifts in the nomenclature, intended to better reflect the experience of children, adolescents, and adults struggling with gender identity issues. The clear separation of this chapter from sexual dysfunctions and paraphilias strongly supports the idea that this diagnosis is not a pathological disorder. In the *DSM-IV-TR*, gender identity disorder, sexual dysfunctions, and paraphilias were classified together under the Sexual and Gender Identity Disorders chapter, which supported the idea that gender dysphoria was a pathological diagnosis. The second symbolic shift is modification of language, which now focuses on "gender incongruence" between biological and expressed gender as opposed to cross-gender identification. The latter, found in the *DSM-IV-TR*, does not adequately highlight the psychological experience individuals with gender dysphoria encounter.

Although specific criteria changes to this section were not extensive, the separation of criteria sets for children versus adolescents and adults and the inclusion of new specifiers (e.g., *with a disorder of sex development* and *posttransition*) to replace the old sexual orientation specifier (i.e., sexually attracted to males, sexually attracted to females, sexually attracted to both, and sexually attracted to neither) are major changes. By separating diagnostic criteria for children, the *DSM-5* does not pathologize developmentally appropriate gender nonconformity in children. Moreover, children and adolescents have unique challenges and treatment options (e.g., puberty-delaying hormones). Also, the requirement that individuals experience a strong desire to live as their expressed gender is no longer required for children because children often do not feel comfortable expressing this desire. Finally, the sexual orientation specifier was removed because critics questioned the relevance to a mental health diagnosis, particularly one that remains in the *DSM* only to assist individuals experiencing persistent and severe internal dysphoria with birth-assigned gender.

To give the reader a better idea of the changes related to gender dysphoria, we list the specific criteria here for gender dysphoria in children, followed by the criteria for adolescents and adults.

Diagnostic Criteria for Gender Dysphoria in Children 302.6 (F64.2)

A. A marked incongruence between one's experienced/expressed gender and assigned gender, of at least 6 months' duration, as manifested by at least six of the following (one of which must be Criterion A1):

1. A strong desire to be of the other gender or an insistence that he or she is the other gender (or some alternative gender different from one's assigned gender).
2. In boys (assigned gender), a strong preference for cross-dressing or simulating female attire; or in girls (assigned gender), a strong preference for wearing only typical masculine clothing and a strong resistance to the wearing of typical feminine clothing.
3. A strong preference for cross-gender roles in make-believe play or fantasy play.
4. A strong preference for the toys, games, or activities stereotypically used or engaged in by the other gender.
5. A strong preference for playmates of the other gender.
6. In boys (assigned gender), a strong rejection of typically masculine toys, games, and activities and a strong avoidance of rough-and-tumble play; or in girls (assigned gender), a strong rejection of typically feminine toys, games, and activities.
7. A strong dislike of one's sexual anatomy.
8. A strong desire for the primary and/or secondary sex characteristics that match one's experienced gender.

B. The condition is associated with clinically significant distress or impairment in social, school, or other important areas of functioning.

Specify if:

With a disorder of sex development: (e.g., a congenital adrenogenital disorder such as 255.2 [E25.0] congenital adrenal hyperplasia or 259.50 [E34.50] androgen insensitivity syndrome).

Coding note: Code the disorder of sex development as well as gender dysphoria.

Diagnostic Criteria for Gender Dysphoria in Adolescents and Adults 302.85 (F64.1)

A. A marked incongruence between one's experienced/expressed gender and assigned gender, of at least 6 months' duration, as manifested by at least two of the following:
1. A marked incongruence between one's experience/expressed gender and primary and/or secondary sex characteristics (or in young adolescents, the anticipated secondary sex characteristics).
2. A strong desire to be rid of one's primary and/or secondary sex characteristics because of a marked incongruence with one's experienced/expressed gender (or in young adolescents, a desire to prevent the development of the anticipated secondary sex characteristics).
3. A strong desire for the primary and/or secondary sex characteristics of the other gender.
4. A strong desire to be of the other gender (or some alternative gender different from one's assigned gender).
5. A strong desire to be treated as the other gender (or some alternative gender different from one's assigned gender).
6. A strong conviction that one has the typical feelings and reactions of the other gender (or some alterative gender different from one's assigned gender).

B. The condition is associated with clinically significant distress or impairment in social, school, or other important areas of functioning.

Specify if:

With a disorder of sex development: (e.g., a congenital adrenogenital disorder such as 255.2 [E25.0] congenital adrenal hyperplasia or 259.50 [E34.50] androgen insensitivity syndrome).

Coding note: Code the disorder of sex development as well as gender dysphoria.

Specify if:

Posttransition: The individual has transitioned to full-time living in the desired gender (with or without legalization of gender change) and has undergone (or is preparing to have) at least one cross-sex medical procedure or treatment regimen—namely, regular cross-sex hormone treatment or gender reassignment surgery confirming the desired gender (e.g., penectomy, vaginoplasty in a natal male; mastectomy or phalloplasty in a natal female).

From *Diagnostic and Statistical Manual of Mental Disorders, Fifth Edition,* 2013, pp. 452–453. Copyright 2013 by the American Psychiatric Association. All rights reserved. Reprinted with permission.

Note

Congenital adrenal hyperplasia is a disease that affects the endocrine system, creating a deficiency or overproduction of sex hormones (Dreger, Feder, & Tamar-Mattis, 2012). In effect, this disease can alter the development of primary and secondary sex characteristics. Androgen insensitivity syndrome involves the development of biological sex either before birth or during puberty (Gottlieb, Beitel, Nadarajah, Palioura, & Trifiro, 2012). Sex development disorders such as these must be diagnosed by a medical professional.

◆ ◆ ◆

Essential Features

A person with gender dysphoria feels there is a "mismatch" between the gender traditionally associated with being male or female and his or her identified gender (i.e., gender identity; Crooks & Baur, 2013). A main feature of gender dysphoria is that there is a significant incongruence between the gender one is assigned at birth and the gender one prefers to express (Crooks & Baur, 2013; Hyde & DeLamater, 2013). APA (2013a) described gender dysphoria as "the distress that may accompany the incongruence between one's experienced or expressed gender and one's assigned gender" (p. 451). The distress experienced must also be visible, meaning there is an evident difficulty in social, occupational, or other significant areas of functioning (APA, 2013a, 2013b).

Individuals diagnosed with gender dysphoria often have a continuous discomfort with their natal gender, feel like they were born the wrong sex, and sense they are different from their peers. They often feel misunderstood; have challenges accessing appropriate mental health care treatment; and have difficulties with social, occupational, and legal issues. APA (2013b) cited a "need for change" (p. 1) and advocated for increased treatment options for individuals experiencing gender dysphoria. In addition to advocacy and increasing access to care, counselors should be aware of confusion and controversy surrounding the terms *sex* and *gender*. *Sex* is characterized as the biological indicators of male and female, typically within a reproductive context, such as testes in males and ovaries in females (APA, 2013a; Crooks & Baur, 2013). Counselors must understand and use the term *sex* in its proper context, which is to describe biological and medical examples. *Gender* is used to describe more cultural situations and contexts (Diamond, 2002). The term *gender identity* indicates which sex one feels represents his or her daily life experience or "lived role as a boy or girl, man or woman" (APA, 2013a, p. 451).

Individuals who experience a conflict between their expressed gender (i.e., gender identity) and biological sex may self-identify as transgender or transsexual. *Transgender* is a broad term for individuals who challenge socially constructed gender norms (Association of Lesbian, Gay, Bisexual and Transgender Issues in Counseling [ALGBTIC], 2009). *Transsexual* is a term for individuals who experience "intense, persistent, long-term discomfort with their body and self-image due to the awareness that their assigned sex is inappropriate" (ALGBTIC, 2009, p. 28). Gender reassignment processes, such as hormone replacement therapy or surgical alterations, are steps transsexual individuals may take toward gender transition, which is a social, psychological, and medical process in which the individuals align themselves with their expressed gender identity (ALGBTIC, 2009).

Children

Gender dysphoria, cutting across all age ranges and genders, presents in different ways. For example, girls who have not yet gone through puberty may state that they wish to be boys or insist that they are boys. They will want to wear boys' clothes and will not want to wear feminine clothes, even at their parents' insistence (APA, 2013a). Diagnosing a child with gender dysphoria can help the child to work on living a life as a transgender person and help decrease incongruence between assigned and expressed gender (Hein & Berger, 2012).

Children with gender dysphoria tend to have increasing rates of same-sex or bisexual orientation than their gender-typical counterparts (Wallien & Cohen-Kettenis, 2008).

Cross-gender behaviors typically present in children between the ages of 2 and 4. This is also the timeframe when children are developing behaviors and interests related to their expressed gender. A person who experiences gender dysphoria in childhood may not necessarily experience it in adolescence or adulthood. The persistence rates in natal males range from 2.2% to 30%; for natal females, the rates range from 12% to 50% (APA, 2013a). Both natal males and females who display persistence are often attracted to their natal sex (APA, 2013a).

Individuals who have a disorder of sex development as well as gender dysphoria often seek medical treatment and attention at an early age. These disorders are often related to gender-atypical behavior that starts in early childhood. It is important to point out that sex development disorders do not always lead to gender dysphoria (APA, 2013a).

Adults

The prevalence for gender dysphoria ranges from 0.005% to 0.014% in natal adult men and from 0.002% to 0.003% in natal adult women; however, not all individuals with gender dysphoria seek treatment at clinics, so these rates may be higher than initially reported (APA, 2013a). Adults who have gender dysphoria regularly experience incongruence between genders and often experience a desire to be rid of their primary and secondary sex characteristics. A strong desire to live as another gender must be present in adults for at least 6 months. As stated previously, this is no longer a requirement for children. Most individuals experiencing gender dysphoria try to reduce the incongruence by living in their expressed gender or incorporating a nontraditional gender role (APA, 2013a). Some adults will have the opportunity for gender reassignment surgery. In these instances, the specifier of *posttransition* will be used.

Adolescents with gender dysphoria may present with characteristics of either children or adults, depending on where they are in their development. They may also be aware that they will be experiencing certain physical changes such as developing secondary sex characteristics (APA, 2013a). However, it is important to point out that adolescents with gender dysphoria are not classified as transgender until they are adults (Diamond, 2002). Adolescents who seek treatment at gender identity clinics are more likely to be diagnosed with gender dysphoria when they are adults compared with their gender-typical peers (Balleur-van Rijn et al., 2012).

Special Considerations

It is essential that counselors do not generalize. Not all individuals who experience incongruence with their assigned gender and expressed gender meet the criteria for gender dysphoria (APA, 2013a; Megeri & Khoosal, 2007; Perrin et al., 2010). Counselors also must not pathologize individuals experiencing gender dysphoria. Counselors can work toward competent practice by learning language that is affirmative to clients and their developmental process; recognizing oppression, even from mental health professionals; and creating an informed, welcoming, and affirmative environment for transgender individuals and their loved ones. Counselors must understand that many individuals with gender dysphoria find themselves isolated from society and experience difficulties in getting their most basic emotional needs met. Male-to-female and female-to-male transsexuals, persons whose gender identity is opposite their biological sex, often put others' needs before their own (Crooks & Baur, 2013; Simon, Zsolt, Fogd, & Czobor, 2011). This could be because they are so used to societal rejection that they would rather do something gratifying for another person who does not reject them, even at the expense of their own needs. Individuals with gender dysphoria may also view the world as negative and threatening. Their self-concept may be affected by their experiences of rejection and the negative reactions from society in general (Simon et al., 2011). Middle and late childhood are vulnerable times, because this is commonly when children start using social comparison as a measure for their own self-concept (Balleur-van Rijn et al., 2012). If a child's behaviors do not match those of his or her peers, the child may start to withdraw and isolate from the peer group.

Counselors should be careful about personal bias and avoid making stereotypical assumptions or buying into parents' or family members' assumptions of sex, gender, and gender identity. Psychoeducation for all parties is critical, as is strict adherence to the *ACA Code of Ethics* (ACA, 2014) relating to values imposition, discrimination and, above all else, promotion of the dignity and welfare of the client.

Cultural Considerations

Individuals with gender dysphoria have been diagnosed across various countries and cultures (APA, 2013a). Determining what is gender atypical for an individual or a cultural group is difficult because what is considered gender appropriate may vary significantly among different individuals and groups. Additionally, gender roles have changed significantly over the years, and roles that may have been viewed as inappropriate years ago are now considered socially acceptable (Langer & Martin, 2004). Furthermore, gender roles are dependent on the way in which society views expectations for men and women. Multicultural awareness is critical for counselors working with these clients and their families; therefore, counselors should remember it might be ineffective to use traditional roles of men and women as a foundation on which to identify and define gender (Kameya & Narita, 2000).

Differential Diagnosis

APA (2013a) included common differential diagnoses for gender dysphoria as nonconformity to gender roles, transvestic disorder, BDD, schizophrenia and other psychotic disorders, and other clinical presentations. Although all of these are diagnoses counselors should consider, the lifetime psychiatric comorbidity in clients with gender-related issues is high. Therefore, counselors should carefully consider co-occurring mental health problems during assessment and treatment planning.

In an investigation of individuals diagnosed with gender identity disorder, Hepp, Kraemer, Schnyder, Miller, and Delsignore (2005) found only 29% of clients had no history of a coexisting mental health disorder. Common comorbid conditions include BDD (Balleur-van Rijn et al., 2012), depression and schizophrenia (Parkes, Hall, & Wilson, 2009), anxiety (Megeri & Khoosal, 2007), substance abuse and personality disorders (Hepp et al., 2005), and trauma-related disorders (Di Ceglie, 2000; Hepp et al., 2005). Many of these conditions may be explained by the diagnostic criteria of gender dysphoria. For example, individuals with gender dysphoria often feel negatively about their bodies, a dissatisfaction that may be a contributing factor to BDD (Balleur-van Rijn et al., 2012). Body dissatisfaction could also be compounded by the fact that these individuals are identifying more with bodies related to their desired gender as opposed to their natal sex. Although evidence is not conclusive, APA (2013a) posited that many individuals who present with gender dysphoria may have anxiety or depressive disorders manifested by disapproval of their bodies. Additionally, by trying to live life in their desired gender, individuals often have to deal with considerable stressors from family, society, and oppressive forces, which may perpetuate symptoms of anxiety or depression (Megeri & Khoosal, 2007). In contrast, Simon et al. (2011) found that there was no evidence of higher rates of depression and anxiety among individuals with gender dysphoria. However, Balleur-van Rijn et al. (2012) pointed out that individuals who internalize a negative self-perception often experience feelings of doubt and worthlessness that may lead to depressive disorders.

Therefore, although awareness of possible comorbidity is important, it is equally important that counselors avoid assumptions when working with the transsexual population and remember that high percentages of psychiatric comorbidity are not always the rule (Gómez-Gil, Trilla, Salamero, Godás, & Valdés, 2009; Haraldsen & Dahl, 2000; Miach, Berah, Butcher, & Rouse, 2000; Seikowski, Gollek, Harth, & Reinhardt, 2008). Counselors need to advocate for individuals diagnosed with gender dysphoria and help them access the support, medical services, and mental health treatments necessary to live a full, satisfactory life.

Etiology and Treatment

It is difficult to pinpoint a particular cause of gender dysphoria (Megeri & Khoosal, 2007). Brain development may be one cause, as some parts of the brain may develop patterns that are similar to those of the opposite sex. Gender development is thought to start at the time of conception, and the environment is also a contributing factor that influences a child's gender development (Dragowski et al., 2011).

Aside from biological origins, it is important to consider the impact of parental influences in the etiology of gender dysphoria (Simon et al., 2011). Many male-to-female and female-to-male transsexuals noted that their mothers were not as caring and affectionate and were described as more controlling. Male-to-female transsexuals found that their fathers were not as caring or available to them. An individual experiencing gender incongruence may be less likely to express these thoughts because of fears of stigma from parents or caregivers. Counselors need to understand that, for many people, gender is socially constructed (not about biological sex), and distress around incongruence is more a reaction to social expectations than one's desire to be another gender. Therefore, the focus of treatment is often on accepting the person and his or her experience and promoting a healthy identity in the face of discrimination or rejection. In contrast to other *DSM* disorders, the focus of treatment for gender dysphoria is not to change one's gendered behaviors but rather to support the client in coping with experiences of incongruence and promote optimal functioning.

Treating gender dysphoria can be complex because there are various kinds of interventions that can be helpful to this population. Children who are gender variant may go on to develop gender dysphoria. Interventions for children should focus on helping to prevent the development of psychosocial problems that may carry into adolescence and adulthood (Balleur-van Rijn et al., 2012). In addition to realizing they are different from their peers, adolescents are also becoming more aware of the general public's reaction to them. Without proper treatment, this could lead to a more negative self-concept.

Counselors can look at how the child sees himself or herself and examine more favorable aspects of the child's self-concept (Balleur-van Rijn et al., 2012). This strength-based approach focuses on what is working rather than on how different the child is from others in his or her peer group. Other interventions may help clients explore and develop awareness of how gender differences affect their identities (Parkes et al., 2009).

Although not all clients will desire medical intervention, counselors may work closely with medical professionals to help clients explore medical treatments available to them. These include surgical alterations of genital anatomy and hormonal treatments that alter body physiology. Whereas other options, such as dressing in accordance to one's preferred gender (i.e., cross-dressing), are available, research indicates that these practices have generally been insufficient in helping individuals reconcile gender incongruence. Crooks and Baur (2008) noted, "In most cases, psychotherapy, without accompanying biological alterations, has been inadequate. . . . For such individuals the best course of action might be to change their bodies to match their minds" (p. 64). Although medical alterations bear high financial and emotional burdens, individuals who undergo such treatments often experience significant improvement in overall quality of life (à Campo, Nijman, Merckelbach, & Evers, 2003; De Cuypere et al., 2005; Lawrence, 2003). Counseling is a strongly recommended and often a mandated part of hormone treatment and other physical interventions (Crooks & Baur, 2013; Parkes et al., 2009).

Implications for Counselors

It is important that counselors take into account the client with gender dysphoria as well as the family. This is even more necessary if the client with gender dysphoria is a child. Parents may need help deciding when and how to set boundaries regarding dress, play with certain playmates, or engagement in other actions in accordance with the child's expressed gender (Balleur-van Rijn et al., 2012). Family therapy sessions may help parents come to terms with letting the child dress as he or she wants to and to be able to explore his or her body like most other children do during this time (Hein & Berger, 2012). Not only will this help the parents, but it will also help the child if he or she sees that his or her parents are willing to take a supportive role.

Counselors should also closely observe parents and children discussing cross-gender identification (Wallien & Cohen-Kettenis, 2008). Parents may dismiss concerns as just a phase or lack awareness of children's experiences outside the home. Parents' account may only provide a glimpse of their behaviors (Wallien, Veenstra, Kreukels, & Cohen-Kettenis, 2010). To have a clear picture of the client's presenting worldview, counselors need to carefully identify what parents are not saying or might be missing.

Counselors should also consider current or past emotional issues in addition to issues related to gender. Parkes et al. (2009) found that many individuals with gender incongruence had been victims of physical and sexual childhood abuse. Counselors can consider whether children experienced signs of gender dysphoria before or after puberty. Some children who experience incongruence with their gender at younger ages may not experience gender dysphoria as they grow older, whereas other children may experience gender dysphoria into adolescence and adulthood (Wallien & Cohen-Kettenis, 2008). The latter is more common, especially when gender incongruence is high, because children who display extreme levels of gender dysphoria are more likely to persist as gender dysphoric as they got older. Those who desisted typically did so once they started secondary school (Dragowski et al., 2011). Finally, gender dysphoria is a sensitive issue for clients and counselors alike. As mental health professionals, counselors need to be cognizant of their own sensitivities and biases.

Finally, it is likely that counselors will encounter clients with gender-related issues (APA, 2013a). Whereas epidemiological studies lack any strong conclusions about the prevalence of gender dysphoria (Zucker & Lawrence, 2009), the *DSM-5* estimates prevalence of 0.005% to 0.014% in natal adult men and 0.002% to 0.003% in natal adult women (APA, 2013a). However, as noted earlier, these are likely underestimates because not all adults who meet criteria for gender dysphoria seek medical alternatives (Byne et al., 2012). It is important for counselors to understand that gender dysphoria exists on a continuum. Although many counselors will not have opportunity to work with clients who meet full diagnostic criteria for gender dysphoria, many will work with clients who experience gender role struggles and conflicts. Therefore, counselors need to clearly understand the needs of clients and remember that etiology and treatment are complex. As with any counseling-related issue, counselors should be open and willing to collaborate with other professionals as necessary.

Counselors must reference the ALGBTIC (2009) *Competencies for Counseling Transgendered Clients*. As with other specialized practices in counseling, counselors must ensure they are adequately prepared and trained to help clients with these issues.

Coding, Recording, and Specifiers

There is only one diagnostic code for gender dysphoria in children, 302.6 (F64.2), and gender dysphoria in adolescents and adults, 302.85 (F64.1). However, it should be specified if the dysphoria is with a disorder of sex development. If this is the case, the disorder should be coded as a disorder of sex development as well as gender dysphoria (APA, 2013a). Counselors should also record *posttransition* if applicable. This specifier indicates that the individual has made the transition to living full time in the desired gender with or without legalization of gender change. For this specifier to be assigned, the individual must also have undergone at least one cross-sex medical procedure or treatment regimen (APA, 2013a).

 Example

Janice is a 4-year-old girl of mixed African and Caucasian American decent. She is the middle child with an older brother and a younger sister and lives with her married, biological parents. Janice's parents describe her as bright, alert, and imaginative. She attends preschool and has many friends there. Although she has friends of both genders, her teacher said that she has more male friends and tends to play with them and participate in male-related activities.

When Janice was 3-years-old, she asked her parents if she could start wearing boy underwear once she started using the toilet. As she got older, she wanted to wear her brother's clothes instead of her own clothes. She hardly plays with her own girl toys anymore and often fights her brother to play with his toys. Lately, she has been saying that she wants to be a boy. Janice's parents are starting to be concerned because she is identifying herself more as a boy as she gets older. They want to be supportive but are unsure of the next steps they should take.

Diagnostic Questions

1. Do Janice's presenting symptoms meet the criteria for gender dysphoria?
2. Based on the disorder identified in Question 1, which symptom(s) led you to select the diagnosis?
3. What would be the reason(s) a counselor may not diagnose Janice with gender dysphoria?
4. What rule-outs would you consider for Janice's case?
5. What other information may be needed to make an accurate clinical diagnosis?

 Example

Tara, a 32-year-old Caucasian woman, has come in seeking private counseling before an elective breast implant surgery. She states that her parents and friends have urged her to speak with someone before the surgery because they feel she has a "problem." Tara states that, although she was born with male genitalia, she has always known she is a woman inside and wants the outside to reflect that. To this end, 4 years ago she changed her name from Terrance to Tara, even though her family strongly objected. Furthermore, her feelings and actions toward becoming fully female are a strong source of family tension since her childhood. She remembers her father walking in on her when she was 9 years old while she was putting on makeup. She was severely punished for this behavior. When she was 18, she met friends who cross-dressed and she began hanging out with them and learning about the transgender community. Her parents and siblings again expressed concern, and, for a while, her father refused to speak to her.

At 32, Tara finally feels empowered not just to dress and behave as a woman but to begin the transformation process. She states that this has caused so much friction within the family that her mother is depressed and calls her almost daily crying and begging her not to follow through. Tara agreed to talk to a counselor before the surgery because her mother is so upset, and she is reconsidering the surgery even though it has been a lifelong dream for her.

♦ ♦ ♦

Diagnostic Questions

1. Do Tara's presenting symptoms meet the criteria for gender dysphoria?
2. What criteria would support giving this diagnosis?
3. What would be the reason(s) a counselor may not diagnose Tara with gender dysphoria?
4. What rule-outs must be considered?
5. What other information may be needed to make an accurate clinical diagnosis?

Part One References

Abramowitz, J. S., Khandker, M., Nelson, C. A., Deacon, B. J., & Rygwall, R. (2006). The role of cognitive factors in the pathogenesis of obsessive-compulsive symptoms: A prospective study. *Behaviour Research and Therapy, 44,* 1361–1374.

Abramowitz, J. S., Wheaton, M. G., & Storch, E. A. (2008). The status of hoarding as a symptom of obsessive-compulsive disorder. *Behaviour Research and Therapy, 46,* 1026–1033.

à Campo, J., Nijman, H., Merckelbach, H., & Evers, C. (2003). Psychiatric comorbidity of gender identity disorders: A survey among Dutch psychiatrists. *American Journal of Psychiatry, 160,* 1332–1336.

Aina, Y., & Susman, J. L. (2006). Understanding comorbidity with depression and anxiety disorders. *Journal of the American Osteopathic Association, 106,* S9–S14.

Akiskal, H. S. (2002). Classification, diagnosis and boundaries of bipolar disorders: A review. In M. Maj, H. S. Akiskal, J. J. López-Ibor, & N. Sartorius (Eds.), *Bipolar disorder* (pp. 33–54). Chichester, England: Wiley.

Alloy, L. B., Abramson, L. Y., Urosevic, S., Bender, R. E., & Wagner, C. A. (2009). Longitudinal predictors of bipolar spectrum disorders: A behavioral approach system (BAS) perspective. *Clinical Psychology: Science and Practice, 16,* 206–226.

American Counseling Association. (2014). *ACA code of ethics.* Alexandria, VA: Author.

American Heritage Medical Dictionary. (2007). Boston, MA: Houghton Mifflin Harcourt.

American Psychiatric Association. (1952). *Diagnostic and statistical manual of mental disorders.* Washington, DC: Author.

American Psychiatric Association. (1968). *Diagnostic and statistical manual of mental disorders* (2nd ed.). Washington, DC: Author.

American Psychiatric Association. (1980). *Diagnostic and statistical manual of mental disorders* (3rd ed.). Washington, DC: Author.

American Psychiatric Association. (1987). *Diagnostic and statistical manual of mental disorders* (3rd ed., rev.). Washington, DC: Author.

American Psychiatric Association. (1994). *Diagnostic and statistical manual of mental disorders* (4th ed.). Washington, DC: Author.

American Psychiatric Association. (2000). *Diagnostic and statistical manual of mental disorders* (4th ed., text rev.). Washington, DC: Author.

American Psychiatric Association. (2013a). *The diagnostic and statistical manual of mental disorders* (5th ed.). Arlington, VA: Author.

American Psychiatric Association. (2013b). *Gender dysphoria.* Retrieved from http://www.dsm5.org/Documents/Gender%20Dysphoria%20Fact%20Sheet.pdf

American Psychiatric Association. (2013c). *Highlights of changes from DSM-IV-TR to DSM-5.* Retrieved from http://www.psychiatry.org/practice/dsm/dsm5

American Psychiatric Association. (2013d). *Major depressive disorder and the "bereavement exclusion."* Retrieved from http://www.dsm5.org/Documents/Bereavement%20Exclusion%20Fact%20Sheet.pdf

Anxiety and Depression Association of America. (2013). *Facts and statistics.* Retrieved from http://www.adaa.org/about-adaa/press-room/facts-statistics

Association of Lesbian, Gay, Bisexual and Transgender Issues in Counseling. (2009). *Competencies for counseling transgender clients.* Alexandria, VA: Author.

Ayers, C. R., Saxena, S., Golshan, S., & Wetherell, J. L. (2010). Age at onset and clinical features of late life compulsive hoarding. *International Journal of Geriatric Psychiatry, 25,* 142–149.

Balleur-van Rijn, A., Steensma, T. D., Kreukels, B. P. C., & Cohen-Kettenis, P. T. (2012). Self-perception in a clinical sample of gender variant children. *Clinical Child Psychology and Psychiatry, 18,* 464–474. doi:10.1177/1359104512460621

Barlow, D. H. (2002). *Anxiety and its disorders: The nature and treatment of anxiety and panic* (2nd ed.). New York, NY: Guilford Press.

Batelaan, N. M., Smit, F., De Graaf, R., Van Balkom, A. J. L. M., Vollebergh, W. A. M., & Beekman, A. T. F. (2010). Identifying target groups for the prevention of anxiety disorders in the general population. *Acta Psychiatrica Scandinavica, 122,* 56–65.

Beard, C., Moitra, E., Weisber, R. B., & Keller, M. B. (2010). Characteristics and predictors of social phobia course in a longitudinal study of primary-care patients. *Depression and Anxiety, 27,* 838–845.

Belmaker, R. H. (2004). Bipolar disorder. *New England Journal of Medicine, 351,* 476–486.

Bjornsson, A. S., Didie, E. R., & Phillips, K. A. (2010). Body dysmorphic disorder. *Dialogues in Clinical Neuroscience, 12,* 221–232.

Black, H. K., Gitlin, L., & Burke, J. (2011). Context and culture: African-American elders' experiences of depression. *Mental Health, Religion & Culture, 14,* 643–657.

Blader, J. C., & Carlson, G. A. (2007). Increased rates of bipolar disorder diagnoses among U.S. child, adolescent, and adult inpatients, 1996–2004. *Biological Psychiatry, 62,* 107–114.

Blatt, S. J., Zuroff, D. C., Bondi, C. M., & Sanislow, C. A. (2000). Short- and long-term effects of medication and psychotherapy in the brief treatment of depression: Further analyses of data from the NIMH TDCRP. *Psychotherapy Research, 10,* 215–234.

Bloch, M. H., Landeros-Weisenberger, A., Kelmendi, B., Coric, V., Bracken, M. B., & Leckman, J. F. (2006). A systematic review: Antipsychotic augmentation with treatment refractory obsessive-compulsive disorder. *Molecular Psychiatry, 11,* 622–632.

Bolin, R. (1986). Disaster characteristics and psychosocial impacts. In B. Sowder & M. Lystad (Eds.), *Disasters and mental health: Selected contemporary perspectives* (pp. 3–28). Bethesda, MD: National Institutes of Mental Health.

Breh, D. C., & Seidler, G. H. (2007). Is peritraumatic dissociation a risk factor for PTSD? *Journal of Traumatic Dissociation, 8,* 53–69.

Bryant, R. A. (2003). Early predictors of posttraumatic stress disorder. *Biological Psychiatry, 53,* 789–795.

Bryant, R. A. (2007). Does dissociation further our understanding of PTSD? *Journal of Anxiety Disorder, 21,* 183–191.

Bryant, R. A., Friedman, M. J., Spiegel, D., Ursano, R., & Strain, J. (2011). A review of acute stress disorder in *DSM-5. Depression and Anxiety, 28,* 802–817. doi:10.1002/da.20737

Burton, N. (2012). *A short history of bipolar disorder.* Retrieved from http://www.psychologytoday.com/blog/hide-and-seek/201206/short-history-bipolar-disorder

Byne, W., Bradley, S. J., Coleman, E., Eyler, A. E., Green, R., Menvielle, E., . . . Tompkins, D. A. (2012). Treatment of gender identity disorder. *American Journal of Psychiatry, 169,* 875–876.

Centers for Disease Control and Prevention, National Center for Health Statistics. (1998). *The international classification of diseases, ninth revision, clinical modification (ICD-9-CM).* Retrieved from http://www.cdc.gov/nchs/icd/icd9cm.htm

Centers for Disease Control and Prevention. (2010). Current depression among adults, 2006 and 2008. *Morbidity and Mortality Weekly Report, 59,* 1229–1235.

Centers for Disease Control and Prevention, National Center for Health Statistics. (2014). *The international classification of diseases, 10th revision, clinical modification (ICD-10-CM)*. Retrieved from http://www.cdc.gov/nchs/icd/icd10cm.htm

Chaffin, M., Hanson, R., Saunders, B. E., Nichols, T., Barnett, D., Zeanah, C., . . . Miller-Perrin, C. (2006). Report of the APSAC task force on attachment therapy, reactive attachment disorder, and attachment problems. *Child Maltreatment, 11,* 76–89. doi:10.1177/1077559505283699

Chamberlain, S. R., Menzies, L., Sahakian, B. J., & Fineberg, N. A. (2007). Lifting the veil on trichotillomania. *American Journal of Psychiatry, 164,* 568–574.

Chatterton, M. L., Ke, X., Lewis, B. E., Rajagopalan, K., & Lazarus, A. (2008). Impact of bipolar disorder on the family: Utilization and cost of health care resources. *Pharmacy and Therapeutics, 33,* 15–16, 23–24, 26–28, 34. Retrieved from http://www.ncbi.nlm.nih.gov/pmc/articles/PMC2730065/

Cohen, J. A., Bukstein, O., Walter, H., Benson, R. S., Chrisman, A., Farchione, T. R., . . . Medicus, J. (2010). Practice parameter for the assessment and treatment of children and adolescents with posttraumatic stress disorder. *Journal of the American Academy of Child & Adolescent Psychiatry, 49,* 414–430.

Comer, J. S., Pincus, D. B., & Hoffman, S. G. (2012). Generalized anxiety disorder and the proposed associated symptoms criterion change for *DSM-5* in a treatment-seeking sample of anxious youth. *Depression and Anxiety, 29,* 994–1003.

Comer, R. J. (2013). *Abnormal psychology* (5th ed.). New York, NY: Worth.

Corey, G. (2013). *Theories and practice of counseling and psychotherapy* (9th ed.). Belmont, CA: Brooks Cole.

Craske, M. G., Rauch, S. L., Ursano, R., Prevoneau, J., Pine, D. S., & Zinbarg, R. E. (2009). What is an anxiety disorder? *Depression and Anxiety, 26,* 1066–1085.

Crooks, R., & Baur, K. (2008). *Our sexuality* (11th ed.). Belmont, CA: Wadsworth.

Crooks, R., & Baur, K. (2013). *Our sexuality* (12th ed.). Belmont, CA: Wadsworth.

Culver, J. L., Amow, B. A., & Ketter, T. A. (2007). Bipolar disorder: Improving diagnosis and optimizing integrated care. *Journal of Clinical Psychology, 63,* 73–92.

Cunningham, J., Yonkers, K. A., O'Brien, S., & Eriksson, E. (2009). Update on research and treatment of premenstrual dysphoric disorder. *Harvard Review of Psychiatry, 17,* 120–137. doi:10.1080/10673220902891836

Das, A. K., Olfson, M., Gameroff, M. J., Pilowsky, D. J., Blanco, C., Feder, A., . . . Weissman, M. M. (2005). Screening for bipolar disorder in a primary care practice. *Journal of the American Medical Association, 293,* 956–963.

Daw, J. (2002). Is PMDD real? *Monitor on Psychology*. Retrieved from http://www.apa.org/monitor/oct02/pmdd.aspx

De Cuypere, G., Tsjoen, G., Beerten, R., Selvaggi, G., De Sutter, P., Hoebeke, P., . . . Rubens, R. (2005). Sexual and physical health after sex reassignment surgery. *Archives of Sexual Behavior, 34,* 679–690.

den Braber, A., Ent, D. V., Blokland, G. A., van Grootheest, D. S., Cath, D. C., Veltman, D. J., . . . Boomsma, D. I. (2008). An fMRI study in monozygotic twins discordant for obsessive-compulsive symptoms. *Biological Psychology, 79,* 91–102.

Diamond, M. (2002). Sex and gender are different: Sexual identity and gender identity are different. *Clinical Child Psychology and Psychiatry, 7,* 320–334. doi:10.1177/1359104502007003002

Di Ceglie, D. (2000). Gender identity disorder in young people. *Advances in Psychiatric Treatment, 6,* 458–466.

Diefenbach, G. J., Reitman, D., & Williamson, D. A. (2000). Trichotillomania: A challenge to research and practice. *Clinical Psychology Review, 20,* 289–309.

Dragowski, E. A., Scharron-del Rio, M. R., & Sandigorsky, A. L. (2011). Childhood gender identity . . . disorder? Developmental, cultural, and diagnostic concerns. *Journal of Counseling & Development, 89,* 360–366. doi:10.1002/j.1556-6678.2011.tb00100.x

Dreger, A., Feder, E. K., & Tamar-Mattis, A. (2012). Prenatal dexamethasone for congenital adrenal hyperplasia: An ethics canary in the modern medical mine. *Journal of Bioethical Inquiry, 9,* 277–294. doi:10.1007/s11673-012-9384-9

Epstein, R. S., Fullerton, C. S., & Ursano, R. J. (1998). Posttraumatic stress disorder following an air disaster: A prospective study. *American Journal of Psychiatry, 155,* 934–938.

Fava, G. A., Rafanelli, C., Tomba, E., Guidi, J., & Grandi, S. (2011). The sequential combination of cognitive behavioral treatment and well-being therapy in cyclothymic disorder. *Psychotherapy and Psychosomatics, 80,* 136–143. doi:10.1159/000321575

Fawcett, J. (2013). Suicide and anxiety in the *DSM-5*. *Depression and Anxiety*. Advance online publication. doi:10.1002/da.22058

First, M. (2010). Clinical utility in the revision of the *Diagnostic and statistical manual of mental disorder (DSM)*. *Professional Psychology: Research and Practice, 41*, 465–473. doi:10.1037/a0021511

First, M., Pincus, H., Levine, J., Williams, J., Ustun, B., & Peele, R. (2004). Clinical utility as a criterion for revising psychiatric diagnoses. *American Journal of Psychiatry, 161*, 946–954.

Flessner, C. A., & Woods, D. W. (2006). Phenomenological characteristics, social problems, and the economic impact associated with chronic skin picking. *Behavior Modification, 30*, 944–963.

Frances, A. (2013). *Essentials of psychiatric diagnosis: Responding to the challenge of DSM-5*. New York, NY: Guilford Press.

Friborg, O., Martinussen, M., Kaiser, S., Overgard, K. T., & Rosenvinge, J. H. (2013). Comorbidity of personality disorders in anxiety disorders: A meta-analysis of 30 years of research. *Journal of Affective Disorder, 145*, 143–155.

Friedman, M. J., Resick, P. A., Bryant, R. A., Strain, J., Horowitz, M., & Spiegel, D. (2011). Classification of trauma and stressor-related disorders in *DSM-5*. *Depression and Anxiety, 28*, 737–749.

Gardner, A. (2011). *U.S. has highest bipolar rate in 11-nation study*. Retrieved from http://www.cnn.com/2011/HEALTH/03/07/US.highest.bipolar.rates/index.html

Gerrity, E. T., & Flynn, B. W. (1997). Mental health consequences of disaster. In E. K. Noji (Ed.), *The public health consequences of disasters* (pp. 101–121). New York, NY: Oxford University Press.

Gershuny, B. S., Keuthen, N. J., Gentes, E. L., Russo, A. R., Emmott, E. C., Jameson, M., . . . Jenike, M. A. (2006). Current posttraumatic stress disorder and history of trauma in trichotillomania. *Journal of Clinical Psychology, 62*, 1521–1529.

Gibson, L. E. (2007). *Acute stress disorder*. Washington, DC: U.S. Department of Veterans Affairs, National Center for PTSD. Retrieved from http://www.ptsd.va.gov/professional/pages/acute-stress-disorder.asp

Girdler, S. S., Leserman, J., Bunevicius, R., Klatzkin, R., Pedersen, C. A., & Light, K. C. (2007). Persistent alterations in biological profiles in women with abuse histories: Influence of premenstrual dysphoric disorder. *Health Psychology, 26*, 201–213. doi:10.1037/0278-6133.26.2.201

Gleser, G., Green, B., & Winget, C. (1981). *Prolonged psychosocial effects of disaster: A study of Buffalo Creek*. New York, NY: Academic Press.

Gómez-Gil, E., Trilla, A., Salamero, M., Godás, T., & Valdés, M. (2009). Sociodemographic, clinical, and psychiatric characteristics of transsexuals from Spain. *Archives of Sexual Behavior, 38*, 378–392.

Gottlieb, B., Beitel, L. K., Nadarajah, A., Palioura, M., & Trifiro, M. (2012). The androgen receptor gene mutations database (ARDB): 2012 update. *Human Mutation, 33*, 887–894.

Grant, J. E., Menard, W., & Phillips, K. A. (2006). Pathological skin picking in individuals with body dysmorphic disorder. *General Hospital Psychiatry, 28*, 487–493. doi:10.1002/humu.22046

Green, B., Grace, M., Lindy, J., Gleser, G., Leonard, A., & Kramer, T. (1990). Buffalo Creek survivors in the second decade: Comparison with unexposed and nonlitigant groups. *Journal of Applied Social Psychology, 20*, 1033–1050.

Green, B., & Solomon, S. (1995). The mental impact of natural and technological disasters. In J. Freedy & S. Hobfoll (Eds.), *Traumatic stress: From theory to practice* (pp. 163–180). New York, NY: Plenum.

Greist, J. H., Jefferson, J. W., Kobak, K. A., Katzelnick, D. J., & Serlin, R. C. (1995). Efficacy and tolerability of serotonin transport inhibitors in obsessive-compulsive disorder: A meta-analysis. *Archives of General Psychiatry, 52*, 53–60.

Guarnaccia, P. J., Martinez, I., & Acosta, H. (2013). Mental health in the Hispanic immigrant community: An overview. In M. Finlayson, M. J. Gonzalez, & G. M. Gonzales-Ramos (Eds.), *Mental health care for new Hispanic immigrants: Innovative approaches in contemporary clinical practice* (pp. 21–46). Hoboken, NJ: Taylor & Francis.

Halpern, J., & Tramontin, M. (2007). *Disaster mental health: Theory and practice*. Belmont, CA: Thompson Brooks/Cole.

Hankin, B. L. (2009). Etiology of bipolar disorder across the lifespan: Essential interplay with diagnosis, classification, and assessment. *Clinical Psychologist, 16*, 227–230. doi:10.1111/j.1468-2850.2009.01161.x

Hanson, R. F., & Spratt, E. G. (2000). Reactive attachment disorder: What we know about the disorder and implications for treatment. *Child Maltreatment, 5*, 137–145. doi:10.1177/1077559500005002005

Haraldsen, I. R., & Dahl, A. A. (2000). Symptom profiles of gender dysphoric patients of transsexual type compared to patients with personality disorders and healthy adults. *Acta Psychiatrica Scandinavica, 102*, 276–281.

Hartl, T. L., Duffany, S. R., Allen, G. J., Steketee, G., & Frost, R. O. (2005). Relationships among compulsive hoarding, trauma, and attention-deficit/hyperactivity disorder. *Behaviour Research and Therapy, 43,* 269–276.

Hasin, D. S., Goodwin, R. D., Stinson, F. S., & Grant, B. F. (2005). Epidemiology of major depressive disorder: Results from the National Epidemiologic Survey on Alcoholism and Related Conditions. *Archives of General Psychiatry, 62,* 1097–1106. doi:10.1001/archpsyc.62.10.1097

Hausmann, A., Hortnagl, C., Muller, M., Waack, J., Walpath, M., & Conca, A. (2007). Psychotherapeutic interventions in bipolar disorder: A review. *Neuropsychiatry, 21,* 102–109.

Hein, L. C., & Berger, K. C. (2012). Gender dysphoria in children: Let's think this through. *Journal of Child and Adolescent Psychiatric Nursing, 25,* 237–240. doi:10.1111/jcap.12014

Hepp, U., Kraemer, B., Schnyder, U., Miller, N., & Delsignore, A. (2005). Psychiatric comorbidity in gender identity disorder. *Journal of Psychosomatic Research, 58,* 259–261.

Hickey, D., Carr, A., Dooley, B, Guerin, S., Butler, E., & Fitzpatrick, L. (2005). Family and marital profiles of couples in which one partner has depression or anxiety. *Journal of Marital and Family Therapy, 31,* 171–182.

Hinton, D. E., & Lewis-Fernández, R. (2010). Idioms of distress among trauma survivors: Subtypes and clinical utility. *Culture, Medicine, and Psychiatry, 34,* 209–218.

Hofmann, S. G., & Smits, J. A. (2008). Cognitive-behavioral therapy for adult anxiety disorders: A meta-analysis of randomized placebo-controlled trials. *Journal of Clinical Psychiatry, 69,* 621–632.

Hollifield, M., Gepper, C., Johnson, Y, & Fryer, C. (2003). A Vietnamese man with selective mutism: The prevalence of multiple interacting "cultures" in clinical psychiatry. *Transcultural Psychiatry, 40,* 329–341.

Hsu, L., Woody S. R., Lee, H.-J., Peng, Y., Zhou, X., & Ryder, A. G. (2012). Social anxiety among East Asians in North America: East Asian socialization or the challenge of acculturation? *Cultural Diversity and Ethnic Minority Psychology, 18,* 181–191.

Hyde, J., & DeLamater, J. (2013). *Understanding human sexuality* (12th ed.). New York, NY: McGraw-Hill.

International Obsessive-Compulsive Disorder Foundation. (2012). *OCD fact sheets.* Retrieved from http://www.ocfoundation.org/materials.aspx

Ivey, A. E., D'Andrea, M. J., & Ivey, M. B. (2012). *Counseling and psychotherapy: A multicultural perspective* (7th ed.). Thousand Oaks, CA: Sage.

Jamison, K. R. (2000). Suicide and bipolar disorder. *Journal of Clinical Psychiatry, 61,* 47–51.

Jenkins, M. M., Youngstrom, E. A., Washburn, J. J., & Youngstrom, J. K. (2011). Evidence-based strategies improve assessment of pediatric bipolar disorder by community practitioners. *Professional Psychology: Research and Practice, 42,* 121–129.

Kameya, Y., & Narita, Y. (2000). A clinical and psycho-sociological case study on gender identity disorder in Japan. *Journal of Sex & Marital Therapy, 26,* 345–350.

Karno, M., Golding, J. M., Sorenson, S. B., & Burnam, M. A. (1988). The epidemiology of obsessive-compulsive disorder in five US communities. *Archives of General Psychiatry, 45,* 1094–1099.

Keller, M. B., McCullough, J. P., Klein, D. N., Arnow, B., Dunner, D. L., Gelenberg, A. J., . . . Zajecka, J. A. (2000). A comparison of Nefazodone, the cognitive behavioral-analysis system of psychotherapy, and their combination for the treatment of chronic depression. *New England Journal of Medicine, 342,* 1462–1470.

Kendler, K. S., Myers, J., & Zisook, S. (2008). Does bereavement-related depression differ from major depression associated with other stressful life events? *American Journal of Psychiatry, 165,* 1449–1455.

Kerns, K. E., Comer, J. S., Pincus, D. B., & Hofmann, S. G. (2013). Evaluation of the proposed social anxiety disorder specifier change for *DSM-5* in a treatment-seeking sample of anxious youth. *Depression and Anxiety, 30,* 709–715. doi:10.1002/da.22067

Kessler, R. C., Berglund, P., Demler, O., Jin, R., Koretz, D., Merikangas, K. R., . . . Wang, P. S. (2003). The epidemiology of major depressive disorder: Results from the National Comorbidity Survey Replication (NCS-R). *Journal of the American Medical Association, 289,* 3095–3105.

Kessler, R. C., Berglund, P., Demler, O., Jin, R., Merikangas, K. R., & Walters, E. E. (2005). Lifetime prevalence and age-of-onset distributions of *DSM-IV* disorders in the National Comorbidity Study Replication. *Archives of General Psychiatry, 62,* 617–627.

Kessler, R. C., Chiu, W. T., Demler, O., & Walters, E. E. (2005). Prevalence, severity, and comorbidity of 12-month *DSM-IV* disorders in the National Comorbidity Survey Replication. *Archives of General Psychiatry, 62,* 617–627.

Kessler, R. C, Petukhova, M., Sampson, N. A., Zaslasvky, A., & Wittchen, H. U. (2012). Twelve-month and lifetime prevalence and lifetime morbid risk of anxiety and mood disorders in the United States. *International Journal of Methods in Psychiatric Research, 21,* 169–184.

Kessler, R. C., Sonnega, A., Bromet, E., Hughes, M., & Nelson, C. B. (1995). Post-traumatic stress disorder in the National Comorbidity Survey. *Archives of General Psychiatry, 52,* 1048–1060.

Ketter, T. A. (2010). Diagnostic features, prevalence, and impact of bipolar disorder. *Journal of Clinical Psychiatry, 71,* e14. doi:10.4088/JCP.8125tx11c

Kleinman, A. (2004). Culture and depression. *New England Journal of Medicine, 351,* 951–953.

Kobak, K. A., Greist, J. H., Jefferson, J. W., Katzelnick, D. J., & Henk, H. J. (1998). Behavioral versus pharmacological treatments of obsessive-compulsive disorder: A meta-analysis. *Psychopharmacology, 136,* 205–216.

Koenig, H. G., & Blazer, D. G. (1996). Minor depression in late life. *American Journal of Geriatric Psychiatry, 4,* S14–S21.

Koran, L. M., Abujaoude, E., Large, M. D., & Serpe, R. T. (2008). The prevalence of body dysmorphic disorder in the United States adult population. *CNS Spectrums, 13,* 316–322.

Kraepelin, E. (1921). *Manic-depressive insanity and paranoia.* Salem, NH: Ayer.

Landaas, E. T., Halmoy, A., Oedegaard, K. J., Fasmer, O. B., & Haavik, J. (2012). The impact of cyclothymic temperament in adult ADHD. *Journal of Affective Disorder, 142,* 241–247.

Landau, D., Iervolino, A. C., Pertusa, A., Santo, S., Singh, S., & Mataix-Cols, D. (2011). Stressful life events and material deprivation in hoarding disorder. *Journal of Anxiety Disorders, 25,* 192–202.

Langer, S. J., & Martin, J. I. (2004). How dresses can make you mentally ill: Examining gender identity disorder in children. *Child and Adolescent Social Work Journal, 21,* 5–23.

Lawrence, A. A. (2003). Factors associated with satisfaction or regret following male-to-female sex reassignment surgery. *Archives of Sexual Behavior, 32,* 299–315.

Leibenluft, E. (2011). Severe mood dysregulation, irritability, and the diagnostic boundaries of bipolar disorder in youths. *American Journal of Psychiatry, 168,* 129–142.

Letiecq, B. L., Bailey, S. J., & Kurtz, M. A. (2008). Depression among rural Native American and European American grandparents rearing their grandchildren. *Journal of Family Issues, 29,* 334–356. doi:10.1177/0192513X07308393

Lewis-Fernández, R., Guarnaccia, P. J., Patel, S., Lizardi, D., & Diaz, N. (2005). Ataque de nervios: Anthropological, epidemiological, and clinical dimensions of a cultural syndrome. In A. M. Georgiopoulos & J. F. Rosenbaum (Eds.), *Perspectives in cross-cultural psychiatry* (pp. 63–85). Philadelphia, PA: Lippincott Williams & Wilkins.

Lin, H., Katsovich, L., Ghebremichael, M., Findley, D. B., Grantz, H., Lombroso, P. J., . . . Leckman, J. F. (2007). Psychosocial stress predicts future symptom severities in children and adolescents with Tourette syndrome and/or obsessive-compulsive disorder. *Journal of Child Psychology and Psychiatry, 48,* 157–166.

Mancebo, M. C., Garcia, A. M., Pinto, A., Freeman, J. B., Przeworski, A., Stout, R., . . . Rasmussen, S. A. (2008). Juvenile-onset OCD: Clinical features in children, adolescents and adults. *Acta Psychiatrica Scandinavica, 118,* 149–159.

Manicavasagar, V., Silove, D., Curtis, J., & Wagner, R. (2000). Continuities of separation anxiety from early life into adulthood. *Journal of Anxiety Disorders, 14,* 1–18.

Manning, J. S. (2010). Tools to improve differential diagnosis of bipolar disorder in primary care. *Primary Care Companion to the Journal of Clinical Psychiatry, 12,* 17–22. doi:10.4088/PCC.9064su1c.03

Marnane, C., & Silove, D. (2013). *DSM-5* allows separation anxiety disorder to grow up. *Australian and New Zealand Journal of Psychiatrists, 47,* 12–15.

Marques, L., Robinaugh, D. J., LeBlanc, N. J., & Hinton, D. (2011). Cross-cultural variations in the prevalence and presentation of anxiety disorders. *Expert Review of Neurotherapeutics, 11,* 313–322.

Martinez, W., Polo, A. J., & Carter, J. S. (2012). Family orientation, language, and anxiety among low-income Latino youth. *Journal of Anxiety Disorder, 29,* 517–525.

Mataix-Cols, D., Pertusa, A., & Leckman, J. F. (2007). Issues for *DSM-V*: How should obsessive-compulsive and related disorders be classified? *American Journal of Psychiatry, 164,* 1313–1314.

Megeri, D., & Khoosal, D. (2007). Anxiety and depression in males experiencing gender dysphoria. *Sexual and Relationship Therapy, 22,* 77–81. doi:10.1080/02699200600565905

Melville, N. A. (2013, April 11). CBT beats adjunctive antipsychotic for refractory OCD. *Medscape Medical News.* Retrieved from http://www.medscape.com/viewarticle/782351

Merikangas, K. R., Akiskal, H. S., Angst, J., Greenberg, P. E., Hirschfeld, R. M., Petukhova, M., & Kessler, R. C. (2007). Lifetime and 12-months prevalence of bipolar spectrum disorder in the National Comorbidity Survey Replication. *Archives of General Psychiatry, 64,* 543–552.

Miach, P. P., Berah, E. F., Butcher, J. N., & Rouse, S. (2000). Utility of the MMPI-2 in assessing gender dysphoric patients. *Journal of Personality Assessment, 75,* 268–279.

Misery, L., Chastaing, M., Touboul, S., Callot, V., Schollhammer, M., Young, P., . . . Dutray, S. (2012). Psychogenic skin excoriations: Diagnostic criteria, semiological analysis and psychiatric profiles. *Acta Dermato-Venereologica, 92,* 416–418.

Mohr, C., & Schneider, S. (2013). Anxiety disorders. *European Child and Adolescent Psychiatry, 22*(Suppl. 1), S17–S22.

Moreno, C., Laje, G., Blanco, C., Jiang, H., Schmidt, A. B., & Olfson, M. (2007). National trends in the outpatient diagnosis and treatment of bipolar disorder in youth. *Archives of General Psychiatry, 64,* 1032–1039.

Morrison, J. (2006). *DSM-IV made easy: The clinician's guide to diagnosis.* New York, NY: Guilford Press.

Myers, J. E., & Harper, M. (2004). Evidence-based effective practices with older adults. *Journal of Counseling & Development, 82,* 207–218. doi:10.1002/j.1556-6678.2004.tb00304.x

National Alliance on Mental Illness. (2009). *Facts about stigma and mental illness in diverse communities.* Retrieved from http://www.nami.org/ContentManagement/ContentDisplay.cfm?ContentFileID=5148

National Institute of Mental Health. (2005). *Dysthymic disorder among adults.* Retrieved from http://www.nimh.nih.gov/statistics/1dd_adult.shtml

National Institute of Mental Health. (2012). *Bipolar disorder.* Retrieved from http://www.nlm.nih.gov/medlineplus/ency/article/000926.htm

National Institute of Mental Health. (2013a). *How is depression diagnosed and treated.* Retrieved from http://www.nimh.nih.gov/health/publications/depression/how-is-depression-diagnosed-and-treated.shtml

National Institute of Mental Health. (2013b). *The number count: Mental disorders in America.* Retrieved from http://www.nimh/nih.gov/health/publications/the-numbers-count-mental-disorders-in-America/index.shtml#Mood

National Institute of Mental Health. (2013c). *Suicide in the U.S.: Statistics and prevention.* Retrieved from http://www.nimh.nih.gov/health/publications/suicide-in-the-us-statistics-and-prevention/index.shtml#Moscicki-Epi

National Institute of Mental Health. (2013d). *Treatment of anxiety disorders.* Retrieved from http://www.nimh/nih.gov/health/publications/anxiety-disorders/treatment-of-anxiety-disorders.shtml

National Institute of Neurological Disorders and Stroke. (2008). *NINDS Williams syndrome information page.* Retrieved from http://www.ninds.nih.gov/disorders/williams/williams.htm

National Library of Medicine. (2013). Obsessive-compulsive disorder. *Medline Plus.* Retrieved from http://www.nlm.nih.gov/medlineplus/ency/article/000929.htm

Nietzel, M. T., Speltz, M. L., McCauley, E. A., & Bernstein, D. A. (1998). *Abnormal psychology.* Needham Heights, MA: Allyn & Bacon.

Norris, F. H., & Elrod, C. C. (2006). Psychological consequences of disaster. In F. H. Norris, S. Galea, M. J. Friedman, & P. J. Watson (Eds.), *Methods for disaster mental health research* (pp. 20–44). New York, NY: Guilford Press.

Norris, F. H., Friedman, M. J., Watson, P. J., Byrne, C. M., Diaz, E., & Kaniasty, K. (2002). 60,000 disaster victims speak: Part I. An empirical review of the empirical literature. *Psychiatry: Interpersonal and Biological Processes, 65,* 207–239.

Odlaug, B. L., & Grant, J. E. (2010). Pathologic skin picking. *American Journal of Drug and Alcohol Abuse, 36,* 296–303.

Office of Applied Research. (2006). *Suicidal thoughts, suicide attempts, major depressive episode, and substance use among adults: The OAS report.* Retrieved from http://www.oas.samhsa.gov/2k6/suicide/suicide.htm

Østergaard, S. D., & Foldager, L. (2011). The association between physical illness and major depressive episode in general practice. *Acta Psychiatrica Scandinavica, 123,* 290–296. doi:10.1111/j.1600-0447.2010.01668.x

Pallanti, S., Grassi, G., Sarrecchia, E. D., Cantisani, A., & Pellegrini, M. (2011). Obsessive-compulsive disorder comorbidity: Clinical assessment and therapeutic implications. *Frontiers in Psychiatry, 2*, 70. doi:10.3389/fpsyt.2011.00070

Paris, J. (2009). The bipolar spectrum: A critical perspective. *Harvard Review of Psychiatry, 17*, 206–213. doi:10.1080/10673220902979888

Paris, J. (2013). *The intelligent clinician's guide to the DSM-5*. New York, NY: Oxford University Press.

Parkes, G., Hall, I., & Wilson, D. (2009). Cross dressing and gender dysphoria in people with learning disabilities: A descriptive study. *British Journal of Learning Disabilities, 37*, 151–156. doi:10.111/j.1468-3156.2008.00538.x

Pearlstein, T., & Steiner, M. (2008). Premenstrual dysphoric disorder: Burden of illness and treatment update. *Journal of Psychiatry & Neuroscience, 33*, 291–301.

Perilla, J. L., Norris, F. H., & Lavizzo, E. A. (2002). Ethnicity, culture and disaster response: Identifying and explaining ethnic differences in PTSD six months after Hurricane Andrew. *Journal of Social and Clinical Psychology, 21*, 20–45.

Perrin, E., Smith, N., Davis, C., Spack, N., & Stein, M. T. (2010). Gender variant and gender dysphoria in two young children. *Journal of Developmental & Behavioral Pediatrics, 31*, 161–164.

Pertusa, A., Frost, R. O., Fullana, M. A., Samuels, J., Steketee, G., Tolin, D., . . . Mataix-Cols, D. (2010). Refining the diagnostic boundaries of compulsive hoarding: A critical review. *Clinical Psychology Review, 30*, 371–386. doi:10.1016/j.cpr.2010.01.007

Phillips, K. A. (2004). Psychosis in body dysmorphic disorder. *Journal of Psychiatric Research, 38*, 63–72.

Phillips, K. A. (1999). Body dysmorphic disorder and depression: Theoretical considerations and treatment strategies. *Psychiatric Quarterly, 70*, 313–331.

Phillips, K. A., & Diaz, S. F. (1997). Gender differences in body dysmorphic disorder. *Journal of Nervous and Mental Disease, 185*, 570–577.

Pilver, C. E., Desai, R. D., Kasl, S., & Levy, B. R. (2011). Lifetime discrimination associated with greater likelihood of premenstrual dysphoric disorder. *Journal of Women's Health, 20*, 923–931. doi:10.1089/jwh.2010.2456

Portzky, G., Audenaert, K., & van Heeringen, K. (2005). Adjustment disorder and the course of the suicidal process in adolescents. *Journal of Affective Disorder, 87*, 265–270.

Prior, V., & Glaser, D. (2006). *Understanding attachment and attachment disorders: Theory, evidence and practice*. London, England: Jessica Kingsley.

Reid, W. H., & Wise, M. G. (1995). *DSM-IV training guide*. New York, NY: Brunner-Routledge.

Riolo, S. A., Nguyen, T. A., Greden, J. F., & King, C. A. (2005). Prevalence of depression by race/ethnicity: Findings from the National Health and Nutrition Examination Survey III. *American Journal of Public Health, 95*, 998–1000. doi:10.2105/AJPH.2004.047225

Robison, J., Schensul, J. J., Coman, E., Diefenbach, G. J., Radda, K. E., Gaztambide, S., & Disch, W. B. (2009). Mental health in senior housing: Racial/ethnic patterns and correlates of major depressive disorder. *Aging & Mental Health, 13*, 659–673.

Rubio, G., & Lopez-Ibor, J. J. (2007). What can be learnt from the natural history of anxiety disorders? *European Psychiatry, 22*, 80–86.

Rubonis, A. V., & Bickman, L. (1991). Psychological impairment in the wake of disaster: The disaster–psychopathology relationship. *Psychological Bulletin, 109*, 384–399.

Ruscio, A. M., Stein, D. J., Chiu, W. T., & Kessler, R. C. (2008). The epidemiology of obsessive-compulsive disorder in the National Comorbidity Survey Replication. *Molecular Psychiatry, 15*, 53–63.

Salmond, C. H., Meiser-Stedman, R., Glucksman, E., Thompson, P., Dalgleish, T., & Smith, P. (2011). The nature of trauma memories in acute stress disorder in children and adolescents. *Journal of Child Psychology and Psychiatry, 52*, 560–570. doi:10.1111/j.1469-7610.2010.02340.x

Samet, S., Fenton, M. C., Nunes, E., Greenstein, E., Aharonovich, E., & Hasin, D. (2012). Effects of independent and substance-induced major depressive disorder on remission and relapse of alcohol, cocaine and heroin dependence. *Addictions, 108*, 115–123. doi:10.1111/j.1360-0443.2012.04010.x

Samuels, J. F., Bienvenu, O. J., Grados, M. A., Cullen, B., Riddle, M. A., Liang, K. Y., . . . Nestadt, G. (2008). Prevalence and correlates of hoarding behavior in a community-based sample. *Behaviour Research and Therapy, 46*, 836–844.

Saveanu, R. V., & Nemeroff, C. B. (2012). Etiology of depression: Genetic and environmental factors. *Psychiatric Clinics of North America, 35*, 51–71. doi:10.1016/j.psc.2011.12.001

Schechter, D. S., & Willheim, E. (2009). Disturbances of attachment and parental psychopathology in early childhood. *Child and Adolescent Psychiatric Clinics of North America, 18,* 665–686.

Seikowski, K., Gollek, S., Harth, W., & Reinhardt, M. (2008). Borderline-personality disorder and transsexualism. *Psychiatrische Praxis, 35,* 135–141.

Shear, K., Jin, R., & Ruscio, A. (2006). Prevalence and correlates of estimated *DSM-IV* child and adult separation anxiety disorder in the National Comorbidity Survey Replication. *American Journal of Psychiatry, 165,* 1074–1083.

Silverman, W. K., Pina, A. A., & Viswesvaran, C. (2008). Evidence-based psychosocial treatments for phobic and anxiety disorders in children and adolescents. *Journal of Clinical Child and Adolescent Psychology, 37,* 105–130.

Simon, L., Zsolt, U., Fogd, D., & Czobor, P. (2011). Dysfunctional core beliefs, perceived parenting behavior and psychopathology in gender identity disorder: A comparison of male-to-female, female-to-male transsexual and nontranssexual control subjects. *Journal of Behavior Therapy and Experimental Psychiatry, 42,* 38–45. doi:10.1016/j.jbtep.2010.08.004

Simpson, H., Foa, E., Liebowitz, M., Ledley, D., Huppert, J., Cahill, S., . . . Petkova, E. (2008). A randomized, controlled trial of cognitive-behavioral therapy for augmenting pharmacotherapy in obsessive-compulsive disorder. *American Journal of Psychiatry, 165,* 621–630.

Solomon, S. D., & Smith, E. S. (1994). Social support and perceived control as moderators of responses to dioxin and flood exposure. In R. J. Ursano, B. G. McCaughey, & C. S. Fullerton (Eds.), *Individual and community response to disaster: The structure of human chaos* (pp. 179–200). Cambridge, England: Cambridge University Press.

Sood, E. D., Mendez, J. L., & Kendall, P. C. (2012). Acculturation, religiosity, and ethnicity predict mothers' causal beliefs about separation anxiety disorder and preferences for help seeking. *Journal of Cross-Cultural Psychology, 43,* 393–409.

Sprock, J., & Fredendall, L. (2008). Comparison of prototypic cases of depressive personality. *Journal of Clinical Psychology, 64,* 1293–1317.

Starcevic, V. (2013). Hyphocondriasis and health anxiety: Conceptual challenges. *British Journal of Psychiatry, 202,* 7–8.

Stein, D. J. (2002). Obsessive-compulsive disorder. *Lancet, 360,* 397–405. Retrieved from http://psych.wright.edu/~ccl/TDW/ReadingsTDW/Stein.pdf

Stein, D. J., Chamberlain, S. R., & Fineberg, N. (2006). An ABC model of habit disorders: Hairpulling, skin-picking, and other stereotypic conditions. *CNS Spectrums, 11,* 824–827.

Stein, D. J., Craske, M. G., Friedman, M. J., & Phillips, K. A. (2011). Meta-structure issues for the *DSM-5*: How do anxiety disorders, obsessive compulsive and related disorders, post-traumatic disorders, and dissociative disorders fit together? *Current Psychiatry Reports, 13,* 248–250.

Stein, D. J., Fineberg, N. A., Bienvenu, O. J., Denys, D., Lochner, C., Nestadt, G., . . . Phillips, K. A. (2010). Should OCD be classified as an anxiety disorder in *DSM-V*? *Depression and Anxiety, 27,* 495–506.

Steinkuller, A., & Rheineck, J. E. (2009). A review of evidence-based therapeutic interventions for bipolar disorder. *Journal of Mental Health Counseling, 31,* 338–350.

Steketee, G., & Frost, R. O. (2003). Compulsive hoarding: Current status of the research. *Clinical Psychology Review, 23,* 905–927.

Substance Abuse and Mental Health Services Administration. (2008). *Results from the 2007 National Survey on Drug Use and Health: National findings* (NSDUH Series H-34, DHHS Publication No. SMA 08-4343). Retrieved from http://www.oas.samhsa.gov/nsduh/2k7nsduh/2k7results.pdf

Sukhodolsky, D. G., Scahill, L., Zhang, H., Peterson, B. S., King, R. A., Lombroso, P. J., . . . Leckman, J. F. (2003). Disruptive behavior in children with Tourette's syndrome: Association with ADHD comorbidity, tic severity, and functional impairment. *Journal of the American Academy of Child & Adolescent Psychiatry, 42,* 98–105.

Swartz, H. A., Frank, E., Frankel, D. R., Novick, D., & Houck, P. (2009). Psychotherapy as monotherapy for the treatment of Bipolar II depression: A proof of concept study. *Bipolar Disorder, 11,* 89–94. doi:10.1111/j.1399-5618.2008.00629.x

Swartz, H. A., Levenson, J. C., & Frank, E. (2012). Psychotherapy for Bipolar II disorder: The role of interpersonal and social rhythm therapy. *Professional Psychology: Research and Practice, 43,* 145–153. doi:10.1037/a0027671

Tenneij, N. H., Van Megen, H. J. G. M., Denys, D. A. J. P., & Westenberg, H. G. (2005). Behavior therapy augments response of patients with obsessive-compulsive disorder responding to drug treatment. *Journal of Clinical Psychiatry, 66,* 1169–1175.

Tolin, D. F., Franklin, M. E., Diefenbach, G. J., Anderson, E., & Meunier, S. A. (2007). Pediatric trichotillomania: Descriptive psychopathology and an open trial of cognitive behavioral therapy. *Cognitive Behaviour Therapy, 36,* 129–144.

Tolin, D. F., Maltby, N., Diefenbach, G. J., Hannan, S. E., & Worhunsky, P. (2004). Cognitive-behavioral therapy for medication nonresponders with obsessive-compulsive disorder: A wait-list-controlled open trial. *Journal of Clinical Psychiatry, 65,* 922–931.

Tundo, A., Salvati, L., Busto, G., Di Spigno, D., & Falcini, R. (2007). Addition of cognitive-behavioral therapy for nonresponders to medication for obsessive-compulsive disorder: A naturalistic study. *Journal of Clinical Psychiatry, 68,* 1553–1557.

Ursano, R. J. (2004). Introduction. In R. J. Ursano, C. S. Fullerton, & A. E. Norwood (Eds.), *Bioterrorism: Psychological and public health interventions* [CD-ROM]. New York, NY: Cambridge University Press.

Ursano, R. J., McCaughey, B. G., & Fullerton, C. S. (1994). *Individual and community responses to trauma and disaster: The structure of human chaos.* New York, NY: Cambridge University Press.

Van de Put, W., & Eisenbruch, M. (2004). Internally displaced Cambodians: Healing trauma in communities. In L. Rasco & K. Miller (Eds.), *The mental health of refugees: Ecological approaches to healing and adaptation* (pp. 133–159). New York, NY: Taylor & Francis.

Van der Kolk, B. A., McFarlane, A. C., & Weisaeth, L. (1996). *Traumatic stress: The effects of overwhelming experience on mind, body, and society.* New York, NY: Guilford Press.

Van der Velden, P. G., Kleber, R. J., Christiaanse, B., Gersons, B. P., Marcelissen, F. G., Drogendijk, A. N., . . . Meewisse, M. L. (2006). The independent predictive value of peritraumatic dissociation for postdisaster intrusions, avoidance reactions, and PTSD symptom severity: A 4-year prospective study. *Journal of Traumatic Stress, 19,* 493–506.

van Grootheest, D. S., Cath, D. C., Beekman, A. T., & Boomsma, D. I. (2005). Twin studies on obsessive-compulsive disorder: A review. *Twin Research and Human Genetics, 8,* 450–458. doi: 10.1111/j.1469-7610.2006.01687.xPMCID: PMC3073143

Van Meter, A. R., Youngstrom, E. A., & Findling, R. L. (2012). Cyclothymic disorder: A critical review. *Clinical Psychology Review, 32,* 229–243. doi:10.1016/j.cpr.2012.02.001

Vázquez, G. H., Kapczinski, F., Magalhaes, P. V., Córdoba, R., Lopez Jaramillo, C., Rosa, A. R., . . . Tohen, M. (2011). Stigma and functioning in patients with bipolar disorder. *Journal of Affective Disorders, 130,* 323–327.

Vontress, C. E., Woodland, C. E., & Epp, L (2007). Cultural dysthymia: An unrecognized disorder among African Americans? *Journal of Multicultural Counseling and Development, 35,* 135–141.

Wakefield, J. C., & First, M. B. (2012). Validity of the bereavement exclusion to major depression: Does the empirical evidence support the proposal to eliminate the exclusion in *DSM-5*? *World Psychiatry, 10,* 1–10.

Wallien, M. S. C., & Cohen-Kettenis, P. T. (2008). Psychosexual outcome of gender-dysphoric children. *Journal of American Academy of Child & Adolescent Psychiatry, 47,* 1413–1423. doi:10.1097/CHI.0b013e31818956b9

Wallien, M. S. C., Veenstra, R., Kreukels, B. P. C., & Cohen-Kettenis, P. T. (2010). Peer group status of gender dysphoric children: A sociometric study. *Archives of Sexual Behavior, 39,* 553–560. doi:10.1007/s10508-009-9517-3

Warren, B. J. (2007). Cultural aspects of bipolar disorder: Interpersonal meaning for clients and psychiatric nurses. *Journal of Psychosocial Nursing and Mental Health Services, 45,* 32–37.

Weinstock, L. M., Strong, D., Uebelacker, L. A., & Miller, I. W. (2009). Differential item functioning of *DSM-IV* depressive symptoms in individuals with a history of mania versus those without: An item response theory analysis. *Bipolar Disorder, 11,* 289–297. doi:10.1111/j.1399-5618.2009.00681.x

Widom C., Czaja S., & Paris J. (2009). A prospective investigation of borderline personality disorder in abused and neglected children followed up into adulthood. *Journal of Personality Disorder, 23,* 433–446.

Wittchen, H. U. (2002). Generalized anxiety disorder: Prevalence, burden, and cost to society. *Depression and Anxiety, 16,* 162–171.

World Health Organization. (2007). *International statistical classification of diseases and related health problems, 10th revision.* Geneva, Switzerland: Author.

World Health Organization. (2010). *International statistical classification of diseases and related health problems, 10th revision* (Version 2010). Geneva, Switzerland: Author.

Wu, K. D., & Watson, D. (2005). Hoarding and its relation to obsessive-compulsive disorder. *Behaviour Research and Therapy, 43,* 897–921.

Zalaquett, C. P., & Stens, A. N (2006). Psychosocial treatments for major depression and dysthymia in older adults: A review of the research literature. *Journal of Counseling & Development, 84,* 192–201. doi:10.1002/j.1556-6678.2006.tb00395.x

Zeanah, C. H., & Gleason, M. M. (2010). *Reactive attachment disorder: A review for DSM-V.* Washington, DC: American Psychiatric Association.

Zisook, S., Shear, K., & Kendler, K. S. (2007). Validity of the bereavement exclusion criterion for the diagnosis of major depressive episode. *World Psychiatry, 6,* 102–107.

Zucker, K. J., & Lawrence, A. A. (2009). Epidemiology of gender identity disorder: Recommendations for the standards of care of the World Professional Association for Transgender Health. *International Journal of Transgenderism, 11,* 8–18.

Part Two

Changes and Implications Involving Addictive, Impulse-Control, and Specific Behavior-Related Concerns

Part Two Introduction

The disorders covered in Part Two are divided into three chapters: Chapter 9: Substance-Related and Addictive Disorders; Chapter 10: Disruptive, Impulse-Control, and Conduct Disorders; and Chapter 11: Specific Behavioral Disruptions. As with Part One, Part Two includes diagnoses commonly seen by most counselors. However, the difference between this section and the previous section is that disorders in Part Two frequently manifest through more visible, external behavioral concerns (e.g., sexual dysfunction) rather than less visible, internal experiences (e.g., depression). The frequency with which counselors work with these concerns varies widely; therefore, we provide detailed information for those diagnoses counselors are more likely to diagnose in practice, such as substance use or disruptive behavior disorders, and provide less detail for those disorders that counselors are less likely to diagnose, such as sleep disorders or sexual dysfunctions. Readers should assume diagnoses that do not include a heading detailing "Major Changes From *DSM-IV-TR* to *DSM-5*" have had no significant changes. Likewise, instances in which differential diagnoses or cultural considerations are sparse or not included indicate a dearth of research on the topic.

Major changes to look for in Chapter 9 include the collapsing of substance abuse and substance dependence into one category. Previous differentiation between abuse and dependence insinuated that abuse was less severe than dependence. In this chapter, readers will find one overarching substance use disorders section with specifiers to indicate the extent of impairment. Another substantive change to substance use and addiction processes in the *DSM-5* is the inclusion of other addictive disorders, such as gambling disorder. Although the manual only identifies one process addiction at this time, this change represents a significant shift in the way in which the mental health community conceptualizes addictive disorders.

Major changes from the *DSM-IV-TR* to the *DSM-5*, including reconceptualization and reorganization of disruptive, impulse-control, and conduct disorders, are highlighted in Chapter 9. Whereas conduct disorder, oppositional defiant disorder, intermittent explosive disorder, kleptomania, and pyromania were included under either the Impulse-Control Disorders Not Elsewhere Specified or the Disorders Usually First Diagnosed in Infancy, Childhood, or Adolescence chapters of the *DSM-IV-TR*, the *DSM-5* now includes these under the new Disruptive, Impulse-Control, and Conduct Disorders chapter. Furthermore, the "not elsewhere specified" section has been removed and other specified disruptive, impulse-control, and conduct disorders and unspecified disruptive, impulse-control, and conduct disorders have been added. Noteworthy is that, for the first time, all mental health disorders evidenced by disruptive behavior and impulse-control problems, including those that go against social norms (i.e., pyromania and kleptomania), have been clustered together in the same chapter.

Finally, as with other parts of this *Learning Companion*, readers will find a description of each disorder or group of disorders that includes essential features and major changes from the *DSM-IV-TR* to the *DSM-5*, special considerations, and case examples to help counselors better apply diagnoses to work with clients. Note, that unlike in Part One, we have not included information for specified or unspecified disorders for each disorder in this section, because the criteria for these diagnoses are similar to those found in Part One. For more detailed information regarding specified and unspecified diagnoses, see Chapter 17.

◆ ◆ ◆

Chapter 9

Substance-Related and Addictive Disorders

After my husband died, I drank more and more to numb the pain. It started out with a few glasses of wine a day, which then turned into a few bottles. I would wake up in the middle of the night and have a glass of wine. I would drink before work and during lunch. That was before I stopped going to work altogether. My family and friends wanted me to get help, but I didn't care. The only thing that made me feel better was drinking. —Susan

Substance-related disorders include 10 classes of drugs (alcohol; caffeine; cannabis; hallucinogens; inhalants; opioids; sedatives, hypnotics, and anxiolytics; stimulants; tobacco; and other/unknown substances) that activate the brain's reward system (APA, 2013a). Use of these substances often leads to impairments in multiple areas of functioning that occur at a clinical level and represent diagnosable disorders. There are three classifications: use, intoxication, and withdrawal (APA, 2013a). Prevalence rates of substance use are extremely high, with 22.6 million individuals in the United States reporting use of illegal substances within the past month; this represents 8.9% of the total population over 12 years of age (SAMHSA, 2011b). Additionally, according to SAMHSA (2011b), a staggering 131.3 million people (51.8%) ages 12 and older had used alcohol and 69.6 million (27.4%) had used tobacco in the past month. During the same year, 23.5 million people ages 12 or older needed treatment for an illicit drug or alcohol abuse problem; this represents 9.3% of the U.S. population age 12 or older (SAMHSA, 2011b).

According to the American Society of Addictive Medicine (ASAM, 2013),

Addiction is a primary, chronic disease of brain reward, motivation, memory, and related circuitry. Dysfunction in these circuits leads to characteristic biological, psychological, social and spiritual manifestations. This is reflected in an individual pathologically pursuing reward and/or relief by substance use and other behaviors. (para. 1)

Addiction is ongoing and often cyclical, with many negative effects on psychological and physiological wellness. Addiction is present and problematic within and across social, cultural, and economic groups (ASAM, 2013; SAMHSA, 2011b). The cost of addiction is enormous, with a price tag of $559 billion annually for illegal substances, alcohol, and tobacco (National Institute on Drug Abuse, 2011).

Because of the devastating impact and high prevalence rates of individuals with diagnosable substance-related and addictive disorders, virtually all counselors—regardless of their professional settings—will work directly with this population or provide services for the family members and loved ones of individuals with the disorders. Substance-related and addictive disorders appear throughout the life span in people of all socioeconomic status levels, educational attainment, gender, culture, ethnicity, and religion. It is critical that counselors possess a strong understanding of criteria for substance-related disorders. To help establish this framework, the following section provides an overview of the changes from the *DSM-IV-TR* to the *DSM-5*.

Major Changes From *DSM-IV-TR* to *DSM-5*

The *DSM-5* includes significant restructuring to the categorization of substance-related disorders. One of the biggest changes in the *DSM-5* is removal of the distinction between abuse and dependence. The prior classification of abuse and dependence was based on the notion that there is a biaxial difference between the two and that abuse was a less severe form of dependence. The bimodal theory did not hold true in research and practice, so the classification was revised to address substance use disorders as existing on a fluid, continuous spectrum (APA, 2013a; Dawson, Goldstein, & Grant, 2013; Keyes, Krueger, Grant, & Hasin, 2011). This resulted in the new substance use disorders section.

Once clinicians note the presence of a substance use disorder, they may specify severity of the addiction using ratings of *mild*, *moderate*, and *severe*. Research supports an increasing spectrum of severity across addictions and addictive behaviors that occurs as a continuous variable; this represents the predominant reason for the move from abuse versus dependence to severity ratings (APA, 2013a; Dawson et al., 2013; Keyes et al., 2011). In addition, the removal of the terms *abuse* and *dependence* supports the fluid and progressive nature of substance use disorders as conceptualized in the manual.

It is important to note that concerns related to specific substances in the Substance-Related and Addictive Disorders chapter of the *DSM-5* (and enumerated in this chapter) are viewed as distinctive disorders. For example, caffeine-related disorders are separate from cannabis-related disorders. However, despite being distinctly separate diagnoses, all substance use disorders are based on the same criteria. Substance use criteria are also separate from substance-specific intoxication and withdrawal criteria. For example, there is alcohol use disorder, alcohol intoxication, and alcohol withdrawal, which are all coded separately. The only exception is hallucinogen-related and inhalant-related disorders, because symptoms of withdrawal have not been sufficiently documented for these substances so the withdrawal criterion has been eliminated. All other criteria for hallucinogen-related and inhalant-related disorders are the same. This modification in the diagnostic process for substance use disorders represents one of the most substantive changes to a diagnostic category in the *DSM-5*.

As discussed in Chapter 2, unlike the discrete categories in the *DSM-IV-TR*, many disorders within the *DSM-5* were revised to represent a continuum. In the Substance-Related and Addictive Disorders chapter of the *DSM-5*, this continuum is represented by replacing distinct categories of substance abuse and dependence with 11 standard enumerated criteria for substance use disorders (APA, 2013a). Two to three criteria must be present for the severity indicator of *mild*, four to five for *moderate*, and six or more for *severe*. Additionally, craving has been included as a criterion, and legal difficulties has been excluded as a criterion.

The APA Substance-Related Disorders Work Group found research that collaborates the development of the substance use spectrum (APA, 2013a). According to Compton,

Dawson, Goldstein, and Grant (2013), 80.5% of individuals who met the criteria for alcohol dependence in the *DSM-IV-TR* also met the criteria for alcohol use disorder (moderate to severe) in the *DSM-5*. Dawson et al. (2013) and Keyes et al. (2011) also found support for this new unimodal, fluid approach.

A second substantive change is that other addictive disorders have been included as part of this chapter, although at this time the *DSM-5* only includes gambling disorder in this category. Pathological gambling was listed in the *DSM-IV-TR* in the Impulse-Control Disorders Not Elsewhere Classified section but has now been relabeled and classified with substance-related disorders. The addition of gambling disorder represents the first time a process-related addictive behavior has been included alongside use of substances. This is due to an abundance of research that shows that gambling activates the brain's reward system in ways that are consistent with substance use (APA, 2013a; Ko et al., 2013; Moran, 2013). The symptoms of gambling disorder also hold similarities to substance use disorders, and gambling disorder possesses similar etiology in terms of presentation, biological underpinnings, and treatment.

Internet gaming disorder, listed in Section III of the *DSM-5* under the chapter Conditions for Further Study, may be added as an addictive disorder to subsequent iterations of the manual. Other types of "behavioral addictions" such as exercise, shopping, or sex addictions have not yet been shown to identify a diagnostic profile or similar developmental course. These may also be considered for inclusion in future editions of the manual (APA, 2013a; Ko et al., 2013; Moran, 2013).

Some scholars have taken umbrage with the wordsmithing of the chapter title, pointing out that Substance-Related and Addictive Disorders implies that being diagnosed with a substance use disorder means the client has an addiction (Kaminer & Winters, 2012). There has also been concern over the removal of the abuse category. Kaminer and Winters (2012) posited that the category of abuse is particularly applicable for adolescents; they discussed a body of knowledge coined the "biobehavioral developmental perspective" that asserts the course of the substance use is heterogeneously progressive and fits a categorical model of abuse versus dependence. The authors worried that removal of the abuse category in the *DSM-5* will affect treatment services for this population. However, other scholars believed modifications will increase access to services (Dawson et al., 2013; Keyes et al., 2011; Mewton, Slade, McBride, Grove, & Teeson, 2011).

Several other changes are reflected in the Substance-Related and Addictive Disorders chapter. Specifically, *early remission* is now defined as at least 3 but not more than 12 months' absence of meeting diagnostic criteria for substance use disorders. Craving can still be present as a symptom, even with remission, because individuals continue to experience craving, or a strong desire, for the substance. The specifier *with physiological dependence* is not included in the *DSM-5* nor is the diagnosis of polysubstance dependence. Newly included codable disorders are caffeine withdrawal and cannabis withdrawal (APA, 2013a).

Substance-Related Disorders

The *DSM-5* includes specific criteria sets for each substance and applicable disorders related to that substance (e.g., use, intoxication, and withdrawal). All diagnostic labels include the name of the specific substance, such as cannabis use disorder, cannabis intoxication, and cannabis withdrawal. If an individual meets the criteria for multiple substance-related diagnoses, they are all listed. The manual is explicit in noting the likelihood of comorbidity of substance-related disorders (APA, 2013a; SAMHSA, 2011b).

Essential Features

According to APA (2013a), "a substance use disorder is a cluster of cognitive, behavioral, and physiological symptoms indicating that the individual continues using the substance despite significant substance-related problems" (p. 483). In severe and long-term use, these changes may be observed through underlying changes in brain circuits (Agrawal et al., 2012). The first four criteria for substance use disorders encompass impaired control, social impairment, risky use, and pharmacological criteria. Criteria 5 to 7 cover social, occupational, and interpersonal problems. Criteria 8 and 9 focus on risk taking surrounding use of the substance, and Criteria 10 and 11 are tolerance and withdrawal, respectively. Assuming an individual meets the general requirement for "clinically significant impairment or distress" related to pattern of use, just two specific criteria must be met to justify assignment of a clinical diagnosis.

The predominant change to the overall diagnostic criteria for substance use disorder is the inclusion of craving and the exclusion of recurrent legal problems. Craving is included in *ICD-10* criteria (WHO, 2007) and has been supported through epidemiological studies as a highly prominent and core feature of substance use disorders (Kavanaugh, 2013; Keyes et al., 2011; Ko et al., 2013; Mewton et al., 2011; Sinha, 2013). Functional magnetic resonance imaging (fMRI) has shown that there are certain brain regions directly related to craving (Ko et al., 2013). Presence of cues, negative moods, and stress reactions often lead to an increase in craving. Mindfulness training has been shown to reduce craving in that it can address awareness of the emotion and redirection of thoughts.

Diagnostic Criteria (Alcohol Use Disorder Example)

A. A problematic pattern of alcohol use leading to clinically significant impairment or distress, as manifested by at least two of the following, occurring within a 12-month period.
1. Alcohol is often taken in larger amounts or over a longer period than was intended.
2. There is a persistent desire or unsuccessful efforts to cut down or control alcohol use.
3. A great deal of time is spent in activities necessary to obtain alcohol, use alcohol, or recover from its effects.
4. Craving, or a strong desire to use alcohol.
5. Recurrent alcohol use resulting in a failure to fulfill major role obligations at work, school, or home.
6. Continued alcohol use despite having persistent or recurrent social or interpersonal problems caused or exacerbated by the effects of alcohol.
7. Important social, occupational, or recreational activities are given up or reduced because of alcohol use.
8. Recurrent alcohol use in situations in which it is physically hazardous.
9. Alcohol use is continued despite knowledge of having a persistent or recurrent physical or psychological problem that is likely to have been caused or exacerbated by alcohol.
10. Tolerance, as defined by either of the following:
    a. A need for markedly increased amounts of alcohol to achieve intoxication or desired effect.
    b. A markedly diminished effect with continued use of the same amount of alcohol.
11. Withdrawal, as manifested by either of the following:
    a. The characteristic withdrawal syndrome for alcohol (refer to Criteria A and B of the criteria set for alcohol withdrawal, pp. 499–500).
    b. Alcohol (or a closely related substance, such as a benzodiazepine) is taken to relieve or avoid withdrawal symptoms.

Note

The diagnostic criteria for alcohol use disorder are used as an example because the criteria are identical for all of the disorders with the exception of Criterion 11, which does not apply to hallucinogen-related and inhalant-related use disorders.

◆ ◆ ◆

Substance Intoxication and Withdrawal

Substance intoxication is a syndrome that develops temporarily after ingestion of a substance. The subsequent psychological changes result from the physiological effects of the substance. Intoxication often includes alterations in attention, thinking, judgment, perception, interpersonal behavior, psychomotor behavior, and wakefulness. The diagnosis of substance intoxication is separate from substance use disorder, and the specific substance of intoxication is listed in the disorder. The *DSM-5* includes criteria sets specific to intoxication for each substance category. *ICD-10-CM* coding will change on the basis of the comorbidity of a substance use disorder. For example, there are different codes for alcohol intoxication with comorbid alcohol use disorder, mild (F10.129), than for alcohol intoxication with comorbid alcohol use disorder, moderate (F10.229), or alcohol intoxication without comorbid alcohol use disorder (F10.929).

Substance withdrawal includes physiological and psychological effects from stopping or reducing substance utilization after significant, prolonged use. Withdrawal can be distinctly unpleasant and trigger a cycle of renewed use to counterbalance the deleterious effects of the withdrawal. An individual can become intoxicated by, and have withdrawal from, more than one substance concomitantly. The *DSM-5* includes criteria sets specific to withdrawal from each substance; generally, withdrawal criteria are opposite what one would expect with substance intoxication for the substance. As with substance intoxication, the diagnosis of substance withdrawal can occur with or without the comorbid diagnosis of a substance use disorder (APA, 2013a).

Coding, Recording, and Specifiers

There are separate diagnostic codes for all substance-related disorders (see list below). In making a diagnosis for a substance-related disorder, counselors must identify specifiers accurately. In addition to specification of substance use disorders as *mild, moderate,* or *severe* as discussed earlier, specifiers include *in early remission, in sustained remission, on maintenance therapy,* and *in a controlled environment,* with the last being an additional specifier for remission. Jails, locked hospital units, and therapeutic living settings are examples of controlled environments.

Counselors use the codes that apply to the specific substances with the name of the specific substance included, for example, alcohol use disorder, mild (*ICD-9-CM,* 305.00; *ICD-10-CM,* F10.10). Other substance use disorder should be used if a substance does not fit into one of the enumerated classes. It should be noted that there are separate codes for use and withdrawal for *ICD-9-CM,* whereas there is one unified code for *ICD-10-CM.*

Diagnostic Codes for Substance Use Disorders

Alcohol-Related Disorders
305.00 (F10.10)	Alcohol use disorder, mild
303.90 (F10.20)	Alcohol use disorder, moderate
303.90 (F10.20)	Alcohol use disorder, severe
303.00 (F10.129)	Alcohol intoxication with use disorder, mild
303.00 (F10.229)	Alcohol intoxication with use disorder, moderate or severe
303.00 (F10.929)	Alcohol intoxication without use disorder
291.81 (F10.239)	Alcohol withdrawal without perceptual disturbances
291.81 (F10.232)	Alcohol withdrawal with perceptual disturbances
291.9 (F10.99)	Unspecified alcohol-related disorders

Caffeine-Related Disorders
305.90 (F15.929)	Caffeine intoxication
292.0 (F15.33)	Caffeine withdrawal
292.9 (F15.99)	Unspecified caffeine-related disorder

Cannabis-Related Disorders

305.20 (F12.10)	Cannabis use disorder, mild
303.90 (F12.20)	Cannabis use disorder, moderate
303.90 (F12.20)	Cannabis use disorder, severe
292.89 (F12.129)	Cannabis intoxication without perceptual disturbance with use disorder, mild
292.89 (F10.229)	Cannabis intoxication without perceptual disturbance with use disorder, moderate or severe
292.89 (F10.929)	Cannabis intoxication without perceptual disturbance without use disorder
292.89 (F12.122)	Cannabis intoxication with perceptual disturbance with use disorder, mild
292.89 (F12.222)	Cannabis intoxication with perceptual disturbance with use disorder, moderate or severe
292.89 (F12.922)	Cannabis intoxication with perceptual disturbance without use disorder
292.0 (F12.288)	Cannabis withdrawal
292.9 (F12.99)	Unspecified cannabis-related disorders

Hallucinogen-Related Disorders

305.90 (F16.10)	Phencyclidine use disorder, mild
304.60 (F16.20)	Phencyclidine use disorder, moderate
304.60 (F16.20)	Phencyclidine use disorder, severe
305.30 (F16.10)	Other hallucinogen use disorder, mild
304.50 (F16.20)	Other hallucinogen use disorder, moderate
304.50 (F16.20)	Other hallucinogen use disorder, severe
292.89 (F16.129)	Phencyclidine intoxication with use disorder, mild
292.89 (F16.229)	Phencyclidine intoxication with use disorder, moderate or severe
292.89 (F16.929)	Phencyclidine intoxication without use disorder
292.89 (F16.129)	Other hallucinogen intoxication with use disorder, mild
292.89 (F16.229)	Other hallucinogen intoxication with use disorder, moderate or severe
292.89 (F16.929)	Other hallucinogen intoxication without use disorder
292.89 (F16.983)	Hallucinogen persisting perception disorder
292.9 (F16.99)	Unspecified phencyclidine-related disorder
292.9 (F16.99)	Unspecified hallucinogen-related disorder

Inhalant-Related Disorders

Specify the particular inhalant

305.90 (F18.10)	Inhalant use disorder, mild
304.60 (F18.20)	Inhalant use disorder, moderate
304.60 (F18.20)	Inhalant use disorder, severe
292.89 (F18.129)	Inhalant intoxication with use disorder, mild
292.89 (F18.229)	Inhalant intoxication with use disorder, moderate or severe
292.89 (F18.929)	Inhalant intoxication without use disorder
292.9 (F18.99)	Unspecified inhalant-related disorders

Opioid-Related Disorders

Specify if on maintenance therapy or in a controlled environment

305.50 (F11.10)	Opioid use disorder, mild
304.00 (F11.20)	Opioid use disorder, moderate
304.00 (F11.20)	Opioid use disorder, severe
292.89 (F11.129)	Opioid intoxication without perceptual disturbance with use disorder, mild

292.89 (F11.229) Opioid intoxication without perceptual disturbance with
use disorder, moderate or severe
292.89 (F11.929) Opioid intoxication without perceptual disturbance
without use disorder
292.89 (F11.122) Opioid intoxication with perceptual disturbance with
use disorder, mild
292.89 (F11.222) Opioid intoxication with perceptual disturbance with
use disorder, moderate or severe
292.89 (F11.922) Opioid intoxication with perceptual disturbance
without use disorder
292.0 (F11.23) Opioid withdrawal
292.9 (F11.99) Unspecified opioid-related disorders

Sedative-, Hypnotic-, or Anxiolytic-Related Disorders
305.40 (F13.10) Sedative, hypnotic, or anxiolytic use disorder, mild
304.10 (F13.20) Sedative, hypnotic, or anxiolytic use disorder, moderate
304.10 (F13.20) Sedative, hypnotic, or anxiolytic use disorder, severe
292.89 (F13.129) Sedative, hypnotic, or anxiolytic intoxication with
use disorder, mild
292.89 (F13.229) Sedative, hypnotic, or anxiolytic intoxication with
use disorder, moderate or severe
292.89 (F13.929) Sedative, hypnotic, or anxiolytic intoxication without
use disorder
292.0 (F13.239) Sedative, hypnotic, or anxiolytic withdrawal without
perceptual disturbance
292.0 (F13.232) Sedative, hypnotic, or anxiolytic withdrawal with
perceptual disturbance
292.9 (F13.99) Unspecified sedative-, hypnotic-, or anxiolytic-
related disorder

Stimulant-Related Disorders
305.70 (F15.10) Amphetamine-type substance use disorder, mild
304.40 (F15.20) Amphetamine-type substance use disorder, moderate
304.40 (F15.20) Amphetamine-type substance use disorder, severe
305.60 (F14.10) Cocaine use disorder, mild
304.20 (F14.20) Cocaine use disorder, moderate
304.20 (F14.20) Cocaine use disorder, severe
305.70 (F15.10) Other or unspecified stimulant use disorder, mild
304.40 (F15.20) Other or unspecified stimulant use disorder, moderate
304.40 (F15.20) Other or unspecified stimulant use disorder, severe
292.89 (F15.129) Amphetamine or other stimulant intoxication without
perceptual disturbance with use disorder, mild
292.89 (F15.229) Amphetamine or other stimulant intoxication without
perceptual disturbance with use disorder, moderate or severe
292.89 (F15.929) Amphetamine or other stimulant intoxication without
perceptual disturbance without use disorder
292.89 (F14.129) Cocaine intoxication without perceptual disturbance with
use disorder, mild
292.89 (F14.229) Cocaine intoxication without perceptual disturbance with
use disorder, moderate or severe
292.89 (F14.929) Cocaine intoxication without perceptual disturbance
without use disorder
292.89 (F15.122) Amphetamine or other stimulant intoxication with
perceptual disturbance with use disorder, mild

292.89 (F15.222)	Amphetamine or other stimulant intoxication with perceptual disturbance with use disorder, moderate or severe
292.89 (F15.922)	Amphetamine or other stimulant intoxication with perceptual disturbance without use disorder
292.89 (F14.122)	Cocaine intoxication with perceptual disturbance with use disorder, mild
292.89 (F14.222)	Cocaine intoxication with perceptual disturbance with use disorder, moderate or severe
292.89 (F14.922)	Cocaine intoxication with perceptual disturbance without use disorder
292.0 (F15.23)	Amphetamine or other stimulant withdrawal
292.0 (F14.23)	Cocaine withdrawal
292.9 (F15.99)	Unspecified amphetamine or other stimulant-related disorders
292.9 (F14.99)	Unspecified cocaine-related disorders

Tobacco-Related Disorders

Specify if on maintenance therapy or in a controlled environment

305.1 (Z72.0)	Tobacco use disorder, mild
305.1 (F17.200)	Tobacco use disorder, moderate
305.1 (F17.200)	Tobacco use disorder, severe
292.0 (F17.203)	Tobacco withdrawal
292.9 (F17.209)	Unspecified tobacco-related disorder

Other (or Unknown) Substance-Related Disorders

305.90 (F19.10)	Other (or unknown) substance use disorder, mild
304.90 (F19.20)	Other (or unknown) substance use disorder, moderate
304.90 (F19.20)	Other (or unknown) substance use disorder, severe
292.89 (F19.129)	Other (or unknown) substance intoxication with use disorder, mild
292.89 (F19.229)	Other (or unknown) substance intoxication with use disorder, moderate or severe
292.89 (F19.929)	Other (or unknown) substance intoxication without use disorder
292.0 (F19.239)	Other (or unknown) substance withdrawal
292.9 (F19.99)	Unspecified other (or unknown) substance-related disorder

Implications for Counselors

The removal of the abuse and dependence categories allows counselors to assess severity on three levels, which lends to enhanced and tailored treatment options. The *mild* level of severity for substance use disorders (two to three criteria met) provides early intervention opportunities; individuals who present with *moderate* (four or five symptoms) or *severe* (six of more symptoms) substance use disorders may require more intensive treatments. In a study addressing the comparability of diagnoses between the *DSM-IV-TR* substance dependence and *DSM-5* substance use disorders, Compton et al. (2013) found excellent correspondence with alcohol, cocaine, cannabis, and opioid use disorders.

Initial substance use typically takes place during the mid-teens for most individuals, and conduct disorder is often comorbid with substance use disorders in adolescents (Crowley, 2007; Vandrey, Budney, Kamon, & Stanger, 2005). Considering the negative psychological, physiological, and environmental effects of substance-related disorders, it is critical to assess thoroughly and engage in treatment modalities early in the course of the disorder.

An important area for counselors to address in treatment is the lingering symptom of substance craving that can present a challenge for client relapse prevention. The desire and yearning for a specific substance or substances is a common symptom that can exist well beyond cessation of use (Sinha, 2013). Instillation of adaptive coping mechanisms and substitution of positive behaviors can be important elements of treatment in working with clients' residual craving. Mindfulness training has also been shown to be beneficial in treatment for substance-related disorders (Brewer, Elwafi, & Davis, 2013).

Specific Substance-Related Disorders Overview

The following sections provide brief descriptions and key elements of substance-related disorders outlined in the *DSM-5*. The manual also contains a section for other (or unknown) substance-related disorders that encompasses substances that fall outside of the specific types enumerated below.

Alcohol-Related Disorders

There is a high prevalence of alcohol use disorder in the United States, with approximately 12.4% of adult men and 4.9% of adult women afflicted (APA, 2013a). The highest prevalence is among Native Americans and Alaska Natives (12.1%) and the lowest is among Asian Americans and Pacific Islanders (4.5%). Age of onset peaks in the late teens, and most individuals who will develop alcohol use disorder do so by their late 30s (APA, 2013a).

Alcohol use and criminal activity are linked, with up to 40% of state prisoners reporting that they were under the influence of alcohol during commission of the crime for which they were incarcerated. Agrawal et al. (2012) found that genetic factors can contribute to alcohol craving, which makes certain individuals particularly vulnerable to alcohol use disorder since craving often exists after cessation of alcohol use (even after it is in sustained remission).

From an environmental standpoint, individuals living in cultures where alcohol availability and use are widespread are more prone to the development of the disorder. This is especially true if there are genetic predispositions to alcohol use disorder as is the case in almost 50% of individuals who develop the disorder. From a physiological standpoint, individuals with bipolar disorder, schizophrenia, and general impulsivity concerns have a heightened risk for alcohol-related disorders (APA, 2013a; Keyes et al., 2011).

Caffeine-Related Disorders

The *DSM-5* does not identify caffeine use disorder. Although evidence supports caffeine use as a condition, there is not yet sufficient information supporting impairment resulting from a problematic pattern of caffeine use. The United States has a high number of caffeine users—more than 85% of adults use caffeine regularly; among those, the average caffeine consumption is about 280 milligrams (two to three small cups of coffee) per day. Thus, caffeine use disorder is included in Section III of the manual as a condition for further study. The *DSM-5* includes caffeine intoxication and withdrawal as diagnosable disorders (APA, 2013a).

Caffeine withdrawal is a newly diagnosable condition and requires stopping caffeine use after prolonged daily consumption, with physical symptoms of headache, fatigue, dysphoric mood, difficulty concentrating, and possible flu-like symptoms that cause clinically significant distress. This is similar to withdrawal criteria for substance-related disorders listed in this chapter. It is interesting to note that excessive caffeine use is often seen in individuals with mental health disorders (e.g., eating disorders and other substance-related disorders) and incarcerated individuals (APA, 2013a). The growing popularity of energy drinks with high caffeine content poses a concern, especially because young people are frequent consumers of those beverages.

Cannabis-Related Disorders

Cannabis, or marijuana, has been known to be a "gateway" drug. According to the United Nations Office on Drugs and Crime (Leggett, 2006), cannabis is used more than any other illegal drug, with a definitive link found between cannabis use and mood disorders (Lynskey,

Glowinski, & Todorov, 2004). Cannabis use is widespread in the United States, and the number of users is projected to increase over the next decade (Alexander & Leung, 2011).

Cannabis withdrawal is new to the *DSM-5* and includes physical symptoms arising after cessation of heavy use, which is defined as daily or almost daily use for a minimum of several months (APA, 2013a). Irritability, anger, aggression, nervousness, restlessness, and sleep disturbance are a few of the symptoms. The inclusion of cannabis withdrawal reflects the plethora of supportive empirical research (e.g., Budney, Hughes, Moore, & Vandrey, 2004; Budney, Moore, Vandrey, & Hughes, 2003; Crowley, 2007; Vandrey et al., 2005). Additionally, genetic factors can contribute to cannabis use and withdrawal, thus providing further rationale for their enumeration in the manual (Verweij et al., 2013).

Hallucinogen-Related Disorders

Hallucinogens are a heterogeneous grouping of substances that can have the same type of alterations of cognition and perception in users. These are most often taken orally, although some are smoked or injected. These types of drugs (e.g., ecstasy; lysergic acid diethylamide [LSD]; 3,4-methylenedioxy-methamphetamine [MDMA or ecstasy]; and psychedelic mushrooms) have a long half-life that can extend from hours to days. Hallucinogen use disorder has an annual prevalence rate of 0.1% in adults, with men more likely than women to engage in use (APA, 2013a). Hallucinogens can have long-term effects on brain functioning. In diagnosing hallucinogen use disorder, counselors should identify the specific substance (e.g., "ecstasy use disorder" rather than the more general "hallucinogen use disorder"). Because withdrawal from hallucinogens has not been clearly documented, the withdrawal criterion is not present for hallucinogen use disorder (APA, 2013a; Kerridge et al., 2011).

Hallucinogens are sometimes used in religious practices (i.e., peyote in the Native American Church). Controlled use during religious observances is not to be considered a diagnosable condition. As with the diagnosis of any mental health disorder, cultural factors must be taken into account during assessment (Pettet, Lu, & Narrow, 2011).

Inhalant-Related Disorders

Inhalants such as glues, paints, fuels, and other "volatile hydrocarbons" are all included in this diagnostic classification. A small percentage (0.4%) of adolescents between the ages of 12 and 17 meet the criteria for inhalant use disorder, although usage rates for young people may be as high as 10% (Dinwiddie, 1994). This disorder is typically not seen in older children or adults (APA, 2013a).

Kerridge et al. (2011) used data from the National Epidemiological Survey on Alcohol and Related Conditions to assess fit for the unidimensional model of substance use disorders for inhalants. Their study found support for the *DSM-5* elimination of abuse and dependence for inhalants. Because of a dearth of documented physiological and psychological effects related to cessation of use, inhalant withdrawal is not included in the manual (APA, 2013a).

Inhalant use is quite dangerous and can be fatal. One author of this *Learning Companion* had a childhood friend who died of inhalant poisoning at 18 years of age. It is important for counselors to effectively identify inhalant-related disorders, especially counselors specializing in adolescent treatment. Counselors should be very concerned about reports of inhalant use. Even reports of "experimentation" can be fatal, as 22% of inhalant abusers who died of sudden sniffing death syndrome (i.e., cardiac arrest) were first-time users (J. F. Williams & Storck, 2007). This problem afflicts children from all socioeconomic backgrounds and from families with both high and low levels of parental education.

Opioid-Related Disorders

Opioid use has multiple deleterious physical effects. Because opioids are frequently injected, there are many risks for infection and disease. Common opioids include morphine, oxycodone, and heroin (APA, 2013a). Counselors must be aware of the risks of needle sharing, which puts opioid users at higher risk for HIV, hepatitis, and tuberculosis. There is a heightened suicide risk and high mortality rate for opioid users (up to 2% yearly). Jim Morrison, Janis Joplin, John Belushi, Chris Farley, River Phoenix, Heath Ledger, and, most recently, Corey Monteith were all young, famous people who died from opioid overdoses. Even prescribed opioid use can be a problem; from 1999 to 2007, the rate of fatal prescription opioid overdoses in the United States increased by 124% (Bohnert et al., 2011).

Opioid use disorder typically develops in early adulthood and spans many years. Rates of opioid use are higher in males than females (APA, 2013a). Problems first occur in adolescence and early adulthood. Opioid use disorder is seen across ethnicities; tolerance and withdrawal are commonly evident criteria. Babies born to mothers who have used opioids during their pregnancy can be born physiologically dependent (APA, 2013a). The severity of negative health effects underscores the need for early and effective interventions for opioid users.

Sedative, Hypnotic, or Anxiolytic-Related Disorders

This class of substances includes all prescription sleeping medications and almost all anxiety medications. One great danger is the swift build-up of tolerance and withdrawal for these substances, often resulting in craving. Individuals in adolescence and early adulthood are at the highest prevalence for the disorder and often engage in concomitant use of other substances (APA, 2013a).

If sedatives, hypnotics, or anxiolytics are prescribed for specific medical purposes and the medication is taken as prescribed, an individual would not meet diagnostic criteria for the use disorder. Sometimes, individuals who receive a prescription will build tolerance and seek out additional access through use of multiple physicians; thus, counselors should be careful to assess for patterns of use even for clients who report accessing substances through medical providers. Sedative, hypnotic, or anxiolytic-related disorders are often comorbid with alcohol and tobacco use disorders, personality disorders, depressive disorders, anxiety disorders, and bipolar disorders (APA, 2013a).

Stimulant-Related Disorders

Substances included in this section include, but are not limited to, amphetamine, dextroamphetamine, methamphetamine, and cocaine. Stimulants can be taken orally, injected, or smoked and typically result in drastic changes in behavior and a concomitant feeling of subjective well-being. Violent and aggressive behavior occurs with stimulant use and can lead to interpersonal and legal difficulties. Withdrawal can cause significant depressive symptoms as well as medical conditions. Examples include cardiac difficulties, seizures, neurocognitive impairment, and respiratory problems, just to name a few. Stimulant-related disorders are likely to co-occur with other substance-related disorders and gambling disorder. It is notable that amphetamines are sometimes medically prescribed to treat ADHD, obesity, and narcolepsy (APA, 2013a).

There has been research supporting a higher diagnostic inclusion of individuals with stimulant-related disorders based on the revised diagnostic spectrum. This can help accurately identify those individuals in need of treatment for stimulant use disorders. Specifically, Proctor, Kopak, and Hoffmann (2012) found that the new criteria assist with inclusivity in meeting the needs of those with cocaine-related disorders.

Tobacco-Related Disorders

Approximately one in five adolescents in the United States will use tobacco on a regular basis; most individuals will develop tobacco use disorder prior to the age of 21. Many tobacco users attempt to quit, with most making multiple attempts before successfully stopping usage (APA, 2013a). Tobacco is linked to a plethora of physical health problems and accounts for approximately one in every five deaths in the United States. Tobacco smokers have a life-span projection that is about 10 years shorter than nonsmokers (CDC, 2008).

Tobacco intoxication is not included in the *DSM-5*. Tobacco withdrawal is a new diagnosis in *DSM-5* and involves symptoms of irritability, anxiety, difficulty concentrating, increased appetite, restlessness, depressed mood, and insomnia. There is a significant comorbidity (22% to 32%) of alcohol, anxiety, depressive, bipolar, and personality disorders (APA, 2013a).

Tobacco use has declined in the United States since the 1960s, in part from heightened awareness of the health risks and restrictions on smoking accessibility. However, the African American and Hispanic populations have seen less of a decline. Those from lower socioeconomic backgrounds are more likely to begin smoking tobacco and less likely to quit successfully (APA, 2013a; CDC, 2008).

 Example

> Maria is a 33-year old Latino American, heterosexual married mother of two young children. Previously employed as a bank manager, Maria has been working as a homemaker since the birth of her second child 2 years ago. Although a social drinker throughout her early adulthood, she began consuming alcohol on a daily basis about a year and a half ago. She started out drinking only wine but quickly progressed to vodka. For close to a year, Maria has been consuming in excess of seven drinks daily.
>
> Maria hides her alcohol use from her family and friends. There have been times when she tried to quit drinking for several days, but those attempts were unsuccessful. Maria often thinks about drinking and admits to driving multiple times under the effects of alcohol, although she denies any impairment or risk. She often starts drinking first thing in the morning several days of the week to get rid of hangover symptoms.
>
> Maria feels stressed by her responsibilities in parenting her two small children and maintaining the household. She also feels unfulfilled in her life and believes that she has wasted her career potential. As a devout Catholic, she also feels her drinking and lying are sinful. This makes her sad and leads to her drinking more to numb the pain.
>
> Maria presents for counseling as a result of her husband confronting her about her drinking. She verbalizes that she loves her husband and family, which is why she sought help from counseling. She denies having a problem and states that she has "everything under control" and can "stop drinking anytime."

◆ ◆ ◆

Diagnostic Questions

1. Do Maria's presenting symptoms meet the criteria for alcohol use disorder?
2. Based on your answer to Question 1, what severity specifier would you assign to Maria's diagnosis?
3. What would be the reason(s), if any, a counselor may not diagnose Maria with an alcohol use disorder?
4. Would Maria be more accurately diagnosed with a mood or personality disorder? If so, why? If not, why not?
5. What rule-outs would you consider for Maria's case?
6. What other information may be needed to make an accurate clinical diagnosis?

312.31 Gambling Disorder (F63.0)

It was like my whole life revolved around being in the casino. I would spend all day there and then dream about it at night. It didn't matter how much money I lost because I just knew that the next time I pulled the slot, I would hit the jackpot. I quit caring about my relationships or the fact that I had been fired from another job. —Johi

Gambling disorder is the only non-substance-related disorder included in the Substance-Related and Addictive Disorders chapter of the *DSM-5*. It replaces pathological gambling from the *DSM-IV-TR*, which was listed in the Impulse-Control Disorders Not Elsewhere Classified section. With criteria almost identical to the previous manual, its movement to this section of the *DSM-5* reflects the similarities in neurocircuitry related to brain reward systems and behavior patterns (APA, 2013a; King & Delfabbro, 2013).

The behavior of gambling activates the brain reward system. It has been posited that most addictions involve the development of a delivery mechanism of some kind; that is, gambling addiction can involve addiction to poker or roulette, which provides the conduit for receiving rewards (King & Delfabbro, 2013). As noted in the *DSM-5*, "gambling involves risking something of value in the hopes of obtaining something of greater value" (APA, 2013a, p. 586). The earlier gambling behaviors begin, the more likely an individual is to develop the disorder. Cultural, environmental, and genetic factors can lead an individual to be at higher risk for the development of gambling disorder. Animal and human research supports a strong neurological basis of addiction, including twin studies that have uncovered a higher prevalence in identical versus fraternal twins.

Cultural Considerations

Males are more likely to develop gambling disorder than females and tend to engage in different types of gambling (APA, 2013a). Playing cards and betting on sports and horse racing are more prevalent gambling activities in males, whereas playing bingo and using slot machines are more common gambling activities for females. Gambling patterns often increase during times of stress or personal difficulty (Moran, 2013).

There is a higher prevalence of gambling disorder among African Americans compared with European Americans and Hispanic Americans; Native Americans have the highest prevalence rates of the disorder (APA, 2013a). Gambling disorder can manifest throughout the life span with occurrences from adolescence through older adulthood (APA, 2013a).

Differential Diagnosis

Nondisordered gambling, manic episodes, personality disorders, and other medical conditions should all be considered as possible differential diagnoses. Examples of nondisordered gambling are professional and social gambling. Discipline and control with minimal and acceptable losses are key elements for professional and social gambling. Gambling issues can be seen in individuals with personality disorders (e.g., antisocial personality disorder, borderline personality disorder). If an individual with a diagnosable personality disorder meets the criteria for gambling disorder, both can be diagnosed (APA, 2013a; Potenza et al., 2013).

Certain medications can enhance urges to gamble (e.g., dopaminergic medications prescribed for Parkinson's disease). Additionally, it is important to rule out disordered gambling that occurs during the course of a manic episode. Manic episodes are often characterized by impaired impulse control, loss of judgment, and engagement in excessive pleasurable activity; for some, gambling may result (APA, 2013a).

Diagnostic Criteria for Gambling Disorder 312.31 (F63.0)

A. Persistent and recurrent problematic gambling behavior leading to clinically significant impairment or distress, as indicated by the individual meeting four (or more) of the following in a 12-month period:
1. Needs to gamble with increasing amounts of money in order to achieve the desired excitement.
2. Is restless or irritable when attempting to cut down or stop gambling.
3. Has made repeated unsuccessful efforts to cut down, control, or stop gambling.
4. Is often preoccupied with gambling (e.g., having persistent thoughts of reliving past gambling experiences, handicapping or planning the next venture, thinking of ways to get money with which to gamble).
5. Often gambles when feeling distressed (e.g., helpless, guilty, anxious, depressed).
6. After losing money gambling, often returns the next day to get even ("chasing" one's losses).
7. Lies to conceal the extent of involvement with gambling.
8. Has jeopardized or lost a significant relationship, job, or educational or career opportunity because of gambling.
9. Relies on others to provide money to relieve desperate financial situations caused by gambling.
B. The gambling behavior is not better explained by a manic episode.

From *Diagnostic and Statistical Manual of Mental Disorders, Fifth Edition*, 2013, p. 585. Copyright 2013 by the American Psychiatric Association. All rights reserved. Reprinted with permission.

Coding, Recording, and Specifiers

There is only one diagnostic code for gambling disorder: 312.31 (F63.0). Specifiers for gambling disorder are *episodic*, which mean symptoms meet diagnostic criteria with amelioration of symptoms for at least several months, and *persistent*, which means symptoms are continuous and ongoing over the course of several years or more. There are both *early remission* and *sustained remission* with duration of 3 months and 12 months, respectively. Levels of severity are *mild* (four to five criteria met), *moderate* (six to seven criteria met), and *severe* (eight to nine criteria met).

Implications for Counselors

The inclusion of gambling disorder as an addictive disorder in the *DSM-5* brings with it a reconceptualization for counselors working with clients who struggle with problematic gambling. Because of its convergent etiology with substance-related disorders, it is important for counselors to be aware of the sequelae of the diagnosis and its psychosocial impact. Clients with gambling disorder frequently face impairment in multiple facets of their lives and often have specific financial hardship as a result of their behaviors (Moran, 2013).

Counselors across settings should be aware of treatment needs, comorbidity, and differential diagnoses for these clients. Lifestyle modifications will often need to be made to alleviate temptation and negative peer influences. If there is a comorbid disorder, the special clinical needs of those clients should be taken into account. Addressing the impact on family members is an important part of treatment because relationships are frequently frayed as a result of the destructive gambling behaviors (Brewer et al., 2013; Moran, 2013; Potenza et al., 2013)

The inclusion of gambling disorder as a nonsubstance addiction holds the potential to assist people with access to treatment. Several treatment modalities have proved efficacious with this population of clients. These include mindfulness training, CBT, behavior modification, contingency management, and motivational interviewing (Brewer et al., 2013; Potenza et al., 2013)

Although gambling disorder is the only non-substance-related disorder in the Substance-Related and Addictive Disorders chapter of the *DSM-5*, Section III of the manual includes Internet gaming disorder as a condition for further study. Internet gaming has been shown to activate the parahippocampus indicated by fMRI scans (Ko et al., 2013). Its inclusion in Section III of the manual reflects the growing body of research showing that excessive engagement with games on the Internet can lead to significant interpersonal challenges and cause impairment in various aspects of one's life. At this time, other potentially addictive behaviors, such as sex, shopping, and exercise addictions, are not included in the manual as codable disorders or conditions for further study (APA, 2013a).

It is important for counselors working across client populations and clinical settings to be aware of the diagnostic criteria, functional impairments, and effective treatment modalities for clients with gambling disorder and Internet gaming difficulties. Counselors who do not work directly with clients who have process addictions may still witness the pervasive and negative impact on family members and loved ones across clinical settings. As with substance-related disorders, gambling disorder (and potentially Internet gaming) has wide-reaching negative consequences.

 Case Example

Akule is a single, Native American, 26-year-old male graduate student living in a metropolitan area. Akule has been a full-time student for all of his adult life and has had to support himself through employment and student financial aid because his family does not have the means to provide financial support. Akule considers himself close to his parents and siblings, although over the last year, he has been avoiding contact with them because he has been "too busy."

Akule originally started gambling during a vacation with a group of friends. Excited by initial winnings and the accolades of his peers, Akule began gambling regularly upon his return home. At first, he was on a lucky streak and was able to pay some bills with his winnings. That soon changed, and he began losing. Over the course of the past year, Akule started gambling multiple days per week, often missing class because he stayed out late at the casino. He would grow irritable and anxious in the days following a string of losses; this began to affect his friendships and his relationship with his girlfriend. She tired of his being out late at night and his irritability. After catching him in a lie about how much money he lost gambling, she broke up with him.

After the break-up, at risk of being put on academic probation, and facing about $10,000 in debt, Akule seeks counseling services. Akule states that he is anxious and depressed but minimizes his gambling behavior, shrugging and saying that it is "not really a problem."

♦ ♦ ♦

Diagnostic Questions

1. Do Akule's presenting symptoms meet the criteria for gambling disorder?
2. Based on the disorder identified in Question 1, what severity specifier would you assign for Akule's diagnosis?
3. What would be the reason(s) a counselor may not diagnose Akule with a personality disorder?
4. Would Akule be more accurately diagnosed with bipolar disorder? If so, why? If not, why not?
5. What rule-outs would you consider for Akule's case?
6. What other information may be needed to make an accurate clinical diagnosis?

Chapter 10

Disruptive, Impulse-Control, and Conduct Disorders

The Disruptive, Impulse-Control, and Conduct Disorders chapter of the *DSM-5* includes problems of self-control and represents the consolidation of all disorders related to emotional or behavioral dysregulation (APA, 2013a). Included in this chapter are oppositional defiant disorder (ODD), intermittent explosive disorder (IED), conduct disorder (CD), pyromania, and kleptomania. Counselors should note this is the first time disruptive, impulse-control, and conduct disorders have been clustered together in the *DSM*. Previously, ODD and CD were listed under disruptive disorders within the Disorders Usually First Diagnosed in Infancy, Childhood, or Adolescence chapter of the *DSM-IV-TR*. IED, CD, pyromania, and kleptomania were previously listed under the Impulse Control Disorders Not Elsewhere Classified chapter. The overuse of the NOS title, poorly defined diagnostic criteria, limited empirical evidence, and questionable comorbidity prompted significant critiques (Coccaro, 2012; Grant, Levine, Kim, & Potenza, 2005; Pardini, Frick, & Moffitt, 2010; Paris, 2013). Some critics called disorders categorized in the Impulse-Control Not Elsewhere Classified chapter in the *DSM-IV-TR* "a number of leftovers" (Morrison, 2006, p. 440) and "orphan[s] left over from previous manuals" (Paris, 2013, p. 150).

Note

Pathological gambling, now called gambling disorder, and trichotillomania, now called trichotillomania (hair-pulling disorder), were previously included within the Impulse Control Disorders Not Elsewhere Classified chapter of the *DSM-IV-TR*. These disorders have been moved in the *DSM-5* to chapters that more appropriately match diagnostic criteria and processes for these disorders. See *DSM-5* chapters Substance-Related and Addictive Disorders for information regarding gambling disorder and Obsessive-Compulsive and Related Disorders for information regarding trichotillomania (hair-pulling disorder).

◆ ◆ ◆

Characteristics of disruptive, impulse-control, and conduct disorders are aggressive or self-destructive behavior, destruction of property, conflict with authority figures, disregard for personal or social norms, and persistent outbursts of anger disproportionate to the situation (APA, 2013a; Grant et al., 2005). Whereas the urge to engage in a behavior that harms oneself or others is common to many mental health concerns (e.g., substance-related and additive disorders), those listed in this diagnostic category include behaviors that either violate the rights of others or diverge significantly from societal norms (APA, 2013a; Coccaro, 2012).

Two disorders within this chapter, pyromania and kleptomania, are characterized by "tension and release" behavior (Morison, 2006, p. 439). Similar to obsessive-compulsive and related disorders, clients feel a sense of affective arousal (i.e., tension) before engaging in the antisocial behavior of fire setting (pyromania) or theft (kleptomania). What differentiates these disorders from obsessive-compulsive related disorders is that individuals with impulse-control disorders are generally sensation-seeking, whereas individuals with obsessive-compulsive related disorders have risk-avoidant behavior such as constantly checking and rechecking locks, repetitive hand washing, or picking at hair and skin (see Chapter 6 for more information; Grant, 2006).

Note

For obsessive-compulsive and related disorders, approximately 70% of individuals in the United States, at some point in their lives, exhibit obsessive-compulsive symptoms (den Braber et al., 2008). The same is true for disruptive, impulse-control, and conduct disorders in that nearly all children and adolescents experience symptoms of defiant, rule-breaking, and disobedient behavior at some point in their development. However, the regularity, pervasiveness, and impairment experienced by some individuals exceed normative behavior for their age, gender, and culture (APA, 2013a).

◆ ◆ ◆

Whereas the underlying cause varies greatly from disorder to disorder, all diagnoses in this chapter share the common characteristic of problems with emotional or behavioral regulation (APA, 2013a). Moreover, all disorders in this chapter are marked by significant impairment associated with symptoms. These disorders are more common in males than females, and age of first onset tends to be in childhood or adolescence (APA, 2013a; Paris, 2013). It is considered rare for disruptive behavior disorders to emerge in adulthood. There is a developmental relationship between ODD and CD, in that individuals diagnosed with CD in preadolescence typically have been diagnosed with ODD previously (Burke, Waidman, & Lahey, 2010; Merikangas, Nakamura, & Kessler, 2009). However, roughly two thirds of children diagnosed with ODD will no longer meet diagnostic criteria after 3 years (Steiner & Remsing, 2007). Risk indicators for CD are earlier onset of ODD, as research indicates the likelihood of ODD progressing to CD is 3 times more likely. Additionally, counselors should closely monitor clients with CD for antisocial personality disorder (ASPD) because 40% of individuals diagnosed with CD eventually meet the criteria for ASPD (Steiner & Remsing, 2007). However, this does not mean that most children with ODD eventually develop CD. Although these individuals are at risk for various mental health concerns, particularly depressive or anxiety disorders, they are not preordained to be diagnosed with CD (APA, 2013a; de Ancos & Ascaso, 2011; Kolko & Pardini, 2010; Nock, Kazdin, Hiripi, & Kessler, 2007; Pardini et al., 2010).

Major Changes From *DSM-IV-TR* to *DSM-5*

As noted previously, the new Disruptive, Impulse-Control, and Conduct Disorders chapter includes a number of disorders previously categorized in the Impulse Control Disorders Not Elsewhere Classified and the Disorders Usually First Diagnosed in Infancy, Childhood, or Adolescence chapters of the *DSM-IV-TR*. As with all diagnostic categories within the *DSM-5*, the Disruptive, Impulse-Control, and Conduct Disorders chapter has criteria for other specified disruptive, impulse-control, and conduct disorder and unspecified disruptive, impulse-control, and conduct disorder. Although ODD and CD have been included in diagnostic nosology since the second edition of the *DSM*, conceptualizations of these disorders have been modified considerably from edition to edition (Pardini et al., 2010). Although the *DSM-5* did not have any significant changes to these diagnoses, this is the first time all mental health disorders marked by disruptive behavior and impulse-control problems, including those which go against social norms (i.e., pyromania and kleptomania), have been clustered together in the same section.

Categorizing these disorders according to common phenomenology has both clinical utility and heuristic value. Because many of these disorders are similar enough to be grouped together but distinct enough to subsist as separate disorders, counselors can more easily distinguish them from one another. For example, including IED and ODD in the same diagnostic classification allows counselors to more easily identify marked differences between these diagnoses. Second, because these disorders are grouped according to symptomatology, researchers can more easily create testable theoretical explanations for disruptive, impulse-control, and conduct-based disorders.

Aside from being an entirely new chapter, there are relatively few changes to the disorders within this section. There have been no changes to diagnostic criteria for CD, but an additional specifier of *with limited prosocial emotions* has been added (APA, 2013a). This is indicated when numerous sources (i.e., parents, teachers, extended family members, peers) report a lack of remorse or guilt, callous behavior, indifference to poor performance, or a lack of emotional expression or superficial affect (APA, 2013a). Placement of CD follows ODD and IED, thus reflecting the developmental relationship between ODD and CD (Paris, 2013).

ODD includes a new clustering of symptoms and new language to further clarify frequency and persistence of observed behavior. Whereas the *DSM-IV-TR* did not allow one to diagnose ODD if CD was present, the *DSM-5* has no such restriction. Consistent with the *DSM-5*'s focus on dimensional rather than categorical assessment, ODD also includes new severity specifiers.

Note

The questionable "rule" that individuals diagnosed with CD cannot be diagnosed with ODD has been removed in the *DSM-5*. Whereas ODD symptoms are undoubtedly associated with CD symptoms over time, individuals with angry or irritable symptoms are more likely to develop emotional disorders such as depressive, anxiety, or substance use disorders. Likewise, individuals with headstrong symptoms (i.e., argues with authority figures) are likely to be diagnosed with ADHD. On the other hand, spiteful or hurtful behavior such as aggression or callousness has been found to be most strongly associated with CD.

◆ ◆ ◆

Finally, IED includes three new criteria for consideration: The recurrent aggressive outbursts must be impulsive and not premeditated, must cause marked distress in occupational or interpersonal functioning, and may not be diagnosed until after the age of 6 (APA, 2013a). As mentioned, counselors should note that pathological gambling—renamed gambling disorder—previously included in the Impulse Control Disorders Not Elsewhere Classified chapter of the *DSM-IV-TR* has been moved to the Substance-Related and Addictive Disorders chapter, and trichotillomania (hair-pulling disorder) has been moved to the Obsessive-Compulsive and Related Disorders chapter.

Differential Diagnosis

It is not uncommon for individuals diagnosed with ODD or CD to also exhibit symptoms of ADHD (APA, 2013a; Paris, 2013). ASPD, because of its close association with CD, is cross-listed in this chapter as well as the Personality Disorders chapter. Symptoms of disruptive, impulse-control, and conduct disorders have commonly been misdiagnosed as pediatric bipolar disorder. Given the addition of DMDD to the *DSM-5*, counselors are advised to consider carefully whether temper outbursts are related to an underlying mood concern such as DMDD or behavior disorders such as IED, ODD, and CD. Although rare, counselors should carefully consider the nurturing environment of any child diagnosed with ODD to rule out RAD (Widom, Czaja, & Paris, 2009).

Disorders in this chapter have high comorbidity with substance use disorders as well as depressive disorders and anxiety disorders (de Ancos & Ascaso, 2011; Nock et al., 2007). Aside from ADHD, disruptive behavior disorders are the most common reason for mental health referrals for children and adolescents (Merikangas et al., 2009). Counselors can differentiate disruptive, impulse-control, and conduct disorders from other disorders by attending to key features of each disorder. For example, IED is related to impaired ability to control one's emotions, ODD tends to be related to one's attitude toward others, and CD may be more intentional and is related to engagement in behavior that violates the rights of others. Whereas ADHD and substance use disorders involve difficulties with impulse management, this is not the primary feature of these other disorders (Ploskin, 2007).

Etiology and Treatment

The literature is quite abundant with regard to the etiological development of disruptive, impulse-control, and conduct disorders. Researchers have identified biopsychosocial (Moeller, Barratt, Dougherty, Schmitz, & Swann, 2001), environmental (Burke, Loeber, & Birmaher, 2002; Burt, Krueger, McGue, & Iacono, 2001), genetic (Eley, Lichtenstein, & Moffitt, 2003; Waldman & Rhée, 2002), emotional (Morrell & Murray, 2003), and familial (Frick et al., 1992; Joussemet et al., 2008) factors. However, despite being grouped together diagnostically, separate pathways for the development of each disorder are found within the literature. Little genetic evidence has emerged as a causal factor for disruptive behavior disorders (Jacobson, Prescott, & Kendler, 2002). Whereas genetic links to ADHD are quite abundant (A. S. Rowland, Lesesne, & Abramowitz, 2002)—and resulted in its controversial placement within the Neurodevelopmental Disorders chapter of the *DSM-5*—biological contributions for disruptive or conduct disorders appear to be relatively small. Likewise, psychobiological studies for these disorders are also inconclusive (Hinshaw & Lee, 2003).

Most researchers have emphasized environmental origins for disruptive behaviors (Burke et al., 2002; Burt et al., 2001; Coie & Dodge, 1998; Hinshaw & Lee, 2003). Familial psychopathology, caregiver substance abuse, caregiver criminality, modeling of aggression, low socioeconomic status, family dysfunction, poor parent–child interactions, and abuse and neglect have been identified as high risk factors for the development of these disorders (Coie & Dodge, 1998; Frick et al., 1992; Joussemet et al., 2008; SAMHSA, 2011b). Other associated factors include cognitive deficits (Moffitt & Lynam, 1994), difficulties in social–cognitive information processing (Crick & Dodge, 1994), and peer rejection (Coie & Dodge, 1998). From a neurological perspective, brain structures within the limbic system (associated with emotions and the formation of memories) and the frontal lobe (linked to planning and controlling impulses) have been connected to disruptive and conduct disorders (Burke et al., 2002; Ploskin, 2007).

There is evidence that neurological irregularities and imbalance of testosterone may play a role in the formulation of disruptive behavioral and impulse-control disorders. In one study, children diagnosed with ODD and CD who had lower levels of testosterone pretreatment were 4 times more likely to respond to treatment and maintain gains compared with those with high levels of testosterone (Shenk et al., 2012). Although controversial, studies that indicate women are predisposed to less aggressive types of impulse-control disorders (i.e., kleptomania) and men to more violent and aggressive types (i.e., pyromania and IED) support this evidence. Researchers have also found connections between certain types of seizure disorders and violent impulsive behaviors (Brower & Price, 2001).

Treatment for these disorders is complex because of the heterogeneity of risk factors and etiological origins. Evidence-based treatments for disruptive behavior disorders tend to fall into several primary categories: parent/family interventions, CBT, and psychopharmacological treatment (Clark & Jerrott, 2012; Eyberg, Nelson, & Boggs, 2008; SAMHSA, 2011b). A systematic review of research regarding evidence-based psychosocial treatments for children and adolescents with disruptive behavioral disorders resulted in identification of 15 potentially efficacious treatments and one well-established treatment (Eyberg et al., 2008). Typically, parent training approaches include fostering positive time between parent and child, modeling of behaviors, introducing rewards and consequences, and teaching coping skills for dealing with difficult behavior. Through CBT, counselors can help clients modify cognitive distortions responsible for the disruptive behavior. This approach helps children and adolescents develop problem-solving skills to improve inhibition, recognize social problems and triggers for disruptive behavior, and pursue more effective alternatives. Parental and psychopharmaceutical interventions are also common (Weyandt, Verdi, & Swentosky, 2010).

Eyberg et al. (2008) concluded that parent training should be a primary approach for young children, noting that counselors may use direct interventions with other children who have the capacity to benefit from the often cognitive–behavioral strategies used in group and individual interventions. For cases in which behavior is more chronic or severe, counselors should consider multicomponent treatment approaches that involve parents, teachers, and mental health providers as change agents. Counselors who are interested in a review of evidence-based treatments for disruptive behavior disorders should refer to the SAMHSA's (2011a) *Interventions for Disruptive Behavior Disorders Kit* or Eyberg et al.'s (2008) review.

Psychopharmacological treatments have been found to be effective for pyromania (Parks et al., 2005) and kleptomania (Koran, Bodnik, & Dannon, 2010). Although no treatment approaches have conclusively been determined as effective, many varied approaches, such as CBT and dialectical behavior therapy (DBT), have been found helpful (Koran et al., 2010). Verheul et al. (2003) cited DBT as "the treatment of choice for patients with severe, life-threatening impulse-control disorders" (p. 139). Other treatment options include training for parents; behavioral therapies that focus on corrective consequences, contracting, and token reinforcement; problem-solving skills training; relaxation techniques to reduce the "urge" to engage in a behavior; overt sensitization; and specific psychoeducation such as fire safety/prevention and knowledge of legal consequences for shoplifting or theft (Koran et al., 2010). Individual and family therapy have also been found helpful.

Implications for Counselors

Counselors across settings will work with clients who engage in behaviors considered deviant and problematic to others. Kleptomania and pyromania are rare, however, with a prevalence of 0.3% to 0.6% in the general population for kleptomania, and among persons within the criminal justice system for fire setting, only 3.3% met the diagnostic criteria for pyromania (APA, 2013a). Disruptive behavior disorders such as ODD and CD are quite common within the general population (American Academy of Child & Adolescent Psychiatry, 2011; SAMHSA, 2011b). Unique challenges in working with individuals with disruptive behaviors include compounded dynamics of working with children and adolescents in general, dynamics of working with offender or nonvoluntary populations, family engagement, assessment considerations, and interdisciplinary collaboration.

Few counselors will argue that the development of a strong therapeutic relationship is essential for counseling success. Counselors may struggle to develop relationships with adolescents in general, and this struggle may be compounded given that the very nature of disruptive behavior and impulse-control disorders means that individuals are most likely engaging in deviant behavior, have difficulty considering others' perspectives, and will not present to counseling voluntarily. Like many offender populations, most youth with disruptive behavior disorders will be mandated into counseling because they have engaged in behavior that adults in their lives find problematic. In many cases, these youth may have difficult and even traumatic relationships with other adults (SAMHSA, 2011b); it would only be normal that they may have difficulty trusting and connecting with other adults. It is critical that counselors consider methods for developing nonjudgmental relationships that do not unintentionally condone defiant or oppositional behavior.

Abuse, neglect, and other unhealthy family dynamics are risk factors for disruptive behavior disorders (SAMHSA, 2011b). Counselors would be wise to consider carefully whether an individual's behavioral difficulties are the result of difficult or even dangerous conditions within the home. At the same time, counselors must take care not to jump to conclusions, pathologize, or otherwise blame caregivers of children with disruptive behavior disorders for their children's difficulty. Certainly, family engagement is difficult yet critical to treatment success (Gopalan et al., 2010), and it is the foundation of nearly all evidence-based treatments for these disorders.

Developmental pathways between ADHD, ODD, CD, ASPD, and adult criminal behavior (Burke et al., 2010) and evidence of striking comorbidity with other disorders (de Ancos & Ascaso, 2011; Nock et al., 2007) make accurate assessment of individuals with disruptive behavior disorders critical. Counselors should consider barriers to accurate assessment, including the likelihood of client underreporting or denying deviant behaviors in manners consistent with those experienced by individuals with substance use disorders. In addition, we urge counselors to look beyond difficult behaviors to consider possible underlying concerns related to learning, mood, and anxiety. Indeed, the National Comorbidity Survey Replication indicated that over 90% of individuals diagnosed with ODD met criteria for another mood, anxiety, impulse-control, and/or substance use disorders (Nock et al., 2007).

As noted previously, ADHD frequently occurs alongside disruptive behavior disorders (Pardini & Fite, 2010), and disruptive behavior at school may also be a result of unrecognized learning difficulties or frustrations. Careful assessment prior to treatment can help counselors and families understand children's developmental, academic, and social needs; co-occurring mental health concerns; barriers to treatment; and treatment preferences (Eyberg et al., 2008). Once the disruptive behaviors are identified, counselors can select from a range of evidence-based treatments to work with both child and family.

Finally, counselors who work with individuals who present with disruptive, impulse-control, and conduct disorders should be prepared to collaborate with professionals in other disciplines. Individuals may present to counseling with a court mandate, with the hopes of reducing legal involvement, or when having substantial problems within school or community settings. Thus, counselors may find themselves members of interdisciplinary treatment teams or in positions to advocate for a child within his or her system.

To help readers better understand changes from the *DSM-IV-TR* to the *DSM-5*, the rest of this chapter outlines each disorder within the Disruptive, Impulse-Control, and Conduct Disorders chapter of the *DSM-5*. As with other chapters in this text, coverage for each disorder includes highlights of key changes, essential features, and special considerations for counselors. Readers should refer to the *DSM-5* to develop a full understanding of diagnostic criteria and features, subtypes and specifiers (if applicable), prevalence, course, and risk and prognostic factors for each disorder.

313.81 Oppositional Defiant Disorder (F91.3)

Everything is an argument, and not just with me. Michael fights with his teachers, his mom, and his siblings. For at least a year now, he has been angry, irritable, and restless. He refuses to follow any rules and seems to deliberately defy his mother and me. Honestly, it is his behavior toward our 8-year-old neighbor Max that worries me the most. Sometimes he just seems cruel, even malicious toward him. —Everett (Michael's dad)

Essential Features

Oppositional defiant disorder (ODD) is characterized by a repetitive pattern of defiant, disobedient, hostile, and negative behavior toward others (Pardini et al., 2010). This disorder consists of three categories of behavior: (a) anger and irritability, (b) quarrelsome and defiant behavior, and (c) vindictiveness (APA, 2013a). Within any of these three categories, at least four symptoms (see diagnostic Criterion A for ODD in the *DSM-5*) must be present for at least 6 months.

Special Considerations

According to the *DSM-5*, prevalence of ODD within the general population is 3.3%; however, the prevalence has been estimated to be as high as 16% in the general population (American Academy of Child & Adolescent Psychiatry, 2011; SAMHSA, 2011b). Results of the National Comorbidity Survey Replication indicated a 10.4% lifetime prevalence of ODD (Nock et al., 2007). Although many studies indicate ODD is more prevalent in boys, especially when diagnosed prior to adolescence (APA, 2013a), some critics argue that existing criteria for ODD is biased against girls (Pardini et al., 2010; Paris, 2013). Nock et al. (2007) reported lifetime prevalence of 11.2% for males and 9.2% for females. New onset of ODD symptoms may begin as early as the preschool years and is rare after early adolescence. Boys presented with more functional impairments in the school and community and were more likely to be expelled from school and to have police involvement compared with girls. Parental reports indicated boys had more difficulty with comorbid ADHD and other attention problems. In contrast, girls with ODD were more likely to report difficulty with mood, self-harm, and thinking; reports from caregivers indicated more comorbid problems with depression, generalized anxiety, and somatic concerns.

Individuals diagnosed with ODD typically are unaware that their attitude and behavior are oppositional (APA, 2013a). Behavior becomes a repetitive pattern, often leading the individual to have significant problems interacting with others. It is not surprising that ODD is more common in families in which child care is interrupted and negligent, caregivers are inattentive, and otherwise harmful child-rearing practices are common (APA, 2013a).

When diagnosing any type of disruptive behavior, counselors need to tread carefully because these diagnoses tend to describe a broad range of behavioral problems, many of which may be developmentally appropriate. When assessing for ODD, counselors should inquire with multiple parties about argumentative behavior. Counselors might start by asking whether the individual gets into power struggles with authority figures and requesting information about the different settings and scenarios in which the behavior occurs. It is not uncommon for ODD to be exclusively present at home or school; when symptoms are present within more than one setting, counselors should consider the behavior to be more severe. Symptoms that occur in a specific setting or circumstance may be normal, developmental, or adaptive responses to difficult environments. Whereas ODD is typically thought of as a developmental antecedent to CD (APA, 2000), counselors need to be aware that not all adolescents diagnosed with ODD will go on to develop CD (Kolko & Pardini, 2010).

When diagnosing ODD, counselors must be sure that behaviors used to make the diagnosis are not age appropriate for the client's developmental stage or normative for the client's gender or culture. For example, it is not unusual for children to display independence-seeking behavior that may be considered disruptive or argumentative (e.g., weekly temper tantrums; APA, 2013a). However, if behavior is persistent, lasts at least 6 months, and is clearly disruptive toward others, counselors may need to consider a diagnosis of ODD. For example, an occasional temper tantrum may not be problematic; however, ODD may be present when tantrums occur alongside many other symptoms and result in educational and social impairment (e.g., being asked to leave a playgroup, suspension from school). Finally, in terms of cultural considerations, manifestations of the disorder have been found to be consistent across cultural backgrounds (APA, 2013a). Still, counselors are advised to consider carefully whether what they perceive to be oppositional behaviors could be actually adaptive and even normative communication patterns within a client's socioeconomic context.

Differential Diagnosis

A diagnosis of ODD cannot be given if an individual meets criteria for DMDD (APA, 2013a). If criteria for DMDD are met, it is assumed that the mood disorder accounts for the child's oppositional behavior and attitudes. Although ODD may be diagnosed alongside CD, ADHD, or IED, it is essential that counselors consider carefully whether symptoms meet criteria for one or both disorders. For example, minor rule-breaking associated with ODD may be more about pushing limits and irritating adults, whereas law-breaking behaviors associated with CD may result in significant injury to individuals or damage to property. As noted in the *DSM-5*, anger in ODD tends to be generalized, whereas anger in IED is characterized by aggression to others. Given that ADHD is commonly diagnosed alongside ODD, counselors should also carefully consider comorbidity with ADHD. Among individuals diagnosed with ODD, 29.0% also met criteria for IED, 35.0% met criteria for ADHD, and 42.3% met criteria for CD (Nock et al., 2007). Finally, it is important to note that children and adolescents may manifest mood concerns with irritability and agitation rather than sadness. Thus, counselors should consider the possibility of coexisting or superseding depressive disorders and bipolar disorders. This is particularly important because individuals diagnosed with ODD had a 45.8% comorbidity with mood disorders, 62.3% comorbidity with anxiety disorders, and 47.2% comorbidity with substance use disorders (Nock et al., 2007).

Coding, Recording, and Specifiers

There is only one diagnostic code for ODD: 313.81 (F91.3). Counselors must indicate current severity of *mild*, *moderate*, or *severe*. There are no codes associated with these specifiers.

Note

If symptoms are present in more than one setting (e.g., school and home), counselors may want to indicate a severity specifier of moderate or severe.

◆ ◆ ◆

312.34 Intermittent Explosive Disorder (F63.81)

I was 23 years old when my best friend from high school told me she was done with our friendship. She said my temper was out of control and she never knew when I was going to "fly off the handle." I thought she was being melodramatic, but 6 months later I had three separate charges for assault. I tried to explain to my lawyer how all of a sudden I just feel rage. Someone would piss me off and bam . . . I would have to hit them or throw something. — Raquel

Essential Features

Intermittent explosive disorder (IED) is characterized by an individual's inability to control his or her response to a stressor or frustration. IED results in excessive, unplanned verbal or physical outbursts among individuals at least 6 years of age. According to the *DSM-5*, less severe outbursts must occur at least twice weekly over a period of 3 months; an individual may also qualify for IED if he or she engages in at least three episodes that resulted in damage to property or injury to others over the period of a year (APA, 2013a).

Special Considerations

Counselors should be aware that some researchers believe little empirical evidence exists for IED (Paris, 2013), and diagnostic criteria for IED have been poorly operationalized (Coccaro, 2012). Coccaro (2012) reported that new *DSM-5* criteria for IED result in better identification of individuals who have concerns with aggression, impulsivity, family risk, and neurobiological markers related to aggression. An epidemiological study regarding IED revealed that, statistically speaking, a categorical or taxonic definition of IED fits data better than a dimensional assessment, thus suggesting that individuals with aggression associated with IED are qualitatively different from individuals with nonpathological levels of aggression (Ahmed, Green, McCloskey, & Berman, 2010). In Ahmed et al.'s (2010) study, those meeting criteria for IED-related anger compared with those with non-IED anger were, respectively, younger at age of onset (14.23 years vs. 17.68 years), more likely to be male (57.22% vs. 41.88%), more likely to seek treatment (28.34% vs. 0.50%), and more likely to report a family history of anger attacks (71.17% vs. 3.46%). They also reported more anger episodes not due to substance use (100% vs. 43.48%), physical illness (63.74% vs. 39.39%), or sadness (56.45% vs. 39.63%). The *DSM-5* includes a notation that IED is more common in individuals who are younger and have lower levels of education.

Some researchers have claimed a lifetime prevalence of 7% among the general U.S. population, but critics posited that this number is inflated given the ambiguous criteria of IED and the considerable challenges of conceptualizing the disorder (Kessler et al., 2008). The *DSM-5* reports a 1-year prevalence of 2.7% (APA, 2013a). Ahmed et al. (2010) reported a prevalence rate of 5.5% and noted that stringent *DSM* criteria may result in underidentification of individuals with IED.

Counselors should also carefully consider the use of this diagnosis in forensic settings when actions of individuals have not been premeditated (Paris, 2013). A good question counselors can ask clients is, "Do you ever become hostile or destructive when you get angry?" Follow-up questions regarding the nature and frequency of anger episodes will help counselors assess for the possibility of IED-related aggression.

Differential Diagnosis

IED includes recurrent behavioral outbursts or disruptions. When assessing for this disorder, counselors would be wise to consider a number of other disorders in which behavioral outbursts are present. These may include disorders within this chapter such as ODD and CD, as well as disorders such as ADHD, DMDD, bipolar and related disorders, and personality disorders in which individuals experience difficulty with impulse control. It is also possible that one experiences aggressive outbursts only when under the influence of a substance; in this case, substance use disorder or substance intoxication may better account for the symptoms. Although counselors should not diagnose IED if another disorder better explains the concern, the *DSM-5* includes a notation that IED can be diagnosed alongside other disorders if "recurrent impulsive aggressive outbursts are in excess of those usually seen in these disorders and warrant independent clinical attention" (APA, 2013a, p. 466).

Coding, Recording, and Specifiers

There is only one diagnostic code for IED: 312.34 (F63.81), and there is only one specifier for this disorder. Counselors must indicate current severity of *mild*, *moderate*, or *severe*. There are no codes associated with these specifiers.

312.8_ Conduct Disorder (F91._)

Jessica was arrested for destruction of property and stealing 4 weeks ago. She and some friends went into a convenience store after it had closed and bashed in the windows, destroyed all shelving, and took everything they could. This isn't the first time either. I found out later she did this at another convenience store and frequently shoplifts at Target and other large stores. Jessica has been charged only once for destruction of property, but she just blamed it on her friends. She doesn't seem to even care about what she is doing. She shows no remorse, even when she has seen her friends get into serious trouble. She just acts like she doesn't care. Honestly, I am afraid to ask her about anything else. I know there is more. For years she has been skipping school, getting into fights, stealing my car, and, although no one has directly accused her, I know she hurt our neighbor's rabbit which used to live in a shed in their backyard. —AJ (Jessica's father)

Essential Features

Conduct disorder (CD) is characterized by "a repetitive and persistent pattern of behavior in which the basic rights of others or major age-appropriate societal norms or rules are violated" (APA, 2013a, p. 469). The *DSM-5* operationalizes this as at least three symptoms over the course of 1 year; because CD is most common among youth, at least one symptom has to be present in the most recent 6 months. Symptoms fall into four clusters involving aggression toward people and animals, destruction of property, deceitfulness or theft, and serious violations of rules. See Criterion A within the *DSM-5* for specific examples of CD symptoms.

Special Considerations

APA (2013a) identified the 1-year prevalence rate of CD as 2% to 10%, consistent across diverse populations and higher among males than females. In a review of research regarding CD risk factors and characteristics, Murray and Farrington (2010) found that 6% to 16% of adolescent boys and 2% to 9% of adolescent girls met criteria for CD at any point in time. Incidence rates increase over time and peak during mid to late adolescence. Similarly, results of the National Comorbidity Survey Replication showed a lifetime prevalence of 12.0% of males and 7.1% of females; median age of onset was 11.6 years (Nock, Kazdin, Hiripi, & Kessler, 2006).

Authors of the *DSM-IV-TR* proposed that CD is part of a developmental pathway from ODD to CD to ASPD; although flawed in some ways, this hypothesis has been supported by numerous researchers (see Burke et al., 2010). Some evidence suggests that earlier onset of CD is associated with less favorable outcomes compared with late-onset CD. In addition, CD is strongly associated with future antisocial outcomes, with individuals who possess callous-unemotional traits of CD more likely to engage in serious and persistent criminal behavior (Pardini & Fite, 2010). Of particular concern to counselors is the fact that severity of CD symptoms is associated with the development of other mental health concerns including mood and substance use disorders (Nock et al., 2006).

CD has been linked to substance abuse, poverty, exposure to violence or traumatic events, and genetic and biological factors (Comer, 2013; Jiron, 2010; Weyandt et al., 2010). Neurobiological researchers have found that individuals who have CD may struggle to associate consequences and are less sensitive to punishment and reward compared with their peers, thus leading some individuals who have CD to respond less to traditional treatments that focus on connecting thoughts, feelings, and behaviors (Matthys, Vanderschuren, Schutter, & Lochman, 2012). A review of research revealed numerous risk factors for CD, including impulsivity, low IQ, low educational attainment, poor parental supervision, history of abuse, parental conflict, antisocial behavior by parents, low socioeconomic status, association with peers engaged in delinquent behavior, negative school environment, and negative community influences (Murray & Farrington, 2010).

When assessing for CD, counselors should inquire with multiple parties about clients' behavior; this is particularly important because individuals who have CD may lie or deceive others as part of their symptomatology or to avoid consequences of their behavior. Counselors should start by asking whether the client gets into trouble at home, in school, at work, or in the community. Once general concerns are identified, counselors may talk with clients, parents, and school officials to determine the likelihood that behavioral concerns meet criteria for CD.

Differential Diagnosis

Individuals who have CD may have remarkably similar diagnosis as individuals who qualify for an ASPD diagnosis. Indeed, diagnosis of CD prior to age 15 is one criterion of ASPD. Fortunately, only about one third of individuals who meet criteria for CD will go on to develop ASPD (Burke et al., 2010). When assessing for CD in an adult, counselors should consider ASPD as a primary differential diagnosis.

As noted previously in this chapter, counselors will also need to consider ADHD and other behavioral disorders when diagnosing CD. In addition, symptoms may be accounted for by DMDD or bipolar disorder. Individuals who have CD may also meet criteria for coexisting substance use disorders.

Coding, Recording, and Specifiers

There is only one general diagnostic code for CD: 312.8_ (F91._); the final digit within the code notes whether the client experienced *childhood-onset type* prior to age 10 years (312.81 [F91.1]), *adolescent-onset type* after age 10 years (312.82 [F91.2]), or *unspecified onset* (312.89 [F91.9]). Depending on the number and seriousness of specific symptoms, counselors must indicate whether the disorder is *mild*, *moderate*, or *severe*. There are no codes associated with these specifiers. Finally, the *DSM-5* includes a new *with limited prosocial emotions* specifier for those who have poorer prognosis as indicated by two or more of the following symptoms across time and setting: lack of remorse or guilt, callous–lack of empathy, unconcerned about performance, and shallow or deficient affect (APA, 2013a).

312.33 Pyromania (F63.1)

Nothing gave me a high like setting fires did. It started off small but eventually I needed to see something just burn and burn. I was sent to prison after the last fire, and that's where I was mandated to therapy. —Demitri

Essential Features

Pyromania, often referred to as "fire setting," occurs in approximately 1% of the population (Grant, Schreiber, & Odlaug, 2013). Identified as an obsessive-compulsive reaction in the first *DSM* (APA, 1952), pyromania today is more aptly defined as an impulse disorder "leading to fire setting without an identifiable motive other than taking pleasure in viewing fire and its effects" (Cermain & Lejoyeux, 2010, p. 255). The change in categorization is a result of conflicting information regarding the origin of the term *pyromania*. Some believe that it originated from the Greek words *fire* and *madness*, thus indicating a driving desire to set fires (i.e., an obsessive-compulsive behavior). Others argue that the origins are from the 19th-century term *monomania*, focusing more on a lack of impulse control (Doley, 2003). It is interesting that pyromania was not included in the *DSM-II* (APA, 1968) but reappeared in the *DSM-III* (APA, 1980) and *DSM-IV-TR* (APA, 2000) as part of the Impulse Control Disorders Not Elsewhere Classified chapter (APA, 2000; Cermain & Lejoyeux, 2010; Doley, 2003). In the *DSM-5*, this diagnosis is no longer part of Impulse Disorders Not Elsewhere Classified but instead has been included as an impulse-control disorder, along with kleptomania, within the Disruptive, Impulse-Control, and Conduct Disorders chapter. Readers should note there have been no conclusive studies linking pyromania to the obsessive-compulsive spectrum (Cermain & Lejoyeux, 2010).

Pyromania, typified by recurrent, purposeful fire-setting behaviors, is characterized by fascination and pleasure from starting or watching fires (APA, 2013a). Although it is not uncommon for people to find pleasure in setting fires, individuals with pyromania often experience intense arousal or tension leading up to the event and high levels of gratification after the fire begins (Cermain & Lejoyeux, 2010). The behavior is deliberate and purposeful, but without ill intention, such as in CD where the aim is to cause serious physical harm to others. Individuals diagnosed with pyromania will demonstrate fascination, curiosity, and attraction to everything related to fire (APA, 2013a). However, this focus is not due to an underlying motivation such as covering up a crime, protesting an injustice, or a psychotic delusion or hallucination.

Special Considerations

Fire starting typically begins in adolescence (Grant et al., 2013), and prevalence has been estimated between 2.4% and 3.5% (Cermain & Lejoyeux, 2010). In adolescents, fire setting is more common in males than in females (Soltys, 1992). Counselors should remember, however, that it is not unusual for children and adolescents to set fires experimentally. Fire starting as an essential feature of pyromania in children is rare (APA, 2013a; Cermain & Lejoyeux, 2010). In cases in which children or adolescents are not simply experimenting or motivated by boredom, counselors do need to act. Pyromania can become chronic over the life span and is associated with high rates of comorbidity with substance use disorders, affective disorders, and anxiety disorders (Cermain & Lejoyeux, 2010; Grant et al., 2013).

Among the general adult population, the lifetime prevalence for pyromania is 1%. Often associated with a wide range of antisocial behavior, individuals diagnosed with pyromania are more likely to be U.S.-born, Caucasian adult males between the ages of 18 to 35 (Vaughn et al., 2010). People living in the Western region of the United States had significantly higher instances of fire-setting behaviors than those living in the Northeast, Midwest, and South.

Counselors need to be aware of the potentially dangerous, even life-threatening, nature of this disorder. Fire setting results in hundreds of fatalities each year, with property losses estimated in the hundreds of millions annually (Vaughn et al., 2010). When engaging these clients in treatment, counselors should apply the *ACA Code of Ethics* (ACA, 2014), especially related to danger to others and duty to warn. In terms of screening, a pragmatic approach is best for pyromania. Counselors should directly ask the client about fire-starting behavior and inquire how many times the client has engaged in this behavior. Counselors should also carefully consider comorbid diagnoses.

As with most disruptive, impulse-control, and conduct disorders, treatment includes psychotherapeutic or psychopharmacological options (Cermain & Lejoyeux, 2010; Grant et al., 2013). Nonpharmacological options that have been established as effective are CBT, outpatient programs, and behavioral therapy. For children and adolescents, psychoeducation has often proved useful, as has collaboration with fire prevention communities and mental health agencies. There is also evidence to support multimodal interventions, including family treatment, individual psychotherapy, psychoeducation, and behavioral interventions (Cermain & Lejoyeux, 2010).

Cultural Considerations

Often associated with underdeveloped social skills and learning issues, pyromania presents in males (82%) much more than females (17%), often emerging between ages 12 and 14 (Dell'Osso, Altamura, Allen, Marazziti & Hollander, 2006; Vaughn et al., 2010). There is little research regarding pyromania within various cultures, although in a study of fire-setting behavior among the general U.S. population, Vaughn et al. (2010) found the prevalence of fire setting was higher among males and lower among African Americans and Hispanics.

Differential Diagnosis

According to the *DSM-5*, true instances of pyromania are very rare (APA, 2013a). Indeed, the APA reported that just 1.13% of the population reported experience with fire setting, and very few of those individuals would actually meet the additional criteria required for pyromania. Counselors working with individuals who set fires should consider whether the behavior was purposeful or accidental. In case of purposeful fire setting, more likely differential diagnoses include CD, ASPD, bipolar disorders, and schizophrenia spectrum and other psychotic disorders (APA, 2013a; Cermain & Lejoyeux, 2010; Vaughn et al., 2010). Counselors should also note that fire setting is strongly correlated with family dysfunction, a history of abuse, and school difficulties,

Coding, Recording, and Specifiers

There is only one diagnostic code for pyromania: 312.33 (F63.1); there are no specifiers associated with this disorder.

312.32 Kleptomania (F63.2)

It started out small. When I was in school, I picked up my friends' pencils. As I got older, I wanted to take things more and more. I would take the entire rack of sunglasses out of a department store. I was really good, until I got caught.—Sharon

Essential Features

Occurring 3 times as often in women as in men, kleptomania refers to continuous theft for pleasure rather than object obtainment or financial reasons (APA, 2013a). The term *kleptomania* originated in the 19th century with French psychiatrists Jean Dominique Etienne Esquirol and Charles Chretien Henry Marc, and cases have been noted in the literature as early as 1878 (Talih, 2011). Whereas this disorder was listed as not elsewhere classified in the *DSM-IV-TR*, it is a stand-alone diagnosis in the *DSM-5*.

Although the act of shoplifting is not uncommon, with as many as one out of 11 individuals shoplifting at some point in their lives (Grant, Odlaug, Davis & Kim, 2009), true kleptomania is very rare. According to the *DSM-5*, instances of kleptomania are highly uncommon, affecting just 0.3% to 0.6% of the population and just 4% to 24% of those who are arrested for shoplifting (APA, 2013a). In one study, only 0.38% of the college population actually met the criteria for this disorder (Odlaug & Grant, 2010).

The etiology of this disorder is not known; however, some theorize that it may be related to neurotransmitter systems, such as serotonergic, dopaminergic, and opioidergic (Grant, Odlaug, & Kim, 2010), or to serotonin levels in the brain (APA, 2013a). Theorists posit a strong correlation between this disorder and substance use disorders, arguing that they could be categorized together (Cermain & Lejoyeux, 2010; Vaughn et al., 2010). Moreover, individuals with this disorder do not typically present for treatment and may be secretive about their behavior because of shame or guilt. Some consequences of kleptomania include poor life quality, social impairment, employment issues, and increased risk of suicide (Kohn, 2006). High rates of incarceration are also associated with this disorder (Grant et al., 2009), and treatment is typically sought after legal action has occurred (Talih, 2011).

Like pyromania, kleptomania is characterized by recurrent, purposeful engagement in stealing for the pure pleasure of it. A sense of tension precedes initiation of the act (APA, 2013a). Unlike other acts of stealing in which there is a concrete or practical motivation for the act, the act itself is the reward in kleptomania. These individuals do not steal as a result of hallucinations or delusions or out of anger or revenge seeking (APA, 2013a).

Special Considerations

Because of the estimated 3:1 female-to-male ratio and lack of need associated with stealing, this disorder is often associated with White, middle- to upper-class women, and almost no data exist on culture or cultural implications (Kohn, 2006). The onset of kleptomania is typically in adolescence, and it can present with varying courses, including chronic, sporadic, and episodic (APA, 2013a). Believed by many to be underreported, kleptomania is usually shameful for the individual and is not talked about or typically addressed in counseling unless there is legal intervention. One clinical study involving individuals diagnosed with kleptomania demonstrated that 68.3% of these individuals had legal involvement, whereas 20.8% experienced incarceration as a result of stealing (Grant et al., 2009).

Although stealing typically begins in adolescence, it is more common for adults to present for treatment as a result of legal consequences (Talih, 2011). In terms of gender, women typically seek treatment around age 35 and men around age 50. As with pyromania, counselors should take a pragmatic approach when screening for kleptomania and should directly ask about theft and inquire how many times the client has engaged in this behavior. There have been few studies on the effectiveness of various treatments with this population, and most theorists base their treatment approaches on etiological beliefs about the disorder. Naltrexone (Grant, 2006) and mood stabilizers have been prescribed for treatment of kleptomania with some success, although they are not indicated for the disorder. Furthermore, CBT and behavioral treatments have been used with some success (Kohn, 2006).

Differential Diagnosis

When working with individuals who are involved in shoplifting, counselors may consider more likely differential diagnoses such as ordinary theft, neurodevelopmental or neurocognitive impairments, CD, ASPD, and manic episodes. Moreover, high comorbidity with many disorders, including substance use disorders (Grant et al., 2009), depressive and bipolar disorders, personality disorders, CD, and other impulse-control disorders, have been noted in the literature (APA, 2013a; Talih, 2011).

Coding, Recording, and Specifiers

There is only one diagnostic code for kleptomania: 312.32 (F63.2); there are no specifiers associated with this disorder. Counselors should note that the original *DSM-5* mistakenly published the code 312.32 (F63.**3**) for kleptomania. This is incorrect, and the code of F63.**2** should be used.

Chapter 11

Specific Behavioral Disruptions

The disorders covered in this chapter are divided into five sections: feeding and eating disorders, elimination disorders, sleep-wake disorder, sexual dysfunctions, and paraphilic disorders. These disorders have been grouped together because they all evidence similar patterns of behavioral disruption. Whereas minor changes have been made to the location of elimination disorders in the *DSM-5*, major changes have been made to feeding and eating disorders, with the revision of diagnostic criteria in anorexia nervosa and bulimia nervosa and the recognition of binge-eating disorder (APA, 2013b) as well as the addition of pica, rumination, and avoidant/restrictive food intake disorder to the section. Because of the desire to enhance the clinical utility, validity, and reliability of the diagnoses and minimize the use of the NOS category, sleep-wake disorders underwent sweeping changes in the *DSM-5*. Insomnia became a stand-alone diagnosis, the subdivision of insomnia into primary and secondary was eliminated (Tucker, 2012), and sleep disorder due to a general medical condition and sleep disorder due to another mental illness were removed (Reynolds & Redline, 2010).

Whereas minor changes were made to paraphilias, with minimal name changes and two new specifiers added, one radical change to the *DSM-5* was the addition of a Sexual Dysfunctions chapter that addresses disturbances in sexual desire or problems related to physiological sexual functioning that were previously included in the Sexual and Gender Identity Disorders chapter of the *DSM-IV-TR*. Furthermore, this chapter includes a paradigm shift in the understanding of sexual arousal and sexual response patterns, more specific criteria than previously given, and a 6-month duration requirement (APA, 2013a).

Feeding and Eating Disorders

Feeding Disorders: Essential Features

Feeding disorders in infants and young children are complex and include pica, rumination disorder, and avoidant/restrictive food intake disorder. For there to be successful feeding, there needs to be an interaction between the child and the caregiver, and maternal psychopathology is a factor in a child developing feeding difficulties (Micali, Simonoff,

Stahl, & Treasure, 2011). Additionally, a child's temperament has been related to feeding difficulties (Lindberg, Bohlin, Hagekull, & Thunström, 1994). Like eating disorders, feeding disorders are often characterized by some type of avoiding or restricting food intake; however, feeding disorders typically manifest in early childhood rather than adolescence (Bryant-Waugh, Markham, Kreipe, & Walsh, 2010). Feeding disorders and short-term feeding issues may present similarly at first. Thus, counselors should pay close attention to diagnostic criteria so they may more accurately differentiate between developmentally appropriate behavior (e.g., a child being a "picky eater") and disordered eating (e.g., a child steering clear of events that entail eating). Prevalence rates for feeding disorders are not clearly identified (Bryant-Waugh et al., 2010).

Eating Disorders: Essential Features

Similar to feeding disorders in infants and young children, eating disorders in adolescents and adults are complex in nature and have a significant, daily impact for those who experience them. An eating disorder is an illness that negatively affects an individual's diet. This can range from eating small amounts of food or nothing at all to eating extremely large amounts of food (NIMH, 2013). Eating disorders can be detrimental to one's physical health, emotional well-being, and interpersonal relationships. Some counselors may struggle to comprehend how eating disorders develop. Given that they can present in a number of ways across age, race, and ethnicity, eating disorders can pose challenges for any mental health professional (Roman & Reay, 2009). Eating disorders covered in this chapter include anorexia nervosa, bulimia nervosa, and binge-eating disorder.

Almost 20 million women and 10 million men have suffered from some kind of eating disorder in their lives (Wade, Keski-Rahkonen, & Hudson, 2011). As high as these figures are, there are many individuals who have eating disorders or are at risk for them but do not seek treatment. The rates of eating disorder cases have increased since the 1950s (Striegel-Moore & Franko, 2003; Wade et al., 2011).

Prevalence rates for eating disorders vary considerably. Over a 12-month period, the prevalence rate of anorexia nervosa is approximately 0.4% among the general population, whereas the prevalence of bulimia nervosa is 1.0% to 1.5% (APA, 2013a). According to the *DSM-5*, the 12-month prevalence of binge-eating disorder is 1.6% among U.S. adult females and 0.8% among U.S. adult males. A study using proposed *DSM-5* criteria for eating disorders revealed the following prevalence rates: 0.8% for anorexia nervosa, 2.6% for bulimia nervosa, and 3.0% for binge-eating disorder (Stice, Marti, & Rohde, 2013). As detailed in the section regarding Major Changes From *DSM-IV-TR* to *DSM-5* (see below), increased prevalence rates are the result of a general lowering of diagnostic thresholds for eating disorders.

Adolescence is the period of greatest risk for developing an eating disorder (Striegel-Moore & Bulik, 2007). However, concerns about body shape, image, and weight that underlie eating disorder processes may begin much younger; 40% to 60% of elementary school girls (ages 6–12) expressed concern about weight or becoming fat (Smolak, 2011). Girls in this age range are forming their self-concepts and may be readily influenced by direct and indirect messages from parents and peers (Linville, Stice, Gau, & O'Neil, 2011). Eating disorders can develop in individuals during the college years and into adulthood as well (Schwitzer, 2012). Estimates of prevalence rates for college students with eating disorders range from 8% to 17% (Eisenberg, Nicklett, Roeder, & Kirz, 2011; Prouty, Protinsky, & Canady, 2002). Although eating disorders are typically prevalent in females, males can also be at risk. Typically, men with eating disorders are more interested in making their bodies more muscular and larger as opposed to women, who are more focused on maintaining a smaller-sized body (Ousley, Cordero, & White, 2008).

Although many feeding and eating disorders have similar psychological and behavioral features, with the exception of pica, only one diagnosis can be given. Diagnostic criteria for the disorders are mutually exclusive, meaning it is not possible to have both binge-eating disorder and bulimia. This ensures differentiation of each disorder and helps counselors target treatment planning and outcome management to unique characteristics of the disorders (APA, 2013a).

Note

Disorders in this section will sometimes resemble substance use disorders (APA, 2013a). For example, symptoms such as craving and compulsive usage are typical to both diagnostic categories. This is because eating and substance use disorders involve the same neural systems that control self-regulation and reward. More research is needed regarding commonalities between development and treatment of eating disorders and substance abuse; however, cognitive-behavioral interventions appear to be effective in the treatment of both eating and substance use disorders.

◆ ◆ ◆

Major Changes From *DSM-IV-TR* to *DSM-5*

The *DSM-5* contains changes in diagnostic criteria and the inclusion of additional disorders from the *DSM-IV-TR*. These changes provide a more representative look at clients' behaviors and symptoms as they deal with these conditions throughout the life span. Some of the more significant changes made by the DSM-5 Eating Disorders Work Group include the revision of diagnostic criteria in anorexia nervosa and bulimia nervosa as well as the recognition of binge-eating disorder (APA, 2013b).

In addition, the following disorders have been added to the Feeding and Eating Disorders chapter: pica, rumination, and avoidant/restrictive food intake disorder. These three disorders were listed in the *DSM-IV-TR* under Disorders Usually First Diagnosed in Infancy, Childhood, or Adolescence; that section has been eliminated in the *DSM-5* (APA, 2013b). Although these three disorders have been moved to the Feeding and Eating Disorders chapter, individuals who seek treatment for pica, rumination disorder, or avoidant/restrictive food intake disorder are more likely to present to a medical clinic as opposed to a mental health clinic (Berg & Peterson, 2013).

Eating disorder NOS was renamed to other specified feeding and eating disorder and unspecified feeding and eating disorder (APA, 2013a). Studies have shown that many individuals being treated for an eating disorder have previously been categorized as eating disorder NOS because, although they display some symptoms of an eating disorder, these individuals did not meet stringent requirements for either anorexia nervosa or bulimia nervosa (Hebebrand & Bulik, 2011; Sysko & Walsh, 2011). By broadening diagnostic criteria for both anorexia nervosa and bulimia nervosa, it is hoped instances of other specified and unspecified feeding and eating disorders will be reduced (Berg & Peterson, 2013; Fairburn & Cooper, 2011). For example, the *DSM-5* criteria reduced the frequency of binge eating from a minimum of twice a week in the *DSM-IV-TR* to once a week. Although critics report instances of diagnostic inflation in the *DSM-5* (Frances, 2013), under the *DSM-IV-TR* criteria at least 50% of clients seen for eating disorders were diagnosed with eating disorder NOS (Fairburn & Cooper, 2011).

Differential Diagnosis

Feeding and eating disorders can present in many different ways. It is important first to understand whether the behavior and accompanying symptoms can be better explained by another medical or psychiatric condition. For all eating disorders, it is important to look at the following variables: weight status, fear of weight gain, dietary restriction, overevaluation of shape and weight, body image disturbance, presence and frequency of binge eating, and presence and frequency of compensatory behaviors (Berg & Peterson, 2013). Although popular culture links anorexia nervosa to restricted eating and bulimia nervosa to binge-purge behavior, both disorders include mention of restriction and compensatory behaviors. Careful assessment regarding disorder processes, underlying thought patterns, and impairments will help counselors identify the eating disorder that best fits the client's experience.

Many individuals who have an eating disorder also have additional pathological behaviors and psychological symptoms. These symptoms include depression, anxiety, substance use, and personality disorders (Choate, 2010; Eisenberg et al., 2011; Kaye, Klump, Frank, & Strober, 2000). In addition, changes in appetite and eating are characteristic of depressive and anxiety disorders, and screening for mood disorders should also be a part of any screening process for eating disorders. In some instances, it might be beneficial for individuals to seek treatment for co-occurring mental health or substance abuse concerns before treatment for the eating disorder (Berg, Peterson, & Frazier, 2012). This way, the client will be able to better manage the symptoms for other co-occurring disorders before working on symptoms and behaviors that are a part of the eating disorder.

Etiology for Feeding Disorders

Feeding difficulties are fairly common among infants and children, and not all difficulties will manifest into feeding disorders (Kerwin, Eicher, & Gelsinger, 2005). However, it is important to make note of such difficulties and use treatment to prevent them from turning into a disorder. Feeding disorders often have different medical and developmental etiologies that call for various interventions (Bryant-Waugh et al., 2010).

It may be difficult to notice if a child has a feeding disorder because the child may still gain weight and not have any medical conditions while symptoms and behaviors of the disorder occur. These children are often seen in different settings and by both medical and mental health professionals. Because there is an overlap of physical and psychological problems, professionals may struggle to determine the cause and effect of feeding disorders (Bryant-Waugh et al., 2010).

As with treatment of other childhood concerns, feeding disorders need to be addressed from a variety of contexts. Counselors should consider characteristics of both the child and caregivers interdependently as opposed to separately (Bryant-Waugh et al., 2010). More detailed assessments may give better insight to the origin of these problems alongside other emotional and behavioral symptoms. It is also important to look at maternal factors and characteristics when examining the etiology of feeding disorders (Maldonado-Duran et al., 2008), especially given the finding that maternal anxiety, depression, and active eating disorder symptomatology in pregnancy predicted feeding difficulties (Micali et al., 2011).

Temperament may also play a role in whether a child has feeding difficulties or disorders. Lucarelli, Cimino, D'Olimpio, and Ammaniti (2012) found that many of the children in their sample were identified as having a difficult temperament. The children displayed some aggressive behavior, including angry moods and temper tantrums, and mothers in the study had higher levels of anxiety and obsessive-compulsive symptoms.

Etiology for Eating Disorders

Disordered eating can be caused by a number of genetic, biological, behavioral, psychological, and social factors (NIMH, 2013). Many times, etiology of eating disorders is seen as black-and-white in that there are either biological or cultural influences that cause these disorders without taking into account possible linkage between other factors (Striegel-Moore & Bulik, 2007). Although some researchers emphasize cultural considerations within eating disorders, it is difficult to determine how much of a role one's culture plays in the development. There is not one specific factor that causes eating disorders, and multiple causal factors may influence each other to differing degrees. These interactions between the different factors, for example, genetic factors interacting with social–cultural influences such as media images, may work in shaping the onset and maintenance of eating disorders (Smolak & Chun-Kennedy, 2013). It is important to look at eating disorders holistically.

Sociocultural models of eating disorders have placed more focus on the extreme thinness and objectification of women. This emphasis on "Western" culture's beauty ideals is considered a risk factor for developing an eating disorder (Striegel-Moore & Bulik, 2007). The mainstream media tends to view anorexia nervosa as a disorder that is caused more in part from viewing thin-ideal media images (Crisafulli, Von Holle, & Bulik, 2008); however, many individuals are exposed to these sociocultural images, and not all of them develop eating disorders. Therefore, the causes and development of eating disorders need to be addressed from a holistic standpoint.

Core features of eating disorders include body image disturbance, control in eating, and exhibiting behaviors to control weight (Striegel-Moore & Bulik, 2007). The body image disturbance can lead to internalizing the thin ideal and can lead one to put greater value on being thin. An individual may then control food consumption by restricting calories. However, if the thin ideal is internalized by someone who is at risk for bulimia nervosa or binge-eating disorder, the individual may lose control over the amount of food consumed.

Treatment of Feeding and Eating Disorders

Complex etiologies of the feeding and eating disorders can make their treatment difficult and multifaceted. Treatment varies based on the disorder as well as the individual presentation of the client but should include attention to physical, behavioral, and emotional health (Roman & Reay, 2009). The disorders are also treated at different levels of care ranging from outpatient to inpatient and residential (Berg et al., 2012). This depends on the level of severity at time of presentation.

Different approaches look at the importance of the therapeutic relationship in treating eating disorders. Oftentimes, clients need to feel a sense of security before beginning the therapeutic process (Ross & Green, 2011). Eating disorders generally isolate a client because many of the behaviors are usually secretive, not discussed, and done in private; therefore, an individual may be reluctant to see a therapist. It is also common for individuals with eating disorders to refuse treatment (Allen, Fursland, Watson, & Byrne, 2011). Typically, this is due to denial or difficulty understanding the need for treatment. Counselors treating clients with eating disorders need to work with the client to develop a therapeutic alliance and help the client understand why treatment may be appropriate.

DBT has been used to treat various eating disorders. DBT is often an effective treatment for individuals who have tried other methods but have been unsuccessful. Using DBT may work with individuals who are ambivalent to change as well as those who present as rigid and perfectionistic. This type of therapy helps individuals see that they can act on their own behalf (Federici, Wisniewski, & Ben-Porath, 2012). In addition to DBT, CBT and interpersonal psychotherapy (IPT) may be effective for the treatment of eating disorders (Murphy, Straebler, Cooper, & Fairburn, 2010). Mental health professionals posit that CBT may be a good match for individuals who experience bulimia and anorexia, whereas IPT may be particularly effective for those battling binge eating (Wilson, Wilfley, Agras, & Bryson, 2010).

Implications for Counselors

Given the high prevalence rates of eating and feeding disorders, it is likely that counselors will encounter clients with eating disorders and disordered eating (APA, 2013a; Hudson, Hiripi, Pope, & Kessler, 2007). Counselors should be particularly concerned with mortality rates of eating disorders: 4% for anorexia nervosa, 3.9% for bulimia nervosa, and 5.2% for eating disorder NOS (Crow et al., 2009). Given the medical consequences of these behaviors, it is essential that counselors collaborate with medical professionals. Furthermore, because eating disorders are complex in both etiology and treatment, counselors will likely collaborate with physicians, dietitians, psychiatrists, and other medical professionals as needed to provide the best possible treatment (Berg & Peterson, 2013). Although there is no one cause of eating disorders, it is necessary that they be looked at from a variety of perspectives, including attention to social and cultural influences that may have facilitated the rise of body image disturbance and eating disorders over the years (Striegel-Moore & Franko, 2003; Wade et al., 2011).

Proper assessment is necessary for accurate identification of individuals with eating disorders (Berg & Peterson, 2013) and selection of effective treatment plans (APA, 2013b). Individuals who are at a normal weight or have not experienced major weight changes may still experience eating disorders or be at risk for developing an eating disorder. Therefore, it is important for counselors to screen for eating disorders even among individuals who appear to be at a normal weight. Asking general questions about various behaviors in terms of self-care can help counselors get a better idea whether an individual might be at risk for an eating disorder (Berg et al., 2012).

Counselors should be aware that individuals with eating disorders are more likely to have other co-occurring psychiatric symptoms. These individuals are at increased risk for suicide and self-injury. Counselors need to be aware of these risks and should take extra time to conduct a thorough suicide risk assessment (Berg et al., 2012). Individuals with anorexia nervosa and bulimia nervosa often deal with low self-esteem, low self-concept, depression, and anxiety (Blank & Latzer, 2004; Cooley & Toray, 2001; Kaye et al., 2000). The assessments used should also incorporate screening questions pertaining to self-esteem (Berg et al., 2012).

Adolescents and adults may experience eating disorders in different ways, including the internalization of maternal messages and communication to be thin, social and peer group comparisons, and birth order issues. It is important for counselors to take these into consideration when evaluating their clients and developing treatment plans (Fisher, Schneider, Burns, Symons, & Mandel, 2001). Because eating disorders are complex and may often involve medical issues, it is also important that counselors develop working relationships with medical providers (Berg et al., 2012).

Individuals who have eating disorders may experience stigma and blame by people who do not understand why they cannot manage their eating behaviors. A study found that those in the general public who were given information on the biological and genetic factors of anorexia nervosa did not blame individuals with the disorder as much as those who were provided information regarding how sociocultural factors can lead to the disorder (Crisafulli et al., 2008).

To help readers better understand changes from the *DSM-IV-TR* to the *DSM-5*, the following sections outline each disorder within the Feeding and Eating Disorders chapter of the *DSM-5*. Readers should note that we have focused on major changes from the *DSM-IV-TR* to the *DSM-5*; however, this is not a stand-alone resource for diagnosis. Although a summary and special considerations for counselors are provided for each disorder, counselors need to reference the *DSM-5* directly when considering a diagnosis. It is essential that counselors understand diagnostic criteria and features, subtypes and specifiers (if applicable), prevalence, course, and risk and prognostic factors for each disorder prior to diagnosis.

Specific Feeding Disorders

307.52 Pica (F98.3 Children; F50.8 Adults)

Essential Features

Pica is a feeding disorder that is characterized by the repetitive eating of nonnutritive, nonfood substances including, dirt, paper, and paint (Shisslak, Swain, & Crago, 1987; Stiegler, 2005). Pica is a common diagnosis in individuals with intellectual disabilities (Danford & Huber, 1982). Individuals with pica may develop serious health problems, including lead poisoning and intestinal blockages (Wiley, Henretig, & Selbst, 1992). Understanding pica can be complex because there is not a single etiology for the disorder (Stiegler, 2005). There were no significant changes to the diagnostic criteria for pica in the *DSM-5*, but the disorder was moved from the Disorders Usually First Diagnosed in Infancy, Childhood, or Adolescence chapter in the *DSM-IV-TR* to the Feeding and Eating Disorders chapter in the *DSM-5*.

An essential feature of pica is eating nonnutritive, nonfood substances for a period of at least 1 month (APA, 2013a). These consumed substances do not aid in the development of the individual. The minimum age for diagnosis is recommended to be 2 years so the developmentally normal practice of mouthing objects is excluded (Stiegler, 2005). It is important to recognize that the consumption is also not part of a cultural or social practice. If pica is present in conjunction with another mental disorder or medical condition, counselors should diagnose pica only if it requires additional clinical attention (APA, 2013a).

Special Considerations

The prevalence of pica is not clear, although it does seem to occur at a higher rate in individuals with intellectual disability and increases with the severity of the condition (APA, 2013a). Because of its self-injurious nature, pica has been known to lead to death in individuals with developmental disabilities (D. E. Williams & McAdam, 2012). Although pica can be diagnosed in otherwise normally developing children, adults who are diagnosed with it typically have an intellectual disability or other mental disorder (APA, 2013a). Pica is also common among children diagnosed with pervasive developmental disorders (Kerwin et al., 2005).

Although feeding disorders are typically seen in medical settings, therapeutic approaches such as CBT have been found effective for treating pica. Typically used in conjunction with parental involvement, strategies such as self-monitoring, behavioral experiments, and cognitive restructuring have yielded successful treatment outcomes (Bryant-Waugh, 2013). In milder cases of pica, behavioral interventions such as positive reinforcement and overcorrection have reduced symptoms (D. E. Williams & McAdam, 2012). Whatever the course of treatment, less restrictive interventions should be applied first (Kerwin & Berkowitz, 1996). In treating pica, however, counselors need to understand how complex the disorder is, because these complexities may lead to different treatment approaches. For example, food aversion has been effective in reducing ingestion of nonnutritive, nonfood substances, but counselors must be competent in using aversion techniques as well as knowing which clients are suited to this type of treatment approach (Ferreri, Tamm, & Wier, 2006).

In terms of cultural considerations, there are some populations for which eating dirt or other nonnutritive substances has spiritual, cultural, or other social value. If the behavior of eating such substances is due to one of these practices, a diagnosis of pica would not be applicable (APA, 2013a). Pathological pica behavior can be seen across cultural, regional, and socioeconomic boundaries (Stiegler, 2005), and the prevalence of pica eating varies widely across diverse social and clinical contexts (Hartmann, Becker, Hampton, & Bryant-Waugh, 2012). In some school-age populations, eating nonfood substances has been reported as a result of medical conditions, such as iron deficiencies (Moore & Sears, 1994). More research is needed to examine the influence of culture on pica in children and adults (Kerwin & Berkowitz, 1996).

Differential Diagnosis

Common differential diagnoses for pica include anorexia nervosa, factitious disorder, and nonsuicidal self-injurious behaviors in personality disorders (APA, 2013a). Pica may also be a symptom in individuals who have a developmental disability or other pervasive developmental disorders (Bryant-Waugh et al., 2010). Pica can also be related to medical conditions. One study found that 33% of children being treated for sickle cell anemia had pica symptoms (Ivascu et al., 2001).

Coding, Recording, and Specifiers

The diagnostic code for pica is 307.52 (F98.3) for children and 307.52 (F50.8) for adults. The *ICD-9-CM* code for pica is 307.52 and is used for children or adults. If, after the full criteria have been met for the disorder, the diagnostic criteria have not been met for a sustained period of time, a person can be considered *in remission* (APA, 2013a). Although the *DSM-5* does not indicate a specific duration for this specifier, counselors can assume that an individual must consistently not ingest any nonnutritive, nonfood substance for at least 1 month.

307.53 Rumination Disorder (F98.21)

Essential Features

Rumination disorder is a feeding disorder that involves repetitive regurgitation of swallowed or partially digested food. The individual may then rechew, reswallow, or spit out the food. Although the disorder is typically found in children, it occurs across age ranges and can develop in healthy adolescents (Schroedl, Alioto, & DiLorenzo, 2013). Rumination disorder occurs most often in infants within the 1st or 2nd year of life. However, it has been known to develop at a later age in individuals with intellectual disabilities. Adults with rumination disorder are more likely to swallow and regurgitate or spit out the food (Bryant-Waugh et al., 2010). When assessing for rumination disorder in infants, it is necessary to look at the length of time between feedings and rumination once the infant begins regurgitating (Franco, Campbell, Tamburrino, & Evans, 1993). More research needs to be conducted to determine if individuals with rumination disorder are more likely to develop an eating disorder later in life (Franco et al., 1993). The only major change to this disorder was moving it from the Disorders Usually First Diagnosed in Infancy, Childhood, and Adolescence chapter in the *DSM-IV-TR* to the Feeding and Eating Disorders chapters in the *DSM-5*.

One of the essential features of rumination disorder is the repeated regurgitation of food. This regurgitation must occur over a period of at least 1 month. The regurgitation occurs frequently, often daily, and at least several times per week. The symptoms should not occur during any other episodes of a different feeding or eating disorder. Symptoms may occur during another mental disorder; however, for a rumination disorder diagnosis, these symptoms should be a main aspect of the presenting issue (APA, 2013a).

Special Considerations

The prevalence for rumination disorder is unclear; however, this disorder is more common among individuals with intellectual disabilities (APA, 2013a). Adults with rumination disorder are less likely to talk about their behaviors with others because they see it as very secretive (Eckern, Stevens, & Mitchell, 1999). It has been pointed out that this is a rare and infrequently identified disorder (Franco et al., 1993; Hartmann et al., 2012). This is likely due to the wide range of clinical terms used to describe rumination, confusion about whether the individual's behavior is voluntary or involuntary, and the fact this behavior typically occurs in private (Hartmann et al., 2012). Because many counselors fail to ask about rumination behaviors, rumination disorder may go undetected. Many professionals may also struggle to determine the clinical boundary between regurgitation and self-induced vomiting among adolescents and adults.

Research does not indicate one specific medical or mental health-based treatment approach to treating rumination disorder. Different behavioral techniques may help lessen symptoms. One treatment method that seems to be effective in infants with rumination disorder is intense nurturing. In older individuals, counselors have found cognitive techniques beneficial in improving self-control. Although interventions do not totally disrupt the behavior, they do offer individuals an improved quality of life and enhanced functioning (Schroedl et al., 2013).

Because rumination disorder is rare, it is difficult to assess cultural considerations. However, research shows that the disorder dates back as early as the 17th century and cuts across social classes (Parry-Jones, 1994). As the world became more industrialized in later centuries, the disorder occurred less and tended to be typically present in settings where there was not enough social and environmental stimulation (Parry-Jones, 1994).

Differential Diagnosis

Common differential diagnoses for rumination disorder include gastrointestinal conditions, anorexia nervosa, and bulimia nervosa (APA, 2013a). Observable behaviors such as tongue thrusting and putting hands in the individual's mouth are still used in determining if one has rumination disorder or if the behaviors are because of other physiological issues (Kerwin & Berkowitz, 1996).

Coding, Recording, and Specifiers

There is only one diagnostic code for rumination disorder: 307.53 (F98.21). It should be specified if the disorder is *in remission*. It is in remission if, after the full criteria were met, the diagnostic criteria have not been met for a sustained period of time (APA, 2013a). As with pica, the *DSM-5* does not clarify duration for this specifier. Counselors should ensure that an individual must consistently not regurgitate or rechew food for at least 1 month.

307.59 Avoidant/Restrictive Food Intake Disorder (F50.8)

Essential Features

Avoidant/restrictive food intake disorder is a feeding condition that typically occurs in middle childhood. As the name implies, this disorder occurs when a child evades or severely limits his or her intake of food. Parents may struggle to notice avoidant or restrictive food processes if children do not have visible weight loss or growth impairment (Bryant-Waugh et al., 2010). Moreover, atypical eating behaviors and disturbances are common in young children (Equit, Palmke, Becker, Moritz, & Becker, 2012), and differentiating between developmentally appropriate behavior and disordered eating behavior is challenging for parents, guardians, or caretakers. One difference between atypical eating behaviors and avoidant/restrictive food intake disorder is that individuals with the disorder are likely to have little interest in eating (Equit et al., 2012).

Core symptoms of restrictive eating and food refusal are avoidance of certain foods, unwillingness to try new foods and only eating certain foods, and consumption of smaller than normal amounts of food as well as the complete refusal of food (Equit et al., 2012). The only major change to this disorder was moving it from the Disorders Usually First Diagnosed in Infancy, Childhood, and Adolescence chapter in the *DSM-IV-TR* to the Feeding and Eating Disorders chapters in the *DSM-5*.

An essential feature of this disorder is avoiding or restricting food intake that leads to persistent failure to meet necessary nutritional needs. The eating disturbance does not occur during the course of anorexia nervosa or bulimia nervosa. There is no disturbance of an individual's body weight or shape (APA, 2013a). The food restriction can be related to a lack of interest in food or eating, avoidance of food for sensory reasons, and avoidance because of feared consequences of eating (Bryant-Waugh, 2013).

Special Considerations

Although this disorder is typically more common in children than adults, there could be a delay between the onset and when it actually presents (APA, 2013a). This disorder can sometimes be confused with other feeding or eating disorders; however, individuals with this disorder do not express concern with weight or body shape (Bryant-Waugh et al., 2010).

Although feeding disorders are typically seen in medical settings, therapeutic approaches such as CBT have been found effective for treating avoidant/restrictive food intake disorder. Typically used in conjunction with parental involvement, strategies such as self-monitoring, behavioral experiments, and cognitive restructuring have yielded successful treatment outcomes (Bryant-Waugh, 2013).

In terms of cultural considerations, it is necessary to make sure that the food disturbance is not part of a culturally approved ritual (APA, 2013a). If it is part of a culturally approved ritual, it would not be considered avoidant/restrictive food intake disorder.

Differential Diagnosis

Common differential diagnoses for avoidant/restrictive food intake disorder are medical conditions including but not limited to gastrointestinal disease and food allergies, specific neurological or congenital disorders, RAD, ASD, specific phobias or anxiety disorders, anorexia nervosa, OCD, MDD, schizophrenia spectrum disorder, and factitious disorder (APA, 2013a). Moving this disorder to the Feeding and Eating Disorders chapter allows it to be looked at across age ranges. Additionally, this disorder has a range of symptoms and presentations, which can make it difficult to diagnosis (Bryant-Waugh, 2013). Selective and restrictive eating behaviors may be associated with anxiety and oppositional symptoms. Equit et al. (2012) found that children who exhibited these restrictive and selective eating behaviors were likely to externalize oppositional symptoms and internalize anxiety symptoms.

Coding, Recording, and Specifiers

There is only one diagnostic code for avoidant/restrictive food intake disorder: 307.59 (F50.8). It should be specified if the disorder is *in remission*. It is in remission if after the full criteria were met, the diagnostic criteria have not been met for a sustained period of time (APA, 2013a). Similar to other disorders in this section, the *DSM-5* does not clarify a specific duration for the *in remission* specifier. Because of the diagnostic criteria for this disorder, counselors can assume that individuals in remission are free of symptoms and have restored all related adverse health effects, such as weight loss and nutritional deficiencies; no longer require enteral feeding or oral nutritional supplements; and have marked improvements in psychosocial functioning.

Specific Eating Disorders

307.1 Anorexia Nervosa (F50.0_)

Essential Features

People with anorexia nervosa often view themselves as being overweight, even if they are visibly underweight. They weigh themselves repetitively, and what they eat and how much they weigh often become obsessions (Kaye et al., 2000; NIMH, 2013). The average age of onset is 19 years (Hudson et al., 2007). Common symptoms of anorexia nervosa include extreme thinness, an unwillingness to maintain a healthy body weight, restricted eating, and disordered body image (NIMH, 2013). Common risk factors for anorexia include gender, ethnicity, socioeconomic status, and psychosocial factors (Lindberg & Hjem, 2003).

Essential features of anorexia nervosa include energy intake restriction, significantly low weight, and an intense fear of becoming fat. In addition, an individual experiences a disturbance based on his or her body weight or shape (APA, 2013a). Predictors of anorexia nervosa include history of eating disorder, sexual problems, and co-occurring disorders (Fichter, Quadflieg, & Hedlund, 2006). Counselors should note that an increased risk is present for clients who have biological relatives who have been diagnosed with anorexia, particularly the binge-eating/purging type (APA, 2013a). Other genetic risk factors include having biological relatives with a history of bipolar or depressive disorders. Children who displayed anxiety or obsessive-compulsive behavior also have a higher risk of developing anorexia nervosa. Finally, environments in which thinness is valued, including occupations or vocational activities such as modeling or sports, are associated with higher rates of anorexia nervosa.

Counselors should not underestimate the seriousness of anorexia nervosa. This disorder has one of the highest mortality rates among all psychiatric disorders (Harris & Barraclough, 1998). Although rates may vary on the basis of how the death is reported (e.g., heart failure, malnutrition), there is an estimated 4% mortality rate for anorexia nervosa (Crow et al., 2009).

Major Changes From *DSM-IV-TR* to *DSM-5*

In the *DSM-IV-TR*, 85% of one's ideal body weight was considered a minimally normal body weight (APA, 2000). However, the DSM-5 Eating Disorders Work Group eliminated this criterion and replaced it with a calculation of body mass index (BMI) and the requirement that an individual be at "significantly low weight . . . defined as a weight that is less than minimally normal or, for children and adolescents, less than minimally expected" (APA, 2013a, p. 338). Individuals who deny having an intense fear of gaining weight will still meet the criterion if they engage in behaviors such as fasting or excessive exercising to prevent or avoid weight gain. The *DSM-IV-TR* criterion of amenorrhea, or the loss of menstrual cycle, is not included in the *DSM-5* (APA, 2013a). However, it is still important to recognize if a girl or woman no longer has a menstrual cycle, as this could be a factor in determining if she is of significantly low weight (Berg & Peterson, 2013).

Special Considerations

The prevalence rate for women with anorexia nervosa ranges from 0.4% to 0.9% (APA, 2013; Hudson et al., 2007). Less is known about prevalence for men with anorexia nervosa, although the rate for lifetime prevalence has been reported at 0.3% (Hudson et al., 2007). The behaviors can keep the individual in a starved state and prevent the transition to more normal functioning in terms of eating and psychological functioning (Hebebrand & Bulik, 2011). Furthermore, some researchers speculate that the lifetime prevalence of eating disorders could increase dramatically under the *DSM-5* because of the relaxed criteria, with estimates around 2.9% for women and 3% for men (Hudson, Coit, Lalonde, & Pope, 2012).

Approximately 33.8% of those with anorexia nervosa are receiving treatment (Hudson et al., 2007). However, the results in treatment can fluctuate over time (Fichter et al., 2006). Over the course of a 12-year study, Fichter et al. (2006) found that there was improvement during therapy, then a decline during the first 2 years after therapy, but more improvement and stabilization during Years 3 to 12. This is important because it shows that the treatment process for anorexia can be a lengthy one. Counselors may wish to incorporate client education regarding the peaks and valleys of the recovery process into treatment.

As stated previously, the 85% ideal body weight criterion was eliminated in the *DSM-5*. This means that counselors will now have to use more clinical judgment to determine whether an individual is considered underweight based on the significantly low weight criterion (Berg & Peterson, 2013). However, the cutoff between a healthy and harmful weight is not drastic and, despite the change from weight to BMI, cannot be defined by a specific number (Hebebrand & Bulik, 2011). Counselors who work with clients who have eating disorders need to be fully aware of risk factors, including previous treatment for an eating disorder, and consult with others when necessary. Individuals who have been treated for, and have recovered from, anorexia nervosa may still display some eating disorder symptoms such as drive for thinness; however, the symptoms are not as strong following recovery (Kaye et al., 2000). Additionally, these individuals are often fixated on their weight. An important therapeutic goal might be to focus more on a healthy weight range because weight often fluctuates (Hebebrand & Bulik, 2011).

According to the NIMH (2013), there are three components in treating anorexia nervosa: (a) restoring the individual to a healthy weight, (b) treating the psychological issues related to the eating disorder, and (c) reducing or eliminating behaviors or thoughts that lead to the eating issue and preventing relapse. CBT is often used in treating clients with anorexia nervosa. Brown, Mountford, and Waller (2013) examined therapeutic alliance and weight gain in clients with anorexia nervosa and found that clients can still experience weight gain despite a therapeutic alliance between the therapist and client. However, the CBT approach could be more effective if the counselor focused more on eating and weight gain issues instead of depending on the therapeutic alliance to bring about the change.

Individuals with anorexia nervosa may experience cognitive inflexibility whereby they are fixated on certain rules about eating. This can also lead to rigid thinking about the disorder. Cognitive remediation therapy helps the client think about the disorder in a broad manner and more holistically as opposed to focusing only on weight or shape (Tchanturia, Lloyd, & Lang, 2013). This type of therapy is newer, and more research needs to be done to determine its effectiveness.

Family-based treatments may also help individuals with anorexia (Chavez & Insel, 2007). These types of treatments may be more beneficial when treating adolescents, although there still needs to be more research done to determine the full effect. Counselors may face some barriers when working with families. These include the time commitment needed from families, parental consistency, and lack of attention to co-occurring symptoms. Additionally, barriers such as not having family meals together can negatively affect treatment. This can stall treatment because the individual with anorexia nervosa needs to be able to work on changing behaviors in real-life situations outside of the counselor's office (Couturier et al., 2013).

Anorexia nervosa occurs across diverse populations but is typically seen more in postindustrialized, high-income countries. It is important to take into consideration weight concerns across different cultures and regions (APA, 2013a). There is evidence that subcultural norms among peer groups can influence attitudes and behaviors about eating (Linville et al., 2011). Although the prevalence of eating disorders in the United States is similar among non-Hispanic Whites, Hispanics, African Americans, and Asians, anorexia nervosa is more common among non-Hispanic Whites (Hudson et al., 2007; Wade et al., 2011).

Differential Diagnosis

Common differential diagnoses for anorexia nervosa are medical conditions, MDD, schizophrenia, substance use disorders, social anxiety disorder, OCD, BDD, bulimia nervosa, and avoidant/restrictive food intake disorder (APA, 2013a). Individuals with anorexia nervosa have reported higher functional impairment and lower BMI scores than individuals without eating disorders (Stice et al., 2013).

Coding, Recording, and Specifiers

There is only one *ICD-9-CM* diagnostic code for anorexia nervosa: 307.1. This coding is assigned regardless of the subtype. However, the *ICD-10-CM* code depends on the subtype, whether the *restricting type* (F50.01) or *binge-eating/purging type* (F50.02). In the restricting type, the individual has not engaged in recurrent episodes of binge eating or purging over the last 3 months. Additionally, the presentation in this subtype typically involves weight loss through dieting, fasting, or excessive exercise. In the binge-eating/purging type, the individual has engaged in repetitive episodes of binge eating or purging over the last 3 months (APA, 2013a).

Counselors should specify if the disorder is *in full remission* or *in partial remission*. It is in partial remission if after full criteria were previously met, the criteria for low body weight has not been met for a sustained period of time but there is still an intense fear of gaining weight or disturbance in self-perception of weight or shape. The disorder is in full remission if no criteria have been met for a sustained period of time (APA, 2013a). The *DSM-5* is unclear about duration needed for remission, but counselors can assume that all physical and medical health concerns, such as low body weight, fear of becoming fat, restriction of food intake, and disturbances in self-perception related to weight, must be reconciled.

Finally, the severity level of the disorder should also be specified. Attained by measuring one's current BMI, these levels are as follows: *mild* (BMI ≥ 17 kg/m²), *moderate* (BMI = 16–16.99 kg/m²), *severe* (BMI = 15–15.99 kg/m²), and *extreme* (BMI < 15 kg/m²; APA, 2013a). For children and adolescents, counselors should use the appropriate BMI percentile. This can be calculated by a physician; a BMI percentile calculator for children and adolescents can be found on the CDC website (www.cdc.gov).

 Example

> Taisha is a 36-year-old, African American heterosexual married woman. She has a successful job in advertising. Taisha has always been worried about her weight. When she was in college, she was worried about getting fat. She exercised a lot and restricted her calories on a regular basis. She was also a picky eater, so she would usually only eat the same things. She said that she exercised a lot because she had always been active as a kid and through high school and played sports. She said that not playing sports in college led her to worry more about gaining weight (or at least the dreaded "freshman 15").
>
> These issues plagued her well into her 20s. When she started graduate school a year after finishing her undergraduate program, she used eating as a way to control some aspects of her life. She was so busy with classes, studying, and being a teaching assistant that she felt like what she ate was the only thing she could control.
>
> Taisha's behaviors have picked up again now that she works nearly 80 hours per week. She said that exercising regularly helps relieve the stress associated with her job. She also said that sometimes she will work out twice a day when she is really stressed and will go to the gym before work and often after pulling a late night at work. She does not eat regularly, and when she does, the portions are very small. She said that watching what she eats is a way to make sure that she does not gain any extra weight.

◆ ◆ ◆

Diagnostic Questions

1. Do Taisha's presenting symptoms meet the criteria for anorexia nervosa?
2. Based on the disorder identified in Question 1, which symptom(s) led you to select the diagnosis?
3. What would be the reason(s) a counselor may not diagnose Taisha with anorexia nervosa?
4. Would Taisha be more accurately diagnosed with bulimia nervosa? Why or why not?
5. What rule-outs would you consider for Taisha's case?
6. What other information may be needed to make an accurate clinical diagnosis?

307.51 Bulimia Nervosa (F50.2)

Essential Features

Individuals with bulimia nervosa often engage in frequent and recurrent episodes of binge eating and then feel a lack of control following those episodes (NIMH, 2013). This lack of control often causes one to engage in behaviors to compensate for the binge eating. These behaviors can include vomiting, excessive exercise, and use of laxatives (NIMH, 2013).

Although some studies have shown a lack of relationship between meal frequency and binge eating, restraint theory models propose that the dietary restrictions will often lead to purging behaviors (Masheb, Grilo, & White, 2011). These behaviors, coupled with feelings of lack of control, can make this a cyclical process. Physical symptoms of bulimia nervosa include but are not limited to inflamed and sore throat, swollen salivary glands, worn tooth enamel, and severe dehydration (NIMH, 2013). Individuals who develop bulimia nervosa may do so after periods of dieting (Kaye et al., 2000). Finally, the mortality rate for bulimia nervosa is high and has been reported at 3.9% (Crow et al., 2009).

There are three essential features of bulimia nervosa: recurrent episodes of binge eating, repetitive compensatory behaviors, and self-evaluation that is influenced by body shape and weight. For a diagnosis to be made, binge eating and engaging in compensatory behaviors must occur at least once a week for 3 months (APA, 2013a). Binge eating is often triggered by negative affect. Episodes may also be set off when there are interpersonal stressors involved along with dietary restraint. After experiencing an episode of binge eating, the individual will engage in an inappropriate compensatory behavior such as purging or excessive exercising (APA, 2013a).

Major Changes From *DSM-IV-TR* to *DSM-5*

The criteria for bulimia nervosa remain mostly unchanged from the *DSM-IV-TR*; however, there is one major change. The DSM-5 Eating Disorders Work Group changed the frequency criterion for binge eating and compensatory behaviors from twice per week for 3 months in the *DSM-IV-TR* to only once per week for 3 months in the *DSM-5* (APA, 2013a).

Special Considerations

The prevalence of bulimia nervosa is 1.0% to 1.5% over a 12-month period (APA, 2013a). Individuals with bulimia nervosa are usually at a healthy or normal weight, so it can be difficult to look at someone and determine whether the individual has the disorder (NIMH, 2013). Between 25% to 30% of individuals presenting to treatment centers with bulimia nervosa have had a prior history of anorexia nervosa (Kaye et al., 2000). Because of morbidity rates, bulimia nervosa has been described as an eating disorder with greater severity compared with binge-eating disorder (Roberto, Grilo, Masheb, & White, 2010). Rates of bulimic symptoms may increase as adolescents moved through young adulthood (Linville et al., 2011).

CBT is often used when treating clients with bulimia nervosa (NIMH, 2013). CBT was found to be effective for at least 60% to 70% of individuals with bulimia nervosa and led to remission of binge eating and purging in 30% to 50% of cases (Kaye et al., 2000). In addition, Kaye et al. (2000) pointed out that CBT helps improve some symptoms including body dissatisfaction and perfectionism. CBT for bulimia nervosa can help individuals establish regular meal and snack patterns, breaking chronic restrained eating that has been shown to lead to cycles of binge eating and purging (Masheb et al., 2011). IPT and DBT have also been shown to be effective interventions for clients with bulimia nervosa (Chavez & Insel, 2007).

Bulimia nervosa is seen in similar frequencies across many industrialized countries. Although it was noted that individuals in the United States who typically present with this disorder are White, it should be pointed out that other ethnic groups have prevalence rates similar to those observed in the White samples (APA, 2013a).

Differential Diagnosis

Common differential diagnoses for bulimia nervosa are anorexia nervosa, binge-eating/purging type, binge-eating disorder, Kleine-Levin syndrome, MDD with atypical features, and borderline personality (APA, 2013a). Individuals with bulimia nervosa noted significantly higher levels of functional impairment, suicidality, and emotional distress than those without bulimia nervosa (Stice et al., 2013). Results from one study show that depressive/negative affect may trigger binge eating among these individuals (Roberto et al., 2010).

Note

Kleine-Levin syndrome, although rare, is a neurological disorder that causes significant problems with cognitive and behavioral functioning (Arnulf, Zeitzer, File, Farber, & Mignot, 2005). One of these disturbances includes bulimic-like cravings for food, or compulsive hyperphagia, which may result in self-induced vomiting. Counselors can differentiate between Kleine-Levin syndrome and bulimia nervosa because individuals diagnosed with Kleine-Levin syndrome do not alternate between periods of self-induced vomiting and voluntary fasting.

◆ ◆ ◆

Coding, Recording, and Specifiers

There is only one diagnostic code for bulimia nervosa: 307.51 (F50.2). It should be specified if the disorder is *in partial remission* or *in full remission*. Partial remission is indicated if some criteria have been met for a sustained period of time after the full criteria had been previously met. Likewise, full remission is indicated if no criteria have been met for a sustained period of time (APA, 2013a). Finally, counselors should indicate the current level of severity. Severity is based on the frequency of compensatory behaviors engaged in per week. The levels of severity are *mild* (an average of one to three episodes of inappropriate compensatory behavior per week), *moderate* (an average of four to seven episodes of inappropriate compensatory behavior per week), *severe* (an average of eight to 13 episodes of inappropriate compensatory behavior per week), and *extreme* (an average of 14 or more episodes of inappropriate compensatory behavior per week; APA, 2013a).

 Case Example

Nisha is a 21-year-old, Indian American female who is in her junior year of college. She is currently seeing a counselor at the college counseling center. She told her counselor that she has had concerns about her weight during adolescence and into her young adult life. Nisha has her sights set on being a professionally trained dancer. She was taught early on to restrict her weight. Looking back, she thinks that her training led to a preoccupation with her weight and body image. She recalls her instructors constantly telling her she was not thin enough even though she dieted continuously. Her friends even began to notice her thinness. Nisha has not really been able to get rid of the feeling that she is too fat even though she weighs 110 pounds and is 5 feet 10 inches tall. Nisha has said that she sometimes gets so hungry after dieting for several days at a time that she would lose control of her eating and eat large amounts of cookies, ice cream, and doughnuts. After she finished eating, she would feel awful about what she just ate and how she broke her diet. She would then force herself to throw up what she had eaten. She disclosed to her counselor that she repeated this cycle once a week for quite a few years.

◆ ◆ ◆

Diagnostic Questions

1. Do Nisha's presenting symptoms meet the criteria for bulimia nervosa?
2. Based on the disorder identified in Question 1, which symptom(s) led you to select the diagnosis?
3. What would be the reason(s) a counselor may not diagnose Nisha with bulimia nervosa?
4. Would Nisha be more accurately diagnosed with binge-eating disorder? Why or why not?

5. What rule-outs would you consider for Nisha's case?
6. What other information may be needed to make an accurate clinical diagnosis?

307.51 Binge-Eating Disorder (F50.8)

Essential Features

Binge eating involves consuming a large amount of food in a certain period of time. Individuals diagnosed with binge-eating disorder lose control over their ability to control food intake. However, unlike bulimia nervosa, the individual with binge-eating disorder does not engage in any compensatory behaviors, such as taking laxatives, purging, or engaging in excessive exercise (APA, 2013a). Past binges may lead to feelings of guilt and shame, which may in turn lead to more binges (NIMH, 2013). Most people who have binge-eating disorder are overweight or obese, but this is not always the case. Obese individuals with binge-eating disorder experience more psychological and medical problems than obese individuals who do not engage in binge eating (Barnes, Masheb, White, & Grilo, 2011).

An essential feature of binge-eating disorder is recurrent episodes of excessive eating in a short period of time. These episodes must occur, on average, at least once per week for 3 months. A binge-eating episode is defined as "eating, in a discrete period of time, an amount of food that is definitely larger than most people would eat in a similar period of time under similar circumstances" (APA, 2013a, pp. 350–351). Counselors should also consider the context of where the eating occurs when determining if the amount of food is excessive. Individuals who are of normal weight, overweight, or obese can be diagnosed with binge-eating disorder.

Major Changes From *DSM-IV-TR* to *DSM-5*

Binge-eating disorder was included in the *DSM-5* as its own category of eating disorder. In the *DSM-IV-TR*, it was listed as a disorder for further study and was only diagnosable by categorizing it as an eating disorder NOS (APA, 2013b). The DSM-5 Eating Disorders Work Group intended for this change to bring awareness and show differences between binge-eating disorder and overeating. Although recurrent binge eating does not occur as frequently as other feeding and eating disorders in this section, it is severe and often includes many physical and psychological problems (APA, 2013b).

Special Considerations

According to the *DSM-5*, the 12-month prevalence of binge-eating disorder in the United States is 1.6% among adult women and 0.8% among adult men. There is higher prevalence of the disorder for those who are in treatment for weight loss compared with the general population (APA, 2013a). When evaluating clients who have been diagnosed with binge-eating disorder, counselors should examine at least two specific examples of their binge-eating behaviors. This will provide information about the food eaten as well as the context in which it was consumed (Berg & Peterson, 2013). Binge eating is somewhat of an abstract concept, so it might be difficult for an individual to be able to conceptualize the amount of food consumed. This could lead to one minimizing how much food is eaten or to deny if a large amount of food has been eaten (Berg et al., 2012).

Treatment for binge-eating disorder is similar to treatment for bulimia nervosa. CBT has been shown to be an effective treatment (NIMH, 2013). Because individuals with binge-eating disorder tend to eat a similar amount of meals but consume a higher frequency of snacks than individuals without binge-eating disorder, CBT techniques can help individuals reduce overeating and atypical behaviors by reducing cognitions associated with their current eating behaviors (Masheb et al., 2011).

In terms of cultural considerations, it has been noted that prevalence rates of binge-eating disorder in ethnic or racial minority groups is similar to the rates for White females. It should also be noted that binge-eating disorder is seen mostly in industrialized countries (APA, 2013a).

Differential Diagnosis

Common differential diagnoses for binge-eating disorder are bulimia nervosa, obesity, bipolar and depressive disorders, and borderline personality disorders. One of the distinguishing differences between binge-eating disorder and bulimia nervosa is that the compensatory behaviors (i.e., purging, excessive exercising) seen in bulimia nervosa are not present in binge-eating disorder (APA, 2013a).

In cases in which bipolar or depressive disorders may also be present, it is important to look for full criteria for both disorders if one is to make a diagnosis of both disorders. Binge eating is part of the impulsive behavior criterion for borderline personality disorder. If full criteria for both disorders are met, a diagnosis for both disorders should be made (APA, 2013a). Individuals who binge eat may also be more likely to display higher depressive or negative affect, which may, in turn, cause greater levels of binge eating. It is important to look at the role mood disturbances play in conjunction with these disorders (Roberto et al., 2010).

Coding, Recording, and Specifiers

There is only one diagnostic code for binge-eating disorder: 307.51 (F50.8). It should be specified if the disorder is *in partial remission* or *in full remission*. The disorder should be specified as in partial remission if binge eating occurs at an average frequency of less than one episode per week for a sustained period of time after the full criteria had been previously met. Full remission should be specified if none of the criteria have been met for a sustained period of time after the full criteria had been previously met (APA, 2013a). Finally, counselors should also indicate the current level of severity. The levels of severity are *mild* (one to three binge-eating episodes per week), *moderate* (four to seven binge-eating episodes per week), *severe* (eight to 13 binge-eating episodes per week), and *extreme* (14 or more binge-eating episodes per week; APA, 2013a).

 **Example**

Mikeal is a 35-year-old, 6-foot, 280-pound man who presented to the clinic to discuss problems with his eating habits over the years. He was an athlete in high school and college; frequent athletic practices allowed him to eat whatever he wanted and not see any changes in his weight. Many of his friends commented on his large appetite. He could eat two pizzas, a bag of popcorn, a gallon of ice cream, and a two-liter soda during a movie. After graduation, Mikeal still ate these large amounts of food. He began to notice that eating these large amounts of food without any physical activity caused him to gain weight. He started to feel unhappy about his appearance, which then led him to feel unhappy about other parts of his life. When he felt unhappy, he turned to food to comfort him.

Over the past few months, Mikeal began to notice some changes in his eating habits. He started to experience a lack of control with his eating. He stated that now he often feels like he cannot stop eating whereas before he would choose to eat larger amounts of food but was able to stop eating. Mikeal has started to feel ashamed about his eating as well as the fact that he has gained more weight recently. His family, originally from Latvia, has even noticed these binges and has encouraged him to try and control his eating. Mikeal tried dieting and would eat only salads and healthy sandwiches while at work. However, he found himself eating large amounts of food by himself whenever he got home from work at night. He states he feels ashamed and doesn't know what to do.

◆ ◆ ◆

Diagnostic Questions

1. Do Mikeal's presenting symptoms meet the criteria for binge-eating disorder?
2. Based on the disorder identified in Question 1, which symptom(s) led you to select the diagnosis?
3. What would be the reason(s) a counselor may not diagnose Mikeal with binge-eating disorder?
4. Would Mikeal be more accurately diagnosed with bulimia nervosa? Why or why not?
5. What rule-outs would you consider for Mikeal's case?
6. What other information may be needed to make an accurate clinical diagnosis?

Elimination Disorders

Elimination disorders involve repeated voluntary or involuntary voiding of urine or passing of feces at inappropriate times. Specifically, enuresis is the act of urinating at inappropriate times; encopresis refers to defecation at inappropriate times (APA, 2013a; Comer, 2013; von Gontard, 2012). The disorders are diagnosed after an age when it is assumed an individual should be able to control these functions. Of the two disorders, enuresis is much more prevalent, occurring in about 12% to 13% of 7-year-olds (van Gontard, 2012). In general, prevalence of the disorder decreases with age; only about 1% of children experience symptoms by age 13 (Comer, 2013).

Major Changes From *DSM-IV-TR* to *DSM-5*

There are no major changes to the diagnostic criteria in this new nomenclature system, although the category itself has been moved from the Disorders Usually First Diagnosed in Infancy, Childhood, and Adolescence chapter in the *DSM-IV-TR* to a separate stand-alone chapter in the *DSM-5*. The Elimination Disorders chapter includes enuresis and encopresis (APA, 2013a). Because there are no major changes to the disorders in this section, we only review essential features and special considerations for each specific disorder.

Differential Diagnoses

Differential diagnoses for elimination disorders center primarily around medical conditions and medication side effects (APA, 2013a). As a result, it is important to ensure that symptoms are not related to medical problems, medications, or normal development. A thorough assessment of the individual's background and medical history is essential, and, if that has not occurred, counselors should refer the individual for a medical examination prior to diagnosing the disorder.

Etiology and Treatment

There are multiple theories as to the etiology of elimination disorders; the research in this area does not clearly endorse one explanation over others (Comer, 2013; Shapira & Dahlen, 2010). Theories regarding enuresis include biological reasons, such as reduced bladder capacity related to developmental delays or inability to produce the normal amount of antidiuretic hormones (Houts, 2010). Enuresis may run along familial lines because children whose fathers reported nighttime issues of bedwetting are 10 times as likely to experience nocturnal bedwetting (APA, 2013a). Additional theories include anxious response to conflict or problematic family situations, abuse (Comer, 2013), and slow or inappropriate toilet training (APA, 2013a; Comer, 2013). The most common theory for etiology of involuntary encopresis seems to be biological, specifically that it relates to intestinal functioning and repeated constipation (Comer, 2013). Whereas environment may also be a factor in involuntary encopresis, voluntary encopresis, which is much less common, may be related to another mental disorder, such as ODD (APA, 2013a).

Elimination disorders will resolve with age for most individuals, but treatments can assist in accelerating this process. Behavioral therapy is often effective in treating nocturnal enuresis. Specific examples of this include the urine alarm treatment (Houts, 2010) and dry-bed training (Comer, 2013). Other therapies include retention control training, stream interruption exercises, overlearning, and cleanliness training (Christophersen & Friman, 2010). A variety of medications can be prescribed to assist in decreasing these symptoms, and alternative therapies such as hypnotherapy and acupuncture have been suggested (Shapira & Dahlen, 2010). Whereas behavioral therapy may be more effective long term than certain types of medications (Glazener, Evans, & Peto, 2005), combination therapies using both tools may be most effective for both enuresis and encopresis. For encopresis, the use of behavioral therapies along with addressing constipation has been shown effective. Constipation can be addressed through medication but also through diet, increasing fiber and water, and cutting out foods such as cheese. Other treatments may include biofeedback and mineral oils (Comer, 2013). Counselors should always consult with medical professionals before making any psychopharmaceutical recommendations, because even over-the-counter medications can have significantly detrimental side effects for some individuals.

Implications for Counselors

Individuals with elimination disorders are likely to present for counseling because of outcomes in the classroom and the emotional toll caused by the disorders. These individuals will likely be young, school-age children and may present first in school counseling settings (Geroski & Rodgers, 1998). It is important that counselors ensure a medical examination has occurred and other diagnoses or medical conditions have been ruled out or addressed. Counselors should identify precipitating events through thorough assessment and address those as appropriate (Geroski & Rodgers, 1998).

Because shame, family problems, social withdrawal, and embarrassment are associated with elimination disorders (APA, 2013a; Comer, 2013), counselors should take care to offer safe and accepting environments in which children can begin to express emotions related to these disorders, which may include behavioral or emotional problems (Geroski & Rodgers, 1998). These children can suffer from self-esteem issues as well as fear of rejection by caregivers or peers. In addition to encouraging positive coping, counselors need to focus on therapies that are shown to be effective with children. Furthermore, counselors can address the family system as appropriate and give information on additional evidence-based treatments such as behavioral therapies and referrals for medication (Geroski & Rodgers, 1998).

307.6 Enuresis (F98.0)

Essential Features

Enuresis is characterized by repeatedly urinating at inappropriate times, either voluntarily or involuntarily. Often referred to as "wetting" or "bed-wetting," this disorder is diagnosed after the age of 5, or when it becomes clear that the individual is developmentally at the level where he or she should be able to control this bodily function. Enuresis affects a surprisingly large number of children. Comer (2013) reported that between 13% and 33% of children have had an experience with bed-wetting, and one in 10 children will meet criteria for enuresis at some point. Nocturnal involuntary urination, sometimes called *monosymptomatic enuresis*, is the most prevalent form of the disorder and affects one in 10 children over the age of 5 (von Gontard, 2012). Voluntary and daytime inappropriate urination occurs at a lower rate (APA, 2013a).

Individuals who experience enuresis either voluntarily or involuntarily urinate repeatedly and inappropriately in the bed or in their clothing. The individual must be at least 5 years of age, and the episodes must occur at least twice a week for 3 consecutive months. This cannot be related to a medical condition, substance, or medication side effects and must be impairing or clinically significant (APA, 2013a).

Special Considerations

Although enuresis has a high prevalence, there continues to be a stigma around these symptoms. Children who have this disorder often experience teasing, restricted social interactions, decreased self-confidence, and embarrassment (Houts, 2010). Counselors should be careful to address the emotional impact of this disorder on the individual and family system. Boys tend to experience nocturnal enuresis more frequently than do girls, whereas girls struggle more with diurnal enuresis than boys. For both, the symptoms diminish greatly with age, with less than 1% of those over 18 years of age continuing to have symptoms (APA, 2013a). Most data suggest that the rate of enuresis does not change with ethnicity or geographic area.

Differential Diagnosis

Differential diagnoses for enuresis typically involve medical conditions or influence of a medication that induces incontinence (APA, 2013a). Counselors should inquire about physical conditions or medications that clients may be taking that could affect urination during the day or night. ODD criteria should also be considered as a differential diagnosis.

Coding, Recording, and Specifiers

There is only one code for enuresis: 307.6 (F98.0). The APA (2013a) allows for three different specifiers: *nocturnal only* (at night), *diurnal only* (waking hours), or a combination of *nocturnal and diurnal*.

 **Example**

Allison is a 6-year-old Caucasian girl who wets the bed almost every night. Her mother is very frustrated, stating that this did not occur with the older siblings whom she potty trained the same way. Allison's father is much more compassionate, reporting that he had the same issues as a child and understands how difficult this must be for Allison. Her parents have brought her to counseling because she cries all morning after the accidents, and they have trouble getting her to go to school. Furthermore, Allison tells you that she had a friend stay over at her house and she wet the bed that night. The friend found out and told other students, who now tease her.

Allison and her parents deny any history of physical or sexual abuse. She is not on medications but hasn't been to a medical doctor in 2 years. She has never been to therapy before and performs very well in school. However, her grades are beginning to suffer because of chronic tardiness. She has begun refusing to talk to her classmates.

♦ ♦ ♦

Diagnostic Questions

1. Do Allison's presenting symptoms meet the criteria for an elimination disorder? If so, which one?

2. Would be the reason(s) a counselor would not diagnose Allison with an elimination disorder?
3. Would she be accurately diagnosed with enuresis?
4. What rule-outs would you consider?
5. What other information may be needed to make an accurate clinical diagnosis?

307.7 Encopresis (F98.1)

Essential Features

Encopresis was listed in the *DSM-IV-TR*; there have been no major changes other than moving it, along with enuresis, to a stand alone-chapter in the *DSM-5*. Encopresis occurs less frequently than enuresis, occurs mainly in males, and has been associated with low socioeconomic status (Comer, 2013).

Encopresis refers to defecating at inappropriate times, either voluntarily or involuntarily. This will occur at least once a month for 3 months or longer. The diagnosis can only be made after the child is 4 years of age and cannot be given if the symptoms can be explained by a medical condition, substance use, or medications (APA, 2013a).

Special Considerations

Encopresis occurs most often in males and is largely due to constipation and intestinal tract issues. For some individuals, the experience of this disorder can be quite painful and shaming. These individuals may experience fear of engaging in normal childhood experiences, social problems, and anxiety or depression (Christophersen & Friman, 2010). These individuals may also experience ongoing urinary tract infections (APA, 2013a). As with enuresis, encopresis does not appear to be associated with ethnicity but is more prevalent in low-income groups.

Differential Diagnosis

Differential diagnoses for encopresis would typically involve medical conditions or the influence of a medication that may induce involuntary defecation (APA, 2013a). Counselors should always inquire about physical conditions or medications that clients may be taking.

Coding, Recording, and Specifiers

There is only one code for encopresis: 307.7 (F98.1). Counselors can specify *with constipation and overflow incontinence* or *without constipation and overflow incontinence*. With constipation and overflow incontinence is typically involuntary in nature, and the related feces may not hold shape. Without constipation and overflow incontinence occurs when incontinence is not present, does not occur frequently, and is often associated with intentional defecation (APA, 2013a).

Sleep-Wake Disorders

Sleeping difficulties can have a profound impact on people's quality of life and can result in major negative effects to their everyday functioning, including mental and physical well-being, productivity, and safety (Szentkirályi, Madarász, & Novák, 2009). The National Highway Traffic Safety Administration (2011) estimates 1,550 fatalities and 40,000 nonfatal injuries annually in the United States are due to drivers who fall asleep or are drowsy behind the wheel. Sleep-wake disorders create a huge emotional as well as financial toll in people's lives. One Australian study reported that the direct and indirect costs of sleep-wake disorders totaled $7,494,000 for Australian citizens (Hillman, Murphy, Antic, & Pezzullo, 2006).

Major Changes From *DSM-IV-TR* to *DSM-5*

Sleep-wake disorders underwent changes in the *DSM-5* to enhance the clinical utility, validity, and reliability of the diagnoses. These changes are also in alignment with the findings of sleep disorder medicine. The new changes facilitated a paradigm shift in the way sleep disorders have been conceptualized and treated (Reynolds & Redline, 2010). The changes in sleep-wake disorders minimized the use of the NOS category by designating restless leg syndrome and rapid eye movement (REM) sleep behavior disorder as stand-alone disorders (Reynolds & Redline, 2010). Insomnia also received a stand-alone diagnosis, and the subdivision of insomnia into primary and secondary was eliminated. This helps clinicians avoid unnecessary confusion between primary insomnia (sleep problems not associated with a medical condition) and secondary insomnia (sleep problems associated with medical conditions such as asthma, depression, or pain; Tucker, 2012). Sleep disorder due to a general medical condition and sleep disorder due to another mental illness have also been eliminated (Reynolds & Redline, 2010). Lastly, counselors should always remember to consult with a medical professional or sleep disorder specialist as needed.

Readers should note that we chose to make this section brief, because most counselors will not be diagnosing sleep-wake disorders. Specifically, we cover essential features and special considerations we feel counselors may need to know when working with clients diagnosed with these conditions. For additional information, we provide some resources at the end of the sleep-wake disorders section. We encourage counselors who are working with sleep disorders to consult with medical professionals and sleep disorder specialists and to seek training in the areas of sleep dysfunction, because this is not an area commonly addressed in counselor training.

780.52 Insomnia Disorder (G47.00)

What is really frustrating is when I am lying there and really want to fall asleep so my body is already tired but I can't shut my mind off enough to fall asleep. When I wake up in the night, time seems really weird and I keep hoping it's earlier in the night so there's a chance I can get sleep. Then I wake up in the morning like that and I am still really tired because I haven't really slept anyway so I can't function at work, even with tons of coffee. —Christa

Essential Features

Previously named primary insomnia in the *DSM-IV-TR*, insomnia disorder has been renamed in the *DSM-5* to avoid the differentiation of primary and secondary insomnia. This is the only major change to this disorder in the *DSM-5*. Insomnia disorder affects about one third of adults (APA, 2013a), and women present about 2 times more than men with this disorder (Espie, 2002). Individuals with insomnia disorder experience great difficulty falling asleep and maintaining sleep as well as early-morning awakening with inability to return to sleep. These symptoms create significant clinical distress in these individuals' lives and must occur at least 3 nights per week for at least 3 months (APA, 2013a).

Special Considerations

Clients will often come to counseling because of problems with their sleep. Oftentimes, they have been having sleep difficulties for months or even years, and it has been negatively affecting their work or personal life. Counselors will often hear clients complain of going to bed at a certain time and lying awake for several hours, sometimes until the early morning, before finally drifting off to sleep. In contrast, some clients might have no difficulties falling asleep at night but wake up 1 to 3 hours before their alarm clock goes off and are unable to fall back asleep.

Insomnia is associated with substantial impairments in an individual's life, such as cognitive impairments, role limitations due to physical health problems, diminished vitality, and social functioning problems (Roth, 2007). Insomnia also contributes to poor physical and emotional health (Johnson, Roth, Schultz, & Breslau, 2006). In diagnosing and treating insomnia disorder, counselors need to explore other contributing factors to the sleep disturbances, including poor sleep hygiene, use of psychostimulants, and other psychosocial stressors such as job loss, divorce, or financial problems. Counselors should also be aware of the high prevalence rate of insomnia with older individuals. Montgomery and Shepard (2010) estimated that 40% to 50% of adults over 60 years of age are dissatisfied with their sleep or have trouble sleeping. Of these individuals, between 12% and 25% suffer from chronic insomnia (Montgomery & Shepard, 2010). Additionally, this disorder is highly comorbid with anxiety disorders, MDD, and other sleep-related disorders (APA, 2013a). Therefore, counselors should pinpoint why the sleep difficulties are occurring in order to find the best treatment. Insomnia disorder has been successfully treated with prescription drugs or CBT with various clients (Jernelöv et al., 2012). There is one diagnostic code for insomnia disorder: 780.52 (G47.00). See the *DSM-5* for specifiers.

780.54 Hypersomnolence Disorder (G47.10) and 347._ _ Narcolepsy (G47.4 _ _)

Sometimes I sleep as much as 14 hours a day. I know I shouldn't be tired but I still am. I feel as though I could never stop sleeping. My coworkers look at me suspiciously and suggest I should see a doctor. I know they think I'm taking drugs, but I'm not. —Philip

Essential Features

Although counselors will most likely not be diagnosing hypersomnolence disorder or narcolepsy, it is important for them to know what the symptoms of these disorders are. Clients displaying these symptoms should be referred to a medical doctor for further evaluation. Previously named primary hypersomnia in the *DSM-IV-TR*, hypersomnolence disorder is characterized by excessive sleepiness despite having a full night's sleep with difficulty being fully awake throughout the day. Narcolepsy is a neurological disorder that has maintained its name in the *DSM-5*. It is characterized by periods of uncontrollable need to sleep, lapsing into sleep, or napping occurring in the same day. Hypersomnolence disorder affects about 4% to 6% of the population (Dauvilliers, 2006), whereas narcolepsy is much more rare, affecting 0.02% to 0.04% of the population (APA, 2013a).

Clients with these two disorders will often complain of feeling overly tired, even after getting a full night's sleep the previous night. Individuals with hypersomnolence disorder may often complain of feeling so tired that they need to nap throughout the day. Another common symptom is that individuals may fall asleep the night before and wake up in the late afternoon the next day, often sleeping through important responsibilities such as work or school. Clients with narcolepsy will frequently complain of an irrepressible need to sleep that comes out of nowhere throughout the day. Some individuals experience this need to sleep while driving and will need to pull over and nap before continuing to drive. These individuals will most likely already be diagnosed with narcolepsy by their medical doctor before coming in to see a counselor.

Special Considerations

Hypersomnolence disorder is comorbid with mood disorders, specifically depressive disorders or episodes (APA, 2013a). Other causes for this disorder can include an inability to cope with stress or the need to fill a void by sleeping (Morrison, 2006). It is important for counselors to treat the depressive symptoms and explore other reasons why clients are experiencing these clinically distressing sleep disturbances. Hypersomnolence disorder is most widely treated with stimulants (Dauvilliers, 2006). However, counselors need to explore the reason for the sleep disorder and may need to refer a client to a medical doctor for medication.

Narcolepsy is strongly hereditary (Morrison, 2006), and the onset is typically in childhood or adolescence (APA, 2013a). Counselors should complete a family history assessment if clients are experiencing symptoms related to narcolepsy and have not yet been diagnosed by a medical doctor. Narcolepsy may co-occur with other disorders such as bipolar disorder, depressive disorders, and anxiety disorders. As with hypersomnolence disorder, narcolepsy is commonly treated with stimulants to promote daytime wakefulness (Dauvilliers, 2006). There is one diagnostic code for hypersomnolence disorder: 780.54 (G47.10). Diagnostic coding for narcolepsy depends on medical conditions such as cataplexy, hypocretin deficiencies, or Type 2 diabetes. See the *DSM-5* for recording criteria.

Breathing-Related Sleep Disorders

Essential Features

In the *DSM-5*, the breathing-related sleep disorders are now divided into three distinct disorders: obstructive sleep apnea hypopnea, central sleep apnea, and sleep-related hypoventilation. This is a major change from the *DSM-IV-TR*, in which breathing-related sleep disorders did not have any distinct disorders within the diagnosis. Obstructive sleep apnea hypopnea is characterized by sleeping disturbances such as snoring, gasping, breathing pauses during sleep, or daytime sleepiness or fatigue despite sufficient sleep the night before. Central sleep apnea is characterized by apneas (temporary suspension of breathing) and hypopneas (abnormally shallow and slow breathing) during sleep caused by inconsistency in respiratory effort. Sleep-related hypoventilation is characterized by decreased respiration associated with elevated CO_2 levels (APA, 2013a). Physicians normally give a polysomnograph to individuals experiencing any of these symptoms to verify any breathing-related sleep disorders diagnosis. Although breathing-related sleep disorders can only be formally diagnosed by medical doctors with a polysomnograph, it is important for counselors to recognize the symptoms of these disorders, because clients who display symptoms of a breathing-related sleep disorder and are not diagnosed with one should be referred to a medical doctor for further evaluation.

Clients suffering from breathing-related sleep disorders often have partners who complain about their snoring or who report that they temporarily stop breathing or have shallow breathing while sleeping. Counselors may hear clients themselves complain of fatigue, morning headaches, impotence, restlessness at night, irritability, cognitive deficiencies, sweating, sleep talking, or sleep terrors associated with these disorders (Morrison, 2006). If clients are displaying these symptoms and have not previously been diagnosed with a breathing-related sleep disorder, counselors should refer them for a medical evaluation as soon as possible.

Special Considerations

Obstructive sleep apnea hypopnea is the most common breathing-related sleep disorder. It is even more common in older adults, affecting more than 20% of these individuals. If an older client complains about sleep disturbances or daytime sleepiness, he or she should be referred to a medical doctor immediately for an evaluation, because breathing-related sleep disorders are potentially lethal (Morrison, 2006). Also, as with other sleep-wake disorders, obstructive sleep apnea hypopnea is strongly hereditary (APA, 2013a), and counselors should complete a full family history during the intake process. Counselors should note that obesity is often a predisposing factor to developing sleep-related hypoventilation.

Unlike obstructive sleep apnea hypopnea, which counselors are likely to see, both central sleep apnea and sleep-related hypoventilation are rare disorders, and the unique prevalence is unknown (APA, 2013a). Counselors will most likely not see these disorders present in their clients. It is important, however, to recognize the implications of these disorders and how their symptoms manifest in clients.

Parasomnias

I could feel my heart pounding and I was sweating. It was always dark and I would run as fast as I could but I never got away. The monster was always right behind me in the shadows. I would wake up with my bed covers wrapped around my legs. I had been running in my sleep again. —Sue

Essential Features

Parasomnias are characterized by abnormal occurrences during sleep. The parasomnias section of the *DSM-5* comprises three separate disorders; non–rapid eye movement (NREM) sleep arousal disorders, nightmare disorder, and REM sleep behavior disorder (APA, 2013a). A major change from the *DSM-IV-TR* is merging the two disorders of sleep-walking and sleep terrors into a distinct disorder, NREM sleep arousal disorders. Also, parasomnia NOS has been removed from the *DSM-5,* and REM sleep behavior disorder is now a distinct disorder.

NREM sleep arousal disorders are characterized by episodes of incomplete awakening from sleep accompanied by either sleepwalking or sleep terrors (abrupt and panicked arousal from sleep; APA, 2013a). Individuals with NREM sleep arousal disorders usually have no recollection of the dream or the episode of sleepwalking or sleep terror. Sleep-walking carries a very high lifetime prevalence of 29.2% in adults, but not all adults who sleepwalk have NREM sleep arousal disorders (APA, 2013a). Episodes of sleep terrors are less common in adults and much more common in children, with a prevalence of up to 36.9% (APA, 2013a).

Nightmare disorder is characterized by extended and dysphoric dreams that the individual can remember vividly. These dreams can be quite frightening and usually involve the individual feeling a threat to his or her safety or security. Nightmares often occur after a traumatic event, forcing the individual to relive the trauma. In adults, there is a 6% prevalence of nightmares occurring at least once per month, whereas frequent nightmares are less common, ranging from 1% to 2% (APA, 2013a). Counselors should note that night-mare disorder should not be diagnosed if an individual only had one nightmare, because nightmares are common among the general population. The reoccurrence and duration of the nightmares must be considered before counselors diagnose nightmare disorder.

Lastly, REM sleep behavior disorder is characterized by repeated episodes of arousal from REM sleep. This often occurs with loud vocalization or violent motor behaviors such as kicking, punching, hitting, or jumping out of bed. These behaviors often reflect the individual's dream and can be quite disturbing to his or her partner. This disorder is rare, occurring in approximately 0.38% to 0.5% of the general population (APA, 2013a).

Special Considerations

Parasomnias can be very disturbing to both the individual and the partner sharing a bed. Individuals coming into counseling might not remember sleepwalking or having sleep terrors, but their partners can certainly testify to these nighttime disturbances. Counsel-ors should be aware that NREM sleep arousal disorders have been associated with serious bodily harm to self and others and have been associated with homicide, automobile ac-cidents, and destruction of property (Shatkin, Feinfield, & Strober, 2002). It is important for counselors to make detailed notes of episodes of sleepwalking in case the individual's records are subpoenaed by a court of law.

Parasomnias have been found to be strongly comorbid with other disorders. Sleepwalking has been associated with major depressive episodes and OCD. Nightmare disorder is frequently comorbid with PTSD, insomnia, schizophrenia, mood disorders, anxiety disorders, adjustment disorders, and personality disorders. REM sleep behavior disorder is also present in approximately 30% of individuals diagnosed with narcolepsy (APA, 2013a). It is important for counselors to distinguish if the parasomnia is occurring due to another psychiatric disorder or if it is a separate diagnosis.

Circadian Rhythm Sleep-Wake Disorders

Circadian rhythm sleep-wake disorders are characterized by the relative absence of a circadian pattern in an individual's sleep-wake cycle (Zee & Vitiello, 2009). The subtypes of circadian rhythm sleep-wake disorders have been expanded to include *delayed sleep phase type, advanced sleep phase type, irregular sleep-wake type, non-24-hour sleep-wake type,* and *shift work type. Jet lag type* has been removed from the *DSM-5*.

Essential Features

Delayed sleep phase type is characterized by delayed sleep onset and awakening without being able to fall asleep and awaken when desired. This type of disorder has a prevalence of 7% in adolescents. Advanced sleep phase type is characterized by advanced sleep onset and awakening times without the ability to remain awake or asleep when desired. This type of disorder has a prevalence of 1% in middle-aged adults. Irregular sleep-wake type is characterized by a disorganized sleep-wake pattern that is variable throughout a 24-hour period. Prevalence of this type is unknown. Non-24-hour sleep-wake type is characterized by sleep-wake cycles not synchronized to the 24-hour environment, consisting of a consistent daily drift of sleep onset and wake times. This type of disorder is very common in individuals who are blind, with prevalence rates of 50%. Lastly, shift work type is characterized by insomnia during major sleep times or sleepiness during major awake times related to an unconventional shift work schedule. This type of disorder is prevalent among 5% to 10% of individuals who work overnight (APA, 2013a).

Special Considerations

Counselors should be aware of comorbidity with some types of circadian rhythm sleep-wake disorders. Delayed sleep phase type is strongly comorbid with depression, personality disorders, somatic symptom disorder, or illness anxiety disorder. Irregular sleep-wake type is comorbid with neurodegenerative and neurodevelopmental disorders such as major neurocognitive disorder, intellectual developmental disorder, and traumatic brain injuries. Non-24-hour sleep-wake type is comorbid with blindness, and shift work type is comorbid with substance use disorders and depression.

Treatment interventions for circadian rhythm sleep-wake disorders can include prescribed sleep scheduling, circadian phase shifting, hypnosis, and stimulant medications. Counselors can plan with clients to ensure that they are getting plenty of sunlight during the day in order to reset their body's natural circadian rhythm and make sure they have a set time to sleep and wake up each day. Also, taking melatonin in the afternoon or evening time can promote a regular sleep cycle (Sack et al., 2007). However, counselors should inform clients that they should always check with a medical professional before taking melatonin or any other sleep aid.

333.94 Restless Legs Syndrome (G25.81)

My experience has been that it usually happens when I'm just about to fall asleep and my leg starts twitching so it wakes me up. I try to relax so the twitching stops, but as soon as I relax the twitching starts again and it's uncontrollable.—Arno

In the *DSM-IV-TR*, restless legs syndrome was classified under dyssomnia NOS. Now a stand-alone diagnosis in the *DSM-5*, restless legs syndrome is a neurological sleep disorder characterized by an irresistible urge to move the legs or arms, which is relieved by movement. This disorder is associated with uncomfortable sensations in the limbs, usually worsening in the evening and at night. The prevalence of this disorder varies widely, with a range of 2% to 7.2% (APA, 2013a). Depressive and anxiety disorders are often comorbid with restless legs syndrome.

Substance/Medication-Induced Sleep Disorder

The key feature of substance/medication-induced sleep disorder is a clinically significant sleep disturbance that is attributable to the effects of a substance (APA, 2013a). There are four type specifiers for this disorder: *insomnia type, daytime sleepiness type, parasomnia type*, and *mixed type*. Specify if *with onset during intoxication* or *with onset during discontinuation/withdrawal*. Females are affected more than males by a 2:1 ratio.

Additional Resources for Sleep Disorders

Ambrogetti, A. (2000). *Sleeping soundly: Understanding and treating sleeping disorders*. Sydney, Australia: Allen & Unwin.

Barion, A., & Zee, P. C. (2007). A clinical approach to circadian rhythm sleep disorders. *Sleep Medicine, 8*, 566–577.

Colten, H. R., & Altevogt, B. M. (Eds.). (2006). *Sleep disorders and sleep deprivation: An unmet public health problem*. Washington, DC: National Academies Press.

Guilleminault, C. (1982). *Sleeping and waking disorders: Indications and techniques*. Menlo Park, CA: Addison-Wesley.

Hunsley, J., & Mash, E. J. (Eds.). (2008). *A guide to assessments that work*. New York, NY: Oxford University Press.

Mahowald, M. W., & Schenck, C. H. (2005). REM sleep behavior disorder. In C. Guilleminault (Ed.), *Handbook of clinical neurophysiology* (Vol. 6, pp. 245–253). New York, NY: Elsevier.

Meltzer, L. J., & Mindell, J. A. (2006). Sleep and sleep disorders in children and adolescents. *Psychiatric Clinics of North America, 29*, 1059–1076.

Stores, G. (2007). Clinical diagnosis and misdiagnosis of sleep disorders. *Journal of Neurology, Neurosurgery & Psychiatry, 78*, 1293–1297.

Sexual Dysfunctions

Sexual functioning is an essential part of well-being. Disturbances in sexual desire or problems with physiological functions that characterize sexual responses are included in the Sexual Dysfunctions chapter of the *DSM-5*. Sexual disturbances, such as delayed ejaculation or erectile disorder, cause marked distress and interpersonal difficulties in those who experience them (APA, 2013a; Simons & Carey, 2001). Simons and Carey (2001) posited, "Sexual dysfunctions are believed to be among the more prevalent psychological disorders in the general population" (p. 177). Prevalence rates of sexual dysfunctions have remained unchanged from the *DSM-IV-TR* to the *DSM-5* (Simons & Carey; 2001; Spector & Carey, 1990). Community samples indicate current prevalence rates of 0% to 3% for male orgasmic disorder, 0% to 5% for erectile disorder, 0% to 3% for male hypoactive sexual desire disorder, 7% to 10% for female orgasmic disorder, and 4% to 5% for premature ejaculation (Simons & Carey, 2001).

These dysfunctions interfere with one's desire to achieve and maintain healthy sexual functioning and can be related to significant distress, including depressive symptoms and lower reported quality of life (Hyde & DeLamater, 2013; Laumann, Paik, & Rosen, 1999). Problems related to sexual disturbances can also be compounded by feelings of shame from individuals who experience them (Crooks & Baur, 2013; Heise, 1995). Seeking help for sexual problems is often difficult; thus, clients do not typically present for counseling until the problem causes hardship in their social or interpersonal relationships (Crooks & Baur, 2013; Hyde & DeLamater, 2013).

Masters and Johnson (1966) outlined a four-stage model of the human sexual response cycle: excitement, plateau, orgasm, and resolution. This model had an enormous influence on the diagnostic criteria for both editions of the *DSM-IV* (Baum, Revenson, & Singer, 2012). As a result of this influence, societal norms surrounding sexuality and medical developments have made significant headway in rethinking how the mental health and medical community defines healthy sexuality. For example, medical advances in addressing erectile dysfunction have aided men in achieving an erection with the use of psychosexual therapies or pharmacological treatments or both. Although these advances are quite significant for men who are diagnosed with sexual dysfunctions, there is still a considerable amount of research that needs to be conducted regarding female dysfunction. There is also a dearth of research focusing on the understanding of sexuality within different cultures (Basson et al., 2000; Tiefer, 2001).

Special Considerations

For assessment purposes, it is important for counselors to always refer clients with sexual problems and dysfunctions to a physician for a medical examination. Additionally, counselors need to address both psychological and biological factors that may contribute to the dysfunction and always be aware that these issues are difficult for people to talk about and are often misunderstood, especially between partners (Crooks & Baur, 2013; Hyde & DeLamater, 2013). For example, when a couple presents for treatment with a history of sexual problems, chances are they have never spoken about these issues before. Thus, the couple might have different viewpoints of the presenting problem. Tiefer (2001) found a 78% discrepancy in reports made by male clients versus their female partners when describing sexual functioning. Furthermore, traumatic sexual experiences have been shown to significantly affect sexual functioning (M. Hall & Hall, 2011).

Sexual dysfunctions can also be a major contributor to a co-occurring mental health disorder such as MDD or a substance use disorder. Therefore, counselors should consider co-occurring conditions in assessment and treatment planning. Finally, counselors must also never fail to take into consideration the clients' cultural worldview and norms within their society about sexual functioning (APA, 2013a).

The Sexual Dysfunctions chapter in the *DSM-5* includes delayed ejaculation, erectile disorder, female orgasmic disorder, female sexual interest/arousal disorder, genito-pelvic pain/penetration disorder, male hypoactive sexual desire disorder, premature (early) ejaculation, and substance/medication-induced sexual dysfunction (APA, 2013a). As with most diagnoses in the *DSM-5*, other specified and unspecified sexual dysfunctions are also listed. Counselors should note these disorders do not occur in isolation; if an individual meets the criteria for several diagnoses, all relevant sexual dysfunctions should be diagnosed (APA, 2013a).

Major Changes From *DSM-IV-TR* to *DSM-5*

The Sexual Dysfunctions chapter of the *DSM-5* is a new chapter dedicated solely to disturbances in sexual desire or problems related to physiological sexual functioning. Previously included in the Sexual and Gender Identity Disorders chapter of the *DSM-IV-TR*, sexual problems were colisted with gender identity disorders (now called gender dysphoria; see Chapter 8 of this *Learning Companion*) and paraphilias. In what is a major structural change, sexual dysfunctions are no longer included with gender dysphoria and are now a stand-alone chapter in the *DSM-5*.

Another appreciable change relating to sexual dysfunction is a shift in how mental health professionals understand sexual arousal and sexual response patterns. In the *DSM-IV-TR*, sexual dysfunctions primarily referred to painful sexual experience or to disturbances in one or more phases of the sexual response cycle (APA, 2013c). Recent research, however, has indicated that sexual responses are not always distinct, clear-cut phases. Therefore, the *DSM-5* takes a more fluid approach to looking at sexual responses. This change is evidenced, for example, by combining sexual desire and arousal disorders for females into one disorder, female sexual interest/arousal disorder (APA, 2013a, 2013c).

All sexual dysfunctions now require a duration of at least 6 months and have more specific criteria than were previously listed in the *DSM-IV-TR*. The increased duration, as well as creation of more distinct criteria, was implemented to help clinicians more clearly distinguish between transitory sexual problems, which most individuals have in their lifetime, and diagnosable sexual dysfunctions (APA, 2013a). Other changes include changing the nomenclature of male orgasmic disorder to delayed ejaculation and premature ejaculation to early ejaculation (APA, 2013a, 2013c). Because of high rates of comorbidity and problems with clinical distinction, dyspareunia and vaginismus were combined and named genito-pelvic pain/penetration disorder (APA, 2013a, 2013c). Finally, sexual aversion disorder was removed from the *DSM-5* because of limited prevalence and a lack of supporting research (APA, 2013c).

Coding, Recording, and Specifiers for All Sexual Dysfunctions

There is only one diagnostic code for each disorder within the sexual dysfunctions chapter of the *DSM-5*.

302.74 (F52.32)	Delayed ejaculation
302.72 (F52.21)	Erectile disorder
302.73 (F52.31)	Female orgasmic disorder
302.72 (F52.22)	Female sexual interest/arousal disorder
302.76 (F52.6)	Genito-pelvic pain/penetration disorder
302.71 (F52.0)	Male hypoactive sexual desire disorder
302.75 (F52.4)	Premature (early) ejaculation

The same subtype indicators are used for each disorder to designate the onset of the difficulty, the level of severity, and whether the disorder occurs in all instances or only in some situations. These indicators include whether delayed ejaculation has been *lifelong* or *acquired*. The acquired specifier indicates whether the problem began after the client had established normal sexual function. Also indicated for each sexual dysfunction disorder are specifiers of *generalized*, meaning they are not situational, and *situational*, which indicates dysfunction with specific stimulations or partners. Counselors will also need to indicate current severity of *mild*, *moderate*, or *severe*, which is indicated by the evidence of distress experienced by the client.

The coding for substance/medication-induced sexual dysfunction is noted for the specific substance/medication (see page 447 of the *DSM-5*). The coding includes the specific substance/medication in the diagnosis and is also accompanied by specifiers in relation to *with onset during intoxication, with onset during withdrawal,* or *with onset after medication use.* Counselors will also need to indicate current severity of *mild, moderate,* or *severe,* which is indicated by the evidence of distress experienced by the client.

To help readers better understand changes from the *DSM-IV-TR* to the *DSM-5*, the rest of this chapter outlines each disorder within the Sexual Dysfunctions chapter of the *DSM-5*. Readers should note that we have focused on major changes from the *DSM-IV-TR* to the *DSM-5*; however, this is not a stand-alone resource for diagnosis. Although a summary and special considerations for counselors are provided for each disorder, when diagnosing clients, counselors need to reference the *DSM-5*. It is essential that the diagnostic criteria and features, subtypes and specifiers, prevalence, course, risk, and prognostic factors for each disorder are clearly understood prior to diagnosis.

302.74 Delayed Ejaculation (F52.32)

My partner eventually got frustrated and left me. At first, he enjoyed that I could go long periods of time without ejaculating but eventually, he would want to discontinue and I didn't. He would stop enjoying himself long before I could finish. We were both frustrated. —Thomas

Major Changes From *DSM-IV-TR* to *DSM-5*

The major change from the *DSM-IV-TR* to the *DSM-5* was the renaming of male orgasmic disorder, formerly inhibited male orgasm in the *DSM-III*, to delayed ejaculation. Waldinger and Schweitzer (2005) reported the *DSM-IV-TR* classification of male orgasmic disorder was found to be "erroneously" labeled because the term did not accurately explain orgasm and ejaculation as different neurobiological processes. Others strongly criticized the name male orgasmic disorder for a lack of precision and specificity (Segraves, 2010).

Essential Features

Delayed ejaculation is the marked delay in or inability to achieve ejaculation, either during intercourse or with manual stimulation (APA, 2013a; Perelman, 2006). Often misunderstood and understudied, delayed ejaculation is considered the least common sexual dysfunction within the *DSM-5,* with a prevalence rate of 3% to 4% (Waldinger & Schweitzer, 2005). During delayed ejaculation, a man is able to attain sexual stimulation and has the desire to ejaculate but is unable to do so. Although the *DSM-5* does not stipulate what length of time is adequate in achieving ejaculation, the delay must not be purposeful or a result of any other physical or psychological problems or be a result of substance/medication use (APA, 2013a). Also referred to as "retarded ejaculation," "inhibited ejaculation," or "anejaculation," the emotional impact of this disorder is severe because it typically results in a lack of sexual fulfillment for both the man and his partner (D. Rowland et al., 2010).

Problems with delayed ejaculation can range from significant delay in ejaculation or a complete inability to ejaculate (D. Rowland et al., 2010). Some men with delayed ejaculation report being able to ejaculate during masturbation but not through intercourse. Symptoms (self-reported) must be present for a minimum duration of approximately 6 months (APA, 2013a). Because the *DSM-5* did not stipulate a length of time when ejaculation should occur, the clinical impression should be made as to the significant distress of the man or his partner. Most men ejaculate after 4 to 10 minutes of genital stimulation (D. Rowland et al., 2010). With delayed ejaculation, however, after prolonged stimulation the man may feel frustrated as he fails to reach orgasm or his partner may feel pain from continued intercourse. In cases such as these, a diagnosis of delayed ejaculation is appropriate.

Special Considerations

The prevalence of delayed ejaculation in the general male population below the age of 65 is 3% to 4% (Waldinger & Schweitzer, 2005). Delayed ejaculation is usually reported in early sexual experiences and continues over the course of a man's life span. Although delayed ejaculation varies across countries and cultures, Asian populations have presented with more complaints than men living in Europe, Australia, or the United States (APA, 2013a). If a man has never ejaculated, through any form of stimulation, including wet dreams, masturbation, or intercourse, counselors should always consult with a medical professional to determine if there is a physical cause. The most common causes for delayed ejaculation are psychological and could include life stressors (i.e., stress at work), lack of attraction for partner, atypical sexual or masturbation patterns, traumatic events, substances or medications, or neurological damage (Corona et al., 2013; D. Rowland et al., 2010). In terms of differential diagnoses, medications, medical illness, injury, and emotional or mental stressors can interfere with ejaculation and should be considered by counselors. In some cases, situational experiences, such as the choice of partner, can contribute to delays or an inability to ejaculate (Corona et al., 2013).

302.72 Erectile Disorder (F52.21)

It's been so embarrassing that I just quit trying to date at all. I told my friends that I'm done with women but honestly, I've tried to have sex different times and just can't keep an erection, even during oral sex. Then I get anxious and it gets worse. I miss the days when I felt like a real man.—Josh

Major Changes From *DSM-IV-TR* to *DSM-5*

Erectile disorder (ED) is the repeated inability to develop or maintain an erection during sexual stimulation or activity (APA, 2013a). The inability to achieve or maintain an erection must occur at least 75% of the time over the course of at least 6 months. The only modification from the *DSM-IV-TR* to *DSM-5* was that the minimum duration of ED was changed from 3 months to 6 months (APA, 2013a).

Essential Features

ED is described as the repeated failure to obtain or maintain an erection during partnered sexual activities (APA, 2013a). As with delayed ejaculation, ED may persist throughout one's lifetime or develop within one's lifetime, hence the specifiers *lifelong* or *acquired*. ED can also be situational, only occurring in certain situations or with certain partners. ED is often extremely disturbing to men and may cause low self-esteem, low self-confidence, a decreased sense of masculinity, and depressed affect (APA, 2013).

Special Considerations

The prevalence of ED in the general population is strongly correlated to age (APA, 2013a). Prevalence is 2% among the general population for men ages 40 to 49 years, 6% for men ages 60 to 69 years, and 39% for men 70 years or older (Inman et al., 2009). The *DSM-5* highlights that 20% of men fear erectile problems, and 8% experience some erectile problems with their first sexual experience. Similar to most sexual dysfunctions, ED can interfere with fertility and further compound individual and interpersonal distress (APA, 2013a). Cultural factors are unknown and have been found to vary across countries. Because ED is a self-report diagnosis, counselors should also consider erectile expectations within the client's cultural background.

Differential Diagnosis

Special consideration should be made as to the man's expectations of what sexual functioning means to him and his partner for a diagnosis of ED. MDD and ED are closely associated (APA, 2013a). Secondary causes of ED can stem from the use of alcohol, substances, and medications that can cause decreases in erectile function. If the cause is due to a medical condition, the individual would not receive a mental health diagnosis (APA, 2013a).

302.73 Female Orgasmic Disorder (F52.31)

I wouldn't say I've never had an orgasm, but it's been so long that I couldn't tell when the last time was. My boyfriend takes it personally. He gets his feelings hurt, especially when I try to pretend. I think he will leave me soon. —Carole

Essential Features

Female orgasmic disorder is defined by the *DSM-5* as a woman's difficulty in experiencing orgasm or markedly reduced intensity of orgasmic sensations on almost all or all (approximately 75% to 100%) occasions of sexual activity (APA, 2013a). The symptoms need to be present for a minimum duration of approximately 6 months. When a woman presents with pronounced strain over her inability to achieve an orgasm, many psychological factors, such as anxiety or relationship factors, as well as her knowledge of her own bodily responses need to be taken into account (APA, 2013a). The only major change from the *DSM-IV-TR* to the *DSM-5* was the addition of the minimum duration of approximately 6 months.

The *DSM-5* describes female orgasmic disorder as the marked delay in, infrequency of, or absence of orgasm with a significant reduction in intensity of orgasmic sensation. The *DSM-5* does not operationally define marked delay in orgasm, and counselors should refer clients presenting with symptoms of female orgasmic disorder for medical evaluation. The *DSM-5* does report that there are measurable physiological changes that occur during female orgasm, including changes in hormones, pelvic floor musculature, and brain activation; however, it is unclear to what degree this affects a woman's overall satisfaction with sexual activity (APA, 2013a).

Special Considerations

The prevalence of female orgasmic disorder in women varies from 10% to 42% depending on multiple factors such as age, culture, duration, and severity of symptoms. Studies have shown that these numbers did not account for distress; only a proportion of women experiencing female orgasmic disorder also reported distress (APA, 2013a). Young women may not feel as comfortable with their own bodies; worry about pregnancy or relationship problems can also be contributing factors.

Cultural Considerations
The importance of orgasm to a woman and its impact on overall sexual satisfaction vary widely by culture (Crooks & Baur, 2013). The *DSM-5* notes there may be marked sociocultural and generational differences in women's orgasmic ability. Inability to reach orgasm ranges from 17.7% (in Northern Europe) to 42.2% (in Southeast Asia; APA, 2013a).

Differential Diagnosis

If symptoms of sexual dysfunction result from interpersonal factors such as partner violence, distress in personal relationships, or other significant stressors, the diagnosis of female orgasmic disorder would not be made (APA, 2013a). Also, the lack of sexual interest or pleasure is a diagnostic criterion for some depressive disorders, such as MDD. Depressive disorders can also contribute to a woman's inability to experience orgasm. However, if the cause of dysfunction is due to another mental health disorder or a medical condition, the woman would not receive the diagnosis. Finally, the use of alcohol, substances, and medications can diminish a woman's overall sexual desire and response.

302.72 Female Sexual Interest/Arousal Disorder (F52.22)

I've wanted to date, but I just don't have much interest in sex. I don't even think about it for the most part. Companionship would be great, but men usually want to be with someone who gets into sex and I haven't had sexual feelings in years, even though I've made out with attractive men. I just don't care about it.—Contra

Major Changes From *DSM-IV-TR* to *DSM-5*

The major change from the *DSM-IV-TR* to the *DSM-5* was combining sexual interest with arousal in a classification for women only. In the *DSM-IV-TR*, hypoactive sexual desire disorder was seen as a one-size-fits-all criteria for low sexual interest. Also, the identifier of *adequate lubrication–swelling response of sexual excitement* was removed. In reviewing sexual dysfunctions in women, Öberg, Fugl-Meyer, and Fugl-Meyer (2004) asserted that women's sexual dysfunctions are not just psychological and should be considered from a biopsychosocial perspective. Oberg and colleagues noted that the *DSM-5* was designed to show increased emphasis on the biopsychosocial perspective.

Essential Features

Female sexual interest/arousal disorder is defined as the marked absence or decrease in sexual activity or sexual/erotic thoughts and fantasies for a minimum of 6 months. The lack of or significantly reduced sexual interest/arousal must be followed by at least three of six criteria, including lack of interest in sex, little or no thoughts or fantasies involving sex, lack of receptivity to sex or no sexual activity at all, no enjoyment of sex or most sexual encounters, limited or nonexistent response to sexual cues, and limited or no response or sensations during almost all sexual encounters (APA, 2013a).

Special Considerations

The prevalence of female sexual interest/arousal disorder, as defined by the *DSM-5*, is unknown and varies with factors such as cultural background, duration of symptoms, relationship history, past traumatic experiences, and presence of distress (APA, 2013a). Also, a woman's sexual problems may decrease with age, because some older women report less distress than younger women (Laumann et al., 1999).

Cultural Considerations
According to the *DSM-5*, there is marked variation in prevalence rates across cultures. East Asian women may have lower sexual desire than Euro-Canadian women. Counselors should always take the woman's cultural influences and background into account (APA, 2013a).

Differential Diagnosis

MDD is marked by the lack of sexual interest or pleasure and may contribute to a woman's sexual desire; if this is the case, then a diagnosis of female sexual interest/arousal disorder would not be made. The use of alcohol, substances, and medications can diminish a woman's overall sexual functioning and response. If the cause is due to a medical condition, the woman would not receive a mental diagnosis. The *DSM-5* highlights contributing interpersonal factors such as partner violence, distress in personal relationships, and other significant stressors; if any of these are present, the diagnosis of female orgasmic disorder would not be made (APA, 2013a).

302.76 Genito-Pelvic Pain/Penetration Disorder (F52.6)

I just don't ever want to feel that way again. It hurt so badly. I don't care if I never have sex again or how my boyfriend feels about it. I'm just too scared. —Hilde

Major Changes From *DSM-IV-TR* to *DSM-5*

The major change from the *DSM-IV-TR* to the *DSM-5* in relation to genito-pelvic pain/penetration disorder is its classification as a female disorder. The *DSM-IV-TR* combined male and female genital pain that is associated with intercourse into one diagnostic classification: sexual pain disorder. However, literature did not support this disorder in males. Also, the previous diagnosis of vaginismus is now included within this category.

Essential Features

Genito-pelvic pain/penetration disorder is the presence of pain with vaginal penetration during intercourse, and the symptoms must persist for a minimum of approximately 6 months. Genital pain during sexual activity typically causes significant distress in the woman, which might be accompanied by tensing or tightening of the pelvic floor muscles during attempted vaginal penetration or marked fear of attempted vaginal penetration. Genito-pelvic pain/penetration disorder can be described as shooting pain, burning, cutting, or throbbing with attempted penetration during intercourse.

Special Considerations

The prevalence of genito-pelvic pain/penetration disorder is unknown. The *DSM-5* reports that approximately 15% of women in North America report recurrent pain during intercourse (APA, 2013a). The *DSM-5* notes that in the past, cultural considerations were related to inadequate sexual education and religious orthodoxy; however, limited research does not support this assumption.

Differential Diagnosis

Inadequate sexual stimulation should be considered as a possible explanation to genito-pelvic pain upon penetration. Also, if a medical condition is present, it might contribute to the genito-pelvic pain/penetration disorder, in which case treating the medical condition might relieve the genito-pelvic pain/penetration symptoms. Counselors should note that a diagnosis cannot be given if symptoms are due to another medical condition.

302.71 Male Hypoactive Sexual Desire Disorder (F52.0)

It's very upsetting at times that I no longer have those thoughts or desires. I can't even remember the last time I really wanted to have sex. I don't even have fantasies. It's not that I can't get aroused, but my wife knows that I'm not into it anymore. She seems hurt.—Connor

Major Changes From *DSM-IV-TR* to *DSM-5*

Male hypoactive sexual desire disorder is defined by two criteria in the *DSM-5* as persistently or recurrently deficient (or absent) sexual/erotic thoughts or fantasies and desire for sexual activity and the symptoms must cause distress in the person. The major change from the *DSM-IV-TR* to the *DSM-5* is its classification as a male-only disorder.

Essential Features

In making an assessment of male hypoactive sexual desire disorder, counselors need to consider interpersonal factors. Although this disorder is primarily identified in aging men, an overall interpersonal assessment should be completed (Brotto, 2010). Symptoms of male hypoactive sexual desire disorder need to be present for a minimum duration of approximately 6 months.

Special Considerations

The prevalence rates for men with hypoactive sexual desire disorder are reported in the *DSM-5* and vary depending on the country of origin and method of assessment. The *DSM-5* notes that approximately 6% of younger men (ages 18 to 24 years) and 41% of older men (ages 66 to 74 years) have problems with sexual desire (APA, 2013a).

Cultural Considerations

The *DSM-5* notes that there is marked variability in prevalence rates of low desire across cultures, ranging from 12.5% in Northern European men to 28% in Southeast Asian men ages 40 to 80 years. Interpersonal conflicts with personal belief systems and culture may contribute to a man's inhibition of sexual desires (APA, 2013a).

Differential Diagnoses

Major depressive disorder is marked by the lack of sexual interest or pleasure and may contribute to a man's sexual desire; if this is the case, then the male hypoactive sexual desire disorder diagnosis would not be made. The use of alcohol, substances, and medications can diminish a man's overall sexual abilities. If the cause is due to a medical condition, the individual would not receive a mental diagnosis. The *DSM-5* points out that if the cause is due to interpersonal factors, such as severe relationship distress or other significant stressors, the diagnosis of hypoactive sexual desire disorder would not be made.

302.75 Premature (Early) Ejaculation (F52.4)

This is really hard for me to talk about, especially since I am only 21, but I feel like I don't know what else to do. As soon as I start having sex, I finish, sometimes in as little as 15 seconds. It has always been this way. I don't know why I even try.—James

Major Changes From *DSM-IV-TR* to *DSM-5*

The major change from the *DSM-IV-TR* to the *DSM-5* is the association of the 1-minute criterion. It was noted in earlier studies that a number of individuals did not want to put a limit on the time criteria for early ejaculation; however, the time length was adopted to align with the International Society of Sexual Medicine, which requires that unwanted ejaculation occur within 1 minute (Binik, Brotto, Graham, & Segraves, 2010).

Essential Features

Persistent or recurrent premature (early) ejaculation disorder is characterized by a pattern of ejaculation within approximately 1 minute of partnered sexual intercourse with vaginal penetration. In order to meet the diagnostic criteria for this disorder, ejaculation must occur before the individual wishes to ejaculate. A diagnosis of premature (early) ejaculation may be considered if early ejaculation occurs only during masturbation or sexual activities that do not include vaginal penetration, however, specific duration criteria have yet to be determined for these activities. Symptoms of this disorder represent the marked lack of control that occurs prior to or shortly after vaginal penetration. The symptoms need to be present for a minimum duration of 6 months. It is important to note that because the diagnostic criteria of premature ejaculation specifically references vaginal penetration, this disorder is not technically applicable to nonvaginal sexual activity. However, this diagnosis still may be applied to these individuals as long as all other criterion for the disorder are met (APA, 2013a).

Special Considerations

According to the *DSM-5*, the prevalence of premature (early) ejaculation varies widely depending on the definition used. Internationally, more than 20% to 30% of men ages 18 to 70 years report concern about how quickly they ejaculate upon penetration. The *DSM-5* notes that with the 1-minute criterion, only 1% to 3% of men would be considered with the diagnosis. It is important for counselors to rule out medical or substance causes and to use self-report on the symptoms, taking into account personal history of sexual experiences. If substance or medication is the cause of premature (early) ejaculation, then substance medication-induced sexual dysfunction should be diagnosed.

Substance/Medication-Induced Sexual Dysfunction

Essential Features

Substance/medication-induced sexual dysfunction is the significant disturbance in sexual function. The *DSM-5* stipulates that two criteria must be met: (a) the symptoms occur during or soon after the substance intoxication or withdrawal or after exposure to medication, and (b) the involved substance/medication is capable of producing the symptoms. With the exception of adding the term *medication* to the name, there is no major change from the *DSM-IV-TR* to the *DSM-5* (APA, 2013a).

The *DSM-5* indicates that sexual dysfunctions can occur in association with intoxication with the following classes of substances: alcohol; opioid; sedative, hypnotic, or anxiolytic; stimulants (including cocaine); and other (or unknown) substances. Medication can cause sexual dysfunction that includes but is not limited to antidepressants, antipsychotics, and hormonal contraceptives (APA, 2013a).

Special Considerations

Whereas antidepressants are widely used to treat a number of disorders, one of the most common side effect of antidepressants, such as Prozac, is difficulty with orgasm or ejaculation (Corona et al., 2013; Hyde & DeLamater, 2013). Because of possible underreporting, the prevalence rates for substance/medication-induced sexual dysfunction are unclear. The *DSM-5* reports the data on prevalence rates vary depending on the agent; approximately 25% to 80% of individuals taking monoamine oxidase inhibitors, tricyclic antidepressants, serotonergic antidepressants, and combined serotonergic-adrenergic antidepressants report sexual side effects. In terms of cultural considerations, there maybe some cultural implications as to how a culture views taking medications for sexual functioning.

Differential Diagnosis

Sexual functioning can be caused by other mental health problems, such as depressive, bipolar, anxiety, and psychotic disorders. A thorough medical and clinical assessment should take place before a diagnosis of substance/medication-induced sexual dysfunction is given by a medical doctor.

Paraphilic Disorders

Paraphilic disorders, formerly known as paraphilias in the *DSM-IV-TR*, consist of eight disorders characterized by abnormal or unnatural sexual tendencies that cause significant impairment to the person or cause harm to others (APA, 2013a). Theorists posit the existence of at least 547 categories of paraphilia, but the term itself originated from the Greek words *para* meaning "beside" and *philia* meaning "love" (Beech & Harkins, 2012). Common paraphilic activities revolve around themes of objects or animals, self- or partner humiliation or suffering, and nonconsenting persons. Although exact etiology is unknown, paraphilias may be biomedical in nature (Beech & Harkins, 2012; Nolen-Hoeksema, 2006).

Rates of paraphilia within the general population are unknown (Marsh et al., 2010). Individuals who exhibit symptoms of paraphilic disorders do not always consider their behavior or sexual tendencies to be problematic. Moreover, paraphilic behaviors typically do not come to the attention of counselors unless the behavior has caused conflict with sexual partners or the individual has been charged with an illegal act. Judging from the large commercial market in paraphilic pornography and paraphernalia, as well as the abundance of websites and online chat rooms devoted to such material, prevalence within the community is believed to be far higher than that indicated by statistics from clinical facilities (Marsh et al., 2010; Nolen-Hoeksema, 2006).

In the *DSM-5*, paraphilic disorders have been organized into distinct categories, including those that are activity specific and those that are target specific (APA, 2013a). Activity-specific disorders loosely reflect courtship, for example, voyeuristic disorder, exhibitionistic disorder, and frotteuristic disorder. Also within the activity-specific category are two disorders involving physical pain that the APA (2013a) refers to as *algolagnic disorders*; these are sexual masochism disorder and sexual sadism disorder. The second category, target-specific disorders, includes pedophilic disorder, fetishistic disorder, and transvestic disorder. Whereas behaviors associated with some of these disorders are clearly illegal (i.e., voyeuristic disorder, exhibitionistic disorder, pedophilic disorder, and frotteuristic disorder), a gray area exists for others. In the context of mutual consent between adults, behaviors involved in sexual masochism disorder and sexual sadism disorder are not illegal by nature (Beech & Harkins, 2012).

It is noteworthy that most individuals with atypical sexual preferences do not have a mental disorder. An individual who has a paraphilia does not necessarily have a paraphilic disorder (APA, 2013a). Counselors should take care to avoid pathologizing sexual interests that do not cause any harm, distress, or impairment to self or others.

Major Changes From *DSM-IV-TR* to *DSM-5*

In an effort to reduce stigma, the *DSM-5* changed the nomenclature of paraphilic disorders. Voyeurism was changed to voyeuristic disorder, exhibitionism to exhibitionistic disorder, frotteurism to frotteuristic disorder, and so on. As with all other categories within the *DSM-5*, new other specified and unspecified disorders were added (APA, 2013a).

Two course specifiers were also included in the *DSM-5*. The specifier *in remission* is now an option to indicate a remission from any paraphilic disorder. The second specifier, *in a controlled environment*, has been added to indicate if the individual is unable to act on certain paraphilic urges because he or she is in a hospital, prison, or other confined environment (APA, 2013a). Aside from semantic changes and the addition of course specifiers, no other major changes have been made to this section. Therefore, we have not included a major changes section within any of the specific diagnoses described below, only essential features, special considerations, differential diagnosis, and coding information.

Differential Diagnoses

Differentiating paraphilias from other disorders is not difficult because this group has distinctive features. However, within the paraphilic disorders grouping, differentiation can be complicated by the tendency for individuals to experience multiple, sometimes related, paraphilias (Comer, 2013). For example, an individual who has transvestic disorder may also have an underwear fetish. Carefully assessing and understanding the individual's symptoms, severity, and consequences can facilitate an appropriate diagnosis (APA, 2013a). Finally, it is critical that counselors differentiate between a diagnosable mental disorder and sexual behavior that is outside of societal norms but does not present clinically significant distress or impairment, such as a foot fetish.

Etiology and Treatment

Although most etiological explanations for paraphilic disorders have a limited research base (Comer, 2013; Nolen-Hoeksema, 2006), theorists typically propose ideas consistent with theoretical belief systems. For instance, psychodynamic theorists, such as Freud, may believe that deviance arises as a result of problems with childhood development;

behaviorists would posit that this is the result of conditioning. Moreover, many contend that paraphilic disorders have both biological and developmental components (Garcia & Thibaut, 2011; Nolen-Hoeksema, 2006).

Treatment options are often based on constructs surrounding etiology. Options include medication, psychotherapy, and a combination of medication and psychotherapy. Psychological treatments are long-standing and can include behavioral techniques, CBT, aversion therapies such as ammonia aversion and olfactory aversion therapy, masturbatory reconditioning, directed masturbation, and verbal satiation (Beech & Harkins, 2012). Multiple options for biologically based treatments have been more recently developed than psychotherapeutic treatments. These are based on reducing sexual arousal level and should only be considered after a full medical examination. These can include antidepressants, such as selective serotonin reuptake inhibitors (SSRIs), and hormones, such as estrogen, steroidal antiandrogens, and gonadotrophin-releasing hormones (Garcia & Thibaut, 2011; Nolen-Hoeksema, 2006). Many of these have negative side effects, and ethical considerations are paramount.

Implications for Counselors

The most common paraphilic disorders counselors will come across are also the most common sexual offenses, and more often than not, clients are in treatment because of involvement of the legal system (Comer, 2013). These include pedophilic disorder (sexual activity with children), exhibitionistic disorder (genital self-exposure to strangers), voyeuristic disorder (watching strangers who are naked, undressing, or having sex), and frotteuristic disorder (touching an unconsenting person). Counselors should note that almost all individuals with these four most common paraphilic disorders are male (Morrison, 2006). The most common psychotherapy modalities include cognitive-behavioral or behavioral approaches. Because of the potential for harm to others, counselors have a responsibility to know and adhere to the state laws regarding mandated reporting and the *ACA Code of Ethics* (ACA, 2014) when working with these clients.

Counselors need to understand that psychosocial impairment is common among individuals diagnosed with paraphilias. Kafka and Hennen (2002) compared individuals with paraphilic disorders with those with nonparaphilic hypersexuality disorders (e.g., compulsive masturbation and dependence on pornography) and found significantly higher rates of physical abuse, lower levels of education, higher instances of hospitalizations for psychiatric or substance abuse problems, higher rates of disability or unemployment, and more legal problems in individuals with paraphilic disorders. Individuals diagnosed with paraphilic disorders also have higher rates of exposure to medical risks such as sexually transmitted infections (Comer, 2013; Hyde & DeLamater, 2013). While being careful to not pathologize individuals diagnosed with these disorders, counselors should always inquire about medical history and whether the client has had a recent physical exam (Crooks & Baur, 2013).

The following sections include descriptions, essential features, differential diagnosis, and case examples for training. In an effort to not stigmatize individuals diagnosed with paraphilias, we have chosen not to include fictitious client testimonials.

302.2 Pedophilic Disorder (F65.4)

Essential Features

Formerly known as pedophilia, pedophilic disorder is the most common type of paraphilia, occurring in an estimated 3% to 5% of men (APA, 2013a). More prevalent in males than females, pedophilic behaviors normally begin during adolescence, and behaviors are escalatory in nature. Characterized by sexual attraction to children, individuals diagnosed with pedophilic disorder prefer to engage in sexual encounters with children as opposed to adults (Nolen-Hoeksema, 2006). Counselors will most likely come across individuals who have been mandated to treatment after engaging in oral sex with a child or touching a child's genitals, as most individuals diagnosed with this disorder do engage in penetration. One important distinction includes whether the individual is exclusively sexually attracted to children, because most individuals diagnosed with pedophilic disorder prefer to have sexual encounters with children. Individuals with this disorder are typically attracted to a specific age range or sex (R. C. W. Hall & Hall, 2007). Most individuals diagnosed with pedophilic disorder are heterosexual men who target female victims (Nolen-Hoeksema, 2006). Substance use also plays a major role in pedophilic behaviors; up to 50% of diagnosed individuals use alcohol before engaging in sexual behaviors with children (Morrison, 2006).

Criteria for pedophilic disorder include recurrent intense sexual desires, fantasies, or behaviors involving sexual activity with an individual age 13 or under. The person must experience these symptoms for at least 6 months, be at least 16 years of age, and be at least 5 years older than the child (Nolen-Hoeksema, 2006). Perhaps the most important criterion for counselors to consider when diagnosing an individual with pedophilic disorder is that the sexual desires, fantasies, or behaviors must cause clinically significant distress or impairment in work, social, or personal functioning or the person has acted on these desires (APA, 2013a).

Special Considerations

As mandated, and in accordance with the *ACA Code of Ethics* (ACA, 2014), counselors should take the criterion of acting on those desires into serious consideration. If a client is currently acting on pedophilic behaviors or states that he or she will act on them, counselors are required to report these actions to the proper authorities. Unless the counselor believes doing so may cause further harm to a child, this should involve a conversation with the client regarding the necessary breach in confidentiality this will entail. Code B.1.d. of the *ACA Code of Ethics* (ACA, 2014) advises that counselors should discuss limitations of confidentiality during the first session with clients so that they are aware of ethical standards. Another important consideration for counselors is the age requirement for this disorder. For example, if a 15-year-old is in a sexual relationship with a 12-year-old, he or she would not fit criteria for pedophilic disorder. It is essential that counselors educate themselves on state laws regarding sexual relationships between children and adolescents.

Beech and Harkins (2012) reviewed the literature on evidence-based treatment for those who have been diagnosed with pedophilic disorder. They reported some success with treatments involving CBT combined with medication, as well as behavioral therapy in combination with medications. Studies involving sexual crimes against children generally indicate that these individuals reoffended at a much lower rate if they had received treatment (Beech & Harkins, 2012). As with all other concerns, counselors need to provide effective, evidence-based treatments for this group.

Many counselors, especially novice counselors, vocalize how difficult it would be for them to work with sex offenders, often stating they would most likely want to refer these clients to another professional. It is important to remember, however, that most individuals diagnosed with pedophilic disorder have experienced neglect and extreme punishment as children (Comer, 2013). As counselors, we must adhere to the *ACA Code of Ethics* (ACA, 2014), which stresses the significance of competence and the professional responsibility we have to our clients (see Section C of the *ACA Code of Ethics*).

Differential Diagnosis

The differential diagnosis for this pedophilic disorder includes ASPD, because individuals with this disorder may be more likely to engage in illegal activities. They may be more willing to approach a minor or engage in activities that could injure others. The impact of alcohol and substance use should be considered as well. Individuals under the influence may be more likely to approach someone who is underage or to engage in related activities. Finally, counselors should consider OCD before giving this diagnosis (APA, 2013a).

Coding, Recording, and Specifiers

There is only one diagnostic code for pedophilic disorder: 302.2 (F65.4). The specifier given for individuals who are only attracted to children is *exclusive type*, and *nonexclusive type* is applied to those who are not attracted only to children. Counselors can use specifiers to identify whether the individual is *sexually attracted to males*, *sexually attracted to females*, or *sexually attracted to both*. In addition, one can specify whether the behavior is *limited to incest* (APA, 2013a).

 Example

Donald, a 45-year-old Caucasian man, is mandated to treatment after being released from prison for a sex offense conviction. Donald reports that his earliest memory includes sexual play with his older female babysitter. As an adult, Donald found himself sexually aroused by the bodies of young girls. Despite this attraction, Donald married at age 24 and had three children (all boys) with his wife, who was his age. Throughout his marriage, Donald began secretly collecting pornographic magazines featuring children. When his sexual tension became too high, Donald would masturbate and think about the pictures in his magazines. By age 30, Donald and his wife began having marital problems, and Donald took up photography. He would invite neighborhood children, specifically 8- to 9-year-old girls, to his house and persuade them to pose for him either partially or fully naked. Donald found satisfaction in taking these pictures and never touched any of the children. His wife found the pictures in his laptop one day and called the police. Donald was arrested; his wife filed for divorce while he was incarcerated. During his intake, Donald stated that he didn't think that taking pictures of children while they were naked could cause them any harm. He also stated, "I'm not proud of it, but it was something that I couldn't resist."

◆ ◆ ◆

Diagnostic Questions

1. Do Donald's presenting symptoms meet the criteria for a paraphilic disorder? If so, which disorder?
2. Based on the disorder identified in Question 1, which symptom(s) led you to select that diagnosis?
3. What rule-outs would you consider for Donald's case?
4. What other information may be needed to make an accurate clinical diagnosis?

302.4 Exhibitionistic Disorder (F65.2)

Essential Features

Exhibitionistic disorder is one of the most common paraphilic disorders. As many as one in three women report having an experience in which a man exposed himself (Comer, 2013). Counselors will most likely come across males with this disorder who expose themselves to females of any age, including children. Individuals with exhibitionistic disorder usually begin exposing themselves to strangers before the age of 18, do not try and contact the person they expose themselves to, and typically do not pose a danger to their targeted victim. The urge to expose self to others often comes in waves, occurring most often when the person is stressed or has free time (Comer, 2013; Morrison, 2006).

Exposing of the self can be quite different for each individual. Men may expose their penis while it is erect or flaccid. Some could masturbate while exposing themselves, craving a reaction from their victims, whereas others may quickly expose themselves and run away. Although individuals with this disorder may fantasize about having intercourse with those they expose themselves to, they seldom act on these fantasies. Many individuals with exhibitionistic disorder lead relatively normal lives, have successful intimate and sexual relationships (Morrison, 2006), and are unlikely to seek treatment unless they experience legal issues.

To be diagnosed with exhibitionistic disorder, the individual must fully meet two criteria outlined within the *DSM-5* (APA, 2013a). The first criterion states that the individual must have recurrent and intense sexual desires, fantasies, or behaviors regarding genital self-exposure to unsuspecting strangers for at least 6 months. The second criterion states that the first criterion must cause significant distress or impairment in the individual's life or the individual must have exposed himself or herself to someone who has not or cannot consent. Examples of distress or impairment can include loss of work, relationship problems, lack of sleep, or legal ramifications due to desires, fantasies, or engagement in exhibitionistic behaviors (APA, 2013a).

Special Considerations

Counselors should note that individuals diagnosed with exhibitionistic disorder may also engage in other paraphilic behaviors such as pedophilic, frotteuristic, or voyeuristic behaviors (Morrison, 2006). It would be prudent for counselors to look for these types of behaviors when working with clients diagnosed with exhibitionistic disorder. Moreover, as with pedophilic disorder, exhibitionistic behaviors are illegal if acted upon. Reporting sexual fantasies about exhibitionistic behavior has been strongly related to the likelihood of engaging in such behaviors (Långström & Seto, 2006). It is important for counselors to discuss confidentiality and the need to breach confidentiality if clients report they will expose their genitals to others, because the individuals could be putting someone else at risk for harm.

Beech and Harkins (2012) identified CBT, behavioral therapy, and empathy training as primary treatment modalities for exhibitionistic disorder. They posited that because there is no physical contact, individuals who engage in this behavior may be less likely to empathize with the people to whom they have exposed themselves. Aspects of behavioral therapy and CBT have been shown to be effective in studies. The most common behavioral treatments include covert sensitization, ammonia aversion, and minimal arousal conditioning.

Differential Diagnosis

As with other paraphilias, counselors should explore the impact of substance use before making a diagnosis. If the behavior is related only to substance abuse, that diagnosis may be more accurate. Furthermore, conduct disorder and ASPD should be explored as alternative or coexisting diagnoses (APA, 2013a).

Coding, Recording, and Specifiers

There is only one diagnostic code for exhibitionistic disorder: 302.4 (F65.2). Specifiers include *sexually aroused by exposing genitals to prepubertal children*, *sexually aroused by exposing genitals to physically mature individuals*, and *sexually aroused by exposing genitals to prepubertal children and to physically mature individuals*. Counselors can identify *in a controlled environment* and *in full remission* as specifiers where appropriate (APA, 2013a).

302.82 Voyeuristic Disorder (F65.3)

Essential Features

Voyeuristic disorder is characterized as sexual arousal from watching unsuspecting strangers engage in private activities. Also known as "peeping toms," a term from 17th-century England, these individuals are almost always men (Comer, 2013); prevalence rates may be as high as 12% in the male population (APA, 2013a). Many individuals with this disorder masturbate while watching unsuspecting victims. They almost never take steps to have any contact, sexual or not, with victims. Similar to those with exhibitionistic disorder, individuals diagnosed with a voyeuristic disorder lead relatively normal lives with intimate relationships and take great precautions to avoid being caught in their paraphilic activities (Morrison, 2006).

A diagnosis of voyeuristic disorder requires two criteria after the age of 18. First, the individual must exhibit at least 6 months of recurrent and intense sexual desires, fantasies, or behaviors regarding the act of watching unsuspecting individuals who are naked, disrobing, or having sex. Second, as with previously mentioned paraphilic disorders, the individual must have engaged in the behavior or the tendencies must cause significant distress or impairment in the individual's life (APA, 2013a).

Special Considerations

Counselors should be aware that voyeuristic disorder tends to be a chronic disorder and normally begins before the age of 15 (Morrison, 2006). As with pedophilic and exhibitionistic behaviors, voyeuristic activities are illegal if acted upon. It is important for counselors to distinguish between individuals who are aroused by watching pornography from individuals who are aroused by watching women undress from their bedroom windows. The latter, of course, is illegal and must be looked at more closely by counselors when clients report that they will engage in illegal behaviors that put others at risk for harm.

As with other paraphilic disorders, counselors must adhere to state laws as well as the *ACA Code of Ethics* (ACA, 2014) regarding confidentiality. Individuals who report voyeuristic behaviors are more likely to report current mental disorders. Exhibitionistic and voyeuristic behaviors have been related to psychological problems, substance use, and sexual risk taking or novelty seeking (Långström & Seto, 2006). Counselors should take note of comorbidity with others paraphilic disorders as well as other mental disorders in the *DSM-5*. Behavioral therapies and CBT are commonly used approaches to treating this disorder (Beech & Harkins, 2012).

Differential Diagnosis

Substance abuse, conduct disorder, and ASPD may have overlapping symptoms with voyeuristic disorder. However, the symptoms of voyeuristic disorder will persist for at least 6 months and are related to intense sexual arousal. Conduct and antisocial symptoms will be related to a pattern of rule-breaking behaviors; single-episode behaviors that occur while intoxicated tend to be related to substance use disorders (APA, 2013a).

Coding, Recording, and Specifiers

There is only one diagnostic code for voyeuristic disorder: 302.82 (F65.3). As with other paraphilias, specifiers can be given to indicate certain conditions such as *in a controlled environment* and *in full remission* (APA, 2013a).

302.89 Frotteuristic Disorder (F65.81)

Essential Features

Frotteuristic disorder, which occurs in an estimated 30% of the male population (APA, 2013a), is the last of the four most common paraphilic disorders counselors will come across in their practice. It is also the final paraphilic disorder for which action or engagement can lead to serious legal ramifications. Unlike exhibitionistic and voyeuristic tendencies, individuals with frotteuristic disorder act out their fantasies and violate the rights of others by molesting unconsenting victims. This disorder is characterized by an individual, almost always a male, who gains sexual pleasure from the act of touching or rubbing a nonconsenting person (who is almost always a female) while sometimes fantasizing about being in a relationship with that person (Comer, 2013).

Frotteuristic disorder is defined as at least 6 months of repeated and intense sexual desires, fantasies, or behaviors involving touching and rubbing a nonconsenting person. As with other paraphilic disorders, this must cause significant distress or impairment in the individual's life or he or she must have acted on such desires (APA, 2013a). An individual with this disorder normally rubs his genitals against a woman's body or fondles a woman's breasts or genitalia. Frotteuristic acts frequently occur in public places such as subways or crowded sidewalks (Morrison, 2006).

Special Considerations

Frotteuristic offenses tend to go underreported, and research in this area is lacking. What is known is that individuals with frotteuristic disorder often begin exhibiting behaviors during adolescence and may have a history of other sexually deviant behaviors such as rape, exhibitionism, pedophilia, sexual sadism, and voyeurism (Morrison, 2006). Research shows that individuals with frotteuristic disorder often experience anxiety, shame, negative self-image, and other emotional concerns related to their diagnosis. Although researchers do not typically address frotteurism separately from other paraphilias, counselors should note that solution-focused therapy might be an effective way to treat this disorder (Guterman, Martin, & Rudes, 2011).

Differential Diagnosis

As with other paraphilic disorders, conduct disorder and ASPD should be considered. If the behaviors are partly related to a pattern of norm-breaking behaviors, frotteuristic disorder may not apply. Isolated episodes that occur with the use of alcohol or other substances will not be part of frotteurism (APA, 2013a).

Coding, Recording, and Specifiers

There is only one diagnostic code for frotteuristic disorder: 302.89 (F65.81). Specifiers for this disorder include *in a controlled environment* and *in full remission* (APA, 2013a).

302.83 Sexual Masochism Disorder (F65.51) and 302.84 Sexual Sadism Disorder (F65.52)

Essential Features

Whereas sexual masochism is characterized by gaining sexual pleasure from receiving pain or suffering, sexual sadism, named such after the infamous Marquis de Sade, is characterized by gaining sexual pleasure from inflicting pain or humiliation (Comer, 2013). These two disorders have much in common and have a high rate of comorbidity with each other (up to 30%); thus, we discuss them together. Unlike the previous four most common paraphilic disorders, sexual masochism and sexual sadism disorders do not usually lead to sexual offenses or legal ramifications. In fact, intimate partners who engage in masochistic and sadistic behaviors are highly consenting and will often have safety words to indicate a time to stop the behaviors (Morrison, 2006).

Both sexual masochistic and sadistic tendencies begin in childhood and are typically chronic. Individuals participate in masochistic and sadistic behaviors in numerous ways, including beating, choking, bondage, blindfolding, spanking, pricking, shocking, hitting, cutting, asphyxiation, or humiliation. Humiliation can be achieved in a variety of ways, including "defecation, urination, or forcing the submissive partner to imitate an animal" (Morrison, 2006, p. 372). Individuals with these disorders commonly require an increase in the severity of these methods to produce the same degree of sexual satisfaction.

Criteria for sexual masochistic disorder and sexual sadism disorder are quite similar. Sexual masochistic disorder requires at least 6 months of fantasies, behaviors, and desires focused on being made to suffer, humiliated, bound, or beaten (APA, 2013a). The sexual urges are persistent and intense in nature and sometimes involve the individual being forced into sex against his or her will (Comer, 2013). In some ways, sexual sadism disorder is the exact opposite. This disorder requires at least 6 months of repeated, intense sexual urges, fantasies, or behaviors in which pain is inflicted by the individual on someone else (APA, 2013a). Both disorders require significant distress or impairment in the individual's functioning. Note that unlike the previous four common paraphilic disorders, an individual cannot be diagnosed for merely participating or engaging in the behaviors with a consenting adult; they must experience clinically significant distress or impairment because of their masochistic or sadistic tendencies (APA, 2013a).

Special Considerations

There are numerous aspects to consider with these two disorders. As with the previously mentioned paraphilic disorders, sexual masochism disorder is predominantly seen in men (APA, 2013a). As with other disorders, treatment tends to focus on behavioral therapy, aversion therapies, and CBT, but research into efficacy is very limited (Beech & Harkins, 2012). Furthermore, some individuals act out sexual sadism with nonconsenting partners. Although there have been cases in which sexual murderers and rapists have been diagnosed with this disorder (Comer, 2013), fewer than 10% of sex offenders who rape can be diagnosed with sexual sadism disorder (Frances & Wollert, 2012). It is of utmost importance that counselors working with this population ensure that the well-being of both partners is protected.

Lastly, the risks of sexual sadistic and masochistic methods should be examined. Methods such as asphyxiation can lead to serious health-related concerns. Also, engagement in asphyxiation leads to a few accidental deaths per million people each year. Counselors can take a psychoeducational role and educate themselves and clients on how to safely engage in these somewhat atypical sexual practices to reduce the risk of health-related concerns and accidental death.

Differential Diagnosis

For both sexual masochistic and sexual sadistic disorders, it is important to differentiate between nonimpairing sexual behaviors and a disorder, which requires distress or impairment that is clinical in nature. When giving the diagnosis, counselors should determine if the urge or behavior is based on giving or receiving pain. Furthermore, counselors should consider substance use, hypersexuality, or antisocial personality symptoms with these disorders. In addition to being potentially different diagnoses, they are often comorbid with sexual masochistic and sexual sadistic disorders (APA, 2013a).

Coding, Recording, and Specifiers

There is only one diagnostic code for sexual masochistic disorder: 302.83 (F65.51). Sexual masochistic disorder has a unique specifier of *with asphyxiophilia*. Sexual sadistic disorder is coded as 302.84 (F65.52) and has no unique specifiers. Both disorders have specifiers of *in a controlled environment* and *in full remission* (APA, 2013a).

302.81 Fetishistic Disorder (F65.0)

Essential Features

Fetishistic disorder, a common paraphilia, is marked by sexual arousal over inanimate objects or nongenital body parts, such as feet, often rejecting all other stimuli (Comer, 2013). Objects vary widely and can include anything from the typical fetish of underwear or shoes to less typical objects such as cars or balloons. This disorder is far more common in men than in women, and the fetishes typically first present in adolescence. The desire to collect the object can result in acts such as stealing women's worn clothing (APA, 2013a; Comer, 2013).

APA (2013a) identified the criteria for fetishistic disorder as intense, repeated sexual fantasies, urges, or behaviors related to the use of an inanimate object or body parts that are not genitals. The object cannot be part of items used or related to cross-dressing or be used solely for genital stimulation. The fantasies, urges, or behaviors must last for at least 6 months, and the individual must experience impairment or clinically significant distress (APA, 2013a).

Special Considerations

There are differing theories as to the etiology of fetishistic disorder, but the exact cause has yet to be determined. Treatments based on different theories have met with some success, particularly CBT and behavioral therapies. Behaviorists posit that conditioning is responsible for fetish behavior. As a result, treatments such as aversion therapy, masturbatory satiation, and orgasmic reorientation have been used (Comer, 2013). Beech and Harkins (2012) reported evidence that these treatments have met with some success. Furthermore, evidence supports the use of CBT and a combined treatment of directive guidance and behavioral modification for reducing symptoms (Beech & Harkins, 2012). When working with individuals diagnosed with fetishistic disorder, counselors need to clearly identify and follow the client's goals. Goals may differ among clients, with some interested in symptom reduction or termination and others desiring relationship improvement or avoidance of legal issues (Beech & Harkins, 2012).

Differential Diagnosis

When differentiating fetishistic disorder from transvestic disorder, counselors should consider the role of the fetish object. If it is an article of clothing or other object used only during cross-dressing, then transvestic disorder is more applicable. Sexual masochistic disorder can be diagnosed along with fetishistic disorder, but if the fetish object is related only to being harmed or coerced, fetishism should not be diagnosed (APA, 2013a). Furthermore, counselors are reminded that having a fetish does not necessarily indicate a disorder. There must be a clinically significant level of distress or impairment for a diagnosis to be given; care and concern should be taken not to stigmatize or shame the individual (Comer, 2013).

Coding, Recording, and Specifiers

There is only one diagnostic code for fetishistic disorder: 302.81 (F65.0). Specifiers for this disorder are related to the type of fetish and include *body parts(s)*, *nonliving object(s)*, or *other*, as well as *in a controlled environment* and *in full remission* (APA, 2013a).

302.3 Transvestic Disorder (F65.1)

Essential Features

Typically beginning in prepubescence and often referred to as "cross-dressing," about 3.2% of the population reports experiencing at least one episode of transvestic disorder. This is primarily a male disorder, occurring in an estimated 2.8% of the male population (Långström & Zucker, 2005). Symptoms range from wearing a single item of other-gender clothing underneath the individual's clothing to fully dressing as a member of the opposite gender (Comer, 2013). For individuals in heterosexual relationships, this can cause distress and conflict within the relationship. Studies have indicated significant correlations between this disorder and other disorders, such as voyeuristic disorder and frotteurism, in which illegal activities could occur (Långström & Zucker, 2005).

The defining characteristics of transvestic disorder include intense sexual arousal resulting from dressing, or fantasies and urges surrounding dressing, in clothing typically associated with the opposite gender (Comer, 2013). This behavior must be recurrent for at least 6 months and result in impairment in functioning or clinically significant distress or both (APA, 2013a).

Note

Cross-dressing does not indicate a diagnosis of transvestic disorder. To qualify for this diagnosis, the individual must experience sexual arousal and excitement almost every time he or she engages in this behavior. The behavior will cause distress or impairment in functioning, often as related to relationships with significant others.

◆ ◆ ◆

Special Considerations

Transvestic disorder typically has onset for boys prior to adolescence and can be episodic over the lifetime. The etiology of the disorder is uncertain; some theorists point to operant conditioning in childhood (Comer, 2013). Furthermore, because these individuals present for treatment infrequently, there is little reported in terms of evidence-based treatments. A few studies indicate effectiveness in medication therapy; however, they involve case studies with limited generalizability (Garcia & Thibaut, 2011). Counselors should be aware of the client's goals and their own personal biases when working with this population. Elimination of the symptoms may not be the client's goal. Instead, the client's ultimate goal may be symptom management, reduction of behaviors, or relationship improvement.

Counselors should also be aware of the potential for comorbidity with other disorders, such as fetishism and sexual masochism (APA, 2013a). There are also indicators that individuals with this disorder may experience pleasure from exposing themselves to others, watching others have intercourse, or using pain as part of sexual arousal (Långström & Zucker, 2005). Careful screening is crucial here, as is awareness of the *ACA Code of Ethics* (ACA, 2014) and potential for harm to others. In addition, harm to self can come into play as individuals with this disorder may also engage in autoerotic asphyxiation (APA, 2013a).

Differential Diagnosis

Differentiating transvestic disorder from fetishistic disorder can be challenging. Whereas those who experience fetishism will focus on an object or body part, an individual with transvestic disorder will have sexual arousal related to the experience of dressing as the opposite gender or imagining himself or herself as a member of the opposite gender. Transvestic disorder can be mistaken for gender dysphoria. However, the differentiating factor between the two disorders is that individuals with gender dysphoria report lack of congruence between physical and emotional gender, whereas those with transvestic disorder experience sexual arousal when cross-dressing. Furthermore, those with gender dysphoria have a desire to change genders, and, typically, those with transvestic disorder do not. These disorders can co-occur, and both should be diagnosed when there is evidence for both (APA, 2013a).

Coding, Recording, and Specifiers

There is only one diagnostic code for transvestic disorder: 302.3 (F65.1). Transvestic disorder specifiers include *with fetishism*, indicating that the individual is aroused by materials, fabrics, or clothing; and *with autogynephilia*, occurring in males and indicating that the individual is aroused by fantasies or pictures of himself as a female (APA, 2013a). Counselors can specify if acts occur *in a controlled environment* or are *in full remission*.

Part Two References

Agrawal, A., Wethrill, L., Bucholz, K. K., Kramer, J., Kuperman, S., Lynskey, M. T., . . . Bierut, L. J. (2012). Genetic influences on craving for alcohol. *Addictive Behaviors, 38,* 1501–1508.

Ahmed, A. O., Green, B. A., McCloskey, M. S., & Berman, M. E. (2010). Latent structure of intermittent explosive disorder in an epidemiological sample. *Journal of Psychiatric Research, 44,* 663–672. doi:10.1016/j.jpsychires.2009.12.004

Alexander, D., & Leung, P. (2011). The *DSM* Guided Cannabis Screen (*DSM-G-CS*): Description, reliability, factor structure and empirical scoring with a clinical sample. *Addictive Behaviors, 36,* 1095–1100.

Allen, K. L., Fursland, A., Watson, H., & Byrne, S. M. (2011). Eating disorder diagnoses in general practice settings: Comparison with structured clinical interview and self-report questionnaires. *Journal of Mental Health, 20,* 270–280. doi:10.3109/09638237.2011.562259

American Academy of Child and Adolescent Psychiatry. (2011, March). *Facts for families: Children with oppositional defiant disorder.* Retrieved from www.aacap.org/App_Themes/AACAP/docs/facts_for_families/72_children_with_oppositional_defiant_disorder.pdf

American Counseling Association (2014). *ACA code of ethics.* Alexandria, VA: Author.

American Psychiatric Association. (1952). *Diagnostic and statistical manual of mental disorders.* Washington, DC: Author.

American Psychiatric Association. (1968). *Diagnostic and statistical manual of mental disorders* (2nd ed.). Washington, DC: Author.

American Psychiatric Association. (1980). *Diagnostic and statistical manual of mental disorders* (3rd ed.). Washington, DC: Author.

American Psychiatric Association. (2000). *Diagnostic and statistical manual of mental disorders* (4th ed., text rev.). Washington, DC: Author.

American Psychiatric Association. (2013a). *Diagnostic and statistical manual of mental disorders* (5th ed.). Arlington, VA: Author.

American Psychiatric Association. (2013b). *Feeding and eating disorders.* Retrieved from http://www.dsm5.org/Documents/Eating%20Disorders%20Fact%20Sheet.pdfS

American Psychiatric Association. (2013c). *Highlights of changes from DSM-IV-TR to DSM-5.* Retrieved from http://www.psychiatry.org/practice/dsm/dsm5

American Society of Addiction Medicine. (2013). *Public policy statement: Definition of addiction.* Retrieved from http://www.asam.org/for-the-public/definition-of-addiction

Arnulf, I., Zeitzer, J. M., File, J., Farber, N., & Mignot, E. (2005). Kleine-Levin syndrome: A systematic review of 186 cases in the literature. *Brain, 128,* 2763–2776.

Barnes, R. D., Masheb, R. B., White, M. A., & Grilo, C. M. (2011). Comparison of methods for identifying and assessing obese patients with binge eating disorder in primary care settings. *International Journal of Eating Disorders, 44,* 157–163. doi:10.1002/eat.20802

Basson, R., Berman, J., Burnett, A., Derogatis, L., Ferguson, D., Fourcroy, J., . . . Whipple, B. (2000). Report of the International Consensus Development Conference on Female Sexual Dysfunction: Definitions and classifications. *Journal of Urology, 163,* 888–893.

Baum, A., Revenson, T., & Singer, J. (2012). *Handbook of health psychology* (2nd ed.). New York, NY: Taylor & Francis.

Beech, A. R., & Harkins, L. (2012). *DSM-IV-TR* paraphilia: Descriptions, demographics and treatment interventions. *Aggression and Violent Behavior, 17,* 527–539.

Berg, K. C., & Peterson, C. B. (2013). Assessment and diagnosis of eating disorders. In L. H. Choate (Ed.), *Eating disorders and obesity: A counselor's guide to prevention and treatment* (pp. 91–117). Alexandria, VA: American Counseling Association.

Berg, K. C., Peterson, C. B., & Frazier, P. (2012). Assessment and diagnosis of eating disorders: A guide for professional counselors. *Journal of Counseling & Development, 90,* 262–269.

Binik, Y. M., Brotto, L. A., Graham, C. A., & Segraves, R. T. (2010). Response of the *DSM-V* sexual dysfunctions subworkgroups to commentaries published in *DSM. International Society for Sexual Medicine, 7,* 2382–2387. doi:10.1111/j.1743-6109.2010.01899

Blank, S., & Latzer, Y. (2004). The boundary-control model of adolescent anorexia nervosa: An integrative treatment approach to etiology and treatment? *American Journal of Family Therapy, 32,* 43–54. doi:10.1080/01926180490255756

Bohnert, A. S., Valenstein, M., Bair, M. J., Ganoczy, D., McCarthy, J. F., Ilgen, M. A., & Blow, F. C. (2011). Association between opioid prescribing patterns and opioid overdose-related deaths. *Journal of the American Medical Association, 305,* 1315–1321.

Brewer, J. A., Elwafi, H. M., & Davis, J. H. (2013). Craving to quit: Psychological models and neurobiological mechanisms of mindfulness training as treatment for addictions. *Psychology of Addictive Behaviors, 27,* 366–379.

Brotto, L. A. (2010). The *DSM* diagnostic criteria for hypoactive sexual desire disorder in women. *Archives of Sexual Behavior, 39,* 221–239. doi:10.1007/s10508-009-9543-1

Brower, M. C., & Price, B. H. (2001). Neuropsychiatry of frontal lobe dysfunction in violent and criminal behavior: A critical review. *Journal of Neurology, Neurosurgery & Psychiatry, 71,* 720–726.

Brown, A., Mountford, V., & Waller, G. (2013). Therapeutic alliance and weight gain during cognitive behavioural therapy for anorexia nervosa. *Behaviour Research and Therapy, 51,* 216–220. doi:10.1016/j.brat.2013.01.008

Bryant-Waugh, R. (2013). Avoidant restrictive food intake disorder: An illustrative case example. *International Journal of Eating Disorders, 46,* 420–423. doi:10.1002/eat.22093

Bryant-Waugh, R., Markham, L., Kreipe, R. E., & Walsh, B. T. (2010). Feeding and eating disorders in childhood. *International Journal of Eating Disorders, 43,* 98–111. doi:10.1002/eat.20795

Budney, A. J., Hughes, J. R., Moore, B. A., & Vandrey, R. (2004). Review of the validity and significance of cannabis withdrawal syndrome. *American Journal of Psychiatry, 161,* 1967–1977.

Budney, A. J., Moore, B. A., Vandrey, R. G., & Hughes, J. R. (2003). The time course and significance of cannabis withdrawal. *Journal of Abnormal Psychology, 112,* 393–402.

Burke, J. D., Loeber, R., & Birmaher, B. (2002). Oppositional defiant disorder and conduct disorder: Part II. A review of the past 10 years. *Journal of the American Academy of Child & Adolescent Psychiatry, 41,* 1275–1293.

Burke, J. D., Waidman, I., & Lahey, B. B. (2010). Predictive validity of childhood oppositional defiant disorder and conduct disorder: Implications for the *DSM-V. Journal of Abnormal Psychology, 119,* 739–751. doi:10.1037/a0019708

Burt, S. A., Krueger, R. F., McGue, M., & Iacono, W. G. (2001). Sources of covariation among attention-deficit/hyperactivity disorder, oppositional defiant disorder, and conduct disorder: The importance of shared environment. *Journal of Abnormal Psychology, 110,* 516–525.

Centers for Disease Control and Prevention. (2008). Smoking-attributable mortality, years of potential life lost, and productivity losses: United States, 2000–2004. *Morbidity and Mortality Weekly Report, 57,* 1226–1228.

Cermain, G., & Lejoyeux, M. (2010). Pyromania: Clinical aspects. In E. Aboujaoude & L. M. Koran (Eds.), *Impulse control disorders* (pp. 255–268). New York, NY: Cambridge University Press.

Chavez, M., & Insel, T. R. (2007). Eating disorders. *American Psychologist, 62,* 159–166. doi:10.1037/0003-066X.62.3.159

Choate, L. H. (2010). Counseling college women experiencing eating disorder not otherwise specified: A cognitive behavior therapy model. *Journal of College Counseling, 13,* 73–86.

Christophersen, E. R., & Friman, P. C. (2010). *Encopresis and enuresis.* Cambridge, MA: Hogrefe.

Clark, S. E., & Jerrott, S. (2012). Effectiveness of day treatment for disruptive behaviour disorders: What is the long-term clinical outcome for children? *Journal of Canadian Academy of Child and Adolescent Psychiatry, 21,* 204–212.

Coccaro, E. F. (2012). Intermittent explosive disorder as a disorder of impulse aggression for *DSM-5*. *American Journal of Psychiatry, 169,* 577–588. doi:10.1176/appi.ajp.2012.11081259

Coie, J. K., & Dodge, K. A. (1998). Aggression and antisocial behavior. In W. Damon (Series Ed.) & N. Eisenberg (Vol. Ed.), *Social, emotional, and personality development: Vol. 3. Handbook of child psychology* (5th ed., pp. 779–862). New York, NY: Wiley.

Comer, R. J. (2013). *Abnormal psychology* (5th ed.). New York, NY: Worth.

Compton, W. M., Dawson, D. A., Goldstein, R. B., & Grant, B. F. (2013). Crosswalk between *DSM-IV* dependence and *DSM-5* substance use disorders for opioids, cannabis, cocaine, and alcohol. *Drug and Alcohol Dependence, 132,* 387–390.

Cooley, E., & Toray, T. (2001). Body image and personality predictors of eating disorder symptoms during the college years. *International Journal of Eating Disorders, 30,* 28–36.

Corona, G., Rastrelli, G., Ricca, V., Jannini, E. A., Vignozzi, L., Monami, M., . . . Maggi, M. (2013). Risk factors associated with primary and secondary reduced libido in male patients with sexual dysfunction. *Journal of Sexual Medicine, 10,* 1074–1089. doi:10.1111/jsm.12043

Couturier, J., Kimber, M., Jack, S., Niccols, A., Van Blyderreen, S., & McVey, G. (2013). Understanding the uptake of family-based treatment for adolescents with anorexia nervosa: Therapist perspectives. *International Journal of Eating Disorders, 46,* 177–188. doi:10.1002/eat.22049

Crick, N. R., & Dodge, K. A. (1994). A review and reformulation of social information-processing mechanisms in children's social adjustment. *Psychological Bulletin, 115,* 74–101.

Crisafulli, M. A., Von Holle, A., & Bulik, C. M. (2008). Attitudes towards anorexia nervosa: The impact of framing on blame and stigma. *International Journal of Eating Disorders, 41,* 333–339. doi:10.1002/eat.20507

Crooks, R. L., & Baur, K. (2013). *Our sexuality* (11th ed.). Belmont, CA: Cengage Learning.

Crow, S. J., Peterson, C. B., Swanson, S. A., Raymond, N. C., Specker, S., Eckert, E. D., & Mitchell, J. E. (2009). Increased mortality in bulimia nervosa and other eating disorders. *American Journal of Psychiatry, 166,* 1342–1346.

Crowley, T. J. (2007). Adolescents and substance-related disorders: Research agenda to guide decisions about *DSM-V*. In J. B. Saunders, M. A. Schuckit, P. J. Sirovatka, & D. A. Regier (Eds.), *Diagnostic issues in substance use disorders: Refining the research agenda for DSM-V* (pp. 203–220). Washington, DC: American Psychiatric Association.

Danford, D. E., & Huber, A. M. (1982). Pica among mentally retarded adults. *American Journal of Mental Deficiency, 87,* 141–146.

Dauvilliers, Y. (2006). Differential diagnosis in hypersomnia. *Current Neurology and Neuroscience Reports, 6,* 156–62. doi:10.1007/s11910-996-0039-2

Dawson, D. A., Goldstein, R. B., & Grant, B. F. (2013). Differences in the profiles of *DSM-IV* and *DSM-5* alcohol use disorders: Implications for clinicians. *Alcoholism: Clinical and Experimental Research, 37,* E305–E313.

de Ancos, E. T., & Ascaso, L. E. (2011). Sex differences in oppositional defiant disorder. *Psicothema, 23,* 666–671.

Dell'Osso, B., Altamura, A. C., Allen, A., Marazziti, D., & Hollander, E. (2006). Epidemiologic and clinical updates on impulse control disorders: A critical review. *European Archives of Psychiatry and Clinical Neuroscience, 256,* 464–475.

den Braber, A., Ent, D. V., Blokland, G. A., van Grootheest, D. S., Cath, D. C., Veltman, D. J., . . . Boomsma, D. I. (2008). An fMRI study in monozygotic twins discordant for obsessive-compulsive symptoms. *Biological Psychology, 79,* 91–102.

Dinwiddie, S. H. (1994). Abuse of inhalants: A review. *Addiction, 89,* 925–939.

Doley, R. (2003). Pyromania fact or fiction? *British Journal of Criminology, 43,* 797–807.

Eckern, M., Stevens, W., & Mitchell, J. (1999). The relationship between rumination and eating disorders. *International Journal of Eating Disorders, 26,* 414–419.

Eisenberg, D., Nicklett, E. J., Roeder, K., & Kirz, N. (2011). Eating disorder symptoms among college students: Prevalence, persistence, correlates, and treatment-seeking. *Journal of American College Health, 59,* 700–707.

Eley, T. C., Lichtenstein, P., & Moffitt, T. E. (2003). A longitudinal behavioral genetic analysis of the etiology of aggressive and nonaggressive antisocial behavior. *Development and Psychopathology, 15,* 383–402.

Equit, M., Palmke, M., Becker, N., Moritz, A., & Becker, S. (2012). Eating problems in young children: A population-based study. *Acta Paediatrica, 102,* 149–155.

Espie, C. A. (2002). Insomnia: Conceptual issues in the development, persistence, and treatment of sleep disorder in adults. *Annual Review of Psychology, 53,* 215–243.

Eyberg, S. M., Nelson, M. M., & Boggs, S. R. (2008). Evidence-based psychosocial treatments for children and adolescents with disruptive behavior. *Journal of Clinical Child & Adolescent Psychology, 37,* 215–237. doi:10.1080/15374410701820117

Fairburn, C. G., & Cooper, Z. (2011). Eating disorders, *DSM-5* and clinical reality. *British Journal of Psychiatry, 198,* 8–10.

Federici, A., Wisniewski, L., & Ben-Porath, D. (2012). Description of an intensive dialectical behavior therapy program for multidiagnostic clients with eating disorders. *Journal of Counseling & Development, 90,* 330–338.

Ferreri, S. J., Tamm, L., & Wier, K. G. (2006). Using food aversion to decrease severe pica by a child with autism. *Behavior Modification, 30,* 456–471. doi:10.1177/0145445504272970

Fichter, M. M., Quadflieg, N., & Hedlund, S. (2006). Twelve-year course and outcome predictors of anorexia nervosa. *International Journal of Eating Disorders, 39,* 87–100. doi:10.1002/eat.20215

Fisher, M., Schneider, M., Burns, J., Symons, H., & Mandel, F. S. (2001). Differences between adolescents and young adults at presentation to an eating disorders program. *Journal of Adolescent Health, 28,* 222–227.

Frances, A. (2013). *Essentials of psychiatric diagnosis: Responding to the challenge of DSM-5.* New York, NY: Guilford Press.

Frances, A., & Wollert, R. (2012). Sexual sadism: Avoiding its misuse in sexually violent predator evaluations. *Journal of the American Academy of Psychiatry and the Law Online, 40,* 409–416.

Franco, K., Campbell, N., Tamburrino, M., & Evans, C. (1993). Rumination: The eating disorder of infancy. *Child Psychiatry and Human Development, 24,* 91–97.

Frick, P. J., Lahey, B. B., Loeber, R., Stouthamer-Loeber, M., Christ, M. A. G., & Hanson, K. (1992). Familial risk factors to oppositional defiant disorder and conduct disorder: Parental psychopathology and maternal parenting. *Journal of Consulting and Clinical Psychology, 60,* 49–55.

Garcia, F. D., & Thibaut, F. (2011). Current concepts in the pharmacotherapy of paraphilias. *Drugs, 71,* 771–790.

Geroski, A. M., & Rodgers, K. A. (1998). Collaborative assessment and treatment of children with enuresis and encopresis. *Professional School Counseling, 2,* 128–135.

Glazener, C. M., Evans, J. H., & Peto, R. E. (2005). Alarm interventions for nocturnal enuresis in children. *Cochrane Database of Systematic Review, 2*(2). doi:10.1002/14651858.CD002911.pub2

Gopalan, G., Goldstein, L., Klingenstein, K., Sicher, C., Blake, C., & McKay, M. M. (2010). Engaging families into child mental health treatment: Updates and special considerations. *Journal of Canadian Child and Adolescent Psychiatry, 19,* 182–196.

Grant, J. E. (2006). Understanding and treating kleptomania: New models and new treatments. *Israel Journal of Psychiatry and Related Sciences, 43,* 81–87.

Grant, J. E., Levine, L., Kim, D., & Potenza, M. N. (2005). Impulse control disorders in adult psychiatric inpatients. *American Journal of Psychiatry, 162,* 2184–2188.

Grant, J. E., Odlaug, B. L., Davis, A. A., & Kim, S. W. (2009). Legal consequences of kleptomania. *Psychiatric Quarterly, 80,* 251–259.

Grant, J. E., Odlaug, B. L., & Kim, S. W. (2010). Kleptomania: Clinical characteristics and relationship to substance use disorders. *American Journal of Drug and Alcohol Abuse, 36,* 291–295.

Grant, J. E., Schreiber, L. R., & Odlaug, B. L. (2013). Phenomenology and treatment of behavioural addictions. *Canadian Journal of Psychiatry, 58,* 252–259.

Guterman, J. T., Martin, C. V., & Rudes, J. (2011). A solution-focused approach to frotteurism. *Journal of Systemic Therapies, 30,* 59–72.

Hall, M., & Hall, J. (2011). *The long-term effects of childhood sexual abuse: Counseling implications.* Retrieved from http://counselingoutfitters.com/vistas/vistas11/Article_19.pdf

Hall, R. C. W., & Hall, R. C. W. (2007). A profile of pedophilia: Definition, characteristics of offenders, recidivism, treatment outcomes, and forensic issues. *Mayo Clinic Proceedings, 82,* 457–471.

Harris, E. C., & Barraclough, B. (1998). Excess mortality of mental disorders. *British Journal of Psychiatry, 173,* 11–53. doi:10.1192/bjp.173.1.11

Hartmann, A. S., Becker, A. E., Hampton, C., & Bryant-Waugh, R. (2012). Pica and rumination disorder in *DSM-5*. *Psychiatric Annals, 42,* 426–430.

Hebebrand, J., & Bulik, C. M. (2011). Critical appraisal of the provisional *DSM-5* criteria for anorexia nervosa and an alternative proposal. *International Journal of Eating Disorders, 44,* 665–678. doi:10.1002/eat.20875

Heise, L. L. (1995). Violence, sexuality, and women's lives. In R. G. Parker & J. H. Gagnon (Eds.), *Conceiving sexuality: Approaches to sex research in a postmodern world* (pp. 109–134). New York, NY: Taylor & Frances/Routledge.

Hillman, D. R., Murphy, A. S., Antic, R., & Pezzullo, L. (2006). The economic cost of sleep disorders. *Sleep, 29,* 299–305.

Hinshaw, S. P., & Lee, S. S. (2003). Conduct and oppositional defiant disorders. *Child Psychopathology, 2,* 144–198.

Houts, A. C. (2010). Behavioral treatment for enuresis. In J. R. Weisz & A. E. Kazdin (Eds.), *Evidence-based psychotherapies for children and adolescents* (2nd ed., pp. 359–374). New York, NY: Guilford Press.

Hudson, J. I., Coit, C. E., Lalonde, J. K., & Pope, H. G., Jr. (2010). By how much will the proposed new *DSM-5* criteria increase the prevalence of binge eating disorder? *International Journal of Eating Disorders, 45,* 139–141. doi:10.1002/eat.20890

Hudson, J. I., Hiripi, E., Pope, H. G., & Kessler, R. C. (2007). The prevalence and correlates of eating disorders in the National Comorbidity Survey Replication. *Biological Psychiatry, 61,* 348–358.

Hyde, J. S., & DeLamater, J. D. (2013). *Understanding human sexuality* (12th ed.). New York, NY: McGraw-Hill.

Inman, B. A., St. Sauver, J. L., Jacobson, D. J., McGree, M. E., Nehra, A., Lieber, M. M., . . . Jacobsen, S. J. (2009). A population-based, longitudinal study of erectile dysfunction and future coronary artery disease. *Mayo Clinic Proceedings, 84,* 108–113.

Ivascu, N. S., Sarnaik, S., McCrae, J., Whitten-Shurney, W., Thomas, R., & Bond, S. (2001). Characterization of pica prevalence among patients with sickle cell disease. *Archives of Pediatrics & Adolescent Medicine, 155,* 1243–1247.

Jacobson, K. C., Prescott, C. A., & Kendler, K. S. (2002). Sex differences in the genetic and environmental influences on the development of antisocial behavior. *Development and Psychopathology, 14,* 395–416.

Jernelöv, S., Lekander, M., Blom, K., Rydh, S., Ljótsson, B., Axelsson, J., & Kaldo, V. (2012). Efficacy of a behavioral self-help treatment with or without therapist guidance for co-morbid and primary insomnia: A randomized controlled trial. *BMC Psychiatry, 12,* 5. doi:10.1186/1471-244X-12-5

Jiron, C. (2010). Assessing and intervening with children with externalizing disorders. In D. C. Miller (Ed.), *Best practices in school neuropsychology: Guidelines for effective practice, assessment, and evidence-based intervention* (pp. 359–386). Hoboken, NJ: Wiley.

Johnson, E. O., Roth, T., Schultz, L., & Breslau, N. (2006). Epidemiology of *DSM-IV* insomnia in adolescence: Life time prevalence, chronicity, and an emergent gender difference. *Pediatrics, 117,* 247–256.

Joussemet, M., Vitaro, F., Barker, E. D., Côté, S., Nagin, D. S., Zoccolillo, M., & Tremblay, R. E. (2008). Controlling parenting and physical aggression during elementary school. *Child Development, 79,* 411–425.

Kafka, M. P., & Hennen, J. (2002). A *DSM-IV* Axis I comorbidity study of males (*n* = 120) with paraphilias and paraphilia-related disorders. *Sexual Abuse: A Journal of Research and Treatment, 14,* 349–366.

Kaminer, Y., & Winters, K. C. (2012). Proposed *DSM-5* substance use disorders for adolescents: If you build it, will they come? *American Journal of Addictions, 21,* 280–281.

Kavanaugh, D. J. (2013). Craving: A research update. *Addictive Behaviors, 38,* 1499–1500.

Kaye, W. H., Klump, K. L., Frank, G. K. W., & Strober, M. (2000). Anorexia and bulimia nervosa. *Annual Review of Medicine, 51,* 299–313.

Kerridge, B. T., Saha, T. D., Smith, S., Chou, P. S., Pickering, R. P., Huang, B., . . . Pulay, A. J. (2011). Dimensionality of hallucinogen and inhalant/solvent abuse and dependence criteria: Implications for *Diagnostic and Statistical Manual of Mental Disorders—Fifth Edition*. *Addictive Behaviors, 36,* 912–918.

Kerwin, M. E., & Berkowitz, R. I. (1996). Feeding and eating disorders: Ingestive problems of infancy, childhood, and adolescence. *School Psychology Review, 25,* 316–329.

Kerwin, M. E., Eicher, P. S., & Gelsinger, J. (2005). Parental report of eating problems and gastrointestinal symptoms in children with pervasive developmental disorders. *Children's Health Care, 34,* 221–234.

Kessler, R. C., Hwang, I., LaBrie, R., Petukhova, M., Sampson, N. A., Winters, K. C., & Shaffer, H. J. (2008). *DSM-IV* pathological gambling in the National Comorbidity Survey Replication. *Psychological Medicine, 38,* 1351–1360.

Keyes, K. M., Krueger, R. F., Grant, B. F., & Hasin, D. S. (2011). Alcohol craving and the dimensionality of alcohol disorders. *Psychological Medicine, 41,* 629–640.

King, D. L., & Delfabbro, P. H. (2013). Issues for *DSM-5* video-gaming disorder. *Australian and New Zealand Journal of Psychiatry, 47,* 20–22.

Ko, C. H., Liu, G. C., Yen, J. Y., Yen, C. F., Chen, C. S., & Lin, W. C. (2013). The brain activations for both cue-induced gaming urge and smoking craving among subjects comorbid with Internet gaming addiction and nicotine dependence. *Journal of Psychiatric Research, 47,* 486–493.

Kohn, C. S. (2006). Conceptualization and treatment of kleptomania behaviors using cognitive and behavioral strategies. *International Journal of Behavioral Consultation and Therapy, 2,* 553–559.

Kolko, D. J., & Pardini, D. A. (2010). ODD dimensions, ADHD, and callous–unemotional traits as predictors of treatment response in children with disruptive behavior disorders. *Journal of Abnormal Psychology, 119,* 713.

Koran, L. M., Bodnik, D., & Dannon, P. H. (2010). Kleptomania: Clinical aspects. In E. Aboujaoude & L. M. Koran (Eds.), *Impulse control disorders* (pp. 34–44). New York, NY: Cambridge University Press.

Långström, N., & Seto, M. C. (2006). Exhibitionistic and voyeuristic behavior in a Swedish national population survey. *Archives of Sexual Behavior, 35,* 427–435. doi:10.1007/s10508-006-9042-6

Långström, N., & Zucker, K. J. (2005). Transvestic fetishism in the general population: Prevalence and correlates. *Journal of Sex & Marital Therapy, 31,* 87–95. doi:10.080/00926230590477934

Laumann, E. O., Paik, A., & Rosen, R. C. (1999). Sexual dysfunction in the United States: Prevalence and predictors. *Journal of the American Medical Association, 281,* 537–544.

Leggett, T. (2006). United Nations Office on Drugs and Crime: Review of the world cannabis situation. *Bulletin on Narcotics, 58,* 1–155.

Lindberg, L., Bohlin, G., Hagekull, B., & Thunström, M. (1994). Early food refusal: Infant and family characteristics. *Infant Mental Health Journal, 15,* 262–277.

Lindberg, L., & Hjem, A. (2003). Risk factors for anorexia nervosa: A national cohort study. *International Journal of Eating Disorders, 34,* 397–408. doi:10.1002/eat.10221

Linville, D., Stice, E., Gau, J., & O'Neil, M. (2011). Predictive effects of mother and peer influences on increases in adolescent eating disorder risk factors and symptoms: A 3-year longitudinal study. *International Journal of Eating Disorders, 44,* 745–751. doi:10.1002/eat.20907

Lucarelli, L., Cimino, S., D'Olimpio, F., & Ammaniti, M. (2012). Feeding disorders of early childhood: An empirical study of diagnostic subtypes. *International Journal of Eating Disorders, 46,* 147–155. doi:10.1002/eat.22057

Lynskey, M., Glowinski, A. L., & Todorov, A. (2004). Major depressive disorder, suicidal ideation, and suicide attempt in twins discordant for cannabis dependence and early-onset cannabis use. *Archives of General Psychiatry, 61,* 1026–1032.

Maldonado-Duran, J. M., Fonagy, P., Helmig, L., Millhuff, C., Moody, C., Rosen, L., & VanSickle, G. (2008). In-depth mental health evaluation of a community sample of nonreferred infants with feeding difficulties. *International Journal of Eating Disorders, 41,* 513–519. doi:10.1002/eat.20538

Marsh, P. J., Odlaug, B. L., Thomarios, N., Davis, A. A., Buchanan, S. N., Meyer, C. S., & Grant, J. E. (2010). Paraphilias in adult psychiatric inpatients. *Annals of Clinical Psychiatry, 22,* 129–134.

Masheb, R. M., Grilo, C. M., & White, M. A. (2011). An examination of eating patterns in community women with bulimia nervosa and binge eating disorder. *International Journal of Eating Disorders, 44,* 618–624. doi:10.1002/eat.20853

Masters, W. H., & Johnson, V. E. (1966). *Human sexual response.* New York, NY: Bantam Books.

Matthys, W., Vanderschuren, L., Schutter, D., & Lochman, J. (2012). Impaired neurocognitive functions affect social learning processes in oppositional defiant disorder and conduct disorder: Implications for interventions. *Clinical Child & Family Psychology Review, 15,* 234–246. doi:10.1007/s10567-012-0118-7

Merikangas, K. R., Nakamura, E. F., & Kessler, R. C. (2009). Epidemiology of mental disorders in children and adolescents. *Dialogues in Clinical Neuroscience, 11*, 7–20.

Mewton, L., Slade, T., McBride, O., Grove, R., & Teeson, M. (2011). An evaluation of the proposed *DSM-5* alcohol use disorder criteria using Australian national data. *Addiction, 106*, 941–950.

Micali, N., Simonoff, E., Stahl, D., & Treasure, J. (2011). Maternal eating disorders and infant feeding difficulties: Maternal and child mediators in a longitudinal general population study. *Journal of Child Psychology and Psychiatry, 52*, 800–807. doi:10.1111/j.1469-7610.2010.02341.x

Moeller, F. G., Barratt, E. S., Dougherty, D. M., Schmitz, J. M., & Swann, A. C. (2001). Psychiatric aspects of impulsivity. *American Journal of Psychiatry, 158*, 1783–1793.

Moffitt, T. E., & Lynam, D. (1994). The neuropsychology of conduct disorder and delinquency: Implications for understanding antisocial behavior. In D. Fowles, P. Sutker, & S. Goodman (Eds.), *Progress in experimental personality and psychopathology research: Psychopathy and antisocial personality* (pp. 233–262). New York, NY: Springer.

Montgomery, P., & Shepard, L. D. (2010). Insomnia in older people. *Reviews in Clinical Gerontology, 20*, 205–218. doi:10.1017/S095925981000016X

Moore, D. F., & Sears, D. A. (1994). Pica, iron deficiency, and the medical history. *American Journal of Medicine, 97*, 390–393. doi:10.1016/0002-9343(94)90309-3

Moran, M. (2013). Gambling disorder to be included in addictions chapter. *Psychiatric News.* doi:10.1176/appi.pn.2013.4b14

Morrell, J., & Murray, L. (2003). Parenting and the development of conduct disorder and hyperactive symptoms in childhood: A prospective longitudinal study from 2 months to 8 years. *Journal of Child Psychology and Psychiatry, 44*, 489–508.

Morrison, J. (2006). *DSM-IV made easy: The clinician's guide to diagnosis.* New York, NY: Guilford Press.

Murphy, R., Straebler, S., Cooper, Z., & Fairburn, C. G. (2010). Cognitive behavioral therapy for eating disorders. *Psychiatric Clinics of North America, 33*, 611–627.

Murray, J., & Farrington D. P. (2010). Risk factors for conduct disorder and delinquency: Key findings from longitudinal studies. *Canadian Journal of Psychiatry, 55*, 633–642.

National Highway Traffic Safety Administration, National Center on Sleep Disorders Research. (2011). *Drowsy driving and automobile crashes.* Retrieved from http://www.nhtsa.gov/people/injury/drowsy_driving1/Drowsy.html#NCSDR/NHTSA

National Institute of Mental Health. (2013). *Eating disorders.* Retrieved from http://www.nimh.nih.gov/health/topics/eating-disorders/index.shtml

National Institute on Drug Abuse. (2011). *Drug facts: Treatment statistics.* Retrieved from http://www.drugabuse.gov/publications/drugfacts/treatment-statistics

Nock, M. K., Kazdin, A. E., Hiripi, E., & Kessler, R. C. (2006). Prevalence, subtypes, and correlates of *DSM-IV* conduct disorder in the National Comorbidity Survey Replication. *Psychological Medicine, 36*, 699–710.

Nock, M. K., Kazdin, A. E., Hiripi, E., & Kessler, R. C. (2007). Lifetime prevalence, correlates, and persistence of oppositional defiant disorder: Results from the National Comorbidity Survey Replication. *Journal of Child Psychology and Psychiatry, 48*, 703–713. doi:10.1111/j.1469-7610.2007.01733.x

Nolen-Hoeksema, S. (2006). The etiology of gender differences in depression. In C. M. Mazure & G. P. Keita (Eds.), *Understanding depression in women: Applying empirical research to practice and policy* (pp. 9–43). Washington, DC: American Psychological Association.

Öberg, K., Fugl-Meyer, A., & Fugl-Meyer, K. (2004). On categorization and quantification of women's sexual dysfunctions: An epidemiological approach. *International Journal of Impotence Research, 16*, 261–269. doi:10.1038/sj.ijir.3901151

Odlaug, B. L., & Grant, J. E. (2010). Impulse-control disorders in a college sample: Results from the self-administered Minnesota Impulse Disorders Interview (MIDI). *Primary Care Companion to the Journal of Clinical Psychiatry, 12*(2), e1–e5. doi:10.4088/PCC.09m00842whi

Ousley, L., Cordero, E. D., & White, S. (2008). Eating disorders and body image of undergraduate men. *Journal of American College Health, 56*, 617–621.

Pardini, D. A., & Fite, P. J. (2010). Symptoms of conduct disorder, oppositional defiant disorder, attention-deficit/hyperactivity disorder, and callous-unemotional traits as unique predictors of psychosocial maladjustment in boys: Advancing an evidence base for *DSM-V*. *Journal of the American Academy of Child & Adolescent Psychiatry, 49*, 1087–1088.

Pardini, D. A., Frick, P. J., & Moffitt, T. E. (2010). Building an evidence base for *DSM-5* conceptualizations of oppositional defiant disorder and conduct disorder: Introduction to the special section. *Journal of Abnormal Psychology, 119,* 683–688.

Paris, J. (2013). *The intelligent clinician's guide to the DSM-5.* New York, NY: Oxford University Press.

Parks, R. W., Green, R. D., Girgis, S., Hunter, M. D., Woodruff, P. W., & Spence, S. A. (2005). Response of pyromania to biological treatment in a homeless person. *Neuropsychiatric Disease and Treatment, 1,* 277–280.

Parry-Jones, B. (1994). Mercyism or rumination disorder: A historical investigation and current assessment. *British Journal of Psychiatry, 165,* 303–314. doi:10.1192/bjp.165.3.303

Perelman, D. (2006). Retarded ejaculation. *World Journal of Urology, 24,* 645–652. doi:10.1007/s00345-006-0127-6

Pettet, J. R., Lu, F. G., & Narrow, W. E. (Eds.). (2011). *Religious and spiritual issues in psychiatric diagnosis: A research agenda for DSM-V.* Washington, DC: American Psychiatric Association.

Ploskin, D. (2007). What are impulse control disorders? *Psych Central.* Retrieved from http://psychcentral.com/lib/what-are-impulse-control-disorders/0001161

Potenza, M. N., Balodis, I. M., Franco, C. A., Bullock, S., Xu, J., Chung, T., & Grant, J. E. (2013). Neurobiological considerations in understanding behavioral treatments for pathological gambling. *Psychology of Addictive Behaviors, 27,* 380–392.

Proctor, S. L., Kopak, A. M., & Hoffmann, N. G. (2012). Compatibility of current *DSM-IV* and proposed *DSM-5* diagnostic criteria for cocaine use disorders. *Addictive Behaviors, 37,* 722–728.

Prouty, A. M., Protinsky, H. O., & Canady, D. (2002). College women: Eating behaviors and help-seeking preferences. *Adolescence, 37,* 353–363.

Reynolds, C. F., & Redline, S. (2010). The *DSM-5* sleep wake disorders nosology: An update and an invitation to the sleep community. *Journal of Clinical Sleep Medicine, 6,* 7–10.

Roberto, C. A., Grilo, C. M., Masheb, R. M., & White, M. A. (2010). Binge eating, purging, or both: Eating disorder psychopathology findings from an Internet community survey. *International Journal of Eating Disorders, 43,* 724–731. doi:10.1002/eat.20770

Roman, M., & Reay, W. E. (2009). Eating dysfunctions: How long can we survive? *Issues in Mental Health Nursing, 30,* 655–657. doi:10.1080/01612840903131818

Ross, J. A., & Green, C. (2011). Inside the experience of anorexia nervosa: A narrative thematic analysis. *Counseling and Psychotherapy Research, 11,* 112–119. doi:10.1080/14733145.2010.486864

Roth, T. (2007). Insomnia: Definition, prevalence, etiology, and consequences. *Journal of Sleep Medicine, 3,* 7–10.

Rowland, A. S., Lesesne, C. A., & Abramowitz, A. J. (2002). The epidemiology of attention-deficit/hyperactivity disorder (ADHD): A public health view. *Mental Retardation and Developmental Disabilities Research Reviews, 8,* 162–170.

Rowland, D., McMahon, C. G., Abdo, C., Chen, J., Jannini, E., Waldinger, M. D., & Ahn, T. Y. (2010). Disorders of orgasm and ejaculation in men. *Journal of Sexual Medicine, 7,* 1668–1686.

Sack, R. L., Auckley, R. D., Auger, R., Carskadon, M. A., Wright, K. P., Vitiello, M. V., & Zhdanova, I. V. (2007). Circadian rhythm sleep disorders: Part II. Advanced sleep phase disorder, delayed sleep phase disorder, free-running disorder, and irregular sleep-wake rhythm: An American Academy of Sleep Medicine review. *Sleep, 30,* 1484–1501.

Schroedl, R. L., Alioto, A., & DiLorenzo, C. (2013). Behavioral treatment for adolescent rumination syndrome: A case report. *Clinical Practice in Pediatric Psychology, 1,* 89–93. doi:10.1037/cpp0000010

Schwitzer, A. M. (2012). Diagnosing, conceptualizing, and treating eating disorders not otherwise specified: A comprehensive practice model. *Journal of Counseling & Development, 90,* 281–289.

Segraves, R. T. (2010). Considerations for a better definition of male orgasmic disorder in *DSM V. Journal of Sexual Medicine, 7,* 690–695.

Shapira, B. E., & Dahlen, P. (2010). Therapeutic treatment protocol for enuresis using an enuresis alarm. *Journal of Counseling & Development, 88,* 246–252. doi:10.1002/j.1556-6678.2010.tb00017.x

Shatkin, J., Feinfield, K., & Strober, M. (2002). The misinterpretation of a non-REM sleep parasomnia as suicidal behavior in an adolescent. *Sleep and Breathing, 6,* 175–179. doi:10.1007/s11325-002-0175-0

Shenk, C. E., Dorn, L. D., Kolko, D. J., Susman, E. J., Noll, J. G., & Bukstein, O. G. (2012). Predicting treatment response for oppositional defiant and conduct disorder using pre-treatment adrenal and gonadal hormones. *Journal of Child and Family Studies, 21,* 973–981. doi:10.1007/s10567-012-0118-7

Shisslak, C. M., Swain, B. J., & Crago, M. (1987). 32 years of persistent pica: A case study. *International Journal of Eating Disorders, 6,* 663–670.

Simons, J. S., & Carey, M. P. (2001). Prevalence of sexual dysfunctions: Results from a decade of research. *Archives of Sexual Behavior, 30,* 177–219.

Sinha, R. (2013). The clinical neurobiology of drug craving. *Current Opinion in Neurobiology, 23,* 1–6.

Smolak, L. (2011). Body image development in childhood. In T. Cash & L. Smolak (Eds.), *Body image: A handbook of science, practice, and prevention* (2nd ed., pp. 67–75). New York, NY: Guilford Press.

Smolak, L., & Chun-Kennedy, C. (2013). Sociocultural influences on the development of eating disorders and obesity. In L. H. Choate (Ed.), *Eating disorders and obesity: A counselor's guide to prevention and treatment* (pp. 3–20). Alexandria, VA: American Counseling Association.

Soltys, S. M. (1992). Pyromania and firesetting behaviors. *Psychiatric Annals, 22,* 79–83.

Spector, I. P., & Carey, M. P. (1990). Incidence and prevalence of the sexual dysfunctions: A critical review of the empirical literature. *Archives of Sexual Behavior, 19,* 389–408.

Steiner, H., & Remsing, L. (2007). Practice parameter for the assessment and treatment of children and adolescents with oppositional defiant disorder. *Journal of the American Academy of Child & Adolescent Psychiatry, 46,* 126–141.

Stice, E., Marti, C. N., & Rohde, P. (2013). Prevalence, incidence, impairment, and course of the proposed *DSM-5* eating disorder diagnoses in an 8-year prospective community study of young women. *Journal of Abnormal Psychology, 122,* 445–457. doi:10.1037/a0030679

Stiegler, L. N. (2005). Understanding pica behavior: A review for clinical and education professionals. *Focus on Autism and Other Developmental Disabilities, 20,* 27–38.

Striegel-Moore, R. H., & Bulik, C. M. (2007). Risk factors for eating disorders. *American Psychologist, 62,* 181–198. doi:10.1037/0003-066X.62.3.181

Striegel-Moore, R. H., & Franko, D. L. (2003). Epidemiology of binge eating disorder. *International Journal of Eating Disorders, 34,* 519–529.

Substance Abuse and Mental Health Services Administration. (2011a). *Interventions for disruptive behavior disorders kit* (SAMHSA Publication No. SMA11-4634). Rockville, MD: Author.

Substance Abuse and Mental Health Services Administration. (2011b). *Results from the 2010 National Survey on Drug Use and Health: Summary of National Findings* (NSDUH Series H-41, HHS Publication No. SMA 11-4658). Rockville, MD: Author.

Sysko, R., & Walsh, B. T. (2011). Does the broad categories for the diagnosis of eating disorders (BCD-ED) scheme reduce the frequency of eating disorder not otherwise specified? *International Journal of Eating Disorders, 44,* 625–629. doi:10.1002/eat.20860

Szentkirályi, A., Madarász, C. Z., & Novák, M. (2009). Sleep disorders: Impact on daytime functioning and quality of life. *Expert Review of Pharmacoeconomics & Outcomes Research, 9,* 49–64. doi:10.1586/14737167.9.1.49

Talih, F. R. (2011). Kleptomania and potential exacerbating factors: A review and case report. *Innovations in Clinical Neuroscience, 8,* 35–39.

Tchanturia, K., Lloyd, S., & Lang, K. (2013). Cognitive remediation therapy for anorexia nervosa: Current evidence and future research directions. *International Journal of Eating Disorders, 46,* 492–495. doi:10.1002/eat.22106

Tiefer, L. (2001). A new view of women's sexual problems: Why new? Why now? *Journal of Sex Research, 38,* 89–96.

Tucker, M. E. (2012). *Insomnia, hypersomnia disorders criteria proposed for DSM-5.* Retrieved from www.familypracticenews.com/news/more-top-news/single.

Vandrey, R., Budney, A. J., Kamon, J. L., & Stanger, C. (2005). Cannabis withdrawal in adolescent treatment seekers. *Drug and Alcohol Dependence, 78,* 205–210.

Vaughn, M. G., Fu, Q., DeLisi, M., Wright, J. P., Beaver, K. M., Perron, B. E., & Howard, M. O. (2010). Prevalence and correlates of fire-setting in the United States: Results from the National Epidemiological Survey on alcohol and related conditions. *Comprehensive Psychiatry, 51,* 217–223.

Verheul, R., van dan Bosch, Koeter, M. W., de Ridder, M. A., Stijnen, T., & van den Brink, W. (2003). Dialectical behaviour therapy for women with borderline personality disorder 12-month, randomised clinical trial in The Netherlands. *British Journal of Psychiatry, 182,* 135–140.

Verweij, K. J. H., Agrawal, A., Nat, N. O., Creemers, H. E., Huizink, A. C., Martin, N. G., & Lynskey, M. T. (2013). A genetic perspective on the proposed inclusion of cannabis withdrawal in *DSM-5. Psychological Medicine, 43,* 1713–1722.

von Gontard, A. (2012). Does psychological stress affect LUT function in children? ICI-RS 2011. *Neurourology and Urodynamics, 31,* 344–348.

Wade, T. D., Keski-Rahkonen, A., & Hudson, J. (2011). Epidemiology of eating disorders. In M. Tsuang & M. Tohen (Eds.), *Textbook in psychiatric epidemiology* (3rd ed., pp. 343–360). New York, NY: Wiley.

Waldinger, M. D., & Schweitzer, D. H. (2005). Retarded ejaculation in men: An overview of psychological and neurobiological insights. *World Journal of Urology, 23,* 76–81. doi:10.1007/s00345-004-0487-8

Waldman, I. D., & Rhee, S. H. (2002). Behavioral and molecular genetic studies. *Hyperactivity and Attention Disorders of Childhood, 2,* 290–335.

Weyandt, L. L., Verdi, G., & Swentosky, A. (2010). Oppositional, conduct, and aggressive disorders. In S. Goldstein & C. R. Reynolds (Eds.), *Handbook of neurodevelopmental and genetic disorders in children* (2nd ed., pp. 151–208). New York, NY: Guilford Press.

Widom, C. S., Czaja, S. J., & Paris, J. (2009). A prospective investigation of borderline personality disorder in abused and neglected children followed up into adulthood. *Journal of Personality Disorders, 23,* 433–446.

Wiley, J. F., Henretig, F. M., & Selbst, S. M. (1992). Blood levels in children with foreign bodies. *Pediatrics, 89,* 593–596.

Williams, D. E., & McAdam, D. (2012). Assessment, behavioral treatment, and prevention of pica: Clinical guidelines and recommendations for practitioners. *Research in Developmental Disabilities, 33,* 2050–2057.

Williams, J. F., & Storck, M. (2007). Inhalant abuse. *Pediatrics, 119,* 1009–1017.

Wilson, G. T., Wilfley, D. E., Agras, W. S., & Bryson, S. W. (2010). Psychological treatments of binge eating disorder. *Archives of General Psychiatry, 67,* 94–101.

World Health Organization. (2007). *International statistical classification of diseases and related health problems, 10th revision.* Geneva, Switzerland: Author.

Zee, P. C., & Vitiello, M. V. (2009). Circadian rhythm sleep disorder: Irregular sleep wake rhythm type. *Sleep Clinic, 4,* 213–218. Retrieved from www.ncbi.nlm.nih.gov/pmc/articles/PMC2768129

Part Three

Changes and Implications Involving Diagnoses Commonly Made by Other Professionals

Part Three Introduction

Part Three covers disorders that are commonly diagnosed by other professionals, including primary care physicians, psychiatrists, and psychologists with specialized training in neuropsychological or neurodevelopmental functioning. We have divided this section into four chapters: Chapter 12: Neurodevelopmental and Neurocognitive Disorders; Chapter 13: Schizophrenia Spectrum and Other Psychotic Disorders; Chapter 14: Dissociative Disorders; and Chapter 15: Somatic Symptom and Related Disorders. Differing from the two previous sections, this part of the *Learning Companion* includes diagnoses that are seen but less commonly diagnosed in a counseling setting. Although counselors certainly work with these concerns, some of these disorders are diagnosed using highly specialized assessments or require an extensive medical examination by a physician or other qualified medical professional.

Readers will note that more detailed information has been given for diagnoses counselors are more likely to see in practice, such as autism spectrum disorder (ASD), and less detail has been given for those disorders that counselors are less likely to diagnose, such as factitious disorder. Diagnoses that have no heading detailing "Major Changes From *DSM-IV-TR* to *DSM-5*" have no significant changes (i.e., global developmental delay).

Furthermore, if special considerations or cultural considerations are scant or not included at all, this indicates there is limited research on the topic.

Major changes to look for in Chapter 12 include the deletion of the Disorders Usually First Diagnosed in Infancy, Childhood, or Adolescence chapter of the *DSM-IV-TR*, because most of these diagnoses are now listed in in the Neurodevelopmental Disorders chapter. Within neurodevelopmental disorders, autistic disorder, Asperger's disorder, childhood disintegrative disorder, Rett syndrome, and pervasive developmental disorder–not otherwise specified (PDD-NOS) have been reconceptualized on a continuum now called autism spectrum disorder (ASD). Also, largely because of Rosa's Law in 2010 and the desire to maintain consistency with the WHO (2007) terminology, the diagnoses previously known as mental retardation has now been reclassified as intellectual development disorder and takes into consideration level of functioning as well as intelligence quotient (IQ). In addition to these changes, neurodevelopmental disorders also present changes to specific learning disorders, combining the separate diagnoses of reading disorder, mathematics disorder, disorder of written expression, and learning disorder NOS (APA, 2013; Wakefield, 2013).

Schizophrenia spectrum disorder takes the place of schizophrenia. Diagnostic criteria of this diagnosis have been reorganized to emphasize the *DSM-5*'s focus on a dimensional conceptualization of diagnosis (see Chapter 2 of this *Learning Companion* for more information about dimensional vs. categorical assessment). Major changes to Criterion A of schizophrenia spectrum disorder include the elimination of special treatment of bizarre delusions and hallucinations, such as when an individual hears two or more voices conversing or hears running commentary regarding his or her behavior. Also eliminated from this disorder was the requirement for two positive symptoms to meet Criterion A. Moreover, subtypes have been removed, and counselors are encouraged to use a dimensional assessment. Various smaller changes to this disorder are covered later, in Chapter 13 of this *Learning Companion*.

Changes to ADHD include a mandate that age of onset must be before age 12. ADHD is also now diagnosable in adults. Furthermore, the cross-situational requirements have been reinforced, all subtypes have been eliminated, specifiers have been added, and the concomitant diagnosis of ADHD and ASD is now permissible (APA, 2013). Whereas the most noteworthy modification to communication disorders is the addition of social (pragmatic) communication disorder, which focuses on verbal and nonverbal social deficiencies in communication, communication disorders now include language disorder and childhood-onset fluency disorder, previously called stuttering.

The Delirium, Dementia, and Amnestic and Other Cognitive Disorders chapter in the *DSM-IV-TR*, now renamed the Neurocognitive Disorders chapter in the *DSM-5*, represents major changes to dementia, while delirium remains the same. Dementia is reconceptualized dimensionally and renamed major neurocognitive disorder. Amnestic and other cognitive disorders have been subsumed under this new category, and a new diagnosis, mild neurocognitive disorder, has been added. In contrast, very few changes have been made to dissociative disorders, which is now located after the Trauma- and Stressor-Related Disorders chapter in the *DSM-5*. For dissociative identity disorder, Criterion A was revised to allow observations or self-reported dissociation as well as experiences of possession, and Criterion B was broadened to include issues with everyday gaps in memory. Depersonalization disorder was renamed depersonalization/derealization disorder, and the dissociative fugue was included as part of dissociative amnesia.

The Somatic Symptom and Related Disorders chapter, previously named Somatoform Disorders, has undergone extensive revisions intended to address multiple concerns identified for these diagnoses (APA, 2013; Dimsdale, 2013). Two new disorders, somatic symptom disorder and illness anxiety disorder, replace somatization disorder, hypochondriasis, pain disorder, and undifferentiated somatoform disorder. In addition, the section on psychological factors affecting other medical conditions was moved from the Other Conditions chapter of the *DSM-IV-TR*, and factitious disorder was also relocated in the *DSM-5*.

In this section, we attempt to address these significant changes in a way that is meaningful for counselors. As with other parts of this *Learning Companion*, readers will find a description of each disorder or group of disorders that includes essential features and major changes from the *DSM-IV-TR* to the *DSM-5*. Where applicable, special considerations, cultural considerations, and case examples will be given to assist counselors in understanding diagnoses and working with clients.

♦ ♦ ♦

Neurodevelopmental and Neurocognitive Disorders

The neurodevelopmental and neurocognitive disorders discussed in this chapter share the commonality of probable biological etiology. Neurodevelopmental disorders tend to appear in the beginning phases of the life span, and neurocognitive disorders are most prevalent toward the end of the life span. The neurodevelopmental disorders enumerated in the *DSM-5* include intellectual disability (intellectual developmental disorder), communication disorders, ASD, ADHD, specific learning disorder, and motor disorders. The neurocognitive disorders encompass delirium and major and mild neurocognitive disorders with multiple etiological subtypes (Addington & Rapoport, 2012; APA, 2013; Bajenaru, Tiu, Antochi, & Roceanu, 2012; Blazer, 2013). Readers should note there are other specified and unspecified disorders associated with each of these categories. We have included a section on other specified and unspecified disorders in the *DSM-5* in Chapter 17: Practice Implications for Counselors, which explains how counselors go about selecting, recording, and coding these diagnoses.

Neurodevelopmental Disorders

> It's my son. I'm a health care professional and kept saying that I knew there was something wrong; on many levels he wasn't developing as he should. It was actually a relief to get the diagnosis. It made me look forward to working with a treatment team to help us. Family counseling was a great benefit too. — Rita

Neurodevelopmental disorders are a cluster of disorders that typically display during early childhood, are assumed to have a neurological basis, and encompass difficulty in multiple areas of functioning, including delays in achieving expected milestones. This grouping of syndromes shares the symptomatology of behavioral deficits and excesses. Neurodevelopmental disorders have varying prevalence rates, with ADHD occurring in up to 5% of the population and ASD extant in between 1% and 2% of children (APA, 2013). Neurodevelopmental disorders are frequently diagnosed in medical and educational settings, although counselors often provide valuable services for diagnosed individuals and their families. Onset during childhood makes these disorders even more relevant to counselors working across multiple agency and school settings.

Recent advances in science show differences in brain development in children and adults with neurodevelopmental disorders, especially within the burgeoning area of molecular genetic research (Addington & Rapoport, 2012). Because individuals with neurodevelopmental disorders possess pervasive impairment in personal, social, occupational, and academic areas, it is important for counselors to understand the nosology of the disorders. The implicit genetic and neurological factors render early identification, effective treatment delivery, and access to support services critical.

Major Changes From *DSM-IV-TR* to *DSM-5*

The *DSM-5* has significant changes to the nomenclature, categorization, and diagnostic criteria of neurodevelopmental disorders. Most of the disorders included in this chapter were previously located in the eliminated Disorders Usually First Diagnosed in Infancy, Childhood, or Adolescence chapter of the *DSM-IV-TR*. The consolidation of the five pervasive developmental disorders (i.e., autistic disorder, Asperger's disorder, childhood disintegrative disorder, Rett syndrome, PDD-NOS) into the umbrella category *autism spectrum disorder* (ASD) received criticism and praise. With awareness of the impact of changes to the autism nomenclature, the Neurodevelopmental Disorders Work Group took great effort to improve the diagnostic process and, specifically, to reduce incidence of the overused PDD-NOS category (APA, 2013; Mandy, Charman, & Skuse 2012).

There has been concern and controversy that heightened levels of diagnostic specificity in the criteria for ASD would leave many individuals in need of treatment undiagnosed. Researchers investigated applicability of the revamped criteria and found conflicting results as to the exclusion of individuals previously diagnosable under the *DSM-IV-TR*. Proponents of the change lauded the heightened specificity of the ASD diagnosis (Kurita, 2011; Lauritsen, 2013; Mandy, Charman, Gilmour, & Skuse, 2011; Mandy et al., 2012; Mazefsky, McPartland, Gastgeb, & Minshew, 2013; McGuiness & Johnson, 2013; Wilson et al., 2013), whereas critics asserted the stringent specificity led to unnecessary exclusion (Barton, Robins, Jashar, Brennan, & Fein, 2013; Frazier et al., 2012; Gibbs, Aldridge, Chandler, Witzlsperger, & Smith, 2012; Mayes, Black, & Tierney, 2013; McPartland, Reichaw, & Volkmar, 2012; Tsai, 2012; Weitlauf, Gotham, Vehorn, & Warren, 2013). In a response to the critics, the Neurodevelopment Disorders Work Group clarified that, under the auspices of the *DSM-5*, individuals previously diagnosed in any of the *DSM-IV-TR* pervasive developmental disorder categories would receive a diagnosis of ASD (APA, 2013; Wakefield, 2013).

Intellectual disability (intellectual developmental disorder) replaces mental retardation in the *DSM-5* as this reflects common professional usage. Public Law 111–256, Rosa's Law, is a 2010 federal statute that legally replaces the term *mental retardation* with *intellectual disability*. Regardless of nomenclature, limitations in pervasive intellectual functioning qualify intellectual disability (intellectual developmental disorder) as a mental disorder in the *DSM-5*. Diagnosis is now rendered by level of functioning as opposed to a specific standardized IQ (APA, 2013; Wakefield, 2013).

Specific learning disorder combines the separate diagnoses of reading disorder, mathematics disorder, disorder of written expression, and learning disorder NOS. Coded specifiers are included for each type. The APA (2013) emphasized that specific learning disorders are highly comorbid with each other (see also Wakefield, 2013).

There are substantial changes to the classification of ADHD. Age of onset has been changed from before 7 years of age to before 12 years of age, and ADHD is now diagnosable in adults. Additional modifications include strengthening the cross-situational requirement; eliminating the subtypes; adding specifiers, including examples to facilitate diagnosis; and allowing for concomitant diagnosis of ADHD and ASD. Consistent with the *DSM-IV-TR*, the same 18 symptoms are used within the domains of inattention and hyperactivity/impulsivity (APA, 2013).

Communication disorders now include language disorder, previously expressive and mixed receptive-expressive language disorder; speech sound disorder, previously phonological disorder; and childhood onset fluency disorder, previously stuttering. The biggest modification to the communication disorders is the addition of social (pragmatic) communication disorder, which focuses on verbal and nonverbal social deficiencies in communication and represents an important differential category for ASD. The key difference between social (pragmatic) communication disorder and ASD is the mandatory absence of repeated restrictive behaviors, interests, and activities in diagnosing the former (APA, 2013).

Implications for Counselors

Counselors working across settings should be comfortable with the revised nomenclature for neurodevelopmental disorders. By definition, symptoms of neurodevelopmental disorders begin in childhood and affect functioning in home and school settings (Addington & Rapoport, 2012). This underscores the importance of assessment and clinical intervention for clients and their families.

It is imperative for counselors to have strong knowledge of diagnostic criteria and differential diagnoses for neurodevelopmental disorders; this is especially relevant because of the controversy surrounding the changes to ASD, the frequency of ADHD diagnoses, and the impact of each of the developmental disorders. Several important areas for counselors to focus on are identifying signs and symptoms indicative of need for assessment referral, providing appropriate clinical treatment services, facilitating client and family education, and working with clients previously diagnosed with a different condition in the *DSM-IV-TR* (e.g., Asperger's disorder, PDD-NOS).

The APA (2013) clarified that the new category of social (pragmatic) communication disorder could more accurately explicate the symptoms and etiology of individuals previously diagnosed with PDD-NOS. The research supports this diagnosis in appropriate identification of this population, which enables provision of a strength-based treatment approach (Lai, Lombardo, Chakrabarti, & Baron-Cohen, 2013; McGuiness & Johnson, 2013).

ASD is lifelong, with adult rates of diagnosis increasing, so clinical interventions and adjunctive support should be emphasized for children, youth, and adults. It is advantageous for counselors to use a spectrum approach depending on each client's level of ability; clinical interventions can then be tailored to specific client needs. The ASD diagnosis is retained, even if the criteria are not currently met, to reflect successful behavioral interventions or environmental changes; this allows for continued treatment services for clients (Greaves-Lord et al., 2013; Kurita, 2011; Mandy et al., 2012).

For ADHD and learning disorders, counselors should achieve a level of comfort with the diagnostic changes and coding. Research-informed practice allows counselors to advocate for clients and implement targeted interventions in their clinical settings. ADHD responds well to structured treatment approaches, including behavioral therapy and CBT (Ghanizadeh, 2013).

Intellectual Disabilities

This category of disorders encompasses deficits in cognitive functioning, typically characterized by limitations in adaptive behaviors such as activities of daily living (e.g., self-management skills such as hygiene, feeding, and organizing life tasks); social skills, including social judgment and interpersonal communication skills; and conceptualization skills, such as language, reading, writing, and memory (APA, 2013). As previously discussed, intellectual disability was referred to as mental retardation in the *DSM-IV-TR*.

This term, however, has been dropped from the diagnostic nomenclature mainly because of the stigma and federal legislation (Rosa's law). This is also more consistent with the *DSM-5*'s developmental emphasis on neurobiological etiology. Because the *DSM-5* does not use multiaxial assessment, it is hoped that intellectual disability will be considered more equally alongside other mental disorders.

31_ Intellectual Disability (Intellectual Developmental Disorder) (F7_)

Essential Features

Intellectual disability refers to deficits in cognitive ability in which expected levels of functioning are not met (e.g., age-appropriate activities of daily living). The parenthetical *intellectual developmental disorder* reflects the WHO (2007) terminology and is an example of the APA harmonizing the *DSM-5* with the *ICD-10*. For this diagnosis to be given, intelligence and adaptive functioning both need to be assessed, which is a departure from the required IQ of 70 or below for a *DSM-IV-TR* diagnosis. The level of adaptive functioning determines severity of the disorder. This diagnosis is only used for individuals old enough to complete standardized assessments measuring intellectual ability; although these ability tests are important, they are not sufficient to render the diagnosis. There is a 1% prevalence rate of the disorder in the general population (APA, 2013).

Differential Diagnosis

If an individual is diagnosed with intellectual disability (intellectual developmental disorder), there is a 3 to 4 times heightened probability of a co-occurring disorder(s). Commonly co-occurring disorders for this diagnosis are major and mild neurocognitive disorders, communication disorders, specific learning disorder, and ASD (APA, 2013).

Coding, Recording, and Specifiers

The *ICD-9-CM* and *ICD-10-CM* codes for intellectual disability (intellectual developmental disorder) are linked with the severity specifiers. Counselors should note that the original *DSM-5* mistakenly published the code as **319** for intellectual disability (intellectual developmental disorder). This is incorrect, and the following codes should be used: 317 (F70) *mild*, 318.0 (F71) *moderate*, 318.1 (F72) *severe*, and 318.2 (F73) *profound*. Severity levels are assigned based on functioning, not intellectual ability, with the assessment of conceptual, social, and practical domains. Readers can refer to Table 1: Severity Levels for Intellectual Disability (Intellectual Developmental Disorder) on pages 34–36 of the *DSM-5* for specific information related to the assessment of each specifier (APA, 2013).

315.8 Global Developmental Delay (F88)

According to the APA (2013), global developmental delay consists of a child's failure to meet milestones across multiple areas of functioning, specifically in children younger than 5 years of age. This diagnosis should be given when a child cannot be fully assessed or participate in standardized testing because of age. Global developmental delay is a temporary diagnosis and requires further assessment; this diagnosis is often viewed as a precursor for intellectual disability (intellectual developmental disorder).

Communication Disorders

This category of disorders encompasses deficits in language, speech, and communication through verbal and nonverbal behaviors and includes language disorder, speech sound disorder, childhood-onset fluency disorder (stuttering), and social (pragmatic) communication disorder. As previously discussed, the new diagnosis of social (pragmatic) communication disorder is intended to encompass individuals with deficiencies in social communication but without restricted repetitive behaviors, interests, and activities extant with ASD. As with all diagnoses, cultural contexts must be taken into account (APA, 2013).

315.39 Language Disorder (F80.9)

Essential Features

Language disorder possesses the core feature of deficits in language acquisition and use that are seen in verbal and written communication. This includes the use of sign language and must be "substantially and quantifiable below that expected for age" (APA, 2013, p. 42). In the *DSM-5*, language disorder is coded as 315.39 (F80.9). There are no specifiers for this disorder.

Differential Diagnosis

The counselor should be aware of normal variations in language, hearing, or sensory impairment. Other differential diagnoses are intellectual disability (intellectual developmental disorder), neurological disorders, and language regression (which could be an indicator of ASD). There is often a family history of language disorder; by the age of 4 years, it becomes a stable diagnosis that typically extends into adulthood (APA, 2013).

315.39 Speech Sound Disorder (F80.0)

Essential Features

The hallmark of speech sound disorder is marked difficulty with the articulation of individual sounds (phonemes). Deficits in knowledge of phonemes and coordination of sound-inducing movements occur. In children without speech sound disorder, speech should be 50% understandable by 3 years of age and completely comprehensible by 7 years of age (APA, 2013). In the *DSM-5*, speech sound disorder is coded as 315.39 (F80.0). There are no specifiers for this disorder.

Differential Diagnosis

Differential diagnoses for speech sound disorder represent normal variations in speech, hearing or other sensory impairment, structural deficits (e.g., cleft palate), dysarthria (when there is a motor disorder affecting speech), and selective mutism (APA, 2013).

315.35 Childhood-Onset Fluency Disorder (Stuttering) (F80.81)

Essential Features

Childhood-onset fluency disorder replaces the term *stuttering* to more accurately reflect the etiology of the disorder and eliminate negative connotations associated with the latter term. Key features represent difficulties with normal fluency and timing of speech that is inappropriate for developmental age. Anxiety can worsen the difficulty, and individuals with this disorder sometimes avoid situations that involve public speaking. Childhood-onset fluency disorder (stuttering) is extant by 6 years of age for 80% to 90% of diagnosed individuals. Prognosis is good, with 65% to 85% recovering from the dysfluency (APA, 2013). In the *DSM-5*, childhood-onset fluency disorder (stuttering) is coded as 315.35 (F80.81). There are no specifiers for this disorder.

Differential Diagnosis

Counselors should be aware of sensory deficits (e.g., hearing), normal speech difficulties, medication side effects, adult-onset dysfluency (not a *DSM-5* disorder), or Tourette's disorder as differential diagnoses (APA, 2013). Referral to a speech-language specialist is recommended.

315.39 Social (Pragmatic) Communication Disorder (F80.89)

Essential Features

The core features of social (pragmatic) communication disorder are deficits in social uses of language and communication that can result from lack of effective communication, social participation, or development of social relationships. Language impairment is the most common feature. This diagnosis is rarely given in children younger than 4 years of age because they are in the natural process of language acquisition and utilization (APA, 2013). In the *DSM-5*, social (pragmatic) communication disorder is coded as 315.39 (F80.89). There are no specifiers for this disorder.

Differential Diagnosis

Social (pragmatic) communication disorder is a new, and important, differential diagnosis for ASD. Individuals with social (pragmatic) communication disorder do not display the restricted, repetitive patterns of behaviors, interests, or activities that are necessary components of ASD. Common differential diagnoses are social anxiety disorder (social phobia), ADHD, intellectual disability (intellectual developmental disorder), and global developmental delay (APA, 2013).

299.00 Autism Spectrum Disorder (F84.0)

> I knew from early on that my daughter was different. My sister's baby boy was close to the same age, and he interacted with family and friends very differently than my child. He smiled and laughed and played while my daughter didn't. It made me very sad, and I didn't know what to do. Her pediatrician was the first person to mention the word *autism* to me; it was a scary time for us. Now, though, my daughter is getting help and my husband and I are in counseling too. We are learning to appreciate the little things that make her unique. —Kathy

The new category of autism spectrum disorder (ASD) replaces pervasive developmental disorders and consolidates previous diagnoses of autism disorder, Asperger's disorder, childhood disintegrative disorder, Rett syndrome, and PDD-NOS. This change reflects scientific understanding that autism encompasses a common set of behaviors that are best represented by a single diagnostic category (APA, 2013; Coolidge, Marle, Rhoades, Monaghan, & Segal, 2013; Mandy et al., 2011, 2012; Mazefsky et al., 2013; Pinborough-Zimmerman et al., 2012). Any client with a previously established diagnosis of autism disorder, Asperger's disorder, or PDD-NOS will now receive an ASD diagnosis.

Prevalence rates for ASD are reported at one in 80, with the diagnosis imperative for access to services (CDC, 2012; Pinborough-Zimmerman et al., 2012). According to Fombonne (2005), diagnostic rates have been increasing and will continue to do so. Because ASD is a lifelong disorder, most individuals living with the diagnosis are adults (Wilson et al., 2013).

Essential Features

The *DSM-5* Neurodevelopmental Disorders Work Group focused on the validity and reliability of the *DSM-IV-TR* diagnoses of autistic disorder, Asperger's disorder, childhood disintegrative disorder, Rett syndrome, and PDD-NOS. The work group reported minimal qualitative differences among them. Thus, the three-tiered *DSM-IV-TR* approach to diagnosing these disorders is now collapsed into dyadic classifications for ASD: (a) deficits in social communication and social interaction across different settings and (b) restricted repetitive behaviors, interests, and activities. Specifically, three criteria address shortcomings in social communication and interaction: deficits in social-emotional reciprocity; nonverbal communication in social interactions; and developing, maintaining, and understanding relationships. All three must be met currently or historically. Two of the following four restrictive behavior criteria must also be met: overly dependent on routines, highly sensitive to changes in their environments, intensely focused on inappropriate items, and sensory input sensitivity (APA, 2013; McGuiness & Johnson, 2013). The APA (2013) lifted the age requirement of symptom detection by 3 years of age; although symptoms were extant, concerns may have gone undetected until the child started school and was faced with increased social demands (McGuiness & Johnson, 2013).

Special Considerations

There has been significant concern over the stringency of the new criteria and collapsing of diagnoses that would exclude individuals from access to treatment (Barton et al., 2013; McPartland et al., 2012). One positive aspect is that more specificity in diagnosis can lend to accuracy in selecting effective treatment interventions. Lauritsen (2013) asserted that the removal of the age restriction represents a warranted change for those previously excluded.

The removal of Asperger's disorder as a diagnosis has sparked controversy, especially for individuals and their families who have learned to embrace the challenges and strengths of the distinctive diagnosis (Mandy et al., 2012). Researchers voiced concern that ASD might have a stronger negative connotation for those previously diagnosed with Asperger's disorder (Wakefield, 2013). Finally, multiple researchers found that fewer children will be diagnosed with ASD under the new criteria (Gibbs et al., 2012; Mayes et al., 2013; Tsai, 2012; Wilson et al., 2013).

Several researchers identified positives from the change (Greaves-Lord et al., 2013; Kurita, 2011; Wakefield, 2013) in that clinicians can now reliably distinguish ASD from other mental disorders, genetic studies support the fluidity of the new approach, and the diagnostic specifiers assist with utility of treatment planning. Social (pragmatic) communication disorder might be a valid and appropriate diagnosis for some individuals because it allows for social difficulties in absence of the restricted repetitive behaviors and would likely include those who would previously have been diagnosed with PDD-NOS.

Diagnostic Criteria for ASD 299.00 (F84.0)

A. Persistent deficits in social communication and social interaction across multiple contexts, as manifested by the following, currently or by history (examples are illustrative, not exhaustive; see text [of *DSM-5*, pp. 50–59]):
  1. Deficits in social-emotional reciprocity, ranging, for example, from abnormal social approach and failure of normal back-and-forth conversation; to reduced sharing of interests, emotions, or affect; to failure to initiate or respond to social interactions.
  2. Deficits in nonverbal communicative behaviors used for social interaction, ranging, for example, from poorly integrated verbal and nonverbal communication; to abnormalities in eye contact and body language or deficits in understanding and use of gestures; to a total lack of facial expressions and nonverbal communication.
  3. Deficits in developing, maintaining, and understanding relationships, ranging, for example, from difficulties adjusting behavior to suit various social contexts; to difficulties in sharing, imaginative play or in making friends; to absence of interest in peers.

  Specify current severity:
  Severity is based on social communication impairments and restricted, repetitive patterns of behavior.

B. Restricted, repetitive patterns of behavior, interests, or activities, as manifested by least two of the following, currently or by history (examples are illustrative, not exhaustive):

1. Stereotyped or repetitive motor movements, use of objects, or speech (e.g., simple motor stereotypies, lining up toys or flipping objects, echolalia, idiosyncratic phrases).

2. Insistence on sameness, inflexible adherence to routines, or ritualized patterns of verbal or nonverbal behavior (e.g., extreme distress at small changes, difficulties with transitions, rigid thinking patterns, greeting rituals, need to take same route or eat same food every day).

3. Highly restricted, fixated interests that are abnormal in intensity or focus (e.g., strong attachment to or preoccupation with unusual objects, excessively circumscribed or perseverative interest).

4. Hyper- or hyporeactivity to sensory input or unusual interest in sensory aspects of the environment (e.g., apparent indifference to pain/temperature, adverse response to specific sounds or textures, excessive smelling or touching of objects, visual fascination with lights or movement).

Specify current severity:

Severity is based on social communication impairments and restricted, repetitive patterns of behavior.

C. Symptoms must be present in the early developmental period (but may not become fully manifest until social demands exceed limited capacities, or may be masked by learned strategies in later life).

D. Symptoms cause clinically significant impairment in social, occupational, or other important areas of current functioning.

E. These disturbances are not better explained by intellectual disability (intellectual developmental disorder) or global developmental delay. Intellectual disability and autism spectrum disorder frequently co-occur; to make comorbid diagnoses of autism spectrum disorder and intellectual disability, social communication should be below that expected for general developmental level.

Note: Individuals with a well-established *DSM-IV* diagnosis of autistic disorder, Asperger's disorder, or pervasive developmental disorder not otherwise specified should be given the diagnosis of autism spectrum disorder. Individuals who have marked deficits in social communication, but whose symptoms do not otherwise meet criteria for autism spectrum disorder, should be evaluated for social (pragmatic) communication disorder.

Differential Diagnosis

According to the APA (2013), common differential diagnoses for ASD are Rett syndrome, selective mutism, language disorders, social (pragmatic) communication disorder, intellectual disability (intellectual developmental disorder) without ASD, stereotypic movement disorder, ADHD, and schizophrenia. Simonoff et al. (2008) found that, out of a population representative study of 12-year-olds diagnosed with ASD, 70% met the criteria for at least one other mental disorder and 41% met the criteria for two.

Coding, Recording, and Specifiers

There are no subtypes for ASD. The assigned specifiers are *with or without accompanying intellectual impairment*; *with or without accompanying language impairment*; *associated with a known medical or genetic condition or environmental factor*; *associated with another neurodevelopmental, mental, or behavioral disorder*; or *with catatonia*. Severity levels are Level 1 (*mild*), requiring support; Level 2 (*moderate*), requiring substantial support; and Level 3 (*severe*), requiring very substantial support (see pp. 51–52 of the *DSM-5*). There has been criticism of unclear severity levels and how comorbid diagnoses would convolute assessment, diagnosis, and treatment (Weitlauf et al., 2013).

 **Example**

Adam is a 5-year-old, African American kindergartner and is the only child of loving, busy career parents who adopted Adam from foster care during infancy. Little is known about his birth parents or their background.

Since Adam was about 18 months old, his parents, Cindy and Samantha, noticed that he acted differently than the other children in his playgroup. Adam did not interact with the other children and rarely responded to play with smiles or laughter. As he got older, it was clear that Adam preferred to play by himself. Because he was rarely upset or caused trouble, Cindy and Samantha didn't worry too much about his preference for solitude until Adam started kindergarten.

Adam's teacher noticed these behaviors and also observed that he would engage in multiple rituals, including rocking back and forth, untying and tying his shoes, and coloring only with blue crayon. Adam's teacher referred him to the school counselor, who recommended that Adam receive follow-up testing for a possible neurodevelopmental disorder.

◆ ◆ ◆

Diagnostic Questions

1. Do Adam's presenting symptoms meet the criteria for ASD?
2. Based on an affirmative answer to Question 1, what specifier(s) would you assign for Adam's diagnosis? What level of severity?
3. What would be the reason(s) a counselor may not diagnose Adam with intellectual disability (intellectual developmental disorder)?
4. Would Adam be more accurately diagnosed with ADHD? If so, why? If not, why not?
5. What rule-outs would you consider for Adam's case?
6. What other information may be needed to make an accurate clinical diagnosis?

314._ _ Attention-Deficit/Hyperactivity Disorder (F90._)

Zach was so precocious as a little boy; he lit up the room and entertained everyone. It wasn't until he started school and his teacher contacted us about her concerns that we realized something was wrong. It's true that Zach can't sit still or focus. Now we are being told he needs medication, and we don't want that. Counseling seems to be our best choice to try and help him. —Tom (Zach's dad)

Attention-deficit/hyperactivity disorder (ADHD) is the most common neurodevelopmental disorder in childhood. According to the APA (2013), 5% of children and 2.5% of adults are diagnosed with ADHD. Along with the high prevalence rates, there has been a marked increase in psychotropic medications for those with ADHD (Pastor & Reuben, 2008) and a 3% increase in the number of children diagnosed in the last 15 years.

Essential Features

ADHD has similar diagnostic criteria from the *DSM-IV-TR* and the same 18 symptoms divided between the domains of inattention and hyperactivity/impulsivity. The main feature of ADHD is ongoing inattention and hyperactivity/impulsivity that are disruptive across many areas of functioning. Symptoms of ADHD must now occur before age 12 instead of the previous requirement of before age 7 (APA, 2013).

DSM-5 enhancements to the criteria include specific examples for diagnosis across the life span and requirement of cross-situational evidence. In adults, five symptoms are required for the diagnosis instead of six; this chronological expansion of ADHD opens up treatment options for diagnosed adults (Wakefield, 2013).

Differential Diagnosis

Language, motor, and social developmental delays are often comorbid with ADHD. Learning disorders also have frequent co-occurrence, with some reports of comorbidity as high as 50% (APA, 2013; Ghanizadeh, 2013). There are multiple additional differential diagnoses: ODD, IED, other neurodevelopmental disorders, specific learning disorder, intellectual disability (intellectual developmental disorder), ASD, RAD, anxiety disorders, depressive disorders, bipolar disorder, DMDD, substance use disorders, personality disorders, psychotic disorders, medication-induced symptoms of ADHD, and neurocognitive disorders (APA, 2013). For counselors, clear understanding of the criteria for ADHD is imperative because of high prevalence rates and pervasive familial, social, and educational impact.

Coding, Recording, and Specifiers

The coding for ADHD is based on presentation type: 314.01 (F90.2) *combined presentation* if inattention and hyperactivity/impulsivity are met for the past 6 months, 314.00 (F90.0) *predominantly inattentive presentation*; and 314.01 (F90.1) *predominantly hyperactive/impulsive presentation*. The *in partial remission* specifier is used if the criteria have been previously met and there is ongoing impairment in social, academic, or occupational functioning. Severity specifiers of *mild*, *moderate*, and *severe* reflect number of symptoms and level of impairment (APA, 2013).

 Example

> Lee is a single, 21-year-old, Asian American college student living with his parents and younger siblings. Although he would like to move out on his own, he has not been able to maintain a job while also keeping his grades high enough to avoid academic probation.
>
> Lee's parents often treat him like a child, and this upsets him. They tell him they will treat him like an adult when he acts like one. Sometimes his friends get angry with him, and he has never really had a girlfriend.
>
> Since Lee was in elementary school, he has struggled with his schoolwork. He is disorganized and has trouble attending to details. Others have constantly told Lee that he is distracted too easily and is extremely forgetful. He is often frustrated with himself but can't seem to change his behaviors.
>
> Lee used to get in trouble at school for talking too much and fidgeting. He still has problems listening and sitting quietly. Lee seeks counseling services at his college counseling center for help with his academic struggles. After speaking with his counselor during the intake session, he realizes that counseling may benefit him in his personal relationships as well.

◆ ◆ ◆

Diagnostic Questions

1. Do Lee's presenting symptoms meet the criteria for ADHD?
2. Based on your answer to Question 1, what presentation and severity specifiers would you assign for Lee's diagnosis?

3. What would be the reason(s) a counselor may not diagnose Lee with ADHD?
4. Would Lee be more accurately diagnosed with ODD? If so, why? If not, why not?
5. What rule-outs would you consider for Lee's case?
6. What other information may be needed to make an accurate clinical diagnosis?

315._ Specific Learning Disorder (F81._)

Essential Features

Specific learning disorder has biological etiology and underlying cognitive deficits and challenges. It is 2 to 3 times more common in males than females. Problems with reading, mathematics, and writing frequently co-occur. In the *DSM-5*, the learning disorders of impairment in reading, in written expression, and in mathematics are collapsed into one disorder and identified with specifiers, which reflects a change from the *DSM-IV-TR* (APA, 2013).

Differential Diagnosis

Differential diagnoses for all three subtypes of specific learning disorder are intellectual disability (intellectual developmental disorder), neurocognitive disorders, normal ability differences, and neurological or sensory disorders. It is important for counselors to make appropriate assessment referrals if a client displays symptoms of specific learning disorder (APA, 2013).

Coding, Recording, and Specifiers

In the *DSM-5*, the diagnostic code for specific learning disorder *with impairment in reading* is 315.00 (F81.0), *with impairment in written expression* is 315.2 (F81.81), and *with impairment in mathematics* is 315.1 (F81.2). There are three severity specifiers: *mild, moderate,* and *severe*. *Mild* represents some deficits in one or two academic domains with limited need for support; *moderate* shows significant difficulty in learning skills in at least one domain with a need for substantial support; and *severe* includes extreme difficulties in learning skills affecting multiple areas existing even with substantial support across school and home environments (APA, 2013).

Motor Disorders

Motor disorders listed in this chapter include developmental coordination disorder, stereotypic movement disorder, and tic disorders. The tic criteria (Tourette's disorder, persistent [chronic] motor or vocal tic disorder, and provisional tic disorder) have been standardized, reflecting a change from the *DSM-IV-TR*. All of the motor disorders must cause impairment or distress and interfere with activities of daily living (APA, 2013). Motor disorders are rarely diagnosed in counseling settings; however, accurate discernment of the diagnoses remains important.

315.4 Developmental Coordination Disorder (F82)

Essential Features

Developmental coordination disorder represents marked deficits in coordinated motor skills that affect daily activities across settings. Symptoms must have onset in early childhood and not be better explained by intellectual disability (intellectual developmental disorder) or attributable to a neurological condition. There is a 5% to 6% prevalence rate in children between the ages of 5 and 11 years, with boys more likely than girls to be diagnosed with the disorder (APA, 2013). The *DSM-5* code for developmental coordination disorder is 315.4 (F82). There are no specifiers for this disorder.

Differential Diagnosis

Differential diagnoses for developmental coordination disorder are impairments due to another medical condition, intellectual disability (intellectual developmental disorder), ADHD, ASD, and joint hypermobility syndrome. ADHD is the most frequent co-occurring disorder, with a 50% comorbidity rate (APA, 2013).

307.3 Stereotypic Movement Disorder (F98.4)

Essential Features

Stereotypic movement disorder consists of repetitive and purposeless motor behavior that appears to be internally driven. These behaviors are often done in a rhythmic way, and the individual may or may not respond to efforts to inhibit them. The movements must interfere with functioning; frequency varies greatly and often changes according to context (e.g., the specific setting or mood). Self-injurious behaviors occur and can include incidents of head banging, face slapping, self-biting, and eye poking (APA, 2013).

Differential Diagnosis

Differential diagnoses for stereotypic movement disorder are ASD, obsessive-compulsive and related disorders, tic disorders, and other neurological or medical conditions. Additionally, body-focused repetitive behavior disorder, listed in the Obsessive-Compulsive and Related Disorders chapter, should be ruled out and normative childhood behavior should be considered (APA, 2013).

Coding, Recording, and Specifiers

The *DSM-5* code for stereotypic movement disorder is 307.3 (F98.4). Specifiers are *with self-injurious behavior*; *without self-injurious behavior*; and *associated with a known medical or genetic condition, neurodevelopmental disorder, or environmental factor*. Use additional coding to identify a medical condition or other neurodevelopmental disorder. Specify also if *mild* (symptoms easily suppressed), *moderate* (symptoms require explicit protective measures), or *severe* (symptoms need continuous monitoring; APA, 2013).

307.2_ Tic Disorders (F95._)

Essential Features

A tic is a "sudden, rapid, recurrent, nonrhythmic motor movement or vocalization" (APA, 2013, p. 81). There are three tic disorder classifications: (a) Tourette's disorder, which possesses both multiple motor and one or more vocal tics; (b) persistent (chronic) motor or vocal tic disorder, which excludes both motor and vocal (must be one or the other); and (c) provisional tic disorder, in which single or multiple motor and/or vocal tics are present for less than 1 year. Onset for all three classifications must be younger than 18 years of age (APA, 2013).

Differential Diagnosis

Differential diagnoses for tic disorders are abnormal movements due to other medical conditions, stereotypic movement disorder, substance-induced and paroxysmal dyskinesias, myonoclus (quick and insuppressible with the lack of a prior urges), and obsessive-compulsive and related disorders (APA, 2013).

Coding, Recording, and Specifiers

The *DSM-5* codes for tic disorders are Tourette's disorder 307.23 (F95.2), persistent (chronic) motor or vocal tic disorder 307.22 (F95.1), and provisional tic disorder 307.21 (F95.0).

The specifier *with motor tics only* or *with vocal tics only* is required for chronic motor or vocal tic disorder (APA, 2013).

Neurocognitive Disorders

I noticed it gradually in mom's behaviors. At first, I would have to repeat myself more and more. The forgetfulness started in earnest shortly after that, and mom had trouble remembering many things. Then, she appeared to have forgotten how to take care of herself. Now, she sometimes doesn't even recognize friends or family. —Nora

Neurocognitive disorders represent mental health disturbances with underlying physical pathology that can sometimes be genetically determined. This differentiates them from other classifications in the *DSM-5*. The term *neurocognitive* stems from the Neurocognitive Disorders Work Group's use of *cognitive*, which has a broad meaning encompassing all information processing, with *neuro* emphasizing brain functioning (Ganguli et al., 2011). Neurocognitive disorders are prevalent, with a staggering 66 million individuals in the United States who will meet the criteria for a major neurocognitive disorder by the year 2030 (Mitchell, 2013).

Although health professionals and laypersons often think of older adults in relation to neurocognitive dysfunction (e.g., Alzheimer's), it is important to remember that these disorders also affect younger individuals. For example, traumatic brain injuries result in 1.4 million emergency room visits annually and occur across the life span (APA, 2013; Bajenaru et al., 2012). Neurocognitive disorders are not limited to memory or cognition problems but also affect complex cognitive processes, language, motor functioning, and social cognition. Early diagnosis and intervention are key. Recent research clearly shows that underlying pathology of these disorders can be seen before symptoms occur (Bajenaru et al., 2012; Blazer, 2013).

Major Changes From *DSM-IV-TR* to *DSM-5*

The unwieldy *DSM-IV-TR* chapter titled Delirium, Dementia, and Amnestic and Other Cognitive Disorders was renamed Neurocognitive Disorders in the *DSM-5*. This change reflects current scientific understanding regarding the neurological pathology and etiology that underlie all disorders in this section. New inclusions represent a unified operationalization of six identified neurocognitive domains—cognitive attention, executive function, learning and memory, language, perceptual-motor, and social cognition—for which APA (2013) provides definitions, examples for major and mild neurocognitive disorder, and corresponding assessments. Thorough comprehension of these domains is imperative to understanding essential features and diagnostic criteria within this section. Refer to the *DSM-5* for more information regarding these neurocognitive domains.

Although delirium remains relatively unchanged, counselors will find substantial modifications to the remainder of the chapter in the *DSM-5*. Specifically, APA (2013) noted a desire to move away from the term *dementia* to a broader conceptualization of cognitive impairments as neurocognitive disorders; in the *DSM-5*, dementia is renamed major neurocognitive disorder. Amnestic disorders and other cognitive disorders have been subsumed under the neurocognitive disorder category. A new diagnosis, mild neurocognitive disorder, appears in the *DMS-5* and was developed to identify individuals early in the etiology of the disease. Amid controversy, the Neurocognitive Disorders Work Group acknowledged the potential for misdiagnosis and unnecessary testing with the new disorder; however, its members believed ongoing research investigations will clearly support the inclusion of mild neurocognitive disorder to the nomenclature (Blazer, 2013). Bajenaru et al. (2012) praised this development and declared the addition of mild neurocognitive disorder important from a nosological perspective to assist with early identification of neurocognitive dysfunction.

Some neurological researchers have criticized the establishment of mild neurocognitive disorder, positing that the diagnosis is too subjective and lacks the needed genetic undergirding. Proponents asserted that early interventions, such as memory enhancement strategies, lend to more accurate diagnosis and allay the progression of symptomatology (Bajenaru et al., 2012). The general criteria sets of major and mild neurocognitive disorder underlie nearly the entire chapter, except delirium, with enhanced focus on the etiology of the neurocognitive disorders.

Etiology and Treatment

Neurocognitive disorders can manifest throughout the life span and may be seen in cognitive functioning concerns resulting from traumatic brain injury or HIV infection. By definition, there must be an acquired decline from previous levels of functioning (Bajenaru et al., 2012). The decline must be clinically determined and must include assessment batteries for primary domains of complex attention, executive ability, learning and memory, language, perceptual-motor ability, and social cognition. Information can be obtained from a client, from a significant other, or by clinical observation (Sorrell, 2013). For neurocognitive disorders, the underlying pathology is often known, which aids in identification of specific etiology. This provides for efficacious treatment development, including health interventions, medication management, and counseling services (Bajenaru et al., 2012; Ganguli et al., 2011).

Implications for Counselors

Neurocognitive disorders represent diagnoses made in medical settings with counselors often working as part of a treatment team for affected individuals and their families. For mild neurocognitive disorders, clients experience initial difficulties performing activities of daily living that can be assuaged by behavioral techniques and supportive counseling. Education and adjustment time can help individuals and their families, providing a critical window whereby course of action can be set, support services identified, and future plans mapped (Mitchell, 2013). The Neurocognitive Disorders Work Group posited that being able to identify a name for the disturbance is often reassuring and can provide an avenue for positive action (Blazer, 2013).

With the new classification system, there is a strong opportunity for counselors to help clients throughout the progression of the disease. We encourage counselors who work with clients living with major and mild neurocognitive disorders to consult with medical professionals, neuropsychologists, and etiological specialists in addition to seeking specialized training, because neurocognitive disorders are not commonly addressed in counselor education. Counselors will likely provide services to loved ones and caretakers of individuals diagnosed with a neurocognitive disorder and need to possess a full understanding of their experiences to provide optimal support.

We urge counselors to thoroughly review the Neurocognitive Disorders chapter in the *DSM-5*. Table 1: Neurocognitive Domains (pp. 593–595 of the *DSM-5*) may be particularly useful for counselors because it highlights symptoms for each of the cognitive domains and gives examples of specific assessments. For example, in the cognitive domain of complex attention, a symptom of mild neurocognitive disorder would be longer time needed to complete tasks with accompanying errors in routine activities; the assessment example would be checking sustained, selective, and divided attention (APA, 2013).

Delirium

Essential Features

Delirium represents a disturbance in attention or awareness with concomitant decline in cognitive functioning inclusive of a "reduced ability to direct, focus, sustain, and shift attention" (APA, 2013, p. 599). This disturbance and decline cannot be better explained by another neurocognitive disorder (either already existing or developing). It is typical for an individual with delirium to have difficulty appropriately responding to questions or orienting to his or her environment.

This decline in functioning happens quickly (within days and sometimes hours) and fluctuates, which is critical in separating delirium from major and mild neurocognitive disorders (Ganguli et al., 2011). There must be evidence that the delirium results from the physiological consequences of a medical condition, substance intoxication or withdrawal, medication usage, or exposure to a toxin. There must also be a change in at least one other area of cognitive functioning, such as memory or language.

Special Considerations

Prevalence rates for delirium are age dependent, with occurrences of up to 14% in adults older than 85 years (APA, 2013). For the overall population, the prevalence rate is 1% to 2%. Early identification and treatment for delirium is critical because it shortens the duration of the disorder and improves prognosis. There are both environmental (e.g., low levels of activity; drug and alcohol use) and physiological risk factors (e.g., major and mild neurocognitive disorders, illness, age; APA, 2013).

Differential Diagnosis

Common differential diagnoses for delirium are psychotic disorders, bipolar and depressive disorders with psychotic features, acute stress disorder, malingering, factitious disorder, and major and mild neurocognitive disorders. Although delirium is diagnosed in a medical setting, with a majority of cases occurring in hospital or nursing care, counselors should be aware of conditions that can commonly be mistaken for delirium so appropriate treatment interventions can be sought (APA, 2013). It is important to note that the presence of delirium almost always indicates the need for immediate medical attention; counselors should assist clients in managing this urgency.

Coding, Recording, and Specifiers

ICD-9-CM codes for delirium are unique to the assigned specifiers. For *substance intoxication delirium* (when there is a disturbance specifically in attention and cognition), the codes are 291.0 for alcohol and 292.81 for cannabis, phencyclidine, other hallucinogen, inhalant, opioid, sedative/hypnotic/anxiolytic, amphetamine, cocaine, or other substance. For *substance withdrawal delirium*, the codes are again specific to the substance as illustrated above.

All *ICD-10-CM* codes are both substance and specifier specific: *with use disorder, mild*; *with use disorder, moderate or severe*; and *without use disorder*. For example, substance intoxication delirium with inhalant use disorder, mild, is F18.121; substance intoxication delirium, moderate (or severe), is F18.221; and substance intoxication delirium without inhalant use disorder is F18.921.

There is also *medication-induced delirium* with an *ICD-9-CM* code of 292.81 and *ICD-10-CM* code depending on the type of medication. With *delirium due to another medical condition*, the name of the condition should be included, for example, 293.0 (F05) delirium due to hepatic encephalopathy. And with *delirium due to multiple etiologies*, separate codes should be used for each etiology.

Clinicians should specify if the diagnosis is *acute* (lasting a few hour or days) or *persistent* (lasting weeks or months) as well as if *hyperactive, hypoactive, or mixed level of activity*. Even though diagnosis of delirium is not made in counseling settings, we encourage counselors working with this population to review the specifiers and recording procedures listed on pages 596–599 of the *DSM-5*.

Major Neurocognitive Disorder

Essential Features

Impairment in only one of the identified cognitive domains (complex attention, executive ability, learning and memory, language, perceptual-motor ability, and social cognition) is required for major neurocognitive disorder, with an emphasis on deterioration from baseline functioning (Mitchell, 2013). For appropriate diagnosis, the decline must be significant. The contributing information is based on two factors: (a) worry from the individual, a "knowledgeable informant," or a clinician and (b) neurological testing or quantitative assessment. This decline in functioning must interfere with activities in daily living, not occur during a delirium, and not be explained by another mental disorder (APA, 2013).

Special Considerations

Some researchers have expressed worry about potential stigma from a major neurocognitive disorder diagnosis as well as subjective decision making on the part of the clinician (Remington, 2012; Sorrell, 2013). However, assessment testing must be done, with clinical significance representing a minimum of two standard deviations below the norm, before a diagnosis of major neurocognitive disorder is made (Ganguli et al., 2011). As with all *DSM-5* diagnoses, age, culture, occupation, and gender are important issues to address during assessment.

Mild Neurocognitive Disorder

Essential Features

The Neurocognitive Disorders Work Group emphasized that research supports a spectrum approach to neurocognitive disorders. There must be evidence of "modest" cognitive decline in at least one of the six previously enumerated cognitive domains. This is in contrast to "substantial" cognitive decline for major neurocognitive disorder (APA, 2013). The information must be based on worry from the individual, a "knowledgeable informant," or a clinician as well as neurological testing/ quantitative assessment. The decline in functioning must interfere with activities of daily living, not occur during a delirium, and not be better explained by another mental disorder (APA, 2013).

Special Considerations

There has been concern that including mild neurocognitive disorder would lead to overdiagnosis of individuals within the typical range of neurocognitive functioning (Obiols, 2012). Remington (2012) discussed the criticism of this "predisease" concept that can lead to stigma, unnecessary intervention, and anxiety. Conversely, early use of medications can sometimes slow down cognitive decline, and insurance companies often only provide reimbursement for diagnosable conditions (Sorrell, 2013). Additionally, supportive counseling services can help individuals and their families enhance coping mechanisms and plan for the future.

Researchers hope to identify biomarkers that can follow the etiological spectrum from normal functioning to mild neurocognitive disorder to major neurocognitive disorder (Geda & Nedelska, 2012). The establishment of mild neurocognitive disorder could spur research initiatives to better assist with identification and early intervention for individuals before they experience significant decline in functioning (Mitchell, 2013).

Major and Mild Neurocognitive Disorders

Differential Diagnosis

Differential diagnoses for major and mild neurocognitive disorders are normal cognition, delirium, MDD, specific learning disorder, and other neurodevelopmental disorders (APA, 2013). Thorough assessment of an individual's previous cognitive functioning will help with effective differential diagnoses because establishment of baseline performance is necessary in assessing major and mild neurocognitive disorders.

Coding, Recording, and Specifiers

For major and mild neurocognitive disorders, specification of an etiological subtype is required. All criteria must be met for major and mild neurocognitive disorders and not be better explained by cerebrovascular disease; another neurodegenerative disease; the effects of a substance; or another mental, neurological, or systemic disorder. Because of the complexity of recording procedures for neurocognitive disorders, we list the *DSM-5* coding of the etiological subtypes in Table 12.1.

Table 12.1

Major and Mild Neurocognitive Disorder Etiological Subtypes

Etiology	Specifier(s) and Descriptor(s)
Alzheimer's disease	
Major	• Causative genetic mutation/factors
	• Decline in memory/learning
	• Decline in cognition
	• Not mixed with other etiologies
Mild	• Exhibits two to four characteristics from major category
Frontotemporal disorder	• Prominent decline in social cognition and/or executive abilities (behavioral variant)
	• Prominent decline in language ability (language variant)
	• Relative sparing of learning and memory and perceptual-motor functioning *Probable if:* Existing evidence of causative genetic mutation or neuroimagery shows frontal/temporal lobe disproportionality
Lewy body disease	• *Core features:* Fluctuating cognition with pronounced variations in attention/alertness, recurrent detailed visual hallucinations, spontaneous features of parkinsonism with onset subsequent to cognitive decline
	• *Suggestive features:* Meets REM (rapid eye movement) sleep behavior disorder requirements, severe neuroleptic sensitivity *Probable if:* two features, with at least one core feature *Possible if:* one core feature or multiple suggestive features
Vascular disease	• Characterized by prominent decline in complex attention and frontal-executive function *Probable if:* onset of cognitive deficits temporally matches one or more cerebrovascular events and/or cerebrovascular disease is evident from medical history or neuroimaging
Traumatic brain injury	• Coupled with loss of consciousness, posttraumatic amnesia, and/or disorientation and confusion, yet neurological anomalies persist after acute postinjury period
Substance/ medication- induced	• Timing of neurocognitive impairments is consistent with long periods of substance use and abstinence, but not limited to exclusive short-term duration of intoxication and withdrawal
HIV infection	• Documented HIV infection
	• Neurological conditions not consistent with non-HIV medical condition
Prion disease	• Insidious onset coupled with rapid progression
	• Motor features of Prion disease documented or biomarkers detected in tests
Parkinson's disease	• Parkinson's disease diagnosis established in client
	• Insidious onset and gradual progression of impairment *Probable if:* no evidence of mixed etiology and Parkinson's disease clearly precedes symptom onset *Possible if:* one of either "probable" conditions met
Huntington's disease	• Clinically established Huntington's disease or risk based on family history/genetic testing
	• Insidious onset with gradual progression
	• Not attributable to another medical condition
Other medical condition	• Evidence that the neurocognitive disorder is the pathophysiological consequence of another medical condition
	• Not attributable to another medical conditions or better explained by another mental disorder
Multiple processes	• Evidence that the neurocognitive disorder is the pathophysiological consequence of more than one etiological process (excluding substances) while not attributable to another medical condition or better explained by another mental disorder

 **Example**

Robbie is an 81-year-old retired, married man who has enjoyed robust physical and mental health throughout his life. Shortly after his 80th birthday, Robbie's wife began to notice changes in his memory and behaviors. At first, it was little things, such as where he had left his glasses. Then he started to forget names of old friends. One day, while his wife was out, he almost burned the kitchen down heating up leftovers.

As the year progressed, Robbie would get angry if his wife mentioned talking to his physician about his forgetfulness and irritability. The final straw came when he pushed her during a fight, which he had never done in their 55 years of marriage. She took the initiative to contact his physician, who requested he come in for an appointment and referred him for neurological testing. In deference to his wife's urgings, Robbie agreed to attend a counseling session with her even though he insisted nothing was wrong and maintained that she was overreacting.

♦ ♦ ♦

Diagnostic Questions

1. Do Robbie's presenting symptoms meet the criteria for a major or mild neurocognitive disorder?
2. Based on an affirmative answer to Question 1, would you select major or mild neurocognitive disorder? What are the reasons for your selection?
3. What would be the reason(s) a counselor may not diagnose Robbie with a neurocognitive disorder?
4. Would Robbie more accurately be diagnosed with delirium? If so, why? If not, why not?
5. What rule-outs would you consider for Robbie's case?
6. What other information may be needed to make an accurate clinical diagnosis?

Chapter 13

Schizophrenia Spectrum and Other Psychotic Disorders

They don't sound like voices at first. One day, maybe I hear someone call my name. Another day, I can hear whispers but I don't know what they are saying. Sometimes it's just sounds. I want it to stop but it won't. It won't let me sleep. The beer helps me sleep. —Ray

Schizophrenia spectrum and other psychotic disorders are "defined by abnormalities in one or more of the following five domains: delusions, hallucinations, disorganized thinking (speech), grossly disorganized or abnormal motor behavior (including catatonia), and negative symptoms" (APA, 2013, p. 87). This chapter includes overviews of delusional disorder, brief psychotic disorder, schizophreniform disorder, schizophrenia, schizoaffective disorder, substance/medication-induced psychotic disorder, psychotic disorder due to another medical condition, and catatonia. The *DSM-5* also includes cross-referencing of schizotypal personality disorder (see Chapter 16 of this *Learning Companion* for more information regarding personality disorders).

To grasp major changes and essential features in this chapter, counselors must understand key elements of characteristic domains. Psychotic disorders involve a constellation of positive, negative, and related cognitive symptoms (NIMH, 2009). Whereas positive symptoms involve introduction of thoughts or behaviors one would not expect, negative symptoms involve absence of expected experiences. Core positive symptoms include delusions, hallucinations, and thought or movement disorders in which a person loses touch with reality (Tandon, 2013b). Delusions are fixed beliefs that are not grounded in reality and for which an individual cannot be convinced otherwise. Hallucinations are sensory experiences in which a person sees (visual hallucinations), hears (auditory hallucinations), smells (olfactory hallucinations), tastes (gustatory hallucinations), or feels (tactile or somatic hallucinations) something for which there is no physical stimulus. Auditory hallucinations are most common, tactile hallucinations are often linked to substance withdrawal or intoxication, and olfactory or gustatory hallucinations may indicate a medical problem. Disorganized thinking, also known as thought disorder, involves disruptions in the flow of thoughts in such a way that makes communication difficult (APA, 2013; NIMH, 2009). Disorganized or abnormal motor behavior, also known as movement disorder, involves agitation, repeated motions, or inability to move or respond to stimuli (i.e., catatonia). Negative symptoms include a lack of pleasure, motivation, engagement in activities of daily living, or emotional experiencing (NIMH, 2009). Finally, cognitive symptoms involve difficulty with executive functioning, attention, or memory. Refer to the *DSM-5* for a more thorough discussion of key symptoms and clinical terminology associated with them.

Psychotic symptoms and psychotic experiences occur across a wide range of medical and mental health concerns; however, psychotic disorders are relatively uncommon. According to the APA (2013), prevalence rates for disorders reviewed in this chapter range from 0.2% to 0.7%. However, we believe this prevalence to be low, because these numbers do not take into account cross-cultural psychotic problems that are not reflected in the *DSM-5* but are commonly found worldwide (Eriksen & Kress, 2005; NIMH, 2009). As we discuss throughout the chapter, individuals who meet criteria for psychotic disorders are diverse and have different experiences. For more than 50% of individuals, a psychotic disorder diagnosis presents a lifelong struggle requiring consistent care and support to maintain even a minimal level of functioning (Gaebel, 2011). A sizable minority, especially those with later age of onset and higher levels of functioning at onset, may remain quite functional in their ability to manage symptoms over time (Rubin & Trawver, 2011).

Counselors in clinical and school settings may encounter clients and family members of clients who are experiencing psychotic disorders. Counselors must be prepared to recognize signs of new onset of psychotic disorders, collaborate with interdisciplinary treatment team members, and support loved ones in providing environments needed to enhance dignity, wellness, and functioning.

Major Changes From *DSM-IV-TR* to *DSM-5*

Many changes to this chapter in the *DSM-5* are conceptual in nature and provide enhanced attention to dimensional assessment. For example, the name of the chapter changed slightly to reference the "schizophrenia spectrum" rather than just "schizophrenia." Like other sections of the *DSM-5*, the chapter was reordered to reflect what is assumed to be a developmental progression of psychotic experiencing. Tandon (2013a, 2013b) noted limitations of the *DSM-IV-TR* as including confusion regarding differences between schizoaffective disorder and schizophrenia, variability in treatment of catatonia, undue special treatment of Schneiderian first-rank symptoms (i.e., bizarre delusions or special hallucinations), and lack of reliability and validity within the schizophrenia subtypes. Most changes to *DSM-5* criteria were designed to facilitate a simpler and more straightforward diagnostic process.

Although not required, clinicians who diagnose psychotic disorders are encouraged to use one of several dimensional assessments printed in the *DSM-5* to determine current severity of disorder. The Clinician-Rated Dimensions of Psychosis Symptom Severity (CRDPSS; see pp. 742–744 of the *DSM-5*) includes attention to eight symptoms associated with psychotic disorders: hallucinations, delusions, disorganized speech, abnormal psychomotor behavior, negative symptoms, impaired cognition, depression, and mania. Clinicians rate the most recent 7-day period using a 5-point severity scale ranging from 0 (*not present*) to 4 (*present and severe*). Overall, the scale shows acceptable psychometric properties and appears to be feasible for use in clinical settings (Ritsner, Mar, Arbitman, & Grinshpoon, 2013). Tandon (2013b) noted that use of the CRDPSS may benefit practice by allowing clinicians to focus on specific domains of concern and track changes in each area. In addition to encouraging use of the CRDPSS throughout this section, we present most disorders with new course specifiers to indicate number of episodes (first or multiple) and current remission status (acute, partial remission, or full remission).

Schizophrenia has undergone many changes in conceptualization over the last century (see Keller, Fischer, & Carpenter, 2010). In the *DSM-IV-TR*, Criterion A for schizophrenia served as the foundation for diagnosis of most psychotic disorders. Major changes to Criterion A included elimination of special treatment of bizarre delusions and hallucinations in which an individual heard two or more voices conversing or heard a running commentary regarding his or her behavior. Tandon (2013b) noted limited impact of this change given that less than 2% of clients diagnosed with schizophrenia met criteria through this provision alone. Similarly, the requirement for two positive symptoms to meet Criterion A should increase reliability of diagnoses without affecting clinical practice.

A major change to schizophrenia involves removal of *DSM-IV-TR* subtypes (Gaebel, Zielasek, & Cleveland, 2012; Tandon, 2013a) based on their "limited diagnostic stability, low reliability, poor validity, and little clinical utility" (Tandon, 2013a, p. 16). Rather than conceptualize differences in presentations as representing catatonic, disorganized, paranoid, residual, or undifferentiated schizophrenia, clinicians will conduct a dimensional assessment using the CRDPSS.

One small yet significant change to schizoaffective disorder includes the specification that depressive and/or manic episodes be present "the majority of the total duration of the active and residual portions of the illness" (APA, 2013, p. 105). This change was implemented in hopes of addressing consistent issues with diagnostic stability for this disorder. Although this may decrease prevalence of schizoaffective disorder, Tandon (2013b) proposed that the change will help clinicians more accurately distinguish among schizophrenia with and without mood symptoms, schizoaffective disorder, and mood disorder with psychotic features.

Counselors will also find various minor changes to disorders throughout the Schizophrenia Spectrum and Other Psychotic Disorders chapter. Schizotypal (personality) disorder is now cross-referenced at the beginning of the chapter to be consistent with *ICD-10* conceptualization as part of the schizophrenia spectrum (see Chapter 16 in this *Learning Companion*). In the past, special treatment of bizarre delusions meant that an individual who experienced bizarre delusions automatically met Criterion A for schizophrenia. Changes to Criterion A now mean that individuals who experience bizarre delusions can be diagnosed with delusional disorder through use of a specifier. The *DSM-5* also clarifies that individuals who have delusional-level concerns as part of OCD or BDD should be diagnosed with the more specific disorder; presence of psychotic symptoms will be noted through a specifier. Finally, changes to catatonia include requirement of a consistent number of symptoms (minimum of three out of 12) across diagnostic contexts. The *DSM-5* also includes catatonia as a stand-alone disorder or as a specifier for disorders both within and outside of this chapter.

Section III of the *DSM-5* includes a proposal of attenuated psychosis syndrome as a condition for further study. Designed to identify those at high risk or vulnerability for developing psychotic disorders among adolescents and young adults, this diagnosis generated controversy during the revision process. On one hand, attention to early detection and treatment of schizophrenia spectrum disorders is essential, and those who meet these criteria are 500 times more likely than the general population to develop a psychotic disorder in the next year. On the other hand, about 70% of those who meet criteria for attenuated psychosis syndrome do not go on to develop a psychotic disorder (Tandon, 2013b). Certainly, there is a need to balance benefits of early intervention with risks of stigma, self-fulfilling prophecy, and unnecessary medication interventions.

Differential Diagnosis

The presence of core positive symptoms of psychosis does not automatically indicate the presence of a psychotic disorder. Rather, psychotic symptoms may be a regular part of substance intoxication or withdrawal, medical conditions, and other mental health disorders. Etiology, precipitating factors, and unique constellation of other symptoms will determine whether a client who presents with psychotic symptoms meets criteria for a disorder in this chapter.

Because medical conditions and substance use can lead to onset or exacerbation of psychotic symptoms, we suggest counselors refer all clients who report new onset of psychotic symptoms for a thorough medical evaluation. This evaluation is critical for informing accurate diagnosis and, in turn, appropriate treatment. A client who experiences brief, new onset of psychotic symptoms in response to a medication will have very different needs compared with a client who hallucinates while withdrawing from alcohol. And both clients will have different needs from someone who experiences a long, slow deterioration in functioning before developing paranoid delusions. Later in the chapter, we will mention specific medical conditions and substances that may trigger psychotic symptoms.

Severe depressive disorders, bipolar disorders, and PTSD frequently involve elements of psychotic process such as delusions and hallucinations. The CRDPSS includes attention to depressive and manic symptoms as a reminder regarding the importance of assessing for preexisting or co-occurring mood concerns that require clinical attention and inform diagnosis. Depression and the negative symptoms of these disorders have much in common, especially as hallmarks of both include a lack of interest or pleasure in everyday living and may result in poor self-care. Negative symptoms and cognitive deficits in schizophrenia spectrum disorders may mirror social impairment associated with ASD and decline associated with neurocognitive disorders. Dissociation common with acute stress disorder and PTSD may also appear as part of thought or speech disorders within the schizophrenia spectrum. Similarly, beliefs associated with some obsessive-compulsive and related disorders and somatic symptom disorders often take on delusional qualities, and individuals who are experiencing psychotic symptoms may find themselves quite anxious and agitated as a result of their hallucinations and delusions. Differential diagnostic concerns include the order in which symptoms developed and core experiences of each.

Individuals with schizophrenia spectrum disorders often experience an array of coexisting health and mental health concerns. Rubin and Trawver (2011) characterized individuals with schizophrenia as having "close to universal" (p. 13) exposure to trauma. Nearly three quarters of these individuals experience depression, half experience anxiety, and half meet criteria for a substance use disorder (Helseth, Lykke-Enger, Johnsen, & Waal, 2009; Potuzak, Ravichandran, Lewandowski, Ongür, & Cohen, 2012; Rubin & Trawver, 2011). Individuals with schizophrenia are 3 times more likely to be addicted to nicotine (NIMH, 2009) than the general population, thus potentially placing them at risk for a plethora of related health concerns. When combined with functional consequences of schizophrenia, decreased engagement in health-related activities (APA 2013; Rubin & Trawver, 2011), and a suicide rate as high as 10% (NIMH, 2009), people with schizophrenia have much lower life expectancies and quality of life than the general population. Counselors who work with this population must remain alert to the likelihood of these concerns.

Etiology and Treatment

Researchers are still working to determine specific causes of psychotic disorders. As mentioned previously, effects of substance use and medical conditions may cause brain changes that lead to psychotic symptoms. Research indicates strong genetic and physiological components of schizophrenia (NIMH, 2009). Individuals with first-degree relatives who have schizophrenia are at 10 times greater risk for developing the disorder, and neuroscience research has revealed that people with schizophrenia have different brain structure, function, and neurotransmitter activity compared with those without (APA, 2013; Gaebel, 2011; NIMH, 2009).

Counselors will likely encounter clients with psychotic disorders in one of two primary locations: (a) crisis stabilization hospitals in which individuals present with new onset of psychotic symptoms or crisis in relation to symptoms and (b) community mental health centers in which clients engage in long-term treatment to manage symptoms and promote functioning (Barrio Minton & Prosek, in press). In both cases, counselors will serve on multidisciplinary teams consisting of psychiatrists, nurses, social workers, case managers, and/or rehabilitation specialists. Counselors' roles vary by setting and are likely to include elements of case management, psychosocial services, and family and caregiver support.

Three pillars of treatment of the schizophrenia spectrum include medications for symptom relief and relapse management, psychosocial interventions to support coping and prevent relapse, and rehabilitation to ensure the highest possible degree of social and occupational functioning (Rössler, 2011). APA's (2004) *Practice Guideline for the Treatment of Patients With Schizophrenia* provides a synthesis of best-practice treatment guidelines tailored to each unique phase of the illness. The principles are often applied to all disorders in the schizophrenia spectrum. For example, during the acute phase, providers will focus on minimizing harm and reducing the most striking of symptoms, often through medication management (Pillar 1) and basic supportive care. In the months following the acute phase, medication will continue, and focus will include introduction of psychosocial treatments designed to reduce stress and educate clients and caregivers regarding elements of the illness (Pillar 2). Once clients are stabilized, clinicians may continue medication and psychoeducation; however, they will turn attention to preventing relapse through psychosocial treatments that include education, skills training, CBT, family intervention, supported employment, and assertive community treatment (Pillar 3; Kopelowicz, Liberman, & Zarate, 2007).

Psychopharmacotherapy for clients with psychotic disorders often focuses on treatment of positive symptoms such as hallucinations, delusions, and disorganized speech and behavior. This trial-and-error process often involves use of atypical antipsychotics such as clozapine (i.e., Clozaril), risperidone (i.e., Risperdal), olanzapine (i.e., Zyprexa), quetiapine (i.e., Seroquel), ziprasidone (i.e., Geodon), aripiprazole (i.e., Abilify), and paliperiodone (i.e., Invega; NIMH, 2012; "Schizophrenia Medications," 2013). Psychiatrists may also integrate other classes of medications, such as antidepressants, antianxiety drugs, lithium, and antiepileptic drugs, for treatment ("Schizophrenia Medications," 2013). Clients may find treatment regiments confusing and overwhelming, especially given that cognitive deficits are quite common within psychotic disorders. In addition, side effects may be quite uncomfortable and lead to problems with medication compliance; strong therapeutic relationships are associated with more positive attitudes and compliance with medication (McCabe et al., 2012). Counselors may find themselves helping educate clients and families regarding medication management and facilitating communication between clients and psychiatrists.

There are several evidence-based psychosocial interventions for schizophrenia and related disorders. SAMHSA (2010) provides a free family psychoeducation evidence-based practices kit that reviews research regarding family education for people with psychiatric disabilities such as schizophrenia and provides guidelines for program development. Similarly, the University of California, Los Angeles Clinical Research Center for Schizophrenia and Psychiatric Rehabilitation used outcome research to develop a number of skills training modules focused on the needs of clients with schizophrenia (see, e.g., Psychiatric Rehabilitation Consultants, 2011). Counselors who specialize in work with this population will likely use several of these resources when developing or providing materials.

Once clients have stabilized, counselors may use CBT for psychosis (CBTp; Beck, Rector, Stolar, & Grant, 2009; Kingdon & Turkington, 2002) to help clients develop insight or understanding regarding the disorder, engage in reality testing of experiences, and participate actively in recovery. Multiple research studies regarding CBTp indicate mild to moderate effectiveness of the approach (Jolley & Garety, 2011).

Finally, rehabilitation resources are essential in treatment and long-term management of schizophrenia spectrum disorders (Rössler, 2011). Evidence-based rehabilitation resources include assertive community treatment (ACT) and focused programs such as supported employment and supportive housing (APA, 2004; Rössler, 2011). ACT is an intensive, multidisciplinary approach focused on providing services that allow individuals with severe and persistent mental illness to function outside of institutional settings (National Alliance on Mental Illness, 2013). Services are tailored to the individual and his or her family, and SAMHSA (2008) provides an ACT evidence-based practice kit in which counselors can learn more about best practices for ACT.

Implications for Counselors

It is highly unlikely that counselors will be providing lead diagnostic services when working with clients who have psychotic disorders. However, counselors may encounter clients with psychotic disorders in front-line service settings, such as mental health crisis and emergency services. They may also provide longer term care as part of their work with community mental health settings. Both situations provide unique challenges and opportunities.

When clients present with active psychotic symptoms, counselors should attend closely to facilitating therapeutic communication while linking clients to levels of care and professionals necessary to respond to acute-phase symptoms. Counselors may struggle to facilitate therapeutic communication when the very nature of psychotic symptoms means clients may be out of touch with reality, struggle to communicate in meaningful ways, be distrustful of the counselor and others in his or her life, and be uninterested in social relationships. Even when symptoms are not grounded in reality, it is essential that counselors remember that hallucinations and delusions are very real to clients; clients may well be confused, agitated, or feel terrorized by these symptoms (Walsh, 2011). For these reasons, Walsh (2011) recommended mental health professionals attend to unique needs of clients experiencing psychosis by engaging in five therapeutic communication strategies: (a) remembering the relationship may provide a link between the client with an essential sense of safety in his or her world, (b) exploring and anchoring thoughts and feelings rather than arguing about reality, (c) processing distress, (d) slowly and gently providing alternative explanations of experiences, and (e) introducing possibilities within the social world.

Counselors may use relationship skills to help clients understand the need for future treatment and link to necessary services. During the acute phase, these services are likely to involve hospitalization in which clients can begin to stabilize on medication and make connections needed to support their long-term recovery and management (APA, 2004). The hospitalization process can be particularly frightening to clients and families who have not yet navigated the process or who have had negative inpatient experiences in the past. Counselors can facilitate this transition through patient reflection and discussion with clients and family members regarding what to expect in the days to come.

When providing services in longer term settings, counselors will best serve their clients if they develop a strong understanding regarding schizophrenia spectrum disorders, evidence-based treatments for the disorders, and interdisciplinary perspectives. At the same time, it is important for counselors to consider how our unique training and perspective equips us to contribute to the treatment team. For example, counselors' focus on strengths and resilience, understanding of family systems and human development, and general facilitation skills may be unique among treatment team members. It is precisely this orientation, along with the creativity that often comes with it, that makes counselors well suited for advocating for client needs and maximizing opportunities for success.

In the remainder of the chapter, we outline major disorders within the Schizophrenia Spectrum and Other Psychotic Disorders chapter of the *DSM-5*. Coverage includes a brief summary of essential features of each disorder as well as notation regarding special considerations such as disorder characteristics, treatment considerations, and coding procedures. In each case, readers should refer to the *DSM-5* for a full explication of diagnostic criteria.

297.1 Delusional Disorder (F22)

Essential Features

Delusional disorder is characterized by a period of 1 month or more during which an individual experiences at least one delusion. Other criteria rule out diagnoses such as schizophrenia; co-occurring mood episodes; or onset caused by substances, medications, or medical conditions. Individuals with delusional disorders do not experience functional impairment or exhibit bizarre behaviors when not experiencing delusions. The nature of delusions can range from experiences that may occur in daily life (e.g., belief that one has a special relationship with another) to those that are completely implausible (e.g., belief that one's thoughts are being stolen by an outside entity). The *DSM-5* includes a number of subtypes to categorize the specific content of the delusion (APA, 2013).

Special Considerations

Delusional disorder is estimated to have a lifetime prevalence of just 0.2% (APA, 2013); there is relatively little research regarding characteristics of individuals with this disorder. Counselors may struggle to detect delusional disorder because functional consequences may be quite low, especially when one is not focused on the delusion. Delusions may also appear quite plausible to those in the outside world, especially when the person with the delusion is the primary source of information regarding related events. For example, counselors may not question reports of events that may be consistent with this disorder (e.g., affairs as in ***jealous type***, workplace harassment or discrimination as in ***persecutory type***).

When assessing for delusional disorder, counselors should take care to assess whether the delusional content is better accounted for by another mental disorder. For example, an individual who has delusional-level beliefs associated with OCD or BDD should receive the more specific diagnosis instead of delusional disorder (APA, 2013). Similarly, delusions are often present in other psychotic, depressive, and bipolar disorders. Counselors must assess fully to make sure one of these more common diagnoses does not better account for the delusion. In addition, presence of negative symptoms or other longer term impairments may mean schizophrenia is a more appropriate diagnosis (APA, 2013).

There is just one code for delusional disorder: 297.1 (F22); however, the *DSM-5* includes a number of specifiers. Subtypes focused on nature of the delusion include *erotomanic type*, *grandiose type*, *jealous type*, *persecutory type*, *somatic type*, *mixed type*, and *unspecified type*. Individuals who experience delusions that could not possibly happen should receive a specifier of *with bizarre content*. Counselors may choose from a variety of course specifiers indicating whether an individual is experiencing *first episode* or *multiple episodes* and whether that episode is currently in *acute episode*, *partial remission*, *full remission*, or *continuous*. Clinicians rate severity using the CRDPSS (APA, 2013).

298.8 Brief Psychotic Disorder (F23)

Essential Features

Brief psychotic disorder is characterized by a 1-day to 1-month time period in which one or more positive psychotic symptoms (e.g., delusions, hallucinations, disorganized speech, and/or disorganized behavior) is present. The APA (2013, p. 94) stressed that symptoms must have sudden onset (i.e., "change from a nonpsychotic state to a clearly psychotic state within 2 weeks, usually without a prodrome") and must involve a full remission and return to functioning at the end of the disturbance. When symptoms continue beyond 30 days, counselors should consider schizophreniform disorder instead.

Special Considerations

Little is known about the lifetime prevalence of brief psychotic disorder; however, the disorder accounts for about 9% of cases of first-onset psychosis, is more common in women, and is more common in developing countries (APA, 2013). Sudden onset of psychotic symptoms is often associated with substance/medication intoxication, substance/medication withdrawal, and medical conditions. For these reasons, counselors should refer clients who appear to meet criteria for this disorder for medical evaluation. Counselors who work with clients who have personality disorders or who may have something to gain from appearing to have mental illness should be alert to the possibility that sudden-onset psychotic symptoms could be intentionally produced or represent a transient response to stressors (APA, 2013).

Brief psychotic disorder has just one diagnostic code: 298.8 (F23). Specifiers include *with marked stressor(s)*, *without marked stressor(s)*, and *with postpartum onset*. Clinicians should note and dual-code if *with catatonia*. Severity is assessed through the use of the CRDPSS.

295.40 Schizophreniform Disorder (F20.81)

Essential Features

Schizophreniform disorder is considered a stepping-stone between brief psychotic disorder and schizophrenia. Essential features of this disorder include 1 to 6 months of disturbance in which an individual experiences two or more psychotic symptoms, including hallucinations, delusions, disorganized speech, disorganized or catatonic behavior, or negative symptoms. Delusions, hallucinations, and/or disorganized speech must be present for an individual to qualify for the diagnosis. When symptoms are present for 6 months or more, counselors must consider schizophrenia as an alternative diagnosis (APA, 2013).

Special Considerations

As with other schizophrenia spectrum disorders, relatively little is known about the prevalence and characteristics of schizophreniform disorder. The APA (2013) noted that characteristics of those affected are similar to those with schizophrenia; however, the incidence rate is likely just 0.2%. Approximately two thirds of those with schizophreniform disorder go on to meet the full criteria for schizophrenia. The other one third of the population diagnosed with schizophreniform disorder experience a decrease or resolution of symptoms.

Treatment considerations for schizophreniform disorder are quite similar to those for schizophrenia, although there is an emerging body of literature regarding treatment for first-episode psychosis. Investigation regarding efficacy of early intervention may provide insights regarding life-changing treatment considerations. For example, results of a random control trial for integrated treatment with individuals with first-onset psychosis indicated that 95% of participants had remission of symptoms compared with just 59% of those in a medication-only treatment group (Valencia, Juarez, & Ortega, 2012). Counselors can use such findings to inspire hope that diagnosis on the schizophrenia spectrum does not automatically imply negative outcomes. Certainly, schizophreniform disorder even includes a specifier to denote the presence of *good prognostic features*, such as rapid onset of symptoms, confusion at the height of symptoms, good functioning at onset, and absence of negative symptoms (APA, 2013). In contrast, those who have slow deterioration in functioning and negative symptoms are more likely to go on to develop schizophrenia.

The *DSM-5* includes just one code for schizophreniform disorder: 295.40 (F20.81). Counselors must specify whether the syndrome is *with good prognostic features* or *without good prognostic features*. A *with catatonia* specifier is available for dual coding, and severity is rated on the CRDPSS. When a diagnosis is made in the initial 6 months and outcome is not known, counselors should note the diagnosis as *provisional* (APA, 2013).

295.90 Schizophrenia (F20.9)

Essential Features

Schizophrenia stands at the heart of this chapter and is characterized by at least 1 month of two or more of the following symptoms: delusions, hallucinations, disorganized speech, grossly disorganized or catatonic behavior, or negative symptoms. As with schizophreniform disorder, delusions, hallucinations, and/or disorganized speech must be present. In addition, the individual must experience deterioration in previous functioning such that the total illness duration is at least 6 months. Exclusionary criteria include consideration of concurrent depressive or manic episodes, physiological effects of a substance, coexisting medical considerations, and preexisting neurodevelopmental disorders.

Special Considerations

Schizophrenia affects about 1% of men and women around the world (NIMH, 2009). In most cases, individuals begin showing signs of schizophrenia by late adolescence or early adulthood. Men display signs of the disorder earlier than women. Onset of symptoms in childhood and early adolescence is associated with longer term and more negative impacts (Gearing & Mian, 2009; Pagsberg, 2013). In contrast, those who experience later onset and higher premorbid development have more positive prognoses (Rubin & Trawver, 2011). Both early and late onset are rare. Although prevalence of schizophrenia appears to be stable across cultures, counselors should be aware that the specific ways in which symptoms manifest may be culturally linked, perhaps contributing to over- or underdiagnosis within certain contexts (APA, 2013; Eriksen & Kress, 2005).

Most individuals who have schizophrenia will experience a degree of lifelong disability related to the condition (Gaebel, 2011). This may be due to neurocognitive deficits that remain present even when individuals are not actively experiencing positive symptoms (Horan, Harvy, Kern, & Green, 2011). Horan et al. (2011) advised clinicians to be alert to four key areas in need of attention: real-world functioning in work, independent living, and social domains; well-being and satisfaction with life; ability to engage successfully in treatment; and functional capacity in social situations. When functioning in these areas is enhanced, clients with schizophrenia will have higher quality of life and lower need for daily supports (Helldin, Kane, Karilampi, Norlander, & Archer, 2007). In all cases, family support, education, and engagement are critical for appropriate treatment and management of schizophrenia (Gearing, 2008; Rössler, 2011).

The *DSM-5* includes just one code for schizophrenia: 295.90 (F20.9). Counselors may use a variety of course specifiers: *first episode, currently in acute episode*; *first episode, currently in partial remission*; *first episode, currently in full remission*; *multiple episodes, currently in acute episode*; *multiple episodes, currently in partial remission*; *multiple episodes, currently in full remission*; *continuous*; and *unspecified*. A *with catatonia* specifier is available for dual coding, and severity may be rated on the CRDPSS (APA, 2013).

295.70 Schizoaffective Disorder (F25._)

Essential Features

Schizoaffective disorder is characterized by concurrent, overlapping psychosis (i.e., Criterion A of schizophrenia) and mood episodes (i.e., major depressive or manic). More precise *DSM-5* criteria require presence of positive symptoms for 2 or more weeks in absence of mood episode as well as presence of mood episode for the majority of the illness. When clients experience only depressive episodes concurrent with the psychosis, the disorder is said to be *depressive type*. Clients who experience manic episodes alone or in combination with depressive episodes are characterized as *bipolar type* (APA, 2013).

Special Considerations

The APA (2013) estimated a lifetime prevalence of just 0.3% for schizoaffective disorder, and characteristics of individuals with the disorder are assumed to be similar to those associated with schizophrenia. Schizoaffective disorder is a historically unstable and unreliable diagnosis, and scholars have argued whether schizoaffective disorder is one distinct disorder or better conceptualized by overlapping schizophrenia and mood disorders (Casecade, Kalali, & Buckley, 2009; Heckers, 2012; Kantrowitz & Citrome, 2011; Lake & Hurwitz, 2008). Gaebel et al. (2012) noted that addition of the lifetime criterion regarding presence of mood symptoms at least half the time may increase clarity and decrease diagnoses of this unique disorder (Gaebel et al., 2012; Tandon, 2013b).

Treatment strategies for schizoaffective disorder tend to be similar to those for schizophrenia and mood disorders. In addition to using the three pillars of treatment for schizophrenia spectrum discussed earlier, treatment may include additional medication to target depressive or manic episodes (Casecade et al., 2009). Counselors and treatment teams may find themselves tailoring treatment strategies to match the most pressing or apparent of symptoms.

The *DSM-5* includes two codes for schizoaffective disorder: 295.70 (F25.0) for *bipolar type* and 295.70 (F25.1) for *depressive type*. Course and catatonia specifiers are identical to those used for schizophrenia. Severity may be rated on the CRDPSS (APA, 2013).

Substance/Medication-Induced Psychotic Disorder

Essential Features

Substance/medication-induced psychotic disorder is diagnosed when an individual has delusions and/or hallucinations; there is evidence that the symptoms were caused by intoxication, withdrawal, or exposure to a medication or substance; and the symptoms cause distress or impairment. The *DSM-5* indicates that psychotic disorders may be induced by substances such as alcohol; cannabis; phencyclidine; other hallucinogen; inhalant; sedative, hypnotic, or anxiolytic; amphetamine (or other stimulant); cocaine; or other (or unknown) substance (APA, 2013).

Special Considerations

A clinician who is qualified to assess both physiological impacts of a substance and psychological after-effects must render the diagnosis of substance/medication-induced psychotic disorder. Treatment may include medical attention to manage effects of the substance, attention to coexisting substance use disorders, and management of psychotic symptoms. The disorder includes specifiers to note *with onset during intoxication* and *with onset during withdrawal*. Clinicians insert the name of the specific substance into the name of the disorder (e.g., alcohol-induced psychotic disorder). Coding depends on the specific substance causing the condition. *ICD-10-CM* coding is even more specific and includes coding to indicate comorbidity with corresponding mild and moderate/severe substance use disorders. Again, severity should be noted using the CRDPSS (APA, 2013).

Psychotic Disorder Due to Another Medical Condition

Essential Features

Psychotic disorder due to another medical condition is diagnosed when an individual has delusions and/or hallucinations; there is evidence that the symptoms were caused by a medical condition; and the symptoms cause distress or impairment. The *DSM-5* includes lists of neurological conditions, endocrine conditions, metabolic conditions, fluid or electrolyte imbalances, hepatic or renal diseases, and autoimmune disorders that may cause psychotic symptoms.

Special Considerations

As with substance/medication-induced disorders, diagnosis of psychotic disorder due to another medical condition must be made by an individual qualified to confirm the presence of the medical condition and the likelihood that the condition caused the psychotic symptoms. Treatment will include attention to the underlying medical condition causing the disorder as well as management of resulting psychotic symptoms. The name of the medical condition is inserted in the name of the disorder (e.g., psychotic disorder due to hyperthyroidism). Disorders characterized by *with delusions* are coded as 293.81 (F06.2), and those characterized by *with hallucinations* are coded as 293.82 (F06.0; APA, 2013).

293.89 Catatonia (F06.1)

Essential Features

Like panic attack, catatonia is not a distinct diagnosis; however, it is a condition associated with a variety of neurodevelopmental, psychotic, bipolar, and mood disorders (APA, 2013) and medical conditions. In essence, catatonia involves psychomotor disturbances that manifest as immobility, decreased engagement, or excessive motor behaviors. The *DSM-IV-TR* included various different criteria sets for catatonia. The *DSM-5* was revised to include one unified criteria set (Tandon, 2013a). To meet criteria for this condition, one must have three or more of the following symptoms: stupor, catalepsy, waxy flexibility, mutism, negativism, posturing, mannerism, stereotypy, agitation, grimacing, echolalia, or echopraxia. Refer to the *DSM-5* for definitions of each symptom.

Special Considerations

Catatonia is designed primarily as a specifier alongside other disorders. It is always coded as 293.89 (F06.1) but will be noted as catatonia associated with another mental disorder, catatonic disorder due to another medical condition, or unspecified catatonia (APA, 2013).

 Example

Cheryl is a 28-year-old mother of two young children who is separated from her husband and lives alone in Section 8 housing. She is referred to the county mental health center for multidisciplinary services as a condition of her release from a behavioral health hospital. The case manager initiating the referral indicated that this was Cheryl's first hospitalization; the stay was precipitated by her presentation to the county hospital emergency room with a bag of pennies and a request that the staff fill her teeth with the pennies to block the FBI from stealing her thoughts. At admission, a drug screen showed evidence of cannabis and alcohol in her system. The case manager indicated that the children were living with their father because of Cheryl's inability to care for them. She was being discharged to home after stabilizing on several atypical antipsychotic medications.

Upon interview, you note Cheryl to be unusually slim with long, greasy hair and tobacco-stained fingers. Although generally cooperative, Cheryl seems to have difficulty engaging in the interview. She makes little eye contact, speaks in monotone, and rarely says more than a few words at a time. At several points during the interview, Cheryl appears to space out, occasionally shaking her head as if to refocus her attention. She responds to your inquiry regarding hallucinations with a shrug and a comment that the "drugs make everything fuzzy." When you ask about the situation that precipitated the hospital stay, Cheryl simply says that "the truth will come to be." She admitted that she occasionally uses alcohol or marijuana when feeling agitated or tense.

Although details are limited, you gather that Cheryl has not had any treatment for prior mental health concerns. During high school, she had several friends and her grades were mostly As and Bs. She graduated from high school, discovered she was pregnant, and married her high school boyfriend. She worked for several years in the retail sector. Her supervisor terminated her employment 2 years ago because she "made others uncomfortable." About that time, her family asked her to get help, presumably for depression. Although Cheryl denied being sad or down, her family members apparently noted her lack of connections with others, lack of motivation, and progressive deterioration of self-care. Cheryl appeared unaffected that her husband left with the children approximately 6 months ago, shrugging and saying, "He knew what he needed to do."

♦ ♦ ♦

Diagnostic Questions

1. Do Cheryl's presenting symptoms appear to meet the criteria for a schizophrenia spectrum disorder? If so, which disorder?
2. Based on your answer to Question 1, which symptom(s) led you to select that diagnosis?
3. What would be the reason(s), if any, a counselor may not diagnose Cheryl with that disorder?
4. Would Cheryl be more accurately diagnosed with a mood disorder? If so, why? If not, why not?
5. What rule-outs would you consider for Cheryl's case?
6. What other information may be needed to make an accurate clinical diagnosis?

Dissociative Disorders

Our child came to us through the foster care system. When they found her, she could not speak, walk, or play. Over the past year, she's learned to do all those things. She does really well most days, but sometimes the smallest things can undo her. We were driving home from a visit with the case manager who helped get her out of that horrid place, and she just checked out. She was staring right at me, but it was like she wasn't even there. Later, she asked me how we got home. She didn't even remember being in the car. —Juan

Dissociation involves a "disconnection or lack of connection between things usually associated with each other" (International Society for the Study of Trauma and Dissociation [ISSTD], 2013b, para. 1) and is a normal part of many life experiences. Everyday dissociation can occur, for example, when an individual is absorbed in an activity, when a child creates an imaginary friend, or when an individual blocks out an unpleasant memory (ISSTD, 2013a). Approximately three quarters of individuals will experience dissociation after a traumatic incident as the brain works to protect itself during times of distress; however, most will not go on to develop dissociative disorders.

Dissociative disorders "are characterized by a disruption of and/or discontinuity in the normal integration of consciousness, memory, identity, emotion, perception, body representation, motor control, and behavior" (APA, 2013, p. 291). Spiegel et al. (2011) described dissociative symptoms as

(a) unbidden and unpleasant intrusions into awareness and behavior, with accompanying losses of continuity in subjective experience: (i.e. "positive" dissociative symptoms); and/or (b) an inability to access information or to control mental functions that normally are readily amenable to access or control: (i.e. "negative" dissociative symptoms). (p. 826)

The ISSTD (2013b) identified five types of dissociation addressed in the *DSM-5*: depersonalization, derealization, amnesia, identify confusion, and identity alteration. Depersonalization is a "sense of being detached from, or 'not in' one's body," whereas derealization is a "sense of the world not being real" (ISSTD, 2013b, para. 4) Amnesia involves a loss of ability to access stored information one would be expected to remember (ISSTD, 2013b). Identity confusion involves an uncharacteristic change in one's sense of self. Identity alteration "is the sense of being markedly different from another part of oneself . . . subtler forms of identity alteration can be observed when a person uses different voice tones, range of language, or facial expressions" (ISSTD, 2013b, para. 7).

There is evidence that dissociative disorders, once considered quite rare or fabricated, are simply missed in clinical settings (Foote, Smolin, Kaplan, Legatt, & Lipschitz, 2006; ISSTD, 2011). Prevalence of this class of disorders is high and estimated at 2% to 10% among the general population (ISSTD, 2013b). Unfortunately, individuals who experience dissociative disorders are among the most vulnerable and high risk of clients. This population experiences near-universal trauma, high rates of comorbid disorders, and suicidal behavior (Brand, Lanius, Vermetten, Loewenstein, & Spiegel, 2012; ISSTD, 2011). This chapter includes a discussion of essential features and special considerations for dissociative identity disorder (DID), dissociative amnesia, and depersonalization/derealization disorder. As with other chapters, the *DSM-5* includes other specified dissociative disorder and unspecified dissociative disorder

Major Changes From *DSM-IV-TR* to *DSM-5*

Dissociative disorders are closely related to trauma, as reflected in APA's decision to place the chapter after the Trauma and Stressor-Related Disorders chapter. Changes to this chapter of the *DSM-5* were modest. DID modifications were designed to address concerns regarding complexity, lack of specificity, expectation for rare yet readily observable shifts between identities, and culturally insensitive exclusion of pathological possession (Spiegel et al., 2011). Thus, Criterion A for DID was revised to allow observations or self-reported dissociation as well as experiences of possession. Criterion B was broadened to include issues with everyday gaps in memory rather than just gaps for traumatic events. Depersonalization disorder was renamed depersonalization/derealization disorder given research suggesting experiences of both are similar (Spiegel et al., 2011), and the rare dissociative fugue was subsumed as a special case of dissociative amnesia.

Differential Diagnosis

Like many other mental health symptoms, dissociative symptoms may be part of other disorders, caused by medical conditions, or triggered by substance use. Neurological conditions leading to symptoms that mimic dissociative disorders may include seizures, traumatic brain injuries, and neurocognitive disorders. In some cases, the presence of what appear to be neurological symptoms may also suggest a diagnosis of conversion disorder. The *DSM-5* listed the following substances as triggering dissociative symptoms: cannabis, hallucinogens, ketamine, ecstasy, and salvia (APA, 2013). Counselors who work with clients experiencing dissociative symptoms should refer them for a complete medical evaluation and psychiatric consultation and consider whether diagnosis is within their scope of ethical practice.

Trauma is almost always at the root of dissociative disorders, so counselors should carefully consider whether a diagnosis of PTSD or acute stress disorder may better account for dissociative experiences. This requires careful assessment to determine whether dissociation occurs only in relation to a traumatic event (e.g., amnesia for trauma, flashbacks, instruction, and avoidance) or in a general manner. Given the strong evidence of a dissociative component of PTSD (Lanius, Brand, Vermetten, Frewen, & Spiegel, 2012), individuals who experience depersonalization and/or derealization in the context of that disorder should be diagnosed accordingly with dissociative symptoms rather than depersonalization/derealization disorder.

ISSTD (2011) recommended special attention to bipolar, affective, psychotic, seizure, and borderline personality disorders when engaging in differential diagnosis. Mood changes may be indicative of identity alteration rather than fluctuations associated with bipolar disorders. Panic attacks have a dissociative quality to them, thus indicating anxiety disorders as potential differential diagnoses. Individuals with dissociative disorders may describe out-of-body experiences, have beliefs regarding possession, or hear different voices that lead one to suspect a psychotic disorder or psychotic features of depression rather than dissociation (Spiegel et al., 2011). Dissociations during times of stress, instability of identity, and history of interpersonal trauma are characteristic of borderline personality disorder as well. Indeed, one study of individuals diagnosed with borderline personality disorder revealed that roughly one quarter met criteria for mild dissociative disorders such as dissociative amnesia and depersonalization disorder, one quarter met the criteria for DID, and one quarter met the criteria for other dissociative disorders (Korzekwa, Dell, Links, Thabane, & Fougere, 2009). Finally, dissociation may be misidentified as behavioral problems (e.g., temper tantrums in ODD, inattention in ADHD) among children (ISSTD, 2013a).

Dissociative disorders are comorbid with a number of concerns, including depressive, anxiety, and substance use disorders (APA, 2013). Counselors should be particularly alert to self-injurious and suicidal behavior, especially given that 70% of those with DID have a history of the latter. Similarly, individuals who experience dissociation also tend to report a number of somatic concerns, thus indicating somatic symptom disorders as differential or comorbid diagnoses (ISSTD, 2011).

Etiology and Treatment

The ISSTD (2013b) characterized dissociation as having both environmental and biological components; there is no evidence of a genetic component. In nearly all cases, dissociative disorders may be linked to experiences of traumatic events, especially early in life. Precipitating experiences leading to dissociation in children and adolescents may include physical, sexual, or emotional abuse; chronic neglect; witnessing violence; loss of loved ones or disruption in caregiving; physical injury, medical conditions, or medical procedures; and accidents or disasters (ISSTD, 2013a). Emerging neurobiological research supports theories that early experiences of trauma and neglect affect brain development in ways that may lead to dissociative disorders (Brand et al., 2012; International Society for the Study of Dissociation [ISSD], 2004). Brain studies regarding individuals with dissociative disorders also provide evidence of divergent brain structure and function (APA, 2013; Brand et al., 2012).

The APA (2013) noted a striking 90% prevalence of childhood abuse and neglect among those with DID. Developmental models of DID posit that

> DID does not arise from a previously mature, unified mind or "core personality" that becomes shattered or fractured. Rather, DID results from a failure of normal developmental integration caused by overwhelming experiences and disturbed caregiver–child interactions (including neglect and the failure to respond) during critical early developmental periods. This, in turn, leads some traumatized children to develop relatively discrete, personified behavioral states that ultimately evolve into the DID alternate identities. (ISSTD, 2011, p. 123)

There is no scientific evidence to support sociocognitive models that proposed clinicians created DID among highly suggestible clients (ISSTD, 2011). Similarly, there is evidence that severity and frequency of trauma are related to dissociative amnesia (APA, 2013). Depersonalization/derealization disorder is linked to experiences of emotional abuse or interpersonal conflicts (Simeon, Guralnik, Schmeidler, Sirof, & Knutelska, 2001), a finding supported by neurobiological research illustrating the relationship between verbal/emotional abuse in childhood and psychobiological brain changes (Spiegel et al., 2011).

Unfortunately, severe dissociative disorders among adults may be among the most difficult, time-intensive, and costly to treat (Brand, 2012; ISSTD, 2011). Childhood and adolescent dissociation appears to be more amenable to treatment than dissociation in adulthood, requiring less time and resulting in more positive outcomes (ISSD, 2004). Research regarding evidence-based treatments for dissociative disorders is rare, and there is a lack of controlled treatment trials (Brand, 2012; Brand et al., 2012). Counselors should be aware that treatments used with acute PTSD (e.g., standard exposure therapy) may be counterproductive and ineffective with this population (Brand et al., 2012). Limited research suggests attention to complex traumas and dissociation may lead to treatment effects ranging from moderate to large across a variety of symptoms such as depression, dissociation, anxiety, somatic symptoms, and substance use. There are mixed findings regarding the degree to which medications are effective for treating dissociative symptoms.

The primary goal of treatment for DID is achievement of integrated functioning (ISSTD, 2011). The ISSTD (2011) advocated for a staged approach to treatment with focus on "1. Establishing safety, stabilization, and symptom reduction; 2. Confronting, working through, and integrating traumatic memories; and 3. Identify integration and rehabilitation" (p. 135). If the client does not present a danger to self, most treatment is conducted on an individual outpatient basis, one to three times weekly, over an extended duration. The ISSTD characterized most treatments as psychodynamic with incorporation of approaches such as CBT, DBT, hypnosis, and eye-movement desensitization and reprocessing. Most individuals with DID receive psychotropic medication focused on specific distressing symptoms. Readers interested in learning more should review the "Guidelines for Treating Dissociative Identity Disorder in Adults" (ISSTD, 2011), "Guidelines for the Evaluation and Treatment of Dissociative Symptoms in Children and Adolescents" (ISSD, 2004), and *ISTSS Expert Consensus Treatment Guidelines for Complex PTSD in Adults* (Cloitre et al., 2012).

Implications for Counselors

Counselors may struggle to detect or diagnose dissociative disorders because clients may not be aware of the dissociation or may minimize the importance of dissociative experiences. Scholars interested in dissociative disorders warn that these are among the most overlooked disorders in clinical practice. Using structured diagnostic assessment tools, Foote et al. (2006) found evidence of dissociative disorders among over one quarter of clients in an inner-city outpatient clinic; only 5% of those meeting criteria for dissociative disorders were diagnosed previously. Counselors may find new assessment and screening tools helpful to detect dissociative experiences in practice (Brand et al., 2012). In addition, the ISSTD (2011) recommended that all clinicians screen routinely for "episodes of amnesia, fugue, depersonalization, derealization, identity confusion, and identity alteration" (p. 124). Counselors who work with youth may wish to consult ISSD (2004) for practical recommendations regarding assessment of dissociative symptoms in children and adolescents.

Opportunities to attend to dissociative experiences are likely to arise during discussion of experiences of trauma or abuse and during screenings conducted in everyday counseling practice. Counselors should be alert to signs of dissociation when initially discussing a client's history of trauma or abuse, when a client provides details related to trauma or abuse, or when a client experiences changes that may serve as triggers to previous experiences. It is important to recognize the protective function of dissociation for many and to refrain from pressing for details if a client appears vulnerable or overwhelmed by the experience.

Experiences related to dissociation may occur during the normal course of other neurological conditions (APA, 2013), and individuals from some cultures may experience dissociation related to highly distressing conflicts or stressors. APA (2013) advised careful consideration for diagnoses based on possession states because such experiences are often a normal part of spiritual practice. Similarly, experiences of depersonalization/derealization may be common in the general population and are often the goal of meditative practices (APA, 2013). Counselors must be careful not to stigmatize these normal experiences.

300.14 Dissociative Identity Disorder (F44.81)

Essential Features

Dissociative identity disorder (DID) was previously known as multiple personality disorder. This disorder is accompanied by usual gaps in everyday recall. Experiences may be recurrent, observed, must cause distress or impairment, must not be culturally accepted, and may not be substance-induced or due to medical conditions. DID specifically involves

> Disruption of identity characterized by two or more distinct personality states, which may be described in some cultures as an experience of possession. The disruption in identity involves marked discontinuity in sense of self and sense of agency, accompanied by related alterations in affect, behavior, consciousness, memory, perception, cognition, and/or sensory-motor functioning. (APA, 2013, p. 292)

Special Considerations

Estimates of DID prevalence vary widely. Although some studies estimate rates as low as 0.01% (ISSTD, 2013b), most studies show general rates of 1% to 3% (ISSTD, 2011). Foote et al. (2006) found that 6% of individuals in a clinical sample met criteria for DID. Men and women appear to experience DID in approximately equal numbers but may vary in their presentation (APA, 2013). It is important to note that DID is likely to be much less dramatic and pronounced than one might believe based on popular cultural representations. There is just one code for DID: 300.14 (F44.81). There are no specifiers associated with this disorder.

300.12 Dissociative Amnesia (F44.0)

Essential Features

Dissociative amnesia is characterized by "an inability to recall important autobiographical information, usually of a traumatic or stressful nature, that is inconsistent with ordinary forgetting" (APA, 2013, p. 298). The amnesia may be localized (focused on a specific period of time), selective (involving loss of memory for some aspects of a period of time), generalized (complete loss of information), systematized (focused on category of information), or continuous (focused on loss of new information; Spiegel et al., 2011). As with other disorders, the amnesia must cause impairment or distress and may not be substance or medically induced. *DSM-5* revisions subsumed dissociative fugue, in which individuals engage in travel or wandering, under this diagnosis.

Special Considerations

APA (2013) estimated a 12-month prevalence of 1.8% among the general population; however, there is evidence of prevalence as high as 7.3% among international samples (Spiegel et al., 2011). Women are more than 2 times more likely to be diagnosed than men (APA, 2013). Now included in the diagnosis of dissociative amnesia, dissociative fugue is believed to be very rare, occurring in 0% to 0.2% of the population (ISSTD, 2013b). When coding only dissociative amnesia, counselors should use 300.12 (F44.0). When coding dissociative amnesia *with dissociative fugue*, counselors should use 300.13 (F44.1).

300.6 Depersonalization/Derealization Disorder (F48.1)

Essential Features

Depersonalization/derealization disorder is characterized by presence of depersonalization and/or derealization with intact reality testing and resulting distress or impairment; the experience cannot be substance induced or medically caused or due to another mental disorder (APA, 2013). In general, depersonalization, the feeling of being outside oneself, involves five elements: "numbing, unreality of self, unreality of other, temporal disintegration, and perceptional alterations" (Spiegel et al., 2011, p. E24). Derealization is characterized by feeling as if the world is unreal.

Special Considerations

Individuals in the general population may experience aspects of depersonalization or derealization on a regular basis, with half of all U.S. adults experiencing at least one lifetime episode (APA, 2013). The ISSTD (2013b) reported that some researchers believe depersonalization disorder follows depression and anxiety as the most common mental disorders; however, estimated lifetime prevalence of the disorder is just 0.8% to 2.8% (Spiegel et al., 2011). There is just one code for depersonalization/derealization disorder: 300.6 (F48.1). The disorder has no specifiers.

 Case Example

Delila is a 35-year-old married woman who lives with her husband, Alex. They have been married nearly 15 years. Delila works full time in the accounting office of a medium-sized company where she is well liked and appreciated for her selfless support of others. Delila reports no contact with her family of origin, disappointed acceptance regarding her inability to have children, and regular engagement in the community. Delila is accompanied to counseling by Alex, who insisted they see a counselor to explore the possibility that she may be experiencing bipolar disorder. Dressed in neatly pressed khakis and a button-up shirt, Delila listens with respect and slight amusement as Alex reports a growing sense of discomfort regarding several recent changes in Delila.

Initially, Alex noted spending sprees during which Delila acquired a wardrobe that was uncharacteristically expensive and revealing. Unconcerned about finances, Alex attributed the changes to Delila's desire to "keep things alive" in their marriage. He became confused and then suspicious when Delila began denying using the credit card and refused to wear the clothes, acting as if she had never seen them before or as if Alex purchased them for her. Delila maintained her innocence yet shrugged off the concern, noting that she had become so busy she must have forgotten a trip to the mall.

Alex noted other times Delila "just wasn't herself." Alex relayed several incidents in which Delila picked fights, sometimes snapping at him and other times mocking him. Hours later, she would deny having the conversation or act as if nothing had happened. Alex wasn't alone in his observations. Delila was recently sent home from work after several altercations with coworkers that led her boss to express concerns about her ability to handle stress. Alex was shocked to come home and find her heavily intoxicated in the middle of the day because she is normally a very light drinker. Delila appeared to be as dismayed as Alex, noting that she would never drink during the day and must have been drugged by a coworker.

◆ ◆ ◆

Diagnostic Questions

1. Do Delila's presenting symptoms appear to meet the criteria for a dissociative disorder? If so, which disorder?
2. Based on your answer to Question 1, which symptom(s) led you to select that diagnosis?
3. What would be the reason(s), if any, a counselor may not diagnose Delila with that disorder?
4. What other diagnoses might you consider for Delila? Why?
5. What rule-outs would you consider for Delila's case?
6. What other information may be needed to make an accurate clinical diagnosis?

Chapter 15

Somatic Symptom and Related Disorders

I am sick and tired of being sick and tired. I have to work to get through the day. The doctors tell me it's all in my head. If I get agitated during an appointment, they use that as more evidence that I'm nuts. Of course I'm upset a lot—I am in pain all the time, and nobody will do nothing about it. I just don't know what to do anymore. —Ayana

Previously known as somatoform disorders, the somatic symptom and related disorders in this chapter are characterized by the presence of physical or somatic complaints; problematic thoughts, feelings, and behaviors in relation to the complaints; and resulting distress and impairment. Individuals who experience these disorders almost always present for medical care to address their very real physical experiences and distress. As many as one third to one half of medical complaints cannot be explained (Sharma & Manjula, 2013). Mergl et al. (2007) investigated prevalence rates of patients in one general health setting and found that more than one quarter met the *DSM-IV-TR* criteria for somatoform disorders. Despite strong evidence of symptoms in everyday practice, very few physicians diagnose these disorders (Dimsdale, 2013).

Given the focus on finding medical explanations for symptoms, individuals with distress regarding somatic concerns may only turn to professional counselors at the urging of multiple physicians and after long, frustrating, unsuccessful attempts to identify the source of their ailments. Substantial comorbidity among depressive disorders, anxiety disorders, and somatic concerns (Mergl et al., 2007; Sharma & Manjula, 2013; Tófoli, Andrade, & Fortes, 2011; Wollburg, Voigt, Braukhaus, Herzog, & Löwe, 2013) means that counselors may find themselves working with clients who experience physical distress alongside other mental health concerns. For better or worse, major changes to these disorders within the *DSM-5* may increase the frequency with which medical and mental health professionals diagnose somatic symptom and related disorders (Dimsdale, 2013; Frances & Chapman, 2013).

Major Changes From *DSM-IV-TR* to *DSM-5*

The name of this chapter was changed from Somatoform Disorders in the *DSM-IV-TR* to Somatic Symptom and Related Disorders in the *DSM-5*. Extensive revisions to this section of the *DSM-5* were designed to address concerns related to stigmatizing and ambiguous terminology, problematic focus on medically unexplained symptoms rather than experiences, unclear boundaries among disorders, unnecessarily complex criteria for somatization disorder, and rare use in practice despite prevalence in the general population (APA, 2013; Dimsdale, 2013). Counselors will find two new disorders in this section: somatic symptom disorder and illness anxiety disorder. These new disorders replace somatization disorder, hypochondriasis, pain disorder, and undifferentiated somatoform disorder. In addition, the category psychological factors affecting other medical conditions was moved from the Other Conditions That May Be a Focus of Clinical Attention chapter of the *DSM-IV-TR*, and factitious disorder was relocated from its own chapter. In all, changes to *DSM-5* criteria may increase the probability that counselors diagnose these disorders.

Clients who have somatic concerns with or without co-occurring medical conditions may be diagnosed with the new somatic symptom disorder if they have both unexplained somatic symptoms and maladaptive responses to those symptoms (APA 2013; Dimsdale 2013; Sirri & Fava, 2013). This diagnosis, discussed in depth below, is intended to replace somatization disorder and undifferentiated somatoform disorder; many individuals who carried previous diagnoses of hypochondriasis and pain disorder will fall within this new diagnosis. Criteria include less emphasis on counting medically unexplained symptoms and more focus on positive symptoms in which a client experiences distressing or disruptive somatic symptoms alongside "excessive thoughts, feelings, or behaviors related to the somatic symptoms" (APA, 2013, p. 311). Although some researchers expressed valid concerns that the changes "mislabel medical illness as mental disorder" (Frances & Chapman, 2013, p. 483), others provided preliminary evidence that the new somatic symptom disorder has increased construct, descriptive, predictive, and clinical utility when compared with *DSM-IV-TR* nosology (Dimsdale, 2013; Voigt et al., 2012; Wollburg et al., 2013).

The APA Somatic Symptoms Disorders Work Group eliminated the diagnosis of hypochondriasis because it believed this nomenclature was stigmatizing to clients (APA, 2013). Clients who have concerns regarding meaning of physical symptoms or experiences will now be diagnosed with somatic symptom disorder (if somatic symptoms are present) or illness anxiety disorder (if no somatic symptoms are present), both new to the *DSM-5*. Similarly, the work group eliminated pain disorder because one cannot reliably determine whether experiences of pain are due to physical or psychological causes (APA, 2013). Clients with pain concerns may be diagnosed with somatic symptom disorder or psychological factors affecting other medical conditions. Finally, conversion disorder carries an additional title of functional neurological symptom disorder, *DSM-5* criteria emphasize neurological examination and deemphasize the assumption that one will readily recognize psychological factors leading to concerns upon initial presentation (Stone et al., 2011).

Differential Diagnosis

Because the signs of somatic symptom and related disorders are medical, initial diagnostic focus must be on medical examination to determine the specific nature of the concern. *DSM-5* criteria allow for the presence of diagnosable health concerns alongside distressing reactions to the concerns. Thus, primary differential diagnosis includes determination regarding (a) which medical conditions are present and (b) whether one's response to the medical concerns are in excess of what would be considered normal. For an individual who is experiencing concerns related to a significant medical diagnosis, an adjustment disorder may be more appropriate (Frances & Chapman, 2013). If one's reaction to medical concerns or symptoms is simply a culturally expected response to a situation, assignment of a V or Z code may be more appropriate.

There is substantial overlap and comorbidity among depressive disorders, anxiety disorders, and somatoform disorders. Mergl et al. (2007) suggested that depressive disorders may be overlooked in many medical settings because these disorders are masked by anxiety or somatic symptoms. In a sample of individuals in a general health setting, 11.9% met the criteria for somatoform disorder whereas only 6.1% met criteria for depressive, anxiety, and somatoform disorders; 5.3% for depressive and somatoform disorders; and 2.3% for anxiety and somatoform disorders. There is strong evidence of a cultural component to expressing anxious or depressive distress somatically (Brown & Lewis-Fernández, 2011; So, 2008; Tófoli et al., 2011). Thus, counselors should consider anxiety and depressive disorders as differential and comorbid diagnoses. Hassan and Ali (2011) found evidence that somatic and anxiety symptoms are common among individuals with substance use concerns. Finally, given evidence that somatic symptoms are a typical response to trauma, counselors should consider the possibility of PTSD as a differential diagnosis (Gupta, 2013).

Etiology and Treatment

Initially, somatoform disorders were viewed as psychodynamic responses to stressors in which an individual converted psychological concerns into physical symptoms as a way of coping or expressing distress. Today, there are various models and explanations regarding etiology of somatic symptom and related disorders, and the APA (2013) identified genetic and biological vulnerability, early traumatic experiences, learning, and cultural/social norms as likely underlying factors. Still,

> Ethnographic fieldwork has long indicated the presence of a specific type of culturally mediated illness where an individual suffering from psychological issues expresses distress in the form of physical symptoms and somatic complaints, with no known organic cause. In western psychiatry, this phenomenon is commonly labeled somatization disorder. (So, 2008, p. 168)

Some argue these disorders are more likely to develop in individuals who do not have strong insight and those who fear psychiatric stigmatization (Hurwitz, 2004). So (2008) advocated for movement toward empirical, neurobiological evidence regarding somatization experiences.

Because somatic symptom and related disorders were considered quite rare, there is a relatively small body of literature regarding treatment considerations. Sharma and Manjula (2013) posited,

> The basic premise of any psychological intervention in disorders with somatic symptoms is that somatization is a universal phenomenon and is a direct consequence of common psychological disorders such as anxiety or depression resulting in autonomic arousal symptoms or somatic complaints; it may be an idiom for help-seeking for severe social adversities such as poverty, domestic violence, stigma, associated with mental illness. (p. 117)

Treatment of somatic symptom disorder in primary care settings may include psychiatric consultation and intervention, reattribution therapy, problem-solving approach, and CBT (Sharma & Manjula, 2013). Among all these treatments, CBT has been found to be most effective for somatic concerns. Similarly, treatment for the *DSM-IV-TR* disorder hypochondriasis (now somatic symptom disorder or illness anxiety disorder) includes psychoeducation, CBT, and medication (Taylor, Asmundson, & Coons, 2005). Psychoeducation may be appropriate for responding to mild concerns and includes a focus on coping strategies, role of stress in bodily sensations, and relaxation training rather than attempts to convince clients their symptoms are not real or provide reassurance regarding medical concerns. Magariños, Zafar, Nissenson, and Blanco (2002) recommended CBT as a first-line treatment for hypochondriasis given findings that it can reduce "disease conviction, need for reassurance, time spent worrying about health, frequency of checking, global problem ratings, and general measures of anxiety and depression" (p. 15). Antidepressants, especially fluoxetine, may be helpful for primary and secondary hypochondriasis; however, providers must be alert to interpretation of side effects in this sensitive population (Magariños et al., 2002; Taylor et al., 2005).

Implications for Counselors

As with all aspects of counseling, strong therapeutic relationships are essential when working with individuals who have somatic symptom and related disorders, especially given the stigma and lack of understanding they may face by frustrated health care providers (Taylor et al., 2005). Because individuals are distressed regarding their symptoms, feeling sensitive, and, in some situations, misunderstood, clients with these concerns may be quick to discontinue treatment if they sense they are not being taken seriously (Sharma & Manjula, 2013). Magariños et al. (2002) encouraged empathy through understanding symptoms as a form of emotional communication.

Frances and Chapman (2013) expressed concerns that in developing a "wildly over-inclusive" diagnostic category, APA "opened the floodgates to the overdiagnosis of mental disorder and promote the missed diagnosis of medical disorder" (p. 483). Counselors can best serve clients in this population by ensuring they receive appropriate medical evaluation and support, remaining alert to potential harms of this diagnosis in terms of access to services, and recognizing that clients who have medically unexplained symptoms can and do develop other medical concerns (Frances & Chapman, 2013; Magariños et al., 2002). Professional counselors will need to take care when determining what types and levels of expression regarding health concerns are "excessive" and "maladaptive" enough to warrant diagnosis (Voigt, 2012).

Hurwitz (2004) suggested mental health professionals conceptualize somatic symptom concerns in three domains: disease (observable medical concerns), illness behavior (subjective experiences, consequences, and symptoms), and predicaments (psychosocial consequences). Counselors can focus interventions on illness behavior and predicaments, regardless of the medical foundations of concerns (Dimsdale, 2013). These may include cognitive, emotional, physical, behavioral, medical, and social experiences (Sharma & Manjula, 2013). For example, somatization is linked to problems such as missed time from work, health care utilization, hypervigilance in detecting and expressing symptoms, and dissatisfaction with treatment (Sharma & Manjula, 2013; Wollburg et al., 2013). The most beneficial approach for an individual with a somatic symptom disorder may be to frame services as focused on helping to cope with stress related to their medical problems (Magariños et al., 2002).

Finally, somatic concerns may be universal phenomena, and there is evidence that specific symptoms experienced vary by culture. Furthermore, symptoms may be culturally normal and expected responses (Brown & Lewis-Fernández, 2011). Somatization is quite stigmatized in Western cultures that focus on mind–body duality; however, a degree of somatization experiences are quite common in cultures in which mind–body holism are accepted and expected (So, 2008). Counselors must be careful not to stigmatize culturally specific ways of expressing distress or difficulties differentiating feelings from bodily sensations as somehow less developed or having less validity. This is particularly important given higher rates of concerns among vulnerable populations, including those with lower socioeconomic status, lower education, poor working conditions, and exposure to violence (Tófoli et al., 2011).

300.82 Somatic Symptom Disorder (F45.1)

Essential Features

Somatic symptom disorder is characterized by the presence of distressing or disruptive somatic symptoms for 6 or more months and "excessive thoughts, feelings, or behaviors related to the somatic symptoms" (APA, 2013, p. 311). These can be considered excessive based on the proportion of time spent thinking about the concern, level of anxiety surrounding the concern, or degree of time and energy devoted to the concern. Counselors may make this diagnosis for cases in which somatic symptoms are or are not medically explained.

Special Considerations

Because somatic symptom disorder is new to the *DSM-5*, there is limited research regarding its prevalence. Lifetime prevalence of *DSM-IV-TR* somatization disorder was as low as 0.13% in general settings and 1.0% in primary care settings (So, 2008), and lifetime prevalence of *DSM-IV-TR* undifferentiated somatoform disorder was approximately 19% (APA, 2013). Dimsdale (2013) cited evidence that prevalence rate of this new disorder may be approximately 6.7% among the general population, and presence of a major medical diagnosis did not inflate this rate. Women are more likely to be diagnosed than men, and the disorder is more common and persistent in individuals who have lower socioeconomic status, lower educational attainment, and more pronounced experiences of stressors (APA, 2013).

There is just one code for somatic symptom disorder, 300.82 (F45.1). The *DSM-5* includes specifiers for *with predominant pain* (replaces *DSM-IV-TR* pain disorder) and *persistent* (for use with severe symptoms, marked impairment, and long duration). Counselors characterize severity as *mild*, *moderate*, or *severe* depending on degree of concern related to Criterion B.

300.7 Illness Anxiety Disorder (F45.21)

Essential Features

Illness anxiety disorder is characterized by a 6-month period in which an individual is preoccupied "with having or acquiring a serious illness" (APA, 2013, p. 315) even though somatic symptoms are absent or very mild. The individual has a high level of anxiety about his or her health and engages in excessive or maladaptive health-related behaviors. Those with illness anxiety disorder are more distressed about having a diagnosis than experiencing the symptoms.

Special Considerations

Approximately 25% of individuals who were previously diagnosed with hypochondriasis will meet criteria for illness anxiety disorder; the remainder may be diagnosed with somatic symptom disorder (APA, 2013; Sirri & Fava, 2013). There is little research regarding prevalence of the new disorder and characteristics of those affected, so the following is based on findings related to hypochondriasis. Prevalence of hypochondriasis ranged from 0.8% to 4.5% in primary care settings, and findings showed few demographic risk factors (Magariños et al., 2002). Although hypochondriasis is chronic for most individuals, one third experience only transient concerns. Differential diagnosis includes medical disorder, phobia of disease exposure, somatic symptoms associated with depressive and anxiety disorders, BDD, and delusional disorder (Magariños et al., 2002). The *DSM-5* also includes the following differential diagnoses: adjustment disorders, somatic symptom disorder, and OCD; APA (2013) estimated that two thirds will have a comorbid mental disorder.

There is just one code for illness anxiety disorder: 300.7 (F45.21). Counselors may use specifiers to note whether an individual has *care-seeking type* or *care-avoidant type*.

300.11 Conversion Disorder (Functional Neurological Symptom Disorder) (F44._)

Essential Features

Conversion disorder, also known as functional neurological symptom disorder, is characterized by symptoms suggesting problems with voluntary motor or sensory function (e.g., paralysis, problems swallowing, speech problems, seizures) in which there is no neurological evidence for the condition. The problem cannot be explained by another concern and must lead to impairment, distress, or medical evaluation (APA, 2013).

Special Considerations

The *DSM-5* criteria removed the requirement that symptoms be preceded by a psychological stressor because stressors may not be evident to or reported by clients (Stone et al., 2011). Focus on medical examination and clinical assessment becomes all the more important when making this diagnosis (Sirri & Fava, 2013; Stone et al., 2011), especially because up to 30% of those diagnosed with conversion disorder have an undetected illness (Hurwitz, 2004). The prevalence of conversion disorder is unknown; however, it appears to account for approximately 5% of neurology clinic referrals (APA, 2013). Brown and Lewis-Fernández (2011) noted that prevalence among men and women varies culturally; however, conversion disorder is consistently more common among women and those with lower socioeconomic status. It is often comorbid with dissociative, depressive, and anxiety disorders. Although there is some evidence in North America that suggests conversion disorder is of short duration, a body of literature shows longer effects in other cultural contexts (Brown & Lewis-Fernández, 2011). Persistent conversion disorder is found in just 0.002% to 0.005% of the population each year.

The *ICD-9-CM* code for conversion disorder is 300.11. The *ICD-10-CM* code (F44._) will vary based on subtype: *with weakness or paralysis, with abnormal movement, with swallowing symptoms, with speech symptom, with attacks or seizures, with anesthesia or sensory loss, with special sensory symptom,* or *with mixed symptoms.* Counselors may specify whether a client is experiencing an *acute episode* (less than 6 months) or *persistent episode* (longer than 6 months) and whether the concern is *with psychological stressor (specify stressor)* or *without psychological stressor* (APA, 2013).

316 Psychological Factors Affecting Other Medical Conditions (F54)

Essential Features

This diagnosis is used when an individual has a medical condition for which psychological or behavioral factors exacerbate symptoms, interfere with treatment, or compound risks. APA (2013) stipulated that the psychological factors cannot be another diagnosable mental disorder. Examples provided in the *DSM-5* include asthma made worse by anxiety, manipulation of insulin for weight loss, or denial of need for treatment of chest pain.

Special Considerations

APA (2013) noted that prevalence for this diagnosis is unknown; psychological factors must be differentiated from cultural differences in help-seeking and may occur throughout the life span. Sirri and Fava (2013) expressed concerns regarding lack of specificity for this diagnosis and, thus, lack of clinical implications. There is one code for this disorder: 316 (F54). Clinicians may use impact on health to rate the disorder as *mild, moderate, severe,* or *extreme.*

300.19 Factitious Disorder (F68.10)

Essential Features

Factitious disorder is characterized by falsification of an illness in the absence of external rewards and other mental disorders explaining the behavior (APA, 2013). Factitious disorder may be diagnosed for individuals who present themselves as ill (factitious disorder imposed on self) as well as individuals who represent others as ill (factitious disorder imposed on another).

Special Considerations

Prevalence of factitious disorder is unknown, although it may present in about 1% of individuals in hospital settings (APA, 2013). There is just one diagnostic code for factitious disorder: 300.19 (F68.10). Clinicians can specify the diagnosis as *single episode* or *recurrent episode*. In cases in which the disorder is imposed on another, the perpetrator receives the diagnosis of factitious disorder, and the victim may be assigned an abuse diagnosis.

 Case Example

Marcos is a single, 34-year-old Latino man who holds a college degree. He presented to counseling for "support and stress management" at the suggestion of his physician. Over the past year, Marcos has experienced a number of medical concerns, especially headaches and light-headedness. He sought assistance from a physician who, upon noting normal blood chemistries and metabolic functioning, prescribed migraine control medication and advised him to be careful about not going too long between meals. When the medication did not bring relief, the physician ordered a complete diagnostic workup including more extensive blood work, an MRI (magnetic resonance imagine), and a CT (computed tomography). All tests were within normal limits; however, Marcos became convinced he had an undiagnosed brain tumor or aneurism. As his work performance decreased because of the effects of the symptoms and worry regarding their implications, Marcos began spending hours each night researching his symptoms and discussing them with others. Convinced his physician did not understand his concerns, he sought a second opinion. At his insistence, the second physician referred him to a neurologist for further evaluation. The neurologist reviewed test results, completed several additional procedures, and did not detect any concerns.

Over the next few months, Marcos developed additional concerns including gastrointestinal upset, shortness of breath, and sleep disturbance. He missed more work, withdrew from family and friends, and stopped going to the gym out of concern that the exertion may not be in his best interest. At this time, his blood pressure became elevated, heightening his concern regarding the possibility of a severe underlying disorder. Referral to a gastroenterologist led to an endoscopy that was normal with the exception of slight esophageal irritation, which the specialist recommended treating with over-the-counter heartburn medication.

In the meantime, Marcos's employer became increasingly frustrated with his lack of reliable attendance and frequent distraction at work. She warned Marcos that she would need to take disciplinary action if the behaviors continued without supporting documentation from his physician. Distraught at the potential loss of health insurance, Marcos visited his physician to explore his options. During a particularly difficult visit, his physician expressed her doubts that they would ever find the "root of the concern" and advised Marcos to attend counseling to learn how to manage his symptoms and distress related to them. Although offended at the suggestion that it was "all in his head," Marcos made the call. After all, he said, the symptoms were distressing and he was realizing he might just have to deal with a lifelong illness.

◆ ◆ ◆

Diagnostic Questions

1. Do Marcos's presenting symptoms appear to meet the criteria for a somatic concern or related disorder? If so, which disorder?
2. Based on your answer to Question 1, which symptom(s) led you to select that diagnosis?
3. What would be the reason(s), if any, a counselor may not diagnose Marcos with that disorder?
4. Would Marcos be more accurately diagnosed with an anxiety disorder? If so, why? If not, why not?
5. What rule-outs would you consider for Marcos's case?
6. What other information may be needed to make an accurate clinical diagnosis?

Part Three References

Addington, A. M., & Rapoport, J. L. (2012). Annual research review: Impact of advances in genetics in understanding developmental psychopathology. *Journal of Child Psychology and Psychiatry, 53,* 510–518.

American Psychiatric Association. (2004). *Practice guideline for the treatment of patients with schizophrenia* (2nd ed.). Retrieved from http://psychiatryonline.org/content.aspx?bookid=28&sectionid=1665359

American Psychiatric Association. (2013). *Diagnostic and statistical manual of mental disorders* (5th ed.). Arlington, VA: Author.

Bajenaru, O., Tiu, C., Antochi, A., & Roceanu, A. (2012). Neurocognitive disorders in *DSM 5* project: Personal comments. *Journal of Neurological Sciences, 322,* 17–19.

Barrio Minton, C. A., & Prosek, E. (in press). Schizophrenia spectrum and other psychotic disorders. In V. E. Kress & M. Paylo (Eds.), *Treating mental disorders: A strength-based, comprehensive approach to case conceptualization and treatment planning.* Upper Saddle River, NJ: Pearson.

Barton, M. L., Robins, D. L., Jashar, D., Brennan, L., & Fein, D. (2013). Sensitivity and specificity of proposed autism spectrum disorder in toddlers. *Journal of Autism Development Disorder, 43,* 1184–1195.

Beck, A. T., Rector, N. A., Stolar, N., & Grant, P. (2009). *Schizophrenia: Cognitive theory, research, and therapy.* New York, NY: Guilford Press.

Blazer, D. (2013). Neurocognitive disorders in *DSM-5. American Journal of Psychiatry, 170,* 585–587.

Brand, B. L. (2012). What we know and what we need to learn about the treatment of dissociative disorders. *Journal of Trauma & Dissociation, 13,* 387–396. doi:10.1080/15299732.2012.672550

Brand, B. L., Lanius, R., Vermetten, E., Loewenstein, R. J., & Spiegel, D. (2012). Where are we going? An update on assessment, treatment, and neurobiological research in dissociative disorders as we move toward the *DSM-5. Journal of Trauma & Dissociation, 13,* 9–31. doi:10.1080/1529 9732.2011.620687

Brown, R. J., & Lewis-Fernández, R. (2011). Culture and conversion disorder: Implications for *DSM-5. Psychiatry, 74,* 187–206.

Casecade, E., Kalali, A. H., & Buckley, P. (2009). Treatment of schizoaffective disorder. *Psychiatry (Edgmont), 6,* 15–17.

Centers for Disease Control and Prevention. (2012). Prevalence of autism spectrum disorders: Autism and Developmental Disabilities Monitoring Network, 14 sites, United States, 2008. *Morbidity and Mortality Weekly Report, 61*(3), 1–19.

Cloitre, M., Courtois, C. A., Ford, J. D., Green, B. L., Alexander, P., Briere, J., . . . Van der Hart, O. (2012). *The ISTSS expert consensus treatment guidelines for complex PTSD in adults.* Retrieved from http://www.istss.org/AM/Template.cfm?Section=ISTSS_Complex_PTSD_Treatment_Guidelines&Template=/CM/ContentDisplay.cfm&ContentID=5185

Coolidge, F. L., Marle, P. D., Rhoades, C. S., Monaghan, P., & Segal, D. L. (2013). Psychometric properties of a new measure to assess autism spectrum disorder in *DSM-5*. *American Journal of Orthopsychiatry, 83,* 126–130.

Dimsdale, J. E. (2013). Somatic symptom disorder: An important change in *DSM*. *Journal of Psychosomatic Research, 75,* 223–228.

Eriksen, K., & Kress, V. E. (2005). *Beyond the DSM story: Ethical quandaries, challenges, and best practices.* Thousand Oaks, CA: Sage.

Fombonne, E. (2005). Epidemiology of autistic disorder and other pervasive developmental disorders. *Journal of Clinical Psychiatry, 36,* 272–281.

Foote, B., Smolin, Y., Kaplan, M., Legatt, M. E., & Lipschitz, D. (2006). Prevalence of dissociative disorders in psychiatric outpatients. *American Journal of Psychiatry, 163,* 623–629.

Frances, A., & Chapman, S. (2013). *DSM-5* somatic symptom disorder mislabels medical illness as mental disorder. *Australian & New Zealand Journal of Psychiatry, 47,* 483–489. doi:10.1177/0004867413484525

Frazier, T. W., Youngstrom, E. A., Speer, L., Embacher, R., Law, P., Constantino, J., . . . Eng, C. (2012). Validation of proposed *DSM-5* criteria for autism spectrum disorder. *Journal of the American Academy of Child & Adolescent Psychiatry, 51,* 28–40.

Gaebel, W. (2011). *Schizophrenia: Current science and clinical practice.* Hoboken, NJ: Wiley-Blackwell.

Gaebel, W., Zielasek, J., & Cleveland, H. (2012). Classifying psychosis: Challenges and opportunities. *International Review of Psychiatry, 24,* 538–548. doi:10.3109/09540261.2012.737313

Ganguli, M., Blacker, D., Blazer, D., Grant, I., Jeste, D. V., Paulson, J. S., . . . Perminder, S. S. (2011). Classification of neurocognitive disorders in *DSM-5*: A work in progress. *American Journal of Geriatric Psychiatry, 19,* 205–210.

Gearing, R. E. (2008). Evidence-based family psychoeducational interventions for children and adolescents with psychotic disorders. *Journal of Canadian Academy of Child and Adolescent Psychiatry, 17,* 2–11.

Gearing, R. E., & Mian, I. (2009). The role of gender in early and very early onset of psychotic disorders. *Clinical Schizophrenia & Related Psychoses, 2,* 298–306.

Geda, Y. E., & Nedelska, Z. (2012). Mild cognitive impairment: A subset of mild neurocognitive disorder? *American Journal of Geriatric Psychiatry, 20,* 821–827.

Ghanizadeh, A. (2013). Agreement between *Diagnostic and Statistical Manual of Mental Disorders, Fourth Edition* and the proposed *DSM-V* attention deficit hyperactivity disorder diagnostic criteria: An exploratory study. *Comprehensive Psychiatry, 54,* 7–10.

Gibbs, V., Aldridge, F., Chandler, F., Witzlsperger, E., & Smith, K. (2012). Brief report: An exploratory study comparing diagnostic outcomes for autism spectrum disorders under *DSM-IV-TR* with the proposed *DSM-5* revision. *Journal of Autism and Developmental Disorders, 42,* 1750–1756.

Greaves-Lord, K., Eussen, M. L., Verhulst, F. C., Minderaa, R. B., Mandy, W., Hudziak, J. J., . . . Hartman, C. A. (2013). Empirically based phenotypic profiles of children with pervasive developmental disorders: Interpretation in the light of the *DSM-5*. *Journal of Autism and Developmental Disorders, 43,* 1784–1797.

Gupta, M. (2013). Review of somatic symptoms in post-traumatic stress disorder. *International Review of Psychiatry, 25,* 86–99. doi:10.3109/09540261.2012.736367

Hassan, I., & Ali, R. (2011). The association between somatic symptoms, anxiety disorders and substance use: A literature review. *Psychiatry Quarterly, 82,* 315–328.

Heckers, S. (2012). Diagnostic criteria for schizoaffective disorder. *Expert Reviews Neurotherapeutics, 12,* 1–3. doi:10.1586/ERN.11.179

Helldin, L., Kane, J. M., Karilampi, U., Norlander, T., & Archer, T. (2007). Remission in prognosis of functional outcome: A new dimension in the treatment of patients with psychotic disorders. *Schizophrenia Research, 93,* 160–168.

Helseth, V., Lykke-Enger, T., Johnsen, J., & Waal, H. (2009). Substance use disorders among psychotic patients admitted to inpatient psychiatric care. *Nordic Journal of Psychiatry, 63,* 72–77.

Horan, W. P., Harvy, P., Kern, R. S., & Green, M. F. (2011). Neurocognition, social cognition and functional outcome in schizophrenia. In W. Gaebel (Ed.), *Schizophrenia: Current science and clinical practice* (pp. 68–107). Hoboken, NJ: Wiley-Blackwell.

Hurwitz, T. A. (2004). Somatization and conversion disorder. *Canadian Journal of Psychiatry, 49,* 172–178.

International Society for the Study of Dissociation. (2004). Guidelines for the evaluation and treatment of dissociative symptoms in children and adolescents. *Journal of Trauma & Dissociation, 5,* 119–150. doi:10.1300/J229v05n03_09

International Society for the Study of Trauma and Dissociation. (2011). Guidelines for treating dissociative identity disorder in adults, third revision. *Journal of Trauma & Dissociation, 12,* 115–187. doi:10.1080/15299732.2011.537247

International Society for the Study of Trauma and Dissociation. (2013a). *Child/adolescent FAQ's.* Retrieved from http://www.isst-d.org/default.asp?contentID=100

International Society for the Study of Trauma and Dissociation. (2013b). *Dissociation FAQ's.* Retrieved from http://www.isst-d.org/default.asp?contentID=76#diss

Jolley, S., & Garety, P. (2011). Cognitive–behavioural interventions. In W. Gaebel (Ed.), *Schizophrenia: Current science and clinical practice* (pp. 185–215). Chichester, England: Wiley-Blackwell.

Kantrowitz, J. T., & Citrome, L. (2011). Schizoaffective disorder: A review of current research themes and pharmacological management. *CNS Drugs, 25,* 317–331. doi:1172-7047/11/0004-0317

Keller, W. R., Fischer, B. A., & Carpenter, W. T. (2011). Revisiting the diagnosis of schizophrenia: Where have we been and where are we going? *CNS Neuroscience & Therapeutics, 17,* 83–88. doi:10.1111/j.1755-5949.2010.00229.x

Kingdon, D. G., & Turkington, D. (2002). *Cognitive–behavioral therapy of schizophrenia.* New York, NY: Guilford Press.

Kopelowicz, A., Liberman, R. P., & Zarate, R. (2007). Psychosocial treatments for schizophrenia. In P. E. Nathan & J. M. Gorman (Ed.), *A guide to treatments that work* (pp. 243–269) New York, NY: Oxford University Press.

Korzekwa, M. I., Dell, P. F., Links, P. S., Thabane, L., & Fougere, P. (2009). Dissociation in borderline personality disorder: A detailed look. *Journal of Trauma and Dissociation, 10,* 346–367. doi:10.1080/15299730902956838

Kurita, H. (2011). How to deal with the transition from pervasive developmental disorders in *DSM-IV* to autism spectrum disorder in *DSM-V. Psychiatry and Clinical Neurosciences, 65,* 609–610.

Lai, M.-C., Lombardo, M. V., Chakrabarti, B., & Baron-Cohen, S. (2013). Subgrouping the autism "spectrum": Reflections on *DSM-5. PLOS Biology, 11*(4), 1–7.

Lake, C. R., & Hurwitz, N. (2008). Schizoaffective disorder—its rise and fall: Perspectives for *DSM-V. Clinical Schizophrenia & Related Psychoses, 2,* 91–97.

Lanius, R. A., Brand, B., Vermetten, E., Frewen, P. A., & Spiegel, D. (2012). The dissociative subtype of posttraumatic stress disorder: Rationale, clinical and neurobiological evidence, and implications. *Depression and Anxiety, 29,* 701–708. doi:10.1002/da.21889

Lauritsen, M. B. (2013). Autism spectrum disorders. *European Child and Adolescent Psychiatry, 22,* S37–S42.

Magariños, M., Zafar, U., Nissenson, K., & Blanco, C. (2002). Epidemiology and treatment of hypochondriasis. *CNS Drugs, 16,* 9–22.

Mandy, W. P., Charman, T., Gilmour, J., & Skuse, D. H. (2011). Towards specifying pervasive developmental disorder-not otherwise specified. *Autism Research, 4,* 1–11.

Mandy, W. P., Charman, T., & Skuse, D. H. (2012). Testing the construct validity of proposed criteria for *DSM-5* autism spectrum disorder. *Journal of the American Academy of Child & Adolescent Psychiatry, 51,* 41–50.

Mayes, S. D., Black, A., & Tierney, C. D. (2013). *DSM-5* under-identifies PDDNOS: Diagnostic agreement between the *DSM-IV* and Checklist for Autism Spectrum Disorder. *Research in Autism Spectrum Disorders, 7,* 298–306.

Mazefsky, C. A., McPartland, J. C., Gastgeb, H. Z., & Minshew, N. J. (2013). Brief report: Comparability of *DSM-IV* and *DSM-5* ASD research samples. *Journal of Autism and Developmental Disorders, 43,* 1236–1242.

McCabe, R., Bullenkamp, J., Hansson, L., Lauber, C., Martinez-Leal, R., Rössler, W., . . . Priebe, S. (2012). The therapeutic relationship and adherence to antipsychotic medication in schizophrenia. *PLoS ONE, 7,* 1–5. doi:10.1371/journal.pone.0036080

McGuiness, T. M., & Johnson, K. (2013). *DSM-5* changes in the diagnosis of autism spectrum disorder. *Journal of Psychosocial Nursing, 51*(4), 17–19.

McPartland, J. C., Reichaw, B., & Volkmar, F. R., (2012). Sensitivity and specificity of proposed *DSM-5* diagnostic criteria for autism spectrum disorder. *Journal of the American Academy of Child & Adolescent Psychiatry, 51,* 369–383.

Mergl, R., Seidscheck, I., Allgaier, A., Möller, H., Hergerl, U., & Henkel, V. (2007). Depressive, anxiety, and somatoform disorders in primary care: Prevalence and recognition. *Depression and Anxiety, 24,* 185–195. doi:10.1002/da.20192

Mitchell, A. J. (2013). Redefining the syndrome of cognitive impairment in *DSM-5. Australian and New Zealand Journal of Psychiatry, 47,* 79–81.

National Alliance on Mental Illness. (2013). *PACT: Program of assertive community treatment.* Retrieved from http://www.nami.org/Template.cfm?Section=ACT-TA_Center&template=/ContentManagement/ContentDisplay.cfm&ContentID=132547

National Institute of Mental Health. (2009). *Schizophrenia* (NIH Publication No. 09-3517). Retrieved from http://www.nimh.nih.gov/health/publications/schizophrenia/

National Institute of Mental Health. (2012). *Mental health medications* (NIH Publication No. 12-3929). Retrieved from http://www.nimh.nih.gov/health/publications/mental-health-medications/nimh-mental-health-medications.pdf

Obiols, J. (2012). *DSM 5: Precedents, present and prospects. International Journal of Clinical and Health Psychology, 12,* 281–290.

Pagsberg, A. K. (2013). Schizophrenia spectrum and other psychotic disorders. *European Child & Adolescent Psychiatry, 22,* S3–S9. doi:10.1007/s00787-012-0354-x

Pastor, C. N., & Reuben, C. A. (2008). Diagnosed attention deficit hyperactivity disorder and learning disability: United States 2004–2006. *Vital Health Statistics, 10,* 1–22.

Pinborough-Zimmerman, J., Bakian, A. V., Fombonne, E., Bilder, D., Taylor, J., & McMahon, W. M. (2012). Changes in the administrative prevalence of autism spectrum disorders: Contribution of special education and health from 2002–2008. *Journal of Autism and Developmental Disorders, 42,* 521–530.

Potuzak, M., Ravichandran, C., Lewandowski, K. E., Ongür, D., & Cohen, B. M. (2012). Categorical vs dimensional classifications of psychotic disorders. *Comprehensive Psychiatry, 53,* 1118–1129. doi:10.1016/j.comppsych.2012.04.010

Psychiatric Rehabilitation Consultants. (2011). *Products and services for the partners in recovery.* Retrieved from www.psychrehab.com

Remington, R. (2012). Neurocognitive diagnostic challenges and the *DSM-5:* Perspectives from the frontlines of clinical practice. *Issues in Mental Health Nursing, 33,* 626–629.

Ritsner, M. S., Mar, M., Arbitman, M., & Grinshpoon, A. (2013). Symptom severity scale of the *DSM-5* for schizophrenia, and other psychotic disorders: Diagnostic validity and clinical feasibility. *Psychiatry Research, 208,* 1–8. doi:10.1016/j.psychres.2013.02.029

Rosa's Law, Pub. L. No. 111-256 (2010).

Rössler, W. (2011). Management, rehabilitation, stigma. In W. Gaebel (Ed.), *Schizophrenia: Current science and clinical practice* (pp. 217–246). Hoboken, NJ: Wiley-Blackwell.

Rubin, A., & Trawver, K. (2011). Overview and clinical implications of schizophrenia. In A. S. Rubin, D. W. Springer, & K. Trawver (Eds.), *Psychosocial treatment of schizophrenia: Clinician's guide to evidence-based practice* (pp. 1–22). Hoboken, NJ: Wiley-Blackwell.

Sharma, M. P., & Manjula, M. (2013). Behavioural and psychological management of somatic symptom disorders: An overview. *International Review of Psychiatry, 25,* 116–124. doi:10.3109/09540261.2012.746649

Schizophrenia medications. (2013, March 8). *The New York Times.* Retrieved from http://health.nytimes.com/health/guides/disease/schizophrenia/medications.html

Simeon, D., Guralnik, O., Schmeidler, J., Sirof, B., & Knutelska, M. (2001). The role of childhood interpersonal trauma in depersonalization disorder. *American Journal of Psychiatry, 158,* 1027–1033.

Simonoff, E., Pickles, A., Charman, T., Chandler, S., Loucas, T., & Baird, G. (2008). Psychiatric disorders in children with autism disorders: Prevalence, comorbidity and associated factors in a population-derived sample. *Journal of the American Academy of Child & Adolescent Psychiatry, 47,* 921–929.

Sirri, L., & Fava, G. A. (2013). Diagnostic criteria for psychosomatic research and somatic symptom disorders. *International Review of Psychiatry, 25,* 19–30. doi:10.3109/09540261.2012.726923

So, J. K. (2008). Somatization as cultural idiom of distress: Rethinking mind and body in a multicultural society. *Counseling Psychology Quarterly, 21,* 167–174. doi:10.1080/09515070802066854

Sorrell, J. M. (2013). *Diagnostic and statistical manual of mental disorders–5*: Implications for older adults and their families. *Journal of Psychosocial Nursing, 51*(3), 19–22.

Spiegel. D., Loewenstein, R., Lewis- Fernández, R., Sar, V., Simeon, D., Vermetten, E., . . . Dell, P. F. (2011). Dissociative disorders in *DSM-5*. *Depression and Anxiety, 28,* 824–852. doi:10.1002/da.20874

Stone, J., LaFrance, W. C., Brown, R., Spiegel, D., Levenson, J. L., & Sharpe, M. (2011). Conversion disorder: Current problems and potential solutions for *DSM-5*. *Journal of Psychosomatic Research, 71,* 369–376.

Substance Abuse and Mental Health Services Administration. (2008). *Getting started with evidence-based practices: Assertive community treatment* (SAMHSA Publication SMA08-4345). Washington, DC: Author.

Substance Abuse and Mental Health Services Administration. (2010). *Getting started with evidence-based practices: Family education* (SAMHSA Publication SMA09-4423). Washington, DC: Author.

Tandon, R. (2013a). Schizophrenia and other psychotic disorders in *DSM-5*: Clinical implications of revisions from *DSM-IV*. *Clinical Schizophrenia & Related Psychoses, 7,* 16–19.

Tandon, R. (2013b). Schizophrenia spectrum and other psychotic disorders: *DSM-5* revisions and their clinical implications. *Psychopharm Review, 48,* 33–39. doi:10.1097/01.PSYPHR.0000430951.60967.d6

Taylor, S., Asmundson, G. J. G., & Coons, M. J. (2005). Current directions in the treatment of hypochondriasis. *Journal of Cognitive Psychotherapy: An International Quarterly, 19,* 285–304.

Tófoli, L. F., Andrade, L. H., & Fortes, S. (2011). Somatization in Latin America: A review on the classification and somatoform disorders, functional syndromes, and medically unexplained symptoms. *Revista Brasileira de Psiquiatria, 33,* 570–580.

Tsai, L. (2012). Sensitivity and specificity: *DSM-IV* versus *DSM-5* criteria for autism spectrum disorder. *American Journal of Psychiatry, 169,* 1009–1011.

Valencia, M., Juarez, F., & Ortega, H. (2012). Integrated treatment to achieve functional recovery in first-episode psychosis. *Schizophrenia Research and Treatment, 2012,* Article ID 962371. doi:10.1155/2012/962371

Voigt, K., Wollburg, E., Weinmann, N., Herzog, A., Meyer, B., Langs, G., & Löwe, B. (2012). Predictive validity and clinical utility of *DSM-5* somatic symptom disorder: Comparison with *DSM-IV* somatoform disorders and additional criteria for consideration. *Journal of Psychosomatic Research, 73,* 345–350. doi:10.1016/j.jpsychores.2012.08.020

Wakefield, J. C. (2013). *DSM-5*: An overview of changes and controversies. *Journal of Clinical Social Work, 41,* 139–154.

Walsh, J. (2011). Therapeutic communication with psychotic clients. *Clinical Social Work Journal, 39,* 1–8.

Weitlauf, A. S., Gotham, K. O., Vehorn, A. C., & Warren, Z. E. (2013). Brief report: *DSM-5* "Levels of support": A comment on discrepant conceptualizations of severity in ASD. *Journal of Autism and Developmental Disorder.* Advance online publication. doi:10.1007/s10803-013-1882-z

Wilson, C. E., Gillan, N., Spain, D., Robertson, D., Roberts, G., Murphy, C. M., . . . Murphy, D. G. (2013). Comparison of *ICD-10R*, *DSM-IV-TR* and *DSM-5* in an adult autism spectrum disorder diagnostic clinic. *Journal of Autism and Developmental Disorder, 43,* 2515–2525. doi:10.1007/s10803-013-1799-6

Wollburg, E., Voigt, K., Braukhaus, C., Herzog, A., & Löwe, B. (2013). Construct validity and descriptive validity of somatoform disorders in light of proposed changes for the *DSM-5*. *Journal of Psychosomatic Research, 74,* 18–24. doi:10.1016/j.jpsychores.2012.09.015

World Health Organization. (2007). *International statistical classification of diseases and related health problems, 10th revision*. Geneva, Switzerland: Author.

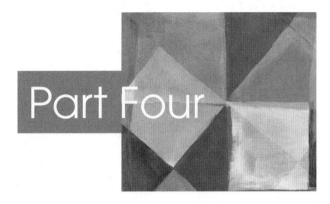

Part Four

Future Changes and Practice Implications for Counselors

Part Four Introduction

In Part Four, we cover personality disorders, highlighting an emerging model of practice to diagnose personality conditions as well as practice implications for counselors using the *DSM-5*. In Chapter 16, Looking Ahead: Personality Disorders, we provide a brief description of each personality disorder and focus the rest of the chapter on a hybrid model of personality disorders proposed for the future. Although we recognize that counselors frequently work with personality dysfunction, we decided to place this chapter at the end of this book because only semantic changes to the diagnostic criteria in the *DSM-IV-TR* (APA, 2000) were made in the *DSM-5* (APA, 2013a). Instead we focus on future changes, which we estimate will significantly modify the way counselors conceptualize and diagnose personality disorders.

In the final chapter, Practice Implications for Counselors, we continue looking ahead but with a focus on clinical practice. This chapter includes philosophical implications for switching from the *DSM-IV-TR* to the *DSM-5* and a detailed discussion of technical considerations, such as how to use other specified and unspecified diagnoses; coding and recording modifications; future changes to coding and recording; and newly available diagnostic assessment and screening tools, including the WHODAS 2.0 (WHO, 2010) and the Cultural Formulation Interview (APA, 2013a). We also describe the potential future direction of diagnostic nosology.

We conclude this section, and this *Learning Companion,* with a sense of urgency for counselors to become advocates for appropriate and empirically based uses of diagnostic nomenclature. We urge counseling professionals to become stewards of diagnostic research, participate in field trials and public comment periods, and have a seat at the table during upcoming modifications to both the *DSM* and *ICD,* as well as other proposed diagnostic formulations such as the Research Domain Criteria project launched by the NIMH (for more information, see Insel et al., 2010; Sanislow et al., 2010). Regardless of the platform, counselors need to find their voice within the future of diagnostic nomenclature so our profession can have a stronger foothold in these discussions.

♦ ♦ ♦

Chapter 16

Looking Ahead:
Personality Disorders

Personality disorders covered in this chapter can be found in both Sections II and III of the *DSM-5*. We first discuss personality disorders found in Section II, which lists all current diagnostic criteria and codes being used by clinicians. Following this brief description, we explain the proposed model for diagnosing and conceptualizing personality disorders found in Section III of the *DSM-5* titled Emerging Measures and Models. We explain the reasoning behind this newly proposed approach, describe various viewpoints regarding the new model, and list practice implications for counselors regarding these proposed changes. Counselors currently in practice should note this model has not been adopted into the general nomenclature system. Currently, this new approach only serves the purpose of stimulating future research endeavors and generating discussion about a dimensional versus hybrid (i.e., containing both categorical and dimensional criteria) approach to personality dysfunction. Readers will find this discussion useful because we anticipate that the diagnostic criteria for personality disorders will soon be replaced.

With the exception of adding diagnostic information related to culture (Peluso, 2013), there were very minor changes to the Personality Disorders chapter within the *DSM-5*. Therefore, we have chosen to cover these disorders in less detail, providing readers with a short description of each disorder that includes essential features, special and general cultural considerations, and common differential diagnoses. We wish to emphasize that counselors who currently understand personality disorder nomenclature as presented in the *DSM-IV-TR* only need to be concerned with very minor, mostly semantic, changes to this section of the *DSM-5*.

Personality disorders permeate an individual's internal and external presentation, are typically rigid and uncompromising, have an onset prior to early adulthood, are chronic dysfunctions (as opposed to episodic), and are very slow to change (APA, 2013a; Durand & Barlow, 2010; Paris, 2013). The disorders discussed in this chapter fall within 10 distinct types: paranoid, schizoid, schizotypal, antisocial, borderline, histrionic, narcissistic, avoidant, dependent, and obsessive-compulsive. All of these disorders share common biological etiology (i.e., inherited traits) and are grouped according to symptomatology. Cluster A disorders are characterized by odd, eccentric thinking or behavior; Cluster B by dramatic, overly emotional thinking or behaviors; and Cluster C by anxious, fearful, or obsessive thinking and behavior (APA, 2013a).

Note

There is no empirical evidence supporting the clustering system used by the APA in the *DSM-5*. This system was maintained in the *DSM-5* for the purpose of clinical utility and to be used in research and academic settings.

♦ ♦ ♦

Disorders found within the Personality Disorders chapter of the *DSM-5* are characterized by persistent maladaptive patterns of behavior, cognition, affect, and interpersonal functioning that deviate from one's cultural norms (APA, 2013a). These traits have a significant negative impact on the client's life, limiting his or her ability to function in essential areas such as work, home, or school. Lifetime prevalence of personality disorders is estimated at 15% (APA, 2013a). However, some claim this number is drastically inflated and merely a product of poorly constructed diagnostic criteria (Paris, 2013).

The APA (2013a) defines *personality disorder* as

An enduring pattern of inner experience and behavior that deviates markedly from the expectations of the individual's culture, is pervasive and inflexible, has an onset in adolescence or early adulthood, is stable over time, and leads to distress or impairment. (p. 645)

This definition seems to have an inherent message that personality disorders are permanent and thus resistant to treatment (Paris, 2013). Individuals diagnosed with personality disorders are generally stereotyped as difficult, unlikable, and extremely challenging (Comer, 2013; Frances, 2013; Nietzel, Speltz, McCauley, & Bernstein, 1998). Although we agree this population is challenging to treat, we side with Paris (2013), who challenged the claim that treatment for these disorders is ineffective. These disorders have been misunderstood primarily because of their complexity; differentiating between normal personality functioning and pathological personality functioning is a complicated task.

Critics of the *DSM-IV-TR* (and subsequently *DSM-5*) nosology have claimed the current categorical diagnoses within this chapter are just as confusing as the definition. Clinicians maintain there is significant overlap and comorbidity between the 10 personality disorder categories (Paris, 2013; Rosenbaum & Pollock, 2002). There is also considerable heterogeneity within diagnostic classifications, as evidenced by some diagnoses that require only five of 10 criteria (Paris, 2013). Finally, clinical utility has traditionally been difficult, as evidenced by overuse of the personality disorder NOS diagnosis (Pagan, Oltmanns, Whitmore, & Turkheimer, 2005; Rosenbaum & Pollock, 2002).

Adding to this challenge is evidence that these disorders typically respond better to psychotherapeutic treatment than to psychotropic medication (Mercer, Douglass, & Links, 2009; Olabi & Hall, 2010). Because research points to the therapeutic alliance as the primary predictor of positive client outcomes (Bachelor, 2013; Lambert & Barley, 2001; Strunk, Brotman, & DeRubeis, 2010), it is difficult for many within the mental health field to conceptualize that counseling is a more effective treatment modality. Aside from the therapeutic alliance, empirical evidence is limited as to the efficacy of different treatment approaches; thus, treatment decisions are typically arbitrary (Rosenbaum & Pollock, 2002).

These controversies fueled the DSM-5 Personality and Personality Disorders Work Group to present a new model for diagnosing personality disorders. The final model, discussed in more detail toward the end of this chapter, proposed a hybrid categorical and dimensional approach. The original proposal, a strictly dimensional model, scored trait dimensions as a way to reduce ambiguous boundaries. Only measuring deviations from normal functioning or "amplifications of normal personality profiles" (Paris, 2013, p. 157), this model was rejected. A second model by the work group was proposed, but this model was also rejected because the new approach minimized personality disorder categories and lacked empirical validation (Paris, 2013). As a result, only minor changes were made to the Personality Disorders chapter of the *DSM-5*, and a proposed model for diagnosing personality disorders is now included within Section III of the *DSM-5*. Before discussing this proposed model and future implications for counselors, we briefly review changes from *DSM-IV-TR* to *DSM-5*.

Major Changes From *DSM-IV-TR* to *DSM-5*

The major change to personality disorders within the *DSM-5* results from the collapse of the multiaxial system into one axis. As a result, personality disorders are not differentiated from other disorders as they have been in the past. The APA (2013d) reported the former distinction as artificial and stated that there are no basic differences between Axis I and Axis II disorders (also see Grohol, 2013). Furthermore, whereas a dimensional approach is applied to other disorders in the manual, personality disorders have not been changed to match this philosophical shift and are still represented categorically (Peluso, 2013). Other changes within these disorders involve subtle changes regarding culture. More predominantly featured in the *DSM-5* is emphasis on cultural factors. For example, antisocial personality disorder tends to be overdiagnosed among individuals of lower socioeconomic status. Acculturation problems may look diagnostically similar to avoidant personality disorder. Finally, high level of productivity and a strong focus on work is a cultural trend within some cultures and could potentially be characteristic of some obsessive-compulsive personality disorder. Including this information in the *DSM-5* can help counselors avoid misdiagnosis and allow for better representation of cultural issues that are not pathological (Peluso, 2013).

Essential Features

Personality disorders are marked by a significant cultural deviation in the pattern of actions and internal focus and require that the individual experience problems in at least two of four areas (APA, 2013a). These areas include a pattern of cognitive distortions as related to perceptions of self, others, and the external world; affective or emotional responses that can be intense, inappropriate, and vary widely in nature; intense difficulty with interpersonal interactions; and impulse control impairment.

Special Considerations

The patterns associated with personality disorders exist in nearly all aspects of clients' lives and vary little in the application to their life roles and relationships (APA, 2013a; Comer, 2013; Nietzel et al., 1998). The onset usually begins in adolescence or early adulthood and results in clinically significant distress and impairment in multiple areas of functioning (APA, 2013a). Furthermore, as with other disorders, the symptoms of personality disorders cannot be attributed to any other disorder or the effects of medication or a medical condition (APA, 2013a). It is important to note that the diagnosis must be given only when a stable, long-term pattern of these behaviors has been established. However, in terms of diagnosing, counselors will not typically be the primary mental health provider assigning a personality disorder diagnosis to a client.

Cultural Considerations

Because personality disorders represent a persistent, marked change from the client's cultural patterns and norms, it is imperative that counselors understand the client's culture, cultural origin, and cultural expectations, including customs, habits, religion, and political views. Additionally, gender is an important consideration in diagnosing, and counselors should carefully watch for gender bias (Durand & Barlow, 2010). For example, antisocial personality disorder is more prevalent in men than in women; however, borderline, histrionic, and dependent personality disorders tend to be diagnosed, perhaps overdiagnosed, more often in women than in men. Again, counselors are encouraged to diagnose in an ethical manner consistent with the *ACA Code of Ethics* (ACA, 2014).

Differential Diagnosis

Because personality disorders are lifelong, pervasive disorders rather than brief changes in personality, counselors need to ensure that the symptoms observed are not related to a change in personality related to substance use, medications, or another medical condition. Counselors should also note the overlap in symptoms among the personality disorders as well as significant comorbidity within this diagnostic class (Durand & Barlow, 2010). Within each disorder, we discuss the distinctive elements in detail to make differentiating these a bit easier.

301.0 Paranoid Personality Disorder (F60.0)

Essential Features

The defining characteristics of paranoid personality disorder include a mistrust and suspicion of other people and their motives that begin in early adulthood and persist across multiple aspects of the individual's life (APA, 2013a; Durand & Barlow, 2010). The mistrust must be manifested in at least four areas, including constant suspicion that others are planning to trick, harm, or exploit the individual; an inability to trust or believe in the loyalty of friends; and/or difficulty confiding in people because of fear that what is shared will be used against the individual. An individual with paranoid personality disorder may have a pervasive pattern of not forgiving others, perceive threats or insults in normal events or conversations, believe that others are engaging in assaults on his or her character and feel the need to attack in response, and chronically believe that his or her spouse or partner is unfaithful (APA, 2013a).

Special Considerations

It is important for counselors to ensure that the symptoms associated with paranoid personality disorder do not only occur during psychosis, a manic episode, or an episode of major depression with psychotic features and that the symptoms are not a result of another medical condition, medications, or substance use (APA, 2013a). Individuals with this disorder will have relationship difficulties and often seem to be argumentative, hostile, aloof, or cold toward others. Family and partner relationship difficulties are not uncommon, as individuals diagnosed with paranoid personality disorder are often extremely self-reliant, controlling, and suspicious. Furthermore, these individuals are not likely to seek treatment and, when they do, have even more difficulty engaging in a trusting relationship with a therapist (Durand & Barlow, 2010).

Cultural Considerations

Paranoid personality disorder occurs more in men than in women (Durand & Barlow, 2010), and it is estimated that about 4.4% of the population has this disorder (APA, 2013a). Symptoms of this disorder should not be confused with reactions related to the experience of disenfranchised or oppressed groups, such as minorities, immigrants, or refugees. Individuals with a family history of psychotic disorders or those who have unique experiences such as being incarcerated are more susceptible to being diagnosed with paranoid personality disorder (Durand & Barlow, 2010).

Note

Throughout this chapter, readers will notice that most personality disorders occur more frequently in men than in women. However, gender bias in diagnosing personality disorders is not uncommon (Durand & Barlow, 2010; Ford & Widiger, 1989). Although prevalence information regarding gender is important, counselors should carefully consider the client's diagnostic profile and watch for gender bias.

◆ ◆ ◆

Differential Diagnosis

Paranoid personality disorder should not be confused with the symptoms of psychotic disorders such as schizophrenia. This diagnosis should be given only if the symptoms occur before psychotic symptoms and continue after psychosis abates. If this occurs, paranoid personality disorders should be listed with the word *premorbid* following the diagnosis. It is important to note that there is a strong comorbidity among personality disorders, and counselors must carefully screen to ensure that another personality disorder, such as schizotypal, is not warranted (APA, 2013a; Durand & Barlow, 2010).

301.20 Schizoid Personality Disorder (F60.1)

Essential Features

Individuals with schizoid personality disorder have little to no interest in relationships, even family relationships (APA, 2013a; Durand & Barlow, 2010; Kosson et al., 2008). They may prefer to engage in activities by themselves, have few or no friends, rarely experience pleasure in activities, and may have little to no interest in sex or intimate relationships. They may have difficulties experiencing emotions or emotional reactions and appear cold or indifferent to others and to assessments of others, such as encouragement or criticism. The symptoms of this disorder should not occur exclusively during a psychotic episode such as those associated with schizophrenia, nor should they be better attributed to ASD (APA, 2013a). Finally, the symptoms of this disorder must impair the individual's functioning significantly for a diagnosis to be made.

Special Considerations

Appearing first in childhood, schizoid personality disorder often results in severe impairment in social, socioeconomic, and occupational functioning. Although it is estimated that 3.1% of the population has this disorder (APA, 2013a), these individuals will not typically seek treatment (Durand & Barlow, 2010; Martens, 2010). Furthermore, it can be argued that schizoid personality disorder receives the least attention of all the personality disorders, both clinically and empirically (Kosson et al., 2008).

In terms of treatment, Parpottas (2012) claimed that when this disorder is conceptualized from an attachment theory lens, CBT partnered with a psychodynamic perspective may be the best approach. Parpottas argued that the role of the counselor is crucial because individuals experiencing this disorder need a model for interpersonal relationships. Additionally, counselors should be aware that individuals with this disorder may experience brief psychotic episodes when under stress or duress (APA, 2013a).

Cultural Considerations

Relatively uncommon in clinical settings, schizoid personality disorder tends to occur more in men than in women (APA, 2013a). Cultural context is essential in the formation of peer relationship and social and behavioral characteristics. Therefore, counselors should carefully consider the client's cultural background when diagnosing schizoid personality disorder, because certain cultures emphasize defensive behaviors or detachment (Martens, 2010). Caldwell-Harris and Ayçiçegi (2006) researched autonomy and interdependence among individuals within individualist (i.e., Boston, Massachusetts) and collectivist (i.e.,

Istanbul, Turkey) cultures. The authors found that individuals who expressed personality characteristics outside their normative cultural group were at risk of psychiatric symptoms that correlated with symptoms of schizoid personality disorder. Of course, having personal attributes that are inconsistent with the values of society is not associated with psychiatric symptoms. However, these results do illustrate that counselors must be very careful, not only when diagnosing schizoid personality disorder but also when assessing clients for all types of personality dysfunction. Finally, special consideration should also be given to individuals who have changed cultures, such as immigrants, or who experience issues with acculturation (APA, 2013a).

Differential Diagnosis

When considering a diagnosis of schizoid personality disorder, counselors should be sure that the symptoms are not related to substance use, medications, or another medical condition such as those that affect the central nervous system (APA, 2013a). Moreover, this disorder should not be diagnosed when the symptoms only occur as a part of psychosis. If there is psychosis, schizoid symptoms should precede this and continue after the episode has resolved in order to be diagnosed. If this does occur, the diagnosis should be written with the word *premorbid* at the end. It is easy to confuse symptoms of other personality disorders and ASD with schizoid personality disorder (APA, 2013a). Careful screening over a period of time is crucial for an accurate diagnosis to be made.

301.22 Schizotypal Personality Disorder (F21)

Essential Features

Schizotypal personality disorder is pervasive and includes bizarre ideation and social constriction or avoidance (APA, 2013a; Paris, 2013). The symptoms of schizotypal personality disorder appear similar in many ways to schizophrenia. Some consider schizotypal personality disorder a milder, nonpsychotic form of schizophrenia; however, manifestations of this disorder do not typically include positive symptoms of hallucinations or delusions (Paris, 2013; Ripoll et al., 2013). Schizotypal personality disorder is characterized by discomfort with any type of close relationships, bizarre or distorted cognitions, and strange behaviors (Comer, 2013). This pattern, which often begins during early adulthood, may include sensations of an external presence, odd physical awareness, magical thinking, or the belief that one's powers may control the behavior of others (APA, 2013a; Comer, 2013; Paris, 2013). Individuals diagnosed with schizotypal personality disorder often think unrelated events pertain to them personally.

Individuals with schizotypal personality disorder exhibit paranoia, flat affect, and odd communication patterns such as loose associations, and they usually have an eccentric appearance (Comer, 2013; Nietzel et al., 1998; Ripoll et al., 2013). Although not formally considered a schizophrenia spectrum disorder, these disorders are actually cross-listed in the *DSM-5*. The primary reason is because of symptom similarity and because clients diagnosed with schizotypal personality disorder have the same biological markers as those with schizophrenia (Paris, 2013). However, because schizotypal personality disorder is not a precursor to schizophrenia, it has been retained in the Personality Disorders chapter of the *DSM-5*.

Individuals diagnosed with schizotypal personality disorder do not have many close friends and continue to be paranoid even when a close relationship does exist (APA, 2013a; Comer, 2013). For example, these individuals tend to appear socially anxious even around family. If symptoms of this disorder only occur as part of depression, bipolar, or schizophrenia disorders, then it is not a true schizotypal personality disorder. If it is diagnosed before the onset of schizophrenia, the word *premorbid* should follow the diagnosis (APA, 2013a). However, as stated previously, schizotypal personality disorder is not a precursor to schizophrenia (Paris, 2013).

Special Considerations

Schizotypal personality disorder occurs in about 3.9% in the general population (APA, 2013a), and individuals with it often present for treatment because of depression or anxiety (Comer, 2013; Nietzel et al., 1998). Because they have difficulty with interpersonal relationships and have few friends, they may feel intensely lonely. Individuals with schizotypal personality disorder are often unemployed or underemployed; have challenges living independently; and experience issues with working memory, attentiveness, inhibition, and abstract thought processing (McClure, Harvey, Bowie, Iacoviello, & Siever, 2013). Comorbidity is not unusual; there is considerable overlap with other personality disorders (APA, 2013a; Rosenbaum & Pollock, 2002), and more than half of the individuals diagnosed with this disorder have also experienced a major depressive episode (Comer, 2013). Whereas antipsychotic medication has been given in low doses with some success, CBT is frequently used to address unusual or inappropriate thoughts and behaviors (Comer, 2013).

Cultural Considerations

Beliefs or behaviors that appear bizarre or outside the norm should always be evaluated within the context of the individual's cultural and religious beliefs. Counselors must fully understand the impact of family, religion, and culture on behavior before making this diagnosis. For example, speaking in tongues, belief in the afterlife, and phenomenon such as voodoo are not considered schizotypal symptoms if these beliefs and behaviors are within the client's cultural context (Peluso, 2013). As with most Cluster A personality disorders, there is evidence that this disorder occurs more in men than in women (APA, 2013a). Finally, individuals who have family members with a history of schizophrenia are more likely to be diagnosed with schizotypal personality disorder (Durand & Barlow, 2010).

Differential Diagnosis

Schizotypal personality disorder should not be diagnosed if the symptoms can be better explained by use of substances or medications or by a medical condition (APA, 2013a). Whereas some individuals with schizotypal personality disorder experience brief moments of psychosis when under stress, this personality disorder should not be confused with delusional, psychotic, depressive, or bipolar disorders. Counselors should look for symptoms that are pervasive and begin before or continue after other types of episodes, such as mania and psychosis. In children, symptoms of a communication disorder or ASD may appear similar to schizotypal personality disorder (APA, 2013a). A thorough assessment over a period of time is necessary to ensure an accurate diagnosis is made.

301.7 Antisocial Personality Disorder (F60.2)

Essential Features

Often referred to as "psychopathy," "sociopathy," or "dissocial" personality disorder (APA, 2013a, p. 659), antisocial personality disorder is characterized by a complete disregard for the feelings, rights, and concerns of others, often resulting in harm to self or others and/or incarceration (Comer, 2013). Individuals with this disorder will have at least three of the following symptoms: illegal behaviors, chronic lying, a lack of regard for personal or others' safety, aggressive behavior frequently leading to fights, a pattern of impulsivity and lack of forethought, problems working and/or meeting financial responsibilities, and chronic indifference to the feelings of others without regret or remorse (APA, 2013a; Comer, 2013; Durand & Barlow, 2010; Frances, 2013). Individuals diagnosed with antisocial personality disorder often receive pleasure from their destructive behavior, such as feeling pleasure when deceiving others. These symptoms cannot be attributed to substance use, another medical condition, or medication use, nor can they occur solely during a psychotic or manic episode. Behaviors must occur before 18 years of age and must be preceded by symptoms of conduct disorder occurring before age 15 (APA, 2013a). Conduct disorder with onset in childhood is nearly a universal occurrence (Paris, 2013).

Special Considerations

Antisocial personality disorder is characterized by deceitfulness, manipulation, anger, irresponsibility, and reckless decision making followed by hazardous behavior (Paris, 2013). Counselors often find that individuals with antisocial personality disorder are often charming, self-assured, and manipulative, particularly in close personal or sexual relationships (Durand & Barlow, 2010). Because of the high rates of criminal activity and incarceration associated with antisocial personality disorder, most of the research on this disorder is conducted on inmates, former inmates, or parolees (Frances, 2013). It is estimated that as many as 30% of those incarcerated have antisocial personality disorders (Comer, 2013). Because of this, and also because of the lack of remorse associated with this disorder, it is unlikely that counselors will see these individuals present voluntarily; most counselors will work with these individuals as a result of court mandate. Furthermore, rates of alcohol and drug use can be very high in this population (Comer, 2013). In general, counseling and therapeutic interventions for this disorder are extremely challenging, largely because these individuals do not see the need to change (Comer, 2013; Paris, 2013). Motivational interviewing or cognitive treatments have been used to increase awareness of behavioral impact. Finally, counselors need to be cognizant of the propensity for violence and suicide in this population and conduct risk and suicide assessments as needed (Frances, 2013).

Cultural Considerations

Although general population estimates for this disorder range from 0.2% to 3.3%, rates are consistently much higher in the male population than in the female population, perhaps as high as four to one (APA, 2013a; Comer, 2013). These rates tend to increase in urban populations and with lower socioeconomic status and sociocultural variables. Although the diagnosis cannot be made prior to age 18, symptoms seem to decrease in later life, with criminal activity in particular decreasing after the age of 40 (APA, 2013a; Comer, 2013; Frances, 2013; Paris, 2013).

Differential Diagnosis

Substance use disorder can be difficult to differentiate from antisocial personality disorder, but symptoms of antisocial personality disorder should begin in younger years, often preceding the substance use (APA, 2013a). When these are co-occurring, they can be diagnosed simultaneously. Symptoms of antisocial personality disorder must occur prior to or outside of a manic or psychotic episode for this diagnosis to be given. There may be overlap with the symptoms of other personality disorders, particularly other Cluster B personality disorders. Antisocial personality disorder can be differentiated by the lack of empathy, aggression, impulsivity, and manipulation of others purely for personal gains (Comer, 2013; Frances, 2013). However, if criteria are met for more than one disorder, counselors may diagnose all applicable disorders (APA, 2013a). Finally, it is important to note the difference between committing a crime and having antisocial personality disorder. Criminal behavior is only one symptom of this disorder, and at least three other symptoms must be met, in addition to age requirements, to make this diagnosis.

301.83 Borderline Personality Disorder (F60.3)

Essential Features

First noted in the *DSM-III* (APA, 1980), individuals with borderline personality disorder "lack a sense of self and engage in intense and unstable relationships" (Montes, 2013, p. 34). This pervasive pattern of instability begins in early adulthood and can be observed through the individual's functioning (Durand & Barlow, 2010; Frances, 2013). At least five out of nine symptoms must be present, and the symptoms can include chronic fear, real or imagined, of impending abandonment by loved ones, friends, or caregivers; intense relationships that vary between idealization of and disappointment in the other person; and unstable or unsure identity patterns, as evidenced by unexpected or sudden changes in career, sense of self, values, or sexual identity (APA, 2013a). These individuals may be impulsive in two, potentially self-damaging, areas, including gambling, sex, spending, or substance abuse. They may frequently threaten and attempt suicide, make gestures indicating suicidal ideation, or engage in self-injurious behaviors such as cutting or burning (Comer, 2013; Durand & Barlow, 2010; Grohol, 2007). Mood instability is not uncommon and can be characterized by change of mood within only a few hours. Symptoms may also include chronic feelings of emptiness, inappropriate expressions of anger including extremely angry or sarcastic outbursts, and even physical aggression and fights. Furthermore, dissociation, depersonalization, and paranoid ideation can occur when the individual is under stress (APA, 2013a; Comer, 2013; Grohol, 2007).

Special Considerations

Individuals with borderline personality disorder frequently present for outpatient services, with estimates at 10% to 20% of those seen in clinics (Biskin, 2013). Counselors need to be aware that there are severe consequences for an individual who has this disorder, including emotional, financial, and interpersonal consequences for the individual and family (Crowell, Beauchaine, & Linehan, 2009). Furthermore, this disorder is related to high rates of suicide, attempted suicide, violence, self-mutilation, and disability (APA, 2013a; Comer, 2013; Frances, 2013). Estimates suggest that 75% of these individuals attempt suicide at least one time (Comer, 2013), and 8% to 10% complete suicides (APA, 2013a; Frances, 2013). As a result, counselors must be vigilant to assess symptoms of this disorder and suicidality in these clients. Counseling these clients can be difficult and emotionally draining because of the lack of boundaries, constant fear of abandonment, and ever-changing emotions (Comer, 2013). Therefore, it is important for counselors working with these clients to practice self-care, be alert to the signs of professional impairment, and engage in services only within the boundaries of their competence, per the *ACA Code of Ethics* (ACA, 2014).

Treatment options for individuals with borderline personality disorder have improved greatly in the past 2 decades (Biskin, 2013). Based on the belief that internal factors (e.g., trouble with emotional regulation caused by neurotransmitter systems) and external factors (e.g., parental abandonment; physical or sexual abuse) combine to explain this disorder, the Biosocial Development Model, developed originally by Marsha Linehan, is frequently used to understand the etiology of this disorder (Comer, 2013; Crowell et al., 2009). Furthermore, dialectical behavior therapy (DBT), based on CBT, has been used with individuals with borderline personality disorder and has documented success (Comer, 2013). Early intervention is emphasized in both the Biosocial Development Model and DBT.

Cultural Considerations

Borderline personality disorder is diagnosed much more frequently in women than in men, with almost 75% of these individuals being female (APA, 2013a). It is important to note that prior to adulthood, symptoms that could be typical teenage behavior can be confused with symptoms of this disorder. The patterns associated with this disorder have been noted in various cultures worldwide (APA, 2013a).

Differential Diagnosis

A diagnosis of borderline personality disorder should not be given if the symptoms occur as a result of another medical condition, substance use, or medication use. Furthermore, if the symptoms occur only during a manic or depressive episode, borderline personality disorder, which is a pervasive pattern of lifelong symptoms, should not be given (APA, 2013a). This disorder often runs concomitant with depressive, bipolar, and some other personality disorders. It is important to ensure that symptoms of this disorder either occur prior to or continue after symptoms of other disorders have subsided. Counselors should be especially cognizant of the high rate of misdiagnoses (i.e., depressive and bipolar disorders) and, as a result, incorrect treatment for individuals with borderline personality disorder (Paris, 2013). Finally, there is significant overlap in the symptoms of this personality disorder and other personality disorders (APA, 2013a). Counselors should remember that borderline personality disorder is uniquely characterized by co-occurring feelings of emptiness, self-destructiveness, and unstable personal relationships.

301.50 Histrionic Personality Disorder (F60.4)

Essential Features

As with all personality disorder, histrionic personality disorder, also referred to as hysterical personality, is pervasive, with lifelong patterns of deviant behavior. Individuals with this disorder will present as attention seeking and excessively emotional (Durand & Barlow, 2010), and they may desperately seek attention through physical appearance, such as dressing in eye-catching colors, grandiose gestures and excessively impressionistic speech, and inappropriate seductive or sexual behaviors (Comer, 2013; Durand & Barlow, 2010). They often act in a theatrical manner (*histrionic* means "theatrical in manner"), as if they are on stage and everyone is watching, and become extremely uncomfortable, even sad or upset, when they are not the center of attention (Comer, 2013; Durand & Barlow, 2010). Their often shallowly expressed emotions shift rapidly, and they are highly suggestible and influenced easily by others. Individuals with this disorder tend to see relationships as more intimate than they are, exchange long-term relationships for more exciting new ones, and seek excitement in romantic partners who may not treat them well (APA, 2013a; Comer, 2013).

Special Considerations

Individuals with histrionic personality disorder tend to embarrass and alienate their friends through their excessive behaviors, have difficulty maintaining long-term romantic relationships, and are more likely to seek treatment than individuals with other personality disorders (Comer, 2013). Although actual suicide risk is not known, these individuals may use suicidal ideation or gestures as part of attention-seeking or manipulative behaviors. Furthermore, counselors may find these clients require a lot of patience because they may act in a sexually seductive manner or become demanding or claim to experience change to gain attention or make the counselor happy (Comer, 2013; Durand & Barlow, 2010). CBT and psychodynamic therapy have been used with individuals who have histrionic personality disorder to encourage insight, independence, and internal satisfaction, with some reported success. For example, clients diagnosed with this disorder tend to view the world in terms of black and white (Durand & Barlow, 2010). Cognitive therapies can help individuals recognize this polarized thinking and take action to refute these self-statements.

Cultural Considerations

Histrionic personality disorder occurs in an estimated 2% to 3% of the population (Comer, 2013). It may be more prevalent in women than in men, but research on this has been equivocal (APA, 2013a; Comer, 2013). Furthermore, culture must be considered when assessing for this disorder. The disorder may be more prevalent in cultures that are accepting of overt sexuality or overdramatization (Comer, 2013; Durand & Barlow, 2010). It is important to note that the symptoms must be pervasive and result in clinically significant functional impairment (APA, 2013a).

Differential Diagnosis

Histrionic personality disorder should not be diagnosed when the symptoms can be attributed to substance use, medications, or another medical condition resulting in personality change (APA, 2013a). Also, there is considerable overlap with other personality disorders, such as narcissistic, borderline, and dependent personality disorders (Comer, 2013; Durand & Barlow, 2010; Paris, 2013). Histrionic personality disorder can be distinguished by the exaggerated emotions and exaggerated intimacy in relationships, by the flamboyant dress and behavior to gain or keep attention, and willingness to be viewed as dependent or fragile to get attention (APA, 2013a).

Note

Because of limited empirical evidence, comorbidity with other personality disorders, and a lack of clinical utility, histrionic personality disorder was proposed to be eliminated from the *DSM-5*. This proposal was rejected but certainly points to a shift counselors are likely to see in the future regarding diagnostic classifications of personality.

◆ ◆ ◆

301.81 Narcissistic Personality Disorder (F60.81)

Essential Features

Initially introduced in the *DSM-III*, narcissistic personality disorder's key components are grandiosity, a desperate need for acknowledgment and admiration of others, and a lack of empathy (Comer, 2013; Nietzel et al., 1998). Individuals with narcissistic personality disorder may also exhibit exaggerated self-importance, as evidenced by an expectation that others will acknowledge them as superior. They may spend time thinking about or reinforcing their belief in personal unlimited success, beauty, or love. Often requiring excessive praise and acknowledgment, these individuals may also hold the firm belief that they are special and their problems are unique to them. They may expect that others will do what they want or comply with their desires automatically, and they often exploit people to get what they want. They may be arrogant, jealous, or believe others are jealous of them, and they will lack empathy, assuming that others should be concerned only for their well-being (APA, 2013a; Comer, 2013).

Special Considerations

Narcissism originates from the Greek word *narkissos* or *Narcissus*, the latter being the name of a man so vain he died while attempting to capture his reflection (Comer, 2013; Nietzel et al., 1998). Individuals with narcissistic personality disorder are "obsessed with overblown notions of self-worth" (Montes, 2013, p. 34), so much so that they are unable to understand others' points of view or empathize with them. Because of this high self-esteem, they may also be vulnerable to narcissistic injury from criticism or lack of success, sometimes resulting in severe disappointment and depression (APA, 2013a; Comer, 2013). These individuals usually come to counseling for depression or another problem not related to the personality disorder.

For counselors, individuals with narcissistic personality disorder can be particularly difficult to treat (Paris, 2013). These clients will not likely see the need to change, they may look down on the counselor as not intelligent enough to help, or they may attempt to manipulate the counselor. They will have difficulty receiving feedback, acknowledging any weaknesses, or caring about the consequences of their behaviors on others (Comer, 2013). Approaches most often used include CBT and psychodynamic therapy, but there is little research to support success for either of these. Diamond and Meehan (2013) argued for the use of transference-focused psychotherapy, a therapeutic approach that integrates object relations theory with attachment theory, an evidence-based treatment for narcissistic personality disorder.

Cultural Considerations

Although estimates for prevalence for narcissistic personality disorder range from around 1% (Comer, 2013) to as high as 6.2% (APA, 2013a), most agree that about 50% to 75% of those with this disorder are men. Studies have indicated an increase in narcissistic traits, such as self-esteem and extraversion, within the United States in the last 13 years (Twenge & Foster, 2010). Although future research needs to investigate the reason for this generational increase, Twenge and Foster (2010) posited that school programs that focus on increasing self-esteem (e.g., "I Am Special" programs) may be a contributing factor. Moreover, Stinson et al. (2008) conducted an epidemiological study on narcissistic personality disorder that revealed a 3.2% lifetime prevalence of this disorder in adults over 65 years of age. As age decreased, lifetime prevalence increased: 5.6% of people age 45 to 64 years, 7.1% of those age 30 to 44 years, and 9.4% of those age 20 to 29 years. Many researchers claim the reason for this change could potentially be an increased focus on individualism within Western society (Roberts & Helson, 1997; Twenge, 2001; Twenge & Foster, 2010).

Differential Diagnosis

A narcissistic personality disorder diagnosis should not be given when persistent substance abuse better accounts for the symptoms (APA, 2013a). Furthermore, grandiosity can be part of mania or hypomania, but symptoms of narcissistic personality disorder will be pervasive and lifelong. Finally, there is overlap in the symptoms of narcissistic personality disorder and other personality disorders. Grandiosity and a stable sense of self are the most distinguishing features of this disorder. Also, those with narcissistic personality disorder need the admiring attention and expect the appreciation of others (APA, 2013a).

301.82 Avoidant Personality Disorder (F60.6)

Essential Features

The hallmark of avoidant personality disorder is persistent and overwhelming fear of being inadequate, negatively evaluated, and rejected, resulting in discomfort in social situations and restriction of interactions with others (APA, 2013a; Comer, 2013; Durand & Barlow, 2010). Symptoms will be noticed in early adulthood and may include fear of criticism or rejection that results in avoidance of work or social activities that involve interpersonal interactions, unwillingness to become involved in a relationship without guarantee of acceptance, and holding back in close or sexual relationships because of fear. These individuals will experience chronic rumination of the thoughts of social rejection and will not fully engage in new relationships because they feel inadequate. They see themselves as fundamentally socially inadequate, inferior, or undesirable and will be reluctant to take risks or try new things for fear of embarrassment (APA, 2013a; Comer, 2013).

Special Considerations

Often referred to as shy or isolated, individuals with avoidant personality disorder are so fearful of criticism or rejection that at times they overly agree with or praise others (APA, 2013a; Durand & Barlow, 2010; Frances, 2013). They frequently pass up social and work engagements or even promotions for fear of being perceived negatively. Some may develop a detailed inner fantasy world and have a strong imagination. When these individuals come in for counseling, they are often looking for acceptance, but they may soon begin avoiding counseling sessions as well. Building trust is important with these individuals. Various treatments have been tried, including CBT, psychodynamic therapy, behavioral therapy, and group therapy, to reinforce skills built (Comer, 2013).

Cultural Considerations

Prevalence of avoidant personality disorder is around 2.4% for the general population, and this disorder seems to occur equally in men and women (APA, 2013a). The perception of avoiding or avoidance will vary in different cultures, so counselors need to consider the individual's culture and acculturation status when considering this diagnosis (Peluso, 2013). As with other personality disorders (e.g., schizoid personality disorder) in which the client is inhibited in social interactions, counselors should pay close attention to whether the client's normative culture is geared toward collectivism (Caldwell-Harris & Ayçiçegi, 2006). A collectivist culture may incite an extreme fear of being rejected by others and personal reticence in clients with this disorder, which might adversely affect them in personal, occupational, or other important areas of functioning.

Differential Diagnosis

The symptoms of social anxiety disorder and avoidant personality disorder can be difficult to differentiate. Counselors need to keep in mind that with avoidant personality disorder, the individual actively avoids social relationships, whereas with social anxiety disorder, the individual avoids the social setting (Comer, 2013). Furthermore, personality disorders, by definition, are pervasive and lifelong.

Counselors also may be confused with the overlap in the symptoms of many personality disorders. Avoidant personality disorder can be distinguished by the avoidance of rejection and humiliation and fear of being embarrassed or perceived as inadequate, as opposed to schizoid personality disorder in which the person is not interested in personal relationships (Durand & Barlow, 2010). Moreover, avoidant personality disorder should not be diagnosed when substance use, medication, or another medical condition can account for the personality change (APA, 2013a).

301.6 Dependent Personality Disorder (F60.7)

Essential Features

Differing from avoidant personality disorder, individuals with dependent personality disorder experience a deep need to be taken care of and an overwhelming fear of being separated from the perceived caretaker (Comer, 2013; Durand & Barlow, 2010; Nietzel et al., 1998). As a result, these individuals may become submissive, needy, and clingy in relationships (Comer, 2013). They struggle with daily decisions and require a lot of reassurance before making any decision and may look to another to take responsibility for daily living decisions. Furthermore, these individuals will not express disagreements and will avoid initiating or completing projects or tasks independently largely because of lack of self-confidence. Individuals with dependent personality disorder will tolerate extreme conditions, such as physical and sexual abuse, and may go great lengths to gain and keep the support of others, even engaging in activities that they do not enjoy. They feel uncomfortable being on their own and, believing that they cannot take care of themselves, will quickly and indiscriminately find another relationship if a close or intimate relationship ends (APA, 2013a).

Special Considerations

One of the most commonly diagnosed personality disorders in mental health clinics (Grant et al., 2004; Newton-Howes et al., 2010), dependent personality disorder is difficult to treat because individuals with this disorder tend to put the responsibility for treatment and outcomes on the counselor (Comer, 2013). Because individuals with dependent personality disorder tend to be submissive and obedient, they may comply with therapy but have no true self-awareness. Furthermore, they may easily become dependent on the counselor (Durand & Barlow, 2010). Various therapeutic treatments have been tried, including psychodynamic, cognitive-behavior, behavioral, and assertiveness training, with some success (Comer, 2013). Counselors need to focus on developing the client's state of independence, such as nurturing problem-solving skills and confidence, and not contribute to the problem by allowing the client to become overly dependent on the counselor.

Cultural Considerations

Some cultures place an emphasis on politeness and passivity, especially for certain age groups (Caldwell-Harris & Ayçiçegi, 2006). Therefore, it is particularly important to consider culture, gender, and age when considering a diagnosis of dependent personality disorder. For example, as discussed with avoidant personality disorder, many individualistic cultures encourage independence, self-service, and confidence. Almost dropped from the *DSM-5*, the diagnostic criteria of this disorder were seen by some mental health professionals as too narrowly geared toward sociocentric males and to pathologize behaviors that are outside this cultural norm (Boeree, 2007). It is noteworthy that although there may be little difference in prevalence rates for men and women, at just around 2% of the population, women are diagnosed with this disorder much more frequently (APA, 2013a; Comer, 2013). As with other disorders described in this chapter, the perception of dependence as pathological will vary in different cultures. Counselors need to consider the client's culture and acculturation status when considering a diagnosis of dependent personality disorder (Peluso, 2013).

Differential Diagnosis

Dependent personality disorder should not be diagnosed if the personality change can be related to substance use, another medical condition, or medications. As with other personality disorders, there are overlaps in symptoms and diagnostic criteria. Counselors can differentiate dependent personality disorder from other personality disorders by the distinguishing characteristics of submissiveness, obedience, clingy behavior, and a desire to maintain a relationship at any cost or replace a lost relationship very quickly (APA, 2013a).

301.4 Obsessive-Compulsive Personality Disorder (F60.5)

Essential Features

Individuals with obsessive-compulsive personality disorder have an all-consuming preoccupation with rules and orderliness, getting "it" perfect, perseveration, and interpersonal and mental control (Comer, 2013; Durand & Barlow, 2010; Paris, 2013). Beginning in early adulthood, compulsions prohibit these individuals from being flexible, productive, and open to new experiences. Individuals with this disorder are unable to see the "big picture," focusing so much on details that they exclude the actual goal of the activity. Decision making can be an arduous, time-consuming process because of rigid perfectionism. These individuals will have difficulty completing projects because they cannot meet their own high standards. Personal or leisure activities, including friendships, may go unattended because the individual is so focused on work or the project. Furthermore, individuals with obsessive-compulsive personality disorder are often reluctant to delegate tasks because others may not live up to their standards. Ideas of right and wrong (i.e., ethics or morality) are inflexible, and others may characterize these individuals as stubborn or rigid (i.e., being stingy with time, money, or personal items; APA, 2013a; Comer, 2013).

Special Considerations

Individuals with obsessive-compulsive personality disorder rarely seek treatment. Similar to those with paranoid personality disorder and schizoid personality disorder, these individuals are not aware that they have a problem and see no reason to change (Comer, 2013; Durand & Barlow, 2010). If they do present for treatment, symptoms of depression or anxiety are often the client's primary reason for seeking counseling. As with many other personality disorders, psychodynamic therapy or CBT is often used to treat these individuals (Comer, 2013). Rational emotive behavior therapy may be appropriate to address the dichotomous thinking and perfectionism that tend to be pervasive in this personality disorder. Despite the name of the disorder, obsessive-compulsive personality disorder is entirely separate from OCD. Also, unlike OCD, there is very limited research and empirical validation for this disorder. Not surprisingly, this disorder was proposed for elimination from the *DSM-5*, so it is likely counselors will not see this disorder in future iterations of the *DSM*.

Cultural Considerations

As with other personality disorders, cultural context must be considered. Some cultures place more value on work and work-related activities, and this should be considered before a diagnosis is given. Some research has indicated a genetic predisposition for this disorder (McKeon & Murray, 1987; Stone, 1993), but most of this has been disregarded for a discussion of individuals who have specific personality traits, such as favoring structure and perfectionism, as more likely to be diagnosed with this disorder (Durand & Barlow, 2010). Finally, twice as many men are diagnosed with obsessive-compulsive personality disorder as women (APA, 2013a).

Differential Diagnosis

Obsessive-compulsive personality disorder should not be diagnosed when long-term substance use, medications, or another medical condition could better account for the personality change (APA, 2013a). As with other personality disorders, there is a considerable overlap in symptoms, especially with Cluster C personality disorders (e.g., avoidant, dependent, and obsessive-compulsive personality disorders). The key features that differentiate this disorder are the extreme perfectionism, inflexible rules, miserly spending habits, and self-criticism not typically found within other personality disorders (APA, 2013a). Counselors are cautioned at confusing this disorder with OCD, which can be differentiated by a lack of obsessive thoughts and the associated compulsive behaviors associated with OCD (Durand & Barlow, 2010). Whereas some symptoms are similar, OCD presents with true obsessions and compulsions. Furthermore, there is an overlap in symptoms with hoarding disorder. When distinguishing between these disorders, counselors need to remember that obsessive-compulsive personality disorder includes a pervasive pattern of lifelong rigidity that is not present with hoarding disorder (APA, 2013a).

Summary

We have outlined personality disorders within the current *DSM-5* that, because all alternative proposals were rejected, are nearly identical to the personality disorders found within the *DSM-IV-TR*. In the following section, we detail an alternative model for diagnosing personality disorders. Although this alternative model has not officially been integrated into the *DSM-5*, it can be found in Section III, Emerging Measures and Models, of the *DSM-5*. Developed by APA for the purpose of providing empirical support for the proposed changes and increasing clinical utility through training and familiarization (Bornstein, 2011), this model has been questioned because of problems with clinical utility and a lack of empirical validation, especially in relation to eliminating four personality disorders from diagnostic nosology (Bornstein, 2011). However, we feel it is important to orient counselors to this alternative model and to discuss the philosophy behind these modifications, varying perspectives of these changes, and implications for counseling professionals who diagnose and work with personality disorders.

Because of controversy surrounding the alternative model, it is our opinion that this proposed approach will change—maybe significantly—before being published within the diagnostic section of the next *DSM*. However, as we highlight in the final chapter of this *Learning Companion*, it is essential for counselors to become involved in future modifications to diagnostic nomenclature for mental health professionals. Without understanding the historical context, philosophy, and research (or lack thereof) behind changes to the

DSM, counselors will be unable to make informed decisions and advocate for appropriate modifications to diagnostic nomenclature. Whether the topic be the *ICD* or the *DSM*, counselors need to have a clear, informed voice in every one of these discussions.

Alternative Model for Diagnosing Personality Disorders

In 1999, APA began working with the NIMH, the WHO's Division of Mental Health, and the World Psychiatric Association on a research agenda for the *DSM-5*. One of the identified priorities in this research agenda was personality and relational disorders (see Kupfer, First, & Regier, 2002, for the full *DSM-5* research agenda). In 2007, the DSM-5 Task Force named Andrew E. Skodol, MD, as chair and John M. Oldham, MD, as co-chair of the Personality and Personality Disorders Work Group. The primary aims of this work group were to move away from categorical assessment, eliminate personality disorder comorbidity, reduce within-disorder heterogeneity, and increase clinical utility. Skodol and Bender (2009) stated,

> The limitations of *DSM* categorical conceptualizations of personality disorders are well known: excessive co-occurrence among disorders, extreme heterogeneity among patients receiving the same diagnosis, arbitrary diagnostic thresholds for the boundaries between pathological and "normal" personality functioning, and inadequate coverage of personality psychopathology such that the diagnosis of personality disorder not otherwise specified (PDNOS) is the most common. (p. 388)

This work group spent nearly 6 years developing (and redeveloping) an alternative model for diagnosing personality disorders (Skodol & Bender, 2009). During this time, an extensive review of the personality and personality disorders literature was conducted by work group members and advisors (APA, 2013a; Bornstein, 2011; Peluso, 2013). Findings revealed that paranoid, schizoid, and histrionic personality disorders lacked significant clinical utility and that only three disorders—antisocial, borderline, and schizotypal—had empirical evidence of validity and clinical utility (Skodol & Bender, 2009). There was also considerable overlap or comorbidity for all 10 personality disorders (Bornstein, 2011). Other issues discussed by the work group included philosophical challenges to the current categorical system, not only for personality disorders but for all disorders in the *DSM* (Brown & Barlow, 2005; Demjaha et al., 2009; First, 2010a; Kraemer, 2007; Paris, 2013). Overuse of personality disorder NOS led researchers Pagan et al. (2005) to state,

> The manner in which the *DSM* classifies [personality disorders] is not optimal. Some variation of a hierarchical model or a dimensional model of personality pathology may be more useful for documenting and conceptualizing the problems and characteristics of personality pathology. (p. 688)

Coined "the poster child" for dimensional assessment, the DSM Task Force and the associated Personality and Personality Disorders Work Group anticipated the creation of a purely dimensional assessment of personality. This was based on the premise that personality dysfunction was mostly a range of trait variation, with normal personality functioning on one end and abnormal personality functioning on the other. Paris (2013) explained,

> A dimensional approach sees personality disorders as dysfunctional amplifications of normal personality profiles. It assumes that there is no fundamental difference between normal and abnormal personality, but a continuum between trait variation and [personality disorders] that can be seen in both community and clinical populations. (p. 157)

A purely dimensional model, a radical change from the current diagnostic structure, was rejected by a majority of the work group and met with significant political opposition (Paris, 2013; Peluso, 2013). After years of deliberation, during which two work group members resigned, an alternative approach was created that introduced a hybrid dimensional–categorical model. This model both assesses symptoms and characterizes five broad areas of personality dysfunction. As opposed to 10 separate diagnostic criteria, this proposed model identifies five personality types with a specific pattern of impairments and traits. In the end, however, this alternative model was rejected by the APA Board of Trustees, "to preserve continuity with current clinical practice, while also introducing a new approach that aims to address numerous shortcoming of the current approach to personality disorders" (APA, 2013a, p. 761).

The reasons for rejection can be summarized into two basic concepts: lack of clinical utility and lack of empirical evidence. The model was difficult for clinicians to use, requiring training most mental health professionals did not possess (Paris, 2013). Additionally, deemed inappropriate for clinical use by the DSM-5 Scientific Advisory Committee, the model significantly lacked empirical validity. Therefore, instead of including this new model in Section II under diagnostic criteria, readers can find the Alternative *DSM-5* Model for Personality Disorders chapter in Section III, Emerging Measures and Models, on pages 761–781 of the *DSM-5*.

The Proposed Model

The alternative model proposes diagnosis of personality disorders as a three-step process. First, counselors must assess elements of personality functioning toward *self* (specifically evaluating identity and self direction) and *interpersonal functioning* (specifically evaluating empathy and intimacy; APA, 2013a). Second, counselors must assess 25 pathological personality traits, grouped into five broad areas: negative affectivity, detachment, antagonism, disinhibition, and psychoticism. Finally, using the information gathered from assessment of personality functioning (Step 1) and pathological personality traits (Step 2), counselors will identify one of six specific personality disorders: antisocial, avoidant, borderline, narcissistic, obsessive-compulsive, or schizotypal personality disorder. For individuals who do not fit into one of these six specific personality disorder, a personality disorder–trait specific (PD-TS) diagnosis may be selected. Although many would consider Step 2, assessing pathological personality traits using a pathological trait taxonomy, a categorical diagnosis, Step 3 is the "categorical" part of the alternative model because counselors will select a specific personality disorder. These six specific personality disorders and PD-TS contain diagnostic criteria relevant to the level of personality functioning and pathological personality traits inherent to the typical features of the specific disorder. Personality functioning (Step 1) can be measured by the Level of Personality Functioning Scale, found on pages 775–778 of the *DSM-5*. Likewise, the five personality disorder trait domains and 25 facets can be found on pages 779–781 of the *DSM-5*.

Counselors will also need to ensure that patterns in personality functioning are pervasive, meaning they occur in multiple contexts, and are stable over time. APA (2013a) emphasized that personality disorders are chronic conditions, beginning almost universally in adolescence. Of course, counselors should not be polarized in their thinking about personality functioning. These dysfunctions are repeated patterns that do not change, but there is some variability in presentation even within the same individual. APA (2013a) stated,

> Impairments in personality functioning and pathological personality traits are *relatively* pervasive across a range of personal and social contexts. . . . The term *relatively* reflects the fact that all except the most extremely pathological personalities show some degree of adaptability. The pattern in personality disorders is maladaptive and relatively inflexible, which leads to disabilities in social, occupational, or other important pursuits, as individuals are unable to modify their thinking or behavior, even in the face of evidence that their current approach is not working. (p. 763)

Finally, as with most disorders in the *DSM-5*, symptoms may not be better explained by another mental disorder, use of a substance, existence of another medical condition, or be due to the individual's developmental stage (APA, 2013a).

Level of Personality Functioning

The first element of personality functioning, *self*, is made up of two factors: identity and self-direction (APA, 2013a). *Identity* is the ability to experience oneself as a unique individual with clear boundaries. Stability of self-esteem and the ability to emotionally regulate oneself are essential. Clients who would have difficulty in this area are those who are overly dependent on others, have low self-esteem, are overtly egocentric, or vacillate between emotional extremes. *Self-direction* is related to motivation; one's ability to pursue meaningful short- and long-term goals; possession of a standard in which one bases one's behaviors (i.e., a moral compass); and the ability for interpersonal reflection (i.e., being able to assess oneself both accurately and productively). Clients who would have difficulty in this area of personality functioning would have extremely high, potentially unrealistic or unstable goals; fail to conform to ethical behavior; have legal problems; or have an inflated sense of morality (APA, 2013a).

Interpersonal functioning, the second element of personality functioning, is also made up of two factors: empathy and intimacy (APA, 2013a). *Empathy* is the ability to appreciate the experience of others, to accept others' views, and to acknowledge that one's behavior can adversely affect others. Clients who would have difficulty in this area of personality functioning are those who lack concern for others or are deceitful, egocentric, or manipulative. *Intimacy* is related to one's ability to form a genuine relationship with another human being. Having a desire for closeness and deep and enduring relationships in one's life is characteristic of someone who possesses intimacy. Clients who would have difficulty in this area of personality functioning are those who fear closeness with others; worry that they will be embarrassed or mocked by others; or tend to control, deceive, or coerce others as opposed to having genuine relationships.

To quantify all the elements, counselors will use the Level of Personality Functioning Scale (see pages 775–778 of the *DSM-5*). This scale uses a Likert-type scale consisting of four choices, ranging from 0 (*little to no impairment*) to 3 (*severe impairment*). APA (2013a) justifies this dimensional scale by claiming that personality, although fluid and unique to each individual, generally allows for appropriate patterns of familial, social, and occupational functioning. Although personality is complex, APA claims that most individuals' personality allows for meaningful relationships; appropriate levels of intimacy; a respect for boundaries and social norms, including laws and moral guidelines; and a care for the well-being of others. Conversely, APA also claims that maladaptive personality functioning contributes to personality pathology that inhibits not only personal relationships but also one's ability to conform to societal standards, perform accurate self-appraisal, and experience empathy for others. APA (2013a) states,

> Like most human tendencies, personality functioning is distributed on a continuum. Central to functioning and adaptation are individuals' characteristic ways of thinking about and understanding themselves and their interactions with others. An optimally functioning individual has a complex, fully elaborated, and well-integrated psychological world that includes a mostly positive, volitional, and adaptive self-concept. . . . At the opposite end of the continuum, an individual with severe personality pathology has an impoverished, disorganized, and/or conflicted psychological world that includes a weak, unclear, and maladaptive self-concept; a propensity to negative, dysregulated emotions; and a deficient capacity for adaptive interpersonal functioning and social behavior. (p. 771)

This fluid conceptualization of personality is what counselors use to indicate whether a client has *little to no impairment*, *some impairment*, *moderate impairment*, or *severe impairment* in terms of self (identity and self direction) and interpersonal (empathy and intimacy) functioning.

Pathological Personality Traits

Stated previously, the *DSM-5* uses a pathological trait taxonomy that consists of five domains: negative affectivity, detachment, antagonism, disinhibition, and psychoticism. Within these domains are 25 facets (see below). These domains and facets are based on the trait-based Five-Factor Model (FFM) of general personality functioning, a widely accepted model used extensively in studies of personality functioning (Samuel & Widiger, 2008; Widiger, 2005; for more information on the FFM, see Digman, 1990). Numerous studies and meta-analytic reviews have concluded that most personality disorders have a meaningful profile of traits that can be linked to these five domains. These traits, or facets, represent different characteristics of the domain. Defined by APA (2013a) as "a tendency to feel, perceive, behave, and think in relatively consistent ways across time and across situations" (p. 772), a personality trait is considered more fluid than a personality function (i.e., identity, self-direction, empathy, or intimacy). For example, individuals with high levels of emotional lability may be able to perform at work without high levels of emotionality. However, they would have a pattern of instability with emotional regulation despite being able to choose situations, such as work, in which they were able to more easily regulate their emotional nature. The alternative model for personality disorders asserts that these 25 personality traits, and subsequentially the five domains, apply to all individuals and that all individuals are "located on the spectrum of trait dimensions . . . personality traits apply to everyone in different degrees rather than being present versus absent" (APA, 2013a, pp. 772–773). See the table titled "Definitions of *DSM-5* Personality Disorder Trait Domains and Facets," on pages 779–781 in the *DSM-5* for a detailed description of the personality trait model. The following is a summary of the domains and associated pathological traits:

Negative affectivity: Emotional lability, anxiousness, separation insecurity, submissiveness, hostility, perseveration, and restricted affectivity (lack of*)

Detachment: Withdrawal, intimacy avoidance, anhedonia, depressivity, restricted affectivity, and suspiciousness

Antagonism: Manipulativeness, deceitfulness, grandiosity, attention seeking, callousness, and hostility

Disinhibition: Irresponsibility, impulsivity, distractibility, risk taking, and rigid perfectionism (lack of*)

Psychoticism: Unusual beliefs and experiences, eccentricity, and cognitive and perceptual dysregulation

The asterisk indicates that low levels as well as high levels are part of the facet definition. For example, a lack of restricted affectivity indicates low levels of negative affectivity and lack of rigid perfectionism indicates low levels of disinhibition.

Specific Personality Disorders

Section III of the *DSM-5* retained six personality types: borderline personality disorder, obsessive-compulsive personality disorder, avoidant personality disorder, schizotypal personality disorder, antisocial personality disorder, and narcissistic personality disorder (APA, 2013a). Four personality disorders (i.e., paranoid, schizoid, histrionic, and dependent) were eliminated because of low clinical utility, inadequate evidence for validity, and high levels of comorbidity with other personality disorders (Bornstein, 2011). Narcissistic personality disorder was originally proposed for elimination, but it was retained because of pushback from clinicians as well as evidence of diagnostic validity, albeit limited, and evidence that incidences of narcissistic personality disorder have increased at unprecedented rates in the last few decades (Montes, 2013; Twenge & Foster, 2010).

The criteria for each personality disorder in the alternative model are diagnostically defined by levels of impairment in personality functioning and typical pathological personality traits. Because of considerable variability and overlap in personality disorders, counselors may also indicate other trait and level of personality functioning specifiers (either domains or facets) that are outside of the diagnostic criteria or considered useful for treatment (APA, 2013a). This allows counselors to highlight additional features, for example, extreme negative affectivity traits such as depression, so these can be focused on during treatment. There are no other specifiers for these disorders, with the exception of a *psychopathy* specifier for antisocial personality disorder, which is used when there is a lack of fear and a general "bold interpersonal style" (APA, 2013a, p. 765) that the individual uses as a screen for manipulative or fraudulent behavior.

Although not included in the specific criteria, these disorders may not be diagnosed if symptoms can be better explained by another mental disorder or are due to the use of a substance, due to existence of another medical condition, or related to the individual's developmental stage (APA, 2013a). Because this model is not currently used within a clinical setting, there are no recording guidance or associated codes for these disorders.

Personality Disorder–Trait Specified

In the event that an individual does not meet the criteria for one of the six proposed personality disorders, but the counselor does note severity of impairment in personality functioning and problematic personality trait(s), the counselor can diagnose a client with PD-TS (APA, 2013a, 2013d). As with other disorders proposed in the alternative model, PD-TS includes an assessment of personality functioning and identification of specific personality traits related to personality pathology. Whereas in some ways this disorder closely represents personality disorder NOS, readers should note that PD-TS is much more precise regarding the extent of the personality pathology. Counselors can list, as specifiers, level of personality functioning (indicative of impairment) and the individual's unique pathological personality traits. APA (2013a) claims diagnoses that were eliminated in the alternative model (i.e., paranoid, schizoid, histrionic, and dependent personality disorders) are represented by this diagnosis.

We remind counselors that good clinical judgment is critical in determining whether a diagnosis of PD-TS can be justified. To do so, counselors should carefully assess an individual's level of distress, as evidenced by extent of time the person has experienced personality dysfunction, level of difficulty experienced by the person, and the influence of these problems on social and occupational adjustment (Pagan et al., 2005).

There are two diagnostic criteria for PD-TS (A and B; APA, 2013a). Criterion A requires moderate or greater impairment in level of personality functioning (i.e., identity, self-direction, empathy, and intimacy). Criterion B requires the individual meet the description for one or more of the five personality trait domains (i.e., negative affectivity, detachment, antagonism, disinhibition, or psychoticism) or express any of the specific trait facets within one or more of the above-listed pathological personality trait domains. Essentially, this means that (a) individuals must receive a score of 2 (moderate impairment) or higher on the Levels of Personality Functioning Scale (see pages 775–778 in the *DSM-5*) in two of the four levels of personality functioning and (b) individuals must meet the descriptive definition found within the pathological trait taxonomy (see pages 779–781 in the *DSM-5*) for either one or more personality disorder trait domains or one or more specific facets within the domains.

Specifiers for PD-TS depend on the specific personality impairments related to Criterion B that an individual is experiencing (APA, 2013a). Counselors would indicate the specific pathological personality trait domain(s) or specific trait facet(s) within the domains. The combination of these pathological personality traits will be unique for each client. For example, an individual who presents with negative affectivity, detachment, and impulsivity would be diagnosed with PD-TS with all of these included as specifiers. There are no subtypes for PD-TS because variations in this disorder are indicated by recording specifiers.

Using the Alternative *DSM-5* Model

To facilitate understanding of the proposed model, we provide readers with a case example and a brief description of diagnosis using the alternative model. We also provide two additional case examples at the end of this chapter to assist counselors in further understanding and applying the proposed model.

> Maurice, a 42-year-old African American, heterosexual, single man, is mandated to treatment because he violated probation. The violation involved stealing his sister's car and credit cards. Maurice explained that many women, including his sister, find him charming, but he has no current girlfriend or any significant history of long-term relationships. His case file indicates he has had extensive legal problems, dating back to early adolescence. These include petty theft, drug possession and distribution, numerous assault charges, and two incidences of domestic violence. Although he denies most charges, when asked about pushing his ex-girlfriend down the stairs 10 years ago, he reports, "She deserved it; she didn't pick up the phone when I called. I just showed her who was boss." Records indicate that Maurice has a long history of manipulation, risky behavior, impulsivity, and problems with anger management. He has never been able to keep a job or manage his financial responsibilities, but he is able to point to his criminal behavior as the reason for his inability to keep employment.

If using the alternative model for personality disorder, the first thing a counselor would do is assess Maurice's level of personality functioning using the Level of Personality Functioning Scale found on pages 775–778 of the *DSM-5*. The counselor finds that Maurice scores a 3 (*severe impairment*) in the areas of empathy and intimacy and a 2 (*moderate impairment*) for identity and self-direction. The counselor gives the justification of severe impairment for empathy because Maurice lacks any concern for others, including his sister whom he stole from and his ex-girlfriend whom he physically abused. In terms of intimacy, Maurice scores a 3 (*severe impairment*) because he has never been able to maintain an interpersonal relationship and his primary means of interaction with others is based on deceit and manipulation. A score of 2 (*moderate impairment*) is given for identity because although Maurice's self-identity depends on others showing him respect, he does not have the weak sense of autonomy or emptiness required for severe impairment. He also scores a 2 (*moderate impairment*) on self-direction because he has some limited insight into his inability to maintain employment.

The next step a counselor would take using the alternative model would be to identify personality disorder trait domains and facets. Referencing the "Definitions of *DSM-5* Personality Disorder Trait Domains and Facets" table found on pages 779–781 of the *DSM-5*, a counselor could see the following traits applied to Maurice's case: manipulativeness, callousness, deceitfulness, risk taking, impulsivity, and irresponsibility. These traits are part of the antagonism and disinhibition domains and relate specifically to the typical features of antisocial personality disorder found in the *DSM-5* alternative model for diagnosing personality disorders. The counselor would also consider the specifier *psychopathy* because Maurice indicates a lack of anxiety or fear and has a façade of being charming to others. Maurice's diagnosis, therefore, would be antisocial personality disorder, severe impairment (empathy and intimacy), with antagonism, disinhibition, and psychopathy.

Note

Because information regarding diagnostic recording using the *DSM-5* alternative model for personality disorders is limited, it is the role of the counselor to determine what specifiers to list (or not list). Counselors may include additional personality features that may be present. Furthermore, although levels of personality functions are required for diagnosis, the actual level of functioning can be included as a specifier if the counselor feels it is appropriate to do so.

◆ ◆ ◆

Case Example

Yosuko is a 43-year-old Japanese American, heterosexual, single woman who lives with her parents. Yosuko works at home as a medical records data-entry clerk and is seeking treatment because her parents are being strongly advised by their physician and Yosuko's older brother to move to an assisted living community. Yosuko strongly disagrees with her brother and is angry at her parents for considering the move, but she reports she is afraid of disagreeing with her family. She alternates between resentment and a "what-about-me" attitude. When asked about her family's health and why her parents' physician would suggest they leave their home, she reports she doesn't really know because her mother is usually the one who takes care of any medical issues regarding the family.

Yosuko's family has seen her turn down multiple job opportunities and even promotions at her current place of employment. She has worked for the same company for 15 years and is viewed as dependable and unassuming. When asked about turning down promotions, she states she doesn't want the responsibility of having to go into the office every day and supervise others. She also said her mother refused to drive her to work every day, so she doesn't see how she could get there on her own. She has one very close friend, a neighbor, whom she has known since childhood. She goes to visit her friend regularly and feels lost if she doesn't see her friend every day. She states the hardest thing she has ever gone through in life was when her friend got married and considered moving to an adjacent neighborhood. She states her parents thinking of leaving her feels similar. She states, "I can't believe they would consider leaving me, I cannot live alone—they know that. I don't see why I can't move with them."

◆ ◆ ◆

Diagnostic Questions

1. Using the current *DSM-5* diagnostic criteria found in Section II, do Yosuko's presenting symptoms meet the criteria for a personality disorder? If so, which one?
2. Using the alternative model proposed for diagnosing personality disorders found in Section III of the *DSM-5*, assess Yosuko's specific level of impairment in personality functioning using the Level of Personality Functioning Scale (pp. 775–778 of the *DSM-5*).
3. Using the alternative model proposed for diagnosing personality disorders found in Section III of the *DSM-5*, assess Yosuko's pathological personality traits using the pathological trait taxonomy found on pages 779–781 of the *DSM-5*.
4. Based on the information gathered in Questions 2 and 3, what personality disorder diagnosis would you assign Yosuko?
5. What specifiers or, if relevant, pathological personality trait combinations would you assign?

Case Example

Born in El Salvador but raised in the United States, Alexis is a 27-year-old bisexual woman who entered therapy because she has a tendency to get involved in relationships with incompatible and disappointing partners. As Alexis talks about these relationships, the counselor begins to recognize a pattern: Alexis tends to idolize her partners early on in the relationship; she then sets unattainable standards for them (e.g., finishing law school or getting a promotion) and is routinely disappointed when these "goals" are not met. She also seems to have considerable problems with boundaries, having lived for a very short time with at least three different partners over the course of 4 years and thinking that calling her partners multiple times a day is appropriate.

When asked about her childhood, Alexis reports people would often call her "intense." She reports having significant problems when her parents divorced and her father remarried. She states her parents still think she is overdramatic, easily upset, sullen, and angry. Her treatment history records are extensive, indicating extreme mood lability and aggressive tendencies toward her parents, siblings, and friends at school. She was suspended from school numerous times for yelling at teachers but was never expelled. According to her own report, she was terrified when she got suspended and, each time, begged the principal and her parents to let her go back to school. Alexis has a history of two suicide attempts and significant scars from cutting herself. She has been on numerous medications but reports, "None of them seem to do anything, but they are a pain in the ass to take so I just take them when I feel like it." She has no history of legal or physical health problems. She admits to using alcohol but does not meet the criteria for a substance use disorder.

♦ ♦ ♦

Diagnostic Questions

1. Using the current *DSM-5* diagnostic criteria found in Section II, do Alexis's presenting symptoms meet the criteria for a personality disorder? If so, which one?
2. Using the alternative model proposed for diagnosing personality disorders found in Section III of the *DSM-5*, assess Alexis's specific level of impairment in personality functioning using the Level of Personality Functioning Scale (pp. 775–778 of the *DSM-5*).
3. Using the alternative model proposed for diagnosing personality disorders found in Section III of the *DSM-5*, assess Alexis's pathological personality traits using the pathological trait taxonomy found on pages 779–781 of the *DSM-5*.
4. Based on the information gathered in Questions 2 and 3, what personality disorder diagnosis would you assign Alexis?
5. What specifiers or, if relevant, pathological personality trait combinations would you assign?
6. What other information would you like to know about Alexis in order to make a more accurate assessment of her presenting problem(s)?

Conclusion

Regardless of model used, careful assessment of the client can reveal a long history of personality dysfunction. Before making a diagnosis, counselors need to assess whether the dysfunction is stable over time, is experienced in multiple contexts, is not better accounted for by another mental health diagnosis, and is not due to the effect of another substance or another medical condition. This dysfunction needs to always involve problems in behavior and emotional and thinking patterns, and personality patterns need to have started early in the client's life. Counselors should ask about patterns in the client's life that relate to personality concerns and be sure to interview family members, friends, teachers, colleagues, and other health professionals to better understand the client's life history.

Chapter 17

Practice Implications
for Counselors

If you made it this far in this *Learning Companion*, you may be wondering how the changes we presented will influence your work as a professional counselor. Although many advocates voiced concerns that the *DSM-5* would lead to a rather drastic shift in conceptualization of mental disorders, assessment procedures, and diagnostic thresholds, this version of the "psychiatric bible" looks remarkably like its predecessor. First (2010b) predicted this lack of change when he noted that the *DSM-5* would keep a descriptive categorical system and that "any future paradigm shift will have to await significant advances in our understanding of the etiology and pathophysiology of mental disorders" (p. 698). Still, those involved in revisions of the *DSM-5* laid the groundwork for future shifts to neurobiological conceptualizations, removal of boundaries between medical and mental disorders, prescription of assessment measures in attempts to document complexities of mental illness, and how counselors will conceptualize schizophrenia spectrum and personality disorders. Indeed, the change from Roman to Arabic numerals is intended to allow for fluid revisions as new information becomes available (e.g., *DSM-5.1, DSM-5.2*).

In this chapter, we review philosophical implications for the counseling profession and address technical considerations such as how to use other specified and unspecified diagnoses, coding procedures, new assessment tools, and the Cultural Formulation Interview (CFI). We conclude the chapter with reflections regarding counselors' roles in the future of the *DSM*.

Diagnosis and the Counseling Profession

As a profession, counseling is uniquely focused on using an empowerment-based approach "to accomplish mental health, wellness, education, and career goals" (20/20: A Vision for the Future of Counseling, 2010, para. 2). Professional counselors should be familiar with philosophical foundations that include a commitment to normal human development; wellness as a primary paradigm (Myers, 1991); and an integrated understanding regarding systemic, social, and cultural foundations. Concerns about the degree to which diagnosis is consistent with a strong professional counseling identity are not new or unique to the

DSM-5. Reflecting on risks and realities within *DSM-IV* (APA, 1994), Ivey and Ivey (1998) asked, "We want to define ourselves as concerned with normal development, but how can we face the reality of pathological and deficit models of child development, managed health care, and the omnipresent *DSM-IV*?" (p. 334). Zalaquett, Fuerth, Stein, Ivey, and Ivey (2008) explained,

> It is important to note that this diagnostic nosology represents a medical model that stands in sharp contrast to many counselors' core values and beliefs. The medical model treats counseling concerns and behavioral symptoms as indicators of underlying diseases, emphasizes the client's deficits, leads to a top-down professional attitude, places the client in a passive (recipient) position, emphasizes individual origin of symptoms, and offers medications as the common mode of treatment. The counseling model, in contrast, treats such symptoms as responses to life challenges, emphasizes the client's strengths and assets in dealing with problems, leads to a more egalitarian relationship in the counseling setting, places the client in an active and engaged (agent) position in the treatment process, directs attention to environmental factors that may be linked to the individual's symptoms, and offers nonpsychopharmacological treatments. (p. 364)

Eriksen and Kress (2006) identified realities; potential benefits of diagnosis within the *DSM*; and key contradictions in values, assumptions, and philosophies and proposed strategies counselors may use to enhance understanding of developmental and contextual considerations in an ethical manner. Similarly, White Kress, Eriksen, Rayle, and Ford (2005) posed a series of questions regarding cultural considerations and formulation within the *DSM-IV-TR*, and more recently, Kress, Hoffman, and Eriksen (2010) addressed ethical dimensions of diagnosis within clinical mental health counseling. These balanced views address issues of professional identity and practice implications well and will continue to be of use to counselors who seek balance in the process. Although most concerns regarding diagnosis and professional identity will remain static, the *DSM-5* presents two new challenges and opportunities as they relate to professional counseling identity: neurobiological foundations and movement to nonaxial diagnosis.

Neurobiological Foundations

The revision process spawned conversations regarding what constitutes a mental disorder, including new conceptualizations regarding the line between medical and mental disorder. Initially, the DSM-5 Task Force proposed a reformulation in the definition of mental disorder to be "a behavioral or psychological syndrome or pattern that occurs in an individual" and "that reflects an *underlying psychobiological dysfunction*" (APA, 2012; italics added). The proposed revision generated a firestorm of controversy regarding the questionable foundation upon which APA could claim all mental disorders as having psychobiological roots. Ultimately, APA rejected the proposed revision in favor of a more balanced definition in which the disturbance "reflects a dysfunction in the psychological, biological, or developmental processes underlying mental functioning" (APA, 2013a, p. 20).

Still, the *DSM-5* includes enhanced attention to neurobiological foundations as evidenced by reconceptualization of most disorders usually first diagnosed in infancy, childhood, and adolescence as neurodevelopmental disorders, and most cognitive disorders as neurocognitive disorders. APA (2013a) noted one purpose of the structural reorganization as to "encourage further study of underlying pathophysiological processes that give risk to diagnostic comorbidity and symptom heterogeneity" (p. 13). It is important to remember that this reorganization was not always clear-cut and without controversy. For example, ADHD is placed with the Neurodevelopmental Disorders chapter rather than relocated to the Disruptive Behavior Disorders chapter as previously conceptualized. Throughout the

DSM-5, narrative descriptions include additional attention to genetic and physiological elements of disorders.

Subtle shifts in language also reflect movement toward biological explanations of disorder within the *DSM-5*. As we discuss below, removal of the multiaxial system means mental disorders will no longer be differentiated from medical disorders in diagnostic formulations. In addition, APA replaced *general medical condition* with *another medical condition* throughout the *DSM-5*. This subtle shift implies that mental disorders are medical disorders at their core.

Ivey and Ivey (1998) were astute in their observation that "developmental orientation, however, does not rule out biological factors—rather environment interacts with personal biology. The issue is finding balance between personal and environmental factors" (p. 336). Miller and Prosek (2013) advocated for renewed attention to the impact of this movement toward biological explanations of emotional problems, especially for vulnerable populations. Certainly, emerging neuroscience research holds much promise for facilitating understanding regarding complexities of the brain, experiences, and disorder. Still, overreliance on biological explanations without attention to the interaction with personal and environmental factors could lead to increased pathologizing, unnecessary pharmacological treatments, and unknown long-term effects on clients. There is also question within the counseling community that this focus may cause counselors to stray from the profession's humanistic roots (Montes, 2013).

For now, we urge professional counselors to seek additional training regarding neuroscience and implications for counseling and remain alert to opportunities and challenges for our profession. Scholars such as Badenoch (2008) and Siegel (2006, 2010, 2011) offer a number of trainings and readings regarding interpersonal neurobiology that are accessible to professional counselors, consistent with our professional foundations, and directly relevant to counseling practice.

Movement to Nonaxial Diagnosis

Beginning with the *DSM-III* (APA, 1980), the multiaxial system was designed to ensure that mental health providers were conceptualizing clients in a biopsychosocial manner. Axes I and II included psychological disorders, Axis III provided space to note medical conditions, Axis IV required attention to psychosocial and environmental stressors, and Axis V provided space for rating degree of distress and impairment in functioning. In contrast, *DSM-5* (APA, 2013a) simply includes a notation that "Axis III has been combined with Axes I and II. Clinicians should continue to list medical conditions that are important to the understanding or management of an individual's mental disorder(s)" (p. 16). In addition to listing all medical and mental health concerns as part of the diagnosis, *DSM-5* users are advised to include separate notations regarding psychosocial stressors, environmental concerns, and impairments or disability.

As noted by APA (2013a), previous iterations of the *DSM* never *required* mental health providers to report diagnoses in a multiaxial manner. Still, multiaxial diagnosis quickly became part of everyday diagnostic decisions and conversations. Insurance companies frequently requested notations for each of the axes and sometimes determined level of care and progress based on Global Assessment of Functioning (GAF) ratings. Scholars concerned with cultural implications of *DSM* diagnosis, context of distress, and professional identity frequently pointed to Axis IV as a place where counselors could ensure attention to external influences on client wellness (e.g., Eriksen & Kress, 2006; Ivey & Ivey, 1998; White Kress et al., 2005; Zalaquett et al., 2008). Some even proposed developing an Axis VI in which practitioners could note theoretical foundations or conceptualizations (Eriksen & Kress, 2006).

Regardless of reporting formats recommended by APA, professional counselors would do well to remember that the *DSM* is a diagnostic guide rather than a theoretical framework or treatment manual. The removal of the multiaxial system in favor of nonaxial diagnosis need not affect how professional counselors make sense of or respond to client concerns. Rather, counselors can still conceptualize clients in manners consistent with our unique foundations, and we can still bring empowerment, strengths-based, and wellness-oriented approaches to all clients, even those who present with significant disruptions in functioning. Counselors who find the *DSM-5* nonaxial diagnostic format incomplete may take steps to incorporate more holistic assessment in routine assessment and treatment planning practices. In the next two sections, we attend more specifically to logistics of coding and recording of diagnoses within the *DSM-5*.

Other Specified and Unspecified Diagnoses

A major goal of the *DSM* revision process was to reduce overreliance on NOS diagnoses, and the DSM-5 Task Force was successful in eliminating NOS from the *DSM-5*. Instead, clinicians who work with individuals who do not meet full criteria for more specific disorders within the *DSM* have options for issuing other specified and unspecified diagnoses. APA (2013a) noted that inclusion of these two options was designed to offer maximum flexibility. Time will tell whether this change in semantics and procedures will lead to enhanced diagnostic specificity over the previous NOS system.

Clinicians will use *other specified* diagnosis to record a concern within a specific diagnostic category and a reason why a more specific diagnosis is not provided. In some cases, the *DSM-5* provides an exemplar list of other specified diagnoses, including conditions for further study. Other times, clinicians may simply indicate, in narrative form, the reason for the other specified diagnosis. For example, a client who met all criteria for bulimia nervosa except frequency requirements could receive a diagnosis of "F50.8 other specified feeding or eating disorder, bulimia nervosa of low frequency."

Clinicians will use *unspecified* diagnoses when they are certain about the category of diagnosis but unable or unwilling to provide additional details. For example, a client who presents to an emergency room in an acutely psychotic state may not be able to provide the history necessary for an accurate diagnosis, and the clinician may not have access to information that might indicate if the disturbance was induced by a substance, medication, or another medical condition. In that case, one may render a diagnosis of "F29 unspecified schizophrenia spectrum and other psychotic disorder."

Coding and Recording

Implementation of *DSM-5*

APA (2013b) noted that the *DSM-5* was "developed to facilitate a seamless transition into immediate use by clinicians and insurers to maintain a continuity of care" (p. 1). Clinicians may begin using the updated manual and diagnostic criteria as soon as they are ready to do so. However, insurance companies, other third-party payers, and community agencies in general may need time to adjust reporting systems from multiaxial to nonaxial formats. At the time the *DSM-5* was published, APA predicted that the insurance industry would transition to *DSM-5* by December 31, 2013. However, this estimate was optimistic, as most third-party billing systems and government agencies are unlikely to formally switch over to the *DSM-5* until October 1, 2014, when a nationwide mandate for the use of *ICD-10-CM* codes goes into effect. This mandate is a result of a final rule, released January 16, 2009, by the Department of Health and Human Services, mandating nationwide conversion to *ICD-10-CM* coding by October 1, 2014.

In cases where organizations such as Medicare and Medicaid only collected single-access data regarding former Axes I, II, and III, this transition should be simple. In other instances, insurance companies will need to decide how they would like to categorize previous Axis IV and which, if any, new documenting procedures should be used in place of GAF to indicate symptom severity and functional impairment. Counselors need to check with their employers and third-party payers to ensure they are coordinating a transition to the *DSM-5* in a manner consistent with local administrative procedures. APA will also make implementation and transition updates available via www.psychiatry.org/dsm.

ICD-9-CM and *ICD-10-CM* Coding

The *DSM-5* includes *ICD-9-CM* (CDC, 1998) codes for current billing use as well as *ICD-10-CM* (CDC, 2014) codes for use after the October 1, 2014, nationwide conversion to *ICD-10* reporting for data collection, payment policy, and research purposes. In the *DSM-5*, *ICD-9-CM* codes appear first, are in black print, and generally include three digits or begin with V. In contrast, *ICD-10-CM* codes appear in parentheses, are in gray print, and generally begin with a letter (F); psychosocial and environmental factors often begin with Z. For example, generalized anxiety disorder includes a notation of coding as 300.02 (F41.1). Clinicians using *ICD-9-CM* codes would report 300.02, and clinicians using *ICD-10-CM* codes would report the disorder as F41.1. Similarly, an individual seeking services related to experiences as a victim of crime would be assigned an *ICD-9-CM* code of V62.89 or an *ICD-10-CM* code of Z65.4. APA (2013b) also noted that "because *DSM-5* and *ICD* disorder names may not match, the *DSM-5* diagnosis should always be recorded by name in the medical record in addition to listing the code" (p. 3). The initial printing of the *DSM-5* contained several coding errors; counselors can obtain a printable desk reference with coding updates by visiting www.dsm5.org.

Subtypes and Specifiers

As readers may have noted, the transition to a more dimensional diagnostic system in the *DSM-5* resulted in a greatly increased number of subtypes and specifiers throughout the manual. For example, a client who has 2 or more years of depressed mood, including the presence of major depressive episodes within the experience, a degree of anxiety, and intermittent panic attacks may be diagnosed with F34.1 persistent depressive disorder; with anxious distress; with panic attacks; late onset; with intermittent major depressive episodes, without current episode; moderate. This is quite a change from the *DSM-IV-TR* diagnosis: 296.35 major depressive disorder, recurrent, in partial remission and 300.00 anxiety disorder NOS.

In most cases, clinicians will include the same diagnostic code regardless of subtypes and specifiers assigned. There are some notable exceptions, especially regarding substance-related disorders. Although we included an outline of coding notes throughout this book, professional counselors should refer to the *DSM-5* for coding instructions and examples. (Refer to Section I of the *DSM-5* for additional details regarding elements of a diagnosis, including coding procedures.)

Nonaxial Reporting Options

Counselors used to reporting diagnoses in a multiaxial format may wonder what nonaxial diagnosis may look like. In short, it can be quite simple. Official *DSM-5* diagnoses will include codes for mental health diagnoses, clinically significant psychosocial and environmental concerns, and relevant medical diagnoses that are part of the official record. These will be reported in a line-by-line manner.

We assume counselors will list disorders or concerns in order of clinical priority or relevance, with the principal diagnosis and reason for visit listed first. When the principal diagnosis and reason for visit are different, APA (2013a) advised users to include a parenthetical notation regarding which is which. For example, a child who is referred for counseling because of numerous disciplinary problems at school and is found to meet criteria for ADHD may receive a diagnosis of

F90.2   attention-deficient/hyperactivity disorder, combined presentation, moderate (principal diagnosis) and

Z55.9   academic or educational problem (reason for visit).

In contrast, someone who meets criteria for depression, uses alcohol excessively, and is unable to control his diabetes as a result of the disturbance may receive a diagnosis of

F32.2   major depressive disorder, single episode, severe;

F10.10   alcohol use disorder, mild; and

E11   type 2 diabetes mellitus.

The second example raises an important consideration regarding counselors' scope of practice. Diagnosis of medical conditions alongside mental health disorders makes sense for psychiatrists who are qualified to diagnose and treat both and for mental health professionals who work in interdisciplinary settings where medical diagnoses are a matter of record. Given that counselors are not qualified to diagnose medical conditions, it may be wise to refrain from including diagnostic mention of specific medical conditions unless information is obtained via official medical record or consultation. Instead, counselors may include mention of client-reported medical conditions elsewhere on the clinical record or qualify self-reported conditions as by client report.

The following points may serve as important reminders regarding rendering of nonaxial diagnoses:

- The *ACA Code of Ethics* (ACA, 2014) notes the right to refuse to diagnose should a counselor believe rendering a diagnosis to be harmful. Refusing to diagnose is different from assigning an inaccurate diagnosis. Braun and Cox (2005) provided an excellent discussion regarding ethical and legal ramifications of upcoding (i.e., assigning a more severe diagnosis so insurance will cover treatment) and downcoding (i.e., assigning a less severe diagnosis to ensure insurance coverage or reduce potential stigma).
- Counselors who are not yet ready to render a diagnosis may defer diagnosis using 799.9 (*ICD-9-CM*) or R69 (*ICD-10-CM*).
- Counselors may use the code V71.09 (*ICD-9-CM*; technically, observation for other suspected mental condition) or Z03.89 (*ICD-10-CM*; technically, encounter for observation for other suspected diseases and conditions ruled out) if they determine no diagnosis is present. In reality, there should always be a reason for a counseling visit or referral, so we recommend using a more specific V or Z code from the Other Conditions That May Be a Focus of Clinical Attention chapter.
- When relatively certain that a client meets or will meet criteria for a diagnosis, counselors may note uncertainty by indicating the diagnosis as provisional. *Provisional* should be placed in parentheses following the diagnosis.
- The *DSM-5* includes a much-expanded list of contextual issues that may be clinically relevant for clients. Given the removal of Axis IV, we encourage counselors to include the V or Z codes when they are important to client conceptualization and treatment planning. Counselors may also use supplemental case documentation formats that include space for enhanced attention to psychosocial and environmental considerations (including strengths and supports in addition to problems).

As discussed previously, the *DSM-5* no longer includes attention to Axis V GAF ratings regarding distress and impairment; however, the text includes directions that clinicians include "separation notations" for disability. To some degree, counselors will indicate degree of distress and impairment using new dimensional assessment severity ratings provided throughout the *DSM-5*. The *DSM-5* also includes a more comprehensive assessment, the WHODAS 2.0 (WHO, 2010), as holding promise for documenting functional impairment. It is currently unknown whether insurance companies will require documentation of degree of concerns via the WHODAS 2.0 or another measure. Regardless of whether one adopts the WHODAS 2.0, counselors need to consider how to attend to impairment in routine assessment and case documentation practices.

Diagnostic Assessment and Other Screening Tools

Early in the revision process, it appeared as if the *DSM-5* would include dimensional assessment measures intended for use with nearly every disorder in the manual. This raised widespread concerns regarding the unknown psychometric properties of the proposed instruments, many of which were constructed by work groups during the revision process. In the end, APA chose to include relatively few assessment tools in the print version of the *DSM*, qualified the assessments as "emerging measures" intended for further study, and provided supplemental assessment tools via www.psychiatry.org/practice/dsm/dsm5. Assessment tools of particular interest include cross-cutting symptom measures, disorder-specific severity measures, the WHODAS 2.0, and personality inventories. In all cases, APA described the purpose of the measures as "to enhance clinical decision-making and not as the sole basis for making a clinical diagnosis" (APA, 2013c, para. 3).

APA (2013a) noted that cross-cutting symptom measures were "modeled on general medicine's review of symptoms" (p. 733). It is best to think of Level 1 cross-cutting symptom measures as very general screening tools. The *DSM-5* includes an adult measure and a child measure to be completed by a caregiver; the supplemental website also includes a self-report measure for children ages 11 to 17. For example, the adult version of the cross-cutting symptom measure includes 23 questions focused on 13 domains of broad concern to clinicians across settings. Domains include areas such as depression, anger, anxiety, and sleep problems. Clients or informants use a scale from 0 (*none/not at all*) to 4 (*severe/nearly every day*) to rate their concern over a 2-week time period. With the exception of suicidal ideation, psychosis, and substance abuse for which any endorsement warrants follow-up, clinicians are advised to further inquire about any domains in which a client endorses items at a level of mild/several days or greater.

To facilitate assessment, most Level 1 domains are associated with Level 2 cross-cutting symptom measures. Level 2 measures for adults include those focused on depression, anger, mania, anxiety, somatic symptoms, sleep disturbance, repetitive thoughts and behaviors, and substance use. These assessment tools and information regarding development, administration, and psychometric properties are available free of charge via the *DSM-5* website. Although most Level 2 measures were developed using well-validated instruments, APA noted that not all formulations have been validated. For these reasons, counselors should use Level 1 and Level 2 measures with caution, considering them just one source of clinical information.

APA also provides a number of disorder-specific severity measures to be used with the *DSM-5*. These measures correspond to specific disorders or categories of disorders. Some are designed as self-report measures, and clinicians complete other measures following a diagnostic interview. With the exception of the Clinician-Rated Dimensions of Psychosis Symptom Severity Scale available in the printed version of the *DSM-5*, these scales are all available through the *DSM-5* website. These scales vary widely in format, quality, and rigor of psychometric validation. For example, APA chose the Patient Health Questionnaire–9, a well-developed instrument in the public domain, as the severity measure for depression. Counselors can easily access information needed to use this scale with a strong degree of integrity. On the other hand, the Severity Measure for Panic Disorder–Adult has face validity but does not include reference to development and validation procedures. Finally, the Clinician-Rated Severity of Oppositional Defiant Disorder measure simply includes one item advising clinicians to rate severity on a 4-point scale based on number of settings in which concerns occur. Counselors who choose to use severity measures in practice are responsible for learning more about development, validation, and psychometric properties of the measures so they may ensure adherence to ethical (ACA, 2014) and best practice (Association for Assessment in Counseling, 2003) guidelines.

As noted before, GAF rating procedures are discontinued in the *DSM-5*, and the WHO-DAS 2.0 is included as an alternative method for assessing disability. The WHODAS 2.0 is a well-established assessment measure appropriate for use with diverse populations and captures the level of functioning in six domains of life:

Domain 1: Cognition—understanding and communicating
Domain 2: Mobility—moving and getting around
Domain 3: Self-care—attending to one's hygiene, dressing, eating, and staying alone
Domain 4: Getting along—interacting with other people
Domain 5: Life activities—domestic responsibilities, leisure, work, and school
Domain 6: Participation—joining in community activities, participating in society. (Üstün, Kostanjsek, Chatterji, & Rehm, 2010, p. 4)

In short, the WHODAS 2.0 may be completed by a client or informant and includes 36 items in which one rates concerns over the past 30 days on a scale ranging from 1 (*none*) to 5 (*extreme*). It takes approximately 5 to 20 minutes to complete and is appropriate for repeat administration. Extensive information regarding scoring, norms, psychometric properties, and the development process is provided in a manual available in the public domain (Üstün et al., 2010). A corresponding measure for children and adolescents is in development.

Finally, APA provides personality inventories designed to "measure maladaptive personality traits in five domains: negative affect, detachment, antagonism, disinhibition, and psychoticism" (APA, 2013c, para 4). Provided online, the measures include brief forms (25 items) and full forms (220 items) for adults and a brief form for children ages 11 to 17. The scales and subscales in the assessment tools are aligned with facets and domains conceptualized within the alternative model for personality disorders printed in Section III of the *DSM-5*. Individuals interested in using this assessment tool should refer to Krueger, Derringer, Markon, Watson, and Skodol (2012).

APA's provision of assessment tools corresponding to key constructs within the *DSM-5* represents a shift in thinking from the *DSM* as a manual that simply describes experiences to one in which a degree of clinical practice is suggested or prescribed. As noted throughout this section, the measures provided in print and online vary widely in their rigor. The degree to which they are usable in everyday counseling practice is likely to vary in accordance with properties of the specific measure, the counselor's work setting and focus, and the counselor's theoretical orientation. The instruments are largely deficit based and grounded in a medical model, and it is not yet known whether counselors will find these instruments useful for practice and feasible in the world of managed care (Jones, 2012). Counselors operating from a wellness and strength-based model may wish to incorporate assessment tools reflective of this orientation in addition to or instead of the tools provided by the APA. To learn more about these assessments in general, refer to Jones (2012). In addition, APA will be releasing measures for further study on a rolling basis, so readers may wish to check back for updates on the *DSM-5* website.

Cultural Formulation Interview

A key criticism of the *DSM* over time has been lack of attention to cultural considerations in diagnostic assessment. The *DSM-IV* was designed with additional attention to culture in mind and included a number of cultural upgrades, including descriptions of cultural features, a cultural formulation outline, and enhanced attention to psychosocial and environmental stressors (Smart & Smart, 1997). The *DSM-5* includes continued attention to cultural considerations through updated diagnostic criteria, text regarding culture-related diagnostic issues for most disorders, additional information about cultural concepts, and a formal Cultural Formulation Interview, or CFI. The CFI was designed to answer questions regarding how one might bring integrated understanding of cultural considerations to assessment, diagnosis, and treatment planning. The CFI client and informant versions are provided on pages 752–757 of the *DSM-5*.

The CFI is a semistructured interview consisting of 16 questions covering domains such as cultural definition of the problem; cultural perceptions of cause, context, and support; cultural factors affecting self-coping and past help seeking; and cultural factors affecting current help seeking. Designed to be completed in about 15 to 20 minutes, the CFI provides concrete direction and tools for bringing culture into diagnostic assumptions. In addition, APA provides a series of 12 supplementary modules to be used as adjuncts to the CFI or independent of the CFI. Addressing topics and populations such as needs of immigrants and refugees; coping and help seeking; and spirituality, religion, and moral traditions, the modules provide a foundation upon which culturally sensitive counselors can build.

During a year-long field trial involving the CFI, Aggarwal, Nicasio, DeSilva, Bioler, and Lewis-Fernandez (2013) identified several barriers to implementing the CFI. From the client perspective, barriers included confusion about how the CFI was different from other assessments, reluctance to discuss the past, confusion over several items, rigidity in conversation, and difficulty participating given the nature of the client's illness. Interdisciplinary clinicians sometimes questioned conceptual connections between the CFI and presenting problems, wondered whether the entire interview was helpful, identified instances in which clients may not be able to participate, and worried about being overly structured in delivery of the interview. They also noted concerns regarding the amount of time needed to complete the entire CFI. Even if counselors simply find the CFI helpful as a guide to facilitating conversations about culture, the CFI provides a step forward in helping counselors move from multicultural awareness to skills when thinking diagnostically.

The Future of the *DSM*

As we discussed in Chapters 1 and 2, the *DSM* is an evolving manual that reflects the particular time in which it was created. Over time, mental health professionals have witnessed the *DSM* shift from explicit psychodynamic foundations in the original document to an implicit supposedly atheoretical medical model in the third revision. APA made a strong statement when it moved from denoting new editions with Roman numerals (e.g., *DSM-III, DSM-IV, DSM-IV-TR*) to indicating editions with Arabic numbers (e.g., *DSM-5, DSM-5.1, DSM-5.2*). This shift indicates plans for ongoing revision of the document as new information becomes available.

Given expansion of national priorities regarding brain-based initiatives and neurobiological research on mental disorders, we expect continued efforts around understanding and classifying etiology of disorders rather than classification of symptom-based experiences (Kupfer & Regier, 2011). Certainly, the NIMH noted such a shift in focus when they endorsed the *DSM-5* as the "contemporary consensus standard for how mental disorders are diagnosed and treated" (Insel & Lieberman, 2013, para. 2) and went on to express plans for "a new kind of taxonomy for mental disorders by bringing the power of modern research approaches in genetics, neuroscience, and behavioral science to the problem of mental illness" (para. 3).

As one of the largest consumers of the *DSM* (Frances, 2011), professional counselors are responsible for ensuring they understand and incorporate the latest advances in related professions while advocating for assessment, diagnostic, and treatment systems that best empower "diverse individuals, families, and groups to accomplish mental health, wellness, education, and career goals" in accordance with ACA's definition of counseling (20/20: A Vision for the Future of Counseling, 2010). In the years to come, professional counselors will need to decide whether to advocate for heightened inclusion in *DSM* revision processes or, deciding that the manual no longer enhances work within the counseling profession, adopt an alternative nosology that is consistent with the philosophical, theoretical foundations and the work that we do as professional counselors.

Part Four References

Aggarwal, K. K., Nicasio, A. V., DeSilva, R., Bioler, M., & Lewis-Fernandez, R. (2013). Barriers to implementing the *DSM-5* Cultural Formulation Interview: A qualitative study. *Culture, Medicine and Psychiatry, 37,* 505–533. doi:10.1007/s11013-013-9325-z

American Counseling Association. (2014). *ACA code of ethics.* Alexandria, VA: Author.

American Psychiatric Association. (1980). *Diagnostic and statistical manual of mental disorders* (3rd ed.). Washington, DC: Author.

American Psychiatric Association. (1994). *Diagnostic and statistical manual of mental disorders* (4th ed.). Washington, DC: Author.

American Psychiatric Association. (2000). *Diagnostic and statistical manual of mental disorders* (4th ed., text rev.). Washington, DC: Author.

American Psychiatric Association. (2012). *Definition of a mental disorder.* Retrieved from http://www.dsm5.org/proposedrevision/Pages/proposedrevision.aspx?rid=465

American Psychiatric Association. (2013a). *Diagnostic and statistical manual of mental disorders* (5th ed.). Arlington, VA: Author.

American Psychiatric Association. (2013b). *Insurance implications of DSM-5.* Retrieved from http://www.psychiatry.org/File%20Library/Practice/DSM/DSM-5/Insurance-Implications-of-DSM-5.pdf

American Psychiatric Association. (2013c). *Online assessment measures.* Retrieved from http://www.psychiatry.org/practice/dsm/dsm5/online-assessment-measures

American Psychiatric Association. (2013d). *Personality disorders.* Retrieved from http://www.dsm5.org/Documents/Personality%20Disorders%20Fact%20Sheet.pdf

Association for Assessment in Counseling. (2003). *Responsibilities of users of standardized tests* (3rd ed.). Retrieved from http://aarc-counseling.org/assets/cms/uploads/files/rust.pdf

Bachelor, A. (2013). Clients' and therapists' views of the therapeutic alliance: Similarities, differences and relationship to therapy outcome. *Clinical Psychology & Psychotherapy, 20,* 118–135. doi:10.1002/cpp.792

Badenoch, B. (2008). *Being a brain-wise therapist: A practical guide to interpersonal neurobiology.* New York, NY: Norton.

Biskin, R. (2013). Treatment of borderline personality disorder in youth. *Journal of the Canadian Academy of Child and Adolescent Psychiatry, 22,* 230–234.

Boeree, G. C. (2007). *Personality disorders.* Retrieved from http://webspace.ship.edu/cgboer/pers-disorders.html

Bornstein, R. F. (2011). Reconceptualizing personality pathology in *DSM-5*: Limitations in evidence for eliminating dependent personality disorder and other *DSM-IV* syndromes. *Journal of Personality Disorders, 25,* 235–247. doi:10.1521/pedi.2011.25.2.235

Braun, S. A., & Cox, J. A. (2005). Managed mental health care: Intentional misdiagnosis of mental disorders. *Journal of Counseling & Development, 83,* 425–433. doi:10.1002/j.1556-6678.2005. tb00364.x

Brown, T. A., & Barlow, D. H. (2005). Dimensional versus categorical classification of mental disorders in the fifth edition of the *Diagnostic and Statistical Manual of Mental Disorders* and beyond: Comment on the special section. *Journal of Abnormal Psychology, 114,* 551–556.

Caldwell-Harris, C. L., & Ayçiçegi, A. (2006). When personality and culture clash: The psychological distress of allocentrics in an individualist culture and idiocentrics in a collectivist culture. *Transcultural Psychiatry, 43,* 331–361.

Centers for Disease Control and Prevention, National Center for Health Statistics. (1998). *The international classification of diseases, ninth revision, clinical modification (ICD-9-CM).* Atlanta, GA: Author.

Centers for Disease Control and Prevention, National Center for Health Statistics. (2014). *The international classification of diseases, 10th revision, clinical modification (ICD-10-CM).* Atlanta, GA: Author.

Comer, R. J. (2013). *Abnormal psychology* (8th ed.). New York, NY: Worth.

Crowell, S. E., Beauchaine, T. P., & Linehan, M. M. (2009). A biosocial developmental model of borderline personality: Elaborating and extending Linehan's theory. *Psychological Bulletin, 135,* 495–510. doi:10.1037/a0015616

Demjaha, A., Morgan, K., Morgan, C., Landau, S., Dean, K., Reichenberg, A., . . . Dazzan, P. (2009). Combining dimensional and categorical representation of psychosis: The way forward for the *DSM-V* and *ICD-11? Psychological Medicine, 39,* 1943–1955. doi:10.1017/S0033291709990651

Diamond, D., & Meehan, K. (2013). Attachment and object relations in patients with narcissistic personality disorder: Implications for therapeutic process and outcome. *Journal of Clinical Psychology, 69,* 1148–1159. doi:10.1002/jclp.22042

Digman, J. M. (1990). Personality structure: Emergence of the five-factor model. *Annual Review of Psychology, 41,* 417–440.

Durand, V. M., & Barlow, D. H. (2010). *Essentials of abnormal psychology.* Belmont, CA: Wadsworth Cengage Learning.

Eriksen, K., & Kress, V. E. (2006). The *DSM* and professional counseling identity: Bridging the gap. *Journal of Mental Health Counseling, 28,* 202–217.

First, M. B. (2010a). Clinical utility in the revision of the *Diagnostic and Statistical Manual of Mental Disorders (DSM). Professional Psychology: Research and Practice, 41,* 465–473. doi:10.1037/a0021511

First, M. B. (2010b). Paradigm shifts and the development of the *Diagnostic and Statistical Manual of Mental Disorders*: Past experiences and future aspirations. *La Revue Canadienne de Psychiatrie, 55,* 692–700.

Ford, M. R., & Widiger, T. A. (1989). Sex bias in the diagnosis of histrionic and antisocial personality disorders. *Journal of Consulting and Clinical Psychology, 57,* 301–305.

Frances, A. (2011, June 8). Who needs *DSM-5*? A strong warning comes from professional counselors. *Psychiatric Times.* Retrieved from http://www.psychiatrictimes.com/couch-crisis/who-needs-dsm-5-strong-warning-comes-professional-counselors

Frances, A. (2013). *Essentials of psychiatric diagnosis: Responding to the challenge of DSM-5.* New York, NY: Guilford Press.

Grant, B. F., Hasin, D. S., Stinson, F. S., Dawson, D. A., Chou, S. P., Ruan, W., & Pickering, R. P. (2004). Prevalence, correlates, and disability of personality disorders in the United States: Results from the National Epidemiologic Survey on Alcohol and Related Conditions. *Journal of Clinical Psychiatry, 67,* 948–958.

Grohol, J. (2007). Characteristics of borderline personality disorder. *Psych Central.* Retrieved from http://psychcentral.com/lib/characteristics-of-borderline-personality-disorder/0001064

Grohol, J. (2013). *DSM-5* changes: Personality disorders (Axis II). *Psych Central.* Retrieved from http://pro.psychcentral.com/2013/dsm-5-changes-personality-disorders-axis-ii/005008.html

Insel, T. R., Cuthbert, B. N., Garvey, M. A., Heinssen, R. K., Pine, D. S., Quinn, K. J., . . . Wang, P. S. (2010). Research domain criteria (RDoC): Toward a new classification framework for research on mental disorders. *American Journal of Psychiatry, 167,* 748–751.

Insel, T. R., & Lieberman, J. A. (2013, May 13). *DSM and RDoc: Shared interests.* Retrieved from http://www.nimh.nih.gov/news/science-news/2013/dsm-5-and-rdoc-shared-interests.shtml

Ivey, A. E., & Ivey, M. B. (1998). Reframing *DSM-IV*: Positive strategies from developmental counseling and therapy. *Journal of Counseling & Development, 76,* 334–350. doi:10.1002/j.1556-6676.1998.tb02550.x

Jones, K. D. (2012). Dimensional and cross-cutting assessment in the *DSM-5. Journal of Counseling & Development, 90,* 481–487. doi:10.1002/j.1556-6676.2012.00059.x

Kosson, D. S., Blackburn, R., Byrnes, K. A., Park, S., Logan, C., & Donnelly, J. P. (2008). Assessing interpersonal aspects of schizoid personality disorder: Preliminary validation studies. *Journal of Personality Assessment, 90,* 185–196. doi:10.1080/00223890701845427

Kraemer, H. C. (2007). *DSM* categories and dimensions in clinical and research contexts. *International Journal of Methods in Psychiatric Research, 16,* S8–S15.

Kress, V. E., Hoffman, R. M., & Eriksen, K. (2010). Ethical dimensions of diagnosing: Considerations for clinical mental health counselors. *Counseling and Values, 55,* 101–112.

Krueger, R. F., Derringer, J., Markon, K. E., Watson, D., & Skodol, A. E. (2012). Initial construction of a maladaptive personality trait model and inventory for *DSM-5. Psychological Medicine, 42,* 1879–1890.

Kupfer, D. J., First, M. B., & Regier, D. A. (2002). *A research agenda for DSM-V.* Washington, DC: American Psychiatric Association.

Kupfer, D. J., & Regier, D. A. (2011). Neuroscience, clinical evidence, and the future of psychiatric classification in *DSM-5. American Journal of Psychiatry, 168,* 672–674.

Lambert, M. J., & Barley, D. E. (2001). Research summary on the therapeutic relationship and psychotherapy outcome. *Psychotherapy: Theory, Research, Practice, Training, 38,* 357–361.

Martens, W. H. (2010). Schizoid personality disorder linked to unbearable and inescapable loneliness. *European Journal of Psychiatry, 24,* 38–45.

McClure, M. M., Harvey, P. D., Bowie, C. R., Iacoviello, B., & Siever, L. J. (2013). Functional outcomes, functional capacity, and cognitive impairment in schizotypal personality disorder. *Schizophrenia Research, 144,* 146–150. doi.org/10.1016/j.schres.2012.12.012

McKeon, P., & Murray, R. (1987). Familial aspects of obsessive-compulsive neurosis. *British Journal of Psychiatry, 151,* 528–534.

Mercer, D., Douglass, A. B., & Links, P. S. (2009). Meta-analyses of mood stabilizers, antidepressants and antipsychotics in the treatment of borderline personality disorder: Effectiveness for depression and anger symptoms. *Journal of Personality Disorders, 23,* 156–174.

Miller, R., & Prosek, E. A. (2013). Trends and implications of proposed changes to the *DSM-5* for vulnerable populations. *Journal of Counseling & Development, 91,* 359–366. doi:10.1002/j.1556-6676.2013.00106.x

Montes, S. (2013, May). Facing a rising tide of personality disorders. *Counseling Today, 56,* 33–39.

Myers, J .E. (1991). Wellness as the paradigm for counseling and development: The possible future. *Counselor Education and Supervision, 30,* 183–193. doi:10.1002/j.1556-6978.1991.tb01199.x

Newton-Howes, G., Tyrer, P., Anagnostakis, K., Cooper, S., Bowden-Jones, O., & Weaver, T. (2010). The prevalence of personality disorder, its comorbidity with mental state disorders, and its clinical significance in community mental health teams. *Social Psychiatry and Psychiatric Epidemiology, 45,* 453–460.

Nietzel, M. T., Speltz, M. L., McCauley, E. A., & Bernstein, D. A. (1998). *Abnormal psychology.* Needham Heights, MA: Allyn & Bacon.

Olabi, B., & Hall, J. (2010). Review: Borderline personality disorder: current drug treatments and future prospects. *Therapeutic Advances in Chronic Disease, 1*(2), 59–66.

Pagan, J. L., Oltmanns, T. F., Whitmore, M. J., & Turkheimer, E. (2005). Personality disorder not otherwise specified: Searching for an empirically based diagnostic threshold. *Journal of Personality Disorders, 19,* 674–689.

Paris, J. (2013). *The intelligent clinician's guide to the DSM-5.* New York, NY: Oxford University Press.

Parpottas, P. (2012). A critique on the use of standard psychopathological classifications in understanding human distress: The example of "schizoid personality disorder." *Counselling Psychology Review, 27,* 44–52.

Peluso, P. (2013, July 30). *DSM-5*: Personality disorders and wrap-up [Webinar]. In *DSM-5: Navigating the new terrain.* Retrieved from http://www.counseling.org/continuing-education/webinars

Ripoll, L. H., Zaki, J., Perez-Rodriguez, M. M., Snyder, R., Sloan Strike, K., Boussi, A., . . . Newa, A. S. (2013). Empathic accuracy and cognition in schizotypal personality disorder. *Psychiatry Research, 210*, 232–241. doi.org/10.1016/j.psychres.2013.05.025

Roberts, B. W., & Helson, R. (1997). Changes in culture, changes in personality: The influence of individualism in a longitudinal study of women. *Journal of Personality and Social Psychology, 72*, 641–651.

Rosenbaum, J. F., & Pollock, R. (2002, June 20). *DSM-V*: Plans and perspectives. *Medscape Psychiatry.* Retrieved from http://www.medscape.org/viewarticle/436403

Samuel, D. B., & Widiger, T. A. (2008). A meta-analytic review of the relationships between the five-factor model and *DSM-IV-TR* personality disorders: A facet level analysis. *Clinical Psychology Review, 28*, 1326–1342.

Sanislow, C. A., Pine, D. S., Quinn, K. J., Kozak, M. J., Garvey, M. A., Heinssen, R. K., . . . Cuthbert, B. N. (2010). Developing constructs for psychopathology research: Research domain criteria. *Journal of Abnormal Psychology, 119*, 631–639.

Siegel, D. J. (2006). An interpersonal neurobiology approach to psychotherapy. *Psychiatric Annals, 36*, 248–256.

Siegel, D. J. (2010). *The mindful therapist: A clinician's guide to mindsight and neural integration.* New York, NY: Norton.

Siegel, D. J. (2011). *Mindsight: The new science of personal transformation.* New York, NY: Bantam Books.

Skodol, A., & Bender, D. (2009). The future of personality disorders in *DSM-V*? *American Journal of Psychiatry, 166*, 388–391.

Smart, D. W., & Smart, J. F. (1997). *DSM-IV* and culturally sensitive diagnosis: Some observations for counselors. *Journal of Counseling & Development, 75*, 392–398. doi:10.1002/j.1556-6676.1997.tb02355.x

Stinson, F. S., Dawson, D. A., Goldstein, R. B., Chou, S. P., Huang, B., Smith, S. M., . . . Grant, B. F. (2008). Prevalence, correlates, disability, and comorbidity of *DSM-IV* narcissistic personality disorder: Results from the Wave 2 National Epidemiologic Survey on Alcohol and Related Conditions. *Journal of Clinical Psychiatry, 69*, 533–545.

Stone, M. H. (1993). *Abnormalities of personality: Within and beyond the realm of treatment.* New York, NY: Norton.

Strunk, D. R., Brotman, M. A., & DeRubeis, R. J. (2010). The process of change in cognitive therapy for depression: Predictors of early inter-session symptom gains. *Behaviour Research and Therapy, 48*, 599–606.

Twenge, J. M. (2001). Birth cohort changes in extraversion: A cross temporal meta-analysis, 1966–1993. *Personality and Individual Differences, 30*, 735–748.

Twenge, J. M., & Foster, J. D. (2010). Birth cohort increases in narcissistic personality traits among American college students, 1982–2009. *Social Psychological and Personality Science, 1*, 99–106.

20/20: A Vision for the Future of Counseling. (2010). *Consensus definition of counseling.* Retrieved from http://www.counseling.org/knowledge-center/20-20-a-vision-for-the-future-of-counseling/consensus-definition-of-counseling

Üstün, T. B., Kostanjsek, N., Chatterji, S., & Rehm, J. (2010). *Measuring health and disability: Manual for WHO Disability Assessment Schedule (WHODAS 2.0).* Geneva, Switzerland: World Health Organization Press.

White Kress, V. E., Eriksen, K. P., Rayle, A. D., & Ford, S. J. W. (2005). The *DSM-IV-TR* and culture: Considerations for counselors. *Journal of Counseling & Development, 83*, 97–104. doi:10.1002/j.1556-6678.2005.tb00584.x

Widiger, T. A. (2005). Five Factor Model of personality disorder: Integrating science and practice. *Journal of Research in Personality, 39*, 67–83.

World Health Organization. (2010). *WHO Disability Assessment Schedule 2.0–WHODAS 2.0.* Geneva, Switzerland: Author.

Zalaquett, C. P., Fuerth, K. M., Stein, C., Ivey, A. E., & Ivey, M. B. (2008). Reframing the *DSM-IV-TR* from a multicultural/social justice perspective. *Journal of Counseling & Development, 86*, 364–371. doi:10.1002/j.1556-6678.2008.tb00521.x

Index

A

Abnormal motor behavior, 257–258
Abuse of substances. *See* Substance-related and addictive disorders
ACA Code of Ethics
    on accessing care, 40
    on assessment instruments, 13
    on competence and professional responsibility, 130, 217, 220, 301
    on diagnosis, 2, 5, 296
    on duty to warn, 176
    on mandated reporting, 109, 110, 176, 216, 217
    on refusal to diagnose, 322
Accreditation standards, 2
ACT (assertive community treatment), 261–262
Acute stress disorder, 106, 119–122
ADAA (Anxiety and Depression Association of America), 33, 34
Addiction, 149–150. *See also* Substance-related and addictive disorders
ADHD (attention-deficit/hyperactivity disorder), 170, 236, 240–241, 247–249
Adjustment disorders, 106–107, 122–124
Adolescents. *See* Children and adolescents
African Americans
    anxiety disorders, 74, 78, 82
    bipolar disorder, 56
    depressive disorders, 34, 40, 41, 42
    gambling disorder, 161
    pyromania, 176
    tobacco use, 160

Aggarwal, K. K., 325
Aging populations. *See* Elderly populations
Agoraphobia, 21, 75, 80–81
Agrawal, A., 157
Ahmed, A. O., 173
Alaska Natives. *See* Native Americans/Alaska Natives
Alcohol-related disorders, 152, 153, 157
ALGBTIC (Association of Lesbian, Gay, Bisexual and Transgender Issues in Counseling), 133
Algolagnic disorders, 215
Ali, R., 279
Amenorrhea, 189
American Counseling Association, role in *DSM-5* revision process, 4–5. *See also* ACA Code of Ethics
American Psychiatric Association. *See Diagnostic and Statistical Manual of Mental Disorders*
American Psychological Association, role in *DSM-5* revision process, 4
American Society of Addictive Medicine (ASAM), 149
Ammaniti, M., 182
Amnesia, dissociative, 269–270, 271, 273
Amphetamines, 159
Androgen insensitivity syndrome, 128
Anejaculation, 208–209
Anorexia nervosa, 180, 188–191
Antagonism, 311
Antidepressants, 214, 280
Antipsychotics, 261
Antisocial personality disorder (ASPD), 166, 174, 175, 299–300
Anxiety, defined, 69

Anxiety and Depression Association of America (ADAA), 33, 34
Anxiety disorders, 69–85
    agoraphobia, 21, 75, 80–81
    case examples, 77–78, 81, 82–83
    in children and adolescents, 72, 73, 76
    coding, recording, and specifiers, 73, 74–75, 77, 79–80, 82, 84, 85
    comorbidity with depressive disorders, 33, 34, 69, 70
    counseling implications, 71
    diagnostic changes, 21, 70
    differential diagnosis, 70, 72–74, 75, 76–77, 78–80, 82, 84–85
    dimensional assessment of, 18
    due to another medical condition, 84–85
    etiology and treatment, 70–71
    gender differences in, 78, 79, 80
    generalized anxiety disorder (GAD), 34, 72, 81–83
    other specified and unspecified, 85
    panic attacks, 21, 79–80, 115
    panic disorder, 21, 72, 75, 78–79
    racial differences in, 74, 76, 78, 82
    selective mutism, 73–74, 76
    separation anxiety disorder, 71–73
    social anxiety disorder, 72, 75–78
    specific phobias, 74–75
    structural changes to classification of, 14
    substance/medication-induced, 83–84
    suicide risk and, 71
Anxiolytic-related disorders, 155, 159
Apneas, 202
ASAM (American Society of Addictive Medicine), 149
ASD. *See* Autism spectrum disorder
Asian Americans/Pacific Islanders
    alcohol-related disorders, 157
    anxiety disorders, 74, 82
    depressive disorders, 40, 41
ASPD. *See* Antisocial personality disorder
Asperger's disorder. *See* Autism spectrum disorder (ASD)
Assertive community treatment (ACT), 261–262
Assessment. *See also specific assessment tools*
    of anxiety disorders, 18
    cross-cutting assessment, 19–20, 323
    of depressive disorders, 18, 34
    philosophical changes in, 17–19, 236, 258, 308–309
    practice implications and, 323–325
    of suicide risk, 18
Association of Lesbian, Gay, Bisexual and Transgender Issues in Counseling (ALGBTIC), 133
Ataque de nervios (attack of nerves), 78, 114
Attention-deficit/hyperactivity disorder. *See* ADHD
Attenuated psychosis syndrome, 21, 259

Atypical antipsychotics, 261
Auditory hallucinations, 257
Autism spectrum disorder (ASD), 20, 236, 240, 241, 244–247
Aversion therapies, 216, 222, 223
Avoidant personality disorder, 304–305
Avoidant/restrictive food intake disorder, 187–188
Ayçiçegi, A., 297–298

B

Badenoch, B., 319
Bajenaru, O., 251
Balleur-van Rijn, A., 131
Baur, K., 132
BDD. *See* Body dysmorphic disorder
Bed-wetting, 196, 197–198
Beech, A. R., 217, 219, 223
Behavioral disruptions, 179–224
    elimination disorders, 196–199
    feeding and eating disorders, 179–196. *See also* Feeding and eating disorders
    paraphilic disorders, 214–224. *See also* Paraphilic disorders
    sexual dysfunctions, 205–214. *See also* Sexual dysfunctions
    sleep-wake disorders, 199–205. *See also* Sleep-wake disorders
Behavior therapy
    anxiety disorders, 71
    elimination disorders, 197
    feeding and eating disorders, 185
    gambling disorder, 162
    neurodevelopmental disorders, 241
    obsessive-compulsive disorders, 99, 100
    paraphilic disorders, 216, 217, 219, 220, 222, 223
    pyromania, 176
Bender, D., 308
Bereavement exclusion criterion, 20, 32, 33, 39
Binge-eating disorder, 21, 180, 194–196
Biobehavioral developmental perspective, 151
Bioecological approach, 16–17
Bioler, M., 325
Biopsychosocial approach, 10
Biosocial Development Model, 301
Bipolar, defined, 53
Bipolar and related disorders, 53–67
    bipolar I disorder, 55–58
    bipolar II disorder, 58–61
    case examples, 57–58, 60–61
    in children and adolescents, 20, 35, 36, 53
    coding, recording, and specifiers, 50, 57, 60, 62, 63, 64, 65–67
    counseling implications, 54–55
    cultural considerations, 56, 59–60, 62
    cyclothymic disorder, 61–62
    diagnostic changes, 21, 33, 53–54

differential diagnosis, 54, 56–57, 60, 62, 63, 64
due to another medical condition, 63–64
etiology and treatment, 54, 56, 59
gender differences in, 56, 59
other specified and unspecified, 64–65
racial differences in, 56
socioeconomic status and, 56
substance/medication-induced, 63
suicide risk and, 53, 55, 59
Blanco, C., 279–280
Body dysmorphic disorder (BDD), 21, 89, 93–95
Body-focused repetitive behavior disorder, 104
Body mass index (BMI), 189, 190, 191
Borderline personality disorder, 300–302
Braun, S. A., 322
Breathing-related sleep disorders, 202–203
Brief psychotic disorder, 263–264
Brown, A., 190
Brown, R. J., 282
Bulimia nervosa, 180, 191–194

C

CACREP (Council for Accreditation of Counseling and Related Educational Programs), 2
Caffeine-related disorders, 153, 157
Caldwell-Harris, C. L., 297–298
Cambodian sickness, 114
Cannabis-related disorders, 154, 157–158
Carey, M. P., 205
Catatonia, 51, 259, 267
Categorical assessment, 17–19
Caucasian Americans
    anxiety disorders, 74, 76, 78, 82
    bipolar disorder, 56
    depressive disorders, 41
    kleptomania, 178
    pyromania, 176
CBT. *See* Cognitive behavior therapy
CD. *See* Conduct disorder
Central sleep apnea, 202–203
CFI (Cultural Formulation Interview), 12, 324–325
Chapman, S., 280
Childhood disintegrative disorder. *See* Autism spectrum disorder (ASD)
Childhood-onset fluency disorder, 20, 236, 243–244
Children and adolescents. *See also* Neurodevelopmental disorders
    anxiety disorders, 72, 73, 76
    autism. *See* Autism spectrum disorder (ASD)
    bipolar and related disorders, 20, 35, 36, 53
    depressive disorders, 20, 35–37
    disruptive, impulse-control, and conduct disorders, 166, 171, 174, 176
    dissociative disorders, 272
    elimination disorders, 196–198, 199

feeding and eating disorders, 179–180, 182, 186, 187–188
gender dysphoria, 126–128, 129, 131
obsessive-compulsive and related disorders, 89, 91, 99, 103
sleep-wake disorders, 203, 204
substance-related disorders, 158
trauma- and stressor-related disorders, 106, 108–111, 113, 117–119, 121, 123
Cigarettes, 156, 159–160
Cimino, S., 182
Circadian rhythm sleep-wake disorders, 204
Clients, implications of *DSM-5* for, 22–23
Clinical judgment, 15
Clinical Research Center for Schizophrenia and Psychiatric Rehabilitation (University of California), 261
Clinician-Rated Dimensions of Psychosis Symptom Severity (CRDPSS), 258, 259, 260, 323
Clinician-Rated Severity of Oppositional Defiant Disorder, 324
Cocaine, 159
Coccaro, E. F., 173
Coding, recording, and specifiers, 205. *See also* *International Statistical Classification of Diseases and Related Health Problems (ICD)*
    anxiety disorders, 73, 74–75, 77, 79–80, 82, 84, 85
    bipolar and related disorders, 50, 57, 60, 62, 63, 64, 65–67
    depressive disorders, 36, 41, 43, 45, 48, 49–51
    disruptive, impulse-control, and conduct disorders, 172, 173, 175, 177, 178
    DSM-5 implementation and, 320–321
    elimination disorders, 198, 199
    feeding and eating disorders, 185–186, 187, 188, 190–191, 193, 195
    gender dysphoria, 133
    neurocognitive disorders, 253, 254, 255t
    neurodevelopmental disorders, 242, 246–247, 248, 249, 250–251
    nonaxial reporting options, 321–323
    obsessive-compulsive and related disorders, 92, 94, 96, 99, 101, 102, 103
    paraphilic disorders, 218, 219, 220, 221, 222, 223, 224
    practice implications on, 320–323
    sexual dysfunctions, 207–208
    sleep-wake disorders, 201, 202, 205
    substance-related and addictive disorders, 150, 151, 153–156, 162
    trauma- and stressor-related disorders, 109, 110, 115, 122, 124
Cognitive behavior therapy (CBT)
    anxiety disorders and, 71
    bipolar disorders and, 54, 56, 59

(Continued)

Cognitive behavior therapy *(Continued)*
depressive disorders and, 34
disruptive, impulse-control, and conduct
disorders and, 168, 169
feeding and eating disorders and, 183, 185, 187,
190, 192, 194
gambling disorder and, 162
kleptomania and, 178
neurodevelopmental disorders and, 241
obsessive-compulsive disorders and, 89, 99
paraphilic disorders and, 216, 217, 219, 220, 222,
223
personality disorders and, 297, 299, 302, 306
pyromania and, 176
schizophrenia spectrum disorders and, 261
sleep-wake disorders and, 201
somatic symptom disorders and, 279–280
Cognitive disorders. *See* Neurocognitive disorders
Cognitive remediation therapy, 190
Cohen, J. A., 109
Collectivism, 72, 297–298, 305
Comer, R. J., 56, 197
Communication disorders, 20, 236, 241, 242–244
Comorbidity. *See also* Differential diagnosis
anxiety and depressive disorders, 33, 34, 69, 70
categorical diagnosis and, 18
OCD and Tourette's syndrome, 89
personality disorders and, 296, 297, 299, 300
Compensatory behaviors, 181, 191, 192
Competencies for Counseling Transgendered Clients
(ALGBTIC), 133
Complex PTSD, 113
Compton, W. M., 150–151, 156
Compulsions. *See* Obsessive-compulsive and related
disorders
Conduct disorder (CD), 166, 167, 173–175. *See also*
Disruptive, impulse-control, and conduct disorders
Congenital adrenal hyperplasia, 128
Conversion disorder, 281–282
Council for Accreditation of Counseling and Related
Educational Programs (CACREP), 2
Counseling. *See also ACA Code of Ethics*; Practice
implications; *specific therapy techniques*
anxiety disorders, 71
bipolar and related disorders, 54–55
defined, 2
depressive disorders, 34–35
disruptive, impulse-control, and conduct
disorders, 169–170
dissociative disorders, 272–273
elimination disorders, 197
feeding and eating disorders, 183–184
gender dysphoria, 132–133
medical information recorded in, 13
neurocognitive disorders, 252
neurodevelopmental disorders, 241

obsessive-compulsive and related disorders,
89–90
paraphilic disorders, implications for, 216
reporting mandates, 109, 110, 176, 216, 217
schizophrenia spectrum and other psychotic
disorders, 262
somatic symptom and related disorders, 280
substance-related and addictive disorders,
156–157, 162–163
trauma- and stressor-related disorders, 107–108
wellness approach, 11
Cox, J. A., 322
Craske, M. G., 70
Cravings, 152, 156–157
CRDPSS. *See* Clinician-Rated Dimensions of Psychosis
Symptom Severity
Crooks, R., 132
Cross-cutting assessment, 19–20, 323
Cross-dressing, 223–224
Cultural considerations. *See also* Gender differences;
Racial and ethnic differences; *specific racial and
ethnic groups*
bipolar and related disorders, 56, 59–60, 62
depressive disorders, 36, 40–41, 42, 45, 48–49
disruptive, impulse-control, and conduct
disorders, 176
feeding and eating disorders, 182–183, 185, 188,
190, 192, 194–195
gambling disorder, 161
gender dysphoria, 130
obsessive-compulsive and related disorders, 91,
94, 96, 100, 103
personality disorders, 295–296, 297–298, 302,
304–305, 306
sexual dysfunctions, 210, 211, 213
structural changes in, 12, 21
trauma- and stressor-related disorders, 109, 110,
114–115, 121, 123
Cultural explanation or perceived cause, 12, 21
Cultural Formulation Interview (CFI), 12, 324–325
Cultural idioms of distress, 12, 21
Cultural syndromes, 12, 21
Cunningham, J., 45
Cyclothymic disorder, 61–62

D

Das, A. K., 54
Dawson, D. A., 151
DBT. *See* Dialectical behavior therapy
Delayed ejaculation, 208–209
Delayed expression, 113, 115, 117, 118
Delirium, 252–253
Delsignore, A., 130
Delusional disorder, 263
Delusions, 257, 259

Dementia. *See* Major neurocognitive disorder

Dependence on substances. *See* Substance-related and addictive disorders

Dependent personality disorder, 305–306

Depersonalization, 113, 115, 117, 118, 269, 274

Depersonalization/derealization disorder, 236, 271, 274

Depression, defined, 33

Depressive disorders, 33–51
    assessment of, 18, 34
    case examples, 37–38, 43–44, 46–47
    in children and adolescents, 20, 35–37
    coding, recording, and specifiers, 36, 41, 43, 45, 48, 49–51
    comorbidity with anxiety disorders, 33, 34, 69, 70
    counseling implications, 34–35
    cultural considerations, 36, 40–41, 42, 45, 48–49
    diagnostic changes, 20–21, 32, 33–34
    differential diagnosis, 34, 36, 41, 42–43, 45, 47, 49
    disruptive mood dysregulation disorder (DMDD), 20, 33, 35–38
    due to another medical condition, 48–49
    in elderly populations, 40
    etiology and treatment, 34
    gender differences in, 34, 40
    major depressive disorder (MDD), 33, 34, 38–41, 50, 51
    other specified and unspecified, 49
    persistent depressive disorder (PDD), 33, 41–44, 50
    premenstrual dysphoric disorder (PMDD), 20, 33, 44–47
    racial differences in, 34, 40–41, 42
    substance/medication-induced, 47–48
    suicide risk and, 40

Derealization, 113, 115, 117, 118, 269, 274. *See also* Depersonalization/derealization disorder

DeSilva, R., 325

Detachment, 311

Developmental coordination disorder, 249–250

Dextroamphetamines, 159

Diagnostic and Statistical Manual of Mental Disorders (1st ed.; *DSM-I*), 9, 17

Diagnostic and Statistical Manual of Mental Disorders (2nd ed.; *DSM-II*), 9–10, 17

Diagnostic and Statistical Manual of Mental Disorders (3rd ed.; *DSM-III* and *DSM-III-R*), 10, 17, 19

Diagnostic and Statistical Manual of Mental Disorders (4th ed.; *DSM-IV* and *DSM-IV-TR*), 10–11, 17, 19

Diagnostic and Statistical Manual of Mental Disorders (5th ed.; *DSM-5*)
    anxiety disorders, 69–85. *See also* Anxiety disorders
    behavioral disruptions, 179–224. *See also* Behavioral disruptions
    bipolar and related disorders, 53–67. *See also* Bipolar and related disorders
    controversy surrounding, 2

    depressive disorders, 33–51. *See also* Depressive disorders
    diagnostic changes in, 20–21
    disruptive, impulse-control, and conduct disorders, 165–178. *See also* Disruptive, impulse-control, and conduct disorders
    dissociative disorders, 269–275. *See also* Dissociative disorders
    future of, 24, 325–326
    gender dysphoria, 125–134. *See also* Gender dysphoria
    history of, 9–11
    implications of, 22–23. *See also* Practice implications
    neurodevelopmental and neurocognitive disorders, 239–256. *See also* Neurocognitive disorders; Neurodevelopmental disorders
    obsessive-compulsive and related disorders, 87–104. *See also* Obsessive-compulsive and related disorders
    personality disorders, 293–315. *See also* Personality disorders
    philosophical changes in, 16–20
    revision process, 3–5
    schizophrenia spectrum and other psychotic disorders, 257–268. *See also* Schizophrenia spectrum and other psychotic disorders
    somatic symptom and related disorders, 179–224. *See also* Somatic symptom and related disorders
    structural changes in, 11–15
    substance-related and addictive disorders, 149–163. *See also* Substance-related and addictive disorders
    trauma- and stressor-related disorders, 105–124. *See also* Trauma- and stressor-related disorders

Dialectical behavior therapy (DBT)
    disruptive, impulse-control, and conduct disorders and, 169
    feeding and eating disorders and, 183, 192
    personality disorders and, 301

Diamond, D., 303

Diaz, S. F., 94

DID. *See* Dissociative identity disorder

Differential diagnosis. *See also* Comorbidity
    anxiety disorders, 70, 72–74, 75, 76–77, 78–80, 82, 84–85
    bipolar and related disorders, 54, 56–57, 60, 62, 63, 64
    depressive disorders, 34, 36, 41, 42–43, 45, 47, 49
    disruptive, impulse-control, and conduct disorders, 167–168, 172, 173, 175, 176–177, 178
    dissociative disorders, 270–271
    elimination disorders, 196, 198, 199
    feeding and eating disorders, 181–182, 185, 187, 188, 190, 192–193, 195

(Continued)

Differential diagnosis *(Continued)*
   gambling disorder, 161
   gender dysphoria, 130–131
   neurocognitive disorders, 253, 254
   neurodevelopmental disorders, 242, 243, 244,
      246, 248, 249, 250
   obsessive-compulsive and related disorders,
      88–89, 91, 94, 96, 99, 100–101
   paraphilic disorders, 215, 217–218, 220, 221, 222,
      223, 224
   personality disorders, 298, 301–302, 303, 304,
      305, 306, 307
   schizophrenia spectrum and other psychotic
      disorders, 259–260
   sexual dysfunctions, 209–210, 211, 212, 213, 214
   somatic symptom and related disorders, 278–279
   trauma- and stressor-related disorders, 107, 109,
      110, 115, 121–122, 124
Dimensional assessment, 17–19, 236, 258, 308–309
Dimsdale, J. E., 281
Disinhibited social engagement disorder (DSED),
   106, 109–111
Disinhibition, 311
Disorganized motor behavior, 257–258
Disorganized thinking, 257
Disruptive, impulse-control, and conduct disorders,
   165–178
   in children and adolescents, 166, 171, 174, 176
   coding, recording, and specifiers, 172, 173, 175,
      177, 178
   conduct disorder (CD), 166, 167, 173–175
   counseling implications, 169–170
   cultural considerations, 176
   diagnostic changes, 166–167
   differential diagnosis, 167–168, 172, 173, 175,
      176–177, 178
   essential features of, 165–166
   etiology and treatment, 168–169
   gender differences in, 166, 174, 176, 177, 178
   intermittent explosive disorder (IED), 167,
      172–173
   kleptomania, 166, 169, 177–178
   oppositional defiant disorder (ODD), 37, 166,
      167, 170–172
   pyromania, 166, 169, 175–177
   racial differences in, 176
Disruptive mood dysregulation disorder (DMDD),
   20, 33, 35–38
Dissocial personality disorder. *See* Antisocial personality
   disorder (ASPD)
Dissociative amnesia, 269–270, 271, 273
Dissociative disorders, 269–275
   case example, 274–275
   in children and adolescents, 272
   counseling implications, 272–273
   depersonalization/derealization disorder, 236,
      271, 274

   diagnostic changes, 270
   differential diagnosis, 270–271
   dissociative amnesia, 269–270, 271, 273
   dissociative fugue, 273
   dissociative identity disorder (DID), 236, 270,
      271, 272, 273
   essential features of, 269–270
   etiology and treatment, 271–272
Dissociative fugue, 273
Dissociative identity disorder (DID), 236, 270, 271,
   272, 273
DMDD. *See* Disruptive mood dysregulation disorder
D'Olimpio, F., 182
Downcoding, 322
Drug-related and addictive disorders, 149–163. *See
   also* Substance-related and addictive disorders
DSED (disinhibited social engagement disorder),
   106, 109–111
*DSM. See Diagnostic and Statistical Manual of Mental
   Disorders*
Dysthymic disorder. *See* Persistent depressive
   disorder (PDD)

E

Early ejaculation, 213–214
Eating disorders. *See* Feeding and eating disorders
Eaton, W. W., 18
ED (erectile disorder), 209–210
Elderly populations
   depressive disorders, 40
   obsessive-compulsive and related disorders, 95
   sexual dysfunctions, 209
   sleep-wake disorders, 201, 202
Elimination disorders, 196–199
Empathy training, 219
Empirically based treatments, 10
Encopresis, 196–197, 199
Enuresis, 196, 197–198
Equit, M., 188
Erectile disorder (ED), 209–210
Eriksen, K., 318
ERP (exposure and response prevention), 89
Ethical guidelines. *See* ACA Code of Ethics
Ethnic differences. *See* Racial and ethnic differences;
   specific racial and ethnic groups
Etiology and treatment. *See also* Counseling; *specific
   therapy techniques*
   anxiety disorders, 70–71
   bipolar and related disorders, 54, 56, 59
   depressive disorders, 34
   disruptive, impulse-control, and conduct
      disorders, 168–169
   dissociative disorders, 271–272
   elimination disorders, 196–197
   feeding and eating disorders, 182–183
   gender dysphoria, 131–132

neurocognitive disorders, 252

obsessive-compulsive and related disorders, 89, 99

paraphilic disorders, 215–216

schizophrenia spectrum and other psychotic disorders, 260–262

somatic symptom and related disorders, 279–280

trauma- and stressor-related disorders, 107

Excoriation disorder, 21, 89, 99–101

Exhibitionistic disorder, 218–219

Exposure and response prevention (ERP), 89

Expressive language disorders, 20

Eyberg, S. M., 169

F

Factitious disorder, 282–283

Family-focused therapy

bipolar disorders, 54, 56, 59

disruptive, impulse-control, and conduct disorders, 169

feeding and eating disorders, 190

gender dysphoria, 132

Farrington D. P., 174

Fava, G. A., 282

Fear, defined, 69

Feeding and eating disorders, 179–196

anorexia nervosa, 180, 188–191

avoidant/restrictive food intake disorder, 187–188

binge-eating disorder, 21, 180, 194–196

bulimia nervosa, 180, 191–194

case examples, 191, 193–194, 195–196

in children and adolescents, 179–180, 182, 186, 187–188

coding, recording, and specifiers, 185–186, 187, 188, 190–191, 193, 195

compensatory behaviors and, 181, 191, 192

counseling implications, 183–184

cultural considerations, 182–183, 185, 188, 190, 192, 194–195

diagnostic changes, 21, 179, 181

differential diagnosis, 181–182, 185, 187, 188, 190, 192–193, 195

essential features of, 179–181

etiology and treatment, 182–183

gender differences in, 180

pica, 184–186

rumination disorder, 186–187

Female orgasmic disorder, 210

Females. *See* Gender differences; Women

Female sexual interest/arousal disorder, 211

Fetishistic disorder, 223

Fichter, M. M., 189

Fire setting. *See* Pyromania

First, M., 19, 317

Five-Factor Model (FFM) of personality functioning, 311

Fluoxetine, 280

fMRI (functional magnetic resonance imaging), 152

Fombonne, E., 244

Food aversion techniques, 185

Foote, B., 272, 273

Ford, S. J. W., 318

Foster, J. D., 304

Frances, A., 280

Friedman, M. J., 70

Frotteuristic disorder, 220–221

Fryer, C., 73

Fuerth, K. M., 318

Fugl-Meyer, A., 211

Fugl-Meyer, K., 211

Functional magnetic resonance imaging (fMRI), 152

Functional neurological symptom disorder, 281–282

G

GAD. *See* Generalized anxiety disorder

Gaebel, W., 266

GAF scale. *See* Global Assessment of Functioning scale

Gambling disorder, 21, 151, 161–163, 165

Gender, defined, 128

Gender bias, 296, 297

Gender differences. *See also* Men; Women

anxiety disorders, 78, 79, 80

bipolar disorder, 56, 59

depressive disorders, 34, 40

in disease prevalence, 48

disruptive, impulse-control, and conduct disorders, 166, 174, 176, 177, 178

elimination disorders, 198, 199

feeding and eating disorders, 180

neurodevelopmental disorders, 249

obsessive-compulsive and related disorders, 91, 94

paraphilic disorders, 216

personality disorders, 295–296, 299, 300, 301, 304, 307

sleep-wake disorders, 200, 205

in socialization, 125

somatic symptom and related disorders and, 281, 282

substance-related and addictive disorders, 157, 159, 161

trauma- and stressor-related disorders, 106

Gender dysphoria, 125–134

case examples, 133–134

in children and adolescents, 126–128, 129, 131

coding, recording, and specifiers, 133

counseling implications, 132–133

cultural considerations, 125, 130

defined, 128

diagnostic changes and criteria, 21, 126–128

differential diagnosis, 130–131

essential features of, 128–130

etiology and treatment, 131–132

special considerations, 129–130

Gender identity, defined, 128
Gender transition, defined, 128
Generalized anxiety disorder (GAD), 34, 72, 81–83
Genito-pelvic pain/penetration disorder, 211–212
Gepper, C., 73
Girdler, S. S., 45
Global Assessment of Functioning (GAF) scale, 12, 13, 324
Global developmental delay, 242
Goldstein, R. B., 151
Grant, B. F., 151
Grief exclusion criterion, 20, 32, 33, 39
Gustatory hallucinations, 257

H

Hair-pulling disorder. *See* Trichotillomania
Hallucinations, 257
Hallucinogen-related disorders, 154, 158
Harkins, L., 217, 219, 223
Hassan, I., 279
Health and Human Services Department, U.S., 15, 320
Hennen, J., 216
Hepp, U., 130
HIPAA (Health Insurance Portability and Accountability Act of 1996), 6, 11
Hispanics. *See* Latinos/Latinas
Histrionic personality disorder, 302–303
Hoarding disorder, 21, 89, 92, 95–98
Hoffman, R. M., 318
Hoffmann, N. G., 159
Hollifield, M., 73
Horan, W. P., 265
Hsu, L., 76
Hurwitz, T. A., 280
Hypersomnolence disorder, 201–202
Hypnotic-related disorders, 155, 159
Hypomanic episodes, 54, 58, 62. *See also* Bipolar and related disorders
Hypopneas, 202

I

ICD. See International Statistical Classification of Diseases and Related Health Problems
Identity alteration, 270
Identity confusion, 270
IED (intermittent explosive disorder), 167, 172–173
Illness anxiety disorder, 281
Impulse-control disorders. *See* Disruptive, impulse-control, and conduct disorders
Income. *See* Socioeconomic status
Individualism, 297–298, 304, 306
Inhalant-related disorders, 154, 158
Inhibited ejaculation, 208–209
Insomnia disorder, 200–201

Intellectual disability, 20, 236, 241–242
Intermittent explosive disorder (IED), 167, 172–173
International Obsessive-Compulsive Disorder Foundation (IOCDF), 89
International Society for the Study of Trauma and Dissociation (ISSTD), 269–270, 271, 272, 274
International Society of Sexual Medicine, 213
International Statistical Classification of Diseases and Related Health Problems (ICD). See also Coding, recording, and specifiers
    blank spaces in codes, 38
    codes included in *DSM-5*, 11, 15, 321
    GAF scale used in, 13
    ICD-10-CM implementation, 11, 13, 320
    mental disorders, inclusion of, 9
    uses of, 16
Internet gaming disorder, 21, 151, 163
Interpersonal therapy (IPT)
    bipolar and related disorders, 54, 56, 59
    depressive disorders, 34
    feeding and eating disorders, 183, 192
Interventions for Disruptive Behavior Disorders Kit (SAMHSA), 169
Intoxication, 153
IOCDF (International Obsessive-Compulsive Disorder Foundation), 89
IPT. *See* Interpersonal therapy
ISSTD. *See* International Society for the Study of Trauma and Dissociation
Ivey, A. E., 318, 319
Ivey, M. B., 318, 319

J

Johnson, V. E., 206
Johnson, Y., 73
Jones, K. D., 18

K

Kafka, M. P., 216
Kahlbaum, K., 61
Kaminer, Y., 151
Kaye, W. H., 192
Kendler, K. S., 39
Kerridge, B. T., 158
Kessler, R. C., 18, 70–71
Keyes, K. M., 151
Kleine-Levin syndrome, 193
Kleptomania, 166, 169, 177–178
Kopak, A. M., 159
Kraemer, B., 130
Kraepelin, E., 53
Kress, V. E., 318
Kupfer, D. J., 3, 4, 16, 23

L

Language disorder, 20, 243
Latinos/Latinas
    anxiety disorders, 74, 76, 78, 82
    depressive disorders, 34, 40–41
    PTSD, 114
    pyromania, 176
    tobacco use, 160
Lauritsen, M. B., 245
Learning disorder, 20, 240, 249
Level of Personality Functioning Scale, 310–311
Lewis-Fernández, R., 282, 325
Lifetime morbid risk (LMR), 70–71
Linde, L. E., 4
Linehan, M., 301
Lithium, 54
Locke, D. W., 4
Lucarelli, L., 182

M

Magariños, M., 279–280
Magee, W. J., 18
Major depressive disorder (MDD), 33, 34, 38–41, 50, 51
Major neurocognitive disorder, 236, 251, 253–256, 255t
Male hypoactive sexual desire disorder, 212–213
Males. *See* Gender differences; Men
Mandated reporting requirements, 109, 110, 176, 216, 217
Manic episodes, 54, 55, 161. *See also* Bipolar and related disorders
Manjula, M., 279
Manning, J. S., 54
Marijuana-related disorders, 154, 157–158
Masochism/sadism, 221–222
Masters, W. H., 206
McGlinchey, J., 19
McGonagle, K. A., 18
MDD. *See* Major depressive disorder
Medical model of behavior, 10, 11, 318
Meehan, K., 303
Melatonin, 204
Men. *See also* Gender differences
    delayed ejaculation, 208–209
    erectile disorder (ED), 209–210
    male hypoactive sexual desire disorder, 212–213
    premature ejaculation, 213–214
Mental disorder, defined, 318
Mental retardation. *See* Intellectual disability
Mergl, R., 277, 278–279
Methamphetamines, 159
Mewton, L., 23
Meyer, A., 9
Mild neurocognitive disorder, 251–252, 254–256, 255t
Miller, N., 130
Miller, R., 319
Mindfulness training, 152, 157, 162
Mixed receptive-expressive language disorders, 20
Monosymptomatic enuresis, 197
Montgomery, P., 201
Mood disorders
    bipolar and related disorders, 53–67. *See also* Bipolar and related disorders
    depressive disorders, 33–51. *See also* Depressive disorders
    diagnostic changes, 20–21, 33
    structural changes to classification of, 14
Mood stabilizing medications, 54, 56
Motor disorders, 249–251
Mountford, V., 190
Movement disorder, 257–258
Multiaxial system, 10–11, 12–14, 13t
Multiple personality disorder. *See* Dissociative identity disorder (DID)
Murray, J., 174
Myers, J. E., 11

N

Naltrexone, 178
Narcissistic personality disorder, 303–304
Narcolepsy, 201–202
National Comorbidity Survey, 34, 72, 106, 170, 171, 174
National Epidemiological Survey on Alcohol and Related Conditions, 158
National Highway Traffic Safety Administration, 199
National Institute of Mental Health (NIMH), 325
    on anorexia nervosa, 189–190
    on bipolar disorder, 53
    on depressive disorders, 34, 38
    DSM-5 revision process and, 3
    on obsessive-compulsive disorder (OCD), 90
    Research Domain Criteria project, 292
National Institutes of Health (NIH), 19
Native Americans/Alaska Natives
    alcohol-related disorders, 157
    anxiety disorders, 76, 82
    depressive disorders, 41
    gambling disorder, 161
Negative affectivity, 311
Negative symptoms of psychotic disorders, 257, 258
Neurocognitive disorders, 251–256
    case example, 256
    coding, recording, and specifiers, 253, 254, 255t
    counseling implications, 252
    delirium, 252–253
    diagnostic changes, 21, 236, 251–252
    differential diagnosis, 253, 254

(Continued)

Neurocognitive disorders *(Continued)*
    etiology and treatment, 252
    major neurocognitive disorder, 236, 251,
        253–256, 255*t*
    mild neurocognitive disorder, 251–252, 254–256, 255*t*
Neurodevelopmental disorders, 239–251
    ADHD, 170, 236, 240–241, 247–249
    autism spectrum disorder (ASD), 20, 236, 240,
        241, 244–247
    case examples, 247, 248–249
    childhood-onset fluency disorder, 20, 236, 243–244
    coding, recording, and specifiers, 242, 246–247,
        248, 249, 250–251
    communication disorders, 20, 236, 241, 242–244
    counseling implications, 241
    developmental coordination disorder, 249–250
    diagnostic changes, 240–241
    differential diagnosis, 242, 243, 244, 246, 248,
        249, 250
    gender differences in, 249
    global developmental delay, 242
    intellectual disability, 20, 236, 241–242
    language disorder, 20, 243
    motor disorders, 249–251
    overview, 239–240
    social communication disorder (SCD), 20, 236,
        241, 244
    specific learning disorder, 20, 240, 249
    speech sound disorder, 20, 243
    stereotypic movement disorder, 250
    tic disorders, 250–251
Neurotic depression. *See* Persistent depressive
    disorder (PDD)
Nicasio, A. V., 325
Nicotine-related disorders, 156, 159–160
Nightmare disorder, 203, 204
NIH (National Institutes of Health), 19
NIMH. *See* National Institute of Mental Health
Nissenson, K., 279–280
Nock, M. K., 171
Nocturnal involuntary urination, 197
Nonaxial system, 12–14, 13*t*, 319–320
Non–rapid eye movement (NREM) sleep arousal
    disorders, 203–204
Not otherwise specified (NOS) diagnosis, 3, 15, 18, 21

O

Öberg, K., 211
Obsessional jealousy, 104
Obsessive-compulsive and related disorders, 87–104
    body dysmorphic disorder (BDD), 21, 89, 93–95
    case examples, 92–93, 94–95, 97–98, 101
    in children and adolescents, 89, 91, 99, 103
    coding, recording, and specifiers, 92, 94, 96, 99,
        101, 102, 103

common obsessions and compulsions, 87, 87*t*
    counseling implications, 89–90
    cultural considerations, 91, 94, 96, 100, 103
    diagnostic changes, 21, 88
    differential diagnosis, 88–89, 91, 94, 96, 99, 100–101
    due to another medical condition, 102–103
    in elderly populations, 95
    etiology and treatment, 89, 99
    excoriation disorder, 21, 89, 99–101
    gender differences in, 91, 94
    hoarding disorder, 21, 89, 92, 95–98
    obsessive-compulsive disorder (OCD), 87, 89,
        90–93, 306–307
    other specified and unspecified, 104
    socioeconomic status and, 91
    substance/medication-induced, 101–102
    trichotillomania (TTM), 21, 89, 98–99, 165
Obstructive sleep apnea hypopnea, 202–203
Oldham, J., 4, 308
Olfactory hallucinations, 257
Opioid-related disorders, 154–155, 158–159
Oppositional defiant disorder (ODD), 37, 166, 167,
    170–172
Other specified disorder diagnosis, 15, 320
Overdiagnosis, 23

P

Pacific Islanders. *See* Asian Americans/Pacific Islanders
Pagan, J. L., 308
PANDAS (pediatric autoimmune neuropsychiatric
    disorder associated with streptococcal infections),
    103
Panic attacks, 21, 79–80, 115
Panic disorder, 21, 72, 75, 78–79
PANS (pediatric acute-onset neuropsychiatric
    syndrome), 103
Paranoid personality disorder, 296–297
Paraphilic disorders, 214–224
    case example, 218
    coding, recording, and specifiers, 218, 219, 220,
        221, 222, 223, 224
    counseling implications, 216
    diagnostic changes, 21, 179, 215
    differential diagnosis, 215, 217–218, 220, 221,
        222, 223, 224
    etiology and treatment, 215–216
    exhibitionistic disorder, 218–219
    fetishistic disorder, 223
    frotteuristic disorder, 220–221
    gender differences in, 216
    overview, 214–215
    pedophilic disorder, 21, 216–218
    sexual masochism/sadism, 221–222
    transvestic disorder, 223–224
    voyeuristic disorder, 220

Parasomnias, 203–204
Parental interventions, 168–169
Paris, J., 294, 308
Parkes, G., 132
Parpottas, P., 297
Patient Health Questionnaire, 34, 323
PD-TS (personality disorder–trait specific), 312
Pediatric acute-onset neuropsychiatric syndrome (PANS), 103
Pediatric autoimmune neuropsychiatric disorder associated with streptococcal infections (PANDAS), 103
Pedophilic disorder, 21, 216–218
Persistent depressive disorder (PDD), 33, 41–44, 50
Personality disorders, 293–315
    alternative model for diagnosing, 12, 294–295, 308–315
    antisocial, 166, 174, 175, 299–300
    avoidant, 304–305
    borderline, 300–302
    case examples, 313–315
    clustering system for, 293–294
    comorbidity and, 296, 297, 299, 300
    cultural considerations, 295–296, 297–298, 302, 304–305, 306
    defined, 294
    dependent, 305–306
    diagnostic changes, 295
    differential diagnosis, 298, 301–302, 303, 304, 305, 306, 307
    essential features of, 293–294, 295
    gender differences in, 295–296, 299, 300, 301, 304, 307
    histrionic, 302–303
    narcissistic, 303–304
    obsessive-compulsive, 306–307
    paranoid, 296–297
    pathological trait taxonomy, 311
    personality disorder–trait specific (PD-TS), 312
    schizoid, 297–298
    schizotypal, 259, 298–299
    suicide risk and, 301
Personality disorder–trait specific (PD-TS), 312
Pervasive developmental disorder, 20
Petukhova, M., 70–71
Phillips, K. A., 70, 94
Phobias, 74–75
Phobic stimulus, 74
Phonological disorder, 20
Pica, 184–186
Pilver, C. E., 45
PMDD. *See* Premenstrual dysphoric disorder
Polysomnographs, 202
Positive symptoms of psychotic disorders, 257
Posttraumatic stress disorder (PTSD), 111–119
    case example, 119

in children and adolescents, 106, 113, 117–119
    coding, recording, and specifiers, 115
    cultural considerations, 114–115
    diagnostic changes and criteria, 21, 106, 111–113, 112t, 115–118
    differential diagnosis, 115
    essential features of, 72, 111, 113–114
    special considerations, 114–115
Practice Guideline for the Treatment of Patients With Schizophrenia (APA), 261
Practice implications, 317–326
    assessment and screening tools, 323–325
    coding and recording, 320–323
    counseling identity and, 317–318
    diagnostic considerations, 23, 317–320
    neurobiological explanations for behavior and, 23, 318–319
    nonaxial diagnosis and, 319–320
    other specified and unspecified diagnosis and, 320
    training needs, 23
Pragmatic communication disorder. *See* Social communication disorder (SCD)
Pregnancy, mood episodes during, 51, 67
Premature ejaculation, 213–214
Premenstrual dysphoric disorder (PMDD), 20, 33, 44–47
Proctor, S. L., 159
Prosek, E. A., 319
Psychobiological approach, 9
Psychoeducation
    bipolar disorders, 54, 56, 59
    pyromania, 176
    schizophrenia spectrum disorders, 261
    somatic symptom disorders, 279
Psychopathy. *See* Antisocial personality disorder (ASPD)
Psychopharmacological treatments, 54, 168–169, 178, 214, 261, 280
Psychotic disorders. *See* Schizophrenia spectrum and other psychotic disorders
Psychoticism, 311
PTSD. *See* Posttraumatic stress disorder
Pyromania, 166, 169, 175–177

R

Racial and ethnic differences. *See also specific racial and ethnic groups*
    anxiety disorders, 74, 76, 78, 82
    bipolar disorder, 56
    depressive disorders, 34, 40–41, 42
    disruptive, impulse-control, and conduct disorders, 176
    substance-related and addictive disorders, 157, 160
    trauma- and stressor-related disorders, 114
Rapid eye movement (REM) sleep behavior disorder, 200, 203, 204

Rational emotive behavior therapy (REBT), 306
Rayle, A. D., 318
Reactive attachment disorder (RAD), 106, 108–109
Recording. *See* Coding, recording, and specifiers
Regier, D. A., 3, 16
Relaxation training, 71
Remington, R., 254
Reporting mandates, 109, 110, 176, 216, 217
Research Domain Criteria project, 292
Research Planning Committee Conference, 3
Restless legs syndrome, 200, 205
Restrictive/avoidant food intake disorder, 187–188
Retarded ejaculation, 208–209
Rett syndrome. *See* Autism spectrum disorder (ASD)
Rogler, L. H., 10
Rosa's Law (2010), 236, 240, 242
Rubin, A., 260
Rumination disorder, 186–187

S

Sadism/masochism, 221–222
Samet, S., 47
SAMHSA. *See* Substance Abuse and Mental Health Services Administration
Sampson, N. A., 70–71
SCD. *See* Social communication disorder
Schizoaffective disorder, 259, 265–266
Schizoid personality disorder, 297–298
Schizophrenia, 265
Schizophrenia spectrum and other psychotic disorders, 257–268
    brief psychotic disorder, 263–264
    case example, 267–268
    catatonia, 51, 259, 267
    counseling implications, 262
    delusional disorder, 263
    diagnostic changes, 20, 236, 258–259
    differential diagnosis, 259–260
    dimensional assessment of, 18–19, 236, 258
    due to another medical condition, 266–267
    essential features of, 257–258
    etiology and treatment, 260–262
    schizoaffective disorder, 265–266
    schizophrenia, 265
    schizophreniform disorder, 264–265
    substance/medication-induced, 266
Schizophreniform disorder, 264–265
Schizotypal personality disorder, 259, 298–299
Schnyder, U., 130
Schweitzer, D. H., 208
Screening tools. *See* Assessment
Sedative-related disorders, 155, 159
Selective mutism, 73–74, 76
Separation anxiety disorder, 71–73
Severity Measure for Panic Disorder–Adult, 323–324

Sex, defined, 128
Sex development disorders, 128, 129
Sexual dysfunctions, 205–214
    coding, recording, and specifiers, 207–208
    consequences of, 205–206
    cultural considerations, 210, 211, 213
    delayed ejaculation, 208–209
    diagnostic changes, 21, 179, 206–207
    differential diagnosis, 209–210, 211, 212, 213, 214
    in elderly populations, 209
    erectile disorder (ED), 209–210
    female orgasmic disorder, 210
    female sexual interest/arousal disorder, 211
    genito-pelvic pain/penetration disorder, 211–212
    male hypoactive sexual desire disorder, 212–213
    premature ejaculation, 213–214
    substance/medication-induced, 214
Sexual masochism/sadism, 221–222
Sexual response cycle, 206
Sharma, M. P., 279
Shell shock, 120
Shepard, L. D., 201
Shoplifting. *See* Kleptomania
Siegel, D. J., 319
Simon, L., 131
Simonoff, E., 246
Simons, J. S., 205
Sirri, L., 282
Skin-picking disorder. *See* Excoriation disorder
Skodol, A., 308
Sleep-related hypoventilation, 202–203
Sleep terrors, 203
Sleep-wake disorders, 199–205
    breathing-related sleep disorders, 202–203
    in children and adolescents, 203, 204
    circadian rhythm disorders, 204
    coding, recording, and specifiers, 201, 202, 205
    consequences of, 199
    diagnostic changes, 21, 179, 200
    in elderly populations, 201, 202
    gender differences in, 200, 205
    hypersomnolence disorder, 201–202
    insomnia disorder, 200–201
    narcolepsy, 201–202
    parasomnias, 203–204
    restless legs syndrome, 200, 205
    substance/medication-induced, 205
Sleepwalking, 203, 204
Smoking, 156, 159–160
So, J. K., 279
Social anxiety disorder, 72, 75–78
Social communication disorder (SCD), 20, 236, 241, 244
Socialization, gender differences in, 125
Social rhythm therapy, 54, 56, 59